Handbook of Child Development and Early Education

RESEARCH TO PRACTICE

Edited by
Oscar A. Barbarin
Barbara Hanna Wasik

THE GUILFORD PRESS
New York   London

57.00

© 2009 The Guilford Press
A Division of Guilford Publications, Inc.
72 Spring Street, New York, NY 10012
www.guilford.com

Printed in the United States of America

This book is printed on acid-free paper.

Last digit is print number: 9 8 7 6 5 4 3 2 1

Library of Congress Cataloging-in-Publication Data
Handbook of child development and early education : research to practice / edited by Oscar A. Barbarin, Barbara Hanna Wasik.
   p. cm.
   Includes bibliographical references and index.
   ISBN 978-1-60623-302-3 (hardcover)
   1. Child development—Handbooks, manuals, etc.   I. Barbarin, Oscar A.   II. Wasik, Barbara Hanna.
   HQ772.H33 2009
   372.21—dc22

                                                        2008054432

About the Editors

Oscar A. Barbarin, PhD, is the Lila L. and Douglas J. Hertz Endowed Chair in the Department of Psychology at Tulane University. He is also a Senior Scientist at the Frank Porter Graham Child Development Institute at the University of North Carolina, Chapel Hill. He served as President of the American Orthopsychiatric Association from 2001 until 2003 and was elected to the Governing Council of the Society for Research in Child Development. Dr. Barbarin's research has focused on the social and familial determinants of ethnic and gender achievement gaps beginning in early childhood. He has developed ABLE, a mental health screening tool for young children. Dr. Barbarin is principal investigator of the PAS Initiative, a national study that focuses on the socio-emotional and academic development of boys of color. His work on children of African descent extends to a 20-year longitudinal study of the effects of poverty and violence on child development in South Africa.

Barbara Hanna Wasik, PhD, holds a William R. Kenan, Jr. Professorship in the School of Education and is a Fellow at the Frank Porter Graham Child Development Institute and Director of the Center for Home Visiting at the University of North Carolina, Chapel Hill. Dr. Wasik also chairs the School Psychology Program. She serves as a consultant to national organizations, is a member of several national boards, and has held office in state and national organizations. For the American Psychological Association, Dr. Wasik has served as chair of the Board of Educational Affairs, a member of the Council of Representatives, and chair of the Task Force on Early Childhood Education. In addition, she was an invited participant to the White House Conference on Child Care and served as a member of the Committee on Early Childhood Pedagogy of the National Academy of Sciences. Since 1999, Dr. Wasik has served as a co-director for the National Forum on Home Visiting. Her research focuses on early childhood interventions, family literacy, social and cognitive development, problem solving, home visiting, and the observational study of children.

Contributors

Nikki Aikens, PhD, Mathematica Policy Research, Inc., Washington, DC

Steve Amendum, PhD, Department of Elementary Education, College of Education, North Carolina State University, Raleigh, North Carolina

Oscar A. Barbarin, PhD, Department of Psychology, Tulane University, New Orleans, Louisiana

Maria G. Bartolini Bussi, PhD, Department of Pure and Applied Mathematics, University of Modena and Reggio Emilia, Modena, Italy

Patricia J. Bauer, PhD, Department of Psychology, Emory University, Atlanta, Georgia

Mara Boni, Department of Pure and Applied Mathematics, University of Modena and Reggio Emilia, Modena, Italy

Marc H. Bornstein, PhD, Child and Family Research, Eunice Kennedy Shriver National Institute of Child Health and Human Development, National Institutes of Health, Bethesda, Maryland

Sue Bredekamp, PhD, Council for Professional Recognition, Washington, DC

Susan D. Calkins, PhD, Department of Human Development and Family Studies and Department of Psychology, University of North Carolina, Greensboro, North Carolina

Beth Casey, PhD, Program in of Applied Developmental and Educational Psychology, Lynch School of Education, Boston College, Boston, Massachusetts

Jennifer L. Coffman, PhD, Department of Psychology, University of North Carolina, Chapel Hill, North Carolina

Catherine Darrow, MAT, Department of Teaching and Learning, Peabody College of Education and Human Development, Vanderbilt University, Nashville, Tennessee

Erik De Corte, PhD, Center for Instructional Psychology and Technology, Department of Educational Sciences, University of Leuven, Leuven, Belgium

Fien Depaepe, PhD, Center for Instructional Psychology and Technology, Department of Educational Sciences, University of Leuven, Leuven, Belgium

David K. Dickinson, EdD, Department of Teaching and Learning, Peabody College of Education and Human Development, Vanderbilt University, Nashville, Tennessee

Lisa A. D'Souza, MEd, Department of Curriculum and Instruction, Lynch School of Education, Boston College, Boston, Massachusetts

Mark Enfield, PhD, School of Education, Elon University, Elon, North Carolina

Rossana Falcade, PhD, Department of Pure and Applied Mathematics, University of Modena, Modena, Italy

Jill Fitzgerald, PhD, School of Education, University of North Carolina, Chapel Hill, North Carolina

Maria Fusaro, EdM, Graduate School of Education, Harvard University, Cambridge, Massachusetts

Kathleen Cranley Gallagher, PhD, School of Education, University of North Carolina, Chapel Hill, North Carolina

Herbert P. Ginsburg, PhD, Teachers College, Columbia University, New York, New York

Miranda Goodman, BA, Department of Psychology, University of California, Davis, California

Jennie K. Grammer, BA, Department of Psychology, University of North Carolina, Chapel Hill, North Carolina

Kelly L. Maxwell, PhD, FPG Child Development Institute and School of Social Work, University of North Carolina, Chapel Hill, North Carolina

Kevin Miller, PhD, Department of Psychology, University of Michigan, Ann Arbor, Michigan

Charles A. Nelson III, PhD, Division of Developmental Medicine, Children's Hospital Boston, and Department of Pediatrics, Harvard Medical School, Boston, Massachusetts

Beth Anne Newman, BA, School of Education, University of North Carolina, Chapel Hill, North Carolina

Sarah M. Ngo, MEd, Department of Curriculum and Instruction, Lynch School of Education, Boston College, Boston, Massachusetts

Erica Odom, PhD, FPG Child Development Institute and School of Social Work, University of North Carolina, Chapel Hill, North Carolina

Samuel L. Odom, PhD, FPG Child Development Institute and School of Education, University of North Carolina, Chapel Hill, North Carolina

Peter A. Ornstein, PhD, Department of Psychology, University of North Carolina, Chapel Hill, North Carolina

Sharon Ritchie, EdD, FPG Child Development Institute and School of Social Work, University of North Carolina, Chapel Hill, North Carolina

Dwight Rogers, PhD, School of Education, University of North Carolina, Chapel Hill, North Carolina

Robert S. Siegler, PhD, Department of Psychology, Carnegie Mellon University, Pittsburgh, Pennsylvania

Anna Stetsenko, PhD, Subprogram in Developmental Psychology, PhD Program in Psychology, The Graduate Center, City University of New York, New York, New York

Paola Strozzi, PhD, Preschool and Infant Toddler Centers, Institute of the Municipality of Reggio Emilia, Reggio Emilia, Italy

Patricia R. Sylvester, PhD, School of Education, University of North Carolina, Chapel Hill, North Carolina

Janet E. Thompson, MA, Center for Child and Family Studies, University of California, Davis, California

Ross A. Thompson, PhD, Department of Psychology, University of California, Davis, California

Kelly K. Twibell, MS, Center for Child and Family Studies, University of California, Davis, California

Lieven Verschaffel, PhD, Center for Instructional Psychology and Technology, Department of Educational Sciences, University of Leuven, Leuven, Belgium

Eduardo Vianna, PhD, Department of Social Science, LaGuardia Community College, City University of New York, Long Island City, New York

Stella Vosniadou, PhD, Department of Philosophy and History of Science, National and Kapodistrian University of Athens, Athens, Greece

Barbara Hanna Wasik, PhD, School of Education and FPG Child Development Institute, University of North Carolina, Chapel Hill, North Carolina

Gordon Wells, PhD, Department of Education, University of California, Santa Cruz, California

Amanda P. Williford, PhD, Center for Advanced Study of Teaching and Learning, University of Virginia, Charlottesville, Virginia

Preface

The idea for this handbook originated in discussions within the International Committee of the Society for Research in Child Development (SRCD) when Oscar Barbarin served as its Chair. The committee identified education as an issue that would be of interest in all corners of the globe. Reflecting both concerns and hopes, education is widely viewed in strikingly similar ways as essential to the advancement of national interests in geographical areas as diverse as Africa and Europe, North America and Asia. The common thread connecting these global hopes and concerns is the recognition of the contribution that quality basic and advanced school education can make to social welfare and economic prosperity in times that demand a well-trained workforce and a well-informed citizenry. Linked to its promise as an engine of economic development is the gnawing concern across countries that their educational systems are failing to deliver and to provide the needed technological competence, creativity, and problem-solving skills. Questions are raised across the board, from the adequacy of pedagogy, curriculum, and teacher training to issues of social, economic, and gender equity in access to quality education. These problems are complex and permit no easy solution.

Developmental science has much to offer in addressing these concerns. However, too little of this body of work has found its way into teacher education and classroom practice. There are many good reasons for this. Applications of research findings to teaching and learning are difficult because they require additional efforts in translating basic research to make it accessible to those who prepare curricula and train teachers. Working seminars that bring researchers and educators into cross-disciplinary conversations offer one way to address this disconnection between development of science and educational practice. The SRCD International Committee pursued such a strategy by creating a Successful Schools Working Group to explore diverse approaches to problems commonly faced in the education of children and adolescents around the world, and to extract principles from existing conceptual models and research that might help to guide the design of education programs. The Successful Schools Working Group, which includes Oscar Barbarin, Kevin Miller, Anna Stetsenka, Chuansheng Chen, and Beth Kurtz-Costes, proposed a series of conferences on the topic of Schooling and Development. The first in the series, a seminar focused on early education, was carried out jointly with the Frank Porter Graham (FPG) Child Development Institute at the University of North Carolina, Chapel Hill. The seminar was made possible through the financial support of First School (FPG) and SRCD. The seminar series took place at FPG and at the SRCD biennial meeting in Boston. Web-based technology made possible global access to the seminar presentations held at the Institute in North Carolina.

The developmental science and early education seminar comprised working meetings, built around invited papers, seminar presentations, and problem-solving discussions. The principal aim of the seminar was to review topics in developmental science (e.g., developmental neuroscience, cognition and memory, socioemotional development, language and literacy development) and to consider their implications for curriculum and instruction in pre-K to third-grade (P–3) schools. A group of distinguished developmental scholars, applied researchers, and practitioners with interest and expertise in P–3 curriculum design and instruction constituted the core members of the working sessions. The working seminar explored ways that knowledge of children's development may be used to inform the design of schools, curriculum, and instruction for young children who might attend these innovative schools. These invited scholars presented their recent research on a topic related to learning, memory, neuroscience, social development, self-regulation, socialization, or emotional health in early childhood. The presenters at the working seminar included Patricia Bauer, Robert Siegler, David Klahr, Peter Ornstein, Rochel Gelman, Susan Calkins, Fred Morrison, Maria Bartolini Bussi, Stella Vosniadou, Catherine Snow, Charles Nelson, Marc Bornstein, Dan Wagner, and Erik de Corte.

In addition, educational scholars and practitioners with expertise in P–3 standards, curriculum development, or instruction, as well as those involved in the planning of the First School curriculum, participated in the working seminar. This group represented different areas of literacy, numeracy, science, socioemotional competence, social studies, and the arts. To accomplish the goal of linking developmental science to early education, seminar participants were asked to prepare papers that summarized research in their area of specialization and to consider how the research might be applied to early education. Along with educational scholars and practitioners, they discussed the implications of development for a wide range of issues, such as school readiness, standards, curriculum, pedagogy assessment, and professional development. The seminar also had a more focused goal. It was intended to glean from developmental research ideas that could be used in the redesign of the children's early school experiences being considered by and planned as the First School initiative at FPG.

This handbook arises from the intellectual fruits of the combined efforts represented in the invited papers, the seminar discussion, and subsequent reflection in the time following the seminar. The *Handbook* draws upon empirical research but focuses less on research methods and more on translation of empirically derived insights and principles, so that they can be applied to the classroom. It represents an effort to make the rich exchange of ideas in the seminar available to a wider audience that could not participate in the seminar but was interested in the design and implementation of curriculum and instruction in early childhood. This includes, of course, early childhood and primary education faculty, researchers, and teachers themselves. The *Handbook* is especially intended to be a resource for those involved in teacher preparation. Moreover, the discussion of critical issues and gaps in our knowledge arouses the interest of early childhood education researchers as well. It is also likely to find use as a supplemental text in undergraduate and graduate courses, and possibly programs of inservice training for professional teachers.

Chapters have been prepared both by renowned developmentalists, whose work has relevance for teaching and learning, and by highly skilled, developmentally oriented scholar-practitioners, who serve as a bridge between developmentalists and classroom teachers. In many ways this latter group had the most difficult task of distilling important research and translating data into ideas that might be applied in the classroom. Their writing complements that of empirical scholars by considering the implications of this body of work for educational practice, particularly curriculum and instruction. Once readers of this volume have read them, we are confident that they will come to the same conclusion we did. The writers rose to the challenge and did an admirable job! If successful, this handbook will help the reader identify important principles emerging from developmental science that are relevant to the learning and teaching of children 3 to 8 years old. The value of this contribution is, of course, attributable to the scholars who generously gave of their time to participate in the seminar and to share the fruits of their reflections for others. Thanks are also due to many people behind the scenes, whose labors have made this work possible, and to Emma Sterritt, whose editorial assistance was invaluable.

OSCAR A. BARBARIN
BARBARA HANNA WASIK

Contents

PART I

DEVELOPMENT AND EARLY EDUCATION

The chapters in this section offer a broad introduction to the context of early childhood education and the role that psychological theory and research can play in resolving some of the key dilemmas confronting early education. In Chapter 1, Oscar A. Barbarin and Kevin Miller review some of the critical problems in contemporary early childhood education and identify significant contributions that developmental science can make to early education.

Sharon Ritchie, Kelly L. Maxwell, and Sue Bredekamp (Chapter 2) identify and discuss four foundational processes that underlie children's developing competence and predict success in school across the span from prekindergarten through third grade (P–3). These predictive processes of early learning and development include self-regulation, representational thought, memory, and attachment. Discussion of these processes prefigures later chapters that focus on specific developmental science advances in each of these areas.

Anna Stetsenko and Eduardo Vianna (Chapter 3) make the case for the utility of developmental theory in guiding educational practice in early childhood. They focus especially on the contributions of Vygotsky and his latter-day disciples. This intellectual tradition has provided important intellectual underpinnings for notions of developmentally appropriate practice commonly invoked in early childhood education. The chapter provides a theoretical background for subsequent chapters on construction of mathematical meaning by Maria G. Bartolini Bussi and Mara Boni (Chapter 20) and on spatial representation by Rossana Falcade and Paola Strozzi (Chapter 22), which derive much of their conceptual inspiration from Vygotsky.

Theoretical insights from this section offer a broad perspective on the current debate on developmentally sensitive practice that is at the heart the para-

1

digmatic clash between preschool viewpoints and those infusing K–12 education. Conceptual traces of the work of Vygotsky and his disciples can be found in many of the assumptions about what constitutes developmentally appropriate practice. This includes notions such as scaffolding, the zone of proximal development, children as active agents in learning, and the importance of child–teacher interactions. Consciously or not, many of the issues that animate discussion of the First School Initiative and other efforts to promote a P–3 continuum in school described here were anticipated by this body of research and theorizing. Notably, the extent to which children acquire knowledge and master skills is as much a consequence of interactions in the child's social world as they are a function of predetermined traits or the preexisting structures of the child's mind. Specifically, variations in developmental outcomes have as much to do with the qualities of interactions with adults, and in the material resources and cultural artifacts to which children have access, as they do to inherited traits. Most importantly, this theory underscores the notion that children develop and master important ideas through mundane experiences and interactions with their social worlds, and the materials available to them in those worlds.

Another aspect of the theory that is widely used in P–3 education is the notion of scaffolding. Here the theory underscores the value of building on the foundation of knowledge that children already possess and connecting new skills to existing competencies. The emphasis here is on how adult intervention matches up with the child's conceptual skills and fund of knowledge. The insights provided by Stetsenko and Vianna constitute ideas that have important implications for curriculum development and for pedagogy.

CHAPTER 1

Developmental Science and Early Education

An Introduction

Oscar A. Barbarin
Kevin Miller

The productivity of any modern society rests heavily on the success of its educational system in preparing its children to become skilled and engaged adults. The major conceptual frameworks developed within developmental science in the early to mid-20th century serve today as the source of inspiration and knowledge for teachers and educators. Much of contemporary education is grounded in these frameworks, in particular those offered by Piaget, Dewey, and Vygotsky. However, in view of the remarkable progress made in recent decades, there is a need today to transfer more recent insights and to upgrade the knowledge base that informs educational practice. Recent research in developmental science has brought about profound changes in our understanding of the conditions that facilitate children's learning and development, demonstrating the fundamentally dynamic and relational nature of learning and development. Recent discoveries regarding brain development, memory, children's early mathematical abilities, and the crucial role of social interactions and use of cultural tools provide startling insights that, if translated into pedagogy, then have the potential of transforming instruction and improving outcomes for all children.

Although spectacular progress has been achieved in developmental science and neighboring disciplines, researchers working at the front lines of science do not always have the time or the incentives to think deeply about the implications of their work for educators, and to translate their ideas and findings into the working tools that can be used in educational practices. This handbook represents a modest contribution toward this much-needed translation. This volume is based on an assumption that basic developmental science has been engaged in theory development and empirical work that has relevance for educational practice. Strong disagreement with this assumption is rare but explicit application of developmental theory and research to questions related to curriculum, standards, pedagogy, and learning requires intentional, intensive, and thoughtful analysis. The *Handbook*'s rationale is precisely to distill innovative ideas of potential educational relevance out of recent research and theories in developmental psychology and to communicate them to the teachers, policymakers, educators, and other professionals concerned with educating children. In a small way, efforts such as these link developmental scientists to the important public policy goal of bringing desperately needed improvements to the ways we educate our young children. Although early childhood education has been identified as a cost-effective investment that potentially benefits children, families, and society, the current system has many problems to be solved before it can realize its promise. In spite of our highest aspirations and substantial investment in pre-K to third grade (P–3) education, we still have a long ways to go in providing consistently high-quality programs as we expand pre-K and place more stringent demands for academic achievement in the early primary grades. The quality of many pre-K programs is disappointingly low. Pre-K programs appear to have difficulty incorporating the demands for cognitive and academic gains with the broader set of needs related to children's physical and social development, and family members' needs for support as they participate in the workforce (Clifford et al., 2005) Many pre-K and primary school programs are neither developmentally appropriate nor family-centered, and they lack effective transition practices and continuity between the grades. The sources of problems in this situation are many. They fall most often within the domains of curriculum, pedagogy, workforce preparation, training, and compensation.

Though deep and serious, these problems can be solved through careful but innovative thought and concerted action. One comprehensive approach to these problems is represented in the P–3 movement, of which the First School Initiative at the University of North Carolina Frank Porter Graham (FPG) Child Development Institute is an example. The seminar whose deliberations formed the basis for this handbook was designed to contribute to those initiatives by reviewing research in developmental science that might inform the conception and planning of First School, an innovative initiative to educate America's young children that requires a radical shift in thinking about how we should educate children ages 3 to 8. First School and P–3 are intended to provide templates for the reform of early educational structures, so that the multiple systems serving young children are integrated into a single system and located in a single setting that provides a seamless transition for children ages 3–8 from one level of learning to the next. This integration requires an organizational and curricular realignment of children's first school experience, with attention to how children vary and change during this developmentally active period. The P–3 movement emphasizes practices that are sensitive to individual developmental needs, and that provide appropriately rich and cognitively engaging curricula to foster childrens' intellectual, physical, and emotional development. Changing the organizational arrangement of early childhood education to join pre-K with K–3 schools is just a first step and is not sufficient by itself to achieve the aims of the P–3 movement. Deeper, more fundamental changes are needed to go to the heart of how schools conceive of their role, how they function, what they teach, and the commitment they have to address the needs of the most vulnerable children, who currently do not benefit as fully from school as they might. Thus, in addition to addressing the developmental needs of the student population as a whole, the P–3 movement must also generate specific ways to address the needs of populations that currently are not being well served in education. These populations include ethnic/minority group, second language learners, and children with special needs, and children from economically disadvantaged households. First School and P–3 must also consider and develop ways to address the wide-ranging cultural and linguistic diversity that now characterizes public schools. To be successful, the design of First School and P–3 must incorporate strategies and processes that promote social inclusion of these diverse groups. To address these issues successfully means that First School and other P–3 efforts must address the broader issues of standards, curriculum, pedagogy, and professional development. These issues have presented significant challenges to schools and can be a source of difficulty at an organizational and interpersonal level. In the end, if the P–3 movement is successful, it will have integrated the best of the developmentally sensitive approaches of preschool with the more coherent and content-rich focus of early elementary education.

First School is not just a pipe dream or the starry-eyed imaginings of romantic fringe groups in education. It embodies a conception of early education that according to many sober observers of education has the potential to address many of the concerns raised about losing children and youth to underachievement and school dropout. Reform of early education along these lines is being considered by many and implemented in a few school districts around the country. In many parts of the United States we can find isolated examples of individual schools that have successfully melded pre-K and early elementary classrooms into a single school serving P–3 students in a single building, with the goal of using an integrated curriculum and developmentally sensitive pedagogy. If successful, the First School movement is likely to spawn prototypes of similar schools that combine early childhood and early elementary education, perhaps paving the way to widespread adoption of one of the most significant changes in public education since the initiation of kindergarten. (For more information about First School go to *www.fpg. unc.edu/~firstschool.*)

Integrating early education and K–12 education is intellectually and politically challenging. What is the need for the innovations proposed by First School? What problem is it intended to solve? The answers to these questions arise from the limitations seen in current approaches to pre-K and early elementary education, and in the gap between approaches used to serve these children with very similar developmental needs. Educators who work with children ages 3–5 often begin with different assumptions and adopt different methods than do educators who work with children ages 5–8, in spite of the striking continuity in issues affecting the education of children across this age range.

Great dismay has arisen among early childhood practitioners over the developmental appropriateness of elementary schools. The concern takes on immediacy in light of efforts to integrate and to make early childhood programs part of elementary school education. Practitioners fear that the procedures, curricula, and organization of K–12 education will be pushed down into preschool and replace the existing emphasis on developmentally appropriate practices with rigidly prescribed curricula and group instruction. The current chasm between early childhood and elementary education neither serves children well nor is it sustainable in the long run. Nevertheless, professionals on the early childhood side are often skeptical that current efforts to make pre-K a part of public elementary schools will result in a smooth transitions for both groups of children throughout their first school experience. Currently, the shift from developmentally appropriate, child-centered pre-K instruction to more formal didactic and curriculum-based K–1 teaching is often abrupt. In simple terms, early childhood professionals fear that the "gold standard" for pre-K classroom organization, curriculum, and pedagogy will be kindergarten and first grade. This possibility is worrisome because kindergarten and first grade rely on curricula and standards that are downward extensions of higher grade curricula that utilize standardized tests, workbooks, ability grouping, and retention, and eschew child-centered practices that are considered appropriate to the developmental stage of 3- to 8-year-old children. This often results in competitive, overly academic environments, with curricula that fail to accommodate the variation of competencies that are often present among children of the same chronological age. Many early childhood practitioners feel that the push toward integration will result in loss of the developmentally appropriate practices that are so fundamental to the way they conceptualize teaching and learning.

The preparation of early childhood teachers has a strong focus on child development, which often sensitizes them to individual differences and the use of exploratory play in their work with children. Consequently, their grounding in theories of child development becomes integral to their professional identities, and they are committed to what is called "developmentally appropriate practice" (DAP). Often the DAP operating principle is that the child will indicate when he or she is ready to acquire some new skill. The working assumption is that until this revelation occurs, the child is incapable and will not learn that new skill, and attempts at direct instruction may be frustrating for the child and, in the end, futile. In this way, DAP may be a handicap because it focuses educators more on the limitations of children's unfolding capacity to acquire information than on what children understand and can learn. As a consequence, teachers may be more attuned to the errors in children's thinking than to the insights that these errors reveal about how children learn. Errors in children's thinking are perceived as a wall arresting progress rather than an opening to facilitate learning and development. Moreover, some early childhood teachers question the value and relevance of curriculum for pre-K when "curriculum" is defined as standardized content presented in an ordered sequence. As a consequence of the beliefs associated with DAP, teachers take an agnostic point of view and let children teach them about what they can know and learn through self-selection of activities and the display of interest; that is, in the absence of fixed notions about what children ought to learn, good teachers following DAP are more often responsive and react to children's invitations or inclinations toward knowledge development. This approach centers on process more than on content. DAP pedagogy often emphasizes the role of the child as active learner and co-constructor of knowledge. In this interactive approach to learning, the role of the teacher is to create settings that are organized and elicit active engagement because they are stimulating and responsive to children's interests and capabilities. The desired outcomes of this approach include thinking critically, working cooperatively, solving problems, and having fun in the process. The strong developmental emphasis can have the unintended consequence of focusing the teacher on what children are unable to do because ostensibly they have not yet developed specific competencies. The operating principle is that children are not ready, and they will let you know when they are ready, to learn. Children's effectiveness in communicating when they are ready to learn rests heavily on teachers' ability to observe and to detect nascent capabilities. However, the developmental lenses through which teachers observe young children may lead them to underestimate what children can know and learn. As a consequence, they may hesitate to stretch or to challenge children sufficiently. In this case, early childhood educators avoid the danger of overwhelming children and demanding more than they can give, but they risk leaving children less stimulated and with fewer skills than they might otherwise have acquired. The danger is lower levels of skills development. Although preschools are beginning to adopt structured curricula developed by publishing companies to achieve these outcomes and to focus on literacy development, this is not yet the norm.

Whereas early childhood programs have traditionally lacked standards-based content, elementary school programs typically use curricula with defined content standards (e.g., in reading, language, math, social studies, science, and the arts) and rely on intentional instructional practices to convey that content (e.g., direct instruction, demonstration and modeling, cooperative learning, skills-based intervention, cognitively guided instruction and inquiry). As a consequence, effective teachers in the K–12 system must be well versed in subject-matter content intended to produce outcomes stated in the learning standards adopted by the state and local school district. This content focus is also reflected in the use of a specific curriculum, lesson plan, and instructional materials provided for teachers' use by the schools.

The approaches used by pre-K and K–12 educators have complementary strengths and corresponding limitations. Though sensitive to developmental and individual differences, early childhood professionals may have limited repertoires of content and methods for use in intentional instruction. More often than not, they lack specific content related, for example, to language, literacy, numeracy, or socioemotional development. Though often knowledgeable about multiple content areas and teaching approaches, elementary school teachers typically lack a developmental lens through which to examine students' readiness for and response to the methods used in curriculum-based work. Their curricular content and teaching methods are largely divorced from, and fail to draw upon, insights about variations, due to individual differences in learning styles and to children's developing capacities.

These differences in pedagogy and curriculum experienced by children as they make the transition from pre-K to elementary school pose difficult adjustment challenges for children and raise questions about whether each approach is doing the best it can for the children it serves. An important contribution to the concept of P–3 education would be to unite the best practices of early childhood and elementary education by bringing a developmental perspective to the content and instructional practices of early elementary education, and by specifying content and intentional pedagogy within the developmentally sensitive practices of early childhood experiences.

A central issue addressed by this handbook is the dilemma represented by the failure to connect basic research findings to educational practice and child outcomes. The divide between research and practice is especially wide for early childhood education. This chapter begins by arguing for a reconceptualization of early schooling, juxtaposing national data that document the burgeoning state-funded pre-K data showing the relatively low quality and isolation of these pre-K programs. The authors describe national efforts to rethink public schooling for children ages 3 to 8, focusing on the theme of uniting knowledge and practice from several fields (e.g., developmental psychology, early childhood education, elementary education) into a more effective blueprint for early schooling. Disappointing educational outcomes and the failure of research to inform practices have led policymakers and research funders to call for harvesting more fully the fruits of basic research for improving P–12 education. Bridging the divide between research and practice is easier said than done. Successful integration requires proper framing of issues and engaging thoughtful people on both sides of the divide in a joint conversation about the implications of research for practice. Distilling useful information from developmental science requires that researchers answer several critical questions. What contributions can developmental science make to educational practice? What are reasonable expectations about what children know and can learn? How is learning best facilitated? How do individual differences moderate childrens' ability to learn and the best methods for teaching them? Creating a dialogue between researchers and educators around these issues is complicated by divergence in language, perspective, knowledge, experiences and worldviews. Often mediation is required by persons in the uneasy position of having a foot on each side of the divide. Many of the authors who contributed to this handbook occupy the space between developmental science and education, and understand the need to remain grounded in the realities of educating young children while they bring knowledge from developmental science to the issues of early childhood.

Critical Questions

How do we improve early childhood education? How can we infuse insights from developmental science into the design and implementation of early education curricula and pedagogy? Differences between early childhood education and K–12 education focus our understanding of children's capacity to learn and help us to appreciate individual differences and abilities, the role of development in the unfolding of children's skills, the appropriateness of educational standards or the content of curricula, the intentionality of pedagogy, and the adequacy of professional development of teachers.

Resolution of the many questions and dilemmas confronting early education may significantly impact the quality of children's early schooling. These critical issues and questions can be categorized into several themes or dimensions: children's capacity to learn, development over time, individual differences, curricula, pedagogy, assessment, professional development, student–teacher relationships, and parental involvement (see Table 1.1). These issues represent gaps in our knowledge, unresolved disagreements, and areas of misunderstanding that result in ill-conceived interventions, mistaken beliefs, half-baked ideas, and misapplication of theory or research. There are problems in each of these domains that continue to undermine or erode the effectiveness of early childhood education.

Development

With respect to the application of developmental theory, early childhood educators' claim that they use developmentally sensitive practices has been open to challenge. Traditional early childhood professionals believe that they are already addressing children's learning and thinking. An important area of concern is what teachers are taught or take away from developmental coursework about children's capacity to learn. There is much to suggest that we have largely underestimated the capacity of young children to develop

TABLE 1.1. Questions Confronting Early Childhood

Capacity to learn	What capabilities do children possess that enable them to acquire knowledge and skills related to literacy, mathematics, and science?
Development	What is developing during the ages 3–8? If we consider developmental changes and variations, what caveats must be observed in curriculum and instruction across the 3- to 8-year-old age span? What key theoretical constructs and empirical findings from developmental science provide a basis for curriculum content and instructional strategies? Do capabilities and limits vary across time? Is there an evolving set of biological, neurological, and experiential processes that interact to determine what children are capable of at a specific point in time?
Individual differences	How do capabilities and limits vary across individuals? When is differentiated classroom instruction warranted for gifted children and children with special needs? What are the special competencies and limitations of English language learners, and how can they be addressed in curriculum and instruction?
Academic standards	What are the critical competencies to be mastered in the area of language, literacy, numeracy, and socioemotional development, and what are the developmental opportunities for mastery during this 3- to 8-year-old age span? What skills should be expected and what knowledge should gained to produce desired outcomes and prepare children for later life? How do we infuse considerations of development into P–3 standards-based curriculum across this age span?
Curricula	Which content areas may be taught across the span of early childhood ages 3–8? Do the ideas and skills build on one another? Is there a specific sequence in which material should be covered? In what areas does the sequence of presentation matter for children's mastery?
Pedagogy	How do children learn, and how should they be taught? What practices help all children develop the knowledge, skills, and confidence necessary to be active citizens in a diverse and democratic society? What are the relative merits/effectiveness of team teaching, and looping (i.e., the same teacher teaches the same children for more than 1 year)? How do we foster and build on literacy, language, and numeracy skills in a systematic and integrated manner across the age span of 3 to 8 years? What instructional approaches might be beneficial for children ages 3–5? How can math and science instruction be introduced to 3- and 4-year-olds?
Assessment	What are the purposes of assessment, and how can assessments be designed to attain their ends? What role does assessment play in instruction?
Professional development	Who should teach? What do they need to know? How should they be prepared? What forms of support are needed to advance teachers' skills? How do we reach those who are teaching? How do we help teachers master effective new procedures?
Relationships	How important are teacher–child relationships to academic achievement? How do child–teacher and home–school relationships contribute to children's mastery of these critical competencies?
Family involvement	What is the proper role of parents in the education of young children? What is meaningful parent participation in schooling? What does participation look like, both in and out of school? How do schools facilitate/sustain family participation across ethnic and economically diverse groups?

competence in a variety of areas, particularly math and language, especially between ages 2 and 5. The problem is that their courses are often limited to a general treatment of Piagetian or Vygotskian ideas, and do not focus in a useful way on what this means for children's understanding and learning. Student teachers are often taught the fixed Piagetian stages of development but may be unaware of the critical role of interactions among prior knowledge, development, and learning. Preservice teachers often conclude that the theory presented in college course, even when it is up to date, is "academic" and irrelevant to what they need to understand and do in the classroom.

Individual Differences

Children are not all made from the same mold. Individual differences are critical to understand and to address. Some of these differences emerge from heritable traits, from experience and prior exposure to information; others emerge from concurrent life circumstances. These all need to be factored into pedagogy and in understanding how children learn. Many children, especially those growing up in poor households, lack experiences that might have prepared them for the language and discourse styles of schools. Children do not begin school on an equal footing. There is mounting evidence of an achievement gap between minority and majority student populations. A number of studies over the past decade have shown that this gap appears early—before children enter kindergarten. One of the most recent studies, which analyzed data from the Early Childhood Longitudinal Study—Kindergarten cohort (ECLS-K), looked at children's achievement scores in literacy and math as they began their kindergarten year. The researchers found that socioeconomic status (SES) accounted for a large proportion of the variance in children's scores—above that accounted for by race or family environment. However, the researchers noted that black and Hispanic children are more likely than white children to come from families in the lowest SES category. Being from one of these minority groups and coming from the lowest SES category accounted for one-half of a standard deviation in achievement scores (Lee & Burkam, 2002). Recognition of this problem was a primary motivation for public sponsored pre-K programs. It has led to the calls to provide high-quality early childhood education for all 3- and 4-year-olds. Although several countries already serve 3- and 4-year-olds in public school, this is now an uncommon practice in the United States, but it is expected to increase as part of the effort to improve the prospects of school success for children at risk of school failure. In this regard, schools face three challenges: (1) responsiveness to cultural and linguistic diversity in early childhood education; (2) inclusion of young learners with disabilities and children with widely varying abilities, ranging from major disabilities to exceptional potential; and (3) inclusion of children from diverse ethnic, linguistic, and racial backgrounds. In attempting to address this diversity and individual difference, educators are confronted with questions about how to think about ability grouping. Are we contributing to inequities, or is the price of separate instruction by ability groups an effective way to respond to and perhaps remedy individual differences? What do we know about the effects of ability grouping? Will the effects differ depending on the age or circumstances of the children?

A perennial problem is the extent to which each state's academic standards set by educational policymakers align with the curriculum and reflect what takes place in every classroom. Alignment is a goal, but few states would claim to have successfully dealt with the issue of making the curriculum reflect the desired and mandated educational outcomes. A "curriculum" is a planned sequence of teaching–learning activity. Curriculum should focus on increased competence in multiple domains: cognitive, motor, behavioral, and socioemotional. The lack of alignment among standards, curricula, and instruction, and the differences across pre-K and K–12 education in each of them, may contribute to the difficulty some children experience in making the transition from pre-K to kindergarten.

Access to effective teaching is also an issue that needs attention. Effective teaching is often considered to comprise coherent development of ideas, supportive feedback, and use of multiple methods of instruction; ongoing assessment is used to individualize or modify instruction; and tasks are targeted to offer a moderate level of challenge for the child. All approaches to pedagogy should begin with the notion that children should be treated as active participants in shaping knowledge and in learning. Few school administrators and educational policymakers would quarrel with the observation that more and better professional development is need both for preservice and inservice teachers. Degrees, by themselves, do not appear to be a sufficient marker of teacher quality. Early and colleagues (2007) found no relationship between teachers' degrees and classroom quality or child academic outcomes. Classroom-relevant training, especially training that focuses on children's development, was related to the quality of instructional interactions in pre-K classrooms. Assessment may play an important role in improving academic outcomes, especially if it enables teachers to provide feedback to students and directs them toward alternative instructional approaches.

Relationships

Family involvement in children's education has come to mean many things. It is clear that conceptions of family involvement need to go beyond volunteering in the classroom or being active in school organizations. Research indicates that children enter school with significant differences in language and reading abilities, differences in home experiences and parental practices that may encourage development of these abilities. Efforts to encourage family involvement in children's education should focus on what parents do at home to nurture and support development of children's skills and involvement in academic activities. Questions remain about specific practices that seem to matter, and how to engage families with limited education and low English language proficiency in children's academic skills development.

Serious questions need to be addressed about how best to insinuate and integrate insights from these advances into educational policy and practice. Questions can be raised about the extent to which development reflects standards set for early childhood education. To what extent do current curricula reflect recent insights from research on brain development and children's thinking, learning, and memory? What does developmental science have to offer with respect to decisions that teachers and curriculum developers make about what to teach children, about the sequence and timing in teaching new skills?

We do not want to overpromise or to be overzealous in our claims about the value of developmental science and its ability to address all the issues facing early education. Clearly, there are some aspects of early education that developmental science has not addressed, and areas that, even when addressed, provide incomplete answers.

What Developmental Science and Early Education Have to Offer to Each Other

As developmental psychology and educational research have developed, an unfortunate division of labor between psychologists and educational researchers has ill-served both our understanding of the nature and limits of child development and our efforts to promote children's healthy cognitive growth. The idea that development and teaching (broadly construed) are inherently bound up in each other is not new, nor is the complaint that researchers have failed to consider learning and development in synchrony. As far back as 1930, Vygotsky (1930/1978) argued that one cannot understand teaching, learning, or development without understanding the relations among them.

Yet the interdependence among developmental processes, learning, and the environmental factors that may promote them is something that is still largely honored in the breach. If, for example, one looks at developmental journal articles on children's literacy or mathematical development, it is rare to find any description of the educational practices of the schools and preschools that children attend. It is also still rare in studies of teachers' thinking and teaching practices to find data on how students interpret those practices or citations about the effects of the relevant literature on student thinking.

The tendency of researchers to focus on development *or* learning *or* educational practices has led to educational advice that leans heavily on one or another of these isolated bodies of research. The titles and to some extent the text of books by developmental researchers (e.g., *The Scientist in the Crib* by Gopnik, Meltzoff, & Kuhl, 1999) have promoted an image of the heroic child who is the author of his or her own development. In some extreme cases this has led to advice such as the following: "Children at different stages cannot learn the same content. They cannot learn about number, for example, until they reach the concrete operational stage" (Copeland, 1984, p. 12).

Yet there are some very encouraging signs that researchers are moving beyond a conceptually suspect division of labor between developmental and educational research, and that these steps toward integration lead to findings that are both theoretically rich and of direct practical significance. One need look no further than this volume to see examples of this emerging synthesis. For example, Siegler (Chapter 19, this volume) has shown that a very brief experience with a board game can produce a massive increase in children's understanding of the magnitude of cardinal numbers, a key insight that not all children bring to school. Because school entry-level mathematical achievement is a strong predictor of later academic success (Duncan et al., 2007) and because this early understanding is associated with social class, research such as Siegler's holds great promise for mitigating some of the massive and increasing achievement gaps related to ethnicity and social class.

The First School provides a key way to help children over a major social threshold, that between "preschool" and "school." It can also help to provide a needed intellectual focus that will both enrich developmental science and make it more useful to society. By understanding the myriad ways in which children slip in moving from home and informal settings to school, and how schools and other social influences can help to ensure a successful transition, developmental science is broadening its scope, from an early focus on the endogenous growth of heroic children to a deeper understanding of how young children traverse the social webs that help them weave their own intellectual development.

Developmental science has much to bring to this partnership. We have a long tradition of taking children's thinking seriously, and understanding the ways in which children may reason consistently and coherently yet reach different conclusions than do adults. Vosniadou's work (Chapter 24, this volume) provides a good example. Vosniadou and Brewer (1992) reported that some children reconcile what they hear about "the Earth" (a blue globe floating in space) with their daily experience of a flat planet by postulating two entities: "the world" where they live, and "the Earth" that is in space. This can be demonstrated by asking them to point to "the Earth" (children with this view will point upward). Only by taking children's thinking seriously will we understand the misconceptions they demonstrate. Only by attending as well to the content and contexts in which they learn about the world will we be able to come up with a deep and helpful understanding of the evolution of children's thinking. The chapters in this volume provide a great illustration of the intellectual and practical promise of this new synthesis.

As a final note, chapters in this handbook are organized into five sections around (1) a general introduction to the theory, context, and processes of early education; (2) brain functioning and learning; (3) socioemotional functioning; (4) language and literacy; and (5) mathematics and science. It reflects the ideas and insight emanating from interactions among developmental researchers and participants in the SRCD-FPG seminar on Developmental Science and Early Schooling. Chapters present developmental research in ways that point to implications for the processes involved in early childhood education, including learning, teaching, teacher preparation and development, and the design of curricula and instructional methods.

References

Clifford, R. M., Barbarin, O. A., Chang, F., Early, D. M., Bryant, D., Howes, C., et al. (2005). What is pre-kindergarten?: Characteristics of public pre-kindergarten programs. *Applied Developmental Science, 9*, 126–143.

Copeland, R. W. (1984). *How children learn mathematics* (4th ed.). New York: Macmillan.

Duncan, G. J., Dowsett, C. J., Claessens, A., Magnusson, K., Huston, A. C., Klebanov, P., et al. (2007). School readiness and later achievement. *Developmental Psychology, 43*, 1428–1446.

Early, D., Maxwell, K., Burchinal, M., Soumya, A., Bender, R., Bryant, D., et al. (2007). Teachers' education, classroom quality and young children's academic skills: Results from seven studies of preschool programs. *Child Development, 76*, 558–580.

Gopnik, A., Meltzoff, A. N., & Kuhl, P. K. (1999). *The scientist in the crib: Minds, brains, and how children learn.* New York: Morrow.

Lee V., & Burkam, D. T. (2002). *Inequality at the starting gate: Social background differences in achievement as children begin school.* Washington, DC: Economic Policy Institute.

Vosniadou, S., & Brewer, W. F. (1992). Mental models of the earth: A study of conceptual change in childhood. *Cognitive Psychology, 24*, 535–585.

Vygotsky, L. S. (1978). Interaction between learning and development. In *Mind in society: The development of higher psychological processes* (M. Cole & V. John-Steiner, Trans. & Eds.). Cambridge, MA: Harvard University Press. (Original work published 1930)

CHAPTER 2

Rethinking Early Schooling

*Using Developmental Science
to Transform Children's Early School Experiences*

**Sharon Ritchie
Kelly L. Maxwell
Sue Bredekamp**

The United States is at a turning point in public education. For many children, school begins before the traditional age of 5 when they enter kindergarten. Public schools across the country are providing early care and education for children as young as age 3. In fact, nearly a million 4-year-olds are served in public schools (Barnett, Hustedt, Hawkinson, & Robin, 2006). State and local governments invest billions of dollars in prekindergarten education. By 2020, it is likely that public school in this country will begin at age 4. We have a unique moment in history to determine thoughtfully and strategically the best approaches to use in educating our young children. The decisions we make today will impact children, families, communities, and the American workforce for generations to come. Instead of thinking about integrating young children into the existing public education system, we need instead to turn the question on its head and ask, "What should schools be like to meet the needs of young children and their families?"

We cannot think about pre-K in isolation from the early elementary grades. The national pre-K to third grade (P–3) movement calls for rethinking public education during children's first years of schooling from ages 3 to 8 (Bogard & Takanishi, 2005; Kauerz, 2006; Maeroff, 2006). This age span represents a unique time in children's development. By age 3, most children have successfully mastered oral language skills, although a wide range of variation in children's language ability is influenced by their home experiences (Hart & Risley, 1995).

Between ages 3 and 8, children learn to read and write, so that they can then use those reading and writing skills to learn academic content across curriculum areas. This acquisition of basic skills provides the foundation for later school achievement. By age

14

9, many children are able to read and write. However, data from the National Assessment of Educational Progress, our nation's report card on education, suggests that a substantial number of children do not acquire basic skills by fourth grade (age 9 for most children). For example, only 41% of white fourth-graders are at or above "proficient" in reading, and only 13% of black and 16% of Hispanic children are considered "proficient" in reading (Perie, Grigg, & Donahue, 2005). The findings for math are similar (Perie, Grigg, & Dion, 2005). These data suggest that we need a new approach to children's first schooling experiences to capitalize on this unique foundational period in children's development and school life.

So what should we do? We believe it is important to move away from the idea of "early childhood education" that is separate from "K–12 education," toward an approach that brings together children ages 3–8 into a single system that reflects the best of early childhood, elementary, and special education. Reform efforts like the First School Initiative at the University of North Carolina, Chapel Hill do just that—change schools by uniting ideas, so that school becomes a place for success for all children, especially those most vulnerable to school failure.

The research base for educating children in these early years should draw upon work from many fields. Historically, early childhood education teacher preparation programs have emphasized child development, whereas preparation programs for elementary school teachers have emphasized academic content (e.g., math, literacy). Research has shown that children are more successful when their teachers understand *both* development *and* content (Siraj-Blatchford, Sylva, Muttock, Gilden, & Bell, 2002).

This integration of developmental science and education is the focus of this handbook. Our purposes in this chapter are to provide an introduction to the topic and to underscore some of the key implications of this work for First School in particular and educational practice in general. We also hope to generate a level of excitement that matches our own. We could truly transform school for young children if we implemented what we know about how children develop and learn best.

In the next section, we identify and describe four foundational processes that are central to young children's development and learning. We then highlight how children's first school experiences would be different if we applied what we know from developmental science. In the final section, we discuss the implications of developmental science for teachers' professional development.

Foundational Processes of Early Learning and Development

Early childhood education has a long association with the study of child development. In fact, the primary professional association of developmental researchers—the Society for Research in Child Development (SRCD)—began as a spin-off from the nation's largest organization of early childhood educators, the National Association for the Education of Young Children (NAEYC; 2001). Throughout its history, NAEYC has advocated teaching practices that are informed by knowledge of child development, a concept that has come to be called "developmentally appropriate practice" (Bredekamp & Copple, 1997).

Despite this historical and mutually beneficial connection, early childhood education and developmental science have developed on two parallel tracks. All too often, advances in developmental science seem unrelated or irrelevant to the issues of educating young children. At the same time, early childhood educational practices tend either to ignore findings from science or to reflect outdated theories and research.

This chapter addresses the disconnect between developmental science and early education. Given advances in knowledge across many disciplines, this is a potentially exciting time in education. But unless this new knowledge is adequately translated into practice principles and disseminated to educators, it is unlikely that current approaches to schooling will change.

Several research strands in developmental science have important implications for early education. These include developmental neuroscience, cognition and memory, socioemotional development, and language and literacy development. In general, findings from developmental science can be classified broadly in one of two categories of research findings:

1. Domain-specific, in which the implications of the research is narrowly applicable to a single or a limited number of domains of knowledge, such as science, mathematics, or literacy learning; or
2. Domain-general, in which findings are applicable across a wide range of developmental areas and/or subject matters.

In reflecting on research across these strands, we identified several foundational domain-general developmental processes. Although other important processes could be explored, we focus on the following four foundations of young children's development and learning: self-regulation; representation; memory; and attachment. These four foundational processes appear to underlie children's developing competence and predict success in school across the span from prekindergarten through third grade.

In the sections that follow, we define and describe each of these key processes and offer basic examples to clarify the concepts. Following this discussion of domain-general processes, we address the realities of individual and cultural differences in young children's development and learning. These realities have important implications for both developmental science and early education. We discuss the application of foundational developmental processes to improvement of school practices in later sections of this chapter.

Self-Regulation

Self-regulation is a broad construct that has come to be understood as the cornerstone of development across all domains (Shonkoff & Phillips, 2000). Self-regulation is an integrated, multidimensional construct that incorporates biological processes, attention, emotion, behavior, and cognition. A basic, working definition of "self-regulation" is the ability to regulate or adapt one's behavior, emotions, and thinking according to the demands of the situation (Bodrova & Leong, 2006; Shonkoff & Phillips, 2000).

Researchers study self-regulation from diverse perspectives—including cognitive, social, and emotional. As a result, the term is used to represent many different aspects of children's functioning. Self-regulation from a socioemotional perspective includes emotion regulation, physical regulation, effortful control, compliance, and delay of gratification (Calkins & Williford, Chapter 9, this volume). From a cognitive perspective, self-regulation includes effortful attention, inhibitory control, planning, abiding by rules, working memory, and the overall cognitive construct that is called executive function (Bodrova & Leong, 2006).

For teachers and parents who lack the technical background of developmental scientists, a more practical definition may prove useful. Self-regulation is "the capacity to control one's impulses both to stop doing something that is unnecessary (even if one wants to continue doing it), and to start doing something that *is* needed (even if one does not want to do it)" (Boyd, Barnett, Bodrova, Leong, & Gomby, 2005, p. 4). This definition explains why children's ability to self-regulate is so strongly related to their success in school. Much of school experience requires that children conform to the social demands of the group, pay attention to the teacher, and engage in "on-demand" learning. For example, every day preschool teachers require that children stop playing (which they usually want to continue) and start cleaning up (which is necessary but not what children prefer to do). Similarly, primary grade teachers demand children's attention during group times or for reading instruction.

Recent research finds that self-regulation abilities strongly predict later success in school and life. Self-regulation measured in preschool has been found to predict children's academic success in the early grades, beyond variations in their intelligence or family backgrounds (Blair & Razza, 2007; McClelland, Acock, & Morrison, 2006). On a cautionary note, failures in self-regulation are strongly related to learning difficulties, problematic social relationships, and various forms of psychopathology (Calkins, 2009).

Children's capacity to self-regulate begins in infancy, and individual differences are soon apparent. The capacity to self-regulate both emotions and cognition appears to be related to biological predispositions, but is also influenced by environmental effects, including parenting practices, relationships with peers, and school experiences (Calkins & Williford, Chapter 9, this volume). Therefore, early intervention for children at risk of self-regulation difficulties is important, as is providing experiences in preschool that promote the development of self-regulation.

Toddlerhood appears to be an important transition point in the development of self-regulation (Calkins, 2009). During this early period of development, children who are at high risk for self-regulation difficulties can be identified, and effective intervention strategies can be implemented to enhance long-term outcomes. During preschool, teacher-supported sociodramatic play has been found to be an effective strategy for developing self-regulation (Bodrova & Leong, 2007). Pretend play in small groups is a particularly effective context for promoting self-regulation because it requires children to regulate their own behavior, and to be regulated by others—all within the same context. A group of children may play grocery store, for example. Each child, whether customer, cashier, or store manager, must conform to the rules of his or her role, as well as stick to the script. The customer can't say, "Paper or plastic?" That's the role of the cashier. For the play grocery store to function effectively, each child must and will engage in high-level self-regulation.

As is evident in the foregoing example, dramatic play promotes children's ability to take another person's perspective (Vygotsky, 1966/1977). Assuming a pretend role—being another person for a while—helps children move to another perspective, then back to their own. In addition, attention to the perspectives of other players is critical for coordinating multiple roles and negotiating play scenarios (Hyson, Copple, & Jones,

2006). This ability to take another's perspective, or to "decenter," as it is called, is essential for success in school, where children must align their perspectives with that of teachers or peers. This ability is also necessary for the development of reflective thinking and metacognition (Elkonin, 1978).

Sociodramatic play during preschool is effective in promoting self-regulation, which is important to later school success. In the next section, we describe another foundational process, representational thought, which also is enhanced by children's play experiences in early childhood.

Representational Thought

Children's ability to engage in symbolic representation begins very early in life and is relatively sophisticated by the early grades of school, if adults support this important developmental process. A layperson's definition of "representation" might be using one thing to stand for another. From the perspective of developmental science, mental representations are crucial for higher-level thinking (Hyson et al., 2006).

Human experience is replete with examples of mental or symbolic representation. Verbal language itself is a representation of physical objects, experiences, feelings, and concepts. For example, in English, we use the word *chair* to represent a four-legged object to sit on. Similarly, different languages represent the diverse cultural experiences of the groups among which they developed. For instance, some languages, such as Arabic, have no word for *privacy*, indicating that without the cultural experience, no word is necessary to represent the concept. Written language is perhaps a more obvious example of symbolic representation. In English, 26 symbols—the letters of the alphabet—are used individually or in combination to represent visually approximately 44 sounds of the spoken language. Learning to read is predicated on children's understanding of this alphabetic principle (National Institute of Child Health and Human Development [NICHD], 2000). Thus, we see that developing symbolic representation is essential to the most fundamental skill for successful negotiation of schooling.

But well before children acquire conventional reading and writing abilities, they begin to develop representational abilities through pretend play (Hyson et al., 2006). Initially, very young children use replicas of real objects in their pretend play, such as when a toddler picks up a toy phone and holds it to her ear. If adults encourage this type of play, children begin to substitute other objects in their pretend play, such as when a preschooler pretends a large block is a guitar (Copple, Cocking, & Matthews, 1984). Finally, experienced players engage in pretending without an object, using gestures or speech to represent an object, such as when a child strums an "air guitar" or swings his arms and says, "I'm a monkey." These play experiences help children move from thought that is controlled by physical action (what Piaget called "sensorimotor") to the ability to use words and other symbols to represent concepts (Piaget, 1945/1962; Vygotsky, 1962).

Graphic representation is another developmental process that both contributes to and also reveals children's thinking. "A picture is worth a thousand words" is an overused cliché, but the phrase accurately describes one of the most effective processes through which children develop and demonstrate conceptual understanding.

Teachers use representation is many ways. For example, to teach the concept of "quantity," a preschool teacher may help children create a graph to see whether there are more girls or boys in class. Each child adds a bar to the side of the graph, indicating his or her gender. The higher bar (girls) visually represents the mathematical concept of "more."

Another powerful use of graphic representation for conceptual development is to engage children in creating their own representations. This activity is a defining characteristic of the internationally known Reggio Emilia approach and one of its major contributions to the knowledge base of early childhood education (Edwards, Gandini, & Forman, 1998; Project Zero & Reggio Children, 2001). In Reggio schools, the purpose of representation is to clarify children's understanding. George Forman, one of the earliest disseminators of the Reggio approach to America, described children's use of graphic representation in Reggio as drawing to learn (Landry & Forman, 1999); he explains that by drawing their theories about how the world works, children and teachers gain a better understanding of children's misconceptions and can move toward more accurate theories.

One example of how representation revealed and challenged a child's thinking is related to a study of rain (from the Hundred Languages of Children exhibit, the Commune of Reggio Emilia, Italy; cited in Landry & Forman, 1999). After many days of rain, teachers asked children, "Where do you think rain comes from?" Children expressed various theories (e.g., that God makes the rain). Simone, age 5½, explained, "The sun heats the rain that has fallen and that's how it goes away afterwards, it goes back into the clouds and then it starts to rain again." From her explanation, it seems that Simone has a good understanding of the rain cycle.

After writing down (representing) the children's theories in words, their teacher asked them to draw pictures of where the rain comes from. Simone's detailed drawing included pipes or tubes going up, from the ground to the sky, to convey the water. Thus, by engaging children in graphic representation of their theories, the teacher got a much clearer picture of Simone's misconceptions, despite her seemingly accurate verbal representation.

Graphic representation has been used effectively to study children's developing scientific theories, as well as to understand and to help children clarify their own learning. For example, studies of older children's theories of gravity (why people don't fall off, if the earth is round) draw on the use of representation (Vosniadou, Chapter 24, this volume). Such studies reveal that children construct similar misconceptions as they strive to understand a complex concept such as gravity. For example, most children in the primary grades readily state that the earth is round because they have been told this fact numerous times. However, when asked to draw the earth, children represent people standing on top of a circle, or other depictions that indicate the limitations of their understanding of this scientific concept. Because misconceptions constructed early in life are highly resistant to change, teachers need to know more about how children think and which strategies, such as representation, are effective in promoting more accurate conceptual development (Gardner, 1991).

One way to think about persistent misconceptions is that they are children's constructed responses to complex questions that make sense to children, and that they remember. But what is memory? We know that memory is an essential foundational process that relates to learning across all domains. But how does memory develop, and what can teachers do to promote its development? We address these questions in the section that follows.

Memory

Developmental science provides useful information to help teachers understand memory, although more needs to be discovered. Studies of learning and memory indicate that these two processes are not the same thing because even in infancy there are age-related memory differences that are unrelated to learning (Bauer, 2009). Nevertheless, memory is essential for new learning to occur and for previous learning to be retrieved when needed.

Neuroscience contributes to our understanding of how memory and learning interact in practice. Two critical processes—consolidation and reconsolidation—must occur if new learning is to be committed to memory. Consolidation is the process of keeping newly learned material alive long enough for it to be integrated into memory (Bauer, Chapter 5, this volume). Consolidation is important because when learning is "new" the child is highly vulnerable to forgetting. Reconsolidation is akin to the process of revisiting what has been learned previously through new learning or experience. Reconsolidation in memory is both a challenge and opportunity for learning. During reconsolidation, the challenge is that new learning can interfere with previous learning and forgetting occurs. The bright side is that reconsolidation offers the all-important and effective opportunity to connect or integrate new learning with prior knowledge—a teaching and learning strategy that is consistently found to be effective (Bauer, Chapter 5, this volume; Bransford, Brown, & Cocking, 2000). Well-known approaches to early childhood education, including the High/Scope curriculum (with its plan-do-review cycle) and the Reggio approach (with its use of representation and documentation of experiences), incorporate the power of revisiting experiences for memory and learning.

Educators can draw a few important conclusions about memory processes from developmental science. Apparently, learning is "fragile" and easily interfered with or forgotten, especially when new learning is introduced. In short, consolidation takes time. Recognizing these basic facts about how memory works leads one to question several aspects of current educational practice. School curricula today are said to be "a mile wide and an inch deep." Such curricula constantly expose children to new facts or concepts well before existing learning has been consolidated. Children have little opportunity or support to relate new learning to what they already know; this is especially difficult for children whose prior experience was gained in diverse cultural contexts. In addition, curricula move along at relentless speed, with little variation for differences in children's ability to keep up. Time tables are set by the graded structure of schools or the date of standardized testing rather than children's need to consolidate learning. Therefore, it is not surprising that children must be taught the same thing year after year, yet still struggle to understand and apply complex concepts. They simply do not recall prior experiences, or they do not understand how new learning is connected to old learning.

More practically based developmental research with preschoolers and elementary age children demonstrates the effectiveness of specific strategies that can promote consolidation and reconsolidation of new learning. Studies of mothers and preschoolers identified several conditions that promote memory in young children (Ornstein, Coffman, & Grammer, Chapter 6, this volume). A meaningful, pretend-play task during which mothers and children engaged in joint verbal exchanges was found to greatly enhance children's comprehension and memory. These situations demonstrated the importance of positive relationships to learning (as in a mother–child dyad), and also the value of particular language strategies to promote memory (Ornstein, Haden, & Hedrick, 2004). Most encouraging was the finding that mothers (and, therefore, presumably teachers) could be trained to use effective language prompts to aid children's remembering of details of experiences. The strategies included (1) using "Wh" questions to call children's attention to details; (2) making connections to what children already know; (3) using follow-ins that connect the experience to children's interests; and (4) encouraging evaluations of the experience ("What did you like best?").

Research conducted in elementary school classrooms supports the findings from studies with mothers and children (Ornstein et al., 2004) Teachers can use specific, deliberate strategies to improve children's memory. These include simple strategies, such as asking children to rehearse new learning and asking children what they remember (deliberate demands for memory). More complex strategies promote metacognition in which children reflect on their own memory processes. Researchers found that focusing on these deliberate memory strategies during first grade (at the outset of children's school career) was especially important for long-term memory and learning success. They also found that most teachers do not intentionally engage in these deliberate memory-enhancing strategies. Adding these skills to teachers' repertoires of effective teaching strategies could go a long way toward improving children's school success, especially for those children who do not receive this kind of assistance in their homes.

In our discussion of each of these fundamental developmental processes—self-regulation, representation, and memory—we have seen the importance of positive relationships between children and parents or teachers. Next, we focus on the essential process of attachment that underlies successful learning and development across domains.

Attachment

From birth, children's development is influenced by the nurturance and care that they receive from adults—first their parents, then members of the extended family, and finally caregivers and teachers. If important adults are responsive and sensitive to their needs, children develop secure attachment relationships that allow them comfortably to explore and learn about the world (Ainsworth, Blehar, Waters, & Wall, 1978; Bowlby, 1969/2000; Sroufe, 1996). These children have a strong foundation not only for building relationships with other people but also for learning (Watson, 2003). Securely attached children see adults as trustworthy and come to see themselves as competent. Secure attachment relationships help children learn self-regulation and social skills.

By contrast, some children grow up in families that, for a variety of reasons, are unable or unwilling to provide reasonably consistent, sensitive, responsive care. Mothers or other caregivers may be depressed, ill, or stressed by economic or other conditions that lead them to be neglectful, punitive, or hostile to their young children. Some children are abused, neglected, or exposed to drugs and violence. In such an environment children may not be able to trust adults to keep them safe, and as a result, they lack social competence. These insecurely attached children may be disruptive in child care centers or schools (Ainsworth et al., 1978).

Although early attachment studies, especially the work of Ainsworth and Bowlby, focused on the mother–child attachment relationship, current research examines the relationships between teachers and children (Birch & Ladd, 1997; Howes & Smith, 1995; Pianta, 1999). This research has found a strong correlation between the quality of teacher–child relationships and children's development and learning across the full age span, from infancy through primary grades. Whereas a secure attachment to a mother or primary caregiver serves as a safe base for exploration and learning, a positive relationship with a teacher also facilitates children's academic, as well as social, success in school.

Fortunately, research also indicates that attachment relationships with parents do not necessarily predict attachment relationships with teachers (Howes & Ritchie, 2002). In fact, children are capable of forming multiple attachments that may differ in quality. A child who is securely attached to parents may be insecurely attached to teachers, or a child may develop a positive relationship with a teacher or caregiver even if he or she is insecurely attached to parents. In a series of studies across the age span from infancy to third grade, Howes and Ritchie (2002) found that positive teacher–child relationships are linked to many positive child outcomes. Moreover, they found that "even if children have not been able to trust prior caregiving adults, current child–teacher relationships can be positive and compensate for difficult previous relationships" (p. 3).

Having examined four different but related foundational processes at various points in development for all children, we now turn to the related topic of how children develop as individuals.

The Role of Individual Differences

A complete discussion of the literature on individual differences is beyond the scope of this chapter. However, developmental science across all the domain-general processes described previously demonstrates that there is a wide range of individual differences in when, how, and to what extent children develop these important abilities. For example, examination of this research strongly supports the interactive relationship between biology and environment in the development of self-regulation. From earliest infancy, children display different degrees of self-regulatory behavior stemming from differences in their ability to control biologically related arousal states, such as the sleep–wake cycle (Calkins & Williford, Chapter 9, this volume). These differences can have long-lasting consequences for children. At the same time, research demonstrates that early intervention strategies implemented by parents and caregivers or teachers can be effective in teaching children many behaviors related to self-regulation. Simple strategies, such as teaching children to take a breath and calm down, are effective because controlling the physical state of arousal helps children begin to control their behavior.

More research is needed to identify patterns of individual differences in children and mechanisms for assessing children's individual strengths as well as needs. Promising research, using a variety of assessment procedures, indicates that even before formal schooling children demonstrate different profiles of abilities (Bornstein, Chapter 7, this volume). When educators only test children's verbal ability, as is often the case, they miss children's strengths in other important areas, such as numeracy, sociability, or psychomotor skills. Attention to the full range of children's capabilities might go a long way toward closing the achievement gap for children from low income families and children of color.

Looking across these processes—self-regulation, representation, memory, and attachment—it is clear that children's experiences in their homes and communities influence individual differences in their development and learning. Some children have many opportunities to represent experience in language, whereas others, especially those living in poverty, have far fewer language-enriching opportunities (Hart & Risley, 1995). Children whose early experience is chaotic and devoid of positive attachments to adults are likely to be at risk for developing all these fundamental processes. Therefore, early childhood programs and schools need to focus as much or more on interventions in these fundamentals as on basic skills. Developmental processes, including self-regulation, representation, memory, and attachment, are the *real basics* of education.

Group Differences

Children develop as individuals, but they also develop as members of groups. All development and learning occurs in, and is influenced by, social and cultural contexts (Bronfenbrenner, 1979). In America's diverse society, schools serve children representing different racial, ethnic, cultural, and linguistic backgrounds. In addition, socioeconomic class intersects with each of these areas of diversity to influence children's identities and abilities.

Given the realities of diversity in our nation, the usefulness of developmental science for education depends on the inclusion of diverse children and families in all research designs. If research within a homogenous population of children (white, middle class) finds a wide range of individual differences (Bornstein, Chapter 7, this volume), similar research with a more diverse population could have wide-ranging implications for educational practice and policy.

Any discussion of research, especially basic research of the kind described here, begs the question, "So what?" In the section that follows, we discuss the implications of developmental science on the classroom for young children.

How Would School Be Different?

If we united developmental science with education and integrated both the best of early childhood education and the best of elementary education, what would school be like for young children ages 3 to 8? This section describes some of the major ways school would differ from what most young children in the United States experience today. Eight differences are highlighted. When describing current practice, we realize that our general statements are not universally true across classrooms in the United States. Please take these statements as they are intended: to paint a general picture of current practices rather than as definitive statements capturing the wide range of current practices.

Experimentation, Explanation, and Explicit Instruction

Many preschool teachers have been taught the Piagetian concept of constructivism, in which children construct knowledge from their own experiences (Piaget, 1952). Teachers often implement this concept by acting in the role of facilitator as young children explore the classroom environment and materials. Teachers may facilitate children's thinking by asking questions, but rarely do the questions probe deeply enough to promote a deep understanding of concepts. There is little explicit instruction except for letter names, counting, and days of the week. By contrast, in elementary schools, teachers engage regularly in explicit instruction and provide little time for exploration. When experiments are included, children are often expected to glean the concepts from their own trial and error.

What would be different if we applied developmental science? Preschool and elementary school teachers would be intentional about when it is best to provide explicit instruction and when to allow experimentation or independent exploration. Teachers would have a full grasp of the content area. Experimentation would include appropriate teacher or peer support. Teachers would provide explanations and be purposeful as to when and how they do so. Explicit instruction would be one of a range of tools teachers would use to build children's knowledge. It would be seen not as the "be all and end all" nor as the "never ever to do" but rather as an efficient way to ensure that children master certain concepts (for more information on exploration and explanation in science instruction, see Klahr & Nigam, 2004).

Understanding Misconceptions

Today, teachers tend to focus on the correct answers. If a child gives an incorrect answer, the teacher may provide the correct answer, with or without an explanation. If we applied knowledge from developmental science, then the teacher would spend considerable time talking with the child and asking questions to understand the child's misconception of the construct. Teachers would also engage children in various forms of representation to reveal children's understanding of complex concepts, as described earlier in this chapter. As is evident in Stella Vosniadou's research (Chapter 24, this volume), effective teachers understand children's naïve or partial thinking so that they can provide the experiences and explanations that specifically address their misconceptions. Thus, spending time to understand children's misconceptions is valued and necessary to teach complex constructs effectively.

Depth Instead of Breadth

Currently, state curricula for the elementary grades often cover a dizzying range of topics within math, language arts, science, and social studies. If we were to implement what we know from developmental psychology about how children learn these topics, curricula for children ages 3–8 would focus on a small array of topics within these content areas. Teachers would spend considerable time and effort to ensure that children have a deep understanding of concepts that are the foundation for later learning.

Deciding What to Teach

Catherine Snow talks about the "problem space" of becoming a competent reader (Snow, Griffin, & Burns, 2005). This space represents the breadth and depth of knowledge and skills necessary to be literate in our society. She recommends that more instructional effort be given to the skills and knowledge that take up larger amounts of this problem space. With regard to literacy, whereas vocabulary is one of these large problem spaces, knowing the names of the letters takes up only a small part of the literacy "problem space." Children need to learn thousands of new words per year to acquire the vocabulary necessary for later reading comprehension and learning across the subject-matter disciplines. By contrast, the alphabet comprises only 26 letters, which most children master within a fairly short period of time. Teachers of young children, however, often spend considerable time on letter knowledge and much less time intentionally teaching new vocabulary words.

If we teachers were to apply what we know from developmental science, we would spend much more time supporting children's vocabulary development and less time teaching specific letter names. Knowing the alphabet is one of the strongest predictors of early reading success, and it should be taught. However, learning the alphabet does not take as much time and effort as expanding vocabulary. Furthermore, teachers and researchers would work together to delineate the "problem spaces" for as many curricular areas as possible, then use them as guides for instructional time in classrooms for children across the 3- to 8-year-old age span.

Development, Content, and Process

As mentioned previously, preschool teachers generally have a better understanding of development than of academic content, and elementary teachers generally have a better understanding of content than of development. Teachers across early childhood and elementary grades typically do not think about the foundational processes of learning, such as memory and problem solving, as something to be taught explicitly (although some may implicitly teach them). If we were to apply what we know from developmental psychology, teachers would have a solid understanding of (1) how foundational processes such as memory, self-regulation, representational thought, and attachment develop between ages 3 and 8; (2) the content of the curriculum in numeracy, literacy, language, and socioemotional competence; and (3) the processes through which children learn. The foundational processes of learning, such as memory and socioemotional competence, would be explicitly addressed in the curriculum.

Play

"Children's work is play," a familiar saying among early childhood educators, is evident in the play-based curricula in classrooms for 3- and 4-year-olds. As discussed earlier, high-level sociodramatic play promotes self-regulation and language competence. Although play is valued by early childhood professionals, there is still insufficient understanding of the benefits of different kinds of play and the critical role of teachers in ensuring that play is beneficial. Additionally, all children are not the "natural" players that some people think they are, and this broadens the role of teachers, who may need to help children learn play skills, if they are to benefit fully.

With the increased accountability demanded by No Child Left Behind, public school for children in kindergarten through third grade looks more like work than play. Engagement with games, props and materials for construction, and art and music is often relegated to recess time on rainy days or saved for special occasions. If teachers of children ages 3 to 8 were to apply developmental knowledge to the classroom, then play would be a regular, intentionally planned, teacher-guided activity across this age spectrum, with the acknowledgment that play for 8-year-olds is different than the play of 4-year-olds. As children become older, play becomes more representational and rule-governed (Piaget, 1945/1962; Vygotsky, 1966/1977). Whereas younger children may create their own dramas in the dramatic play area that is set up like a grocery store or dentist office, older children might act out a play or dramatize a story they've read. By understanding the development of children's play and the role of play in children's learning across this age span, teachers can effectively use play as another instructional tool.

Relationships

Early childhood research has long emphasized the importance of positive relationships between a teacher and a child as foundational to all work with young children. Research has consistently demonstrated an association between positive teacher–child relationships and children's social, emotional, and intellectual competence (Cost, Quality and Child Outcomes Study Team, 1995; Howes, Smith, & Galinsky, 1995; NICHD Early Child Care Research Network, 1999, 2005; Whitebrook, Howes, & Phillips, 1990). Internalized dispositions toward learning, such as competent exploration and self-reliance. are also linked to secure attachment organizations (Cohn, 1990; Pianta & Harbers, 1996). Systems theory takes the notion of relationships one step further to suggest that children are motivated by adults who support their need to be competent and encourage them to interact positively with others (Connell & Wellborn, 1991; Ryan & Deci, 2000; Skinner, Connell, & Zimmer-Gembeck, 1998).

If we apply what we know about the importance of positive relationships, a classroom may look different in several ways:

- Social development would not simply be scheduled into the day, or ignored outright; rather, teachers would utilize the opportunities for prosocial development that emerge throughout the day, such as conflict resolution, and expressions of feelings.
- Teachers would be willing and able to explore more effective ways to interact with challenging children.
- Difficult behavior would be viewed as a child's way of communicating problems rather than as misbehavior or as an opportunity for discipline.
- There would be frequent opportunities for children to engage in meaningful and extended conversations with teachers and peers.

Addressing the Whole Child

Currently, the bulk of a young child's day in kindergarten and primary school comprises literacy and math. There is often little or no time for physical activity, art, music, and even social studies and science. A concern for knowing far more about children's skills and abilities would call for a far more balanced day than what is generally found today. Marc Bornstein's work (Bornstein, Chapter 7, this volume) addresses the question, "What about the child's mind should we consider when interacting with and teaching the child?" His simple answer is that we currently focus on a far too limited and limiting view of children's abilities. Bornstein helps teachers expand their notions of skills, talent, and expertise in children by emphasizing strengths in three domains—physical, cognitive, and socioemotional. If teachers utilized Bornstein's ideas, then both the priorities for a school day and assessment would look very different. Teachers would draw on children's unique strengths and interests to help them achieve in the important areas of literacy and math, as well as broaden the curriculum to allow for development in more domains.

If we want school for 3- to 8-year-olds to look different than it does now, we must implement multiple strategies to spark and sustain the needed changes. One of the most important strategies for supporting long-term change is working with institutions of higher education to change the way they prepare teachers of children in this age span. In the next section we discuss some of the changes that developmental science suggests for teacher preparation.

Teacher Preparation

This is a reflective time for teacher-educators and teacher education programs. With the No Child Left Behind (NCLB) Act of 2001 (Public Law 107-110) and its complementary early childhood initiative, Good Start, Grow Smart (Office of the White House, 2002), as well as scientific evidence about the importance of quality teacher–child interaction in the early years (e.g., Shonkoff & Phillips, 2000), increasing attention has been turned to professionals who work with young children. However, the research base is unable to offer policymakers and practitioners specific strategies and systems that may develop a highly qualified early childhood workforce (Zaslow & Martinez-Beck, 2006). The very usefulness of teacher education has been publicly challenged in both research and political areas (e.g., Ballou & Podgursky, 2000; Darling-Hammond & Youngs, 2002; U.S. Department of Education, 2003). The U.S. Secretary of Education, for example, suggested that teachers' content knowledge and verbal abilities are more critical than education training and field experiences (U.S. Department of Education, 2003). A joint data analysis project of seven major studies examining early childhood classrooms, teachers, and children revealed few linkages between classroom quality and teacher education (Early et al., 2007). One of the possible explanations for this lack of association is that teacher preparation programs vary widely in their content and quality. At the same time, the changing demographics in our society are pushing us to examine culture and inclusion of all children, and this certainly provides real challenges to current teacher education (Isenberg, 2001). Finally, and most importantly, the educational needs of our most vulnerable children continue not to be met (Ray, Bowman, & Robbins, 2006).

The focus on empirically supported pedagogy is essential for the optimal preparation of professional educators. Scholars argue that teachers who understand how learning occurs are better able to select and develop curricula that support the learning process (Bransford, Darling-Hammond, & LePage, 2005). Teachers who understand child development and learning are more likely to select learning experiences, tasks, materials, and instructional strategies that meet children where they are, maintain their motivation, and move them toward greater competence (Horowitz et al., 2005). The blending of sound elementary education teaching strategies that focus on content knowledge with the child development pedagogies of early childhood education is needed to provide the early educator with the skills and knowledge to engage in meaningful and productive teaching. The early educator needs to possess a wide repertoire of skills to help education professionals respond to the individualized learning strengths and challenges of children. Research suggests that the varied use of strategies is the hallmark of the versatile teacher, who is able to select among teaching approaches to match students' learning styles and competencies (de Kruif, McWilliam, Ridley, & Wakely, 2000; Kontos & Wilcox-Herzog, 1997).

Teacher-educators are being called upon to reexamine their programs to be responsive to research findings. Teacher-educators who seek change can benefit from knowledge gained from programs involved in change processes; from inclusion community members, family members, and school faculty in program planning; from the evaluation of faculty competence; from the close scrutiny of the knowledge and skills developed through the examination of teacher and student outcomes; and from the ability of the program structure to sustain and to convey the program mission and values.

In response to some of these issues, a task force of researchers and developmental scientists convened in December 2005 and March 2006 to discuss the topic *Child and Adolescent Development Research and Teacher Education: Evidence-Based Pedagogy, Policy, and Practice.* James Comer, Chair of the task force, wrote of an important moment:

> Over the years, the numbers of teachers who had taken child and adolescent development courses in their pre-service training increased to almost all. But even now, few have had applied child development courses or experiences. The most powerful moment of our roundtable time together for me occurred when the teachers of teachers identified this major continuing problem—we teach the theory, but not enough about how to apply it. It was this kind of insight that I had long hoped that discussions between child development scientists and educators would bring about. (NICHD & National Council for the Accreditation of Teacher Education [NCATE], 2007, p. iv)

This group concluded with three recommendations for teacher educators:

1. Training teachers in development should not be a one-course solution.
2. Training approaches should be different for teachers at elementary, middle, and high school levels.
3. Emphasis should be on the centrality of development rather than passing on information.

We have used these recommendations as a platform to expand thinking about the implications for teacher education practices that focus on fundamental processes as the real basics of education.

Training Teachers in Development

Four strategies for changing the program structure of teacher preparation programs are described.

Communities of Practice

Scholars argue that the knowledge teachers need to teach well emanates from systematic inquiries about teaching, learners and learning, curricula, and schools and schooling. This knowledge is constructed collectively in local and broader communities (Cochran-Smith & Lytle, 1999). A community of practice promotes meaningful teaching and learning through regular engagement of education professionals in an inquiry process to examine and refine instructional practices to improve teaching and learning processes for children. A community of practice approach promotes a mindset that pushes practitioners past the notion that a simple right answer or a formula will solve the complex problems they encounter in classrooms, to one wherein situations they encounter drive them to seek new information, value the knowledge and experience of other professionals, and inquire into their own practice. These kinds of established networks need to start during preservice and be facilitated as an essential aspect of ongoing professional development.

An Interdisciplinary Focus

The community of practice approach merits an interdisciplinary and collaborative focus in the preparation of teachers. To become an effective collaborator, professional education students need opportunities to practice and learn about shared communication and decision making across the education disciplines in the school community. Models and strategies for collaboration across the education disciplines must include teaming and collaboration with literacy specialists, special educators, allied health professionals, school counselors and psychologists, and school administrators. Interdisciplinary collaboration promotes the integration of instructional strategies that help professionals move toward an integrated and holistic approach to children's learning.

Joining Preservice and Inservice Efforts

Better informed ways to approach children's learning need to shape not only the novice but also the veteran teacher and other education professionals. Schools provide the best possible forum for interactions. Novice teachers simply cannot be the only ambassadors for change. An approach to lifelong learning based on shared expertise and multiple perspectives has multiple benefits. It allows preservice teachers to get out of college classrooms and inside schools to grapple with these issues with people who encounter them daily. It allows for discourse between university/college people and professionals who have not recently been engaged with higher education. It facilitates teachers' buying into new notions of how to think about children and their learning styles.

It is often difficult for preservice/student teachers and novices to bring their enthusiasm and newly gained knowledge and ideas into environments where they are the new kid on the block. They are too often quickly silenced by their own inability to articulate their knowledge, and by teachers who assure them that none of what they learned in college really works. On the other side of that coin, university faculty would do well to encounter the realities of classrooms and the complexity of making changes in classroom practices or school policy.

Transcending the Survey Method of Teacher Education

As programs reexamine the content of their courses, using the principles of cognitive science provides a lens through which to view the traditional focus on breadth rather than depth in methods and content courses. Cognitive science guides us to narrow the number of topics in science and math to those that are foundational to subsequent learning. Helping teachers acquire knowledge that more adequately develops conceptual understanding of scientific principles will enable them to respond fully to children's misconceptions and help children to expand and clarify their thinking.

Emerging and veteran educators need program structure to be responsive to what we know about what teachers need. A professional development model characterized by a social process, in which novice and expert education professionals across the schools, community, and university collaborate to solve common problems and challenges within schools (Rogoff, 1990; Tharp & Gallimore, 1988), makes needed room for the integration of emerging knowledge on cognitive science and foundational processes.

Differentiating Training Approaches

The foundational processes focus on children ages 3–8; thus, we not only support the notion of differentiating training approaches but also advocate for fully adapting teacher education to prepare educators to work with children across this particular age span and developmental period. Most children develop substantial oral language skills by age 3, and by the time they reach third grade, schools expect them to be relatively competent in written language. Because success beyond third grade is highly dependent on children's skills in writing and understanding written language, their early school experiences should ensure that they have optimal opportunities to become competent readers and writers. Schools typically increase and alter expectations for children at about age 7 or 8, which underscores the need to prepare teachers to help children reach these goals.

Language and literacy, however, cannot be the only focus. Teachers of young children must also facilitate the development of the foundational processes that support memory development, representational thinking, mathematical reasoning, self-regulation, and attachment. Success in these areas will support children's acquisition of critical thinking skills and knowledge, skills, and concepts across content areas. Children must develop physically, socially, and emotionally, and become increasingly competent in practices that will keep them healthy and safe. These are all critical tasks for children's early school years.

Race, social class, and culture must be part of the conversations about effective teacher preparation. Teacher preparation must embody a social justice agenda that pushes educators to take responsibility for responding to the ongoing conditions that contribute to a national crisis that perpetuates situations in which racial minority children and children in poverty are more likely to attend programs with teachers who lack subject content knowledge, have lower academic achievement, and are inexperienced (Peske & Haycock, 2006). Racial and cultural minority children, and children from low-income families, are more likely to enter kindergarten behind their middle-class European American peers; to have lower educational achievement in reading and math; and to be assigned disproportionately to special education classes. Even when their incomes are similar, ethnic/minority children fare more poorly on standardized tests (Denton & West, 2002; Riegle-Crumb, 2006); African American boys are more likely to be expelled from preschools (Gilliam, 2005), and African American and Latino boys have higher rates of grade failure (U.S. Department of Commerce, 2005). Educators must be prepared to think beyond traditional practices that relegate the most vulnerable populations to repeated failure.

Preparation approaches need to correspond closely in method and content to what is being asked of teachers. Just as teachers are prepared to link children's new learning to prior knowledge, they need opportunities to experience new learning in a variety of contexts and to engage in metacognitive reflection upon their learning. Opportunities for teachers should include linking new knowledge about foundational processes of memory, self-regulation, representation, and attachment to their own knowledge and experience, practical application and practice in classrooms, and a forum for inquiry and refinement.

Novice and veteran educators and university faculty need to work with one another to explore some of the following questions:

- What is the effect of ongoing difficulties in classrooms for children who struggle with repeated failures due to difficulty with relationships, memory, and self-regulation?
- What are teachers' varying roles in offering emotional and instructional support for the development of foundational processes?
- How does language acquisition/vocabulary development support children's foundational processes?
- How do teachers become intentional in their application of skills and knowledge?
- How does a lens that makes central the questions of race, class, and culture refine practices that truly meet the needs of all children?

Emphasizing the Centrality of Development

Educators who focus on children's development "match content with children's developmental levels and emerging abilities" (Epstein, 2007, p. 128). In today's schools, content tends to equate to objectives of the school/district/state curriculum that mandates what children will learn and, more often than not, how they will learn it. Moving toward a more developmental approach will not be popular among administrators who are pressured by NCLB and who do not have a background or experience in child development. A developmental approach is not prescriptive, it is not didactic, and it is not one size fits all. A developmental approach respects teacher knowledge and decision making and recognizes individual difference in children. Because most schools—and therefore most teachers—are preoccupied with making sure that children meet accountability standards, it is important that the links between these approaches and positive outcomes for children become more apparent. Administrators' concerns are real, and their perspective is valid; thus, empirical research that supports a developmental approach, and educators who can articulate their developmental practices, must be part of the dialogue that helps all education professionals struggle to make choices on behalf of children, and their social and academic success in school. Evidence that curricular and instructional practices support the development of children's foundational processes will contribute significantly to this discussion.

Implementing the ideas voiced throughout this section is not a simple charge. Developmental science historically has not been a strong part of teacher preparation programs. Assuming the burden of rethinking the content, structure, and process of teacher education will require proactive thinking and planning that includes the voices of the faculty and the commitment of the group to developing and implementing shared values and vision.

Recommendations

In this chapter, we addressed three fundamental questions:

1. Based on current research in developmental science, what are the foundational developmental processes that underlie achievement across all areas from age 3 through grade 3?
2. How would early schooling look different if developmental science were broadly applied in practice?
3. What are the implications of developmental science and its practical applications for teacher preparation?

Developmental science holds relevance for every dimension of early schooling—curriculum design, assessment, and instructional practice, as well as initial teacher preparation and ongoing professional development of teachers. In earlier sections of the chapter we discussed each of these questions in some detail, along with implications for changes to practice. We conclude by offering a few crosscutting recommendations.

• *Update child development studies at every level to reflect current developmental science.* Although early childhood teacher preparation tends to include more child development study than does elementary education, the content of courses is not always current. The emphasis is often on ages and stages or theories without clear connections to practice. Teachers need deeper understanding of domain-general and domain-specific developmental and learning processes. They also need a repertoire of effective strategies and interventions for applying this important knowledge across the age span. For example, self-regulation is a far broader and more complex developmental process than self-control, which is more likely to be a goal of early childhood programs at present. Similarly, the importance of representation, when it is discussed at all, tends to be connected only to reading and writing, rather than more broadly as a competence that applies across domains and subject-matter disciplines.

• *Apply current knowledge of developmental science to curriculum design.* It is time that early childhood and elementary education move away from stereotyping of curriculum as either canned and totally prescribed or emergent and nonintentional to a broader based effort to ensure that whatever the source, curriculum design reflects developmental science about how children learn. Domain-specific research in areas such as science and mathematics indicates that teachers need curricular support to teach concepts accurately and sequentially, where necessary, to build children's understanding (Ginsburg, Chapter 18, this volume). The same is true of language and literacy learning. Such curricular resources, which may include scripts or prompts that do not restrict teachers but rather guide teachers' explanations or launch conversational exchanges, can be effective ways to move current knowledge into practice.

• *Provide teachers with more curriculum resources, assessment tools, and guidance for individualizing instruction.* Evidence of individual differences permeates developmental science, yet most educational practice ignores the reality of individual and cultural variation among children. This is not an easy reality to address, yet the large achievement discrepancies between groups of children will never be eliminated unless specific solutions are forthcoming.

• *Eliminate simplistic, either–or solutions to educational questions while expanding and deepening teachers' understandings of complex developmental processes.* This recommendation refers to the unfortunate tendency in education to oversimplify teaching and learning, which are complex processes indeed. This tendency leads to the overuse of bromidic phrases, such as "Play is children's work," "Children construct their own knowledge," or "Direct instruction leads to rote memorization." Even a cursory summary of developmental science such as that provided in this chapter demonstrates that these statements are half-truths at best and gross misrepresentations at worst. Under certain supportive conditions, play is a highly effective context for developing important processes, including self-regulation and language, but such a positive outcome is not automatic. Similarly, although it is true that children construct understanding, left to their own devices, children cannot discover all that is important for them to know. Children's own experimentation, supported by teacher explanation and at times, explicit instruction, is perhaps the most effective teaching strategy. Likewise, memory is essential for learning and should not be stereotyped as "rote." At the same time, teachers can explicitly instruct children in deliberate strategies to improve memory.

• *Promote positive teacher–child relationships across the educational spectrum.* Current developmental science more than ever supports the importance of positive, responsive relationships between teachers and parents for children's learning and development (Mashburn et al., 2008). Given that such relationships are not the norm for every child and are actually rare in many elementary classrooms, concerted effort must be made to incorporate relationship-building strategies in teacher preparation and ongoing professional development (Pianta, Belsky, Vandergrift, Houts, & Morrison, 2008). The power of joint verbal exchanges—interesting, engaging conversations between teachers and children—to effect learning also provides a strong foundation for personal relationships.

• *Build collaborations between developmental scientists, educational researchers, and teachers.* An inherent conundrum exists in the call for scientifically based educational practice. Good science controls as many variables as possible to identify cause–effect relationships accurately. By contrast, classrooms are messy structures in which variables and conditions cannot be controlled. Good teaching tends to be responsive and is adapted to the inherent individual variation among children rather than applying the same solution to all problems. Bringing scientists into the "messy" world of classrooms is essential if their work is truly to be applicable to practice.

Implementing these broad recommendations along with the more focused recommendations included in previous sections of this chapter would go a long way toward bridging the ever-widening gap between developmental science and early education. At the same time, such efforts would undoubtedly transform early schooling, resulting in improved educational achievement for all children.

References

Ainsworth, M. D. S., Blehar, M. C., Waters, E., & Wall, S. (1978). *Patterns of attachment.* Hillsdale, NJ: Erlbaum.

Ballou, D., & Podgursky, M. (2000). Reforming teacher preparation and licensing. *Teachers College Record, 102*(1), 5–27.

Barnett, W. S., Hustedt, J. T., Hawkinson, L. E., & Robin, K. B. (2006). *The state of preschool: 2006 state preschool yearbook.* New Brunswick, NJ: National Institute for Early Education Research.

Bauer, P. (2009). Learning and memory: Like a horse and carriage. In A. Woodward & A. Needham (Eds.), *Learning and the infant mind* (pp. 3–28). New York: Oxford University Press.

Birch, S. H., & Ladd, G. W. (1997). The child–teacher relationship and children's early school adjustment. *Journal of School Psychology, 35,* 61–79.

Blair, C., & Razza, R. C. (2007). Relating effortful control, executive functional and false belief understanding to emerging math and literacy ability in kindergarten. *Child Development, 78*(2), 647–663.

Bodrova, E., & Leong, D. J. (2006). Self-regulation as a key to school readiness: How early childhood teachers can promote this critical competency. In M. Zaslow & I. Martinez-Beck (Eds.), *Critical issues in early childhood professional development* (pp. 203–224). Baltimore: Brookes.

Bodrova, E., & Leong, D. J. (2007). *Tools of the mind: The Vygotskian approach to early childhood education.* New York: Merrill/Prentice-Hall.

Bogard, K., & Takanishi, R. (2005). PK–3: An aligned and coordinated approach to education for children 3 to 8 years old. *SRCD Social Policy Report, 19*(3), 3–23.

Bowlby, J. (2000). *Attachment and loss: Vol. 1. Attachment.* New York: Basic Books. (Original work published 1969)

Boyd, J., Barnett, W. S., Bodrova, E., Leong, D. J., & Gomby, D. (2005, March). *Promoting children's social emotional development through preschool* (Preschool Policy Report). New Brunswick, NJ: National Institute for Early Education Research.

Bransford, J. D., Brown, A. L., & Cocking, R. R. (Eds.). (2000). *How people learn: Brain, mind, experience, and school* (Expanded ed.). Washington, DC: National Academy Press.

Bransford, J. D., Darling-Hammond, L., & LePage, P. (2005). Introduction. In L. Darling-Hammond & J. D. Bransford (Eds.), *Preparing teachers for a changing world: What teachers should learn and be able to do* (pp. 1–39). San Francisco: Jossey-Bass.

Bredekamp, S., & Copple, C. (Eds.). (1997). *Developmentally appropriate practice in early childhood programs* (rev. ed.). Washington, DC: National Association for the Education of Young Children.

Bronfenbrenner, U. (1979). *The ecology of human development: Experiments by nature and design.* Cambridge, MA: Harvard University Press.

Calkins, S. D. (2007). The emergence of self-regulation: Biological and behavioral control mechanisms supporting toddler competencies. In C. A. Brownell & C. B. Kopp (Eds.), *Socioemotional development in the toddler years: Transitions and transformations* (pp. 261–284). New York: Guilford Press.

Cochran-Smith, M., & Lytle, S. L. (1999). The teacher research movement: A decade later. *Educational Researcher, 28*(7), 15–25.

Cohn, D. A. (1990). Child–mother attachment of six-year-olds and social competence at school. *Child Development, 61*(1), 152–162.

Connell, J. P., & Wellborn, J. G. (1991). Competence, autonomy, and relatedness: A motivational analysis of self-system processes. In M. R. Gunnar & L. A. Sroufe (Eds.), *Self processes and development* (pp. 43–77). Hillsdale, NJ: Erlbaum.

Copple, C. E., Cocking, R. R., & Matthews, W. S. (1984). Objects, symbols, and substitutes: The nature of the cognitive activity during symbolic play. In T. D. Yawkey & A. D. Pellegrini (Eds.), *Child's play: Developmental and applied* (pp. 105–124). Hillsdale, NJ: Erlbaum.

Cost, Quality and Child Outcomes Study Team. (1995). *Cost, quality, and child outcomes in child care centers.* Denver: University of Colorado, Center for Research in Economics and Social Policy, Department of Economics.

Darling-Hammond, L., & Youngs, P. (2002). Defining "highly qualified teachers": What does "scientifically-based research" actually tell us? *Educational Researcher, 31*(9), 113–125.

de Kruif, R. E. L., McWilliam, R. A., Ridley, S. M., & Wakely, M. B. (2000). Classification of teachers' interaction behaviors in early childhood classrooms. *Early Childhood Research Quarterly, 15,* 247–268.

Denton, K., & West, J. (2002). *Children's reading and mathematics achievement in kindergarten and first grade.* Washington, DC: National Center for Education Statistics.

Early, D. M., Maxwell, K. L., Burchinal, M., Alva, S., Bender, R. H., Bryant, D., et al. (2007). Teachers' education, classroom quality, and young children's academic skills: Results from seven studies of preschool programs. *Child Development, 78*(2), 558–580.

Edwards, C., Gandini, L., & Forman, G. (1998). *The hundred languages of children: The Reggio Emilia approach.* Greenwich, CT: Ablex.

Elkonin, D. (1978). *The psychology of play.* Moscow: Pedagogika.

Epstein, A. S. (2007). *The intentional teacher: Choosing the best strategies for young children's learning.* Washington, DC: National Association for the Education of Young Children.

Gardner, H. (1991). *The unschooled mind: How children think and how schools should teach.* New York: Basic Books.

Gilliam, W. S. (2005). *Prekindergarteners left behind: Expulsion rates in state prekindergarten systems.* New Haven, CT: Yale University Child Study Center.

Hart, B., & Risley, T. R. (1995). *Meaningful differences in the everyday experiences of young American children.* Baltimore: Brookes.

Horowitz, F. D., Darling-Hammond, L., Bransford, J., Comer, J., Rosebrock, K., Austin, K., et al. (2005). Educating teachers for developmentally appropriate practice. In L. Darling-Hammond & J. Bransford (Eds.), *Preparing teachers for a changing world* (pp. 88–125). San Francisco: Jossey-Bass.

Howes, C., & Ritchie, S. (2002). *A matter of trust: Connecting teachers and learners in the early childhood classroom.* New York: Teachers College Press.

Howes, C., & Smith, E. (1995). Children and their child care teachers: Profiles of relationships. *Social Development, 4,* 44–61.

Howes, C., Smith, E., & Galinsky, E. (1995). *The Florida Child Care Quality Improvements Study: Interim report.* New York: Families and Work Institute.

Hyson, M., Copple, C., & Jones, J. (2006). Bringing developmental theory and research into the early childhood classroom: Thinking, emotions, and assessment. In W. Damon & R. M. Lerner (Series Eds.) & K. A. Renninger & I. E. Sigel (Vol. Eds.), *Handbook of child psychology: Vol. 4. Child psychology in practice* (6th ed., pp. 3–47). New York: Wiley.

Isenberg, J. P. (2001). The state of the art in early childhood professional preparation. In National Institute on Early Childhood Development and Education (Ed.), *New teachers for a new century: The future of early childhood professional preparation* (pp. 15–48). Washington, DC: U.S. Department of Education.

Kauerz, K. (2006, January). *Ladders of learning: Fighting fade-out by advancing PK–3 alignment* (Issue Brief No. 2). Washington, DC: New America Foundation Early Education Initiative.

Klahr, D., & Nigam, M. (2004). The equivalence of learning paths in early science instruction: Effects of direct instruction and discovery learning. *Psychological Science, 15,* 661–667.

Kontos, S., & Wilcox-Herzog, A. (1997). Influences on children's competence in early childhood classrooms. *Early Childhood Research Quarterly, 12*(3), 247–262.

Landry, C. E., & Forman, G. (1999). Research on early science education. In C. Seefeldt (Ed.), *The early childhood curriculum: Current findings in theory and practice* (pp. 133–158). New York: Teachers College Press.

Maeroff, G. (2006). *Building blocks: Making children successful in the early years of school.* New York: Palgrave/Macmillan.

Mashburn, A. J., Pianta, R. C., Hamre, B. K., Downer, J. T., Barbarin, O. A., Bryant, D., et al. (2008). Measures of classroom quality in prekindergarten and children's development of academic, language, and social skills. *Child Development, 79*(3), 732–749.

McClelland, M. M., Acock, A. C., & Morrison, F. J. (2006). The impact of kindergarten learning-related skills on academic trajectories at the end of elementary school. *Early Childhood Research Quarterly, 21*(4), 471–490.

National Association for the Education of Young Children. (2001). *NAEYC at 75: Reflections on the past, challenges for the future.* Washington, DC: Author.

National Institute of Child Health and Human Development. (2000). *Report of the National Reading Panel: Teaching children to read: An evidence-based assessment of the scientific research literature on reading and its implications for reading instruction.* Washington, DC: Author.

National Institute of Child Health and Human Development & National Council for the Accreditation of Teacher Education (NICHD & NCATE). (2007). *Child and adolescent development research and teacher education: Evidence-based pedagogy, policy, and practice* (Summary of Rountable Meetings, December 1–2, 2005, and March 20–21, 2006). Washington, DC: NCATE. Retrieved September 17, 2008, from *www.ncate.org/documents/research/childadoldevteachered.pdf*

NICHD Early Child Care Research Network. (1999). Child outcomes when child-care center classes meet recommended standards for quality. *American Journal of Public Health, 89,* 1072–1077.

NICHD Early Child Care Research Network. (2005). Early child care and children's development in the primary grades: Follow-up results from the NICHD Study of Early Child Care. *American Educational Research Journal, 42*(3), 537–570.

No Child Left Behind Act of 2001, Public Law 107-110 (2002).

Office of the White House. (2002). *Good Start, Grow Smart: The Bush Administration's early childhood initiative.* Retrieved August 8, 2007, from *www.whitehouse.gov/infocus/early-childhood/earlychildhood.html*

Ornstein, P. A., Haden, C. A., & Hedrick, A. M. (2004). Learning to remember: Social-communicative exchanges and the development of children's memory skills. *Developmental Review, 24,* 374–395.

Perie, M., Grigg, W., & Dion, G. (2005). *The nation's report card: Mathematics 2005* (NCES 2006-453; U.S. Department of Education, National Center for Education Statistics). Washington, DC: U.S. Government Printing Office.

Perie, M., Grigg, W., & Donahue, P. (2005). *The nation's report card: Reading 2005* (NCES 2006-451; U.S. Department of Education, National Center for Education Statistics). Washington, DC: U.S. Government Printing Office.

Peske, H. G., & Haycock, K. (2006). *Teaching inequality: How poor and minority students are shortchanged on teacher quality.* Retrieved August 7, 2007, from *www2.edtrust.org/edtrust/press+room/teacherquality2006.htm*

Piaget, J. (1952). *The origins of intelligence in children.* New York: International Universities Press.

Piaget, J. (1962). *Play, dreams, and imitation in childhood.* New York: Norton. (Original work published 1945)

Pianta, R. C. (1999). *Enhancing relationships between children and teachers.* Washington, DC: American Psychological Association.

Pianta, R. C., Belsky, J., Vandergrift, N., Houts, R., & Morrison, F. J. (2008). Classroom effects on children's achievement trajectories in elementary school. *American Educational Research Journal, 45*(2), 365–397.

Pianta, R. C., & Harbers, K. L. (1996). Observing mother and child behavior in a problem-solving situation at school entry: Relations with academic achievement. *Journal of School Psychology, 34*(3), 307–322.

Project Zero & Reggio Children. (2001). *Making learning visible: Children as individual and group learners.* Reggio Emilia, Italy: Reggio Children.

Ray, A., Bowman, B., & Robbins, J. (2006). *Preparing early childhood teachers to successfully educate all children: The contribution of 4-year undergraduate teacher preparation programs.* New York: Foundation for Child Development.

Riegle-Crumb, C. (2006).The path through math: Course sequences and academic performance at the intersection of race–ethnicity and gender. *American Journal of Education, 113*(1), 101–122.

Rogoff, B. (1990). *Apprenticeship in thinking: Cognitive development in social context.* New York: Oxford University Press.

Ryan, R. M., & Deci, E. L. (2000). Self-determination theory and the facilitation of intrinsic motivation, social development, and well-being. *American Psychologist, 55,* 68–78.

Shonkoff, J. P., & Phillips, D. A. (Eds.). (2000). *From neurons to neighborhoods: The science of early childhood development.* Washington, DC: National Academy Press.

Siraj-Blatchford, I., Sylva, K., Muttock, S., Gilden, R., & Bell, D. (2002, June). *Researching effective pedagogy in the early years* (Research Brief No. 356). Norwich, UK: Queen's Printer.

Skinner, E. A., Connell, J. P., & Zimmer-Gembeck, M. J. (1998). Individual differences and the development of perceived control. *Monographs of the Society for Research in Child Development, 63*(2–3), 1–220.

Snow, C., Griffin, P., & Burns, M. S. (2005). *Knowledge to support the teaching of reading: Preparing teachers for a changing world.* San Francisco: Jossey-Bass.

Sroufe, L. A. (1996). *Emotional development: The organization of emotional life in the early years.* New York: Cambridge University Press.

Tharp, R. G., & Gallimore, R. (1988). *Rousing minds to life: Teaching and learning in social context.* New York: Cambridge University Press.

U.S. Department of Commerce, Census Bureau, Current Population Survey (CPS). (2005, December). *Percentage of youth ages 16–19 who had never been retained in a grade in their school career, by current enrollment status and selected characteristics: 1995, 1999, and 2004.* Retrieved February 2, 2009, from *http://nces.ed.gov/programs/coe/2006/section3/table.asp?tableID=506*

U.S. Department of Education, Office of Policy Planning and Innovation. (2003). *Meeting the highly qualified teachers challenge: The Secretary's annual report on teacher quality.* Washington, DC: Author.

Vygotsky, L. S. (1962). *Thought and language.* Cambridge, MA: MIT Press.

Vygotsky, L. S. (1977). Play and its role in the mental development of the child. In M. Cole (Ed.), *Soviet developmental psychology* (pp. 76–99). Armonk, NY: Sharpe. (Original work published 1966)

Watson, M. (2003). Attachment theory and challenging behaviors: Reconstructing the nature of relationships. *Young Children, 58*(4), 12–20.

Whitebrook, M., Howes, C., & Phillips, D. (1990). *Who cares?: Child care teachers and the quality of care in America* (Final report: National Child Care Staffing Study). Oakland, CA: Child Care Employee Project.

Zaslow, M. J., & Martinez-Beck, I. (2006). *Critical issues in early childhood professional development.* Baltimore: Brookes.

CHAPTER 3

Bridging Developmental Theory and Educational Practice

Lessons from the Vygotskian Project

Anna Stetsenko
Eduardo Vianna

This chapter makes the case for a bidirectional interdependence and mutual utility of *developmental theory* and *educational practice* based on the view that these two seemingly disparate endeavors are essentially intertwined—representing two dimensions of one and the same continuously evolving process of sociocultural practices (or human praxis). We focus on the contribution of Vygotsky and his followers (what we term "the Vygotskian project") and discuss how insights from this approach inform current debates on the relationship between theory and practice, while helping to bridge the gap between them. In particular, we show, on the one hand, how Vygotskian novel theory about the dynamic links among the processes of teaching, learning, and development represents a crucial step in devising educational practices that meet the needs and demands of the learners, and on the other hand, how these very practices serve as an important vehicle that helps to advance theorizing about human development. We also comment on the question of developmentally sensitive practice that is at the heart of the paradigmatic clash between direct instruction and discovery-based learning models.

Our argument proceeds in the following way. We first address the question about how theory and practice relate to each other and expose some long-standing stereotypes that still exist in today's approaches, as well as comment on the recently emerging, important trends in this area of inquiry. With the goal of drawing attention to the agentive and transformative power of theory and knowledge at large, in the next section, we discuss Vygotsky's cultural–historical theory and show how it offered a perspective in which theory and practice are closely aligned—to the effect that they are essentially intertwined. Our position (Stetsenko, 2004) can be briefly summarized in a two-part statement that whereas there is nothing more practical than a good theory, at the same time, there is nothing more theoretical than a good practice. In the final section, we address the cultural–historical viewpoint on the relationship between teaching, learning, and development (including a brief historical overview), and focus on how Vygotsky's initial theoretical formulations have been expanded and elaborated by his followers. Our aim is to demonstrate that by dispelling the unfortunate stereotypes that still prevail in traditional thinking about learning, teaching, and development, a more dynamical theory of these processes (as proposed in the Vygotskian project and expanded herein) directly embodies ways to conduct educational practices that lead to profound developmental changes, with these improved practices reciprocally enacting theory of human development and serving as a vehicle to advance this theory in a unified cycle of human praxis engendering seamless "theory–practice–theory" transitions.

Theory and Practice: The Traditional Divide and Advances in Overcoming It

A deep divide exists between theory and practice—as well as, concurrently, between basic and applied types of research and knowledge—in the eyes of many researchers and practitioners, including those working in the field of education. According to the still prevalent traditional or "classical" view inherited from ancient Greek philosophy and consolidated at the dawn of modern sciences in the 17th century (Stokes, 1997), theory has to do with abstract notions of little practical relevance, derived mostly through contemplation, whereas practice is little concerned with and hardly useful for advancing theoretical constructions and fundamental knowledge. Within this strictly dichotomous (split) view, theory and practice are two separate realms, with no immediate connections between them and no easy way to traverse the gap that divides them. One of the hallmarks of this view is that basic research is considered to be the only avenue to achieve "pure" and genuine knowledge. Such knowledge is thought to be emancipated from considerations of practical relevance and independent of procedures through which it is obtained (including dimensions related to researchers' goals, interests, motivations, and their overall positioning vis-à-vis research topics). In addition, this kind of "pure" or basic research and knowledge are often seen as having priority (being more significant and "truly scientific") over applied research and knowledge, entailing the view that research should always proceed in a linear fashion from a search for basic knowledge to its application.

The position that theory and practice are incontrovertibly divided is underpinned by no less than a deeply entrenched and all-encompassing system of assumptions and beliefs shared by many in the scientific and educational communities—a de facto coherent *worldview* that often remains unarticulated and largely implicit in research and theorizing. In this worldview, the reality is split into all sorts of separate and totally independent realms, such as knowing and doing, external and internal, ideal and material, subjective and objective, and so forth. One important ingredient of this worldview is the notion that knowledge is a purely "mental" phenomenon contained in and confined to a separate space of ideas (or representations), and divorced from the tangible and material "messy" processes out in the world associated with doing things rather than thinking about them or getting to understand them. In other words, "knowledge" is defined as the inner depiction of outer, mind-independent realities and phenomena that have very little to do with practical (i.e., tangible and material) actions in and on the world.

Closely associated with this is the traditional notion that the major mission of science is to explain and, at best, predict phenomena and events in the world (e.g., see *The American Heritage Dictionary of the English Language*) rather than to play any significant role in influencing, shaping, and constructing these phenomena and events. Indeed, it is not unusual for representatives of fundamental sciences to take pride in their research being categorically *a*practical and completely devoid of any considerations of usefulness. For example, as one mathematician states, "I have never done anything 'useful.' No discovery of mine has made, or is likely to make, directly or indirectly, for good or ill, the least difference to the amenity of the world. ... Judged by all practical standards, the value of my mathematical life is nil" (G. H. Hardy, quoted in Schoenfeld, 1999, p. 4).

That the view about knowledge and practice being separate has persisted through centuries—from the time of Galileo, Descartes, and Newton until today—is actually quite ironic, especially given the sharp contrast between the realities of life during that distant historical epoch (when common diseases were untreatable and the steam engine had not yet been invented) and present-day life, which is influenced by the powerful effects of science, knowledge, and technology at each and every level. It is quite misleading to think of science as being a totally "purist" and *a*practical endeavor aimed at merely achieving knowledge and testing ideas, and of knowledge as merely ephemeral and ineffectual, when the very air we breath, the food we eat, the environment we inhabit, and indeed the whole fabric of life as we experience it today—with science heavily involved at all of its phases from inception to death—have been altered, for better or worse, in truly profound ways by this very science and knowledge. Indeed, it is seemingly impractical science, such as mathematics (the idea endorsed by many basic researchers and epitomized in the earlier quote from Hardy), that in fact is directly implicated in advances in modern technology, including computers and magnetic resonance imaging, that have radically altered human life and communication (Schoenfeld, 1999).

The traditional views on theory and knowledge are mirrored in how scholars working within the basic research paradigm on the one hand, and practitioners working in classrooms and other practical settings on the other, organize and structure their pursuits. Basic research typically focuses on understanding phenomena in their "essence," that is, in abstraction from all the unpredictable influences and variations that potentially occur within real-world contexts. Accordingly, an indispensable part of basic research is believed to be selection and operational specification of variables that often represent isolated aspects of some complex phenomena or processes. Researchers then pursue validity and replicability of these isolated aspects, without much concern for a more holistic approach that could do justice to the real-life complexity of these phenomena. In sharp contrast to this, in actual educational practices, problems tend to be complex and ill-structured, with phenomena being fluid and interdependent, as well as highly contingent on surrounding contexts and circumstances, demanding solutions that avoid piecemeal, isolationist approaches.

As a result, developmental psychology and educational practice so far have not profited from each other as much as they potentially could given their common concern for understanding and supporting the processes implicated in human growth and development. On the one hand, discoveries about learning processes have not contributed much to our understanding of how children's minds develop. For example, new teaching methods are rarely discussed in terms of their implications for general theories of human development. On the other hand, psychological theories of development so far do not have a large impact on the practice of teaching and learning (Strauss, 1998). Although some ideas from cognitive psychology have influenced educational practice (e.g., the emphasis on metacognition), too often these ideas have not been supported by explicit strategies for implementing them in school. It is a height of irony that arguably the greatest contribution of cognitive psychology to education is sometimes summed up as "Think less about teaching and more about learning," as if the two processes can be viewed in isolation from each other. Indeed, we believe that the impassable wall between teaching and learning inadvertently encouraged by such views can hardly benefit our understanding of either one of these processes (Stetsenko & Arievitch, 2002).

Recently, the traditional "dualist" views on science and knowledge have been challenged in a number of ways. Motivated by thought-provoking work by Donald Stokes (1997), researchers in education have intensified debates on how to bring theory and research closer together, and how to traverse the interface between basic and applied fields to bridge the gap that separates fundamental understanding and considerations of use (e.g., Klahr & Li, 2005; Schoenfeld, 1999). Exciting developments are also taking place in applied developmental psychology (ADP)—a discipline that seeks to advance the integration of research with policies and programs striving to improve the life chances and conditions of vulnerable populations and communities (e.g., see Lerner, Fisher, & Weinberg, 2000; Pearce & Larson, 2006). This discipline defines itself as a major means to foster science "for and of the people," while contributing to community life and social justice. What these disparate research directions have brought to the fore is a realization that knowledge and its application need not be seen as two separate enterprises, and that instead the findings from use-inspired basic research can directly inform the practice and at the same time generate insights that help to advance theoretical knowledge.

Furthermore, there is an upsurge of approaches to science and research that are inclusive of history, context, politics, and practices of knowledge production in psychology and other social sciences (e.g., Danziger, 1990; Morawski, 2001; Narayan & Harding, 2000; Walkerdine, 2002), as well as in participatory approaches that place issues of power and politics at the center (e.g., Fine & Harris, 2001; Reason & Bradbury, 2001). These diverse works, united in their quest to increase practical relevance of science, build upon many previous perspectives in philosophy of science and science studies that capitalize on (1) facts and observations being contingent on scientific theory and intimately entangled with it, (2) the role of social factors in shaping science, and (3) the historicized nature of knowledge (e.g., see classical works by Kurt Lewin, Thomas Kuhn, Karl Popper, Charles Tolman, and more recently Latour [2007], Knorr-Cetina [1999], feminist epistemology, and others). In these approaches, science is revealed to be much more than a purely intellectual enterprise, separate from contexts and practices in which knowledge comes to life and to which it contributes. Instead, theories and knowledge are understood to arise from the practices of scientific communities that are saturated with social relationships between researchers and their wider social context, including, importantly, participants in research. Theory itself is understood to be originating from and transformative of these practices. What is highlighted in these approaches, in other words, is the reciprocal link between human involvement in the making of scientific knowledge, including theory, and the sciences' involvement in the making of human life and history. As Jill Morawski (2001, p. 434) puts it, "Largely unrecognized by most practicing scientists is that theory is not a universally fixed term but a historically contingent practice. ... Theory and practice can be more commodious yet still distinct phenomena." Drawing on insights from Dewey and Lewin, Morawski reinstates the centrality of the notion of *praxis*—as practice informed by theory and also theory informed by practice, while arguing for the need to relate the two more intimately together.

However, all the exciting developments of recent years in discussions about theory and practice notwithstanding, much of the debate suffers, in our view, from one considerable shortcoming, namely, that in many works (especially in philosophy of science and science studies) one can notice a reliance on the old-fashioned psychological notions of mind and knowledge, for example, based in interpretations—and often misinterpretations—of narrowly conceived cognitive approaches. In science studies and philosophy of science, the Piagetian stage-dominated understanding of how the mind develops, for example, has been and often still is taken for granted (e.g., in works by prominent scholars such as Thomas Kuhn, Jürgen Habermas, and Margaret Archer; see Driver-Linn [2003] on Kuhn's reliance on Piaget). In many other works, the notion of mind and its development remain undertheorized and therefore vulnerable to interpretations that are still grounded in the dualistic worldview in which knowing and doing are seen as fundamentally incompatible processes. Because understanding how science and knowledge function is impossible without a thorough account of human mind, its origins, and its development through the lifespan, the disciplines dealing with the issues of theory and practice (as well as with broader issues related to the status of knowledge) can benefit from what developmental psychology can offer today. As suggested in the next section, the Vygotskian project can be used as a springboard for developing viable concepts of mind and knowledge that are suited for the larger purpose of overcoming the split between theory and practice.

Vygotsky's Cultural–Historical Theory

Vygotsky's theory (e.g., Vygotsky, 1997a, 1997b, 1999, 2004) is now widely known to psychologists and educators around the world as one of the seminal approaches to the issues of human development and learning in the 20th century. This system of views, often referred to as cultural–historical (also known as sociocultural) theory, was originally proposed by Lev Vygotsky in the 1920s and 1930s in collaboration with Alexej N. Leontiev, Alexander R. Luria, and several other scholars. After Vygotsky's untimely death in 1934, this theory was continued within the gradually expanding investigative project of what became Vygotsky's school of thought, embracing several generations of researchers (e.g., Galperin, Zaporozhets, Elkonin, Davydov). Initially developed during a revolutionary time in Russia, marked by much turbulence and turmoil, yet also imbued with social activism and hope, this approach offered—well ahead of its time—a new vision on the most profound questions pertaining to human development. It also suggested a new mission for psychology as a discipline that can be put to use for the betterment of society and, in particular, its educational system. Below we reconstruct major tenets of this approach (especially its deep-seated grounding assumptions; cf. Stetsenko, 2004, 2005; Stetsenko & Arievitch, 2004), while also drawing comparisons to two other seminal theories of human development of the 20th century—those by Jean Piaget and John Dewey. Our central goal in this section is to draw attention to

Vygotsky's unique conceptualization of mind and knowledge as stemming from, participating in, and embodying collaborative social practices, contingent on mediation by cultural tools and, therefore, as encompassing dimensions of knowing and doing in one inseparable blend.

Cultural–historical theory can be characterized by its central claim that human psychological processes develop as a result of continuous interactions (or engagements) of individuals with their social world—the world of people who do things with and for each other, who learn from each other and use experiences of previous generations to meet successfully the continuously changing demands of life. In this sense, at the level of its broad grounding assumptions, cultural–historical theory replaces the metaphor of separation and dualism (typical of the mechanistic worldview) with the dynamical metaphor of the person–world mutual co-construction, coevolution, continuous dialogue, and participation—all underscoring relatedness and interconnectedness, blending and meshing, in one word, the "coming together" of individuals and their world that transcends the split between them. In this logic, development and learning are not seen as products of solitary individuals endowed with internal machinery of cognitive skills that only await the right conditions to unfold. Instead, they are seen as existing in the flux of individuals relating to their world, driven by these relations and their unfolding logic and, therefore, as not being constrained by any rigidly imposed, preprogrammed scripts or rules.

The focus on interactions with the environment marks the Vygotskian approach, as well as those of Piaget and Dewey, by a transactional, relational, dynamical, and contextualized mode of thinking about human development (cf. Stetsenko & Arievitch, 2004; Vianna & Stetsenko, 2006), and entails at least two important implications. First, all three theories place human action, understood as a process that relates and links individuals with their world, at the foundation of analysis. The growth of human action in its increasingly complex transformations, and as something that takes place *between* human beings and their world, and not just "in the head," is considered by all three scholars to be the origin of psychological processes. These processes appear to be part and parcel of ongoing activities that individuals perform in life, positing no split between action and knowledge. Therefore, for Vygotsky, Piaget, and Dewey, the mind is not a container that stores memories and knowledge, but is instead a dynamic system formed and expressed in actions. Because development is a contextually embedded process of interactions with the world, it is understood as being not preprogrammed; innate, blueprinted mechanisms are by definition inappropriate for tackling the tasks imposed by an emergent, constantly changing reality of humans acting in contexts. It is here that all three scholars stand in opposition to strictly nativist (i.e., Chomsky) and one-sidedly mentalist (i.e., many in the mainstream cognitive approaches) frameworks.

Second, all action-centered theories implicate growth through increasing elaborateness of actions and therefore concern themselves with the issues of learning and development (although much more directly in Vygotsky's and Dewey's than in Piaget's works). Here, all three scholars again converge, in that they imply that children *learn by doing, that is, through acting in and on the environment*. This view places Vygotsky, Piaget, and Dewey in clear opposition to traditional views on mind as a passive container of knowledge, on teaching as transmission of knowledge, and on learning as a process of acquiring fixed facts and rules that are thought to exist independently of human activity.

However, the Vygotskian approach is marked by a much stronger (compared to Piaget and Dewey) emphasis not simply on individuals acting in the world and exploring or experiencing it, but instead on *shared, collaborative activities* (or practices) as the core reality in which and through which development and learning take place and operate, and from which they stem. Human development is understood as grounded in such collaborative (i.e., social and communal) activities because they represent a unique relation of humans to the world determinant of their emergence as species in phylogeny, their development in ontogeny, and their cultural–historical evolution as a human civilization. Importantly, these collaborative practices serve the goals of *transforming* the world (instead of adapting to it, as in the nonhuman world) and involve creating, accumulating, and passing on from generation to generation the collective experiences of engaging with the world—meeting environmental demands, facing challenges, and solving problems encountered in the course of such engagements. Each new generation—and, in fact, each individual human being—learns from these experiences, comes to use them as their own "habits of mind," and potentially contributes to collaborative experiences in what is the ever-expanding, dynamic process of human cultural–historical practices or cultural evolution (cf. the notion of "ratchet effect"; see Tomasello, 2000).

These collective experiences of engaging particular aspects of environment, solving particular classes of problems, and making sense of events and phenomena in the world become, in the course of human history, crystallized in what is termed "cultural tools" or artifacts. Cultural tools, in other words, embody collective experiences—ways of thinking and knowing, rules of conduct, templates of solving problems—discovered in collective practices by previous generations of people and passed down to the next ones in often abbreviated and symbolic forms (e.g., as in traffic signs that stand for and direct the conduct of traffic participants). Organized in systematic ways, these tools together comprise human culture—the unique dimension of human life that has to do with the profoundly collaborative and collective (communal) character of how humans act in the world in the sense of their fundamental interdependence and reliance on each other—and rely on cultural artifacts that embody experiences of other people, including those from previous generations. Cultural tools, as embodiments of collective experiences (or collaboratively discovered ways of solving problems) can come about in various forms, such as (1) material objects (e.g., items of kitchenware that crystallize specifically human ways of eating; computers that represent lengthy history of technological discoveries and afford complicated activities), (2) patterns of behavior specifically organized in space and time (e.g., bedtime or meal rituals and other sets of rules for conduct), and (3) concepts that stand for ways of knowing and thinking about various phenomena in the world. Most often, however, cultural tools are combinations of elements of a different order, with human *language* being a multilevel combination of culturally evolved arrangements of meanings, sounds, grammar, rules of communication, and so forth.

According to Vygotsky, learning to use such tools is not something that simply helps the mind to develop; instead, this learning leads to and essentially gives rise to specifically human (i.e., cultural) forms of psychological functioning—thinking, knowing, reasoning, arguing, remembering, feeling, self-regulating, perceiving, and so on (Falcade & Strozzi, Chapter 22, this volume). Thus, in the case of learning the language, this process calls into being—and in effect shapes and forms—new facets of the learner's mind, such as higher-order thinking, self-regulation and self-awareness. For example, a child who learns the words to call for attention gets a powerful new tool for regulating first other people's and then his or her own behavior and relations. Another example is a child who learns to memorize events of the past by applying memory tools (so-called mnemonic techniques) such as a storyline that helps to unite these events in one coherent and meaningful overarching sequence, thus greatly enhancing capacities for memory. By learning the cultural tool of storytelling, the child is thereby advancing to more sophisticated—deliberate and efficient—levels of his or her memory capacities and overall cognitive functioning (for further examples, see Bodrova & Leong, 1995). Thus, the structures and procedures of acting with cultural tools are turned into the structures and procedures of the mind.

Closely related to the notion of cultural tools is the idea of cultural *mediation* of psychological processes that conveys the following points. Human beings are not isolated, lone agents who directly respond to their environment in immediate ways (i.e., in spontaneous and "natural," self-created ways, as in a stimulus–response schema adopted in behaviorism); instead, human beings are *social* agents who act as participants in collaborative sociocultural practices—bound by the rules and norms of these practices, yet also benefiting from their collective achievements, inventions, and means. Therefore, specifically human (i.e., cultural) ways of dealing with and acting upon the world necessarily build on and continue experiences of other people and entail employment of cultural tools that mediate (i.e., "intervene" or become inserted) between individuals and the relevant aspects of their environment, thereby shaping and affecting ways of interacting with (responding to and acting in) this environment. Thus, the notion of cultural mediation underscores the importance of social interactions, connections, bonds, and filaments that determine the ways humans engage with the world; it also specifies the concrete mechanism—namely, the collaborative invention and employment of cultural tools as intermediate devices of acting—that makes these interactions and filaments possible and sustainable through the history of human society.

To summarize, the central notion of the cultural–historical theory is that people develop through collaboratively transforming and creating their environment with the help of cultural tools that unfold and cumulatively grow through history of human communities, thus greatly expanding each community member's capacities and horizons of development. It is in these processes that people create and constantly transform their very lives, thereby also changing themselves in fundamental ways and, through this change, gaining self-knowledge and knowledge about the world. Importantly, cultural–historical practices (or activities) are neither ancillary nor complementary to development and learning. Instead, they are *the very realm* (or the very "matter" and fabric) that these processes serve, stem from, belong to, and are carried out in, with no ontological gap posited between people actively engaging their world on the one hand, and their knowing, learning, and becoming on the other.

These broad ideas are reflected in all of Vygotsky's major concepts. For example, they are exemplified in his "general law" of development, according to which psychological processes (e.g., cognition, emotion, self-regulation, and motivation) emerge out of social, collective activity (see Vygotsky, 2004, p. 83) and never completely break away from this activity. They are also reflected in a particular emphasis on cultural tools that runs as a common thread through all of Vygotsky's and his followers' works. These ideas are also implicated in Vygotsky's notion that teaching–learning leads development. These processes take place in the "zone of proximal development," where individuals cooperate and are mutually involved in actively co-constructing their knowledge and identities and, thus, their very development. What these notions imply is no less than a novel worldview on human development as a cultural–historical practice in which individuals *develop together*—through participating in and contributing to collaborative pursuits—and in which other people are intimately involved, including through teaching each other and learning from each other, while drawing on and simultaneously contributing to common experiences and human cultural–historical heritage.

These novel ideas about development and learning, as well as the notion of knowledge in Vygotsky's project, can be extended to bear, through a number of implications, on the "theory versus practice" debate discussed in the previous chapter. In particular, based on Vygotsky's premises, and in view of collaborative activities mediated by cultural tools being the core source and the very fabric of the mind, it can be stated that knowing and acting are never separate; instead they belong together as they form inherent aspects (or dimensions) of one and the same process of people collaboratively engaging with their world. In this sense, to know something is not to have some inert facts stored in the mind; instead, it is an ability of an intentional human being to carry out, participate in, continue, and ultimately contribute to collaborative practices through one's actions. Therefore, knowledge (including its theoretical forms) does not merely reflect the world. Instead, knowledge embodies templates of past practices at a given point in history, and in a given sociocultural context, to represent these past practices in symbolic forms amenable for further use in what essentially are continuously expanding cycles of "practice–theory–practice." In this sense, knowledge is an alive, generative, and deeply historical process that is engendered by and itself engenders active engagement in collaborative sociocultural practice. Knowledge appears then as a social process rather than a mere product of solitary explorations—a dynamical phenomenon that needs to be collaboratively performed and enacted rather than stored and then retrieved from some inner individual space "in the mind"; that is, knowledge can be seen as a social activity in the world because it always comes out of sociocultural transformative practices and always returns into them, serving as an important step in carrying out these practices and having its grounding, its mode of existence, and its ultimate relevance within these broader transformative practices. And in view of the radical reappraisal of the link between knowledge and action, theory and practice too appear as intertwined—as arising from and giving rise to each other in one essentially inseparable blend of a "theory–practice–theory" cycle.

Continuing Vygotsky's Legacy

In this section, we discuss how Vygotsky's ideas have been continued and expanded by his followers, especially Galperin and Davydov, who helped to bring to life many of his insights and creatively expanded on them. Importantly, they did so while working at the interface of developmental theory and the practice of schooling. In particular, they focused their efforts on exploring and conceptualizing the links among the processes of teaching, learning, and development, while working in the midst of classroom practices, actively shaping and transforming these practices and drawing theoretical implications from these transformative engagements—thereby putting forth, with unusual clarity, the message about theory and practice being intertwined. To create a wider context for our argument, we first briefly discuss how the links among these three processes have been approached in the history of psychology, then present the Vygotskian account.

The relationship among the processes of teaching, learning, and development is not a topic that has attracted much attention throughout the history of psychology. This history is characterized more by a shifting of attention from one to the other process rather than focusing on how they depend on or influence each other. With some notable exceptions, such as the work of John Dewey and Lev S. Vygotsky, these relationships were largely ignored in psychological theories through much of the last century. For example, behaviorism had made learning its focal point (in terms of stimulus–response contingencies), yet it never concerned itself with the issues of how learning could lead to development of psychological processes and what teaching has to do with either one of these processes. With the rise of cognitive psychology, learning ceased to attract attention altogether (cf. Siegler, 2000; Stetsenko & Arievitch, 2002; Strauss, 1998), and research focused instead on discovery of deep universal laws of mind that were presumed to be practically independent from any external influences, including teaching and learning. Cognitive approaches primarily aimed, and continue to aim, at describing context-independent processes (e.g., information-processing modules) common to all humans, regardless of the culturally specific activities in which people engage. The issue of how cognitive-developmental change comes about has been central in Jean Piaget's "genetic epistemology." This theory can be credited with the discovery of important regularities in how the human mind develops through the individual's active engagement with the world. However, this theory largely attributed children's progress in developing cognitive capacities, such as conceptual understanding and problem solving, to their own independent experiences and explorations, irrespective of what children learn through participating in cultural–historical collaborative practices, such as learning.

Thus, the question of how specific activities in which learners engage, and the cultural tools that they are provided in classrooms, affect the development of their minds has rarely been clearly formulated, let alone sufficiently explored. Today, teaching, learning, and development continue to be viewed by many as processes that are essentially different from each other, or only superficially related. For example, despite growing evidence that intelligence can be learned and taught (e.g., Perkins, 1995), there is little debate about the mechanisms that could underlie and possibly link all three processes.

The reason why researchers concerned with teaching, learning, and development are not finding common grounds on which their findings might be integrated, we believe, has to do with a dearth of conceptual space in which the relationship between these processes might be conceived and theorized (cf. Stetsenko & Arievitch, 2002). Indeed, when learning is regarded only as the forming of links between stimuli and responses (as in behaviorism), or when the developing mind is viewed as largely governed by internal and for the most part innate regularities (as in many branches of cognitive psychology), or when the impact of teaching on development is ignored (as in most of developmental psychology), there is simply no room for the three processes to be conceptually brought together and explored for their complementary effects.

However, it is precisely the exploration into the links among teaching, learning, and development that became a pivotal element in cultural–historical theory of human development and learning. Already Vygotsky's own early works not only allowed for a synthesis of teaching, learning, and development but they also actually actively called for it. In particular, Vygotsky proposed that teaching–learning (with his original term *obuchenie* connoting precisely the unity of teaching and learning) leads to development because it allows children to learn to use cultural tools, thus participating in and potentially contributing to evolving cultural–historical practices at the foundation of human development and society. Development was therefore seen as inherently linked to processes of teaching and learning, with the three together comprising a threefold process in which cultural tools are provided, learned, and transformed into the building blocks of the mind, all within the ever-expanding cultural–historical practices that entail active interaction and cooperation in the zone of proximal development.

To illustrate this with the memory example again: *Teaching* children to use cultural tools and strategies for memorizing materials is the pathway for the children to develop, through *learning* to apply these tools, the higher-order capacities in which these cultural tools for memorization represent the key *building blocks of the child's mind*. As a result, the child's new capacities associated with the newly acquired tools open up ways for novel activities and more sophisticated social interactions—including learning ever more complex tools introduced through teaching—within the conjoined and expanding processes of teaching, learning, and development.

A wealth of further examples of how these theoretical ideas work in practice of early education has been recently reported in *Science* (and widely disseminated; e.g., by the National Institute for Early Education Research [NIEER], 2007) from a study by Diamond, Barnett, Thomas, and Munro (2007). This study examined the effects of *The Tools* curriculum for preschoolers developed by Elena Bodrova and Deborah Leong, based on Vygotsky's insights into teaching, learning, and development. This curriculum, used in several U.S. states, has been shown to improve psychological processes, such as the self-regulation and cognitive control skills important for success in school and life in at-risk preschoolers, without costly interventions but, rather, through introducing efficient cultural tools through teaching–learning practices.

In addition to the main tenets of Vygotsky's theory that have been shown to be efficient in early education, there is one more line of research carried out by Vygotsky's followers that is also of great potential, we believe, to serve the same purposes. In particular, Vygotsky's followers, most notably Galperin (1985) and Davydov (1990), focused their efforts on specifying and further expanding Vygotsky's ideas about the relationship between teaching–learning and development. Their point of departure was the notion that teaching–learning leads development; therefore, to better understand the mechanisms of development, including cognitive growth, they turned to classroom practices and began exploring how various methods of teaching and various curricular materials—including those they endeavored to devise together with teachers—led to differential learning and developmental outcomes (cf. Arievitch, 2003). Their mode of research is notable in that it represents perhaps the first deliberate attempt to bridge the gap between applied and basic research at the intersection of developmental theory and education, by bringing together the goals of explanation, exploration, and transformation. In particular, this research implemented the following sequence of steps, encompassing these three goals in one research design termed "the formative study": (1) devising theoretically driven methods of teaching and cultural tools for learning as the cornerstones of instruction (in line with Vygotsky's theory); (2) implementing these methods in naturalistic settings, such as classrooms; (3) testing, exploring, and documenting whether and how these methods enhance learning and development to produce differential developmental outcomes to then (4) draw theoretical implications from these instructional interventions for the theory of teaching, learning, and development (as the centerpiece of developmental theory at large). Importantly, the last design component was seen as the stepping-stone for devising new instructional practices for these methods to again be tried out and tested in classrooms to further advance theory in one seamless theory–practice–theory cycle. Thus, this work essentially predated attempts to bridge the gap between fundamental understanding (i.e., theory) and considerations of use (i.e., application in practice)—much in line with the recent developments in and recommendations for research in education including intervention studies and design experiments (e.g., Cobb, 2005; Klahr, Chen, & Toth, 2001; Klahr & Li, 2005).

Based on the theoretical premise that teaching and learning lead development and that cultural tools play indispensable role in this process, Galperin, Davydov, and their coworkers (for an overview of this research extending through several decades, see Arievitch & Haenen, 2005; Arievitch & Stetsenko, 2000) aspired to construct and design curricular content in ways that would most efficiently facilitate the learning of cultural tools by students, thus leading to better developmental outcomes. The solution they gradually came to in their practical work in schools was to immerse students in meaningful sociocultural practices whereby they could be introduced to efficient cultural tools for addressing and solving problems they encountered while participating in these practices. Importantly, they realized that cultural tools need to be introduced not as some separate and self-sufficient devices (or pieces of information) but as practically valuable means to solve various problems inherent in particular sociocultural practices—as these means have been discovered and gradually elaborated upon in the course of human history. In other words, the central breakthrough in this research had to do with the realization that students come to develop knowledge and psychological processes through learning by immersion in sociocultural practices in which the cultural tools can be revealed, in the course of instruction, as meaningful components serving the purposes of solving problems encountered in human practices.

One illustrative example is the program developed by these scholars for elementary mathematics, which dramatically differs from traditional teaching of this subject (for a detailed description, see Arievitch & Stetsenko, 2000). The traditional teaching is typically based on learning numbers that are introduced through discrete objects (one apple, two cups, etc.) that students explore through hands-on manipulation, then directly apply to counting tasks. In contrast, Galperin's and Davydov's approach is based on systematically introducing children to the *meaningful practice of measurement* as the core activity in which numbers emerge and make sense as its tools. As children master measurement (i.e., by exploring how various objects can be compared and assessed through this operation), they discover the need to keep track of results of their activities in some form, at which point the teachers introduce the concept of number and help children use it as an analytical tool with which they can record the relations between objects of measurements (i.e., A greater or smaller than B by certain amount X, A equal to B, etc.).

Children are introduced to the concept of number as a stand-in for relations between objects that are revealed through the practice of measurement. In other words, the concept of number is taught through introducing children to the genuine practice from which this concept has emerged, and which it continues to serve. In this approach, then, to learn the concept of number is not reduced to learning to count discrete objects or to learning the words for various numbers. Instead, the concept of number is introduced as a way to solve problems that the learners face while carrying out tangible and meaningful activities—in this case, activities of quantitative comparisons and other types of measurement. In this way, students come to understand numbers from the viewpoint of how numbers serve *as tools in solving practical problems* within meaningful practices rather than as abstract symbols; therefore, they also come to see how this knowledge can be put to use in their own practice.

One related, and equally important, finding from this line of research is that knowledge (including concepts) needs to be introduced to students not only as a tool that has emerged and makes sense within certain practice (i.e., as part and parcel of a meaningful activity) but also as itself representing the ways of carrying out various activities; that is, knowledge and concepts need to be taught in ways that reveal how they stand for certain ways of doing things and represent abbreviated embodiments of activity (templates for action) that entail knowledge of how to act within certain problem areas. A revealing example is teaching about the geometrical notion of circle. The traditional teaching might involve learning how circles differ from other figures and also memorizing relevant verbal definitions (i.e., circles are shapes comprising those points in a plane that are at a constant distance, called the "radius," from a fixed point, called the "center"). However, this verbal definition is quite complicated and difficult to memorize, especially for younger learners. An alternative to this traditional teaching is based on a definition of a circle as "a figure described by the rotation of a line with one end free [moving] and the other fixed" (quoted in Davydov, 1990, p. 251). This description precisely lays bare the construction and method of operation of the pair of compasses that allows the learners to grasp major regularities of circles (e.g., the constancy of the radius) based on understanding actions that make circles possible—that is, to understand the notion of a circle in a tangible and practical way. Learning the concept of a circle based on this definition dispenses with the need for anyone learning geometry to memorize a ready-made fact that does not, by itself, make much sense.

Importantly, in Davydov's (1990) approach, rendering concepts meaningful through revealing activities and practices "hidden" behind them makes learning tangible and practical, and at the same time truly "theoretical." Specifically, this kind of learning was shown to allow students to (1) grasp the often ostensibly abstract, utmost theoretical generalities within a given subject domain through (2) understanding how various components of knowledge "are made" and "come to be" as tools in human practices, and therefore simultaneously (3) grasping how this knowledge can be applied in practice. That is, viewing knowledge as a form of practice in this approach did not entail trivializing knowledge as merely hands-on manipulation of objects; instead, this view brought about a focus on practical relevance and origins of concepts as a way to reveal their most general (i.e., theoretical) regularities and features. Understanding concepts in this "theoretical" way in turn entailed knowing the utmost *practical ways* of dealing with issues and phenomena, and solving problems involving them. Thus, theory was seen not as a separate way of knowing, superior to practice, but as a form of practice that encapsulates the most efficient ways of acting and doing. Therefore, this approach highlighted how truly porous the boundary between the practical and theoretical types of knowing are and opened up ways to move beyond portraying them as incompatible modes that exist in opposition to each other.

In addition, this approach sought to move beyond the opposition between traditional forms of instruction, characterized by unidirectional transmission of facts and rules on the one hand, and Piagetian constructivist approaches that emphasize children's independent construction of knowledge, without direct instruction, on the other. In place of this opposition, this approach employed teaching models that introduced knowledge through instruction, not in a passive form but through active participation in various practices. In this type of instruction, knowledge and various cultural tools, while being introduced by teachers, had to be actively reconstructed (or reenacted) by each student in her or his own activity. The *active appropriation (or creative reconstruction) of cultural tools* was the linchpin of Galperin's and Davydov's approach, with this notion essentially bridging the gap between direct instruction (entailing provision of cultural tools) and independent discovery (entailing learners' active reconstruction of these tools). Thus, this ground-breaking approach potentially opened ways for effectively synthesizing top-down (teacher-centered) and bottom-up (child-centered) approaches by fostering active participation of children in the construction of knowledge through exploration and inquiry into established sociocultural practices and relevant cultural tools introduced by teachers.

Finally, this practical research in classroom contexts served as important fodder for further development of theoretical ideas and premises. For example, the notion of cultural tools became refined and elaborated through this research. In particular, because cultural tools were shown to be most efficiently appropriated by learners through acting upon and with them, the very notion of cultural tools was redefined as representing and embodying specifically human ways of acting (including doing and knowing) rather than as merely static "things" (for details, see Stetsenko, 1999). Another theoretically significant outcome of this work was that to be a leading force in development, the process of teaching and learning needs to integrate high-quality cultural tools that embody the most efficient ways of solving problems. Thus, in this approach, theory building was integral to the work of devising curricular materials and implementing them in classroom practices, while this work in turn was integral to theory building, with no gap between these two complementary facets within a unified endeavor of engaging the world and solving problems encountered in the course of such engagements.

Conclusions: Implications for Developmental Psychology and Education

The Vygotskian approach integrates the analysis of teaching–learning and development by (1) conceptualizing all three as historically evolving cultural practices grounded in collaborative endeavors by human communities to which all individual human beings have an important contribution to make, and (2) capitalizing on an element that is central to all three of these processes. This element concerns activities mediated by the cultural tools provided by teachers and learned by students, thereby allowing students to transform these tools into powerful new instruments of their minds that can be put to use in further expanding these collaborative endeavors. These new instruments instigate development and bring it in motion, in the full sense, as they empower learners to become active participants in and potential contributors to cultural–historical practices and, therefore, to be engaged and motivated explorers and thinkers. In this sense, the Vygotskian approach fills the gaps so typical of previous frameworks in both psychology and education, in which teaching, learning, and development are viewed as disconnected.

In contrast to traditional theories, which often ignore how development is contingent on teaching and learning practices, thus confusing developmental outcomes achieved within particular educational systems with universal developmental regularities, the Vygotskian approach draws attention to a self-perpetuating "vicious circle," namely, *inadequate theories of development → poor educational practices → poor development outcomes → inadequate theories of development*. For example, many traditional theories posit that young children lack the ability to reason in a reflective way with abstract categories. Given this view, many educators think that children need to be taught in a fashion that best accommodates this allegedly fixed, age-related feature of their thinking capacities. Thus, traditional instruction typically includes the requirement to teach young children in a "piecemeal" fashion, whereby they are exposed to small bits of information supported by concrete illustrative examples, with no attempt to reveal the general rules and connections that lie behind these examples. As a result, children indeed do not develop the ability to operate with abstract (i.e., generalized, systematic) concepts. In contrast, research findings by Vygotsky and his colleagues demonstrate that when knowledge is taught as tools that stem from meaningful practices and can be used in solving practical tasks, as described earlier, there are spectacular developmental changes, including progress in abstract reflective thinking, self-regulation, and cognitive control (for further examples, see Arievitch & Stetsenko, 2000; Bodrova & Leong, 1995; Diamond et al., 2007; Karpov & Haywood, 1998). In this sense, then, the traditional instructional restrictions thought to be grounded in inherent limitations of children's minds in fact themselves produce these limitations!

Furthermore, a cultural–historical approach gives an instructive, albeit counterintuitive, answer to what is perhaps the most pressing issue concerning education today: Is direct instruction or is independent discovery a better model for schools? From a Vygotskian perspective, the very dichotomy between these two models is misguided. In place of this dichotomy, the demarcating line needs to be drawn between *inert knowledge* (cf. Vosniadou, Chapter 24, this volume) and learning on the one hand, and *generative knowledge* on the other. Emphasis on inert knowledge—whether gained through "hands-on" and vivid but too often fortuitous and unsystematic experiences or through direct instruction that follows a transmission, "top-down" model in which the learners are passive—is what stymies learning and development. Unlike inert facts and knowledge, generative knowledge that embodies historically evolved cultural practices, and serves as its instrument, empowers children with methods for expansively continuing these practices and for constructing *new* knowledge. Therefore, it is also this kind of knowledge that can be actively used by learners in the cycles of exploration and discovery within cultural–historical practices. Arguably, there is nothing more practical than such knowledge, especially in the 21st century, which is increasing likely to value innovation, expansion, and creativity.

In summary, the Vygotskian approach, while predicated on highly abstract, theoretical premises, such as the notion of mediation by cultural tools and the leading role of teaching and learning in development, is at the same time a very practical guide for acting. In particular, this approach makes imperative research that is grounded and carried out in the form of transformative work in classrooms empowering students to learn, with this research serving as the vehicle to further develop and expand theoretical ideas about cultural mediation. The very theory that teaching–learning leads development (based in broad ideas about human development) compelled the scholars in Vygotsky's tradition to turn to practical organization of classroom practices to explore cultural mediation *through understanding how it works*. We would argue, therefore, that cultural–historical theory represents a key development in research on teaching, learning, and development at the interface of theory and practice. Ultimately, it is in this sense that this theory is a contribution *simultaneously* to fundamental knowledge in developmental psychology and to classroom practices—one powerful and instructive exemplar of how the gap between the two can be bridged.

References

Arievitch, I. M. (2003). A potential for an integrated view of development and learning: Galperin's contribution to sociocultural psychology. *Mind, Culture, and Activity, 10*, 278–288.

Arievitch, I. M., & Haenen, J. P. P. (2005). Connecting sociocultural theory and educational practice: Galperin's approach. *Educational Psychologist, 40*, 155–165.

Arievitch, I. M., & Stetsenko, A. (2000). The quality of cultural tools and cognitive development: Galperin's perspective and its applications. *Human Development, 43*, 69–93.

Bodrova, E., & Leong, D. (1995). *Tools of the mind: A Vygotskian approach to early child education.* Upper Saddle River, NJ: Prentice-Hall.

Cobb, P. (2005). Supporting the improvement of learning and teaching in social and institutional context. In S. M. Carver & D. Klahr (Eds.), *Cognition and instruction: 25 years of progress* (pp. 455–478). Mahwah, NJ: Erlbaum.

Danziger, K. (1990). *Constructing the subject: Historical origins of psychological research.* New York: Cambridge University Press.

Davydov, V. V. (1990). Types of generalization in instruction: Logical and psychological problems in the structuring of school curricula. In *Soviet studies in mathematics education* (Vol. 2). Reston, VA: National Council of Teachers of Mathematics.

Diamond, A., Barnett, W. S., Thomas, J., & Munro, S. (2007). Preschool program improves cognitive control. *Science, 318*, 1387–1388.

Driver-Linn, E. (2003). Where is the psychology going?: Structural fault lines revealed by psychologists' use of Kuhn. *American Psychologist, 58*, 269–278.

Fine, M., & Harris, A. (Guest eds.). (2001). Under the covers: Theorising the politics of counter stories [Special issue]. *Critical Psychology, 4.* London: Lawrence & Wishart.

Galperin, P. (1985). *Metody obuchenija i umstvennoe razvitie rebenka* [Methods of instruction and mental development of the child]. Moscow: Izdatelstvo MGU.

Karpov, Y. V., & Haywood, C. H. (1998). Two ways to elaborate Vygotsky's concept of mediation. *American Psychologist, 53*, 27–36.

Klahr, D., Chen, Z., & Toth, E. E. (2005). Cognitive development and science education: Ships passing in the night or beacons of mutual illumination? In S. M. Carver & D. Klahr (Eds.), *Cognition and instruction: 25 years of progress* (pp. 75–119). Mahwah, NJ: Erlbaum.

Klahr, D., & Li, J. (2005). Cognitive research and elementary science instruction: From the laboratory, to the classroom, and back. *Journal of Science Education and Technology, 14*, 217–238.

Knorr-Cetina, K. (1999). *Epistemic cultures: How the sciences make knowledge.* Cambridge, MA: Harvard University Press.

Latour, B. (2007). *Reassembling the social: An introduction to actor–network theory.* New York: Oxford University Press.

Lerner, R. M., Fisher, C. B., & Weinberg, R. A. (2000). Toward a science for and of the people: Promoting civil society through the application of developmental science. *Child Development, 71*, 11–20.

Morawski, J. G. (2001). Gifts bestowed, gifts withheld: Assessing psychological theory with a Kochian attitude. *American Psychologist, 56*, 433–440.

Narayan, U., & Harding, S. (Eds.). (2000). *Decentering the center: Philosophy for a multicultural, postcolonial, and feminist world.* Bloomington: Indiana University Press.

National Institute for Early Education Research (NIEER). (2007). Preschool program shown to improve key cognitive functions (including working memory and control of attention and action). Retrieved September 1, 2008, from *nieer.org/mediacenter/index.php?pressid=79*

Pearce, N. J., & Larson, R. W. (2006). How teens become engaged in youth development programs: The process of motivational change in a civic activism organization. *Applied Developmental Science, 10*, 121–131.

Perkins, D. N. (1995). *Outsmarting IQ: The emerging science of learnable intelligence*. New York: Free Press.

Reason, P., & Bradbury, H. (Eds.). (2001). *Handbook of action research: Participative inquiry and practice*. London: Sage.

Schoenfeld, A. H. (1999). Looking toward the 21st century: Challenges of educational theory and practice. *Educational Researcher, 28*, 4–14.

Siegler, R. S. (2000). The rebirth of children's learning. *Child Development, 71*, 26–35.

Stetsenko, A. (1999). Social interaction, cultural tools, and the zone of proximal development: In search of a synthesis. In M. Hedegaard, S. Chaiklin, S. Boedker, & U. J. Jensen (Eds.), *Activity theory and social practice: Proceedings of the ISCRAT 1998: Keynote speeches and panels* (pp. 235–253). Aarhus: Aarhus University Press.

Stetsenko, A. (2004). Introduction to "Tool and sign" by Lev Vygotsky. In R. Rieber & D. Robbinson (Eds.), *Essential Vygotsky* (pp. 499–510). New York: Kluwer Academic/Plenum Press.

Stetsenko, A. (2005). Activity as object-related: Resolving the dichotomy of individual and collective types of activity [Special issue]. In V. Kaptelinin & R. Miettinen (Guest eds.), *Mind, Culture, and Activity, 12*(1), 70–88.

Stetsenko, A., & Arievitch, I. (2002). Teaching, learning, and development: A post-Vygotskian perspective. In G. Wells & G. Claxton (Eds.), *Learning for life in the 21st century: Sociocultural perspectives on the future of education* (pp. 84–96). Malden, MA: Blackwell.

Stetsenko, A., & Arievitch, I. M. (2004). Vygotskian collaborative project of social transformation: History, politics, and practice in knowledge construction. *International Journal of Critical Psychology, 12*, 58–80.

Stokes, D. E. (1997). *Pasteur's quadrant*. Washington, DC: Brookings Institution Press.

Strauss, S. (1998). Cognitive development and science education: Toward a middle level model. In W. Damon, I. E. Sigel, & K. A. Renninger (Eds.), *Handbook of child psychology: Vol. 4. Child psychology in practice* (5th ed., pp. 357–399). Hoboken, NJ: Wiley.

Tomasello, M. (2000). *The cultural origins of human cognition*. Cambridge, MA: Harvard University Press.

Vianna, E., & Stetsenko, A. (2006). Embracing history through transforming it: Contrasting Piagetian versus Vygotskian (activity) theories of learning and development to expand constructivism within a dialectical view of history. *Theory and Psychology, 16*, 81–108.

Vygotsky, L. S. (1997a). The historical meaning of the crisis in psychology: A methodological investigation. In R. W. Rieber & J. Wollock (Eds.), *The collected works of L. S. Vygotsky: Vol. 3. Problems of the theory and history of psychology* (pp. 233–343). New York: Plenum Press.

Vygotsky, L. S. (1997b). The problem of the development of higher mental functions. In R. W. Rieber (Ed.), *The collected works of L. S. Vygotsky: Vol. 4. The history of the development of higher mental functions: Cognition and language* (pp. 1–26). New York: Plenum Press.

Vygotsky, L. S. (1999). Tool and sign in the development of the child. In R. W. Rieber (Ed.), *The collected works of L. S. Vygotsky: Vol. 6. Scientific legacy* (pp. 3–68). New York: Plenum Press.

Vygotsky, L. S. (2004). Thinking and speech. In R. Rieber & D. Robbinson (Eds.), *Essential Vygotsky* (pp. 33–148). New York: Kluwer Academic/Plenum Press.

Walkerdine, V. (Ed). (2002). *Challenging subjects: Critical psychology for a new millennium*. Hampshire, UK: Palgrave.

PART II

BRAIN FUNCTIONING AND LEARNING

A growing body of neuroscience research about the developing brain offers new possibilities for understanding and supporting student learning during the school years. Fusaro and Nelson (Chapter 4) present an overview of the neurobiology of brain development, and of the points of connection between neuroscience and education, using language accessible to educators. They begin with general principles of brain development during the prenatal period and the first years of life. Then they introduce the concept of neural plasticity, drawing on the twin themes of experience-expectant and experience-dependent plasticity. One of the important take-home points to be gleaned from this review is how experience, particularly experience at school, weaves its way into the structure of the brain, particularly during sensitive periods of development. In addition the discussion demonstrates and underscores the contribution of the neurosciences to understanding important phenomena for schooling. These phenomena include control of attention and behavior, reading, and mathematics. They describe what happens in the brain as children use skills in each of these areas, and how these processes change as a result of experience, practice, and maturation.

Bauer (Chapter 5) points out how learning and memory are inextricably linked to one another. At the same time, memory processes themselves seem to shape and impact learning and performance. Bauer places the study of learning in the context of recent developments in our understanding of the neurobiology of memory. Of special note is the postencoding process of consolidation, and the complementary process of reconsolidation. These processes involve active changes that occur in the brain and influence what is retained after the processes of teaching and learning have ceased. The implications of these postencoding processes for learning and performance are considered, as are developmental changes in the processes and how they might relate to age-associated differences in learning.

Children who learn by employing specific mnemonic strategies retain information much better than children who do not rely on strategies. But how do children acquire these strategies? This issue is taken up by Ornstein, Coffman, and Grammer (Chapter 6), who review basic memory research and address the question of whether and how adults, such as parents and teachers, contribute to the development of children's use of strategies to remember what they are taught. This work points to the important role of dialogue between adults and children around shared events in children's development of strategies to remember the details surrounding those shared events. They also pinpoint the behaviors that differentiate between teachers whose students learn to employ effective mnemonic strategies and teachers whose students do not develop and employ such strategies.

The wide use and acceptance of the concept of intelligence in common parlance conceal the sometimes contentious debate about what intelligence really is. Bornstein (Chapter 7) reviews in detail the long-standing debate on the nature and assessment of intelligence. The arguments are clearly laid out and presented in a fair and balanced manner. Bornstein concludes that intelligence comprises multiple domains, and that efforts to rank-order or categorize children on the basis of a single global or general intelligence factor is misplaced. This may lead to possible errors of classification, sometimes with dire consequences for children. Bornstein points out how prominent theories contrast the nature and structure of intelligence and its development. This chapter briefly reviews the ways specific and general intelligences can be viewed. The structure of children's minds before they are enrolled in formal education is best understood in terms of a single general intelligence factor that is complemented by several specific and relatively independent faculties. Bornstein reports on prominent patterns of individual differences supporting the view that early child intelligence has both general and domain-specific manifestations organized in a hierarchical structure.

CHAPTER 4

Developmental Cognitive Neuroscience and Education Practice

Maria Fusaro
Charles A. Nelson III

Early childhood educators and those specializing in early intervention have come to recognize the importance of human brain plasticity for educational practice. For example, early speech and language intervention programs operate under the general principle that the developing system is particularly malleable in its first years (National Research Council and Institute of Medicine, 2000). This early malleability justifies efforts to provide support for very young children facing various risks to keep developmental trajectories on a normative track. Although less public attention has been placed on brain changes between 3 and 8 years of age, this period of early to middle childhood continues to be vitally important for brain development. It is not the case that the brain stops changing after age 3. Indeed, for education to take root, changes in brain anatomy, chemistry, physiology, and function need to occur over many years.

There is strong agreement across disciplines that learning occurs as a person interacts with the environment. For example, students learn by manipulating educational materials (both physical and abstract), engaging in literacy-based activities, and interacting with adults and peers. Teachers foster learning by providing experiences that are seen as beneficial, or optimal, for the young student. The complementary goal of many developmental neuroscientists is to understand how biological and environmental factors interact in typical and atypical development. The distinction between scientist and educator, though, is not simply a matter of emphasis on research versus practice. Instead, educators face a weighty challenge of making explicit the larger purpose of education: What student characteristics or behaviors should we promote, and which should we aim to reduce? What subject matter is worth learning? On these culturally embedded matters, the neuroscientist remains relatively silent.

Developmental neuroscience can help to explain changes in children's behavior and skills, which are simultaneously shaped by maturation and experience. To review this knowledge base, we begin with a brief overview of early brain development, describing those developmental processes that become active during the prenatal period and several of which continue in postnatal life. Findings from animal and human studies are combined, as similar, largely gene-driven developmental processes take place across species to form the basic architecture of the brain. We then discuss two related concepts, experience-expectant plasticity and experience-dependent plasticity, and their relation to education's requirement of effortful learning. These sections help to clarify the time course of brain development and the role of experience during the childhood years. These general principles also provide important background for the reader as we go on to review current research on the development of executive function (attention and behavioral inhibition), literacy, and numeracy during early to mid-childhood.[1] Throughout the chapter, we draw connections to educational practice and, as needed, describe how future research is needed to clarify outstanding questions.

Overview of Brain Development

The earliest stages of brain development are largely gene-driven; that is, the formation of brain cells and the laying down of the basic architecture of the brain are processes set in motion by genetic events that are common across humans and many other species. Even with this strong role for biology, the developing embryo is always susceptible to environmental factors, such as the well-known toxic effects of alcohol overconsumption during pregnancy. Here, and in Table 4.1, we focus on the processes involved in building the brain's basic structure under normative conditions (for review, see Nelson, Thomas, & de Haan, 2006; Stiles, 2008).

Within a week or two of conception, the human brain begins to form. Once the zygote has formed its three layers of tissue (endoderm, mesoderm, and ectoderm), the outer (ectodermal) layer begins to undergo a transformation. Cells in the ectodermal layer multiply, and the tissue thickens to form a pear-shaped neural plate. By day 24 (week 4), the neural plate buckles and folds in onto itself (*neurulation*), creating the neural tube. The tube closes first at the bottom end, then a few days later at the top end. The top end will come to form the brain itself, whereas the tail (caudal) end of the tube becomes the spinal cord. Once the neural tube has formed, cell division continues at a rapid pace, quickly leading to the formation of three vesicles (fluid-filled sacs). The topmost vesicle, referred to as the forebrain, will give rise to the telencephalon (cerebral hemispheres) and the diencephalon (thalamus and hypothalamus). The middle vesicle gives rise to the midbrain (pons, medulla), and the caudalmost vesicle to the hindbrain (brain stem). These three structures are formed by the end of the sixth prenatal week.

Initially, relatively few stem cells populate these structures. However, these cells soon begin to proliferate at an astounding rate. This process of neurogenesis yields many more cells than will eventually survive to support the organism. Roughly 40–60% of all neurons that are initially produced will be pruned back around the time of birth, a largely gene-driven process referred to as "apoptosis."

TABLE 4.1. Time Line of Early Brain Development

Weeks postconception	Developmental process
1 to 2	Initial formation of neural plate
3 to 4	Formation of neural tube
6	Development of three, fluid-filled vesicles
7 to birth[a]	Neurogenesis (proliferation of neurons)
7 to 8 weeks to 5th–7th prenatal month	Construction of the cerebral cortex via cell migration
23 to first months of life	Differentiation of cells; synapse formation; beginning of myelination

Period	Developmental events occurring after birth
Birth through midadolescence; completion timing varies	Competitive elimination of synapses
Primarily early childhood through late adolescence	Myelination (insulation) of short and long-distance connections

[a]An exception is that in the olfactory bulb and dentate gyrus of the hippocampus, new neurons continue to be born into at least middle age.

Once the brain has obtained an initial number of immature neurons, the construction of the cerebral cortex begins, generally around the seventh to eighth week after conception. In humans, the cerebral cortex is a thin (2–4 mm) sheet of cells that makes up the outermost layers of the brain. The actual surface area of the cortex is larger than one might expect because the tissue is folded in the characteristic pattern of bulges and wrinkles depicted in most images of the brain. In humans, the cortex has six discernable layers of cells, which are constructed by waves of migrating neurons that move from their initial position in the brain (generally the ventricular zone) until they reach their final destination. These cells migrate in an inside-out direction: thus, a deep, initial layer of cells is formed (layer 6), followed by the formation of the next layer (layer 5), and then the next (layer 4), until finally all six layers of the cortex are complete, generally by the fifth or sixth prenatal month.

Once a neuron has migrated to its final destination, it begins the process of differentiation. Here the cell body forms, along with cellular processes, or outgrowths, known as axons and dendrites. Once differentiation has occurred, the next monumental event can begin: the formation of synapses (*synaptogenesis*). Synapses are the point of contact between two neurons, allowing signals to travel from one cell to the next. Connections generally (although not always) form between dendrites and axons. Neurons will eventually form multiple connections, becoming organized into networks that support the many functions of the brain. The first synapses generally appear by about the 23rd prenatal week and increase rapidly through the end of gestation and into the first postnatal year. In the visual cortex, for example, the peak of overproduction occurs around the third or fourth postnatal month. In the prefrontal cortex (the seat of all higher cognitive functions and emotion regulation) the peak does not occur until about the 12th postnatal month.

Postnatally the next phase of brain development commences: the competitive elimination of synapses. As a rule, synapses that do not receive appropriate coordinated signals from incoming neurons are eliminated. The timing of synaptic pruning varies across brain regions. For example, in the parts of the cortex involved with visual and auditory perception, pruning ends by approximately the fourth to sixth year of life. In contrast, in areas involved with higher cognitive functions (the prefrontal cortex), synaptic pruning continues through midadolescence (Huttenlocher & Dabholkar, 1997).

The initial overproduction of synapses, hand in hand with the selective pruning of connections, is adaptive for the developing organism. This flexibility in the specification of connections allows the organism to adapt to its unique environment by maintaining those synapses that prove useful, that is, those that receive incoming chemical signals that help the connection to stabilize. In this way, networks of neurons can be fine-tuned and changed as needed.

One final developmental and anatomical process involving cell communication is referred to as "myelination." Myelin is a fat-based substance that coats axons, essentially insulating them. Myelinated axons transmit electrical signals more rapidly than do nonmyelinated axons (for discussion, see Webb, Monk, & Nelson, 2001). This developmental process also occurs over an extended period and is subject to a nonuniform time course. Axons in some regions of the brain, such as sensory and motor areas, are myelinated earlier than others, such as those subserving higher cognitive abilities (Gibson & Petersen, 1991). Myelination in the sensory and motor areas is complete by the preschool period. In contrast, myelination in the prefrontal cortex is not complete until late adolescence or early adulthood (for recent reviews, see Nelson et al., 2006; Nelson & Jeste, 2008).

Brain Development during the Elementary School Years

Unfortunately, much of what is known about brain development is constrained to the prenatal and immediate postnatal period, and the adolescent period. Very little is known about the elementary school years, in part because of the challenges involved with studying this age group. We do know that by the time a child enters kindergarten, the basic architecture of the brain has been established, and that sensory and perceptual functions are adult-like. Structurally, regions within the medial temporal lobe concerned with memory (e.g., hippocampus) and emotion (e.g., amygdala) are also adult-like, although, functionally, declarative memory continues to develop through age 9–10 years. However, a rather dramatic physiological change occurs during the elementary school years, namely, a change in the overall ratio of gray matter volume (cell bodies) to white matter volume (primarily myelinated axons); that is, there is an increase in gray matter, which is followed, into the adolescent years, by a decrease in gray matter and an increase in white matter. This means that long-distance myelinated connections appear to be developing during childhood, permitting one region of the brain to communicate within another more efficiently. These changes are subtle at first, but they increase rapidly during the adolescent years. Perhaps the classic example is the relation between the "amygdala"—the seat of emotion and emotional experience—and the prefrontal cortex, the region of the brain that controls and oversees emotion, and behavior regulation generally. Although this example is suggestive of a brain-based explanation for the development of emotion regulation, the relationship between changes in neural connectivity and changes in behavior are currently poorly understood.

Summary

In general, brain development begins a few weeks after conception and is complete by late adolescence or early adulthood. The structure of the brain is laid down primarily during the prenatal period and childhood, whereas the formation and refinement of neural networks continue over the longer term. The brain's many functions do not develop at the same time. Basic sensation and perception systems are fully developed by the time children enter kindergarten. By that age, the brain structures involved in memory and emotion are also adult-like, but functionally, memory continues to develop through approximately age 10. Finally, the formation of neural networks, which begins before birth, continues throughout life.

It is misleading to think that by the end of the early childhood years, or even the teen years, the brain is fully formed: Quite the contrary, the human brain continues to change across much of the lifespan, particularly in the domains of learning and memory. Prenatal changes in the brain are primarily gene-driven and progress in a relatively predictable sequence. In contrast, much of the change that occurs in the brain postnatally is heavily dependent on experience. The notion of experience-induced changes in brain function is generally referred to as "plasticity" and is the topic to which we next direct our attention.

Experience-Expectant and Experience-Dependent Plasticity

William Greenough and colleagues (for reviews, see Black, Jones, Nelson, & Greenough, 1998; Greenough, Black, & Wallace, 1987) have discussed two types of experience-induced changes in brain function: experience-expectant and experience-dependent changes. The former refers to experience-induced changes in the brain that are common to all members of the species and that typically occur during a sensitive period of development. For example, our ability to use our two eyes to derive information about depth ("binocular depth perception") requires access to patterned light information at a time in development when synapses in the visual cortex are still malleable. In other words, most infants have access to normal visual input that allows neural networks to become organized to support visual depth perception. Based on our knowledge of synaptogenesis (reviewed earlier), this sensitive period ends toward the end of the preschool period, when adult numbers of synapses in the visual cortex are present. Thus, for a child to obtain normal binocular vision requires access to a normal visual world by the time a child is 4–5 years old. It is for this reason that visual disorders such as "strabismus" (i.e., cross-eyed) must be corrected before the end of the preschool period.

Other examples of experience-expectant development include speech and face processing, and the formation of attachment relationships with caregivers. In all cases the principle is the same: The genome simply codes for the development of a general circuit that becomes specialized by exposure to experience during a particular period of time. The assumption is that all members of the species are exposed to, and can thus *expect* the same basic experiences (e.g., patterned light; speech input; interactions with adult caregivers) at the same period of time. The young child picks up on regularities in the environment to learn, for example, differentiated sounds in the language environment.

Experience-dependent changes are unique to the individual and not subject to sensitive periods. The classic example of this form of plasticity is learning and memory. Barring damage to the brain from injury or disease, we are all capable of learning and remembering new things throughout the entire lifespan. Exactly what we learn and remember, however, depends on our unique experiences. Learning how to read and to compute using symbols both capitalize on experience-dependent plasticity; assuming an intact neural system, learning these skills depends on whether a child is exposed to and internalizes these symbol systems. Unfortunately, given limits of spatial resolution of current imaging technologies, it is not yet possible to look closely at children's functioning neural networks before, during, and after learning a new skill. However, based on existing knowledge, some of the mechanisms thought to underlie experience-dependent plasticity include formation of new synapses, axon regrowth, formation of new dendritic spines, and an increase in capillaries (leading to increased blood flow to support the functioning of neural networks). In all these ways, networks of neurons are shaped by children's learning experiences in and out of school.

Summary

In general, experience-expectant functions are those that (1) occur very early in the life span and (2) are constrained to the establishment of the basic functional architecture of the brain (e.g., basic sensory, perceptual, and emotional functions). For development of these functions to proceed normally, children need access to the relevant environmental input during sensitive periods. In contrast, experience-dependent development occurs throughout the lifespan and is perhaps most relevant to education. Learning of academic subject matter, for example, capitalizes on this form of plasticity, and individuals vary in what they learn based on their unique experiences in school and other contexts.

Executive Functions

The period from age 3 to age 8 years is one of extraordinary development of "executive functions" (EFs), or skills needed to control one's thinking and behavior. These skills include inhibiting behavior impulses, controlling attention, problem solving, changing one's behavior in flexible ways, planning, decision making, and maintaining information in working memory (for further review, see Nelson et al., 2006). These effortful processes in part comprise a "supervisory attention system" (Shallice, 1988)—a system for inhibiting or overriding routine or reflexive behaviors in favor of more controlled or situation-appropriate behaviors. Similarly, this system allows us to pay attention to relevant information in the environment, while we inhibit irrelevant information. EFs are important for success on schoolwork that requires higher-order thinking, focused attention, and manipulation of multiple pieces of information in memory. Posner and Rothbart (2007) argue that EF skills, as measured in laboratory settings, are associated closely with the self-control processes that facilitate good learning behaviors in the classroom. Here we focus on the protracted development of attention control and behavior regulation as two executive functions that are particularly relevant for school-based learning.

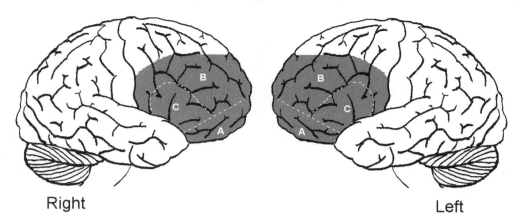

Right   Left

FIGURE 4.1. Primary brain regions within the frontal cortex that are activated during executive function tasks. A, orbitofrontal cortex; B, dorsolateral prefrontal cortex; C, ventrolateral prefrontal cortex. Not shown: ventromedial prefrontal cortex, deeper in the folds beneath area C.

The vast majority of EFs are supported by a distributed network of structures in the prefrontal cortex, toward the front of the brain (see Figure 4.1). These skills are still emerging during the early school years and do not reach their highest level until middle to late adolescence, the end of the long period of prefrontal cortex development, when myelination and synapse formation have also obtained adult levels in this region. Advancement in EFs may arise from the physiological development of prefrontal cortex, as well as the developing integration of this region with other parts of the brain that provide input and feedback to it. Presumably, interactions with the environment shape these developmental processes, though more research is needed to understand precisely how experience weaves its way into the systems underlying executive processing skills.

Behavioral Inhibition

Behavioral inhibition, an important example of an EF, may be of particular interest to educators of young children. Difficulties with it can explain, for example, young children's limitations in delaying gratification and waiting their turn for a desirable object. Inhibitory skills are also required for games like Simon Says, in which children must hold back from carrying out an action (e.g., touch your head) in the minority of cases, when the leader does not say "Simon says" before modeling the action. In that game, the dominant response is to mimic the modeled action. Relative immaturity of prefrontal brain networks may be associated with behaviors that fail to suppress dominant responses and to demonstrate self-control. Although the urge to reach for an object of desire may be strong throughout life, and may vary in intensity depending on the context, the period from approximately age 3–6 years is one in which children can increasingly inhibit dominant responses and carry out more appropriate behaviors.

Behavior inhibition can be systematically tested in a laboratory setting using a "go/ no-go" paradigm. In this task, participants press a button in response to every image presented on a screen *except* one (e.g., all letters except *X*). Since most trials are "go" trials, a tendency is built up to respond every time a letter appears on the screen. Inhibitory control is measured by the child's ability to refrain from responding on "no-go" trials. This form of self-control increases across the preschool- and school-age years (e.g., Levin et al., 1991).

Adults and school-age children differ in the patterns of brain activity elicited by the go/no-go task. Imaging studies measure changes in blood flow throughout the brain to identify the neural structures that show heightened activation during a task. Researchers have found that adults experience signal increases in ventral prefrontal cortex (PFC) during no-go trials—periods high in inhibitory demand—and lower levels during go trials, when there is no need to inhibit button pressing (Casey et al., 1997, 2001; Konishi et al., 1999). Children show reduced signal levels compared to adults in the ventral PFC but increased activity in adjacent brain areas (ventrolateral PFC) with increasing inhibitory demands (Bunge, Dudukovic, Thomason, Vaidya, & Gabrieli, 2002; Durston, Thomas, & Yang, 2002). Brain structures beyond the prefrontal cortex, such as the basal ganglia, are also recruited for response inhibition (e.g., Luna et al., 2001). This may especially be the case for children (Bunge et al., 2002; Casey et al., 1997; Durston et al., 2002). In other words, children seem to recruit a more widespread network of neurons to inhibit an action, whereas adults use a more restricted, presumably efficient network of neurons. This pattern of change has also been found in one longitudinal study of go/no-go activation, with children at 11 years of age showing more focal activation than they did on the same task at age 9 (Durston et al., 2006). These developmental changes may help us to understand why students in the early grades, compared to older ones, have particular difficulty inhibiting their behavior—waiting for one's name to be called, for example, when the dominant response is to "go" line up at the door for art class.

Control of Attention

To perform virtually any effortful academic task, a student must be able to focus attention on it, which requires control of attention resources. The notion of a "searchlight of attention" at the brain level (Crick, 1984) is often used to describe the narrowing of the focus of one's attention, and suppression of interference or conflict from other, irrelevant information. A simple assessment of this executive function is the Eriksen flanker task. Participants are shown a series of arrows (e.g., ← ← ← ← ← or ← ← → ← ←) and are asked to press a button to indicate the direction of the center arrow. Doing so requires focusing attention on the central item, while ignoring the direction of the nearby (i.e., flanking) arrows, which, for this task, are irrelevant and misleading when they face the opposite direction. This and other tasks that require focusing attention and managing cognitive conflict recruit the anterior cingulate gyrus and the left PFC (Fan, Flombaum, McCandliss, Thomas, & Posner, 2003). Higher conflict levels, that is, trials in which the nearby arrows face the wrong direction, are associated with greater levels of activation in these frontal brain regions.

Child-friendly versions of this task have been used to test attention control among younger children. For instance, the arrows can be replaced with colorful pictures of fish; children indicate with a button press in which direction the center fish is swimming. Overall, children respond more slowly and make more mistakes than do adults. Rueda, Posner, Rothbart, and Davis-Stober (2004; Rueda, Fan, et al., 2004) found that performance on the child version of the task improves between ages 4 and 7 years, reflecting development of the frontal brain regions important for success. Development of attention control skills during the school years leads to fewer errors even on the difficult trials, when the flanking items are misleading.

These researchers are also examining whether and how to enhance the attention control skills of young children using computer-based training (Rueda, Rothbart, McCandliss, Saccamanno, & Posner, 2005). They tested 4- and 6-year-old children before and after participation in an attention-training program, and compared their performance to that of children in a control condition. The training involved five sessions, lasting 45 minutes each, during which individual children played computer-based games that required focused attention. Even though dose and duration of this training were minimal, modest group differences were found in posttraining performance on the child flanker task, and in patterns of brain activity associated with the task. Further research is needed, however, to determine whether training effects from this program were large enough to generalize to enhanced performance in school tasks. Importantly, questions about the duration of effects are needed to understand whether this level of training brings about long-term change.

Executive Function in School

The experimental tasks described earlier are each designed to isolate one or a small number of skills to study their development and brain basis systematically. In school, activities more often tap multiple executive processes, as well as students' language, memory, and other cognitive systems. For example, consider a student who notices that one of her answers during a class spelling test is not quite accurate but cannot remember the correct spelling. She may find it difficult to shift her attention away from the distracting error and focus on the next words the teacher presents. Therefore, a student's difficulties with such an activity could stem from troubles with the content being assessed, or from the attention demands required for good performance.

The protracted development of EF can help us understand children's difficulties with school activities that otherwise seem within their range of academic ability. Studies using a child version of the Wisconsin Card Sorting Task demonstrate this idea. In this task, children first sort a set of cards by one salient feature, such as the color of the pictured items (e.g., *blue* trucks and stars in one pile, and *yellow* trucks and stars in another). Even 3-year-olds typically find this to be an easy "rule" for piling cards. Indeed, in preschool to grade 2 mathematics, young students are expected to "sort, classify, and order objects by size, number, and other properties" (Algebra standard; National Council of Teachers of Mathematics, 2000). However, when a change is made to the rule, requiring the cards to be sorted by an alternative feature, such as shape (e.g., trucks and stars, regardless of color), 3-year-olds tend to make many mistakes. Like adults with damage to the dorsolateral PFC (Milner, 1963) young children tend to persevere in using the original sorting criterion (e.g., Frye, Zelazo, & Palfai, 1995). Though they tend to pass this simple test, 4- to 5-year-olds' performance falls apart once a third sorting dimension (e.g., size: big and small) is added to the rule. Of course, the problem is not due to misunderstanding the new rule. Young children who fail to switch to the new sorting rule can often verbalize it accurately, revealing an intriguing distinction between explicit knowledge of the instructions and behavioral success.

Summary

During the early school years, children enjoy an improvement in attention control and in the suppression of irrelevant information. They develop an increasing ability to inhibit actions associated with one learned rule to guide behavior by another. They become more flexible at modifying their actions in light of changes in instructions. They can also increasingly juggle two or more pieces of information in working memory (e.g., color, shape, and size), facilitating performance on increasingly complex tasks. General skills such as behavioral and attention control are needed for successful performance in very many school contexts. Knowing that young children struggle in these areas, teachers may be able to make better sense of children's uneven performance in school; that is, features of class activities that demand higher levels of executive control might be obscuring young children's mastery of the academic skills the assignments primarily aim to assess. In their planning, teachers may find it helpful to consider the general cognitive demands of a lesson, in addition to its content-specific requirements. That way, the errors that students make might be more clearly identified as either a misunderstanding of content or a general limitation in executive function.

Reading

During the primary school years, young students face a significant challenge in learning to read. Literacy acquisition is an effortful and complex endeavor, and requires direct instruction and practice. Spoken language, on the other hand, is relatively easy to learn and does not typically require intentional teaching. Insights from neuroscience help us understand this discrepancy in the difficulty of learning spoken versus written language (for review, see Dehaene, 2004).

Over evolutionary time, humans have evolved brains that favor speech-relevant sounds over nonlinguistic sounds from the environment. Very early in life, infants pay more attention to the human voice than to other sounds. Provided that a child has an intact sensory system and experiences a language environment that is within the normal range, the brain becomes organized to carry out language processing efficiently. We do not yet know whether the qualities of language input a child receives affect the brain's efficiency in processing language. Debate continues on defining what is "innate" versus "learned" in language. Nonetheless, the consensus is that certain brain networks, primarily in the left hemisphere, become specialized to process language stimuli, from the smallest units of sound ("phonemes") to meaningful streams of words. This specialization is made possible by experience with the sounds of language and communicative interactions with other language users. Assuming intact cognitive starting points, children will typically comprehend and produce vocal speech in the early years of life. Similarly, deaf children typically acquire fluent signed speech when raised in the context of adequate input from, and communicative interaction with, skilled signers. Therefore, learning to speak or sign is relatively easy for the human brain using these early emerging skills of perceiving and processing verbal or signed language.

In contrast to spoken and signed languages, written language systems are a relatively new cultural invention. Natural selection has not shaped any single part of the human brain to be particularly facile with acquiring symbolic literacy skills (Dehaene,

2004). Instead, reading relies on processing capacity from a coordinated network of brain areas that must work in concert to translate written text viewed on a page into comprehended meaning. Therefore, achieving efficiency, or "fluency," in reading is a more challenging endeavor, and children cannot master this skill without some instruction. During the period from ages 3 to 8 years, English-speaking children typically learn to identify alphabetic letters, map each letter to corresponding sounds, decode words and memorize irregular sight words, and eventually read text fluently. After learning to read, older children make important progress in reading to learn about school subjects and other topics of interest and value. Here, we elaborate on the process of decoding text.

Much of what we know about the brain processes underlying reading comes from the study of skilled adult readers, adults with brain damage who have lost the ability to read, and people who face difficulties reading, such as those with dyslexia. As of this writing, no longitudinal studies have examined neurological processing of written text before, during, and after typically developing children are first taught to read. Nonetheless, studies with adults and with dyslexic individuals, as well as a handful of cross-sectional imaging studies with children, have shed light on brain processes underlying typical and atypical reading. When examined in light of cognitive theories of reading and a broader understanding of brain development, these brain-based studies may prove useful for educators.

Dual-route theories of reading from cognitive science and psychology provide some guidance for interpreting patterns of brain activity associated with word reading (Jobard, Crivello, & Tzourio-Mazoyer, 2003). These theories identify component skills in word reading, from the visual perception of a string of letters to the recognition of their meaning. Dual-route models propose two different pathways in the brain for reading words. These routes will seem familiar to primary school educators. One route to reading is an indirect one: Printed letters are visually processed (e.g., *c-a-t*), converted into their respective sounds, then blended to decode the word phonetically. Acquiring this phonological route begins with an understanding of the alphabetic principle, that is, an awareness that written letters represent particular spoken sounds. The reader will understand the word if its "sound" matches a word that he or she already knows, most likely through oral language. The second proposed route is more direct, though its mode of functioning in the brain remains controversial. This "word form area" of the brain (at the base of the left temporal lobe) seems to become specialized for word recognition. In typical adult readers, this area is sensitive to groups of letters in a word, processed visually, that obey the spelling rules ("orthography") of one's language. For example, the letters *ight* would elicit more activity in this region for a reader of English than would the same letters presented as *gtih*, because the latter pattern does not commonly occur in the language. When a word or word part does follow the rules of a reader's language, it does not matter in what font style, size, or case the words are presented—skilled readers seem to have developed expertise for visually recognizing and abstracting linguistically meaningful chunks of words. This type of processing is particularly important when the pronunciation of a word is ambiguous and the spelling is irregular (e.g., *cough, who, cousin*). Dual-route models posit that emerging readers must acquire this direct route to reading, as well as the indirect phonological route, to achieve fluency.

According to this general model, educators support young readers by teaching both letter–sound correspondences and notable exceptions (i.e., sight words), facilitating acquisition of both the phonological (indirect) and lexical (direct) routes to reading. They also support reading by helping to build children's vocabulary, which facilitates the recognition of word meanings from text; that is, a child demonstrates better fluency reading text that presents words with which he or she is already familiar, most often from oral language experience. This suggests that curricula aimed at exposing children to new words may also be advantageous for children's reading fluency by establishing or strengthening connections between a written word and its meaning.

Implicit in a dual-route model is the notion that no single "reading area" of the brain is activated in response to text perception. Instead, a network of connected brain regions is called upon during reading, reflecting the complexity of this cognitive activity (Joseph, Noble, & Eden, 2001; McCandliss & Noble, 2003). These regions include the base of the temporal lobe for the lexical route to reading (Figure 4.2, area A), as well as the left angular gyrus for the phonological route (Figure 4.2, area B), near the juncture of the parietal and temporal lobes in the left hemisphere. Additionally, a frontal region important for producing spoken language is also recruited reliably while reading aloud or silently (Figure 4.2, area C, Broca's area). Brain activity can be detected in many regions while reading words, but these areas seem to be particularly important for skilled readers. Connections between the areas, as well as the integrity of the brain tissue in these areas themselves, are typically essential for reading success.

In English, mapping letters to sounds is relatively difficult because the approximately 40 phonemes used to verbalize words can be spelled in over 1,100 ways (Nyikos, 1988). For example, multiple alphabetic combinations convert into the same sound in the words *neigh, hay*, and *hey*. Other languages, such as Italian and Spanish, have a smaller set of possible sounds and fewer irregular words. Indeed, compared to English readers, Italian readers show increased levels of activity in brain areas associated with phonological processing when reading words (Paulesu et al., 2000), reflecting the sound-based strategy that is effective for word reading in the Italian language. Readers of English, on the other hand, show more activation of the orthographic route even

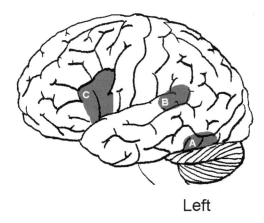

Left

FIGURE 4.2. Brain regions corresponding to a dual-route model of reading. A, lexical route, base of the left temporal lobe; B, phonological route, region of left angular gyrus; C, frontal activity supporting skilled reading, Broca's area.

when reading regular words. Although the multicomponent reading system is largely similar across cultures, the demands of different writing systems seems to shape the organization of effective reading circuits by modifying the relative involvement of various components.

Many argue that, with reading practice, more words are recognized and processed automatically using the direct route (Dehaene, 2004; Shaywitz et al., 2002). Increasing automaticity is one factor that facilitates fluent reading. Indeed, skilled readers cannot help but read words presented to them. For example, when a color word, like *green*, is typed in an opposing ink color, such as *red*, it is difficult to ignore the written word and simply report the color of the ink. The automatic tendency to read the word interferes with identification of the print color, and color-naming time is slowed as a result. In everyday contexts, even when spellings are somewhat scrambled or letters are missing, the skilled reader's ability to decode meaningful words is relatively robust:

The childern play in the shcool gym.
Cla_ _ _f '08

Many questions remain open regarding our understanding of neural networks underlying reading and how they develop. For example, how do experiences with literacy (both formal instruction and informal reading) get "under the skin" to help organize these neural connections? How robust are these circuits, once established? To what extent is repeated activation necessary to stabilize them (in practical terms, how do breaks from formal instruction impact circuit formation)? How do emotional processes, such as enjoyment of or engagement in reading and motivation to learn to read, shape this process of neural specialization? Finally, are there benefits or drawbacks associated with exposing children to formal instruction in reading during preschool, in terms of fine-tuning reading circuits to function efficiently?

Recent imaging studies with children have elucidated some of the developmental processes underlying improvement in basic word reading. As mentioned earlier, one way in which the brain changes with development is in the increasing specialization of neural networks. A growing body of literature suggests that this type of change occurs in word reading. For example, a cross-sectional study of readers ages 7–17 years by Shaywitz and colleagues (2002) found both right- and left-hemisphere activation during word reading among younger and less skilled readers, but greater levels of left-localized brain activity among more skilled readers. This suggests that what starts off as a task that calls on widely distributed parts of the brain eventually becomes one that is handled by more focalized and efficient networks of neurons.

Further evidence for increasing specialization of reading circuits comes from the Turkeltaub, Gareau, Flowers, Zeffiro, and Eden (2003) study of brain activation in an implicit reading task. These authors studied 6- to 22-year-old subjects cross-sectionally. Participants were asked to identify whether a word or symbol string had any "tall letters" or symbols, like *k, h,* or *d,* as opposed to having only short letters, like *c, o,* and *a.* If reading were an automatic process, then even though they were not asked to read the words, participants would have done so in this task. Age-related differences associated with this implicit reading included lower levels of right-hemisphere activity (right lower temporal sulcus and the back region of the fusiform gyrus) among older and more skilled participants. Additionally, greater levels of left-lateralized activity in the lower frontal gyrus were documented among older subjects, suggesting that this region takes on more importance as the reader becomes skilled.

Summary

Currently, research findings are consistent with the view that whereas beginning reading draws upon an individual's widely distributed brain network to decode text, skilled word reading is associated with increasing specialization of a largely left-hemisphere network. This specialization facilitates more automatic and efficient processing of printed text. However, as with spoken language, right-hemisphere structures likely continue to play a role in reading, particularly as we go beyond single-word processing. For instance, in spoken language, "prosodic information" (i.e., the melodic qualities of speech) is processed in the right hemisphere. This processing helps a listener to understand the emotional tone and intentions of a speaker, such as when a speaker uses sarcasm. More research is needed to understand how these brain systems interact to enable the reader to make sense of more complex texts.

An important point is that reading is always associated with multiple brain structures working together to support reading; there is no *single* brain region that can be characterized as a center for reading. Minimally, both phonetic and word recognition strategies are at work when a fluent reader encounters words. Longitudinal and experimental studies will help to tease apart the effects of maturation and experience in the organization of reading circuits. Future studies will examine how the brain functions during word processing before, during, and after reading instruction. Furthermore, practice-relevant studies might capitalize on the neuroscientist's tools for additional, sensitive measures of the effectiveness of varied teaching approaches. Careful analysis of the type and quantity of instruction will help to clarify the role of experience in the development of literacy skills and further our understanding of how to intervene when children have trouble learning to read.

Numeracy and Mathematics

Numeracy, like literacy, is one of the essential foundations for academic learning. In the early grades, children learn to understand and use numbers across varied types of representations (National Council of Teachers of Mathematics, 2000, Number & Operations Standard). By the end of second grade, they are expected to be able to count, link numerals and number words to quantities, and grasp the relative magnitudes of whole numbers (i.e., understand the number line). They also learn the basic operations of addition and subtraction, using multiple methods and tools for developing a concrete understanding of arithmetic. Developing a flexible understanding of number lays the groundwork for the learning of more complex operations and math concepts in later grades. Also as in literacy instruction, effort and time eventually lead to the automatization of several aspects of number knowledge, as students become more "fluent" in the language of numerals. These skills build on children's early understanding of quantity and develop with the effortful practice of mastering a symbolic system of numerals and notations.

Reasoning about numbers, like reading text, recruits a distributed network of cognitive systems. Research with patients with brain damage and neuroimaging studies suggest that separate components of the neural system are specialized for at least two different aspects of numeracy, understanding quantity and retrieving learned calculations. For adults, structures in the parietal lobe tend to be recruited for these forms of reasoning.

Understanding Quantity: The Number Line

One component of the cognitive system for numeracy underlies our understanding of quantity (Dehaene & Cohen, 1997; for review, see Dehaene, Piazza, Pinel, & Cohen, 2003). Comparing the relative magnitude of two numbers, for example, taps this system. Understanding relative quantity goes hand in hand with our ability to think about numbers along a number line and to make numeric approximations (see Siegler, Chapter 19, this volume). Dehaene and colleagues (2003) refer to this system as a "nonverbal semantic representation of the size and distance relations between numbers" (p. 488). That is, neural networks become organized to code the magnitude and order of the numbers, reflecting the central features of the number line. This number sense seems to apply across modes of representation, such as numerals, number words, and collections of objects or dots; that is, in each format, parietal lobe activity in both hemispheres is associated with reasoning about abstract quantity information (Figure 4.3, area A). In adults, greater levels of activity are generated when comparisons are more difficult, such as when two close numbers (e.g., 21 vs. 24) rather than distant numbers (e.g., 17 vs. 46) are compared for relative magnitude (Pinel, Dehaene, Riviere, & LeBihan, 2001).

In a standard numeric comparison task, participants are presented with a numeral from 1 to 9, or a dot pattern of 1 to 9 dots. They indicate by pressing buttons whether the value is greater than or less than a target value, such as five. Adults are faster at making these decisions when the test number is farther from 5 (e.g., 1 or 9, as opposed to 4 or 6). This response pattern reflects the organization of neural circuits in the parietal lobe, such that numerals representing values closer together are more difficult to distinguish than are two digits farther from each other along the number line. Temple and

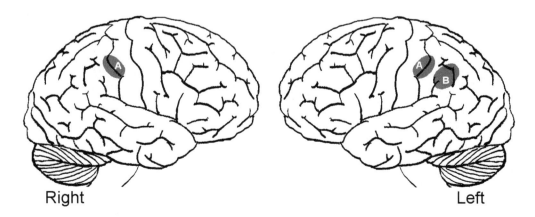

Right   Left

FIGURE 4.3. Brain regions activated during numeric estimation (A, region of parietal lobe on each side) and arithmetic (B, region of left angular gyrus).

Posner (1998) measured brain activity, using event-related potentials (ERPs), during this number comparison task with adults and a small group of typically developing 5-year-olds. The patterns of brain activity evident during both numeral and dot comparison were quite similar across the age groups. Both groups showed larger responses during close, versus far, comparisons (N1 amplitude) over parietal electrodes. The time course of this neural response was only slightly delayed for children (194–224 msec poststimulus) compared to adults (124–174 msec poststimulus), even though button presses were very delayed in children (overall average: 1,576 msec; adults: 498 msec). These results suggest that, at least for small whole numbers, young children closely resemble adults in their neural processing of relative quantity. Thus, some of the building blocks for mathematics seem to be in place by age 5 years. Much more research is needed, however, given the small final sample size of 13 children, and the potential for individual variation among 5-year-olds with different levels of experience working with numbers in symbolic (numeral) form.

It is not clear yet whether most typically developing 5-year-olds demonstrate an overlap in brain areas associated with processing of symbolic and nonsymbolic representations of numbers (e.g., numeral symbols and dot arrays). It may be that the overlap arises only through experiences in translating numerals into quantities and vice versa. Indeed, although young children may be able to reason about number in concrete forms, such as using dots or real objects, they may differ in their ability to reason using numerals. Achievement gaps in math, evident even at kindergarten entry, might have a counterpart in neural processing of numbers specifically in a numeral format. Future research can illuminate whether differences derived from variation in exposure to and communication about *symbolic* representations of number explain differences in early math skills. Such research would help to clarify the basis of the early achievement gap, and the scope of "number sense" that must be taught in the classroom (e.g., understanding of quantity per se, or the mapping of number symbols to quantities).

Early "number sense," that is, an understanding of quantity in nonsymbolic formats, may support students' learning of calculation using numbers (Barth et al., 2006). Barth and colleagues (2006) tested 5-year-olds' performance on "arithmetic" problems using arrays of dots rather than number symbols. This way, they could examine children's ability to add, without using numerals that children did not yet fully understand. On a computer screen, 5-year-olds were briefly shown, for example, a set of 13 blue dots, which was then covered up to prevent counting. Another set of 8 blue dots was "dropped" behind the screen, to be added together with the others. Then, a set of 19 red dots was presented, and children reported whether there were more red or blue dots. Even though children could not perform symbolic addition (i.e., "What is 13 + 8?"), they were quite successful at this nonsymbolic version, choosing the right color 70% of the time. Thus, before they learn symbolic arithmetic, young children seem to be able to use nonsymbolic number sense for arithmetic processing. The authors argue that children's understanding of quantity in nonsymbolic formats can serve as a bridge to an understanding of formal math skills. This idea is consistent with the use of manipulables in early grades math lessons to help children practice reasoning about quantities as a gateway into formal math. Future education-minded studies might illuminate whether and how to use concrete objects to support children's more abstract understanding of number concepts. New questions may be raised, such as whether a child's actual actions involved in manipulating materials facilitates number processing at the brain level, compared to instruction based on observation of a teacher's use of objects (e.g., in a whole-group activity).

To make advances in math, young children need to integrate their understanding of how quantities map onto symbolic numbers, much like young readers need to sort out letter–sound correspondences. Siegler and Booth (2004) argue that by 6 years of age, children integrate their quantity and counting systems into a mental number line that they can then use to reason with numbers. One mathematics curriculum program for early grades instruction, Number Worlds, is designed to promote formal understanding of the number line, particularly among children from disadvantaged backgrounds (Griffin, Case, & Siegler, 1994). The researchers who developed the program did so based on studies suggesting that emphasis on the number line would be particularly useful as an intervention for children from low-income families because children from middle- and high-income families generally tend to have more informal instruction in numbers and enter kindergarten with better developed number knowledge (e.g., discriminating which of two numbers is bigger) (Griffin et al., 1994). In this curriculum, students use board games and group activities to build an understanding of the number line and the symbols used to represent it. Evidence from experimental studies shows that participation in the kindergarten program can help children from disadvantaged backgrounds perform as well as their more advantaged peers, applying their understanding of number in a variety of ways. Future studies by this group will begin to examine changes in the neural processing of numbers associated with use of this program, and extensions of this program into the primary school grades.

Arithmetic

Making comparisons and estimates of numerical quantities only takes us so far in our understanding and use of numbers. Skill in carrying out exact calculations also needs to be practiced and learned in elementary school. For adults and older students, "solving" simple arithmetic problems means retrieving learned math facts (e.g., $5 + 3 = 8$; $3 * 4 = 12$). Circuits in the left hemisphere of the brain associated with language appear to be recruited for this type of recall (Dehaene et al., 2003). More specifically, Dehaene and his colleagues (2003) propose that a region of the left angular gyrus is part of the language system that is essential for retrieving math facts stored in verbal memory (Figure 4.3, area B). Thus, a verbal circuit may be recruited for retrieving multiplication and addition facts from memory, whereas the quantity circuit described earlier is more heavily recruited for subtraction and other true manipulations of quantity.

A neuroimaging study examined age-related changes in brain activity associated with carrying out one-digit addition and subtraction problems (Rivera, Reiss, Eckert, & Menon, 2005). Participants ranging in age from 8 to 19 years were asked to indicate whether a given arithmetic problem was solved correctly (e.g., $4 + 3 = 7$, $9 - 3 = 5$). The researchers compared brain-related activation elicited by this and a nonquantitative task in which participants identified whether a zero (0) was present in a string of five digits. Age-related differences in activation during the math task were consistent with a pattern of increased specialization with age. In particular, age-related decreases in brain activity were found in areas considered to underlie secondary processes involved in addition and subtraction, such as working memory and attention. Decreased activation in frontal areas of the brain over developmental time, as well as in the basal ganglia and hippocampal structures, accords with the notion that simple calculations are quite effortful for younger children but become more automatic during the later school years.[2]

In general, automaticity in important skills such as simple arithmetic is an advantage, in that these computations become less taxing on one's attention and memory, freeing up these resources for other, potentially competing challenges. For example, fluency in single-digit arithmetic would free up working memory resources needed to solve multidigit math problems, or algebra problems for which multiple calculations need to be held in mind simultaneously.

Summary

In summary, the study of math processing at the level of the brain has begun to shed light on the neural processes involved with number sense and basic arithmetic. Adults use a specialized neural network to process relative quantity, regardless of whether the values are presented as abstract symbols or concrete objects. Although there is initial evidence that this convergence is apparent among 5-year-olds, much more research is needed to know whether and how early experience with numeric symbols facilitates this mapping process. Additional careful research in the future can address educationally relevant follow-up questions regarding more abstract mathematics concepts that are difficult for many students, such as fractions, roots, and negative numbers. For example, certain teaching approaches may be more effective for helping children flexibly switch strategies when subtraction problems involve negative numbers. As this example suggests, more advanced math concepts will, at least initially, require students to use working memory and attention resources effectively to solve problems. Thus, at the neural level, the development of EF likely goes hand in hand with students' increasing facility with numbers during the school years.

Conclusions

Advances in developmental neuroscience are helping us understand, at the biological level, some of the major changes in the developing brain, and in children's skills and behavior during the school years. We know that although the basic architecture of the brain is laid down relatively early in life, genes and environments interact over time as children act in the world and develop more advanced abilities. Consideration of biological perspectives sheds new light on how children learn the foundational academic and self-regulatory skills important for school success, such as focusing attention, reading printed words, and reasoning about numbers. Although considerable work has been done to examine how environmental influences shape development, many questions remain open about how specific interactions between the child and the environment, in and out of school, organize the developing child into a cognitively efficient, skilled adult. Developmental neuroscience, a relatively new and growing field, will continue to provide important insights for considering how the whole child develops and learns in the early school grades.

Notes

1. Here we focus on normative development to inform readers about typical changes in the brain that are common to most children. Studies of atypical development, reviewed elsewhere, are beginning to reveal the relationship between atypical brain development and learning disabilities that impact school learning.
2. Unfortunately, findings regarding addition and subtraction were not reported separately, precluding conclusions about developmental change in processing associated with these different math skills.

References

Barth, H., La Mont, K., Lipton, J., Dehaene, S., Kanwisher, N., & Spelke, E. (2006). Nonsymbolic arithmetic in adults and young children. *Cognition, 98*, 199–222.

Black, J. E., Jones, T. A., Nelson, C. A., & Greenough, W. T. (1998). Neuronal plasticity and the developing brain. In N. E. Alessi, J. T. Coyle, S. I. Harrison, & S. Eth (Eds.), *Handbook of child and adolescent psychiatry: Vol. 6. Basic psychiatric science and treatment* (pp. 31–53). New York: Wiley.

Bunge, S., Dudukovic, N., Thomason, M., Vaidya, C., & Gabrieli, J. (2002). Immature frontal lobe contributions to cognitive control in children: Evidence from fMRI. *Neuron, 33*, 301–311.

Casey, B. J., Forman, S. D., Franzen, P., Berkowitz, A., Braver, T. S., Nystrom, L. E., et al. (2001). Sensitivity of prefrontal cortex to changes in target probability: A functional MRI study. *Human Brain Mapping, 13*, 26–33.

Casey, B. J., Trainor, R. J., Orendi, J. L., Schubert, A. B., Nystrom, L. E., Giedd, J. N., et al. (1997). A developmental functional MRI study of prefrontal activation during performance of a go–no-go task. *Journal of Cognitive Neuroscience, 9*, 835–847.

Crick, F. H. C. (1984). Function of the thalamic reticular complex: The searchlight hypothesis. *Proceedings of the National Academy of Science USA, 81*, 4586–4590.

Dehaene, S. (1996). The organization of brain activations in number comparisons: Event-related potentials and the additive-factors method. *Journal of Cognitive Neuroscience, 8*, 47–68.

Dehaene, S. (2004). Evolution of human cortical circuits for reading and arithmetic: The "neuronal recycling" hypothesis. In S. Dehaene, J. R. Duhamel, M. Hauser, & G. Rizzolatti (Eds.), *From monkey brain to human brain* (pp. 133–158). Cambridge, MA: MIT Press.

Dehaene, S., & Cohen, L. (1997). Cerebral pathways for calculation: Double dissociation between rote verbal and quantitative knowledge of arithmetic. *Cortex, 33*, 219–250.

Dehaene, S., Piazza, M., Pinel, P., & Cohen, L. (2003). Three parietal circuits for number processing. *Cognitive Neuropsychology, 20*, 487–506.

Durston, S., Davidson, M. C., Tottenham, N., Galvan, A., Spicer, J., Fossella, J. A., et al. (2006). A shift from diffuse to focal cortical activity with development. *Developmental Science, 9*, 1–8.

Durston, S., Thomas, K., & Yang, Y. (2002). Development of neural systems involved in overriding behavioral responses: An event-related fMRI study. *Developmental Science, 5*, 9–16.

Fan, J., Flombaum, J. I., McCandliss, B. D., Thomas, K. M., & Posner, M. I. (2003). Cognitive and brain consequences of conflict. *NeuroImage, 18*, 42–57.

Frye, D., Zelazo, P. D., & Palfai, T. (1995). Theory of mind and rule-based reasoning. *Cognitive Development, 10*, 483–527.

Gibson, K. R., & Petersen, A. C. (Eds.). (1991). *Brain maturation and cognitive development: Comparative and cross-cultural perspectives.* New York: Aldine de Gruyter.

Greenough, W. T., Black, J. E., & Wallace, C. S. (1987). Experience and brain development. *Child Development, 58*(3), 539–559.

Griffin, S. A., Case, R., & Siegler, R. S. (1994). Rightstart: Providing the central conceptual prerequisites for first formal learning of arithmetic to students at risk for school failure. In K. McGilly (Ed.), *Classroom lessons: Integrating cognitive theory and classroom practice* (pp. 25–49). Cambridge, MA: MIT Press.

Huttenlocher, P. R., & Dabholkar, A. S. (1997). Regional differences in synaptogenesis in human cerebral cortex. *Journal of Comparative Neurology, 387,* 167–178.

Jobard, G., Crivello, F., & Tzourio-Mazoyer, N. (2003). Evaluation of the dual route theory of reading: A metanalysis of 35 neuroimaging studies. *NeuroImage, 20,* 693–712.

Joseph, J., Noble, K., & Eden, G. (2001). The neurobiological basis of reading. *Journal of Learning Disabilities, 34,* 566–579.

Konishi, S., Nakajima, K., Uchida, I., Kikyo, H., Kameyama, M., & Miyashita, Y. (1999). Common inhibitory mechanism in human inferior prefrontal cortex revealed by event-related functional MRI. *Brain, 122,* 981–999.

Levin, H. S., Culhane, K. A., Hartmann, J., Evankovich, K. Mattson, A. J., Harward, H., et al. (1991). Developmental changes in performance on tests of purported frontal lobe functioning. *Developmental Neuropsychology, 7*(3), 377–395.

Luna, B., Thulborn, K., Munoz, D., Merriam, E., Garver, K., Minshew, N., et al. (2001). Maturation of widely distributed brain function subserves cognitive development. *NeuroImage, 13,* 786–793.

McCandliss, B. D., & Noble, K. G. (2003). The development of reading impairment: A cognitive neuroscience model. *Mental Retardation and Development Disabilities Research Reviews, 9,* 196–205.

Milner, B. (1963). Effects of different brain lesions on card sorting. *Archives of Neurology, 9,* 90–100.

National Council of Teachers of Mathematics. (2000). *Principles and standards for school mathematics.* Retrieved June 30, 2007, from *standards.nctm.org/document/chapter4/*

National Research Council and Institute of Medicine. (2000). *From neurons to neighborhoods: The science of early childhood development* [Committee on Integrating the Science of Early Childhood Development, Jack P. Shonkoff & Deborah A. Phillips (Eds.), Board on Children, Youth, and Families, Commission on Behavioral and Social Sciences and Education]. Washington, DC: National Academy Press.

Nelson, C. A., & Jeste, S. (2008). Neurobiological perspectives on developmental psychopathology. In M. Rutter, D. Bishop, D. Pine, S. Scott, J. Stevenson, E. Taylor, et al. (Eds.), *Textbook on child and adolescent psychiatry* (5th ed., pp.145–159). London: Blackwell.

Nelson, C. A., Thomas, K. M., & de Haan, M. (2006). *Neuroscience of cognitive development: The role of experience and the developing brain.* Hoboken, NJ: Wiley.

Nyikos, J., (1988). A linguistic perspective of illiteracy. In S. Embleton (Ed.), *The 14th LACUS Forum 1987* (pp. 146–163). Lake Bluff, IL: Linguistic Association of Canada and the United States.

Paulesu, E., McCrory, E., Fazio, F., Menoncello, L., Brunswick, N., Cappa, S. F., et al. (2000). A cultural effect on brain function. *Nature Neuroscience, 3,* 91–96.

Pinel, P., Dehaene, S., Riviere, D., & LeBihan, D. (2001). Modulation of parietal activation by semantic distance in a number comparison task. *NeuroImage, 14,* 1013–1026.

Posner, M. I., & Rothbart, M. K. (2007). *Educating the human brain.* Washington, DC: American Psychological Association.

Rivera, S. M., Reiss, A. L., Eckert, M. A., & Menon, V. (2005). Developmental changes in mental arithmetic: Evidence for increased functional specialization in the left inferior parietal cortex. *Cerebral Cortex, 15,* 1779–1790.

Rueda, M. R., Fan, J., Halparin, J., Gruber, D., Lercari, L. P., McCandliss, B. D., et al. (2004). Development of attention during childhood. *Neuropsychologia, 42,* 1029–1040.

Rueda, M. R., Posner, M. I., Rothbart, M. K., & Davis-Stober, C. P. (2004). Development of the time course for processing conflict: An event-related potentials study with 4 year olds and adults. *BMC Neuroscience, 5,* 39.

Rueda, M. R., Rothbart, M. K., McCandliss, B. D., Saccamanno, L., & Posner, M. I. (2005). Training, maturation, and genetic influences on the development of executive attention. *Proceedings of the National Academy of Sciences of the USA, 102,* 14931–14936.

Shallice, T. (1988). *From neuropsychology to mental structure.* Cambridge, UK: Cambridge University Press.

Shaywitz, B. A., Shaywitz, S. E., Pugh, K. R., Mencl, W. E., Fulbright, R. K., Skudlarski, P., et al. (2002). Disruption of posterior brain systems for reading in children with developmental dyslexia. *Biological Psychiatry, 52,* 101–110.

Siegler, R. S., & Booth, J. L. (2004). Development of numerical estimation in young children. *Child Development, 75,* 428–444.

Stiles, J. (2008). *Fundamentals of brain development: Integrating nature and nurture.* Cambridge, MA: Harvard University Press.

Temple, E., & Posner, M. I. (1998). Brain mechanisms of quantity are similar in 5-year-old children and adults. *Proceedings of the National Academy of Sciences USA, 95,* 7836–7841.

Turkeltaub, P. E., Gareau, L., Flowers, D. L., Zeffiro, T. A., & Eden, G. F. (2003). Development of neural mechanisms for reading. *Nature Neuroscience, 6,* 767–773.

Webb, S. J., Monk, C. S., & Nelson, C. A. (2001). Mechanisms of postnatal neurobiological development: Implications for human development. *Developmental Neuropsychology, 19,* 147–171.

CHAPTER 5

Neurodevelopmental Changes in Infancy and Beyond
Implications for Learning and Memory

Patricia J. Bauer

One of the most significant factors in learning—and, therefore, in the growth of knowledge—is memory. This "truth" is patently obvious. Unless all knowledge is built into the organism, it must be acquired. The means through which it is acquired is learning. Learning can be accomplished in a number of ways (observation, study, practice, direct tuition, etc.), and it may be intentional or unintentional. Regardless of the source and the objective, the products of learning must be stored in memory to be maintained over time. As such, it is inevitable that discussions of learning must include discussions of memory.

In the course of this chapter, I elaborate on relations between learning and memory, with special focus on age-related differences therein. A guiding principle of the review is that although learning and memory are close siblings, they are not identical twins, that is, equal learning does not result in equal remembering. This observation leads to consideration of memory and related processes that occur after a learning episode, and of the developmental status of the neural structures and network that support the processes. Consideration of these factors helps to explain some of the vulnerabilities in young children's learning and memory. It also opens a window on educational practices that may aid students in overcoming—and even capitalizing on—these vulnerabilities. The chapter ends with suggestions for future research that will further integrate basic cognitive and developmental psychological principles with educational practice.

Relations between Learning and Memory

It is well known that prior learning influences memory, and that memory influences the learning or acquisition of new knowledge. There are many examples of the effects of domain knowledge on memory. One that had an enormous impact on our understanding of the dynamic interaction of these two domains comes from the developmental psychology of the late 1970s. Half of the story came as no surprise. Micheline Chi (1978) administered to children and adults a task requiring them to remember string of digits of various lengths (e.g., 7-4-3, 8-6-1-9, 3-2-5-4-7, 1-6-8-3-5-2, 7-4-2-5-9-1-8). She found precisely what she expected, namely, that adults remembered more digits than children. The other half of the story provided quite a jolt, however. The children in the study had been selected because they were experts in the game of chess; the adults (graduate students) knew how to play chess but were not experts. When Chi challenged the young chess experts and the adults to remember not strings of digits but chess positions, she found that the children outperformed the adults. In the years since this demonstration, effects of expertise on memory have become commonplace. Yet, at the time, they were not widely appreciated. They contributed to a new perspective on "what develops," one that deemphasized domain-general cognitive structures (e.g., Inhelder & Piaget, 1958, 1964) and emphasized specific domains of knowledge.

There also are demonstrations of the influence of memory on learning and acquisition of new knowledge. An example comes from the literature on relations between working memory, as measured by listening span, and reading comprehension. "Listening span" is the number of successive short sentences that a person can recall verbatim. Daneman and Carpenter (1980) found that from the preschool through the college years, listening span correlates with reading comprehension. Similar relations are found between working memory, as measured by the number of final words in sentences a child or adult is able to remember, and reading comprehension. In addition, differences in working memory capacity differentiate reading-disabled from non-reading-disabled readers (e.g., Siegel & Ryan, 1989). These simple illustrations serve to make the point that if we are to understand learning, we must think about memory. Furthermore, if we are to understand age-related or developmental differences in learning, we must understand developmental differences in memory.

Age-Related Differences in Learning and in Memory: Examples from Infancy Research

We know that there are age-related differences in learning and in memory. The question is how they are related at the level of behavior, and at the underlying neural level. I address these questions by using specific examples from the infancy literature not because I believe readers of this volume are especially interested in infancy, but because the infancy literature is one domain in which these questions have been asked in a systematic way. The expectation is that the lessons are generalizable, within limits, to learning and memory in preschool- and school-age children.

Learning and Memory in Infancy

Numerous challenges are associated with testing learning and memory in infants. The most salient one is that we cannot rely on the measures of these processes that we use with older, verbal children. Infants do not play chess. They obviously do not read, which makes it impossible to test them with reading span or reading comprehension tasks. In fact, because infants by definition are nonverbal (*infantia*, Latin for "inability to speak"), they cannot be tested with any of the language-based assessments designed for use with older children and adults. Thus, assessments of learning and memory in infancy require nonverbal tasks.

The learning and memory task that we have used in our laboratory is elicited imitation of multistep sequences. In elicited or deferred imitation, props are used to produce a sequence of actions that the infant (or older child; Riggins, Miller, Bauer, Georgieff, & Nelson, 2009) is invited to imitate either immediately (elicited imitation), after a delay (deferred imitation), or both. Although the task is nonverbal and depends on behavior, there is ample reason to believe that it taps the same type of memory as that assessed through verbal report in language-using children and adults (for discussions, see Bauer, 2004, 2005b, 2007). A sample sequence is to "make a gong" by (1) folding a bar across a swing-set-shaped base, thus forming a crosspiece; (2) hanging a metal disk from the bar; and (3) striking the metal disk with a small mallet, thus causing it to "gong."

Use of this technique with infants as young as 6 months of age (e.g., Barr, Dowden, & Hayne, 1996), and throughout the second year of life (e.g., Bauer, Wenner, Dropik, & Wewerka, 2000), has revealed a number of age-related differences in memory. First, based on a single learning trial, infants learn and remember. For example, as reflected in Figure 5.1, relative to an uninstructed baseline (during which we observe spontaneous production of target actions and their order), immediately after seeing sequences demonstrated, 16- and 20-month-old infants produce both more actions of sequences, such as the gong (i.e., folding the bar, hanging the disk from the bar, striking the disk with the mallet), and more actions in the demonstrated order. This provides strong evidence of learning based on a single experience of an event. After a delay of 2 weeks, they still remember the sequences, though some forgetting is apparent (i.e., performance after 2 weeks was lower than performance immediately after the demonstration; Bauer &

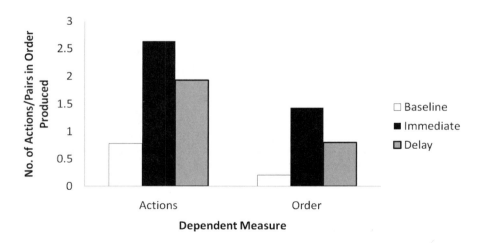

FIGURE 5.1. The number of actions and pairs of actions in correct temporal order produced by 16- and 20-month-old infants in an uninstructed baseline condition, at immediate recall and after a 2-week delay. Data from Bauer and Mandler (1989).

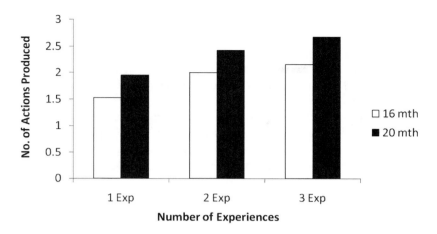

FIGURE 5.2. The number of actions produced by 16- and 20-month-old infants after a 1-month delay, as a function of the number of experiences with the sequences (1, 2, or 3) prior to imposition of the delay. Data from Bauer (unpublished).

Mandler, 1989). Thus, even preverbal infants learn and remember multistep sequences of action.

Second, as reflected in Figure 5.2, with more learning trials, memory is more robust; that is, when tested after a 1-month delay, infants remember more of the actions (reflected in Figure 5.2) and more information about the order of actions they have seen demonstrated three times relative to two times, and two times relative to one time. Thus, learning accrues with experience. Third, also apparent in Figure 5.2, regardless of the number of learning trials, older infants remember more than do younger infants. Although these basic effects are illustrated with data from infants in the second year of life, throughout development, children benefit from multiple experiences of events or to-be-remembered material, and older children learn more rapidly than do younger children (Howe & Brainerd, 1989).

Do Differences in Learning Explain Differences in Memory?

The tight coupling of learning and memory throughout infancy and childhood raises the question of whether age-related differences in memory reflect nothing more than age-related differences in learning. If that were the case, then if we equalized learning, we could also equalize remembering. Because learning accrues over trials, we could give younger children more learning trials, relative to older children, and watch age-related differences melt away.

Although the coupling is tight, it is not perfect. Age-related differences in memory are not explained by differences in learning, at least not as we typically conceive of learning. Illustration of this point comes from another infant study from my laboratory (Bauer, 2005a). This research involved three groups of 16-month-old and three groups of 20-month-old infants. All of the infants learned multistep sequences, such as "make a gong," prior to imposition of 1-, 3-, or 6-month delays (the delay interval was between subjects). To examine age-related differences in remembering, we controlled age-related differences in learning. Specifically, we matched the 16- and 20-month-olds for the amount learned prior to the delay. For example, a younger infant who produced three actions prior to the delay was matched with an older infant who produced three actions, and so forth. Thus, the infants of different ages entered the delay interval with equal learning.

In spite of the fact that the infants learned the same amount about the events, they did not remember the same amount; age differences were especially apparent at the longer delays. When retested after 1 month, the older and younger infants had forgotten approximately the same amount about the events: They had lost about 1 in 4 of the individual actions they had learned. After both 3 months and 6 months, age-related differences were pronounced. After 3 months, younger and older infants forgot roughly 2.5 and 1.4 actions, respectively; after 6 months, younger and older infants forgot roughly 3.1 and 2.2 actions, respectively (for details, see Bauer, 2005a). Clearly, equal learning does not result in equal forgetting (or its complement, remembering).

But might the younger and older infants have retained the same amount, and the older infants were simply better at retrieving what they remembered, especially after the long delays? To address this possibility, after the test trial, we demonstrated the sequences once again, then tested the infants' recall. If the groups of infants had equal amounts of information about the events in memory storage, but the younger infants were simply having more trouble accessing it (retrieving), then in this classic test of "savings in relearning" (Ebbinghaus, 1885/1964) they should perform equally. With the burden of retrieval lifted (by demonstration of the event), younger infants should have been able to "show what they know." Contrary to this possibility, on the relearning trial, the older infants outperformed the younger infants. Thus, the difference in long-term recall could not be attributed to differences in accessibility at retrieval (for details and discussion, see Bauer, 2005a). With both "bookends" eliminated (initial learning and retrieval), we must look to the middle (the period between learning and testing) to find the source of age-related differences.

The Importance of the Postlearning Process of Consolidation

To understand how equal learning can produce unequal retention, we must look to processes that take place after learning but before the long-term retrieval test. What happens during this period that might help explain differential retention over the long term? A candidate answer to this question is a postlearning process that has received relatively little attention in the contemporary literature, namely, "consolidation," the process by which an initially labile memory trace is stabilized and integrated into long-term storage. The process is subserved by a particular neural substrate, one that undergoes substantial postnatal developmental change throughout infancy and into the school years. This makes it an attractive candidate as a source of age-related differences in retention of newly learned information in memory.

The process of consolidation originally was hypothesized by Müller and Pilzecker (1900) to account for retroactive interference. In laboratory tests they observed that new material learned shortly after (but not long after) old material produced deficits in subjects' memory for the old material. Consider two testing situations, both of which involve learning and remembering lists of words. In one situation, subjects learn List 1, time is allowed to pass, then they learn List 2. In this situation, Müller and Pilzecker observed high levels of subjects' memory of both lists. In the other situation, subjects learned List 1, then very shortly thereafter were presented List 2. In this case, the researchers observed good recall of List 2 but poor recall of List 1. It seemed that in the short-delay situation, List 2 retroactively interfered with List 1. Müller and Pilzecker advanced the hypothesis that there was retroactive interference because at the time that List 2 was learned, List 1 had not yet been stabilized or integrated into storage, a process they termed "consolidation."

Müller and Pilzecker's (1900) work served to illustrate an important principle about learning and memory: processes that take place after learning influence later remembering. It also illustrated an important features of the postlearning process of consolidation: It takes time. In the years since the introduction of the concept of consolidation, we have learned more about this critical process. We have learned that it involves multiple steps, and that it depends on a network of neural structures. In the next sections, I provide a summary of "how the brain builds a memory," followed by discussion of the implications of these processes for learning and memory in development.

Neural Structures Involved in Learning and Memory

Early "hints" as to the neural structures that subserve the process of consolidation and memory trace construction more generally came from observation of patients with brain damage, such as the famous H. M. In 1953, for treatment of otherwise intractable seizures, 27-year-old H. M. underwent bilateral removal of major portions of his medial temporal lobes (i.e., the interior surfaces of the lobes of the brain that sit above one's ears; Scoville & Milner, 1957). In that era, experimental brain surgeries were almost common. They were heralded as treatments for a range of disorders, including schizophrenia and depression. The surgery was successful as a control for the H. M.'s seizures. After the surgery, H. M. had significantly less seizure activity (he was reported to experience no more than two major seizures per year: Corkin, 2002). From the standpoint of memory, however, the surgery was a personal tragedy for H. M., even as it was a boon for researchers.

From the time of the surgery, which took place when he was a young adult, H. M. had great difficulty learning new facts and forming memories of new private or public events (Milner, Corkin, & Teuber, 1968; Scoville & Milner, 1957). For example, he was unable to remember a list of words he studied only minutes before. His recognition of a word on the list paired with a word that was not on the list was no better than chance. H. M.'s difficulty in learning new things extended to many different types of materials, including strings of digits; series of musical tones; faces of famous people; public events; and even private events and personal facts, such as how old he was, that his hair had grayed, or how many years had passed since his surgery. Although H. M. showed some ability to remember new information that he encountered over and over again, such as the spatial layout of the house in which he went to live 5 years after his surgery (Corkin, 2002), he was unable to acquire new information on the basis of a single exposure or a small number of exposures to it. It is not that information did not register in H. M.'s conscious mind: He was able to remember over a matter of seconds (i.e., his short-term memory was preserved), but he failed to establish new long-term memories.

The case of H. M. gave researchers a lot of guidance in identifying the neural structures involved in learning and memory. Through work with other patients, animal models of lesion and disease, and, more recently, the aid of neuroimaging techniques such as positron emission tomography (PET) and functional magnetic resonance imaging (fMRI), we have learned even more. The work has made clear that encoding, consolidating, storing, and later retrieving the products of learning depends on a multicomponent neural network involving structures in the medial temporal lobes and the frontal lobes of the brain. Briefly, the perceptual experience of an event impinges on and produces excitation across multiple brain regions distributed across the cortex (see Figure 5.3). Certain areas of cortex, termed "association areas" (e.g., the front portion of the frontal lobe, known as the anterior or prefrontal cortex) bring the information together (thus the name "association" areas), giving rise to conscious awareness of the experience. Neural structures on the medial surface of the temporal lobe are involved in the consolidation of the distributed representation into a durable memory trace. Over the long term, memories are stored in the same cortical areas that participated in initial registration of experience. Prefrontal cortex is implicated in retrieval of memories from long-term stores (e.g., Kandel & Squire, 2000). In the sections that follow, I outline in greater detail each of these steps in "how the brain builds a memory," namely, initial registration, consolidation, storage, and retrieval of information.

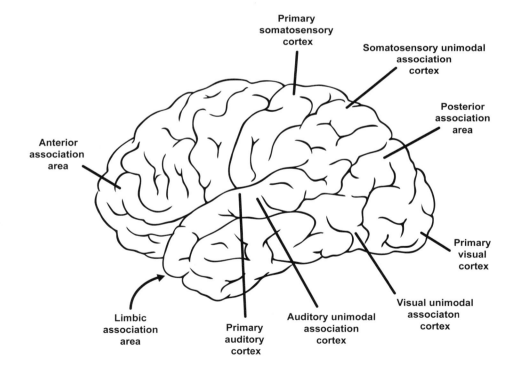

FIGURE 5.3. Lateral view of the association areas of the human brain. Drawing by Ayzit O. Doydum.

Initial Registration

Information about events and experiences does not impinge upon the brain all at once in the same time and place. Rather, it is distributed across multiple cortical areas; that is, neurons in primary visual cortex (see Figure 5.3) respond to the form, color, and motion of an object or event. In parallel, neurons in primary somatosensory cortex respond to inputs from the skin (registering information about light touch) and muscles and joints (registering information about the position and movement of our extremities), and neurons in primary auditory cortex respond to various attributes of the sounds made by the object or event. Inputs from these primary sensory areas are sent (projected) to sensory association areas that are dedicated to a single modality (vision, somatic sensation, or audition), where they are integrated into whole percepts of what the object or event looks, feels, and sounds like, respectively. These unimodal sensory association areas in turn project to polymodal (also termed "multimodal") posterior–parietal, anterior–prefrontal, and limbic–temporal association areas, where inputs from the different sense modalities are integrated.

Studies with humans and nonhuman primates have shown that over very brief time intervals (on the order of seconds), information about objects or events is maintained in the cortical association areas. When normal function of association cortices is disrupted by lesion or disease, forgetting sets in after delays as short as a few seconds (for a review, see Diamond, 2001). Research with nonhuman primates sheds light on how information is maintained in cortical areas over the short term. In monkeys, neurons in the prefrontal cortex begin to fire when a visual stimulus is presented. If the stimulus is hidden from view, the neurons continue to fire during a short delay interval (typically less than 30 sec). When the delay is over, the animal is able to make a correct reach or look to where the object or cue had been. Thus, the neurons "represented" the object in the brain even after the sensory stimulation was gone. In contrast, if the neurons stop firing during the delay period, the monkey is unable to locate the stimulus (e.g., Fuster & Alexander, 1971; for a review, see Eichenbaum & Cohen, 2001). Such findings indicate clearly that the association cortices play a role in the initial registration and temporary representation of information.

Consolidation

Cortical association areas are involved in the short-term registration of experience. They permit us to hold in mind information, such as a phone number just long enough to dial it, for example. In addition, the association areas are ultimately the long-term storage sites for memories: It is from association areas that we retrieve our own home phone number. Yet between initial registration and commitment to long-term storage there is substantial additional processing. That processing generally is described as involving stabilization and integration of the various inputs from different cortical regions, and is thought to be performed by structures within the temporal lobes (i.e., in the medial aspect of the lobe). Whereas stabilization and integration processes begin upon registration of a stimulus, they do not end there. By some estimates, the process of consolidation of a memory trace continues for hours, days, months, and even years. Importantly, throughout the consolidation period, memories are vulnerable to disruption, interference, and, therefore, forgetting.

Two major types of evidence imply that for memory traces to live on beyond immediate experience, they must undergo additional processing. The first source comes form
patients like H. M., who suffer from "anterograde amnesia": an inability to form new
explicit memories. Patients with damage in the medial temporal lobe have normal intelligence (as measured by standardized IQ tests) and normal short-term memory (e.g., over
intervals of a few seconds, they can remember a series of digits as well as can healthy
control subjects). However, they perform at levels below normal control participants on
a variety of memory tasks that require new learning, including reproducing a diagram
after a 5- to 10-minute delay, recalling and recognizing individual words presented on
lists, and recognizing words and faces after a 24-hour delay (Reed & Squire, 1998). The
memory deficits of these individuals cannot be accounted for by problems with retrieval
alone: Lower levels of performance are apparent on tests of recognition, as well as recall,
even though tests of recognition make lower retrieval demands relative to the demands
of recall. These observations imply that for new memories to be effectively stored, they
must undergo additional processing after initial registration.

The second source of evidence that memories must undergo a process of consolidation to live on is the observation of "temporally graded retrograde amnesia": Memory for
more recent events is impaired relative to memory for more remote events (for a review,
see Brown, 2002). Notice that this pattern is precisely the opposite of normal forgetting. The phenomenon is observed in humans whose amnesia is the result of Korsakoff's
syndrome (attributed to chronic alcohol abuse), as well as in patients whose amnesia is
acute due to lesion, infarction, or anoxia. It also can be induced in nonhuman animals
(including rabbits, mice, and monkeys; for reviews, see Eichenbaum & Cohen, 2001;
Squire & Alvarez, 1995) by creating a lesion in medial temporal structures at different
points after learning of a novel association, for example (e.g., an association between a
tone and an electrical shock). Lesions made shortly after learning produce a large deficit
in performance; lesions made well after training produce only mild or no disruption
of performance (e.g., Kim & Fanselow, 1992; Takehara, Kawahara, & Kirino, 2003).
Together, the data on temporally graded retrograde amnesia and on anterograde amnesia provide strong evidence that to be preserved over the long term, memories must
undergo additional processing for some time after the experience of an event.

What is the nature of the processing that traces of experience must undergo to be
maintained over the long term? There is general consensus that consolidation actually involves two processes that occur in parallel: (1) stabilization of a memory trace
through formation of associations among the individual elements of experience, and
(2) integration of the memory trace in cortical association areas (e.g., Zola & Squire,
2000). Stabilization of a memory trace begins as inputs from the association areas are
projected to structures in the medial temporal lobes (see Figure 5.4). As noted earlier,
at the time of experience, inputs from different sensory modalities are processed by different association cortices (i.e., unimodal and polymodal association areas). The neural
codes of the representations of these inputs come together in the perirhinal and parahip-
pocampal cortices of the medial temporal lobes. These cortices then relay the information to another medial temporal structure, the entorhinal cortex, which in turn relays it
into the hippocampus itself (by way of the dentate gyrus). It is in the hippocampus that
enduring links between the different elements of experience are forged. By way of analogy, this aspect of the consolidation process is akin to forming a bouquet out of single
cut flowers, with each flower representing an element of experience. A principal role of

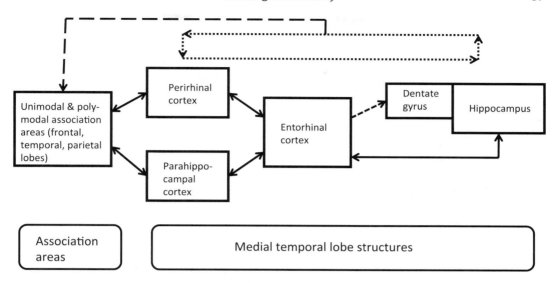

FIGURE 5.4. Schematic representation of the temporal–cortical network implicated in encoding, consolidation, storage, and retrieval of memories. Adapted from Kandel, Schwartz, and Jessell (2000, p. 1232) and Zola and Squire (2000, p. 487). Copyright 2000 by the McGraw-Hill Companies and by Oxford University Press. Reprinted by permission.

the hippocampus is to join the individual stems of experience into a unified bundle (a single event or episode).

Even as it is being processed in the hippocampus, new information is being associated with old information in cortical storage areas (note in Figure 5.4 the bidirectional nature of information flow into and out of the hippocampal formation). The basis for association is shared elements: A "rose" in the current bundle of "flowers" shares elements with roses already in storage. As a result, "roses"—those in the current experience and those stored in memory—are simultaneously activated. Simultaneous activation is the presumed means by which information comes to be established in cortical areas, through the mechanism of "synchronous convergence": Neurons that are repeatedly activated together tend to become associated. The result is an entire pattern of interconnection of new information with old. Throughout the period of consolidation, the pattern is regularly "refreshed" by additional neural signaling within the hippocampus and surrounding cortices, and between the medial temporal structures and the association areas (depicted by dashed lines at the top of Figure 5.4). Eventually, the connections between cortical neurons become "cemented," after which medial temporal activity is no longer necessary for the continued existence of the representation (Alvarez & Squire, 1994; McClelland, McNaughton, & O'Reilly, 1995).

We may think of the entire consolidation process as analogous to gelatin setting. At first, gelatin is liquid, and the only way to hold it in one place is with a mold. With refrigeration, the gelatin hardens to the point that the mold can be removed and the gelatin will maintain its shape. New memories are like gelatin, the hippocampus is the mold, and the coordinated processing within the medial temporal lobes (to bind the elements together) and between the medial temporal structures and the neocortex (to bind new elements to old) is the refrigeration. Once refrigeration (coordinated processing) has done its work, the mold (hippocampus) is no longer necessary to maintain the integrity of the gelatin (the memory). Unlike gelatin, which sets in a matter of hours, the process of consolidation of new memories may require days, weeks, or even years to complete.[1]

Storage

As just reviewed, consolidation involves establishing memory representations in cortical areas. This process is essential because the cortex, rather than the medial temporal lobes, is the long-term storage site for explicit memories. The first suggestion that memories must be stored outside the hippocampus came from evidence of temporally-graded retrograde amnesia (discussed earlier). That organisms with medial temporal lobe damage have intact memories from the distant past, with impaired memory for more recent experiences, is strong evidence that after some period of time, memories are no longer dependent on medial temporal lobe structures.

Neuroimaging studies provide another source of evidence of a time-limited role for medial temporal structures in memory storage. Petersson, Elfgren, and Ingvar (1997) found that even over a short time interval, medial temporal lobe activation decreases in humans as a function of repeated encoding and recall. Conversely, functional connectivity across cortical areas (as indicated by statistical modeling of fMRI data) increases as a function of repeated performance of a task (Büchel, Coull, & Friston, 1999). There also is evidence of lower levels of medial temporal involvement in memories from the remote relative to the more recent past. For example, Haist, Gore, and Mao (2001) tested 60- to 70-year-old participants for recognition of the faces of people who had been famous during different decades, ranging from the 1990s to the 1940s. The results suggested greater neural activity in the hippocampus in response to faces of people famous in the 1990s relative to faces of people famous in the more distant past.

Finally, consistent with the suggestion that memories eventually are stored in neocortical association areas, it has been found that lesions in such areas impair recall of information acquired before the damage. For instance, individuals with lesions in association cortex show impaired long-term memory for familiar objects and faces (e.g., Hodges & Patterson, 1995, 1996). Such patients have higher levels of recognition of names of famous people from the recent relative to the remote past (Hodges & Graham, 1998). This pattern suggests that as long as maintenance of the information is supported by intact medial temporal structures, memories are accessible. As the responsibility for storage is given over to cortical structures, however, accessibility is lost (for discussion, see Mayes, 2000).

Retrieval

The *raison d'être* for the consolidation and storage of memories is so that they can be retrieved at some later time. But just what is retrieval? Joaquin Fuster (1997) suggests that "retrieval" is, in essence, a reactivation of the neural network that represents the event. Reactivation occurs because "an internal or external stimulus, whose cortical representation is part of the network by prior association, will reactivate that representation and, again by association, the rest of the network" (Fuster, 1997, p. 455). It is increasingly clear that retrieval of information from long-term stores is accomplished by the same circuits that were involved in initial registration of the experience, namely, the association cortices in general, and the prefrontal cortex in particular. Damage to the prefrontal cortex disrupts long-term memory retrieval of both post- and premorbidly experienced facts and episodes (e.g., Janowsky, Shimamura, & Squire, 1989). Prefrontal involvement also is implied by neuroimaging studies (fMRI and PET), which reveal increased activation in prefrontal cortex during memory retrieval. The findings generalize across many kinds of retrieval tasks, including auditory and visual stimuli, and recall and recognition (for a review, see Maguire, 2001).

For Children, Increased Vulnerability and Opportunity during Consolidation

As just described, the process of consolidation takes time. In addition, as illustrated by the phenomenon of temporally-graded retrograde amnesia, while newly-learned information is being consolidated, the information is vulnerable to forgetting. The result is the opposite of normal forgetting, such that memory for recently learned material is impaired, relative to memory for information learned long ago. My suggestion that the period of consolidation may be especially critical for children does not stem from an assumption that they suffer temporally-graded retrograde amnesia. Rather, it stems from the expectation that consolidation processes may represent a challenge for the developing child, due to relative immaturity of the neural structures and network involved in memory trace construction (for discussion, see Bauer, 2006).

Development of the Temporal–Cortical Network

The period of consolidation may be especially "perilous" for children because the structures involved in the process—medial temporal and cortical areas—undergo a protracted course of development. Although we have a great deal to learn about the development of the structures and connections of the temporal–cortical network that supports construction and maintenance of memories, critical pieces of information are in place. They lead to expectations of relations between changes in brain and in behavior throughout childhood.

In terms of brain development in general, there are changes in both gray matter (neurons) and white matter (myelinated axons) well into adolescence (e.g., Giedd et al., 1999; Sowell et al., 2004). By 5 years of age the child's brain is roughly 90% of adult volume (Kennedy, Makris, Herbert, Takahashi, & Caviness, 2002), with an additional 5% increase in volume by the end of the second decade (Caviness, Kennedy, Richelme, Rademacher, & Filipek, 1996). Beyond puberty, gray matter volume actually declines (Gogtay et al., 2004). In contrast to gray matter, the volume of which changes in a curvilinear pattern (with overshot of adult levels, followed by reduction), white matter volume increases linearly with age (Giedd et al., 1999). Increases in white matter volume are associated with greater connectivity between brain regions and with myelination processes that continue into young adulthood (e.g., Johnson, 1997; Klingberg, Vaidya, Gabrielli, Soseley, & Hedehus, 1999; Schneider, Il'yasov, Hennig, & Martin, 2004).

In terms of the temporal–cortical memory network, there are documented postnatal and, in some cases, protracted developments. In primates, much of the hippocampus matures early, with adult levels of synapses and glucose use by age 6 months (Seress,

2001). Yet there are gradual increases in hippocampal volume into adolescence (e.g., Gogtay et al., 2004; Pfluger et al., 1999; Utsunomiya, Takano, Okazaki, & Mistudome, 1999). In dentate gyrus (which links the temporal cortices and hippocampal cell fields; see Figure 5.4), as many as 30% of the cells proliferate, migrate, and establish connections postnatally. Whereas much of the work is accomplished by the second year of life (e.g., the rise to peak numbers of synapses occurs at 8–20 months), there is evidence that neurogenesis continues throughout childhood and into adulthood (Altman & Das, 1965; for discussion, see Tanapat, Hastings, & Gould, 2001). Functional maturity of the structure is expected to be reached by 16–20 months of age, coincident with the rise to peak number of synapses. Full maturity—associated with achievement of the adult number of synapses—is delayed until at least 4–5 years (for discussion, see Eckenhoff & Rakic, 1991; Webb, Monk, & Nelson, 2001). Myelination in the hippocampal region continues throughout childhood and adolescence (Arnold & Trojanowski, 1996; Benes, Turtle, Khan, & Farol, 1994; Schneider et al., 2004).

In prefrontal cortex, the rise to peak number of synapses occurs at 8–24 months. Pruning to adult levels does not begin until late childhood, and adult levels are not reached until late adolescence or even early adulthood (Huttenlocher, 1979; Huttenlocher & Dabholkar, 1997). As noted, as a result of pruning and other regressive events (i.e., loss of neurons and axonal branches), by adolescence, there are declines in the thickness of the cortical mantle (e.g., Giedd et al., 1999; Gogtay et al., 2004; Sowell, Delis, Stiles, & Jernigan, 2001; for discussion, see Van Petten, 2004). Coincident with decreases in gray matter volume are increases in connectivity between brain regions and myelination processes that continue well into adolescence or young adulthood (e.g., Johnson, 1997; Klingberg et al., 1999; Schneider et al., 2004). Although there are well-documented reciprocal connections between the hippocampus and frontal lobes, the development of these connections has not been fully elucidated (see Barbas, 2000; Fuster, 2002). Finally, not until adolescence do neurotransmitters, such as acetylcholine, reach adult levels (discussed in Benes, 2001).

Although much of the attention to developmental changes had been focused on the medial–temporal and prefrontal regions, changes in the lateral temporal and parietal cortices also likely have implications for memory and its development. Longitudinal data indicate that the nonlinear changes in cortical gray matter occur earlier in the frontal and occipital poles, relative to the rest of the cortex, which matures in a parietal-to-frontal direction. The superior temporal cortex is last to mature (though the temporal poles mature early; Gogtay et al., 2004). The late development of this portion of cortex is potentially significant for memory because it is one of the polymodal association areas that play a role in integration of information across sense modalities.

Implications for Consolidation

The relative immaturity of the structures and connections of the temporal–cortical network implies that consolidation processes may be less effective and less efficient in infancy and early childhood in particular. Continued development of cortical association areas implies that vulnerability may extend well into adolescence. As a result, even after successful learning, material remains vulnerable to forgetting. The younger the child, the more vulnerable the trace. To further complicate matters, there is increasing evidence that at both the cellular and systems level, memory traces undergo "reconsolidation"; that is, each time a memory trace is activated, it becomes vulnerable all over again. There is a "silver lining" though, in that each time a trace is activated, it can be strengthened, and new elements can be added.

Reconsolidation

The necessity that newly learned material be consolidated for long-term storage, and the fact that the neural network implicated in consolidation processes has a protracted course of development, presents challenges for learning and memory in infancy and childhood. To make matters "even worse," there is strong evidence at both the cellular and systems levels that traces undergo "reconsolidation" each time they are reactivated; that is, each time a stored trace is cued—typically by elements of the present situation that overlap with elements that are part of the stored trace (cueing may be either intentional or unintentional)—it is reactivated and undergoes consolidation all over again. The process of reactivation and reconsolidation is a double-edged sword. On the negative side, each time a memory trace is reconsolidated, it returns to a state of increased vulnerability (though for a shorter period of time). On the positive side, reconsolidation affords an opportunity to integrate new learning with old learning. After describing some of the recent data on reconsolidation at the cellular and systems levels, I discuss the implications of reconsolidation for learning and memory in development.

Cellular Reconsolidation

There is evidence that the cellular events involved in establishing new long-term memories are repeated whenever old traces are reactivated. Briefly, long-term storage of information depends on new protein synthesis, which supports structural changes that enhance functional connectivity, including changes in the morphology and growth of new dendritic spines on postsynaptic neurons. This process occurs the first time a memory is stored, and as suggested by the results of research by Debiec, LeDoux, and Nader (2002), is repeated when memories are reactivated.

Debiec and colleagues (2002) conditioned rats to expect a shock when placed in a distinctive context, a type of learning that is known to be dependent on the hippocampus. Three days after learning, different subgroups of trained rats underwent different treatments. Rats in one subgroup had their memories of the contingency reactivated: They were placed back in the distinctive context, though no shocks were administered. Rats in the other subgroup did not have their memories reactivated. Rats in both subgroups then were injected with anisomycin, a compound known to block the new protein synthesis necessary for long-term memory. Later the rats were tested for long-term memory of the contingency by placing them back in the conditioning chamber once again. The rats that had not had their memories reactivated showed evidence of retention of the conditioned response. When they were placed in the conditioning chamber they froze, an indication of fear induced by the distinctive environment. In contrast, the rats whose memories had been reactivated showed little evidence of memory, as indicated by high mobility and low freezing. These results strongly suggest that memory traces undergo protein synthesis–dependent reconsolidation after reactivation. When reactivation occurs, the processes that originally converted a temporary pattern of activation into an enduring trace must occur once again. If they are blocked, the memory is, in effect, functionally erased.

Systems Reconsolidation

As evidenced by the work of Takehara and colleagues (2003; see also Kim & Fanselow, 1992), memories eventually become independent of the hippocampus. Yet the work of Debiec and colleagues (2002) indicates that hippocampal dependence is reinstated by reactivation of the memory. Evidence of a return to hippocampal dependence at the neural systems level comes from another study of contextual fear conditioning. In this study, Debiec and his colleagues conditioned rats to fear a particular context, then waited 45 days, to allow the memory to consolidate fully and become independent of the hippocampus. Half of the rats then had their memories reactivated by reexposure to the distinctive context. All of the rats then underwent hippocampal surgery. Days later, the rats were once again placed in the distinctive context and their behavior was observed. The rats whose memories had not been reactivated exhibited retention of the contingency, as evidenced by the observation that they spent about half of their time freezing. In contrast, the rats whose memories had been reactivated before the hippocampal lesion spent only about 10% of their time freezing, suggesting loss of memory for the contingency. These results indicate that even once memories have been safely tucked away for long-term storage, when they are reactivated, they are vulnerable all over again.

Summary and Implications

It is clear that learning and memory are intimately related. Yet learning does not explain remembering. The fact that these two foundational processes cannot be reduced to one another is made clear by findings of age-related differences in memory in the face of equivalent levels of learning. To explain the differences we must consider processes that take place postlearning. An excellent candidate process is consolidation: the means by which initially labile memory traces become stabilized and integrated into long-term storage. Work with animal models makes clear that memory traces are vulnerable throughout the period of consolidation. In the developing human, consolidation may be especially perilous because the neural structures implicated in it (medial temporal and cortical structures) are relatively immature. As a result, newly learned information may never make it to long-term storage. Further complicating the matter is the apparent fact that even once they have been successfully stored, memory traces may return to a period of lability (thus, vulnerability) when they are reactivated by exposure to some element that cues the stored trace. Whereas consolidation and reconsolidation represent periods of vulnerability, as outlined in the next section, they also provide an opportunity for growth and cognitive development.

Capitalizing on Consolidation and Reconsolidation Processes

The phenomenon of consolidation initially was identified as a result of memory failure; that is, it was hypothesized to account for retroactive interference of one set of to-be-remembered stimuli with another. Two different types of memory failure—anterograde and temporally-graded retrograde amnesia—provide additional evidence for the process. Disruptions of memory also serve as the source of evidence that reactivated memory traces undergo reconsolidation. And most of the discussion of the developmental implications of consolidation and reconsolidation in this chapter has been on the darker side, emphasizing that newly formed memory traces are vulnerable throughout the period of consolidation. Is there any hope that understanding these process will do more than illuminate the potholes in learning and remembering?

The good news is that consolidation and reconsolidation also have a "lighter side." In fact, consideration of these processes provides means to understand a number of well-established phenomena in learning and memory, and includes the following findings: (1) Memory traces are strengthened with repetition; (2) once established, memory traces can be embellished or elaborated upon; and (3) memory traces become integrated with one another, thereby forming a broader or more general base of knowledge. I discuss each in turn, followed by some suggestions for how we might capitalize on these phenomena to facilitate learning and remembering in the classroom, and what additional research needs to be done to maximize the potential.

The Possible Engine behind Three Effects

We have long known that repetition facilitates retention. In other words, additional learning trials can strengthen existing memory traces (see Figure 5.2). In fact, for very young infants, repetition may be necessary to ensure long-term retention. In a study in my laboratory, 9-month-olds were exposed to events (e.g., "make a gong") once, twice, or three times prior to imposition of a 1-month delay. The infants in the three-experience condition had higher levels of recall 1 month later relative to infants in the one- and two-experience groups (which did not differ from one another). In fact, only infants in the three-experience condition demonstrated memory for the order in which the events occurred (Bauer, Wiebe, Waters, & Bangston, 2001). The process of consolidation provides a neural mechanism for the strengthening of the representation. We can think of each trial as a "pulse" that keeps the material reverberating through the medial–temporal system (see Figure 5.4), increasing the likelihood that it will stabilize and become integrated into long-term storage.

It also is apparent that once established, memory traces can be embellished or elaborated upon by repeated experience. Evidence of elaboration of an existing trace is provided in Figure 5.5. In this study, we found that with each additional learning trial, infants recalled more actions (reflected in Figure 5.5). They also were increasingly accurate in production of the actions in the correct temporal order, thus indicating better organized memory traces with additional learning trials. The processes of consolidation and reconsolidation provide a possible neural means by which this is accomplished. With experience of an event, the process of stabilization of a memory trace begins. Hours, or days, later the event can be reactivated by a cue; there is no better cue than to reexperience the same event. Once reactivated, the memory trace is open to incorporation of new elements, such as an action that was not adequately encoded on an earlier learning trial, or additional information about the temporal order of actions. Thus, with each reconsolidation, initially "sparse" memory representations can become augmented with additional information. The new elements become part of the reconsolidated trace, leaving it "new and improved," relative to the original.

The phenomena of consolidation and reconsolidation also provide possible mechanisms by which separate learning episodes can be integrated with one another. Consider

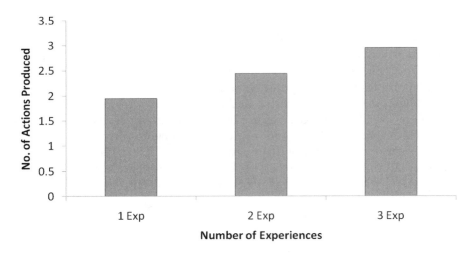

FIGURE 5.5. The number of actions produced by 16- to 20-month-old infants after one, two, or three experiences with a sequence. Data from Bauer (unpublished).

that an initial learning episode sets into motion the process of encoding and consolidation. A subsequent episode of a similar—but not identical—kind sets into motion its own process of encoding and consolidation. Assuming that some elements are shared between the episodes, a demand for retrieval of either will cause both to be reactivated. Once activated simultaneously, the two episodes will "intermingle" and be reconsolidated, each embellished by the other.

We are currently in the process of testing this simple model. Children participate in three interactions with an experimenter. In the first, they learn a novel fact, such as that "dolphins communicate by clicking and squeaking." In a separate episode, on a different day, they learn that "dolphins live in groups called *pods*." Our expectation is that because the two episodes share mention of the feature "dolphin," Learning Episode 2 will reactivate Learning Episode 1. As a result, Learning Episode 1 will be strengthened and also become integrated with Learning Episode 2. We are testing this possibility through a third interaction, in which children are challenged to answer the question "How does a pod communicate?" If the separate learning episodes do not become integrated, there is no basis for address of this question, since children are not explicitly taught that pods communicate by clicking and squeaking. However, if, as expected, the episodes become integrated through simultaneous activation, then not only will the children be able to provide an answer to the question but also all three bits of information will be strengthened in the process. It is a simple experiment, but one that stands to make a significant contribution to our understanding of how learning takes place, and how newly learned information becomes transformed through integration into a larger knowledge network.

In summary, learning involves storing new facts and experiences, and also relating them to old facts and experiences. Each time a memory trace is reactivated, it can be strengthened. Each reactivation also provides an opportunity for new information to be added to previously acquired knowledge, leaving it "new and improved" relative to the original. Once reactivated, a memory trace also is open to linkage or integration with information already stored in memory, based on shared (or similar) elements that result in simultaneous activation of memory traces containing them.

Implications for the Classroom

We have much to learn about the processes of consolidation and reconsolidation, especially in developmental populations. Yet the need for additional research should not stop us from considering possible classroom implications of what we already know about these processes. Indeed, articulation of possible implications of these basic memory processes for educational settings could help to shape the course of future research, some suggestions for which I outline in the next section.

As I launch this section, I am painfully aware of the numerous constraints under which educators, especially in the primary and secondary grades, must operate. The number of curricular choices that are no longer a matter of choice is staggering, and the demands are unlikely to recede any time soon. That said, with the processes of consolidation and reconsolidation in mind, there are two basic principles around which curricula seemingly should be organized to achieve the maximum bang for our educational buck. In bumper sticker form, the principles are "Repeat, with variation on the theme," and "Link early, link often."

The mandate for repetition comes from what we know about the process of consolidation. To invoke an analogy I used earlier in the chapter, the elements of memory traces must remain refrigerated long enough for the gelatin to set. But what if our refrigerator is in a developing country, and electricity to operate it is only available a few hours at a time? In this case, on the basis of a single bout of refrigeration, only a thin layer may form on the surface of the mold. For the gelatin to solidify all the way through, we may need several bouts of refrigeration, distributed over time. So it goes with learning and memory, especially in the developing brain. A learning episode that seems to have "taken" may really be only skin deep, such that it cannot endure without reinforcement (as in Bauer et al., 2001). For the young child, a single learning episode may be sufficient to give the *illusion* that the lesson has been learned, but like the gelatin, it loses its integrity quickly (it does not survive consolidation). Reinforcement in the form of repetition serves to keep the lesson reverberating long enough for consolidation to occur. Variations on a theme serve to ensure that the resulting memory trace has a strong core, with multiple different associates.

The mandate for links comes from what we know about the process of reconsolidation. A single learning episode established a trace that is comprised of elements *A*, *B*, and *C*, for example. A subsequent episode establishes a trace that is comprised of elements *C*, *D*, and *E*. Establishment of the second trace means that element *C* is reinstated, which simultaneously serves to reinstate elements *A* and *B*. The result is that the links in the original episode are strengthened and linked to the subsequent episode. By "linking early," the new associate serves almost as a separate learning trial for the original trace. By "linking often" the network of associations grows, strengthening and elaborating along the way.

Though no doubt there are other elements not captured in the equation, the principles of "Repeat, with variation on the theme" and "Link early, link often" are consistent with Jerome Bruner's (1960) conceptualization of a "spiral curriculum." Bruner suggested that an effective curriculum is one that, as it develops, revisits basic ideas repeatedly, "building upon them until the student has grasped the full formal apparatus that goes with them" (p. 13). The curriculum is a spiral (rather than a circle) because although it exposes students to a concept over and over again, it does not stay at the same level of complexity or demand over time. Rather, concepts are introduced and reintroduced, each time in different contexts with different neighbors, and at different levels of sophistication. Some students may grasp the concept the first time around and use subsequent "passes" to elaborate on it. For other students, the first pass (or two) may have little impact, but the concept is revisited, granting them another opportunity. When activities with similar educational functions are repeated and coordinated with one another, and when learning experiences in one course or subject matter are coordinated with those in another, the spiral widens. A spiral curriculum seems ideally suited to reveal the "silver lining" in what might otherwise be the dark cloud of consolidation and reconsolidation.

Suggestions for Future Research

If we take seriously the educational implications of the processes of consolidation and reconsolidation, then two research questions need to be addressed in the near term. The first question concerns the optimal timing of repeated lessons of a similar kind. Ideally, learning episodes are timed such that they do not interfere with one another (remember Müller & Pilzecker, 1900!), but such that the trace from Learning Episode 1 is still maximally available, so that upon Learning Episode 2, the first trace is effectively reinstated. Unfortunately, because the topics of consolidation and reconsolidation have not been at the forefront of concern in cognitive psychology, we know little about timing or spacing effects, even in adults. Although we might assume that the amount of time required to consolidate (or reconsolidate) a memory trace is relatively constant over development, we actually have very little to go on in making that assumption. Thus, major questions for research are the timing or spacing of episodes to optimize strengthening, elaboration, and integration of traces based on shared elements—and possible developmental differences therein.

The second question concerns the levels of similarity of elements that are minimally necessary and optimal. The benefits of consolidation and reconsolidation for strengthening learning and memory will be realized only if the repeated episodes of a similar kind are indeed perceived as "similar." In the absence of overlap in features, episodes will not reinstate one another. There is a long tradition of research in analogical reasoning and problem solving (applying a well-known domain of knowledge, the base, to a lesser known target domain) that makes clear that analogies are facilitated by high surface similarity between the base and the target domain. For example, analogical problem solving is reasonably successful when 5-year-old children hear a base story about a Genie who must transport her jewels from her current bottle to a new one (from her current "home" to her new "home") across a barrier (e.g., Brown, Kane, & Echols, 1986). The Genie succeeds by rolling a piece of paper (her "magic carpet") into a tube, placing the tube at the mouth of the new bottle, and rolling the jewels through the tube.

The children are then faced with the problem of an Easter Bunny, who needs to transport eggs from his basket on one side of a river to a friend's basket on the other side of the river. Children are more successful at solving the second task (i.e., suggesting that the Easter Bunny roll his blanket into a tube and pass the eggs through it) when both the surface and the underlying, deep characteristics of the problems are similar (Brown et al., 1986). Surface similarity is increased by manipulating the elements of the problems, such as changing the identity of the main characters (so that both are four-legged animals), the objects to be transported (so that they are from the same category, such as fruit), or the mode of transportation (both problems can be solved by rolling a piece of fabric). The deep characteristics are the goals of the problem (i.e., moving small objects from one location to another), the obstacles that must be overcome (an impassable barrier), and the potential solutions (creating a conduit).

Although the situations are only "analogous," it is reasonable to hypothesize that episodes will be successfully reinstated when there is high similarity in the surface features between or among the individual episodes. Thus, teaching children that *dolphins* communicate by clicking and squeaking, and that *dolphins* live in groups called pods, might be more likely to encourage integration of the separate episodes than teaching them how *dolphins* communicate and that *porpoises* live in pods. In the latter case, the question of how a pod communicates may go unanswered because the amount of overlap in the traces is not sufficient to cause Learning Episode 1 to be reinstated during presentation of Learning Episode 2. The amount of overlap in surface and deep features that is minimally necessary and optimal is an empirical question. It is likely that the answer will vary as a function of the age of the child, the amount of domain knowledge the child possesses (i.e., whether the child is aware that dolphins and porpoises are synonymous), and even perhaps as a function of the amount of time or space between learning episodes (as memory traces begin to fail, more surface similarity might be necessary for successful reinstatement).

Summary and Conclusions

Learning and remembering are intimately related to one another. We measure learning by testing remembering; remembering is requisite for a body of knowledge to accrue. There are many examples in the literature of the influence of domain knowledge on memory, and of memory on the acquisition of new information. Yet although the processes are "siblings," they are not identical twins. We have learned many things that we no longer remember; we remember things that we have no idea how we learned. My major purpose in this chapter was to consider the implications for new learning and the growth of knowledge of memory processes that take place "behind the scenes," after a learning episode or experience has taken place.

The process of forming a new memory—and thus of acquiring new information—involves several steps, beginning with initial registration of the information across distributed cortical regions. For the event or experience to live on beyond the immediate present, the initially labile representation of the experience must be stabilized, and the resulting trace must be integrated with information already in storage. Retrieval of a stored memory trace occurs when an internal or external stimulus that shares elements with the trace reactivates it. Every act of retrieval is an opportunity to strengthen and elaborate upon the original trace, and also to create new linkages between it and other traces with elements in common. Thus, every act of retrieval of previously stored information is an opportunity to solidify and expand the knowledge base.

The means by which memory traces are born and develop, and the processes that take place each time they are retrieved or reactivated, have implications for learning and memory in the classroom. In sound-bite terms, they suggest that educators "Repeat, with variation on the theme" and "Link early, link often." These mandates stem from what we know about the processes of consolidation and reconsolidation, and the developmental status of the neural structures and network that subserves them. Even for the young child, a single lesson or learning episode may be sufficient to support retention over the short term. However, essential elements of the representation likely will be lost as the trace undergoes consolidation. Reinforcement in the form of repetition serves to keep the lesson-related trace alive long enough for it to be successfully consolidated and integrated with existing knowledge. Variations on the lesson theme serve to increase the number of associations to the trace and thus the number of routes to retrieval (and reactivation) of it. The mandate for links stems from the observation that shared elements—and their associates—are strengthened each time they are activated. Thus, a new association that shares elements with an old one strengthens the original trace in much the same manner as an additional learning trial. By "linking often" the network of associations grows, strengthening and elaborating along the way.

The principles of "Repeat, with variation on the theme" and "Link early, link often" are consistent with conceptualization of *spiral curricula* (Bruner, 1960). In such curricula, students are introduced and reintroduced to key concepts, in different contexts and at different levels of sophistication. When learning experiences in one course or subject matter are coordinated with those in another, the spiral widens, providing a firm foundation for continued learning and expansion. Spiral curricula have potential for students of all ages, from those in kindergarten to those in graduate school. They can be used for the full range of subjects, from beginning concepts in mathematics to engineering and medical training (Bruner, 1992).

Optimization of the potential of consideration of basic memory and neural processes for enhancing educational practice will require us to address a number of questions. One question for future research is the optimal timing and spacing for repetition of lessons and concepts. Because the processes of consolidation and reconsolidation have not been a central focus in cognitive or developmental psychology, we know little about the timing of them in adults or children. A second question is the level of similarity of elements that is minimally necessary and optimal to ensure that separate episodes, perhaps experienced in different contexts, serve to strengthen and enhance one another. No doubt the answers to both of these questions will be different for younger and older children, and for students with different levels of expertise in a domain. Thus, we have much ground to cover. Fortunately, addressing these questions provides an excellent opportunity for collaboration across the aisles of basic and applied research because answers to them will further both agendas.

Note

1. Discussion of the specific cellular and molecular events that accomplish the "linkage" of elements to one another is beyond the scope of this chapter. See, for example, Eichenbaum and Cohen (2001) and Kandel, Schwartz, and Jessell (2000) for reviews.

References

Altman, J., & Das, G. D. (1965). Autoradiographic and histological evidence of postnatal hippocampal neurogenesis in rats. *Journal of Comparative Neurology, 124*, 319–335.

Alvarez, P., & Squire, L. R. (1994). Memory consolidation and the medial temporal lobe: A simple network model. *Proceedings of the National Academy of Sciences, 91*, 7041–7045.

Arnold, S. E., & Trojanowski, J. Q. (1996). Human fetal hippocampal development: I. Cytoarchitecture, myeloarchitecture, and neuronal morphologic features. *Journal of Comparative Neurology, 367*, 274–292.

Barbas, H. (2000). Connections underlying the synthesis of cognition, memory, and emotion in primate prefrontal cortices. *Brain Research Bulletin, 52*, 319–330.

Barr, R., Dowden, A., & Hayne, H. (1996). Developmental change in deferred imitation by 6- to 24-month-old infants. *Infant Behavior and Development, 19*, 159–170.

Bauer, P. J. (2004). Getting explicit memory off the ground: Steps toward construction of a neuro-developmental account of changes in the first two years of life. *Developmental Review, 24*, 347–373.

Bauer, P. J. (2005a). Developments in declarative memory: Decreasing susceptibility to storage failure over the second year of life. *Psychological Science, 16*, 41–47.

Bauer, P. J. (2005b). New developments in the study of infant memory. In D. M. Teti (Ed.), *Blackwell handbook of research methods in developmental science* (pp. 467–488). Oxford, UK: Blackwell.

Bauer, P. J. (2006). Constructing a past in infancy: A neuro-developmental account. *Trends in Cognitive Sciences, 10*, 175–181.

Bauer, P. J. (2007). *Remembering the times of our lives: Memory in infancy and beyond*. Mahwah, NJ: Erlbaum.

Bauer, P. J., & Mandler, J. M. (1989). One thing follows another: Effects of temporal structure on one- to two-year-olds' recall of events. *Developmental Psychology, 25*, 197–206.

Bauer, P. J., Wenner, J. A., Dropik, P. L., & Wewerka, S. S. (2000). Parameters of remembering and forgetting in the transition from infancy to early childhood. *Monographs of the Society for Research in Child Development, 65*(4, Serial No. 263).

Bauer, P. J., Wiebe, S. A., Waters, J. M., & Bangston, S. K. (2001). Reexposure breeds recall: Effects of experience on 9-month-olds' ordered recall. *Journal of Experimental Child Psychology, 80*, 174–200.

Benes, F. M. (2001). The development of prefrontal cortex: The maturation of neurotransmitter systems and their interaction. In C. A. Nelson & M. Luciana (Eds.), *Handbook of developmental cognitive neuroscience* (pp. 79–92). Cambridge, MA: MIT Press.

Benes, F. M., Turtle, M., Khan, Y., & Farol, P. (1994). Myelination of a key relay zone in the hippocampal formation occurs in the human brain during childhood, adolescence, and adulthood. *Archives of General Psychiatry, 51*, 477–484.

Brown, A. L., Kane, M. J., & Echols, C. H. (1986). Young children's mental models determine analogical transfer across problems with a common goal structure. *Cognitive Development, 1*, 103–121.

Brown, A. S. (2002). Consolidation theory and retrograde amnesia in humans. *Psychonomic Bulletin and Review, 9*, 403–425.

Bruner, J. (1960). *The process of education*. Cambridge, MA: Harvard University Press.

Bruner, J. (1992). Science education and teachers: A Karplus lecture. *Journal of Science Education and Technology, 1*, 5–12.

Büchel, C., Coull, J. T., & Friston, K. J. (1999). The predictive value of changes in effective connectivity for human learning. *Science, 283*, 1538–1541.

Caviness, V. S., Kennedy, D. N., Richelme, C., Rademacher, J., & Filipek, P. A. (1996). The human brain age 7–11 years: A volumetric analysis based on magnetic resonance images. *Cerebral Cortex, 6,* 726–736.

Chi, M. T. H. (1978). Knowledge structures and memory development. In R. S. Siegler (Ed.), *Children's thinking: What develops?* (pp. 73–96). Hillsdale, NJ: Erlbaum.

Corkin, S. (2002). What's new with the amnesic patient H. M.? *Nature Reviews, 3,* 153–160.

Daneman, P., & Carpenter, P. (1980). Individual differences in working memory and reading. *Journal of Verbal Learning and Verbal Behavior, 19,* 450–466.

Debiec, J., LeDoux, J. E., & Nader, K. (2002). Cellular and systems reconsolidation in the hippocampus. *Neuron, 36,* 527–538.

Diamond, A. (2001). A model system for studying the role of dopamine in the prefrontal cortex during early development in humans: Early and continuously treated phenylketonuria. In C. A. Nelson & M. Luciana (Eds.), *Handbook of developmental cognitive neuroscience* (pp. 433–472). Cambridge, MA: MIT Press.

Ebbinghaus, H. (1964). *On memory* (H. A. Ruger & C. E. Bussenius, Trans.). New York: Dover. (Original work published 1885)

Eckenhoff, M., & Rakic, P. (1991). A quantitative analysis of synaptogenesis in the molecular layer of the dentate gyrus in the rhesus monkey. *Developmental Brain Research, 64,* 129–135.

Eichenbaum, H., & Cohen, N. J. (2001). *From conditioning to conscious recollection: Memory systems of the brain.* New York: Oxford University Press.

Fuster, J. M. (1997). Network memory. *Trends in Neuroscience, 20,* 451–459.

Fuster, J. M. (2002). Frontal lobe and cognitive development. *Journal of Neurocytology, 31,* 373–385.

Fuster, J. M., & Alexander, G. E. (1971). Neuron activity related to short-term memory. *Science, 173,* 652–654.

Giedd, J. N., Blumenthal, J., Jeffries, N. O., Castellanos, F. X., Liu, H., Zijdenbos, A., et al. (1999). Brain development during childhood and adolescence: A longitudinal MRI study. *Nature Neuroscience, 2,* 861–863.

Gogtay, N., Giedd, J. N., Lusk, L., Hayashi, K. M., Greenstein, D., Vaituzis, A. C., et al. (2004). Dynamic mapping of human cortical development during childhood through early adulthood. *Proceedings of the National Academy of Sciences USA, 101,* 8174–8179.

Haist, F., Gore, J. B., & Mao, H. (2001). Consolidation of human memory over decades revealed by functional magnetic resonance imaging. *Nature Neuroscience, 4,* 1139–1145.

Hodges, J. R., & Graham, K. S. (1998). A reversal of the temporal gradient for famous person knowledge in semantic dementia: Implications for the neural organisation of long-term memory. *Neuropsychologia, 36,* 803–825.

Hodges, J. R., & Patterson, K. (1995). Is semantic memory consistently impaired early in the course of Alzheimer's disease?: Neuroanatomical and diagnostic implications. *Neuropsychologia, 33,* 441–459.

Hodges, J. R., & Patterson, K. (1996). Non-fluent progressive aphasia and semantic dementia: A comparative neuropsychological study. *Journal of the International Neuropsychological Society, 2,* 511–525.

Howe, M. L., & Brainerd, C. J. (1989). Development of children's long-term retention. *Developmental Review, 9,* 301–340.

Huttenlocher, P. R. (1979). Synaptic density in human frontal cortex: Developmental changes and effects of aging. *Brain Research, 163,* 195–205.

Huttenlocher, P. R., & Dabholkar, A. S. (1997). Regional differences in synaptogenesis in human cerebral cortex. *Journal of Comparative Neurology, 387,* 167–178.

Inhelder, B., & Piaget, J. (1958). *The growth of logical thinking from childhood to adolescence.* New York: Basic Books.

Inhelder, B., & Piaget, J. (1964). *The early growth of logic in the child*. New York: Norton.

Janowsky, J. S., Shimamura, A. P., & Squire, L. R. (1989). Source memory impairment in patients with frontal lobe lesions. *Neuropsychologia, 27*, 1043–1056.

Johnson, M. H. (1997). *Developmental cognitive neuroscience*. Oxford, UK: Blackwell.

Kandel, E. R., Schwartz, J. H., & Jessell, T. M. (2000). *Principles of neural science* (4th ed.). New York: McGraw-Hill.

Kandel, E. R., & Squire, L. R. (2000). Neuroscience: Breaking down scientific barriers to the study of brain and mind. *Science, 290*, 1113–1120.

Kennedy, D. N., Makris, N., Herbert, M. R., Takahashi, T., & Caviness, V. S. (2002). Basic principles of MRI and morphometry studies of human brain development. *Developmental Science, 5*, 268–278.

Kim, J. J., & Fanselow, M. S. (1992). Modality-specific retrograde amnesia of fear. *Science, 256*, 675–677.

Klingberg, T., Vaidya, C. J., Gabrielli, J. D., Soseley, M. E., & Hedehus, M. (1999). Myelination and organization of the frontal white matter in children: A diffusion tensor MRI study. *NeuroReport, 10*, 2817–2821.

Maguire, E. A. (2001). Neuroimaging studies of autobiographical event memory. *Philosophical Transactions of the Royal Society of London, 356*, 1441–1451.

Mayes, A. R. (2000). Selective memory disorders. In E. Tulving & F. I. M. Craik (Eds.), *The Oxford handbook of memory* (pp. 427–440). New York: Oxford University Press.

McClelland, J. L., McNaughton, B. L., & O'Reilly, R. C. (1995). Why there are complementary learning systems in the hippocampus and neocortex: Insights from the successes and failures of connectionist models of learning and memory. *Psychological Review, 102*, 419–457.

Milner, B., Corkin, S., & Teuber, H. L. (1968). Further analysis of the hippocampal amnesic syndrome: 14-year followup study of H. M. *Neuropsychologia, 6*, 215–234.

Müller, G. E., & Pilzecker, A. (1900). Experimentelle Beitrage zur Lehre vom Gedachtnis. *Zeitschrift für Psychologie, 1*, 1–300.

Petersson, K. M., Elfgren, C., & Ingvar, M. (1997). A dynamic role of the medial temporal lobe during retrieval of declarative memory in man. *NeuroImage, 6*, 1–11.

Pfluger, T., Weil, S., Wies, S., Vollmar, C., Heiss, D., Egger, J., et al. (1999). Normative volumetric data of the developing hippocampus in children based on magnetic resonance imaging. *Epilepsia, 40*, 414–423.

Reed, J. M., & Squire, L. R. (1998). Retrograde amnesia for facts and events: Findings from four new cases. *Journal of Neuroscience, 18*, 3943–3954.

Riggins, T., Miller, N. C., Bauer, P. J., Georgieff, M. K., & Nelson, C. A. (2009). Electrophysiological indices of memory for temporal order in early childhood: Implications for the development of recollection. *Developmental Science, 12*, 209–219.

Schneider, J. F. L., Il'yasov, K. A., Hennig, J., & Martin, E. (2004). Fast quantitative difusion-tensor imaging of cerebral white matter from the neonatal period to adolescence. *Neuroradiology, 46*, 258–266.

Scoville, W. B., & Milner, B. (1957). Loss of recent memory after bilateral hippocampal lesions. *Journal of Neurological and Neurosurgical Psychiatry, 20*, 11–12.

Seress, L. (2001). Morphological changes of the human hippocampal formation from midgestation to early childhood. In C. A. Nelson & M. Luciana (Eds.), *Handbook of developmental cognitive neuroscience* (pp. 45–58). Cambridge, MA: MIT Press.

Siegel, L. S., & Ryan, E. B. (1989). The development of working memory in normally achieving and subtypes of learning disabled children. *Child Development, 60*, 973–908.

Sowell, E. R., Delis, D., Stiles, J., & Jernigan, T. L. (2001). Improved memory functioning and frontal lobe maturation between childhood and adolescence: A structural MRI study. *Journal of International Neuropsychological Society, 7*, 312–322.

Sowell, E. R., Thompson, P. M., Leonard, C. M., Welcome, S. E., Kan, E., & Toga, A. W. (2004). Longitudinal mapping of cortical thickness and brain growth in normal children. *Journal of Neuroscience, 24,* 8223–8231.

Squire, L. R., & Alvarez, P. (1995). Retrograde amnesia and memory consolidation: A neurobiological perspective. *Current Opinion in Neurobiology, 5,* 169–177.

Takehara, K., Kawahara, S., & Kirino, Y. (2003). Time-dependent reorganization of the brain components underlying memory retention in trace eyeblink conditioning. *Journal of Neuroscience, 23,* 9897–9905.

Tanapat, P., Hastings, N. B., & Gould, E. (2001). Adult neurogenesis in the hippocampal formation. In C. A. Nelson & M. Luciana (Eds.), *Handbook of developmental cognitive neuroscience* (pp. 93–105). Cambridge, MA: MIT Press.

Utsunomiya, H., Takano, K., Okazaki, M., & Mistudome, A. (1999). Development of the temporal lobe in infants and children: Analysis by MR-based volumetry. *American Journal of Neuroradiology, 20,* 717–723.

Van Petten, C. (2004). Relationship between hippocampal volume and memory ability in healthy individuals across the lifespan: Review and meta-analysis. *Neuropsychologia, 42,* 1394–1413.

Webb, S. J., Monk, C. S., & Nelson, C. A. (2001). Mechanisms of postnatal neurobiological development: Implications for human development. *Developmental Neuropsychology, 19,* 147–171.

Zola, S. M., & Squire, L. R. (2000). The medial temporal lobe and the hippocampus. In E. Tulving & F. I. M. Craik (Eds.), *The Oxford handbook of memory* (pp. 485–500). New York: Oxford University Press.

CHAPTER 6

Learning to Remember

Peter A. Ornstein
Jennifer L. Coffman
Jennie K. Grammer

Children's abilities to remember their past experiences and to plan deliberately for later assessments of memory are central to successful school performance (Ornstein, Coffman, Grammer, San Souci, & McCall, in press; Ornstein & Haden, 2001). As such, studies of the development of memory are of critical importance for understanding children's learning in school and for the generation of instructional strategies that will maximize their achievement in the classroom. The research on children's memory reported here is directly relevant to these issues because it contributes to our understanding of the mnemonic skills of both preschool and elementary school children, and examines factors in the social context that influence age-related changes in these competencies. In an effort to address both of these issues, we make use of tasks drawn from the information-processing tradition to characterize children's skills, and we draw upon social constructivist approaches to examine social interchanges—in the form of parent–child and teacher–child conversation—that we feel are associated with developmental changes in mnemonic skill (Ornstein & Haden, 2001).

As will be seen, our research program is based on a commitment to a set of assumptions about the nature of both memory and development (Ornstein, Haden, & Elischberger, 2006; Ornstein, Haden, & San Souci, 2008). We accept the basic utility of characterizing remembering in terms of the interrelated processes that are involved in the encoding, storage, retrieval, and reporting of information, and we apply a developmental perspective to understanding these processes. To illustrate, we see the encoding of information as being driven by the activities in which a child is engaged as an event is experienced or a set of materials is being studied for a subsequent test of memory. Attentional focus—whether achieved by visual examination, physical manipulation, or linguistic means—serves to highlight some of the features of the event/materials being remembered and, accordingly, to facilitate encoding and the establishment of representations in memory. Information from these representations, moreover, must be retrieved and reported when remembering is requested, and these operations are governed by both the deployment of effective search routines and the knowledge of appropriate narrative conventions.

Given our theoretical orientation, we are particularly interested in factors that govern developmental changes in the encoding, retrieval, and reporting of information (Ornstein et al., 2006, 2008). In terms of preschoolers' encoding, we focus on child and maternal behaviors that regulate understanding of ongoing activities and interaction with to-be-remembered materials, and hence can influence the establishment of coherent representations. We see mother–child conversations about events and activities that are to be remembered as potential opportunities for children to gain experience in retrieving information from memory and using language for reporting the past, and for the acquisition of some general principles regarding retrieval and reporting. Extending our work to the elementary school years, we examine the role of the classroom context in supporting the emergence and refinement of deliberate strategies for remembering, such as rehearsal, organization, and study skills. Although teachers do not provide direct instruction in these techniques for remembering, they nonetheless differ markedly in the memory-relevant language they use in the course of instruction, and we focus on the implications of teachers' "mnemonic style" for the children's developing repertoires of skills.

This research perspective has led to the design of two longitudinal investigations, one focusing on children's developing memory for events in the preschool years, and the other dealing with parallel changes in children's deliberate memory skills in the elementary school years (Coffman, Ornstein, McCall, & Curran, 2008; Ornstein, Haden, & Hedrick, 2004). In both investigations there is a commitment to the exploration of social factors—such as interactions with parents and teachers—that are associated with developmental changes in children's abilities to remember. However, it should be noted that we feel strongly that as important as longitudinal work is for documenting developmental changes in skill within individual children and examining the impact of adult–child conversation on these developmental patterns, it is only the starting point for a thorough developmental analysis of children's memory. As such, we emphasize the importance of linking our observational methods with experimental procedures in which the nature of adult–child social interaction is brought under experimental control, so that presumed causal connections can be evaluated and potential intervention studies launched (see, e.g., Boland, Haden, & Ornstein, 2003; Ornstein & Haden, 2001).

In this chapter we discuss our work in the context of the extant literature on the factors associated with children's developing repertoires of mnemonic skills. We first examine linkages between adult–child social interaction in the home and children's reports of events they have experienced, and then turn to the classroom, focusing on associations between teachers' "mnemonic styles" and children's deliberate skills for remembering.

The Impact of Mother–Child Conversation as Events Unfold

Parent–child conversation has been widely discussed in the literature as one potential mediator of change in young children's autobiographical memory skills. Consider, for example, investigations that examine the role of verbal exchanges between mothers and children as they discuss shared experiences. Findings from studies focusing on mother–child dyads have demonstrated that maternal conversational style when talking about recently experienced, shared events has been linked to children's independent skills for remembering (e.g., Fivush, Haden, & Reese, 2006). For example, children of "high-elaborative" mothers exhibit elevated recall in comparison with peers whose mothers make use of a "low-elaborative" conversational style. Moreover, longitudinal work reveals that these differences in remembering are associated with differences in later independent recall, suggesting that the high-elaborative conversations may facilitate the development of generalized skills for remembering. In addition, a growing parallel line of work focusing on parent–child interactions as events unfold suggests that these conversations affect how children understand and represent experiences (e.g., Ornstein et al., 2004).

In this section, we present a brief summary of two studies that illustrate the impact of mother–child conversations as events unfold on children's subsequent reports of these experiences. To illustrate the paradigm that we employ to explore potential linkages between parental conversational style and children's remembering, we consider first a short-term longitudinal investigation in which young children took part in three specially constructed "adventures" with their mothers when they were 2½ to 3½ years of age (Haden, Ornstein, Eckerman, & Didow, 2001). We then turn to data from a larger longitudinal investigation, our Developmental Pathways to Skilled Remembering project, to provide a more in-depth analysis of linkages between aspects of parent–child conversation and children's subsequent memory performance.

Haden and colleagues (2001) arranged for mother–child dyads to experience three unique events when the children were 30, 36, and 42 months of age: a camping outing, a birdwatching activity, and the opening of an ice-cream shop, respectively. These activities took place in the living rooms of the participating families, with the aid of props that the researchers provided. For example, the mothers and their children were given (1) backpacks, fishing equipment, and play food for grilling during the camping trip; (2) binoculars, a tree full of stuffed birds, and worms and other food in the bird-watching adventure; and (3) an ice-cream stand, with scoops and serving dishes, in the ice-cream shop event. These three events were created to provide mothers and children with novel experiences that would be fun and engaging, and also prompt conversation; the mother–child interactions were videotaped for subsequent analysis. Observations of the video records focused on the types of verbal and nonverbal interactions that mothers and children had as the events unfolded with the specific features of each activity (e.g., backpacks in the camping adventure). Of particular interest was whether each component feature of the activities was talked about, on the one hand, or handled physically (e.g., manipulated, touched) by the mother, the child, or both participants, on the other hand, and whether these patterns of interaction were related to later recall of the features, assessed after delays of 1 day and 3 weeks.

Haden and colleagues' (2001) basic findings are depicted in Figure 6.1, which displays for each event the percentage of features recalled that had been jointly handled and jointly discussed, jointly handled and talked about only by the mother, and jointly handled and not discussed. Inspection of Figure 6.1 indicates a dramatic effect of joint talk as the events unfolded on the information that children provided in response to open-ended questions of the interviewers. As can be seen, those features of the activities

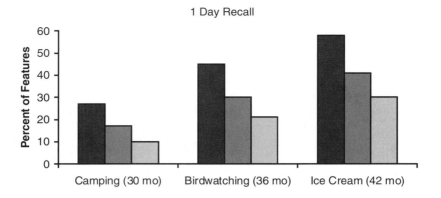

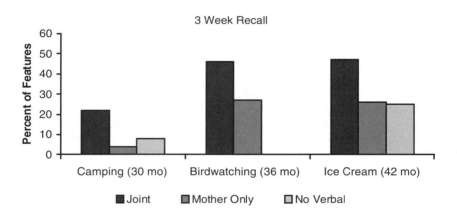

FIGURE 6.1. Percentage of features recalled in response to open-ended questions of those jointly handled during the camp, birdwatching, and ice-cream events.

that were handled and discussed by both mother and child than those that were handled jointly but talked about only by the mother, which, in turn, were better recalled than those not discussed. This pattern was observed at both memory interviews for each of the activities, with some indication of a drop in recall over the 3-week delay interval for features that had been jointly handled but only discussed by the mother.

The findings of Haden and colleagues' (2001) preliminary study indicate clearly that the nature of mother–child interaction as an experience takes place is associated with differences in children's later reports of that experience. Further evidence of the importance of these interactions can be seen in the findings of our larger-scale *Pathways* study, in which we tracked two cohorts of children—one enrolled in the longitudinal investigation at 18 months and the other at 36 months of age—through the transition to school. In this study (see Ornstein et al., 2004), we employed a wide battery of measures to assess participating children on a range of indicators, including event and deliberate memory performance and language skills. The same camping and birdwatching events described earlier were a part of this battery, and Hedrick, San Souci, Haden, and Ornstein (in press) observed the joint verbal exchanges of 89 mother–child dyads as they took part in these novel adventures when the children were 36 and 42 months of age.

Based on these observations, Hedrick, San Souci, and their colleagues (in press) were able to characterize the conversations of the dyads as either high or low in "joint talk," which they defined according to the number of instances in which a mother used open-ended questions (*who, what, where, when, why,* or *how*) to ask her child for new information, and her child's responses. Within the sample, 36 high joint talk dyads were identified as those in which the children were more likely to respond correctly to the open-ended questions and less likely not to respond to these questions. The remaining 53 mother–child pairs were classified as low joint talk dyads because they had lower proportions of correct responses to the mothers' open-ended *Wh-* questions, coupled with higher proportions of mothers' *Wh-* questions to which children did not respond at all. To illustrate these two types of conversation, we present in Table 6.1 examples of two dyads that took part in the birdwatching adventure.

As can be seen in these exchanges, the high joint talk dyad is characterized by instances in which the mother asks open-ended questions and her child accurately responds, whereas the child responds less frequently to her open-ended questions in the low joint talk dyad. To explore the extent to which these differences in interactional style were associated with differences in recall, the children's reports were obtained at 1 day and at 3 weeks. In contrast to the analyses carried out by Haden and colleagues (2001), in which the children's recall was evaluated for specific groups of features that had been engaged in different ways (e.g., joint conversation), Hedrick, San Souci, and colleagues (in press) carried out separate analyses of the children's recall of *features* and

TABLE 6.1. Sample Dyadic Exchanges during the Birdwatching Adventure

High-joint-talk dyad	Low-joint-talk dyad
As the mother and child begin their birdwatching adventure, the mother points toward an egg that she sees, and says:	*In this example, the mother and child have just found a stuffed eagle, and are on the hunt for new birds to add into their bag as they walk along the trail. As the mother holds up the stuffed eagle, she says:*
M: Hey, what do you see down here?	
C: An egg.	
M: An egg, that's right. Does that mean maybe a bird was close by?	M: That's an eagle. Look, he's got long wings. That's an eagle with a white head. Want to put him in the bag too?
C: Yeah.	C: Uh huh.
M: What else do you see around that might show that a bird is around?	M: We're finding lots of birds aren't we!
C: That (*pointing to feather*).	C: Yeah.
M: Oh, what do you see? Do you want to go get it?	M: Shove him in the bag. That's good. You found another one, didn't you? What is it?
C: Yeah. Come.	*The child does not respond. The mother picks up the guide book.*
The child walks across room and picks up a feather, then finds a stuffed bird, and the mother follows.	M: Let's look through the book and see if we can figure out which one this is. Is that it?
M: Which bird is that, do you remember?	C: No.
C: A bluejay.	M: It's a duck. What do ducks say?
M: A bluejay, exactly. Good! Let's see what else we see.	C: Quack, quack, quack.

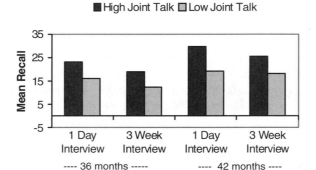

FIGURE 6.2. Children's event elaborations at 36 and 42 months as a function of dyadic style.

their recall of *event elaborations* (e.g., "The backpack was red" and "The fish was big"). Consistent with expectation, the children in the high joint talk dyads reported more features than did their peers in the low joint talk dyads. They also produced more event elaborations than did their peers in the low joint talk dyads, as can be seen in Figure 6.2. Indeed, at both the 36- and 42-month assessments, the children in the high joint talk dyads produced more event elaborations than did their peers after delays of 1 day and 3 weeks. These results provide additional evidence about the importance of enriched conversational interactions as events are jointly experienced for children's subsequent remembering.

Experimental Manipulations of Mother–Child Conversation

The two studies just described illustrate the naturally occurring associations between mother–child exchanges and children's memory performance. Haden and colleagues (2001) have shown that even when both members of a dyad attend to a given feature of an unfolding event (as assessed by joint manipulation), joint conversation about that feature is associated with greater recall than is the case when only the mother talks about it. Moreover, Hedrick, San Souci, and colleagues (in press) have demonstrated that dyads differ in the extent to which they communicate with each other as events unfold and high joint talk—defined in terms of maternal questioning and child responding—facilitates recall. To be sure, these investigations illustrate the ways in which social interaction is associated with children's enhanced memory performance, but we must emphasize that the linkages that have been observed are correlational in nature. To make causal statements about the presumed impact of joint conversation, it is necessary to carry out experimental studies in which the conversations to which children are exposed are manipulated. We turn now to a treatment of two such experiments, each of which provides support for the causal connections between conversational style and remembering.

In the first of these studies, Boland and colleagues (2003) trained a group of mothers in the use of four specific conversational techniques designed to enhance their children's understanding of the camping event discussed earlier. Each mother was asked to use: (1) *wh- questions* to elicit her child's linguistic participation in the activity, (2) *associations* to relate that which was being experienced to what her child already knew, (3) *follow-ins* that encouraged discussion of aspects of the event in which her child showed interest, and (4) *positive evaluations* to praise her child's verbal and nonverbal contributions to the interaction. After the mothers were instructed in the use of these techniques, they interacted with their children as they took part in the camping "adventure." Another group of mothers did not receive the training in conversational style prior to experiencing the camping event with their children.

Boland and her colleagues (2003) were interested in two things. First, would the mothers who received the training actually incorporate the suggested conversational techniques into their discussions with their children? And second, would the children of the trained mothers evidence enhanced recall? Both of these questions can be answered in the affirmative. Figure 6.3 indicates that the mothers who received the training made greater use of the targeted conversational techniques on the camping adventure with their children than did the mothers in the untrained group. Moreover, Figure 6.4 indicates that the children of the trained mothers recalled more information about the camping event than did children of untrained mothers when they were assessed both 1 day and 3 weeks after the activity. Indeed, as can be seen in Figure 6.4, children of trained mothers not only recalled more features of the event but also provided more elaborated accounts of their experiences.

Boland and colleagues (2003) demonstrated clear causal linkages between the nature of mother–child conversation as events unfold and children's subsequent memory performance. However, as suggested earlier, a rich literature—composed of both longitudinal/observational and experimental/training studies—attests to the importance of maternal conversational style during conversations about the past (e.g., Bauer & Burch, 2004; Fivush et al., 2006; Peterson, Jesso, & McCabe, 1999; Reese, Haden, & Fivush, 1993). Given that children are naturally exposed to conversation with their parents both during and after events have taken place, it becomes important to examine the combined effects of conversations about the present and past on memory performance, and we present here a study in which Hedrick, Haden, and Ornstein (in press) manipulated

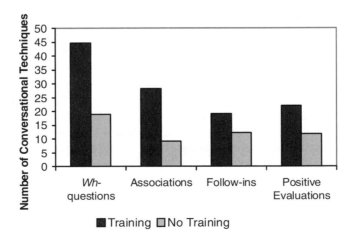

FIGURE 6.3. Mean number of conversational techniques used by mothers as a function of training.

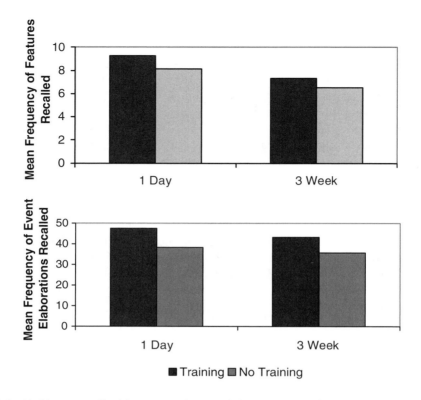

FIGURE 6.4. Children's recall of features and event elaborations as a function of maternal training.

elaborative style during an ongoing event and in postevent conversations (see McGuigan & Salmon, 2004, 2005).

The children who took part in Hedrick, Haden, and Ornstein's (in press) study experienced the camping adventure with a researcher (not a parent), then discussed the event a day later with another researcher, and finally, after a delay of 3 weeks, provided an account of what they could remember. The researchers' conversations with the children both during and after the camping event were manipulated experimentally to be either elaborative or nonelaborative, as described below, but the delayed memory assessment was carried out with our standard, neutral interview.

One-half of the 4-year-olds in the Hedrick, Haden, and Ornstein (in press) study were assigned to a *high elaborative event talk* condition in which the experimenter asked *Wh-* questions requesting information, made associations between the camping activity and what the child might already know or have previously experienced, and offered positive evaluations that directly praised the child's behaviors and verbalizations. In contrast, the other children were assigned to a *low elaborative event talk* condition in which the researcher used repetitive comments that did not add new information to the conversation, asked basic yes–no questions (e.g., "Do you want to carry this?"), and offered very general evaluative comments (e.g., "Cool," "Neat"). The children were then exposed to one of two contrasting types of a memory conversation on the day after the camping event. After prompting the participants to provide information about the camping event ("Tell me what you did on your camping adventure"), the researcher used an elaborative reminiscing style in conversations with half of the children and a nonelaborative style in conversations with the other children. More specifically, the researcher evaluated positively the responses of the children in the high elaborative memory conversation condition, provided them with scripted new details about the event, and requested new information by posing additional follow-up *Wh-* questions. In contrast, the researcher confirmed the memory information provided by the children in the low elaborative memory conversation condition and followed up with yes–no questions and repetitions of the same general request for more information (e.g., "Cool! Tell me more"), but did not provide any additional details about the event.

Thus, the four groups of children varied in their exposure to high elaborative conversation about the camping adventure: One group experienced both the event and the postevent conversation with an elaborative experimenter, another group participated in both, with a nonelaborative experimenter; and the two remaining groups had one elaborative and one nonelaborative experience. Importantly, the nature of the conversation both during and after the event impacted the children's reports when they were interviewed in a neutral fashion after 3 weeks. Indeed, as can be seen in Figure 6.5, the children in the high elaborative event talk condition recalled more items and provided more elaborative details about their experience than did those in the low elaborative event talk condition. In addition, when examining the combined impact of elaborative talk, both during and after the event, there was some evidence to suggest that the effects of elaborative talk may be additive. It appears that children exposed to an elaborative conversational style during the event and in the subsequent conversation remembered more than did those in any other group; moreover, those participants who had one elaborative experience—either during the event or in the conversation a day later— outperformed peers who had only been exposed to a nonelaborative conversation. These findings emphasize the impact of elaborative conversational exchanges on enhancing memory performance.

Children's Deliberate Memory Strategies:
The Impact of Teachers' Memory-Relevant Language

Given the impact of mother–child conversations on preschoolers' memory skills, the notion that *parent talk* about an event can influence children's remembering suggests that *teacher talk* may also be relevant for the development of early memory skills. Indeed, generalizing on the basis of studies of children's event memory that suggest that preschoolers learn general skills for talking about the past in the context of elaborative parent–child conversations (e.g., Reese et al., 1993), it seems likely that older children acquire deliberate strategies for remembering in the social context of the elementary school classroom. Although we know less about factors that influence the development of children's deliberate strategies for remembering, such as rehearsal (e.g., Ornstein & Naus, 1978), organization (e.g., Lange, 1978), and elaboration (e.g., Rohwer, 1973), it is apparent from a wide body of literature that children become more proficient in the use of these mnemonic strategies over the elementary years (Kail & Hagen, 1977;

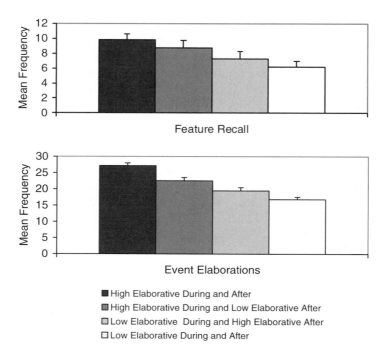

FIGURE 6.5. Children's recall of features and event elaborations during the neutral interview as a function of event talk and memory conversation.

Schneider & Bjorklund, 1998). With an increase in age there is a very systematic transition from relatively passive to more active techniques of remembering in tasks involving deliberate memorization of words or pictures, and these strategies are linked clearly to success in remembering (Schneider & Bjorklund, 1998). Thus, given the substantial growth in children's repertoires of mnemonic strategies during the elementary school years, it seems likely that these accomplishments are influenced by interactions with teachers in the school setting that are analogous to elaborative parent–child conversations.

The Importance of the School Context
for Understanding Children's Memory Development

Support for this perspective can be seen in a number of lines of work that point to the potential impact of formal schooling on the development of memory strategies (e.g., Moely et al., 1992; Morrison, Smith, & Dow-Ehrensberger, 1995; Wagner, 1978). To illustrate, consider a series of comparative-cultural explorations of the cognitive skills of children who differed in terms of whether they had or had not attended Western-style schools. Conducted in countries such as Liberia (Scribner & Cole, 1978), Mexico (Rogoff, 1981), and Morocco (Wagner, 1978), these investigations revealed that children who attended school demonstrated superiority in the memory skills that have typically been studied by Western psychologists. Although it is important to point out that these findings do not suggest in any way that "schooled" children outperform their "unschooled" peers on everyday memory tasks that are embedded in activities central to their cultures, the findings do indicate that something in the formal school context most likely is related to the children's deliberate memory performance.

Additional support for the view that formal schooling is important for the development of mnemonic skills comes from the work of Morrison and his colleagues (e.g., Christian, Bachman, & Morrison, 2001), who examined the influence of the elementary school classroom on aspects (e.g., reading, memory) of children's cognitive development. This research complements the cross-cultural work, and suggests more precisely that the first-grade experience is particularly important for the development of children's memory skills (Morrison et al., 1995). Capitalizing on a mandated school entry date, Morrison and his colleagues studied two groups of children who were close in age but differed in their grade in school. More specifically, their participants were students who had either just made the cutoff for school entry and thus were old enough to be in the first grade ("young" first-graders), or had just missed the date and therefore were the same age but enrolled in kindergarten classrooms ("old" kindergartners). Taking performance at the start of the school year as a baseline, the first-graders evidenced substantial improvement in their memory skills over the course of the year. In contrast, the performance of the older kindergartners did not change over the year, although improvement was noted the next year, following the children's experience in the first grade. These findings imply that something in the first-grade context is supportive of the development of children's deliberate memory skills.

Given that schooling is identified as a potential facilitator of developmental change in mnemonic skill, what is it about the classroom context that is important? As a result of extensive observations in elementary school classrooms, Moely and her colleagues (1992) identified specific aspects of classroom instruction that they thought might be important for children's mnemonic growth. They focused on instances in which teachers provided general information about cognitive processes or gave specific strategy suggestions. Although Moely and colleagues found that explicit instruction in the use of strategies was quite rare, they were nonetheless able to group first-, second-, and third-grade teachers on the basis of the amount of strategy suggestion they provided in the course of their teaching. Importantly, the children in the first-grade classes of teachers who provided more suggestions about strategy use in their lessons were more likely to generate organizational strategies spontaneously in recall tasks than were children whose teachers gave fewer strategy suggestions. This differentiation in strategy usage was not found among second- and third-grade children of high versus low strategy teachers.

The teachers in the Moely and colleagues (1992) investigation did not invest a great deal of time on instruction in deliberate memory techniques, but when they did so, at least in the first grade, it seemed to be associated with children's use of strategies for remembering. Moreover, teachers at all grade levels reported that memory played a central role in their classrooms. In a similar fashion, the teachers with whom we have worked have indicated that memory is essential to many of the tasks in which children are engaged in the classroom (see, e.g., Ornstein, Coffman, & Grammer, 2007). Consider a few sample responses from first-grade teachers with whom we have worked:

- "Children use their memory to recall information that relates to social and academic progress. ... They are constantly using their memory to retrieve this information."

- "We are constantly building on previous experiences to learn new skills. The children must be able to retain information from the past in order to associate new material."
- "Whether we are working on math with facts or literacy, memory plays a vital role. As a teacher I am continuously calling on my students to recall information and to relate learned information to newly introduced facts."

Linking the Classroom Context and Children's Memory Performance

We therefore arrive at something of a paradox. The comparative cultural literature (e.g., Wagner, 1978) suggests that deliberate memory strategies emerge in the context of the classroom, and interviews with teachers and administrators (Coffman et al., 2008; Moely et al., 1992) indicate clearly that memory is important for success in school. However, the findings of Moely and her colleagues (1992; see also Mercer, 1996) indicate clearly that strategy instruction in the classroom is relatively infrequent, although when it does takes place it seems to have an impact on children's developing skills. But if the classroom setting is important for children's strategy development, and if instruction in mnemonic techniques is rare, then just what are teachers doing that is associated with the emergence and refinement of children's skills? In an effort to investigate this critical issue, we decided to launch an investigation of aspects of teachers' instructional styles that we thought might have implications for the development of children's memory skills. We were particularly interested in broadening the focus to include teachers' expectations for remembering (i.e., the "memory demands," both implied and expressed, that may be woven into lessons, as well as the extent to which teachers either provided or solicited metacognitive information from their students).

With these goals in mind, our research team conducted a longitudinal study that was aimed at tracing children's developing memory skills across the elementary school years, while simultaneously making in-depth observations of the participants' teachers as they provided instruction. Beginning in the first grade, we assessed the children's memory skills with a multitask battery and used two parallel coding systems to characterize each teacher's instructional style during 2 hours of instruction, one in language arts and the other in mathematics. We developed the Taxonomy of Teacher Behaviors to describe the nature of instruction, primarily on the basis of classifying teachers' in-class conversations into four categories: those having to do with instruction; those reflecting "cognitive structuring activities" (encouraging children to engage the materials in ways that are known to facilitate encoding and retrieval of information); those involving memory requests (asking students to retrieve information already acquired or to prepare for future activities); and those providing metacognitive information (providing or soliciting information that might facilitate performance on a range of cognitive tasks in the classroom). Furthermore, we supplemented the Taxonomy with a Narrative Coding System that yielded a detailed contextual narrative of each lesson, including descriptions of the content, the dominant teacher and child activities, and the children's verbal responses, to enable us to make judgments about the nature of the memory "demands" or goals, both implied and deliberate, that the teachers were communicating to their students. Moreover, on the basis of these two systems, we were able to develop a measure of each teacher's mnemonic style or orientation.

Characterizing the Classroom Context

Using the Taxonomy and the Narrative Coding System, two researchers observed 2 hours of instruction in each participating classroom. The first observer used the Taxonomy to make judgments every 30 seconds, while the second observer prepared the narrative of each lesson as it unfolded. Although, taken together, the coding systems enable us to capture many features of classroom instruction that are likely important for the development of children's mnemonic skills, we (see Coffman et al., 2008) focused on the construction of an index of teachers' "mnemonic orientation" that was based on a subset of component codes. As indicated in Table 6.2, this composite index was based on a consideration of teachers' strategy suggestions and metacognitive questions (even though these are relatively low-frequency activities), and on the occurrence of deliberate memory demands in the context of (1) instructional activities, (2) cognitive structuring activities, and (3) the provision of metacognitive information. The selection of these activities for the index was based primarily on their presumed role in memory and its development. Thus, for example, cognitive structuring activities affect the depth to which information is processed (Craik & Lockhart, 1972), whereas memory requests, and the provision of strategy suggestions and metacognitive information, impact encoding, retrieval, or both (Schneider & Pressley, 1997).

To illustrate these two different styles of engagement in the classroom, in Tables 6.3 and 6.4, we provide four excerpts from first-grade classroom instruction, two from high-mnemonic teachers and two from low-mnemonic teachers. As can be seen in Table 6.3, "high-mnemonic" in contrast to "low-mnemonic" instruction in language arts and mathematics is characterized by more instances of the memory-relevant language described earlier, such as asking children whether a word selection makes sense or eliciting a specific strategy for answering a mathematics problem. Alternatively, as can be seen in the next two lesson excerpts in Table 6.4, the "low-mnemonic" instruction is characterized by fewer instances of memory-relevant language. The teachers are still engaging the students in the topics being discussed, although, in contrast to the high-mnemonic teachers illustrated earlier, they pose more basic questions, focus less on strategy use, and do not emphasize understanding *why* a specific answer may be correct.

TABLE 6.2. Teacher-Relevant "Talk": Component Codes in Teacher Measure

Individual taxonomy codes	Definitions
Strategy suggestions	Recommending that a child adopt a method or procedure for remembering or processing information.
Metacognitive questions	Requesting that a child provide a potential strategy, a utilized strategy, or a rationale for a strategy he or she has indicated using.

Co-occurring codes	Definitions
Deliberate memory demands and instructional activities	Intervals that contain both requests for information from memory and the presentation of instructional information by the teacher.
Deliberate memory demands and cognitive structuring activities	Intervals that contain both requests for information from memory and teacher instruction that could impact the encoding and retrieval of information, such as focusing attention or organizing material.
Deliberate memory demands and metacognitive information	Intervals that contain both requests for information from memory and the provision or solicitation of metacognitive information.

TABLE 6.3. Sample Instruction from High-Mnemonic Classrooms in Language Arts and Mathematics

High-mnemonic language arts example	High-mnemonic math example
In this example, a first-grade teacher is leading students in a word game, in which students have been asked to guess the words that are covered up in several sentences. She wants them to use the context of the surrounding words to make informed guesses as to what the covered word could be. As the teacher pulls the names of students out of her "magic bag," she asks each one to provide a word that will make sense in the sentence and that follows the theme of In My Classroom.	*The teacher is standing in front of the chalkboard teaching a lesson about place value and how numbers can be demonstrated visually using tally marks. On the overhead are math manipulatives (rods and squares, where the rods equal 10 and the squares equal 1). She tells the class that each individual tally mark equals 1, and each "box" of tally marks equals 5. There is a student at the overhead demonstrating how to write a number using 10's and 1's. The teacher asks the class whether the student will need to make another "box" to complete the number.*
T: Let's see if you guys can help me figure out what the covered up word is. ... So let's see, let's choose four words for each sentence, and see if you guys can make it make sense because this is why we learn to read. These words have to make sense or they don't mean anything to us. So let's read it together.	T: And each box is worth how much?
	S1: Five.
All: On the teacher's desk, there are ...	T: Five, so each tally mark is worth one, each box is worth five. And she's doing a wonderful strategy of putting the amount underneath, counting by fives. Five, 10, 15, and now she's going to add the rest. Will she make another box?
T: OK, what could be on the teacher's desk? Just look back there and see what's back there. Look, what could be back there on that teacher's desk?	
	S2: No.
S1: Pencils.	T: No, she does not have enough to make a box, but she has her amount. Beautiful! That's how your tally boxes should look for that number. Five, 10, 15, and then 16, 17. *(The teacher is showing the students each box/tally on the board as she calls out the numbers.)* Who will take a risk, and show us that number using place values?
T: Pencils! Ok, on the teacher's desk, there are pencils. *P-E-N-C-I-L-S.* Does that make sense in the sentence? Let's see if it makes sense.	
The teacher and students all read the sentence again together.	*The students raise their hands. The teacher looks around and calls on a student, and he comes up to the overhead.*
All: On the teacher's desk, there are *pencils.*	T: You have two choices. You can use the overhead rods if you'd like, or you can draw them if you'd like. What's a good strategy to do with the number 17 before he even starts with the place values? Is there a good strategy?
T: Would that make sense?	
Students: Yes!	S3: Yes.
	T: Yes. What's a good strategy?
	S3: You ... do the 10's and then the 1's.

TABLE 6.4. Sample Instruction from Low-Mnemonic Classrooms in Language Arts and Mathematics

Low-mnemonic language arts example	Low-mnemonic math example
In this example, a teacher is leading students in a lesson in which she is asking them to assist her in making sentences on the board. As the teacher writes sentences on the board she intentionally leaves out letters for the students to fill in.	*In this lesson, a first-grade teacher is leading her students in addition problems involving two-digit numbers. The teacher presents the problems to the class on the overhead projector, and the students are called on to answer them.*
T: OK, let's see. *Last October, ws my birthday. i had so much fn.* What's wrong?	T: Let's count again, let's do 92 + 8. We have 92, we have 93 ..
S1: There should be a *u* in *fun.*	All: 94, 95, 96, 97, 98, 99, 100.
T: A *u* in *fun?* Are you sure?	T: 100. You got close, Mara, good job, but the answer is 100. Now, who had number two?
S1: Yes.	
T: All right, before we fix anything else, what happened to my words though? What did I do?	*The teacher moves on to the next problem.*
S2: You were going too fast.	T: 89 + 9 equals 98. How about this, is this correct?
T: I was going too fast, *and* what did I do?	S: Yes.
S3: You messed up on getting letters.	T: All right, good job. Just look at number three. 54 + 10 equals 64.
T: But what did I forget in general? We talked about it yesterday. What did I forget? I forgot to always take my time, and I forgot what?	All: 64.
S4: The vowels.	T: Who had this one? Is this correct?
T: I forgot the vowels! Because without the vowels, do you know what it sounds like?	*Some students respond with yes and others with no.*
The teacher tries to say the sentence using no vowels. The class giggles when she reads "ws."	T: Class, do we agree?
	Students again respond with yes and no.
T: *A,* I'm just going to squeeze it in. *O-c-t-o-b-e-r.* You hear how that opens it up? Last October was my *b-i-r-t-h-d-a-y,* and I can be excited about that. I couldn't be excited without the vowels. I need the vowels to be excited. Last October was my birthday!	T: Let's see, we have 54 plus 10 more. 5 plus 1 is what?
	S: 64.
	T: 64 is correct. Good job.

Importantly, from the perspective of examining associations between the classroom context and the children's performance, there was considerable variability among participating teachers in these aspects of their memory-related talk. To illustrate this variability, consider the extent to which the first-grade teachers varied in their use of the coded memory-relevant language in the course of instruction. These teachers' *strategy suggestions* ranged from 0.8 to 13.8% of the 30-second intervals that were observed, and their use of *metacognitive questions* varied from 0.8 to 9.6%. Interestingly, large differences were also seen in the combination codes that include both *deliberate memory demands* and either *instructional activities* (ranging from 25.8 to 50.0% of the intervals), *cognitive structuring activities* (ranging from 10.0 to 35.4%), or *metacognitive information* (ranging from 1.3 to 12.1%). Moreover, because of this variability across classrooms, we were able to characterize each teacher's mnemonic style as being either "high mnemonic" or "low mnemonic," based on the extent to which the teachers made use of memory-relevant language in instruction; that is, we divided the teachers into two groups (high- vs. low-mnemonic orientation) using a median split relative to other teachers in the same grade.

Linking the Classroom Context and Children's Memory Strategy Performance

Based on this measure of mnemonic orientation, we then examined the patterns of a range of indices of children's memory performance as a function of their classroom assignment. To illustrate this approach, consider children's use of an organizational strategy on a sort–recall task in the first and second grades, in which they were presented with 16 picture cards with line drawings taken from four conceptual categories, allowing for the assessment of organizational strategies at both input (e.g., sorting or grouping) and output (e.g., categorical clustering). In this task, children's sorting scores were calculated using the Adjusted Ratio of Clustering (ARC) measure (Roenker, Thompson, & Brown, 1971), resulting in ARC scores ranging from –1 (below chance organization) to 0 (chance) to 1 (complete categorical organization). As can be seen in Figure 6.6, the sorting performance of the children in the two types of classrooms did not differ initially on either the baseline or generalization trials at the first assessment point (Time 1) of grade 1, but by the winter, the groups had diverged, with differences evident at both Time 2 and Time 3. Furthermore, these differences continue across grade 2, indicating that not only did the mnemonic orientation of the first-grade teachers have an impact on the performance of the children in their classes but it also evidenced a sustained impact even when the children were taught by other teachers.

The Interplay of Classroom Context and Children's Academic Achievement

In addition to examining the impact of the classroom context on children's mnemonic skill, we have also explored child-level factors that may moderate the influence of teachers' mnemonic styles. For example, we have been able to track over time the mem-

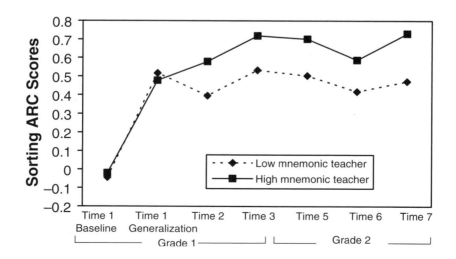

FIGURE 6.6. Sorting ARC scores as a function of first-grade teacher mnemonic orientation.

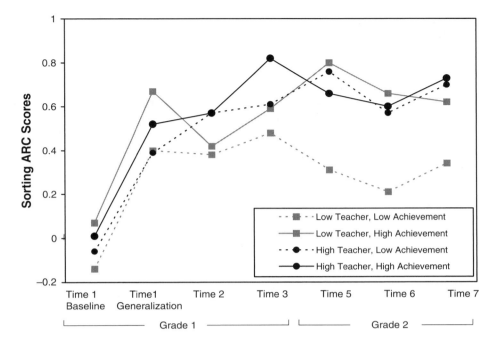

FIGURE 6.7. Sorting ARC scores as a function of first-grade teacher mnemonic orientation and children's academic achievement.

ory skills of groups of children identified as higher or lower in academic achievement level, as assessed by the Woodcock–Johnson Tests of Achievement (WJ-III; Woodcock, McGrew, & Mather, 2001), and taught by either high- or low-mnemonic first-grade teachers. The memory performance of these two groups of children was then examined as a function of the mnemonic style of the classrooms in which they were embedded, and, as can be seen in Figure 6.7, although higher-achieving students had elevated patterns of sorting regardless of their first-grade teachers' mnemonic orientation, lower-achieving children's performance was strongly linked to teacher style. Lower-achieving students who were placed into a lower, mnemonically oriented classroom sorted less, whereas those who were taught by high-mnemonic teachers sorted at levels equivalent to those evidenced by their higher-achieving peers. Moreover, the interplay of first-grade teacher orientation and children's academic achievement persisted through the second grade (Ornstein et al., 2007).

Summary and Future Directions

The research outlined here focuses on the importance of contextual factors that influence the development of children's memory. We now know a considerable amount about aspects of mother–child conversation at home and teachers' memory-relevant language in the classroom that influence children's developing skills for remembering. Beginning with longitudinal studies of autobiographical memory, we have identified important associations between adult–child conversations about ongoing and prior events, and children's abilities to provide information about these experiences (Haden et al., 2001; Hedrick, San Souci, et al., in press). We then extended this observational work with experimental interventions to establish causal linkages between aspects of adult–child conversation and children's memory reports (Boland et al., 2003; Hedrick, Haden, & Ornstein, in press; Ornstein et al., 2004). Moreover, paralleling our observational studies of autobiographical memory, we carried out a large-scale longitudinal investigation in the classroom, in which we focused on linking aspects of the instructional context and children's deliberate memory strategies (Coffman et al., 2008; Ornstein et al., in press). The next step in this program of work is to move forward with small-scale interventions that enable us to make causal connections between teachers' memory-related talk and children's use of deliberate strategies for remembering.

Our ongoing work is designed to implement these interventions in the form of experiments in which teachers are trained to use conversational techniques employed spontaneously by teachers with high- and low-mnemonic styles. If the results of these studies confirm the correlational findings we obtained in our longitudinal work in the classroom, with children taught by teachers instructed to use a high-mnemonic style outperforming their peers taught by teachers using a low-mnemonic style, then we will be able to make causal statements regarding linkages between instructional context and children's developing deliberate memory skills. If this is the case, then the findings will have important educational implications and can lead to the development of interventions that may affect teacher instructional style in the classroom. Ultimately, our goals are to develop instructional programs for teachers that in turn can have a meaningful impact on children's cognitive development.

References

Bauer, P. J., & Burch, M. M. (2004). Developments in early memory: Multiple mediators of foundational processes. In J. M. Lucariello, J. A. Hudson, R. Fivush, & P. J. Bauer (Eds.), *The development of the mediated mind* (pp. 101–125). Mahwah, NJ: Erlbaum.

Boland, A. M., Haden, C. A., & Ornstein, P. A. (2003). Boosting children's memory by training mothers in the use of an elaborative conversational style as an event unfolds. *Journal of Cognition and Development, 4*, 39–65.

Christian, M. K., Bachman, H., & Morrison, F. J. (2001). Schooling and cognitive development. In R. J. Sternberg & E. L. Grigorenko (Eds.), *Environmental effects on cognitive abilities* (pp. 287–336). Mahwah, NJ: Erlbaum.

Coffman, J. L., Ornstein, P. A., McCall, L. E., & Curran, P. J. (2008). Linking teachers' memory-relevant language and the development of children's memory skills. *Developmental Psychology, 44*, 1640–1654.

Craik, F. I. M., & Lockhart, R. S. (1972). Levels of processing: A framework for memory research. *Journal of Verbal Learning and Verbal Behavior, 11*, 671–684.

Fivush, R., Haden, C. A., & Reese, E. (2006). Elaborating on elaborations: Role of maternal reminiscing style in cognitive and socioemotional development. *Child Development, 77*, 1568–1588.

Haden, C. A., Ornstein, P. A., Eckerman, C. O., & Didow, S. M. (2001). Mother–child conversational interactions as events unfold: Linkages to subsequent remembering. *Child Development, 72*, 1016–1031.

Hedrick, A. M., Haden, C. A., & Ornstein, P. A. (in press). Elaborative talk during and after an event: Conversational style influence children's remembering. *Journal of Cognition and Development*.

Hedrick, A. M., San Souci, P. P., Haden, C. A., & Ornstein, P. A. (in press). Mother–child joint conversational exchanges during events: Linkages to children's event memory over time. *Journal of Cognition and Development*.

Kail, R. V., & Hagen, J. W. (1977). *Perspectives on the development of memory and cognition*. Hillsdale, NJ: Erlbaum.

Lange, G. (1978). Organization-related processes in children's recall. In P. A. Ornstein (Ed.), *Memory development in children* (pp. 101–128). Hillsdale, NJ: Erlbaum.

McGuigan, F., & Salmon, K. (2004). The time to talk: The influence of the timing of adult–child talk on children's event memory. *Child Development, 75*, 669–686.

McGuigan, F., & Salmon, K. (2005). Pre-event discussion and recall of a novel event: How are children best prepared? *Journal of Experimental Child Psychology, 91*, 342–366.

Mercer, J. G. (1996). *Developing a taxonomy of memory relevant classroom experiences*. Unpublished honors thesis, University of North Carolina at Chapel Hill.

Moely, B. E., Hart, S. S., Leal, L., Santulli, K. A., Rao, N., Johnson, T., et al. (1992). The teacher's role in facilitating memory and study strategy development in the elementary school classroom. *Child Development, 63*, 653–672.

Morrison, F. J., Smith, L., & Dow-Ehrensberger, M. (1995). Education and cognitive development: A natural experiment. *Developmental Psychology, 31*, 789–799.

Ornstein, P. A., Coffman, J. L., & Grammer, J. K. (2007, April). Teachers' memory-relevant conversations and children's memory performance. In P. A. Ornstein & F. J. Morrison (Chairs), *The impact of the classroom context on children's cognitive development: Memory, mathematics, and literacy*. Symposium conducted at the biennial meeting of the Society for Research in Child Development, Boston, MA.

Ornstein, P. A., Coffman, J. L., Grammer, J. K., San Souci, P. P., & McCall, L. E. (in press). Linking the classroom context and the development of children's memory skills. In J. Meece & J. Eccles (Eds.), *The handbook of research on schools, schooling, and human development*. New York: Routledge.

Ornstein, P. A., & Haden, C. A. (2001). Memory development or the development of memory? *Current Directions in Psychological Science, 10*, 202–205.

Ornstein, P. A., Haden, C. A., & Elischberger, H. B. (2006). Children's memory development: Remembering the past and preparing for the future. In E. Bialystok & F. I. M. Craik (Eds.), *Lifespan cognition: Mechanisms of change* (pp. 143–161). New York: Oxford University Press.

Ornstein, P. A., Haden, C. A., & Hedrick, A. M. (2004). Learning to remember: Social-communicative exchanges and the development of children's memory skills. *Developmental Review, 24*, 374–395.

Ornstein, P. A., Haden, C. A., & San Souci, P. P. (2008). The development of skilled remembering in children. In J. H. E. Byrne (Series Ed.) & H. Roediger III (Vol. Ed.), *Learning and memory: A comprehensive reference: Volume 4. Cognitive psychology of memory* (pp. 715–744). Oxford, UK: Elsevier.

Ornstein, P. A., & Naus, M. J. (1978). Rehearsal processes in children's memory. In P. A. Ornstein (Ed.), *Memory development in children* (pp. 69–99). Hillsdale, NJ: Erlbaum.

Peterson, C., Jesso, B., & McCabe, A. (1999). Encouraging narratives in preschoolers: An intervention study. *Journal of Child Language, 26*, 49–67.

Reese, E., Haden, C. A., & Fivush, R. (1993). Mother–child conversations about the past: Relationships of style and memory over time. *Cognitive Development, 8*, 403–430.

Roenker, D., Thompson, C., & Brown, S. (1971). Comparison of measures for the estimation of clustering in free recall. *Psychological Bulletin, 76*, 45–48.

Rogoff, B. (1981). Schooling and the development of cognitive skills. In H. C. Triandis & A.

Heron (Eds.), *Handbook of cross-cultural psychology* (Vol. 4, pp. 233–294). Boston: Allyn & Bacon.

Rohwer, W. D. (1973). Elaboration and learning in childhood and adolescence. In H. W. Reese (Ed.), *Advances in child development and behavior* (Vol. 8, pp. 1–57). New York: Academic Press.

Schneider, W., & Bjorklund, D. F. (1998). Memory. In D. Kuhn & R. S. Siegler (Eds.), *Handbook of child psychology* (Vol. 2, pp. 467–521). New York: Wiley.

Schneider, W., & Pressley, M. (1997). *Memory development between 2 and 20*. New York: Springer-Verlag.

Scribner, S., & Cole, M. (1978). Literacy without schooling: Testing for intellectual effects. *Harvard Educational Review, 48*, 448–461.

Wagner, D. A. (1978). Memories of Morocco: The influence of age, schooling, and environment on memory. *Cognitive Development, 45*, 389–396.

Woodcock, R. W., McGrew, K., & Mather, N. (2001). *The Woodcock–Johnson Tests of Achievement: Third Edition*. Itasca, IL: Riverside.

CHAPTER 7

The Mind of the Preschool Child
The Intelligence–School Interface

Marc H. Bornstein

Intelligence at School

> To judge well, to comprehend well, to reason well,
> these are the essentials of intelligence.
> —BINET AND SIMON (1905, p. 196)

When a teacher looks out over his or her classroom, what does the teacher see? Is there a blooming, buzzing confusion of one *mass* of young children to be instructed according to a fixed curriculum? Or does the teacher see in that mass a group of unique children to be instructed using individualized plans? And, if the latter, then are those individual children to be instructed as though they aligned themselves along a *continuum* or hierarchy of intelligence, with smart at the top? Or are teachers to instruct individual children, recognizing that each child offers a *profile* of differing intellectual strengths (presumably to be exploited) and weaknesses (presumably to be remediated)? Based on contemporary empirical developmental science, teachers should look out and see the children in their classroom as individuals who may generally distribute themselves along a continuum of intelligence but who, at the same time, have distinctive profiles of intellectual strengths and weaknesses.

The odyssey that leads to this conclusion starts with a brief consideration of what intelligence is, how it has been assessed traditionally, and the deductions about the mind to which historical evaluations of intelligence have pointed. Precise definition and measurement of intelligence are long-standing goals of psychology and its allied fields (Sattler, 1992; Sternberg & Detterman, 1986). As a result, there is agreement that human beings possess intelligence, but there is less agreement about what intelligence is. What we purport to know tends to originate in and reflect theoretical views that shape the way intelligence is defined, measured, and studied. This chapter begins with a critical discussion of two traditional conceptions of intelligence. In a nutshell, a general factor theory of intelligence (g) posits that a single common factor underlies all mental abilities. In contrast, some authorities hold that there is no general factor that is common to all mental abilities. Instead, intelligence is made up of multiple, more or less unrelated mental abilities or faculties (F). An implication of the first view (intelligence as a general factor) is that persons who are high on one facet of intelligent behavior will be high on every facet of intelligence. The second view (intelligence as unique specific abilities) implies that just because a person is high on one aspect of intelligence, he or she is not necessarily high on every aspect. A resolution of this disagreement can be found in a third view, which integrates the single general factor view with the multiple unique factor view, namely, that g is a higher-order factor that appears in several ability F factors, thus admitting roles for both general intelligence and multiple, domain-specific intelligences. The chapter then proceeds to a consideration of relevant empirical work with young children based on the foregoing theoretical frameworks. We administered several traditional and purpose-made novel tasks to 4-year-old preschool children that have resulted in measures of general intelligence and numeracy/spatial, verbal, sociability, psychomotor, and literacy faculties. The chapter reviews the multiple child measures we administered, briefly recounts our model-building strategy, and provides results of modeling that supports the view that early child intelligence has both general and domain-specific manifestations organized in a hierarchical structure. The hierarchical model applies to girls and to boys equally, as well as to children who are in child care and those who are not. It all applies across levels of socioeconomic status. To complement this mass view, we also analyzed prominent patterns of individual differences in Fs. The chapter concludes by drawing attention to a variety of issues related to the meaning of this model for understanding childhood intelligence, as well as its implications for education.

This chapter leaves aside many central questions and controversies about intelligence even if they cannot be entirely neglected. Few questions in the social sciences stir as much passionate public interest and as much controversy as whether intelligence is a valid concept, how important intelligence actually is, the genetic versus experiential bases of intelligence, the modifiability of intelligence, and so forth. These have been the predominant issues in the history of criticism of the intelligence testing movement.

These central issues notwithstanding, intelligence has been entangled implicitly or explicitly with school throughout its history. Generally speaking, intelligence tests were originally developed and designed to measure those aspects of mental ability that are important for success in school (at least as classroom requirements tend to be assessed in middle-income communities in the Western World), as well as in similar activities outside of school. Indeed, a return to their very beginnings, around the turn of the 20th century, brings to mind the story of the forward-thinking Commission on the Education of Retarded Children in Paris engaging Alfred Binet to develop a test with the well-intentioned aim of identifying children in the public schools who would fail in normal schools and who might benefit from remedial education. To meet this goal, Binet and several collaborators—Simon, Piaget, and others—developed an economical, manageable, impartially graded test whose objective was to predict children's performance in the classroom. Binet recognized that parents and teachers alike underestimate or overestimate the accomplishments of children. So, Binet's test was intended to provide a more consistent and less biased means to assess children than subjective parental description or teacher intuition. Binet's test initiated major developments in the fields of mental assessment and school evaluation alike. By the 1920s, intelligence tests were used in schools to measure intellectual capacity and to serve as a basis for ability grouping, selection into special classes, and so forth, and tests of this type have increasingly been used in connection with admission to higher education. Indeed, tests of intelligence are administered in the traditional ways of the classroom: Examinees seated at desks answer by marking in test booklets or on answer sheets and are given uniform time limits to complete their work.

In part because of their original aim, to predict academic performance, intelligence tests traditionally focus on a narrow band of linguistic and logical–mathematical skills that customarily have helped students succeed in school. Reciprocally, educational attainment has been among the most popular external validators of intelligence tests. They have largely succeeded. Correlations between intelligence test scores and formal tests of reading, mathematics, or other subjects, and between intelligence test scores and school exam performance or grades, range between .40 and .70 (Brody, 1992; Jensen, 1980; Lavin, 1965; Vernon, 1947). Intelligence test performance correlates about .60 with total number of years of education (Jencks, 1972; McCall, 1977).

Intelligence: Three Views

People are perennially interested in intelligence. In the words of one prominent observer: "No concept in the history of psychology has had or continues to have as great an impact on everyday life in the Western world" as intelligence (Scarr, 1989, p. 75). As vital as intelligence is, however, the concept itself has eluded consensual definition. A symposium on the meaning of intelligence, published by Thorndike in 1921, produced a plethora of definitions: Intelligence was variously described as "ability to learn" (Buckingham, cited in Thorndike, 1921), as "the power of good responses from the point of view of truth or fact," as "the ability to carry on abstract thinking" (Terman, cited in Thorndike, 1921), as "the ability of the individual to adapt himself adequately to relatively new situations in life" (Pintner, cited in Thorndike, 1921), as "involving two factors—the capacity for knowledge and the knowledge possessed" (Henmon, cited in Thorndike, 1921), and as "the capacity to acquire capacity" (Woodrow, cited in Thorndike, 1921). Fifty years on, when two dozen prominent theorists were asked to define "intelligence," they gave two dozen somewhat different definitions (Sternberg & Detterman, 1986). Later still, Sattler (1992) discussed more than 20 separate (if somewhat overlapping) definitions of intelligence, many of which led to the development of distinct scales to measure a wide variety of skills and abilities. Even if scientists cannot agree as to what intelligence is, many (as we shall see) have agreed that it can be measured.

The Structure of Intelligence

One of the most basic (and controversial) questions about intelligence is whether individual differences in performance can be understood best in terms of a single, underlying general ability or in terms of a collection of many independent, if (more or less) related, abilities. One kind of theory is essentially monistic; the other is pluralistic. These two models have tended to dominate modern understanding of the structure of intelligence. Theoreticians and researchers in one school contend that basically one general ability accounts for individual differences in mental performance in a wide variety of tasks, jobs, and instructional and training programs. This psychometric model of intelligence (*qua* IQ) includes the assumption that the mind is best represented as a single complex entity or unified set of processes. Dissatisfied with the view that intelligence entails only one or perhaps two (linguistic and logical–mathematical) abilities, another school of researchers and theoreticians holds that IQ provides an incomplete description of cognition and contends for multiple specialized abilities, each perhaps particular to a specific performance situation. These schools of thought divide into those (historically, following Spearman) who believe in a "general factor" and those (historically, following Thurstone) who posit a family of "primary mental abilities." The question of whether intelligence is general or specific is actually a debate about the structural nature of intelligence. For our hypothetical classroom teacher, resolution to that debate has startling consequences in terms of how to think about children and how best to teach them.

The principal method of assessing the structural nature of intelligence has been to examine relations among different measures of it. Researchers in the IQ tradition have consistently reported substantial positive correlations among diverse tests of child and adult mental ability. They cite these findings as clear evidence that intelligence is a general ability. Challenging this view, other researchers find that intelligence in the same studies only appears to reflect a general ability, and only because the tested types of ability are all of a kind.

g: *The General Intelligence View*

People who are good at one test are good at other tests as well, and so it seems reasonable to infer that there is some ability being tested that is common to all the tests. All branches of intellectual activity have in common one fundamental function. ... This *g*, far from being confined to some small set of abilities whose intercorrelations have actually been measured and drawn up in some particular table, may enter into all abilities whatsoever.
—SPEARMAN (1904, p. 201)

Galton (1883), the founder of psychometrics and differential psychology, claimed that a single source of individual differences in mental abilities could be traced to differences in performances on rather simple tests of the acuity of the senses, speed of reaction, and the like. Cattell (1890), who later became interested in individual differences in speeds of reaction, sensory discrimination, word association, and other equally uncomplicated mental tasks, introduced the term "mental test." It was Spearman (1904), however, who published a prescient and original interpretation of some data that he had collected in a village school in Hampshire, England. Spearman observed that children who were highly developed in one intellectual ability tended to be, on average, highly developed in other, different intellectual abilities as well. In other words, intellectual tasks show a "positive manifold," whereby all tasks positively correlate with each other, albeit to varying degrees. Children who received high scores on a test of vocabulary were likely to receive high scores on a test of memory. This led to the idea that a single process—he called it *general intelligence*, often symbolized as *g*—underlies human cognitive capability. From this analysis, Spearman concluded that different abilities share a general factor that is common to all tests of intellectual ability. The initial empirical base for

Spearman's theory of g comprised the grades and teacher evaluations of a handful of schoolchildren in a few English village schools.

Spearman's argument that there is a single, fundamental process of g that permeates all intellectual activities, and determines performance on any test thought to constitute a measure of intelligence, provided a simple and satisfying explanation of the finding of positive correlations between a wide variety of different tests. The so-called "positive manifold" has been hailed as "one of the most remarkable findings in all of psychology ... that scores on all mental ability tests of every variety was positively intercorrelated in any representative sample of the general population" (Jensen, 1981, p. 52) and "one of the most reliable, replicable, and important empirical discoveries about human ability yet found" (Detterman & Daniel, 1989, p. 349).

In Spearman's theory of g, a single structural factor permeates performance on all the various tests and tasks used to assess intelligent behavior. The main purpose of the IQ test is, therefore, to measure the amount of that intelligence an individual has. This goal anticipates the study of individual differences in intellectual abilities. Designed to be a differential variable, IQ is meant to discriminate among individuals and place them in ordinal relation to one another. Thus, individuals who respond correctly to one item in a test should have a higher probability of correctly responding to a second item in the same or a different test than individuals who respond incorrectly to the first item.

IQ tests have since evolved to measure this g factor that is to reflect or indicate a single factor that underlies performance in many different intellectual tasks. In both Spearman's own work and that which followed in his wake, the g factor has been viewed as critical to understanding the nature of intelligence. Jensen (1980), for example, would contend that g is the most fundamental feature of intelligence. Yet psychometric test theory includes certain critical assumptions: that different tasks yield reliable measures of characteristic behaviors of the individuals who perform the tasks; that individuals may be ordered on a unidimensional scale reflecting different degrees of their competence; and that the characteristic underlying IQ performance is real (Brody, 1992; Jensen, 1998; Neisser et al., 1996). Given these assumptions and deductions, it is remarkable that there has never been concord as to what g actually is: in its history, it has variously been thought of as a type of mental energy (Spearman, 1927), a statistical regularity (Thomson, 1939), a generalized abstract reasoning ability (Gustafsson, 1984), and a measure of neural processing speed (Reed & Jensen, 1992). Perhaps the most common view is that intelligence test scores reflect some (innate) capacity of the individual to think in abstract terms, to learn in school, and to adapt to the requirements of an increasingly complex technological society. Despite the many shortcomings of IQ theory and an IQ score, no other measure has been found to relate to so many other behaviors of theoretical and practical significance (Kohlberg & Zigler, 1967; Mischel, 1968). As a predictor, IQ scores account for up to half the variance in many different developmental measures (which means that other individual characteristics, such as interpersonal skills or personality, are of equal or greater importance).

Current versions of the Wechsler scales of intelligence represent the fulfillment of this psychometric approach. They include three scales, the Wechsler Adult Intelligence Scale–III (WAIS-III; Wechsler, 1997), the Wechsler Intelligence Scale for Children—Fourth Edition (WISC-IV; 2003), and the Wechsler Preschool and Primary Scale of Intelligence—Third Edition (WPPSI-III; 2002). The Wechsler scales are typically considered to be the best standardized measures in the field (Kaufman, 1993). Not surprisingly, the Wechsler scales are the most frequently used instruments for the assessment of intelligence and have been translated into numerous languages, including Chinese, Dutch, French, German, Hebrew, Italian, Korean, Portuguese, Spanish, and Swedish. Consider the Wechsler Preschool and Primary Scale of Intelligence—Revised (WPPSI-R). Verbal subtests include scales on Information, Comprehension, Arithmetic, Vocabulary, Similarities, and Sentences; and Performance subtests include scales on Object Assembly, Geometric Design, Block Design, Mazes, Picture Completion, and Animal Pegs. Factor analysis of the data from its standardization sample age 3–7 years yields a Verbal factor and a Performance factor, in addition to a Total or Full Scale IQ score. According to Wechsler (1958), the Verbal and Performance subtests are different measures of the same intelligence, not measures of different kinds of intelligence. All WPPSI-R subtests, for example, load relatively high on g (Sattler, 1992).

g does not account for all the variance in IQ test performance. In his later writings, Spearman (1923, 1927) developed a so-called "two-factor theory of intelligence." Spearman's ultimate model assumed that an observed IQ score for an examinee may be accounted for in terms of a weighted sum of scores on two underlying unobservable variables; a general one that is common and enters in to all tasks (g), and another that is specific to each task (s).

F: The Multiple Faculties View

If anyone insists on having a single index such as an I.Q., it can be obtained by taking an average of all the known abilities. But such an index tends so to blur the description of each man that his mental assets and limitations are buried in the single index.
—THURSTONE (1946, p. 110)

Classical scholars commonly distinguished among reason, will, and feeling, and Medieval sages had their trivium of grammar, logic, and rhetoric, and their quadrivium of mathematics, geometry, astronomy, and music. "Faculty psychology" views the mind as congeries of independent abilities. The evolutionary psychology view is that, over the course of evolution, human beings have come to possess a number of special-purpose information-processing devices, or "computational mechanisms." Some are decidedly molecular (line detection); others are far more molar (control of voluntary action). We could hardly have survived as a species for many thousands of years without a secure likelihood that we would all be able to speak, perceive, and remember many forms of information in relatively similar ways. Furthermore, it has been argued that these faculties are self-governing in two senses: First, each mechanism operates according to its own principles and is not "yoked" to any other one; second, these information-processing devices operate simply in the presence of certain forms of information to be analyzed, and without being directed to do so. For example, mechanisms used to process language, and the neural structures mediating language, represent a self-contained, functionally autonomous faculty.

Even though there is virtually no situation in which the concept of g may be completely disregarded, there also are many situations in which more specialized abilities should be considered alongside g. Gardner (1983, 1987, 1990) has pointed out that intelligence comprises many different abilities, and that intelligence tests omit much relevant information about an individual's intellect. Undeniably, intelligence tests sample from a rather narrow band of the true range of intellectual potential. Whereas Spearman (1927) emphasized the importance of a general factor that represents what all tests have in common, others, like Thurstone (1938), focused on specific groups of factors, such as memory, verbal comprehension, and number facility. The identities of such specific factors differ across theories, and theoreticians and researchers with the best intentions disagree regarding what dimensions are both necessary and sufficient for specialized abilities, or even for clear operational definitions that might lead to the development of specific test contents for them. Guilford (1967) favored 120 vectors of mind; the Cattell–Horn theory (Cattell, 1971) divided g into two subfactors, g_f (fluid ability) and g_c (crystallized ability). Here, I discuss two of the most prominent faculty theories.

During the 1930s, multidimensional alternatives to Spearman's unidimensional theory appeared. Thurstone (1931, 1938, 1947) pioneered the ideas and methods for the most prominent, primary mental abilities (PMA) theory. Thurstone dismissed the notion of g and in its stead proposed that intelligence comprises a set of independent or "primary" abilities. The fundamental idea of a primary mental ability was that "it behaves as a functional unity that is strongly present in some tests and almost completely absent in many others" (Thurstone & Thurstone, 1941, p. 9).

To identify PMA, Thurstone (1938) used the statistical technique of factor analysis to examine the performance of an intellectually heterogeneous group of public school-children. Whereas, overly simply put, the positive manifold stops at identifying the principal component in a correlation matrix, factor analysis concerns the structure of correlations among variables; that is, the question of how many "factors" or "latent traits" are indicated by a set of correlations arranged in a matrix, such that all the correlations among variables are shown systematically. Following the administration of a battery of tests, Thurstone analyzed the intercorrelations among the tests to determine which factors were measured by several, but not all, of the tests. His analysis did not converge on a general factor, but on several separate factors. According to PMA theory, intelligence does not comprise a single general factor, g. Rather, the theory posits that intelligence comprises seven somewhat independent primary mental abilities, which Thurstone designated by capital letters: V for verbal comprehension, W for word fluency, N for number (computational), S for spatial visualization, M for associative memory, P for perceptual speed, and R for reasoning. More formal versions of the PMA battery were published subsequently (Thurstone & Thurstone, 1941). Thurstone's results supported a rather different concept of intelligence from the one that had theretofore dominated the mental testing movement; that is, his analysis supported the argument that, rather than one, there are many kinds of intelligence.

However, Thurstone's results also showed that primary abilities were themselves correlated, reraising the possibility of a general factor (Thurstone & Thurstone, 1941). This admission represented a partial convergence between Thurstone's PMA theory and Spearman's two-factor theory. Thurstone acknowledged the existence of correlations among his PMAs and allowed for the existence of a second-order g (Snyderman & Rothman, 1988; Sternberg & Powell, 1983), but he retained the view that the primaries were of fundamental interest (Thurstone, 1947).

Gardner (1983; Gardner & Hatch, 1989) later argued that a positive manifold is to some extent an artifact of testing. He pointed out that most measures of intelligence are

paper-and-pencil tests of linguistic and logical skills. In consequence, the positive manifold may reflect the measurement of restricted content with similar techniques rather
than the true structure of intelligence. Gardner rejected the model of a central organization that controls the functioning of the mind, and his eventual classification of abilities
did not admit a general ability. He contended that the tendency to view the mind as
a single entity, or even a set of coordinated processes, lacks plausibility and is unsupported by diverse (e.g., neurophysiological, developmental, evolutionary) data. Rather,
cognition is better accounted for by a framework that posits a number of (fairly) specific and (fairly) independent computational mechanisms. In *Frames of Mind*, Gardner
proposed a theory of "multiple intelligences," each informed by eight "signs": studies of
patients with brain damage, prodigies, gifted individuals, idiots savants, normal children, normal adults, experts in different lines of work, and individuals from diverse cultures. Thus, an intelligence exists to the extent that one can find evidence for its separate
developmental pathway, its organization in specific regions or systems in the nervous
system, its isolation in special populations, its occurrence across a range of cultures,
its evolutionary history within and across species, and its susceptibility to codifica-
tion within a symbol system. Meeting these criteria provides converging evidence from
diverse sources that an intelligence is relatively autonomous. Gardner proposed seven
separate intelligences: "linguistic intelligence," fluency in the production of language;
"logical–mathematical intelligence," the ability to solve computation and word problems; "musical intelligence," thoughtful fluency in musical terms, the core components
of which are pitch, rhythm, and timbre; "spatial intelligence," the ability to generate,
retain, retrieve, and transform well-structured visual images; "bodily–kinesthetic intelligence," the ability to solve problems or fashion products by using the whole body or
parts or the body, such as hands or mouth; "interpersonal intelligence," the ability to
understand other individuals and to use this understanding to work effectively with
them; and "intrapersonal intelligence," the ability to form an accurate working model
of oneself and to make effective decisions based on that model. Gardner did not claim
that the seven intelligences are definitive; rather, his aim was to support a pluralistic
view of intelligence. In 1984, Feldman and Gardner initiated a research effort (Project
Spectrum—Malkus, Feldman, & Gardner, 1988; Wexler-Sherman, Gardner, & Feldman, 1988) to assess preschool children's cognitive activity as it is reflected in the seven
intelligences. Gardner's intelligences may be refined through education. According to
Gardner, it is through the educational process that "raw" intellectual competencies are
developed and individuals are prepared to assume mature cultural roles.

g and F: Hierarchical Integrative Models of Intelligence

One theory of mental logic postulates a general system of intelligence that will operate
on any information presented to it. Domain specificity has often been interpreted as evidence for an "opposite modularity of mind," the idea that human beings posses domain-
specific modules for different types of input, rather than one, general-purpose problem
solver. But the two ideas are not mutually exclusive. There is nothing self-contradictory
about a theory of human cognition that acknowledges that the mind contains a number
of modules specialized for particular tasks (e.g., language learning) but at the same time
is resolute that the mind also contains a general system that is not domain-specific. We
may have not only an innate language acquisition device that allows us to become com-

petent in the grammar of language but also a more general-purpose cognitive system that contributes to solving both language and other types of problems. Our knowledge and expertise may be domain-specific, but the means by which we become knowledgeable and expert may be entirely general.

Spearman based his psychological interpretation on a belief that g was dominant and real, a general intelligence that marks a person's essential intelligence. Thurstone professed that there are many ways in which a person can be intelligent. The difference between the two theories is primarily one of emphasis, with either the general factor or the specific abilities considered more important in explaining intelligence. Both Spearman (top-down) and Thurstone (bottom-up) ultimately admitted the validity of some of the other's view. It would appear that performance on a variety of cognitive tasks relates in some but not total degree. So, in mathematical terms, the solutions to the positive associations of performance on different tasks are equally acceptable; in theoretical terms, however, interpretations of the two solutions are somewhat contradictory. Because the solutions are mathematically equivalent, neither theoretical view is definitively supported by the results of factor analysis. Historically, however, a resolution has been achieved through the development of theories of intelligence that include both a general factor and various specific abilities.

One kind of hybrid theory is essentially hierarchical. Let's say that we have measures of children's performance on several tasks. This is the most specific level of the variable. Now, it turns out that some measures of some performance vary together in a way that makes a single, first-order factor, and other measures of other performance covary in a way that makes another, first-order factor. Thus, the first-order factors account for the intercorrelations among specific measures. Now, suppose a "second-order" factor accounts for some variance in the two first-order factors. With this approach a hierarchy of factors is constructed, starting from below, with a larger number of narrow measures, and ending at the top of the hierarchy with (one or a few) broad, higher-order factors. Such higher-order analyses yield hierarchical models, in which specific factors at lower levels are subsumed under more general factors at higher levels. In consequence, a resolution of the tension between proponents of monistic and pluralistic theories of intelligence is achieved by accommodating both conceptions of the nature of intelligence. Hierarchical theories of intelligence (e.g., Burt, 1940; Cattell, 1971; Holzinger, 1938; Horn, 1968; Royce, 1973; Vernon, 1971) restore the concept of general ability and combine the perspective of those emphasizing several narrower dimensions of cognitive ability with that of those emphasizing one general cognitive ability. Vernon (1950, 1971) presented an integration of results achieved in several studies in the form of just such a hierarchical model. At the top of his model was a g factor. The model also included two major group factors underneath: a verbal–numerical–educational ($v{:}ed$) factor and a practical–mechanical–spatial–physical ($k{:}m$) factor. Given a sufficient number of tests, these major group factors may be subdivided into several minor group factors. Thus, the $v{:}ed$ factor subdivides into different scholastic factors such as v (verbal) and n (number) group factors. The $k{:}m$ factor may be subdivided into minor group factors, such as perceptual, spatial, and mechanical abilities.

Another hierarchical model that includes two general dimensions (crystallized intelligence, g_c, and fluid intelligence, g_f) was developed by Cattell and Horn (Cattell, 1943, 1963; Horn, 1968; Horn & Cattell, 1966, 1967). "Fluid intelligence" represents basic capacity, and "crystallized intelligence" represents abilities acquired through learning, practice, and exposure to education. Crystallized abilities tend to be measured by tests of knowledge and skills that are related to formal education. Fluid ability measures tend to be related to abstract reasoning skills that are not formally taught in school but that might be influenced by exposure to formal education. The fact that G_f and G_c tend to correlate supports the existence of a single higher-order factor g (Kail & Pellegrino, 1985).

A consensus hierarchical organization was presented by Carroll (1993) on the basis of a heroic survey and reanalysis of than 400 datasets collected over 70 years of studies on the nature, identification, and structure of human cognitive abilities. Carroll's three-stratum theory includes factors of three degrees of generality: narrow, broad, and general. The general factor, a single factor at the third and highest level of the model, influences performance in each domain below it. General ability is related to different kinds of abilities at the second stratum. The abilities are arrayed from left to right, in decreasing degree of relation to the single common ability at the third stratum (see Figure 7.1).

Carroll's analysis indicates that intelligence may be conceived as a single general ability and as many specialized abilities related to each other in a hierarchical structure. A detailed description of this theory as it pertains to the different domains of ability appears in *Human Cognitive Abilities* (Carroll, 1993). It implies that individual profiles of ability levels are much more complex than previously thought, but at the same time it offers a way of structuring such profiles by classifying abilities in terms of strata. The general factor is close to former monistic conceptions of intelligence, whereas second-stratum factors summarize abilities in individual domains thought to be specialized phylogenetically or experientially.

Summary

In overview, some theories about the structure of intelligence emphasize one general ability; other theories emphasize several specialized abilities. The clash between these

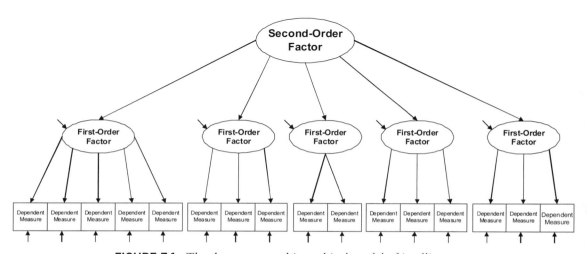

FIGURE 7.1. The three-stratum hierarchical model of intelligence.

approaches is resolved in hierarchical theories, which accommodate both general and specialized abilities. Many theorists now agree that at least three categories of ability dimensions should be recognized: general cognitive ability, broad abilities, and narrow abilities. Most factor-analytic models are hierarchical. Usually, they suggest that at the top of the intellectual abilities hierarchy there is a single general factor of intelligence (g). Below g are lower-order factors representing more specific mental abilities. At the bottom of the hierarchy are the most specific abilities, which cannot be broken down any further into factors. Inherent in a hierarchical model, however, is the idea that because some mental abilities are related, they converge on a higher-level ability.

An Empirical Approach to the Hierarchical Model with Young Children

With these ideas in mind, Bornstein, Putnick, and Haynes (2008) developed a wide-ranging test battery. Children and their mothers participated in an experimental protocol around the time of the child's fourth birthday. While the child was involved in completing her or his parts of the protocol, the child's mother normally sat nearby or in the adjacent room and completed sociodemographic and other questionnaires; she was also interviewed.

Each child engaged in a variety of activities with an administrator, each completed in a predetermined order. Extensive pretesting determined that order to maintain the child's interest and to minimize fatigue: They examined (1) verbal and performance psychometric intelligence, (2) numeracy, (3) literacy, (4) mechanics, (5) artistry, (6) psychomotor ability, (7) sociability, and (8) adaptive behavior. These domains were selected because of their importance in our culture, and because they represent a range of abilities as they are expressed in young children. Together, the activities yielded a variety of dependent variables that were used in subsequent modeling. In some cases, there was a one-to-one correspondence between a dependent variable and a faculty; in other cases, an activity yielded a small variety of dependent variables that related to different faculties. The several measures used in this study proved stable in a 1-week retest assessment, and they maintained their group mean level across that time as well. These findings support the psychometric adequacy of the measures as distributed, stable, and continuous.

Bornstein and his colleagues (2008) then modeled the hierarchical structure of g and Fs derived from 4-year-olds. The best-fitting solution resembled the three-stratum model of Carroll, with specific dependent variables at the bottom that converged on five first-order factors that loaded on one second-order factor. They called the five first-order factors numeracy/spatial, linguistic, interpersonal, bodily–kinesthetic, and literacy, and the second-order factor, general intelligence. They also tested two alternative models (one that omitted the five first-order factors, and another that omitted the one second-order factor), concluding that the a priori hierarchical model was the best and most parsimonious fit to the data. They further determined that the hierarchical model applied to girls and to boys equally well (although girls perform better than boys in several domains). The final model also fit the data, while accounting for variance associated with family socioeconomic status and maternal verbal intelligence. Notably, children who attended preschool outscored their counterparts who did not attend preschool in general intelligence, as well as numeracy/spatial, linguistic, interpersonal, and bodily–kinesthetic intelligence; however, when sociodemographic factors that also distinguished preschool attendees from nonattendees were controlled, some differences in intelligences attenuated.

The findings revealed two kinds of processing systems, one global and five local. As to the global, it appears from Spearman and the positive manifold that whenever a battery of tasks is factor-analyzed, a common ingredient can be shown to exist that all the tasks seem to share, over and above their unique ingredients. So, for example, a vocabulary test may not only reflect a set of specific skills (e.g., verbal fluency, inferring meaning from context) but also the operation of some common or general intelligence resource. Some cognitive systems are nonmodular and central, and can plausibly be assumed to cut across specific cognitive domains. Even if some systems are domain-specific, some cognitive mechanisms are not. They are relatively domain-nonspecific and nondenominational, and appear to function across information that input systems provide. As to the local processing systems, "faculty psychology" is the view that many fundamentally different kinds of psychological mechanisms are required to explain mental life. These theories claim the existence of multiple subcomponents of cognition, each capable of functioning relatively independently of each other (e.g., language vs. spatial skills).

Individual Differences

> In a variable approach, the lawfulness of structures and processes in individual functioning and development is studied in terms of statistical relations among variables. ... Individuals differ only quantitatively, not qualitatively, along the dimension for a certain variable.
> —MAGNUSSON (1998, pp. 45–46)

> With reference to the goal for psychological research—namely, to understand and explain how and why individuals think, feel, act, and react as they do in real life—a great advantage of the person approach is that generalizations of empirical results refer to persons, not to variables.
> —MAGNUSSON (1998, p. 51)

To this point, the analyses that Bornstein and colleagues (2008) undertook focused on group mean–level statistics. Although these techniques proved useful to elucidate patterns of relations among variables, they ignored individual variation. The identification of individual differences in intelligence has long been of interest. Galton's (1869) original survey of British scientists addressed this issue, as did Goddard (1911) and Terman (1916). Certainly, the configuration of individual variables in a system also has meaning other than overall group representations.

The dominant approach to assessment in developmental science uses single variables, combinations of variables, or relations among variables as the main conceptual and analytical units (Hartmann & Pelzel, 2005). In this so-called "variable approach," a single datum for an individual derives psychological meaning from its position relative to the positions of data from other individuals on a given dimension. The variable approach to measurement posits that individuals assume positions on latent dimensions for relevant factors and undertakes to locate individuals on those dimension(s); the appropriate measurement technique is one that discriminates along the entire range of possible positions. By contrast, the so-called "person approach" undertakes to assign individuals to clusters within a total system; the appropriate measurement technique is one that clusters information about the individual with other, like individuals. The person approach is based on a wholistic–interactionistic research paradigm to development and functioning, meaning that it sees the individual as an organized whole, functioning and developing as a totality (Magnusson & Allen, 1983). The totality derives its characteristic features and properties from interactions among its elements (the whole is more than the sum of the parts) rather than from the effect of isolated parts of the totality or as an integration of variables. In the person approach, each datum derives its psychological meaning from its place in a pattern of data representing positions on latent dimensions. The variable approach uses methods that focus on values on a scale; the person approach uses methods that focus on patterns or configurations of values in variables in individuals.

With this variable–person distinction in mind, Bornstein and colleagues (2008) revisited the data and analyzed prominent patterns of individual differences among children in terms of the distributions of faculties. To isolate the specific abilities associated with each F, and remove the effect of shared general intelligence, each faculty factor score derived from the hierarchical g and F model was residualized for the higher-order general intelligence factor score. These residualized scores were then standardized to ease interpretation and comparison. Using a cut point of 1 standard deviation above and below the mean, each standardized faculty factor score was recoded into three groups: low intelligence, average intelligence, and high intelligence. The patterns were quite similar on all Fs, with roughly 16% of the sample falling 1 or more standard deviations above the mean, 68% falling within 1 standard deviation of the mean, and 15% falling 1 or more standard deviations below the mean.

At the individual level, approximately 22% of the sample scored within 1 standard deviation of the mean on all five faculties factor scores; approximately 18% scored in the high range on one or more faculties factor scores and in the average range on the others; approximately 13% scored in the low range on one or more faculties factor scores and in the average range on the others; and approximately 47% had a mixture of high, average, and low faculties. No child scored 1 standard deviation above or below the mean on more than three faculties factor scores.

Looking at children with one special or one deficient faculty to see how they scored on other faculties, children could score high on any F, and when they did, their scores tended to be average or slightly below average on all other faculties. The same held true for children with one deficiency; those who showed a deficiency in one F tended to score average or slightly above average in the other faculties. Looking at children with two specialties or two deficiencies, similar patterns emerged in the sense that children could have any pair of specialty or deficiency Fs, and, if they did, tended to score around average in the other faculties. Finally, looking at the pattern of individual differences in children with both one specialty and one deficiency, again, these could occur in any combination, and children tended to score at average on all the other faculties.

When a wide range of abilities is assessed, individuals tend to display an uneven profile of abilities; that is, they are more competent in some areas and less so in others. Children did not perform at the same level on most tasks; that is, children performed at different levels on different tasks when levels of performance within each child's set of scores was examined. Indeed, 4-year-olds displayed configurations that were domain-specific, and virtually no children showed precisely the same "profile" of intelligences. A comparison among children's varied patterns of performance revealed many different patterns. The varying levels of performance on the tasks were specific, and each child's pattern of expressed *F*s was unique.

To describe differences in intelligence, children are customarily rank-ordered on the basis of their IQ. Calling this approach into question, the results of the study just recounted indicate that an individual child's rank, based on a domain-specific task score, actually varies depending on the domain. Therefore, the rank of an individual child that is based on a single score fails to describe accurately the range and the pattern of that child's abilities. As a result, such ranks also distort relations among individual children. By extension, the results suggest that more informal characterizations of intellectual ability, such as "smart," "average," and "below average" are also potentially misleading and inaccurate. When a range of areas is considered, children are likely to have strengths in some specific area(s) and average performance or slight difficulties in some other specific area(s). Rather than being general, these abilities appear to be differentiated. To the extent that they are, it is not possible to predict reliably an individual child's ability in one area based on performance in other areas. Because abilities are specific, the description of a child should also be specific. For the description to be accurate, the child's abilities across a range of distinct domains must be determined. Based on multiple assessments, however, a revealing profile detailing an individual child's capabilities can be constructed. This profile provides a comprehensive and more detailed portrait of each individual child's capabilities at a particular point in time. The essence of each child is her or his individual profile.

Individual-difference patterns among intelligences tend to support a modularity perspective on the child's mind. That individual children exhibit varying levels of competence when abilities from distinctive areas are evaluated supports the claim that some intelligences are domain-specific. This finding also has implications for the description of individual differences in intelligence. Specifically, when individuals are described in terms of either a single numerical score (e.g., IQ) or a global category (e.g., a Piagetian stage), meaningful variations within an individual's repertoire of abilities are obscured. Vital information about the individual child is lost.

Intelligence Returns to School

This chapter began, as did Binet, Spearman, and Thurstone, in school. School systems have long since discarded the use of IQ tests per se in devising educational policy, as did teachers in their instruction, for many good reasons. Teachers can be unjustifiably prejudiced by them; test scores can be used to label children unfairly; the tests are insufficiently accurate; and assessments often yield information about skills that are tied to membership in certain groups or classes. Historically, simple and biased approaches to intelligence measurement may have shortcomings that warrant their being discredited. However, we should entertain the revisionist notion of newer approaches that are sensitive to dimensions of individual differences in a diverse array of mental abilities, and pay closer attention to skills that can be differentially identified in performance may merit our consideration and classroom application. Our hypothetical school teacher surely recognizes individual differences in the room and may even wish to be responsive to them, but indentifying them more precisely and determining how to be individually responsive have proven challenging. Part of the problem may lie in the need for fitting measures that adequately describe individual children. Children can be characterized as unique, or they are described in terms of their global ability, or both. Some educators may see and respond to some children as generally more intelligent (and worthy) than others, and they implicitly adopt a unitarian view of intelligence. Other educators, however, seem to see and respond to children as more or less intelligent in different ways (hence, worthy of equal respect) because every child is capable in her or his own way. Those teachers recognize that individual children are unique constellations of abilities, but seeing them in this light makes it difficult to meet their needs or reconcile a fixed curriculum with such individual differences. When children can be described only in terms of their global abilities (level of general intelligence or broad developmental stages), it may be easier to respond to them or to the group, but what is distinguishing about each individual child is misplaced. When children are portrayed only in terms of specialized proficiencies or deficiencies, equivalent risks arise in terms of labeling and mischaracterization. Thus, further information is needed on domain-general and individual intellectual abilities and skills.

The philosophy espoused in this chapter, along with the study data presented earlier, have twin concrete implications for education. One concerns teachers, and the other, curriculum. For some years now, the National Association for the Education of Young Children (NAEYC; 2001), perhaps the preeminent U.S. professional association of early childhood educators, has encouraged the development of instructional systems that are informed by developmental science. Indeed, the Society for Research in Child Development, perhaps the preeminent international professional association of developmental researchers, derived originally from NAEYC; so early childhood education has a long-standing alliance with the science of child development. It is also widely recognized in a natural history known as "developmentally appropriate practice" (Bredekamp & Copple, 1997). Nonetheless, these two intellectual silos normally stand apart. Historically, educational practices pay little heed or fall behind fast-paced scientific theory and research. For its part, developmental science too often fails to take full advantage of real-world classroom experience. What is most unfortunate in this light, of course, is how much each discipline stands to benefit from the other. How much would educators profit from a deeper understanding of both the domain-general and domain-specific abilities of their pupils? How much would developmental scientists gain from a deeper appreciation of how children in the classroom perform at multiple activities (and how their developing brains map on to their performance)? One cannot help but think that developmental researchers would be better at formulating their problems and refining their empirical work if they were better informed by the child in the schoolroom, just as educators would be more successful in communicating style and content of learning if they better understood child development theory and substance.

The other instructional domain for which the philosophy and data discussed in this chapter have relevance is the curriculum. What we have found is that young children, at an age just before they start school, possess both domain-general and domain-specific competencies that likely play key roles in their performance on tasks and in situations that are pertinent to school curricula. Thus, these findings beg a syllabus that moves well beyond "reading, 'riting, and 'rithmetic." Our research showed, first, that children can and do perform across a variety of cognitive domains and, second, even among relatively similar young children, substantial individual differences in performance in these domains emerge (imagine the variation that describes more diverse samples).

Then, should not curricula, even with young children, first reflect their diverse abilities, and should not teachers use curricula, second, to identify areas where children excel or fail, to capitalize on their strengths, and to remediate their weaknesses? Essentially, admission of such a multivocal course calls for depth and breadth alike in the would-be revised school curriculum. Children would experience a very different kind of daily routine, one that would include a much richer variety of topics that tap a wider range of their talents. It might alter what is taught, where, and how as the main concerns of the day change and evaluations of children are transformed.

This chapter is about theory and research in developmental science, so it approaches the science–education nexus from only one side. Developmental science historically has not been a strong part of teacher preparation programs, and it does not normally hold forth on implications for other fields. Here, however, the connections seem so intimate and artless that guild canons might be temporarily suspended.

Finally, school readiness is a topic of perennial interest to parents, researchers, and policymakers (National Association for the Education of Young Children, 2001; Swick, Brown, & Boutte, 1994). School readiness predicts later academic success (Entwisle & Alexander, 1996). Researchers have long recognized that factors within the home environment foster school readiness and children's preparation to master readiness tasks (Bluestone & Tamis-LeMonda, 1999; Brooks-Gunn & Markman, 2005; Entwisle & Alexander, 1996). School readiness comprises many factors (e.g., communication, cognitive, motor, social, and adaptive) that have been measured (McAllister, Wilson, Green, & Baldwin, 2005), and the multidimensional definition of school readiness is supported by federal initiatives (e.g., No Child Left Behind Act), as well as other research findings on early interventions (e.g., Good Start, Grow Smart and the Head Start National Reporting System). Early education programs (e.g., Head Start) are designed to enhance children's competencies and contribute to their readiness for school. If the early acquisition of specific skills forecasts or enhances later achievement, it may be beneficial to add domain-specific early skills (e.g., that we have studied) to the definition of school readiness, and to promote interventions aimed at improving those skills prior to the start of school (Duncan et al., 2007). Thus, understanding which skills are linked to children's academic achievement also has important implications for early education programs. Developing appropriate means of multidimensional intelligence assessment will demand much from researchers and educators alike. When more appropriate appraisals are formulated, the description of individual children's abilities will become more complete and accurate.

Conclusions

> IQ testing has had momentous consequences.
> —GOULD (1981, p. 150)

Two models have dominated our understanding of intelligence. The monistic view holds that the mind is best represented as a single (if complex) entity or unified set of processes. The pluralistic view maintains that intelligence is more than coordinate linguistic and logical–mathematical abilities that without more specialized systems provide an incomplete description of cognitive capacity. The development of the psychometric

IQ test to identify general aptitude was a landmark in the field of intelligence research. However, multiple cognitive abilities are, at best, only imperfectly measured by tests of general intelligence. In addition to the general-purpose skills measured by IQ tests, human beings also possess several specific-purpose cognitive systems that are somewhat independent of IQ. Perhaps, then, existing IQ measures evaluate only a meager bit of intelligence. With the advent of more sophisticated multidimensional assessments, both general and domain-specific abilities will be identified. The developers of mental tests have always acknowledged that more predictive instruments would come from more exact and advanced knowledge of the nature of human abilities.

Many traits that human beings use in solving problems—determination, imagination, leadership, social understanding—are not addressed by intelligence tests. Moreover, in addition to intelligence, personality, motivation, interest, and other characteristics are important determinants of success in school and in life. The hierarchical (three-stratum) approach to mental functioning, spelled out in this chapter, is intended to provide guidance for further research concerning cognitive abilities and their structure. Procedural details and statistical methods aside, the take-home message for educators like our hypothetical classroom teacher may be relatively straightforward. To wit, we need to see in the forest of students in front of us the individual saplings, and appreciate the unique nature and structure of each one. Thus, hierarchical theory has major implications for the practical assessment and tuition of children in educational settings. If the stance of educators and researchers toward the nature and role of intelligence were that intellectual competencies represent positive forces, and that their development and application could be advanced through education and training, perhaps objections to intelligence tests would fall away, and their validity and utility would be further enhanced.

Acknowledgments

This chapter summarizes selected aspects of my research, and portions of the text have appeared in previous scientific publications cited in the references. This research was supported by the Intramural Research Program of the National Institutes of Health, Eunice Kennedy Shriver National Institute of Child Health and Human Development. I thank O. M. Haynes, D. Putnick, and T. Taylor.

References

Binet, A., & Simon, T. (1905). Méthodes nouvelles pour le diagnostic du niveau intellectuel des anormaux [New methods for the diagnosis of intellectual level in abnormal people]. *L'Année Psychologique, 11*, 191–336.

Bluestone, C., & Tamis-LeMonda, C. S. (1999). Correlates of parenting styles in predominantly working- and middle-class African American mothers. *Journal of Marriage and the Family, 61*, 881–893.

Bornstein, M. H., Putnick, D. L., & Haynes, O. M. (2008). *The mind of the preschool child.* Unpublished manuscript, Eunice Kennedy Shriver National Institute of Child Health and Human Development.

Bredekamp, S., & Copple, C. (Eds.). (1997). *Developmentally appropriate practice in early childhood programs* (rev. ed.). Washington, DC: National Association for the Education of Young Children.

Brody, N. (1992). *Intelligence* (2nd ed.). San Diego, CA: Academic Press.

Brooks-Gunn, J., & Markman, L. (2005). The contribution of parenting to ethnic and racial gaps in school readiness. *The Future of Children, 15,* 139–168.

Burt, C. (1940). *The factors of the mind.* London: University of London Press.

Carroll, J. B. (1993). *Human cognitive abilities.* New York: Cambridge University Press.

Cattell, J. M. (1890). Mental tests and their measurement. *Mind, 15,* 373–381.

Cattell, R. B. (1943). The measurement of adult intelligence. *Psychological Bulletin, 40,* 153–193.

Cattell, R. B. (1963). Theory of fluid and crystallized intelligence: A critical experiment. *Journal of Educational Psychology, 54,* 1–22.

Cattell, R. B. (1971). *Abilities: Their structure, growth, and action.* Boston: Houghton Mifflin.

Detterman, D. K., & Daniel, M. H. (1989). Correlations of mental tests with each other and with cognitive variables are highest for low IQ groups. *Intelligence, 13,* 349–359.

Duncan, G. J., Dowsett, C. J., Claessens, A., Magnuson, K., Huston, A. C., Klebanov, P., et al. (2007). School readiness and later achievement. *Developmental Psychology, 43,* 1428–1446.

Entwisle, D. R., & Alexander, K. (1996). Family type and children's growth in reading and math over the primary grades. *Journal of Marriage and the Family, 58,* 341–355.

Galton, F. (1869). *Hereditary genius: An inquiry into its laws and consequences.* London: Macmillan.

Galton, F. (1883). *Inquiries into human faculty and its development.* London: Macmillan.

Gardner, H. (1983). *Frames of mind: The theory of multiple intelligences.* New York: Basic Books.

Gardner, H. (1987). The theory of multiple intelligences. *Annals of Dyslexia, 37,* 19–35.

Gardner, H. (1990). Assessment in context: The alternative to standardized testing. In B. R. Gifford & M. C. O'Connor (Eds.), *Future assessments: Changing views of aptitude, achievement, and instruction* (pp. 2–44). Boston: Kluwer.

Gardner, H., & Hatch, T. (1989). Multiple intelligences go to school: Educational implications of the theory of multiple intelligences. *Education Researcher, 18,* 4–10.

Goddard, H. H. (1911). Two thousand normal children measured by the Binet Measuring Scale of Intelligence. *Pediatric Seminars, 18,* 232–259.

Gould, S. J. (1981). *The mismeasure of man.* New York: Norton.

Guilford, J. P. (1967). *The nature of human intelligence.* New York: McGraw-Hill.

Gustafsson, J. E. (1984). A unifying model for the structure of intellectual abilities. *Intelligence, 8,* 179–203.

Hartmann, D. P., & Pelzel, K. E. (2005). Design, measurement, and analysis in developmental research. In M. H. Bornstein & M. E. Lamb (Eds.), *Developmental science: An advanced textbook* (pp. 103–184). Mahwah, NJ: Erlbaum.

Holzinger, K. J. (1938). Relationships between three multiple orthogonal factors and four bifactors. *Journal of Educational Psychology, 29,* 159–164.

Horn, J. L. (1968). Organization of abilities and the development of intelligence. *Psychological Review, 72,* 242–259.

Horn, J. L., & Cattell, R. B. (1966). Refinement and test of the theory of fluid and crystallized intelligence. *Journal of Educational Psychology, 57,* 253–270.

Horn, J. L., & Cattell, R. B. (1967). Age differences in fluid and crystallized intelligence. *Acta Psychologica, 26,* 107–129.

Jencks, C. (1972). *Inequality: A reassessment of the effect of family and schooling in America.* New York: Basic Books.

Jensen, A. R. (1980). *Bias in mental testing.* New York: Free Press.

Jensen, A. R. (1981). *Straight talk about mental tests.* New York: Free Press.

Jensen, A. R. (1998). *The g factor: The science of mental ability.* Westport, CT: Praeger.

Kail, R., & Pellegrino, J. W. (1985). *Human intelligence*. New York: Freeman.

Kaufman, A. S. (1993). King WISC the third assumes the throne. *Journal of School Psychology, 31*, 345–354.

Kohlberg, L. N., & Zigler, E. (1967). The impact of cognitive maturity on the development of sex-role attitudes in the years 4 to 8. *Genetic Psychology Monographs, 75*, 89–165.

Lavin, D. E. (1965). *The prediction of academic performance: A theoretical analysis and review of research*. New York: Russell Sage Foundation.

Magnusson, D. (1998). The logic and implications of a person-oriented approach. In R. B. Cairns, L. R. Bergman, & J. Kagan (Eds.), *Methods and models for studying the individual* (pp. 33–64). Thousand Oaks, CA: Sage.

Magnusson, D., & Allen, V. L. (Eds.). (1983). *Human development: An interactional perspective*. New York: Academic Press.

Malkus, U., Feldman, D. H., & Gardner, H. (1988). Dimensions of mind in early childhood. In A. D. Pellegrini (Ed.), *The psychological bases for early education* (pp. 25–38). Chichester, UK: Wiley.

McAllister, C. L., Wilson, P. C., Green, B. L., & Baldwin, J. L. (2005). "Come and take a walk": Listening to early Head Start parents on school-readiness as a matter of child, family, and community health. *American Journal of Public Health, 95*, 617–625.

McCall, R. B. (1977). Childhood IQ's as predictors of adult educational and occupational status. *Science, 197*, 482–483.

Mischel, W. (1968). *Personality and assessment*. Hoboken, NJ: Wiley.

National Association for the Education of Young Children. (2001). *NAEYC at 75: Reflections on the past, challenges for the future*. Washington, DC: Author.

Neisser, U., Boodoo, G., Bourchard, T. J., Boykin, A. W., Brody, N., Ceci, S. J., et al. (1996). Intelligence: Knowns and unknowns. *American Psychologist, 51*, 77–101.

Reed, T. E., & Jensen, A. R. (1992). Conduction velocity in a brain nerve pathway of normal adults correlates with intelligence level. *Intelligence, 16*, 259–272.

Royce, J. R. (1973). *Multivariate analysis and psychological theory*. New York: Academic Press.

Sattler, J. M. (1992). Assessment of children's intelligence. In C. E. Walker & M. C. Roberts (Eds.), *Handbook of clinical child psychology* (2nd ed., pp. 85–100). Oxford, UK: Wiley.

Scarr, S. (1989). Protecting general intelligence: Constructs and consequences for interventions. In R. L. Linn (Ed.), *Intelligence* (pp. 74–118). Urbana: University of Illinois Press.

Snyderman, M., & Rothman, S. (1988). *The IQ controversy, the media and public policy*. New Brunswick, NJ: Transaction.

Spearman, C. (1904). "General intelligence," objectively determined and measured. *American Journal of Psychology, 15*, 201–293.

Spearman, C. (1923). *The nature of "intelligence" and the principles of cognition*. London: Macmillan.

Spearman, C. (1927). *The abilities of man*. London: Macmillan.

Sternberg, R. J., & Detterman, D. K. (Eds.). (1986). *What is intelligence?: Contemporary viewpoints on its nature and definition*. Norwood, NJ: Ablex.

Sternberg, R. J., & Powell, J. S. (1983). Comprehending verbal comprehension. *American Psychologist, 38*, 878–893.

Swick, K. J., Brown, M., & Boutte, G. (1994). African American children and school readiness: An analysis of the issues. *Journal of Instructional Psychology, 21*, 183–191.

Terman, L. M. (1916). *The measurement of intelligence*. Boston: Houghton Mifflin.

Thomson, G. H. (1939). *The factorial analysis of human ability*. London: University of London Press.

Thorndike, E. L. (1921). Intelligence and its measurement: A symposium. *Journal of Educational Psychology, 12*, 123–147.

Thurstone, L. L. (1931). Multiple factor analysis. *Psychological Review, 38*, 406–427.

Thurstone, L. L. (1938). *Primary mental abilities.* Chicago: University of Chicago Press.

Thurstone, L. L. (1946). Theories of intelligence. *Scientific Monthly, 62*, 101–112.

Thurstone, L. L. (1947). *Multiple factor analysis.* Chicago: University of Chicago Press.

Thurstone, L. L., & Thurstone, T. G. (1941). Factorial studies of intelligence. *Psychometric Monographs, 2.*

Vernon, P. E. (1947). Research on personnel selection in the Royal Navy and the British Army. *American Psychologist, 2*, 35–51.

Vernon, P. E. (1950). *The structure of human abilities.* London: Methuen.

Vernon, P. E. (1971). *The structure of human abilities.* London: Methuen.

Wechsler, D. (1958). *The measurement and appraisal of adult intelligence.* Baltimore: Williams & Wilkins.

Wechsler, D. (1997). *Weschsler Adult Intelligence Scale–III.* San Antonio, TX: Psychological Corporation.

Wechsler, D. (2002). *Wechsler Preschool and Primary Scale of Intelligence—Third Edition.* San Antonio, TX: Psychological Corporation.

Wechsler, D. (2003). *Wechsler Intelligence Scale for Children—Fourth Edition.* San Antonio, TX: Psychological Corporation.

Wexler-Sherman, C., Gardner, H., & Feldman, D. H. (1988). A pluralistic view of early assessment: The Project Spectrum approach. *Theory Into Practice, 27*, 77–83.

PART III

SOCIAL AND EMOTIONAL DEVELOPMENT

The socioemotional domain is intertwined with that of children's academic development. Out of necessity we often separate the two domains to examine them in depth. In this section, the authors address social and emotional development, beginning with the initial manifestations of these behaviors in home settings, then moving to the preschool and primary classroom settings.

To begin this section, Ross A. Thompson and Miranda Goodman (Chapter 8) provide a detailed examination of the development of self, relationships, and socioemotional competence as the foundation for early school success. They organize their work into three sections. First is the element of self-development and its relevance to early learning. Here the authors take the reader through a detailed analysis of self-awareness, self-regulation, social and emotional understanding, and initiative in learning. Second, they focus on social interaction skills and strategies that might be especially important to competence in group learning, discussing how children learn to interact with adults who are not their primary caregivers, and with peers. As part of the analysis of interaction skills, they discuss cooperation and responsibility, noting that children are motivated to cooperate because of not only rewards or punishments but also their emotional attachments to their caregivers. Third, the authors examine the importance of relationships within the classroom and at home that influence early learning, and describe how these relationships evolve over time to become more stable and sophisticated.

Following on this work, Susan D. Calkins and Amanda P. Williford (Chapter 9) provide an in-depth analysis of the construct of self-regulation, and demonstrate how self-regulation is related to school readiness. They conceive of self-regulation as a set of specific processes, namely, control mechanisms that function at the biological and behavioral levels. These control mechanism enable an individual to manage arousal, attention, emotion, behavior, and cognition in an adaptive way. Self-regulation begins early in life and continues across the early childhood years. Self-regulation occurs through the acquisition of an integrated set of domain-specific self-regulatory mechanisms, namely, biological, attentional, emotional, behavioral, and cognitive. Each of these mechanisms is examined in depth, and its impact on school functioning is described. Following these descriptions, the authors provide a translation of the research on these domains for educational practices, especially in the preschool setting. Two intervention programs that are effective in preschool and primary grades are then described as accessible tools for teachers and administrators to promote children's self-regulation.

Following these two chapters that present complementary analyses of children's social development, Janet E. Thompson and Kelly K. Twibell (Chapter 10) move the reader into considerations of curriculum principles that can contribute to the growth of many of the capacities identified by Thompson and Goodman in Chapter 8. They illustrate how a well-designed early childhood curriculum can help teachers facilitate the growth of children's cognitive skills and their socioemotional skills, arguing that these two goals are not only compatible but also essential in preschool classrooms. They first present general foundations for the kind of curriculum that can enhance children's social and emotional development. Next, they present three specific foundations that can be used to promote social and emotional development in an early childhood classroom: (1) the design of the classroom environment, (2) important elements of the program's daily routine, and (3) the child's interactions with teachers. Through their presentation, they identify curriculum practices that can encourage the development of specific aspects of social and emotional growth, and illustrate one constructivist curriculum approach that effectively addresses both socioemotional and cognitive skills development.

Taking a much more detailed look within early education classrooms, Kathleen Cranley Gallagher and Patricia R. Sylvester (Chapter 11) examine aspects of children's classroom-based peer relationships and pull from the developmental science findings that suggest ways teachers can support children's social and academic development. They describe four theoretical perspectives that help to frame their discussions: social learning, social information processing, social network, and ecological perspectives. First they consider classroom-based peer relationships among typically developing children ages 3–8 years. They examine the meaning and role of children's friendships, identifying the factors that influence friendships during this time period. Next, they discuss peer groups and the influence of play in children's development. As part of their presentation, they include information on problems in peer relationships, such as bullying and social isolation. They also include a detailed discussion of family, home, and child characteristics (e.g., ability, gender) that influence the development of peer relationships. Specific recommendations are made for teachers and schools for supporting positive peer relationships.

To bring Part III to a close, Oscar A. Barbarin and Erica Odom (Chapter 12) focus our attention on subtle forms of stigmatization and intolerance that take place very early in the lives of young children, resulting in many children's experiences of exclusion from groups and negative evaluations. Going into more depth on issues raised by Gallagher and Sylvester (Chapter 11) on bullying and social isolation, they challenge the reader with questions about how to prepare children to "embrace life in a multicultural world in which differences are respected and getting along with those who are different is valued" (p. 248). They offer definitions of social acceptance and respect for diversity that have implications for educators of young children. In particular, they offer a way of thinking about the attitudes, dispositions, and behaviors related to social acceptance and respect for diversity that leads to positive interventions in the lives of children by sensitive adults. They conclude with a set of specific strategies and activities that teachers can implement to support the development of children's positive attitudes and behaviors, including positive attitudes such as altruism, empathy, tolerance, and fairness toward others, as well as strategies to help children learn to value diversity among their peers and in their lives.

CHAPTER 8

Development of Self, Relationships, and Socioemotional Competence

Foundations for Early School Success

Ross A. Thompson
Miranda Goodman

W hat are the foundational skills that contribute to school readiness and early academic success? This question has been at the heart of public discussion of early achievement for more than a decade. As national attention has focused on how the achievement gap in cognitive and linguistic skills emerges surprisingly early, and as public policy has increasingly focused on standards-based accountability in schools, understanding the determinants of early school success has become increasingly important. From the beginning of this national discussion, educators and researchers have recognized that social and emotional skills are central to early school achievement.

The National Education Goals Panel (1997) was inaugurated in the 1990s, with the national consensus that school children in the United States were poorly prepared for the scientific and technological challenges of the future. In urging that, by the year 2000, "all children shall enter school ready to learn," the Panel outlined five dimensions of school readiness based on the child's (1) health and physical development, (2) emotional well-being and social competence, (3) approaches to learning, (4) communication skills, and (5) cognition and general knowledge. Building on this effort, a consortium of 17 states created the National School Readiness Indicators Initiative (2005) to identify assessments of school readiness that could be used for policymaking and evaluation purposes. Their core readiness indicators comprised six domains—children, families, communities, health services, early care and education, and schools—to emphasize that school readiness is a characteristic of not only young children but also the social systems that surround the child. Within the child domain, indicators of school readiness focused on the child's physical well-being and motor development, social and emotional development, approaches to learning, language development, and cognition and general knowledge. In these two important national initiatives and in other ways, school readiness has been perceived as a function of not only cognitive skills but also socioemotional competence, motivational factors, and other influences.

These broad conceptualizations of school readiness by national panels are not mirrored, however, in how school readiness is presented in state-level early learning standards that shape early childhood education programs and primary grades instruction. In a recent analysis, Scott-Little, Kagan, and Frelow (2006) reported that early learning standards adopted by 46 states strongly emphasize cognitive and language competence, and devote much less attention to socioemotional skills and children's approaches to learning. In some respects, it is understandable that state education administrators who are concerned with boosting early academic achievement would emphasize cognitive and linguistic skills, especially in an era of No Child Left Behind federal legislation that holds schools accountable for student achievement in these areas. Education administrators likely feel that it is best to emphasize the kinds of skills that are crucial to assessments of children's academic success. Indeed, the best predictors of early school reading and math achievement are reading and math test scores taken late in the preschool years (Duncan et al., 2007; LaParo & Pianta, 2000). But the emphasis on cognitive and linguistic abilities does not account for *why* children develop such disparate competencies in learning achievement during the preschool years, nor the factors that can help narrow the early-emerging achievement gap (for an authoritative review of research on this issue, see Bowman, Donovan, & Burns, 2000).

Indeed, quite a different picture of school readiness emerges when kindergarten teachers and the parents of young children are interviewed (National Center for Education Statistics, 1993, 1994). For parents and teachers, two of the three most important qualities for early learning are being "enthusiastic and curious in approaching new activities" and "communicates needs, wants, and thoughts verbally in the child's primary language." Teachers also highly rate "can follow directions," while parents listed "takes turns and shares" and "sits still and pays attention" as essential qualities. The *lowest* rated qualities for both parents and teachers are traditional academic skills such as "knows the letters of the alphabet," "can count to 20 or more," and "able to use pencils or paint brushes," perhaps because these skills can be easily taught in a kindergarten or primary grade classroom. Other surveys of kindergarten teachers indicate that difficulty in emotional or behavioral self-control, limited social skills, and lack of enthusiasm or interest in learning are some of the challenges to school readiness in the young children they teach (see Lewit & Baker, 1995; Rimm-Kaufman, Pianta, & Cox, 2000). Consistent with these concerns, behavioral and emotional problems account for serious problems in the early childhood education classroom and can provoke the removal of the child from the group (Gilliam, 2008; Yoshikawa & Knitzer, 1997).

The importance of socioemotional competencies for school readiness and early academic success remains, therefore, somewhat uncertain. Although national panels and the experience of teachers and parents together indicate that these competencies are important to school success, state-level early learning standards are focused more narrowly on cognitive and language skills. Our purpose in this chapter is to explore the significance of socioemotional development to early school achievement. We address the following questions: Is the development of self, social interaction skills, and relational competencies important to school achievement? What does developmental research indicate about how children grow in these areas during the preschool and early school years? What do we know about their relevance to school readiness and school success? Is there value in efforts to foster these competencies along with the cognitive and linguistic skills that are more typically encouraged in preschool and the early primary grades? How, in general, should we conceptualize school readiness?

This chapter is organized in three sections. The first focuses on elements of self-development (including motivational qualities) relevant to early learning. The second concerns social interaction skills and strategies that might be especially important to competence in group learning. The third section focuses on the importance of relationships within the classroom and at home as influences on early learning. We conclude the chapter with comments that draw together the implications of this discussion for how we should think about school readiness and the foundations of early school success.

This chapter is based on work conducted for the development of the California Preschool Learning Foundations (California Department of Education, 2008), for which Ross A. Thompson was primary author. This state learning foundation document is unusual in that it articulates to early childhood educators the dimensions of socioemotional development relevant to school readiness. Together with companion documents from the California Department of Education on infant–toddler learning foundations and early learning standards in the primary grades, it underscores the multidimensional origins of school success. Although in this chapter we do not discuss the implications of this work for early education practice and instruction, J. Thompson and Twibell (Chapter 10, this volume) describe curricular strategies and classroom practices that can enhance socioemotional growth in an early learning environment that also fosters cognitive, language, and other academic skills.

Development of Self

At the core of learning is the child and the personal qualities that motivate or inhibit new understanding. Children approach new challenges enthusiastically and with confidence in their capabilities or, less often, with disinterest and uncertainty about whether they can discover the answers to the questions that interest them. They approach the classroom environment with capacities for behavioral, cognitive, and emotional self-control and understanding of other people that significantly color their learning experiences. In this section, we consider five aspects of the development of self that are especially relevant to early learning and school success. First, a child's *self-awareness* is important to the self-confidence, conceptions of ability, and self-concept that motivate new learning. Second, classroom learning requires *self-regulation* of attention, thinking, behavior, feelings, and impulses, so that children can cooperate with peers and adults. Third, classroom success also requires *social and emotional understanding*, by which children are able to comprehend and to respect how they differ and are similar to those with whom they learn and work. Fourth, a capacity for *empathy and caring* enlists this understanding into compassionate responses when peers are distressed. Fifth, but perhaps most important to early learning, a child's *initiative in learning* denotes the qualities of curiosity, enthusiasm, and pleasure in discovery that make children active learners and engaged participants in classroom activities. Each of these qualities is discussed in this section.

Self-Awareness

Developmental research shows that early learning is motivated by how children regard themselves as learners, particularly the self-confidence with which they approach new challenges (Dweck & Leggett, 1988). This early-emerging "mastery motivation" can be readily observed in infants and toddlers (MacTurk & Morgan, 1995), and is part of what motivates very young children eagerly to explore their surroundings, to figure out how things work, to persist when initial efforts fail, and to master new skills. This early form of self-awareness grows as children mature through the preschool and early primary grade years to incorporate expanding awareness of themselves as unique physical and psychological individuals (Harter, 1999). A young preschooler's self-awareness is initially based on simple, observable, external and physical attributes and skills (e.g., "I have red hair," "I run fast"). Preschoolers also at times reveal an unrealistically optimistic and positive self-regard that may place them at risk for engaging in behaviors they are not actually capable of completing successfully (e.g., 3-year-olds may try to climb higher on playground equipment than they can safely navigate, or try and fail to solve problems that are not age-appropriate) (Harter & Pike, 1984).

Older preschoolers exhibit a more sophisticated self-awareness that includes internal, psychological characteristics (e.g., "I am nice"). Research has indicated an emerging awareness of these internal traits in children as young as 4 to 5 years old (Marsh, Ellis, & Craven, 2002; Measelle, Ablow, Cowan, & Cowan, 1998). By the kindergarten years, social comparison (e.g., "Tony is bigger than me") has also become an important part of self-awareness and will become ever more important during the elementary school years (Pomerantz, Ruble, Frey, & Greulich, 1995). Taken together, self-concept and self-confidence develop significantly during the preschool and early school years, with significant implications for children's motivation to succeed in academic (and nonacademic) contexts.

How is self-concept shaped? Throughout this period, young children are very sensitive to how significant adults evaluate their behavior and performance, and how adults comment on their characteristics and value (Stipek, 1995; Stipek, Recchia, & McClintic, 1992). Consistent with classic concepts of the "looking-glass self," young children readily incorporate into their self-awareness the evaluations they receive from parents, as well as from teachers and other adults who matter to them. As they become more sensitive to social comparison information and make spontaneous evaluations of themselves in relation to peers, grade schoolers become vulnerable to challenges to self-esteem arising from the discovery that they cannot do the things other children can do, especially if these are valued skills in the classroom or playground (e.g., "Her drawing is nicer than mine"). In these situations, teachers support children's academic motivation when they encourage them to view *progress* in skills development as an important and desirable goal, emphasize their abilities to succeed, and attribute children's failures to lack of effort or persistence—which can be improved—rather than intrinsic ability, which is more difficult to change (Dweck & Leggett, 1988).

Self-Regulation

"Self-regulation" can be viewed as the ability to suppress a dominant response and to perform instead a subdominant response. Thus, it is relevant to a variety of essential capabilities in classroom learning, including concentration of attention (and ignoring distractions from elsewhere or from the child's own impulses), focused thinking (and suppressing irrelevant thoughts or desires), behavior management (and subduing contrary impulses), regulation of sociability (and suppressing antisocial impulses; e.g., aggressive responses), and control of emotions (Kopp, 2002; Thompson, 2002; Thompson & Raikes, 2007). Indeed, several studies have shown that differences in these self-regulatory abilities are predictive of children's math and reading achievement in the early elementary school years (Alexander, Entwisle, & Dauber, 1993; National Institute of Child Health and Human Development [NICHD] Early Child Care Research Network, 2003). In one study, a behavioral measure of attentional self-regulation predicted first-graders' reading achievement scores independently of vocabulary and a prior measure of kindergarten reading ability (Howse, Lange, Farran, & Boyles, 2003). Other studies have shown significant associations between children's self-regulatory skill and independent measures of social competence, conscience development, and psychological adjustment (see, e.g., Eisenberg, Hofer, & Vaughan, 2007; Kochanska & Knaack, 2003; Zelazo & Cunningham, 2007).

The preschool and early grade years witness significant advances in self-regulatory capability in all areas, as reflected in the difference between a toddler's impulsivity and the more socialized, self-controlled conduct of a second-grader. Advances in brain development are one explanation for these achievements, particularly in higher brain regions relevant to self-control (Bunge & Zelazo, 2006; Diamond & Taylor, 1996). Parents also guide the development of strategies of self-control (e.g., coaching children to look away from a forbidden treat or to use words rather than hitting when angry) that children can later use on their own. Parents and teachers also foster the growth of self-regulation as they increasingly use explanations, negotiation, appeals to self-image, and other strategies to enlist children's behavioral cooperation through self-control rather than through the adult's proactive intervention or rewards alone. As a consequence, by the end of the preschool years, young children have begun to master a widening variety of strategies of self-control. With respect to emotion regulation, for example, young children begin to comprehend how their feelings can be managed by seeking another's assistance, avoiding or ignoring emotionally arousing situations (e.g., going to another room when a scary TV show is on), redirecting attention or activity in more emotionally satisfying ways (e.g., quitting a game that one is losing), using reassuring self-talk and, later, through psychological means, such as internal distraction (Thompson, 1990).

As parents and teachers know, however, self-regulatory skills are not well consolidated even by middle childhood, and children of any age vary considerably in their self-control. Beyond parental coaching and other specific strategies, research shows that the general support and sensitivity of parental care foster self-regulatory competence in children; conversely, adult punitiveness and overcontrol undermine it (Fox & Calkins, 2003; see Calkins & Williford, Chapter 9, this volume). Children who live in difficult circumstances may reveal the effects of stress in their deficits in emotional and behavioral self-control in the classroom, playground, or elsewhere (Brooks-Gunn & Duncan, 1997; Shaw, Gilliom, & Ingoldsby, 2003). For this reason, it is important for teachers to be aware that the difficult behavior of a child who cannot pay attention or sit still may arise for many reasons, including family stress, developmental immaturity, inappropriate expectations, or other factors independent of willful obstinacy. Teachers can also encourage competency in the many domains affected by self-regulatory abilities by being mindful of the dramatic differences in self-management between children entering preschool and those getting ready to enter kindergarten. Kindergartners are more persistent in problem-solving tasks, for example, and more capable of following directions (e.g., cleaning up in preparation for another activity), although they still have a long way to go in self-regulatory growth. Moreover, recent research indicates that carefully designed classroom strategies can improve overall levels of self-regulation in preschoolers, which may lead to improved academic and social performance (see Diamond, Barnett, Thomas, & Munro, 2007). Teachers who use activities involving self-regulation, such as encouraging children to talk through their problem-solving strategies and promoting sociodramatic play, may strengthen these skills, and the academic and social competencies with which they are associated.

Social and Emotional Understanding

For a long time, scientists and practitioners believed that young children are egocentric and have considerable difficulty distinguishing their own thoughts and feelings from those of others. New research refutes this view, however, and presents an image of young children who care deeply about the thoughts and feelings of others, and are interested in how those thoughts compare to their own (see Thompson, 2008). With this transformed view of the young child has come the recognition that social and emotional understanding is an essential part of early social competence. Children who are more socially and emotionally perceptive are superior playmates and get along better with adults, and the association between socioemotional understanding and social competence extends from preschool into elementary school (see reviews by Denham, 2006; Denham & Weissberg, 2004). These findings are relevant to school readiness and early academic achievement because of the connections between children's social and scholastic lives. Young children who are more competent in understanding others' feelings have been found, for example, to become more academically competent in elementary school, perhaps because of their more successful peer and adult relationships (Izard, 2002; Izard et al., 2001; see also Raver, 2002; Raver & Knitzer, 2002).

Developmental researchers portray the growth of social and emotional understanding in terms of an emerging "theory of mind"—that is, a child's developing understanding of other people's internal mental states and how these states motivate behavior. Between the ages of 3 and 5, children progress from a theory of mind primarily concerned with how simple desires, feelings, and goals motivate behavior to a more advanced understanding of how people's thoughts and beliefs also contribute to behavior (see Harris, 2006; Wellman, 2002). Children learn that beliefs can be mistaken, which leads to the realization that people can be misled or fooled. Young children also learn that *they* can fool others, and that they can conceal or mask their own feelings and beliefs (e.g., when denying wrongdoing or conveying appreciation for an undesirable gift).

A developing theory of mind leads to other achievements in psychological understanding. One is growth in understanding others' *emotions*. During the preschool years, children become increasingly aware of the psychological basis of emotional experiences (e.g., Joey is mad because he can't go outside to play) (Denham, 1998, 2006; Thompson & Lagatutta, 2006). This awareness leaves them better equipped to understand and interact with their classmates in an increasingly sophisticated fashion. Another significant gain during the later preschool years involves children's *event knowledge*. Children begin to understanding and predict familiar routines, such as those they encounter in their classroom, which contributes to their sense of predictability and control in daily experience (Hudson, 1993; Nelson, 1993). Growing awareness of *diversity* in gender, culture, and ethnicity is another significant development of children's social understanding during the preschool years (Aboud, 2005; see also Chapter 12 by Barbarin & Odom, this volume). Finally, young children begin to grasp the concept of *personality* and how it contributes to stable features of individual behavior (Giles & Heyman, 2005; Heyman & Gelman, 2000).

There are many examples of children's burgeoning social and emotional understanding throughout the preschool and early primary grade years. Although younger preschoolers may notice and comment on their peers' emotional states, their descriptions are likely to be behavioral and focused on external factors (e.g., Sally was *crying* because her toy broke). As children approach the primary school years, however, they become more capable of describing emotions directly and can attribute more complex psychological motives for them. A kindergartner, for example, would be able to recognize that her classmate felt *sad* because he *thought* his mother was not going to arrive to get him, whether or not it was actually true. Children's efforts to describe and explain others' feelings provide opportunities for teachers to discuss children's feelings and their causes, and to help children understand why their peers feel and respond as they do.

Empathy and Caring

An important consequence of young children's increasing social and emotional understanding is their capacity to respond empathically to others in distress. "Empathy" concerns a person's resonant emotional response to another's distress, a response that can be observed even in infants and toddlers. "Caring" concerns a person's efforts to help that distressed person, which often (but not always) derives from empathy. The distinction is important because young children may feel empathy but not yet be capable of acting in a helpful, caring manner. Knowing how to respond to a peer in distress is a difficult task for a young child (more difficult still is responding to a distressed adult), but a failure to help should not be interpreted as a lack of emotional concern in a young child. A 3-year-old may pay close and questioning attention to a crying peer, and may even become mildly upset, but he or she may not reliably offer any genuine assistance to help the situation. Older children, however, may work to cheer a distressed classmate by offering a favorite toy or a hug. As children enter elementary school, their capacity for appropriate and situation-dependent responses increases (Eisenberg, Spinrad, & Sadovsky, 2006; Thompson, 1998). A 5-year-old may offer to help repair a broken toy or to verbally comfort another child by addressing specifically what is bothering the child (e.g., "Don't be scared. It's just a puppet").

Gains in empathy and caring lead to greater social competence and to children who are more actively engaged in the well-being of their classmates, teachers, and the greater school environment. Late in preschool and into the primary grades, children also become more aware of what they perceive as unjust or unfair behavior (Killen, Pisacane, Lee-Kim, & Ardila-Rey, 2001). If a peer is being teased, for example, they may actively come to their defense. Children at the transition between preschool and the primary grades also become more interested in caregiving, whether bringing a special treat for the class pet or offering water to a classmate who is coughing. Teachers can encourage competencies in this domain by allowing their students to be involved in comforting and providing care for other people.

Initiative in Learning

How young children approach the challenges of learning and problem solving is an essential component of their academic success and school competence. Their "initiative in learning," which can be defined as the child's classroom engagement, motivation, and participation, is an important predictor of classroom achievement in kindergarten and throughout elementary school (Alexander et al., 1993; Duncan, Claessens, & Engel, 2005). Children bring to the classroom their natural curiosity and interest in learning, and through positive educational experiences gain confidence in their abilities to make their own intellectual discoveries (Thompson, 2002). This is especially true when parents and teachers actively solicit children's ideas and questions, encourage them to take the lead in investigating a new discovery, and positively affirm their eagerness to learn. There are also important developmental changes in children's initiative, persistence, and enthusiasm in the classroom. Although younger preschoolers approach novel learning situations with confidence and enthusiasm, they are also more likely to experience frustration when confronting difficult problems and give up. Older preschoolers and children in the primary grades show greater persistence and also greater creativity and initiative in their problem solving (Bowman et al., 2000; Renninger, Hidi, & Krapp, 1992).

Though most children have a natural interest in learning and discovery, they bring considerable individual differences, beginning in early childhood, in self-confidence, enthusiasm, and motivation to new learning situations. Several studies have shown that children develop unique learning styles that influence the initiative they take in their learning experiences and how persistent they will be when faced with difficult challenges (Burhans & Dweck, 1995; Dweck, 2002; Dweck & Leggett, 1988). Much of the research has focused on two different orientations toward learning: performance orientation and learning orientation. For a child with a "performance orientation," the primary goal of learning is to elicit positive evaluations from others and to avoid negative judgments. As a consequence, these children may avoid or fail to persist in situations where success is unlikely, and they may miss important educational opportunities. Furthermore, performance-oriented children are vulnerable to developing learned helplessness, whereby they tend to give up after failing due to a lack of confidence in their ability ever to succeed.

For children with a "learning orientation," on the other hand, the purpose of learning is to increase their abilities. A learning-oriented child is more likely to tackle difficult challenges and to persist even if early efforts are unsuccessful. For these reasons, a strong learning orientation best predicts classroom achievement. Differences in learning orientation have been found to emerge as early as the late preschool years (Burhans & Dweck, 1995; Smiley & Dweck, 1994) and may arise from a variety of influences. One of the most important influences is how teachers and parents respond to children's achievement successes and failures: Adults who emphasize children's efforts and intrinsic abilities contribute to the development of a learning orientation in children. Extrinsic motivators, such as stickers or other rewards for good performance, should be used only sparingly, and strong effort should be valued even if it results in initial failure. Young children also need encouragement to persist in their efforts to solve difficult learning challenges.

Another way for adults to encourage persistence and a strong learning orientation in young children is to structure carefully the achievement challenges they offer children. It is important to ensure that these challenges not only are within children's capabilities but also contribute to the development of new knowledge and skills. The development of complex skills can be fostered by teachers who reinforce partial achievements and approximate competence, provide clear explanations and prompts as children are working, and exhibit confidence in the children. In these and other ways, young children have successful learning experiences and develop the self-regard that is part of a strong learning orientation.

Development of Social Interaction Skills

The personal qualities we discussed earlier that contribute to academic achievement are important. But classroom learning is also a group activity in which children's capacities to interact constructively with teachers and peers, and to understand their shared roles and responsibilities as group members are also essential qualities to academic achievement. A young child who cannot cooperate with other children, follow the teacher's instructions, manage transitions in the daily classroom routine, or who fails to perceive him- or herself as both an individual and a member of a "classroom community" is unlikely to benefit as well from classroom instruction as children who can. In this section, therefore, we consider four kinds of social interaction skills that are relevant to classroom competence and early learning. First, children's *interactions with familiar adults* are important for understanding the social skills, trust, and mutual respect that underlie their encounters with teachers, volunteers, and other adults. Second, *interactions with peers* are also important for young children's abilities to work and play constructively with other children in the classroom. Third, we consider children's developing capacities for *cooperation and responsibility*, which involve following instructions and responding appropriately to the behavioral expectations of adults. Finally, we discuss skills of *group participation*, which involve understanding how to participate with other children and adults in shared activity and one's role as a classroom member. Each of these four kinds of social interaction skills is discussed in the pages that follow.

Interactions with Familiar Adults

During the preschool and early school years, children must adjust to regularly interacting with adults who are not their primary attachment figures. These teachers and teacher aides, volunteer staff, center directors or principals, parent volunteers, and other adults are part of the constellation of people with whom children interact in their preschools or early primary grade classrooms. Although these adults do not necessarily serve as sources of comfort and security in the way that children's attachment figures do, children must be able to navigate interactions with them competently to succeed in school because adult–child interactions are essential contributors to classroom learning.

The social capabilities of young children with familiar adults build on many of the developing capacities we discussed earlier (Thompson, Goodvin, & Meyer, 2006).

Interactions with adults require self-regulatory skills, including children's focused attention and behavioral self-control when working with another on a learning activity. Children must be capable of understanding and behaving according to what is expected of them; communicating clearly their ideas, feelings, and experiences; asking questions about things they do not understand; seeking assistance, when necessary; and responding cooperatively as a member of the classroom group. Advances in self-awareness and in socioemotional understanding enable children to function better in a group and to respond more perceptively and appropriately to the behavior of adults and other children—although, as indicated earlier, this ability may be enlisted for purposes of deception and manipulation as children begin to understand how they may deliberately mislead others' thoughts.

Important developmental changes in these capacities occur during the preschool years and early primary grades. A young preschooler shows increasing ease in interacting with adults who become familiar to the child. Children of this age may show off their accomplishments, seek the adult's assistance, and respond to the adult's initiatives or requests with increasing self-confidence. Older preschoolers are capable of greater initiative and engage in more sustained interactions with an adult, such as cooperating with a classroom aide in the give-and-take of solving a problem set, or participating in an extended conversation about the morning's events, with the child contributing new and relevant information. By the primary grades, children understand better the roles of the various adults in the classroom and engage these adults in appropriate ways throughout the day. Adults contribute to these skills when they respond with interest and enthusiasm to children's initiatives, model respectful social interaction and communication, coach children about how to interact with other adults, and encourage children to share their ideas and experiences with confidence.

Interactions with Peers

Beyond the academic skills they acquire, classroom learning presents unparalleled opportunities for young children to develop social skills with peers. Unfortunately, developmental scientists and practitioners have tended to underestimate the skills and sophistication of young children's interactions with peers, focusing instead on episodes of peer conflict as confirmation of young children's egocentrism and limited social interest. Current research has revealed, however, that considerable social understanding underlies preschoolers' capacities to read the cues of other children and respond appropriately, whether in shared tasks, brief conversations, or pretend play. We described the advances in social understanding that enable these peer interaction skills as deriving from young children's developing "theory of mind" and its contributions to greater insight into other children's feelings, goals, desires, thoughts, and ideas. In addition, the preschool years and early primary grades witness significant advances in conflict resolution skills, such that children become more adept and resourceful in their efforts to manage social conflict with other children in a constructive manner. Indeed, rather than an indication of their limited social understanding, conflict with peers is actually an important forum for the development of social understanding and social skills in early childhood.

Because peers are such a significant feature of the classroom environment, interactions with peers are an important influence on academic achievement. Children who have positive peer relationships look forward to coming to school and become more involved in learning activities, thus benefiting more from them. Studies have shown that students with high peer acceptance participate in more classroom activities and achieve more in the classroom (Ladd, Birch, & Buhs, 1999; Ladd, Kochenderfer, & Coleman, 1996, 1997). Peer rejection is a problem not only because of children's feelings of loneliness but also because rejection causes children to withdraw from involvement with peers in the classroom, express a desire to avoid school, and perform more poorly on academic achievement measures (Buhs & Ladd, 2001).

The preschool years and early primary grades are a period of rapid growth in the breadth and sophistication of peer interaction skills (Rubin, Bukowski, & Parker, 2006). Young children advance from simple activity in parallel with one or two playmates to more complex and genuinely interactive activity with several other children. Older preschoolers and kindergartners also become more adept at the skills that make peer interaction go smoothly, including better communication skills, emotional understanding, sharing, and mutual cooperation (e.g., spontaneous turn taking), which are based on the previously discussed advances in social understanding. These are important foundations for elementary school, where classroom group size is typically larger and children are expected to participate in group activities. During the early primary grades, children add to their social repertoires a growing comprehension of fairness in peer interactions (Killen et al., 2001), an expanding range of social problem-solving skills (Crick & Dodge, 1994), and greater emotional understanding and sensitivity (Denham & Weissberg, 2004; Izard et al., 2001). However, it is important to note that in one longitudinal study, kindergarten teacher ratings of social skills *and* aggressiveness were each positively associated with first-grade teachers' ratings of student achievement (Dowsett & Huston, 2005). One interpretation of this finding is that assertiveness, as well as cooperation, may be important to peer acceptance.

Changes in pretend play also reflect these developing social skills. Pretend play is itself a complex activity involving the coordination of behavior of several children in multiple pretend roles according to a shared sociodramatic "script." Yet this hallmark of preschool peer play blossoms in sophistication as young children proceed from brief episodes of pretense to longer, unfolding dramas involving well-coordinated roles, self-correction, and mutual responsiveness (Goncu, 1993; Howes, 1992). By the end of the preschool years, children plan complex pretend-play scenarios, correct each other for deviations from the roles they have assumed, stage-manage new directions in the story flow, and easily integrate new children (and roles) into the activity. That older preschoolers are capable of this kind of complex sociodramatic play confirms our new appreciation of their social understanding and self-regulatory competencies.

Early childhood also witnesses changes in the nature of peer conflict and growth in conflict resolution strategies. Younger preschoolers are more likely to respond to disagreements with physical aggression, whereas older preschoolers may rely more on verbal aggression, such as teasing, that reflects growth in self-control (Tremblay, 2000). When disagreements arise, an older preschooler may also be capable of suggesting simple strategies to alleviate conflict (e.g., offering to take turns playing with the toy truck that several children are fighting over), alternative activities, or negotiation (Howes, 1987, 1988). These conflict resolution strategies, which continue to develop during the elementary school years, are essential to children's social competence and, therefore, to school competence. For this reason, educators should strive to support and assist children in developing and utilizing these skills, as well as help them understand the feelings and viewpoints of other children, suggest and model constructive interaction skills, and reinforce cooperative efforts.

Cooperation and Responsibility

For many years, guided by the theories of Piaget and Kohlberg, researchers viewed young children as being motivated to cooperate by the rewards and punishments of adult authorities (e.g., a preschooler cleans up the art materials so the teacher doesn't get annoyed). However, just as recognition of children's social and emotional competence has evolved in recent decades, so has a new view of the early growth of cooperation and responsibility emerged. Studied under the term "conscience development," this new approach recognizes that children are motivated to cooperate based on not just rewards and punishments but also their emotional attachments to their caregivers, a desire to view themselves with positive regard, and their sensitivity to the feelings of others (Kochanska, 1997, 2002; Thompson, Meyer, & McGinley, 2006).

Because of their strong emotional connections to caregivers, preschoolers seek to cooperate with the adults' expectations from a desire to maintain a mutually cooperative relationship. An adult's disapproving vocal tone after child misbehavior may provoke an apology not only to avert anticipated punishment but also to restore a positive relationship with an adult on whom the young child relies emotionally. Thus, positive relationships with parents, teachers, and other adults are an important resource for the growth of conscience. Furthermore, as young children become increasingly sensitive to the feelings and needs of others, they also are motivated to behave in a way that will not cause distress to other people. By the end of the preschool years, another important resource for conscience development emerges. Young children come to view *themselves* more positively when they cooperate and act responsibility, which further motivates these behaviors. Their positive self-regard when acting in an approved fashion derives in part from the adult approval they obtain, but it is an internal rather than external reward. In short, young children are motivated toward cooperative, responsible conduct because of not only external motivations (rewards and punishments) but also an internal standard of behavior based on a desire to maintain positive relationships with adults who matter, and to view themselves as cooperative and good individuals. This internal standard is a much more mature and reliable basis for cooperative conduct because it does not depend on the responses of adult authorities, and its foundations develop during the preschool years.

The capacity to behave cooperatively and responsibly (an important component of group participation) is a significant predictor of early school success because responsible behavior not only fosters better relationships with teachers and peers but also enhances children's involvement in learning activities (teachers may also pay more attention to children who are cooperative). Research has shown that individual differences in children's cooperation are directly associated with children's early academic achievement. McClelland, Morrison, and Holmes (2000) found, for example, that "work-related skills" in kindergartners (e.g., compliance with instructions; completion of work) predicted children's academic achievement 3 years later, even after they controlled for earlier academic achievement (see also Alexander et al., 1993; Yen, Konold, & McDermott, 2004). Of course, the development of cooperation and responsibility is built on many of the other developmental domains discussed in this chapter. Self-regulation plays a particularly key role because cooperation often requires one to suppress an initial response to comply with a behavioral standard. Developing self-awareness also plays a key role because it enables older preschoolers to view themselves positively and approvingly when they behave cooperatively.

Because much cooperative behavior is directed toward teachers and caregivers, it is relatively easy to witness developmental changes in cooperation and responsibility. Adult support is especially important early in the preschool years, when young children may strive to behave cooperatively but lack the self-regulatory capacities to do so consistently or when strong contrary impulses are involved (e.g., when distressed or frustrated by a peer). Teachers and adult caregivers can provide regular prompts about expected behavior, comment gently about inappropriate conduct, reinforce desirable behavior, and draw attention to children's cooperative conduct as a model for others. Another important contribution that adults provide to the growth of cooperation and responsibility is to ensure that behavioral expectations are developmentally appropriate. When young children are asked to comply with requirements that significantly stretch their capabilities (e.g., expecting 3-year-olds to sit quietly for an extended period), the result is frustration for children, as well as their teachers, and a breakdown in the positive relationships that can be a foundation for cooperative conduct. Children's cooperation is enhanced by a mutually positive adult–child relationship. By contrast, when relations are coercive or adversarial (which can occur when children's behavioral problems are particularly challenging), children may comply when adults are monitoring them but misbehave on other occasions.

Group Participation

In preschool and primary grades, children become part of a "classroom community" that requires them to participate as group members. Children may be expected to practice reading skills in pairs, create small groups for science projects, and participate in whole-group activities. Understanding and applying the roles and responsibilities of group membership contributes to the growth of social interaction skills and include knowing what to do during group routines (e.g., circle time or recess) or games (e.g., Follow the Leader), helping to prepare for and clean up group tasks, understanding and applying rules for classroom behavior (e.g., sharing and taking turns), managing transitions in classroom activities, and participating in group projects. Because most of these aspects of group participation require children to take other children's interests into consideration, they are an important basis for the social skills required of a primary grade classroom. In these ways, group participation skills are essential components of school success.

Fortunately, many of the developmental achievements discussed earlier provide a foundation for these group participation skills. Developing memory skills and event knowledge enables older children to remember daily routines and the behavior that is expected of them (Hudson, 1993; Nelson, 1993). As a result, children anticipate gathering and dismissal activities at the beginning and end of each day, are aware that cleanup activities must precede (and follow) snacks, know what to do before free-play or painting projects, understand how the class prepares for mealtimes, and know what they must do for each activity. Developing event knowledge also helps older children manage transitions better because they can mentally anticipate the activities that follow each transition. Growth in self-regulatory skills in turn enables older children to stay on task better, apply behavioral expectations to their own conduct, and spontaneously self-correct to maintain compliance (Bronson, 2000; Kopp & Wyer, 1994). In addition, advances in behavioral and attentional self-control enable children to focus their interest deliberately on the task at hand, sit still for longer periods of time without fidgeting or becoming distracted, and participate in social activities in which specific timing and turn taking are important (e.g., singing activity songs or playing a board game in which players alternate moves) (Zelazo, Müller, Frye, & Marcovitch, 2003). Furthermore, with growth in self-awareness, young children can view themselves as not just individuals in the classroom but as members of a group (the entire class, a small study group, or a collaborating pair) with cooperative goals and purposes. This capacity also builds on growth in social and emotional understanding that enables children, in the context of group activity, to coordinate their interests and goals with those of other children and adults (Harris, 2006; Thompson, 2006). Finally, their developing sense of cooperation and responsibility, motivated by the desire for adult approval and positive self-regard, enhances older preschoolers' commitment to cooperate with classroom procedures, to anticipate them before being reminded and, at times, to remind other children about them (e.g., "We wash our hands before lunch").

Taken together, a variety of developing capacities contribute to young children's ability to participate constructively as group members. Because these skills are not fully developed, however, children benefit from adults' efforts to offer guidance and coaching, including reminders about expected behavior, explanations about why the procedures are the way they are, prompts (e.g., songs, games, or picture cards) to support effective group participation, and praise and reinforcement of constructive conduct.

Development of Relationships

A central ingredient to school readiness and academic success is the quality of the relationships that young children share with others who are important to them. In their first experience with child care or a classroom, preschoolers arrive with the legacy of a parent–child relationship that has influenced their sense of themselves as learners, their enthusiasm for discovery, and their interactions with other people. As their social worlds expand, close relationships with special teachers, caregivers, and peers color children's experience of learning and motivation to succeed. Because these relationships are important to learning, in this section we consider the influence of three kinds of relationships that are central to early learning. First, we consider *attachments to parents* and the foundation they provide to children's self-confidence, learning skills, and social competence. Second, we examine *close relationships with teachers and caregivers* as a critical feature of the classroom environment to young children. Third, we discuss *friendships with peers* because of the importance of peer acceptance to school adjustment and classroom competence. Each of these three kinds of relationships is discussed below.

Attachments to Parents

Decades of research on early parent–child relationships have shown that young children rely on their attachment figures for emotional security and well-being, and that these relationships influence developing personality, social skills, self-concept, and understanding what other people are like (see Thompson, 2006). Experiences in close relationships tutor young children in understanding and respecting others' views and feelings, in negotiating differences of opinion, in learning to get along with other people, in gaining self-confidence, and in valuing discovery. Perhaps for these reasons attachment relationships also play an important role in the development of early school readiness and school achievement. Children with more secure and supportive parent–child relationships subsequently exhibit greater academic success in kindergarten and the early primary grades, have better work habits, are more socially competent in the classroom, and show fewer conduct problems (Burchinal, Peisner-Feinberg, Pianta, & Howes, 2002; Morrison, Rimm-Kauffman, & Pianta, 2003; NICHD Early Child Care Research Network, 2005; Pianta, Nimetz, & Bennett, 1997). In one longitudinal study, Estrada, Arsenio, Hess, and Holloway (1987) found that a measure of the emotional quality of the mother–child relationship was associated with the child's cognitive competence at age 4, and was predictive of school readiness measures at ages 5 and 6, IQ at age 6, and school achievement at age 12.

Most of this research focuses, of course, on the mother–child relationship in light of mothers' greater involvement in the lives of young children, but it is likely that these conclusions extend also to father–child relationships. Moreover, the significant attachment figures in a child's life do not necessarily have to be biological parents. In some cases nonbiological parents may take full responsibility for the child (e.g., when a child whose biological parents are absent is raised by an aunt and uncle or a grandparent) and these adults become "psychological parents" to the child. On other occasions, nonparents (e.g., a stepparent) may raise the child alongside a biological parent. Any adult who assumes a parenting function in a child's life, regardless of biological ties, can serve as an attachment figure.

As children develop, their relationships with their caregivers change: Children become less dependent on physical proximity and can better tolerate separations, and they become more focused on building a relationship of mutual positive cooperation (Marvin & Britner, 1999). At all ages, of course, children show clear preferences for their primary caregivers, specifically seeking them out for comfort when distressed, taking pleasure in demonstrating their achievements to them, seeking their assistance in problem-solving tasks, enjoying shared activities and experiences with them, and being able to talk about troubling topics that they do not feel comfortable discussing with others. These and other behaviors reflect children's emotional reliance on their attachment figures at every age. As they mature, however, children take greater initiative in seeking the support of their caregivers, and in striving to please and to cooperate with them. They also become capable of better managing separations from their caregivers. Young preschoolers may have difficulty coping with the parent's departure in the morning, especially if they are new to the classroom, and may require comfort from their teachers and support throughout the day. Older preschoolers and children in the primary grades can better cope with separations because they are more able to maintain satisfying mental representations of attachment figures, and the relationship they share sustains them while they are away from their parents. Older children are also more capable of predicting the parent's return, maintaining emotional self-control, and engaging in classroom activities and peer relationships while they are in the classroom.

Although teachers rarely have opportunities to observe directly the quality of children's interactions with their attachment figures, except when parents bring their children to school and later pick them up, their recognition of the importance of these relationships to their students can influence their interactions with children throughout the day. Teachers can make family activities and relationships a topic of discussion in the classroom, encouraging children to bring items from home to share and making the family's culture and language a focus of interest for the class. These activities can contribute significantly to the growth of self-awareness when children are encouraged to take pride in their family identity and experiences. Teachers also respect the importance of attachment relationships when they aid children in managing separations by encouraging children to talk about their family caregivers and when they will return. At times, family relationships are an important source of assistance when children exhibit behavioral or emotional problems in class. On these occasions, consultation with children's attachment figures may create an important bridge between the family and the classroom, helping teachers work with parents in identifying sources of assistance for the child or the family.

Close Relationships with Teachers and Caregivers

Young children develop close relationships with not only nonparental figures at home (e.g., grandparents) but also adults outside the home (Dunn, 1993; Howes, 1999). They rely on their close relationships with certain teachers, caregivers, or other adults for a sense of security, comfort when upset, and support for the challenges of the classroom. This can be observed when a preschooler seeks the assistance of a particular teacher for help (sometimes refusing the assistance of other adults), or when a first-grader eagerly shares an experience at home with a classroom teacher to whom he or she has developed a special attachment. These relationships can motivate excitement about learning, support self-confidence, and foster social development in many of the same ways that parent–child attachments do.

Perhaps for this reason, a number of studies have found that the security and warmth of a preschooler's relationship with the teacher is predictive of subsequent classroom competence, attentional skills, and social competence in the kindergarten and primary grade classroom (Pianta et al., 1997; for reviews, see Bowman et al., 2000; Lamb, 1998). In a similar manner, the quality of the teacher–child relationship in kindergarten and the primary grades is important in children's adaptation to school and their success in the classroom, with conflict in the child–teacher relationship predicting poorer academic performance and greater behavioral problems, sometimes much later in the school years (Birch & Ladd, 1997; Hamre & Pianta, 2001; LaParo & Pianta, 2000; Pianta & Stuhlman, 2004a, 2004b). Children who develop warm, positive relationships with their teachers are more excited about learning, more positive about coming to school, more self-confident, and achieve more in the classroom. A positive teacher–child relationship may be especially important for young children who are otherwise at risk of academic difficulty because of the support it can provide for classroom participation and self-confidence (Pianta, Steinberg, & Rollins, 1995). Thus, there is considerable value in the growth of warm, close relationships between teachers and young children.

The behaviors that indicate a young child has developed a special relationship with a preschool or primary grade teacher are similar to those reflecting parent–child attachment. Children seek comfort, security, and support from the adults with whom they have a close relationship, and prefer that person for shared activity when seeking assistance or approval, displaying accomplishments, and sharing conversation, especially about troubling topics. Children are particularly responsive to these adults' behavioral expectations and expressions of disappointment when they misbehave. This is not to say that young children's close relationships to teachers are the same as parent–child attachments, nor that teacher–child relationships are as important to young children as their relationships with parents (they are not). Rather, children seek support from significant adults in multiple settings, and these special relationships often have shared—as well as unique—meaning for the child. Multiple close relationships with adults at home and elsewhere contribute significantly to young children's social development and psychological well-being, and do not diminish the strength of their parental attachments.

As with the parent–child relationship, children take greater initiative and responsibility for maintaining a mutually positive association with their special teachers as they mature. Preschool and primary grade teachers can respect the importance of the relationships they develop with children by responding positively and supportively to children's initiatives, being enthusiastic about their accomplishments, paying attention when children need assistance or comfort, and recognizing that different adult–child relationships are not interchangeable in young children's worlds. Another way that teachers respect the significance of these relationships to children is by working to develop a friendly, cooperative association with children's attachment figures at home. In these and other ways, close relationships with teachers and adult caregivers provide support for young children's self-confidence and enthusiasm for school.

Friendships with Peers

Friendships with other children provide a foundation for school readiness and academic success because they contribute to children's positive classroom experiences, give them a reason to look forward to coming to school, and contribute to academic achievement (Ladd et al., 1996, 1997, 1999). Interactions with peers are, as we indicated earlier, significant influences on children's classroom experiences, and friendships enhance the significance of peer associations through children's close relationships with one or more special peers.

The sophistication of these friendships increases with age (Parker & Gottman, 1989; Rubin, Coplan, Chen, Buskirk, & Wojslawowicz, 2005; Rubin et al., 2006). During the preschool years, friendships become increasingly stable, exclusive (i.e., a group of friends playing tag may not allow another child to join in the activity) and reciprocal (e.g., mutual assistance when a child is teased by other children). Because older children are also more psychologically aware of the friendships they share, they place a greater value on relationships (e.g., telling a parent that they want to go to school so that they can see their friend). Children engage in more sophisticated forms of play (e.g., complex imaginative play) and greater prosocial behavior with their friends. Somewhat paradoxically, preschoolers direct more affectionate and positive behaviors toward their friends but also engage in more conflict with their friends than with nonfriend peers. Such elevated levels of conflict probably arise because friends spend more time together than do nonfriends. Conflict may also arise because there is greater emotion invested in the interactions of friends, and such emotions can be difficult for young children to manage. As children enter kindergarten, however, they are more likely to negotiate with friends or adopt other strategies to keep conflict from escalating. They are also more capable of maintaining friendships and allowing those relationships to recover from conflict (Gottman, 1983; Hartup, 1996; Parker & Gottman, 1989).

Teachers contribute to the value of friendships when they encourage young children to enjoy shared activities with friends (while remaining vigilant to the consistent exclusion of other children who may wish to join them), helping children to recognize and respond appropriately to the feelings of their friends, and assisting them in conflict resolution. Teachers should also remain watchful for students, particularly near the end of their preschool years, who seem to have formed few close relationships with their peers. Because friendship is such an important predictor of social competence and school success, problems in this area should be taken seriously.

Concluding Comments

There is no doubt that linguistic, literacy, numeracy, and other cognitive skills are essential to school achievement. To acquire the skills needed for success in a complex information and technological society, children must master foundational cognitive skills early in life. But the growth of the mind does not occur independently of other features of early childhood development. Whether children are being home-schooled or tutored, have extensive or no preschool experience, or are being educated in a private or public primary grade school, learning is a social activity that involves skills for interacting with others. Learning also enlists the motivational qualities of the self, particularly the child's curiosity and interest in discovering new things, and the confidence that he or she can succeed in doing so. And because early childhood development depends so significantly on close relationships, the quality of those relationships has significant implications for how children learn. Our conclusion in this chapter is that school readiness and early school achievement enlist significant social and emotional capacities that make early learning a multifaceted process.

Such a conclusion is consistent with research in developmental neuroscience, which indicates the developing brain is a highly integrated organ that does not have independently functioning regions to govern cognition, emotion, sociability, and other basic human capacities (see Eichenbaum, 2003; LeDoux, 1996). Rather, brain areas are mutually influential, such that memory function and cognition are affected by the individual's experience of emotion and stress, and the growth of neurobiological self-regulatory capacities in the prefrontal cortex has implications for cognitive, emotional, attentional, and behavioral self-control (for a review, see Thompson, 2008). This means that a focus on cognitive and linguistic skills alone, without concern for children's social and emotional functioning, risks undermining early learning by ignoring important influences on cognitive growth, especially when children are in stressful or challenging living circumstances. Neurobiologically, as well as developmentally, early learning depends on socioemotional and motivational influences, and the cognitive capacities of the child.

Such a conclusion is also consistent with emerging ideas from economics, particularly the economic science of human capital development (e.g., Cunha, Heckman, Lochner, & Masterov, 2006; Heckman, 2007). Contrary to earlier work in this field, which focused primarily on IQ as an index of early human capital relevant to workforce capability, contemporary economists have devoted increased attention to the influence of "noncognitive abilities," including motivation, self-esteem, self-regulation, and perseverance as important features of the human capital necessary for a skilled workforce. According to these economists, these noncognitive abilities are also important contributors to early cognitive achievement, and have their origins in early childhood development.

Independent of whether schools should strive to foster children's curiosity, self-confidence, prosocial motivation, social skills, and ability to get along with others for their own sake, therefore, a concern with early social and emotional competencies is important to achieving even the core cognitive and linguistic outcomes of school achievement. This is especially true for children at greatest risk of educational failure, who help to account for the early-emergent achievement gap and often live in troubled families, dangerous neighborhoods, poverty, or other conditions of social and emotional challenge. As preschoolers, children from difficult and disadvantaged circumstances show early learning problems coupled with emotional and behavioral difficulties and social skills problems that make it difficult for them to get along with other children in the classroom (Gilliam, 2008). As they enter the primary grades, these children are at greatest risk of being identified as having behavioral problems that are associated with their learning difficulties. To conclude that their school achievement problems are primarily a matter of difficulty in literacy and numeracy skills misses how significantly the emotional, behavioral, motivational, and self-related problems of these children undermine the learning process.

School readiness is multifaceted and unfolds developmentally based on not only the child's competencies but also the support provided for healthy development in the family and other social institutions that surround the young child. In this light, fostering early school achievement is a matter of ensuring that young children have not only acquired mental skills that prepare them for later learning but also the sense of self, competent social skills, and supportive relationships that will help them succeed—and that families, schools, and communities are well-prepared to help them with these accomplishments.

References

Aboud, F. E. (2005). The development of prejudice in childhood and adolescence. In J. F. Dovidio, P. Glick, & L. A. Rudman (Eds.), *On the nature of prejudice: Fifty years after Allport* (pp. 310–326). Malden, MA: Blackwell.

Alexander, K. L., Entwisle, D. R., & Dauber, S. L. (1993). First grade classroom behavior: Its short- and long-term consequences for school performance. *Child Development, 64,* 801–814.

Birch, S., & Ladd, G. W. (1997). The teacher–child relationship and children's early school adjustment. *Journal of School Psychology, 35,* 61–79.

Bowman, B. T., Donovan, M. S., & Burns, M. S. (Eds.). (2000). *Eager to learn: Educating our preschoolers* (Report of the Committee on Early Childhood Pedagogy, National Research Council). Washington, DC: National Academy Press.

Bronson, M. B. (2000). *Self-regulation in early childhood: Nature and nurture.* New York: Guilford Press.

Brooks-Gunn, J., & Duncan, G. J. (1997). The effects of poverty on children. *The Future of Children, 7,* 55–71.

Buhs, E. S., & Ladd, G. W. (2001). Peer rejection as an antecedent of young children's school adjustment: An examination of mediating processes. *Developmental Psychology, 37,* 550–560.

Bunge, S. A., & Zelazo, P. D. (2006). A brain-based account of the development of rule use in childhood. *Current Directions in Psychological Science, 15,* 118–121.

Burchinal, M. R., Peisner-Feinberg, E., Pianta, R., & Howes, C. (2002). Development of academic skills from preschool through second grade: Family and classroom predictors of developmental trajectories. *Journal of School Psychology, 40,* 415–436.

Burhans, K. K., & Dweck, C. S. (1995). Helplessness in early childhood: The role of contingent worth. *Child Development, 66,* 1719–1738.

California Department of Education. (2008). *California preschool learning foundations: Vol. 1. Social–emotional development, language and literacy, English-language development, mathematics.* Sacramento: Author.

Crick, N. R., & Dodge, K. A. (1994). A review and reformulation of social information processing mechanisms in children's social adjustment. *Psychological Bulletin, 115,* 74–101.

Cunha, F., Heckman, J. J., Lochner, L., & Masterov, D. V. (2006). Interpreting the evidence on life cycle skill formation. In F. Welch & E. Hanushek (Eds.), *The handbook of the economics of education* (pp. 697–812). Amsterdam: North Holland.

Denham, S. A. (1998). *Emotional development in young children.* New York: Guilford Press.

Denham, S. A. (2006). The emotional basis of learning and development in early childhood education. In B. Spodek & O. N. Saracho (Eds.), *Handbook of research on the education of young children* (2nd ed., pp. 85–103). Mahwah, NJ: Erlbaum.

Denham, S. A., & Weissberg, R. P. (2004). Social–emotional learning in early childhood: What we know and where to go from here? In E. Chesebrough, P. King, T. P. Gullotta, & M. Bloom (Eds.), *A blueprint for the promotion of prosocial behavior in early childhood* (pp. 13–50). New York: Kluwer Academic/Plenum Press.

Diamond, A., Barnett, W. S., Thomas, J., & Munro, S. (2007). Preschool program improves cognitive control. *Science, 318,* 1387–1388.

Diamond, A., & Taylor, C. (1996). Development of an aspect of executive control: Development of the abilities to remember what I said and to "do as I say, not as I do." *Developmental Psychobiology, 29,* 315–334.

Dowsett, C., & Huston, A. (2005, April). The role of social–emotional behavior in school readiness. In G. Duncan (Chair), *Hard skills and socioemotional behavior at school entry: What matters most for subsequent achievement?* Symposium presented to the biennial meeting of the Society for Research in Child Development, Atlanta, GA.

Duncan, G. J., Claessens, A., & Engel, M. (2005, April). The contributions of hard skills and socioemotional behavior to school readiness in the ECLS-K. In G. Duncan (Chair), *Hard skills and socioemotional behavior at school entry: What matters most for subsequent achievement?* Symposium presented to the biennial meeting of the Society for Research in Child Development, Atlanta, GA.

Duncan, G. J., Dowsett, C. J., Claessens, A., Magnuson, K., Huston, A. C., Klebanov, P., et al. (2007). School readiness and later achievement. *Developmental Psychology, 43,* 11428–1446.

Dunn, J. (1993). *Young children's close relationships: Beyond attachment.* Newbury Park, CA: Sage.

Dweck, C. S. (2002). The development of ability conceptions. In A. Wigfield & J. S. Eccles (Eds.), *Development of achievement motivation* (pp. 57–88). San Diego, CA: Academic Press.

Dweck, C. S., & Leggett, E. L. (1988). A social-cognitive approach to motivation and personality. *Psychological Review, 95,* 256–273.

Eichenbaum, H. (2003). Learning and memory: Brain systems. In L. R. Squire, F. E. Bloom, S. K. McConnell, J. L. Roberts, N. C. Spitzer, & M. J. Zigmond (Eds.), *Fundamental neuroscience* (2nd ed., pp. 1299–1327). New York: Academic Press.

Eisenberg, N., Hofer, C., & Vaughan, J. (2007). Effortful control and its socioemotional consequences. In J. J. Gross (Ed.), *Handbook of emotion regulation* (pp. 287–306). New York: Guilford Press.

Eisenberg, N., Spinrad, T. L., & Sadovsky, A. (2006). Empathy-related responding in children. In M. Killen & J. G. Smetana (Eds.), *Handbook of moral development* (pp. 517–549). Mahwah, NJ: Erlbaum.

Estrada, P., Arsenio, W. F., Hess, R. D., & Holloway, S. D. (1987). Affective quality of the mother–child relationship: Longitudinal consequences for children's school-relevant cognitive functioning. *Developmental Psychology, 23,* 210–215.

Fox, N., & Calkins, S. (2003). The development of self-control of emotion: Intrinsic and extrinsic influences. *Motivation and Emotion, 27,* 7–26.

Giles, J. W., & Heyman, G. D. (2005). Preschoolers use trait-relevant information to evaluate the appropriateness of an aggressive response. *Aggressive Behavior, 31,* 498–509.

Gilliam, W. S. (2008). *Implementing policies to reduce the likelihood of preschool expulsion* (FCD Policy Brief No. 7). New York: Foundation for Child Development.

Goncu, A. (1993). Development of intersubjectivity in the dyadic play of preschoolers. *Early Childhood Research Quarterly, 8,* 99–116.

Gottman, J. M. (1983). How children become friends. *Monographs of the Society for Research in Child Development, 48*(Serial No. 201).

Hamre, B. K., & Pianta, R. C. (2001). Early teacher–child relationships and the trajectory of children's school outcomes through eighth grade. *Child Development, 72,* 625–638.

Harris, P. (2006). Social cognition. In W. Damon & R. M. Lerner (Series Eds.) & D. Kuhn & R. Siegler (Vol. Eds.), *Handbook of child psychology: Vol. 2. Cognition, perception, and language* (6th ed., pp. 811–858). New York: Wiley.

Harter, S. (1999). *The construction of the self: A developmental perspective.* New York: Guilford Press.

Harter, S., & Pike, R. (1984). The pictorial scale of perceived competence and social acceptance for young children. *Child Development, 55,* 1969–1982.

Hartup, W. W. (1996). The company they keep: Friendships and their developmental significance. *Child Development, 67,* 1–13.

Heckman, J. J. (2007). The economics, technology, and neuroscience of human capability formation. *Proceedings of the National Academy of Sciences USA, 104,* 13250–13255.

Heyman, G. D., & Gelman, S. A. (2000). Preschool children's use of trait labels to make inductive inferences. *Journal of Experimental Child Psychology, 77,* 1–19.

Howes, C. (1987) Social competence with peers in young children: Developmental sequences. *Developmental Review, 7,* 252–272.

Howes, C. (1988). Peer interaction of young children. *Monographs of the Society for Research in Child Development, 53*(Serial No. 217).

Howes, C. (1992). *The collaborative construction of pretend.* Albany: State University of New York Press.

Howes, C. (1999). Attachment relationships in the context of multiple caregivers. In J. Cassidy & P. R. Shaver (Eds.), *Handbook of attachment* (pp. 671–687). New York: Guilford Press.

Howse, R. B., Lange, G., Farran, D. C., & Boyles, C. D. (2003). Motivation and self-regulation as predictors of achievement in economically disadvantaged young children. *Journal of Experimental Education, 71,* 151–174.

Hudson, J. (1993). Understanding events: The development of script knowledge. In M. Bennett (Ed.), *The child as psychologist: An introduction to the development of social cognition* (pp. 142–167). New York: Harvester Wheatsheaf.

Izard, C., Fine, S., Schultz, D., Mostow, A., Adkerman, B., & Youngstrom, E. (2001). Emotion knowledge as a predictor of social behavior and academic competence in children at risk. *Psychological Science, 12,* 18–23.

Izard, C. E. (2002). Emotion knowledge and emotion utilization facilitate school readiness. *Social Policy Report, 16,* 7.

Killen, M., Pisacane, K., Lee-Kim, J., & Ardila-Rey, A. (2001). Fairness or stereotypes?: Young children's priorities when evaluating group exclusion or inclusion. *Developmental Psychology, 37,* 587–596.

Kochanska, G. (1997). Mutually responsive orientation between mothers and their young children: Implications for early socialization. *Child Development, 68,* 94–112.

Kochanska, G. (2002). Committed compliance, moral self, and internalization: A mediated model. *Developmental Psychology, 38,* 339–351.

Kochanska, G., & Knaack, A. (2003). Effortful control as a personality characteristic of young children: Antecedents, correlates, and consequences. *Journal of Personality, 71,* 1087–1112.

Kopp, C., & Wyer, N. (1994). Self-regulation in normal and atypical development. In D. Cicchetti & S. L. Toth (Eds.), *Disorders and dysfunctions of the self: Rochester Symposium on Developmental Psychopathology* (Vol. 5, pp. 31–56). Rochester, NY: University of Rochester Press.

Kopp, C. B. (2002). School readiness and regulatory processes. *Social Policy Report, 16,* 11.

Ladd, G. W., Birch, S. H., & Buhs, E. S. (1999). Children's social and scholastic lives in kindergarten: Related spheres of influence? *Child Development, 70,* 1373–1400.

Ladd, G. W., Kochenderfer, B. J., & Coleman, C. C. (1996). Friendship quality as a predictor of young children's early school adjustment. *Child Development, 67,* 1103–1118.

Ladd, G. W., Kochenderfer, B. J., & Coleman, C. C. (1997). Classroom peer acceptance, friendship, and victimization: Distinct relational systems that contribute uniquely to children's school adjustment? *Child Development, 68,* 1181–1197.

Lamb, M. E. (1998). Nonparental child care: Context, quality, correlates. In W. Damon (Ed.) & I. E. Sigel & K. A. Renninger (Vol. Eds.), *Handbook of child psychology: Vol. 4. Child psychology in practice* (5th ed., pp. 73–134). New York: Wiley.

LaParo, K. M., & Pianta, R. C. (2000). Predicting children's competence in the early school years: A meta-analytic review. *Review of Educational Research, 70,* 443–484.

LeDoux, J. E. (1996). *The emotional brain.* New York: Simon & Schuster.

Lewit, E. M., & Baker, L. S. (1995). School readiness. *The Future of Children, 5,* 128–139.

MacTurk, R. H., & Morgan, G. A. (Eds.). (1995). *Mastery motivation: Origins, conceptualizations, and applications.* Norwood, NJ: Ablex.

Marsh, H., Ellis, L., & Craven, R. (2002). How do preschool children feel about themselves?: Unraveling measurement and multidimensional self-concept structure. *Developmental Psychology, 38,* 376–393.

Marvin, R. S., & Britner, P. A. (1999). Normative development: The ontogeny of attachment. In J. Cassidy & P. R. Shaver (Eds.), *Handbook of attachment: Theory, research, and clinical applications* (pp. 44–67). New York: Guilford Press.

McClelland, M. M., Morrison, F. J., & Holmes, D. L. (2000). Children at risk for early academic problems: The role of learning-related social skills. *Early Childhood Research Quarterly, 15,* 307–329.

Measelle, J., Ablow, J., Cowan, P., & Cowan, C. (1998). Assessing young children's views of their academic, social, and emotional lives: An evaluation of the self-perception scales of the Berkeley Puppet Interview. *Child Development, 69*, 1556–1576.

Morrison, E. F., Rimm-Kauffman, S., & Pianta, R. C. (2003). A longitudinal study of mother–child interactions at school entry and social and academic outcomes in middle school. *Journal of School Psychology, 41*, 185–200.

National Center for Education Statistics. (1993). *Public school kindergarten teachers' views on children's readiness for school* (NCES 93-410). Washington, DC: U.S. Department of Education.

National Center for Education Statistics. (1994). *National Household Education Survey of 1993: School readiness data file user's manual* (NCES 94-193). Washington, DC: U.S. Department of Education.

National Education Goals Panel. (1997). *The National Education Goals Report, 1997: Building a nation of learners*. Washington, DC: U.S. Government Printing Office.

National School Readiness Indicators Initiative. (2005). *Getting ready: Findings from the National School Readiness Indicators Initiative*. Providence: Rhode Island Kids Count.

Nelson, K. (1993). Events, narratives, memory: What develops? In C. Nelson (Ed.), *Memory and affect in development: Minnesota Symposia on Child Psychology* (Vol. 26, pp. 1–24). Hillsdale, NJ: Erlbaum.

NICHD Early Child Care Research Network. (2003). Do children's attention processes mediate the link between family predictors and school readiness? *Developmental Psychology, 39*, 581–593.

NICHD Early Child Care Research Network. (2005). Predicting individual differences in attention, memory, and planning in first graders from experiences at home, child care, and school. *Developmental Psychology, 41*, 99–114.

Parker, J. G., & Gottman, J. M. (1989). Social and emotional development in a relational context: Friendship interaction from early childhood to adolescence. In T. J. Berndt & G. W. Ladd (Eds.), *Peer relations in child development* (pp. 15–45). New York: Wiley.

Pianta, R. C., Nimetz, S. L., & Bennett, E. (1997). Mother–child relationships, teacher–child relationships, and school outcomes in preschool and kindergarten. *Early Childhood Research Quarterly, 12*, 263–280.

Pianta, R. C., Steinberg, M. S., & Rollins, K. B. (1995). The first two years of school: Teacher–child relationships and deflections in children's classroom adjustment. *Development and Psychopathology, 7*, 295–312.

Pianta, R. C., & Stuhlman, M. W. (2004a). Conceptualizing risk in relational terms: Associations among the quality of child–adult relationships prior to school entry and children's developmental outcomes in first grade. *Educational and Child Psychology, 21*, 32–45.

Pianta, R. C., & Stuhlman, M. W. (2004b). Teacher–child relationships and children's success in the first years of school. *School Psychology Review, 33*, 444–458.

Pomerantz, E. M., Ruble, D. N., Frey, K. S., & Greulich, F. (1995). Meeting goals and confronting conflict: Children's changing perceptions of social comparison. *Child Development, 66*, 723–738.

Raver, C. C. (2002). Emotions matter: Making the case for the role of young children's emotional development for early school readiness. *Social Policy Report, 16*, 3–18.

Raver, C. C., & Knitzer, J. (2002). *Ready to enter: What research tells policymakers about strategies to promote social and emotional school readiness among three- and four-year-old children*. New York: National Center for Children in Poverty.

Renninger, K. A., Hidi, S., & Krapp, A. (Eds.). (1992). *The role of interest in learning and development*. Hillsdale, NJ: Erlbaum.

Rimm-Kaufman, S. E., Pianta, R. B., & Cox, M. J. (2000). Teachers' judgments of problems in the transition to kindergarten. *Early Childhood Research Quarterly, 15*, 147–166.

Rubin, K. H., Bukowski, W. M., & Parker, J. G. (2006). Peer interactions, relationships, and groups. In W. Damon & R. M. Lerner (Eds.) & N. Eisenberg (Vol. Ed.), *Handbook of child psychology: Vol. 3. Social, emotional, and personality development* (6th ed., pp. 571–645). New York: Wiley.

Rubin, K. H., Coplan, R. J., Chen, X., Buskirk, A. A., & Wojslawowicz, J. C. (2005). Peer relationships in childhood. In M. H. Bornstein & M. E. Lamb (Eds.), *Developmental science: An advanced textbook* (5th ed., pp. 469–512). Mahwah, NJ: Erlbaum.

Scott-Little, C., Kagan, S. L., & Frelow, V. S. (2006). Conceptualization of readiness and the content of early learning standards: The intersection of policy and research? *Early Childhood Research Quarterly, 21*, 153–173.

Shaw, D. S., Gilliom, M., & Ingoldsby, E. M. (2003). Trajectories leading to school-age conduct problems [Special issue: Violent children]. *Developmental Psychology, 39*, 189–200.

Smiley, P. A., & Dweck, C. S. (1994). Individual differences in achievement goals among young children. *Child Development, 65*, 1723–1743.

Stipek, D. (1995). The development of pride and shame in toddlers. In J. P. Tangney & K. W. Fischer (Eds.), *Self-conscious emotions* (pp. 237–252). New York: Guilford Press.

Stipek, D., Recchia, S., & McClintic, S. (1992). Self-evaluation in young children. *Monographs of the Society for Research in Child Development, 57*(Serial No. 226).

Thompson, R. A. (1990). Emotion and self-regulation. In R. A. Thompson (Ed.), *Socioemotional development: Nebraska Symposium on Motivation* (Vol. 36, pp. 383–483). Lincoln: University of Nebraska Press.

Thompson, R. A. (1998). Empathy and its origins in early development. In S. Braten (Ed.), *Intersubjective communication and emotion in early ontogeny* (pp. 144–157). Cambridge, UK: Cambridge University Press.

Thompson, R. A. (2002). The roots of school readiness in social and emotional development. *Kauffman Early Education Exchange, 1*, 8–29.

Thompson, R. A. (2006). The development of the person: Social understanding, relationships, self, conscience. In W. Damon & R. M. Lerner (Eds.) & N. Eisenberg (Vol. Ed.), *Handbook of child psychology: Vol. 3. Social, emotional, and personality development* (6th ed., pp. 24–98). New York: Wiley.

Thompson, R. A. (2008). The psychologist in the baby. *Zero to Three, 28*(5), 5–12.

Thompson, R. A. (2008, December). Connecting neurons, concept, and people: Brain development and its implications. In National Institute for Early Education Research (Ed.), *NIEER Preschool Policy Brief*, issue 17.

Thompson, R. A., Goodvin, R., & Meyer, S. (2006). Social development: Psychological understanding, self understanding, and relationships. In J. L. Luby (Ed.), *Handbook of preschool mental health: Development, disorders, and treatment* (pp. 3–22). New York: Guilford Press.

Thompson, R. A., & Lagatutta, K. (2006). Feeling and understanding: Early emotional development. In K. McCartney & D. Phillips (Eds.), *The Blackwell handbook of early childhood development* (pp. 317–337). Oxford, UK: Blackwell.

Thompson, R. A., Meyer, S., & McGinley, M. (2006). Understanding values in relationship: The development of conscience. In M. Killen & J. Smetana (Eds.), *Handbook of moral development* (pp. 267–297). Mahwah, NJ: Erlbaum.

Thompson, R. A., & Raikes, H. A. (2007). The social and emotional foundations of school readiness. In D. F. Perry, R. F. Kaufmann, & J. Knitzer (Eds.), *Social and emotional health in early childhood: Building bridges between services and systems* (pp. 13–35). Baltimore: Brookes.

Tremblay, R. E. (2000). The development of aggressive behaviour during childhood: What have we learned in the past century? *International Journal of Behavioral Development, 24*, 129–141.

Wellman, H. (2002). Understanding the psychological world: Developing a theory of mind. In U. Goswami (Ed.), *Handbook of childhood cognitive development* (pp. 167–187). Oxford, UK: Blackwell.

Yen, C.-J., Konold, T. R., & McDermott, P. A. (2004). Does learning behavior augment cognitive ability as an indicator of academic achievement? *Journal of School Psychology, 42,* 157–169.

Yoshikawa, H., & Knitzer, J. (1997). *Lessons from the field: Head Start mental health strategies to meet changing needs.* New York: National Center for Children in Poverty.

Zelazo, P. D., & Cunningham, W. A. (2007). Executive function: Mechanisms underlying emotion regulation. In J. J. Gross (Ed.), *Handbook of emotion regulation* (pp. 135–158). New York: Guilford Press.

Zelazo, P. D., Müller, U., Frye, D., & Marcovitch, S. (2003). The development of executive function. *Monographs of the Society for Research in Child Development, 68*(Serial No. 274).

CHAPTER 9

Taming the Terrible Twos
Self-Regulation and School Readiness

Susan D. Calkins
Amanda P. Williford

Overview: The Construct of Self-Regulation

Developmental science is continually evolving to reflect new ways of thinking about development and new methodologies for studying it. For instance, our knowledge of factors that affect children's development has changed considerably with the advent of methods for studying genetic and biological contributions to this development. And as the understanding of the role of these genetic and biological processes has grown, a shift in focus has occurred in our understanding of *how* specific behavioral developments emerge and influence children's outcomes. Researchers have come to see development as a dynamic process involving interactions between the child and his or her environment that affect development at both a biological and behavioral level (e.g., Blair, 2002; Wachs, 1999). Thus, not only does a child's genetic and biological makeup affect how he or she approaches the environment, but the interaction with the environment also affects the child's biological system.

As an illustration of how biology affects children's early behaviors and may be shaped by the environment, consider a toddler who has a very reactive physiology (i.e., is hypersensitive, easily alarmed, and very tentative when approaching new things) and is faced with the task of entering a neighbor's home for the first time. The child reacts with increased vigilance and clings to the mother. Rather than becoming frustrated with her toddler, the mother can hold the child, calmly state that they are "in a new house but it's a safe place," and sit down to let the child observe the surroundings. The mother can talk quietly with the neighbor, while continuing to hold the child (rather than forcing the child out of her lap), and give the child adequate time to relax physically and become stimulated by the new environment. Eventually the toddler will tentatively leave the mother's lap to explore the living room. Over time, these repeated experiences with new environments, coupled with the mother's sensitive responsiveness allow the child's biological system to adapt, and the child develops coping mechanisms when faced with new environments. Eventually, the child takes less time to begin independently interacting with new stimuli. And these early environmental experiences shape how this toddler will approach entering the new preschool environment—we hope with interest and engagement as opposed to fearfulness and disengagement. The fundamental processes that are important for this transition to take place center on the child's emerging ability to self-regulate and illustrate why it is important for such shifts in our understanding of children's development to translate into practices that encourage children's adaptive adjustment and achievement via a focus on this set of skills.

Domains of Self-Regulation

An important dynamic process in developmental psychology that has been the focus of considerable recent theorizing and research is the development of *self-regulation*. Very broadly, "self-regulation" can be defined as one's *own* ability to control emotions and behaviors to cope effectively with environmental demands. Although the term "self-regulation" has been used as a rubric for a wide range of behaviors, we use the term to refer to a *specific* set of processes: control mechanisms functioning at the biological and behavioral level that enable an individual to manage arousal, attention, emotion, behavior, and cognition in an adaptive way (Baumeister & Vohs, 2004).

Figure 9.1, a visual depiction of the elements of self-regulation that we view as critical to children's early functioning in a wide variety of situations, illustrates that the development of self-regulation is marked by the acquisition of an integrated set of domain-specific (biological, attentional, emotional, behavioral, cognitive) self-regulatory mechanisms that are hierarchical in nature, and that build upon each other. Figure 9.1 also emphasizes that self-regulatory skills begin to develop very early in life and substantially across all domains during the early childhood years. Children use

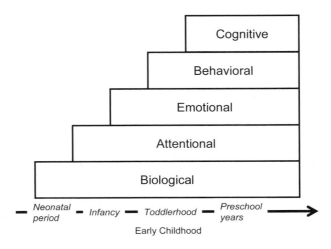

FIGURE 9.1. Self-regulation conceptualized and measured across multiple domains during early childhood.

self-regulatory processes to control fear, to pay attention during school, to follow directions, and to negotiate with parents. From a translational perspective, understanding
how these skills develop is critical to facilitating their development and deployment in
the school setting.

Toddlerhood provides a compelling window to self-regulation because its characteristically challenging behavior stems largely from the newfound ability of the toddler to
exercise control over him- or herself. This ability to self-regulate enables the toddler to
be autonomous from the caregiver in many ways; this autonomy is reflected by the defi-
ance so frequently observed in toddlers during this time. Additionally, self-regulatory
skills within the emotional and behavioral domains are just becoming part of the child's
repertoire and have not fully developed. Most toddlers can delay gratification for a few
moments (e.g., by being able to wait momentarily while the mother retrieves her keys,
rather than running out the door). However, the ability to regulate behaviors and emotions at this age is fragile and short-lived (e.g., if the mother now decides to answer the
ringing phone and take a call, then the toddler's ability to wait is challenged and he or
she may run out the door or display a temper tantrum). The transition through toddlerhood to preschool, and the subsequent transition to the early primary school years, is
marked by the substantial development of self-regulation, particularly in the emotional,
behavioral, and cognitive domains. In this chapter, we provide a description of each
of the different domains of self-regulation, how these domains appear and function in
toddlerhood and early childhood and, importantly, how these domains relate to early
school success.

Self-Regulation as an Element of School Readiness

"School readiness" can be broadly defined as the skills observable at school entry that
are necessary for later school success (Snow, 2006). Whereas the focus of school readiness has often been on preliteracy and premath skills, more recently school readiness
has been recognized as a multidimensional construct that also includes early social
and emotional competence (Bierman, Nix, Greenberg, Blair, & Domitrovich, 2008;
Webster-Stratton, Reid, & Stoolmiller, 2008). Kindergarten teachers report that the
mastery of basic skills, such as working independently, understanding and following
classroom rules and routines, and sharing and taking turns, is more important than
the mastery of academic skills for future school readiness (Rimm-Kaufman, Pianta, &
Cox, 2000). Moreover, researchers have demonstrated that social competence in young
children serves as a protective factor against later academic, behavioral, and/or emotional problems (Barkley et al., 2002; Repetti, Taylor, & Seeman, 2002), and that early
socioemotional skills predict later academic achievement (see Raver & Knitzer [2002]
for a review; Shields et al., 2001; Trentacosta & Izard, 2007).

This broad conceptualization of readiness underscores the importance of self-
regulatory processes for future school success and of the development of self-regulatory
skills during early childhood as critical components of school readiness (Bierman et al.,
2008; Blair, 2002; Webster-Stratton et al., 2008). Blair (2002) describes self-regulation
as a core feature of school readiness—one that "underlie[s] many of the behaviors and
attributes that are associated with successful school adjustment" (p. 112). In the following pages, we highlight research that illustrates how the development of the different
domains of self-regulation relate to early school functioning.

A Longitudinal Study of the Development of Self-Regulatory Processes

To help frame our discussion on self-regulation we provide a brief overview of our own longitudinal research as a concrete example of how the development of self-regulation is studied in children and as an introduction to how self-regulation impacts children's development across a broad array of areas, including early school functioning. The RIGHT Track research project began with a group of 450 two-year-olds and their mothers (Calkins, Blandon, Williford, & Keane, 2007; Calkins & Keane, 2004; Williford, Calkins, & Keane, 2007). Children were recruited from the community by having mothers complete a behavior problems questionnaire that emphasized *externalizing* or *acting-out* problems seen in toddlers (Child Behavior Checklist for Ages 2–3 [CBCL/2–3], Achenbach, 1991). We oversampled for children who were behaviorally at risk, and 29% of these toddlers were identified by their mothers as being particularly difficult to manage (more temper tantrums, more difficult to soothe, more easily frustrated, and cried more frequently compared to the typical 2-year-old). When the children were age 2, mothers and toddlers participated in laboratory assessments that measured the different domains of self-regulation. Each mother was asked to report on her child's, her own, and her family's functioning. We conducted similar visits at later ages. The self-regulation tasks were adapted at each time point, so that they were age appropriate.

In addition to laboratory assessments, we also assessed children's functioning in the classroom when children entered day care, preschool, or formal schooling (kindergarten) (Keane & Calkins, 2004). We asked teachers to report on children's behavioral, emotional, and academic functioning; beginning in kindergarten, we added a peer assessment to measure how socially successful children were in making and keeping friends. Thus, we have used a multimethod, multi-informant approach to gather information about children's ability to control themselves in individual tasks and in the school and peer settings.

The data collected to this point have provided evidence of the importance of self-regulation skills for children's development across many areas of functioning. Of particular relevance to this chapter are results indicating that children who displayed deficits in emotion regulation in preschool also displayed problems with behavioral regulation in the kindergarten classroom, which predicted quality of academic performance in literacy and math at the end of the kindergarten year (Howse, Calkins, Anastopoulos, Keane, & Shelton, 2003). In a follow-up study, we found that kindergartners who were reported by their parents to regulate their emotions effectively had greater early math and literacy skills, and their teachers reported that they were more academically successful in the classroom (Graziano, Reavis, Keane, & Calkins, 2007). These examples of our findings emphasize that self-regulation skills are important for early school success.

Summary

This review of the current science and our own research points to the utility of understanding self-regulatory processes and using specific strategies to encourage the development of specific self-regulation skills to promote successful achievement during early childhood. Below we describe the normative development of self-regulation within the separate domains and provide evidence for the importance of self-regulation in the school domain. We follow this normative description with a discussion of how knowledge about the early development of self-regulation can translate into classroom practices during preschool, kindergarten, and the early primary grades. Finally, we suggest areas of new knowledge that might be explored by developmental scientists as a way to refine our understanding of how self-regulation in young children may be fostered within the classroom to increase children's success in school.

The Development of Self-Regulation and Its Impact on School Functioning

In this section we examine how marked developments in a broad range of adaptive skills that are characteristic achievements of toddlerhood, including self-control, autonomy, and compliance, are a function of foundational regulatory developments in biology, attention, and emotion. As depicted in Figure 9.1, developments across these domains are hierarchically organized, with basic biological processes contributing to developments in emotional and cognitive functioning (Calkins, 2007; Calkins, Graziano, & Keane, 2007). Toddlerhood is a developmental period marked by an emerging self-concept that allows children to see themselves as capable of independent action, and by linguistic and motor developments that support the production of such actions. These changes in the way children see themselves, and the accompanying skills that support autonomous behavior, are a function of fundamental changes at both a biological and a behavioral level in their ability to regulate the self.

Recent developmental neuroscience work suggests that because the development of self-regulatory processes is dependent on the maturation of prefrontal–limbic connections that occurs relatively later in childhood compared to other brain development, development of these processes is relatively protracted; that is, these processes develop slowly across childhood (Beauregard, Levesque, & Paquette, 2004), from the basic and automatic regulation of physiology in infancy and toddlerhood to the more self-conscious, sophisticated, and intentional regulation of cognition in middle childhood (Ochsner & Gross, 2004). From a developmental perspective then, opportunities for success and failure of self-regulation are numerous over the course of early childhood, particularly given the potential of environmental factors, such as parenting and teaching, to facilitate or disrupt development across the domains (Calkins, Smith, Gill, & Johnson, 1998). In infancy, the child focuses on regulating basic functions of eating, sleeping, and arousal, and success at regulation depends heavily on parental awareness, flexibility, and responsivity to the child's emotional expression—realizing when intervention is needed, such as providing a consistent sleeping and eating schedule based on the infant's cues of hunger and fatigue. During toddlerhood, the ability to initiate use of a greater repertoire of self-regulating behaviors becomes critical as the child is gaining independence, control, and an identity separate from the caregiver (e.g., the ability of a toddler to walk away from a child who is playing with a toy that he or she wants and to play instead with an adjacent, available toy). Importantly, failures of early self-regulation are considered to be both core features of childhood psychological problems and factors that constrain the child's subsequent development and response to later developmental challenges, such as the transition to school, positive peer relationships, and academic achievement (Calkins & Fox, 2002; Keenan, 2000). Below we describe early normative processes in each of these domains (biological, attentional, emotional, behavioral, and cognitive) with a brief reference to the nature of the general problems associated with the failure to acquire these basic regulatory skills and evidence of their importance for academic and socioemotional competence.

Biological Regulation

Biological regulation includes the body's ability to control basic physiological processes, such as heart rate and respiration. Recent developmental psychophysiological work emphasizes that certain underlying biological processes and functions play an important role in the underpinnings of later developing regulatory behaviors in the attentional, emotional, behavioral, and cognitive domains (Fox, 1994; Fox & Card, 1999; Porges, 1991, 1996). Thus, theories of self-regulation that focus on underlying biological components of regulation assume that maturation of different biological support systems lays the foundation for increasingly sophisticated emotional and behavioral regulation observed across childhood. Fox (1989, 1994), for example, has noted that the frontal lobes of the brain are differentially specialized for approach and avoidance, and that these tendencies influence children's behaviors when they are emotionally and behaviorally aroused (e.g., the decision whether to interact with or to shy away from an unfamiliar adult, such as a new teacher or visitor within a classroom). Other researchers have emphasized the role of biological stress responses (Stansbury & Gunnar, 1994) and physiological regulation as processes that support behavioral manifestations of regulation (Calkins, 1997; Calkins & Dedmon, 2000).

Researchers interested in testing these theories often use measures of heart rate to assess arousal and control of arousal. However, Porges (1996; Porges, Doussard-Roosevelt, & Maita, 1994) argues that isolation of parasympathetic from sympathetic processes of the autonomic nervous system is needed to interpret most accurately the nature of the physiological regulation. During a stressful event, the sympathetic nervous system prepares the body for the "fight or flight" response through arousal (increased respiration and heart rate, dilated pupils), whereas the parasympathetic nervous system works to bring the body back to homeostasis after the event ends or is no longer perceived as dangerous. Porges notes that maturation of the parasympathetic nervous system in particular plays a key role in the regulation of state, motor activity, and emotion, and that such functioning may be indexed by measures of heart rate variability. He and his colleagues (Porges, 1991; Porges, Doussard-Roosevelt, Portales, & Greenspan, 1996) developed a method to assess the variability in heart rate that occurs with changes in the frequency of breathing (i.e., respiratory sinus arrhythmia, RSA) and is thought to reflect the parasympathetic influence on heart rate variability (via the vagus nerve). Using this measure of physiological regulation, an infant with a high resting RSA would have greater heart rate variability under conditions of minimal environmental challenge, indicating that this child has a responsive parasympathetic nervous system. We would expect that such an infant's biology would support a greater physiological and behavioral response, or "reactivity," when a response to an environmental event is needed. Indeed, studies have linked high RSA in newborns and children with good developmental outcomes, suggesting that it may be an important physiological component of appropriate environmental engagement (Hofheimer, Wood, Porges, Pearson, & Lawson, 1995; Richards & Cameron, 1989; Stifter & Fox, 1990; Suess, Porges, & Plude, 1994).

Moreover, Porges proposes that "vagal regulation" (regulation of the heart) may be more directly related to the kinds of regulatory behaviors that children begin to display in toddlerhood and early childhood (Porges et al., 1996). Vagal regulation is measured by a decrease in RSA during situations in which coping is required. It is thought that vagal regulation (as indexed by RSA suppression) during demanding tasks reflects physiological processes that allow the child to shift focus from internal homeostatic demands to external demands (i.e., the environment) that require internal processing or the generation of coping strategies to control affective or behavioral arousal. Thus, suppression of RSA is an unconscious biological strategy permitting sustained attention and behaviors, indicative of active coping, that are mediated by the parasympathetic nervous system (Porges, 1991, 1996; Wilson & Gottman, 1996). Strong evidence suggests that RSA does change under conditions in which the individual must cope with a variety of external challenges (Blair, Peters, & Granger, 2004; Calkins, 1997; Calkins et al., 1998; Calkins & Dedmon, 2000; Calkins, Graziano, et al., 2007; Calkins & Keane, 2004; Donzella, Gunnar, Krueger, & Alwin, 2000; Moore & Calkins, 2004). And RSA suppression seems to be an indicator of both the degree of challenge the task imposes on the child's regulatory ability and the extent to which the child can generate a coping response independently rather than with environmental support.

One interesting and important finding within this area of research is that young children's physiological response to challenge (vagal regulation) is often enhanced when the caregiver helps the child manage the task as opposed to the child dealing with the challenge alone (Calkins & Dedmon, 2000; Calkins & Keane, 2004). In short, the finding that children's physiological regulation is better when they are assisted by a caring adult has significant implications for classroom instruction. Finally, research clearly indicates that this response is observable in early infancy, and that biological regulation abilities vary significantly across very young children (Calkins, Dedmon, Gill, Lomax, & Johnson, 2002). Early in life, some children's biological systems make it easier for them to regulate arousal, and these differences continue to be evident as children develop. Given its early appearance in the child's repertoire, and because it is influenced by caregiver support, physiological regulation most likely provides a foundation for later appearing regulatory competencies in the attentional, emotional, behavioral, and cognitive domains.

Impact on School Functioning

Research examining biological reactivity and regulation has indicated that these processes are linked to skills necessary for school success. For example, researchers using a different measure of biological reactivity (salivary cortisol) found that preschoolers who evidenced moderate arousal displayed greater executive functioning (cognitive self-regulation), and were reported by their teachers to have better attentional and behavioral control within the classroom (Blair, Granger, & Razza, 2005). Also, recent research from our longitudinal study indicates that kindergartners with better vagal regulation tend to display more adaptive social skills, as reported by their teachers and their classmates (Graziano, Keane, & Calkins, 2007). These results support the notion that regulation at the biological level facilitates one's ability to engage and disengage with the environment (Porges et al., 1996), whether that environment comprises social or cognitive challenges.

Attentional Regulation

"Attentional regulation" can be defined as the ability to organize, attend to, and maintain focus on selected stimuli while resisting distraction from extraneous stimuli. During early infancy, attentional self-regulation efforts are thought to be controlled by innate biological mechanisms (Derryberry & Rothbart, 1997; Kopp, 1982; Posner & Rothbart, 1998). But by 3 months of age, primitive and more reactive attentional self-regulatory mechanisms of orienting and attentional persistence assist in simple control of behavioral state and emotional reactivity (Eisenberg et al., 2004). For example, an infant may orient to and persist in watching a mobile to facilitate a state of calm arousal. The period between 3 and 6 months of age marks a major transition in infant development. Sleep–wake cycles, eating, and elimination processes become predictable, and the infant begins *voluntarily* to control its own arousal. This control depends largely on attentional control mechanisms and simple motor skills (Rothbart, Ziaie, & O'Boyle, 1992; Ruff & Rothbart, 1996), and leads to coordinated use of attention engagement and disengagement, particularly in contexts that evoke negative affect. Infants are now capable of engaging in self-initiated distraction, and of moving attention away from sources of negative arousal toward more neutral, nonsocial stimuli.

The emergence of voluntary control of attention during the infant's first year coincides with the development of several related attentional systems of the brain (for detailed descriptions of these systems, see Calkins, 2007). The development and integration of these attentional systems provide the neural mechanisms necessary for the young child to regulate reactivity through orienting, redirecting, and maintaining attentional focus; allowing attention to move from one location to another through engagement and disengagement; allowing the adjustment of the breadth of attention to focus closely on details or to give a broader picture of the information to be processed (Posner & Rothbart, 1992); and, finally, allowing conscious, willful, or *effortful* control of behavior through which the individual can regulate more reactive motivational functions. The attentional system in the brain that is responsible for effortful control is relatively late to develop, with the most rapid maturation occurring during toddlerhood and the preschool years (Derryberry & Rothbart, 1997). Effortful control of attention permits the young child to engage in a broader array of cognitive tasks, such as initiating, inhibiting, and monitoring behavior (Eisenberg et al., 2004; Rothbart & Bates, 1998).

Considerable research indicates that attentional regulation in infancy and toddlerhood is important for the development of later self-regulation processes. Attention regulation in infancy, for instance, predicts better emotion regulation in toddlerhood (Morales, Mundy, Crowson, Neal, & Delgado, 2005). Also, effortful control of attention during toddlerhood plays a key role in delay behaviors, and in suppressing and slowing down behaviors (Kochanska, Murray, & Harlan, 2000) that are components of the behavioral regulation necessary for successful social and academic functioning. However, not all children are able to control reactivity successfully, to inhibit a behavioral response, or to carry out a planned activity. For example, some children are unable to shift their attention away from a negative event (e.g., something frightening) toward a positive distracter (e.g., something familiar), which leads to increased experiences of negative affect. As with physiological regulation, there are clear individual differences in children's abilities to utilize attention skills of engagement and disengagement successfully to maintain control of emotion, cognition, and behavior. To illustrate, some children's lack of attentional control is severe enough to cause further impairments in the later development of emotion and behavioral self-regulation that are significant enough to warrant a diagnosis of attention-deficit/hyperactivity disorder (ADHD) (Nigg & Huang-Pollock, 2003; Sethi, Mischel, Aber, Shoda, & Rodriguez, 2000). In this way, early attention problems associated with ADHD, such as the inability to sustain attention, may act to constrain the normal development of self-regulation (Barkley, 2004).

Impact on School Functioning

Recent research has linked aspects of self-regulation of attention to various aspects of early school success. One study found that children with better effortful control abilities during preschool had subsequently better math and literacy achievement scores in kindergarten (Blair & Razza, 2007). With regard to social competence, effortful control of attention has been linked to socially appropriate behavior in the context of emotionally challenging situations (Kieras, Tobin, Graziano, & Rothbart, 2005). Similarly, in another study, first- and second-graders who evidenced high attentional competence within the classroom, as rated by their teachers, were reported by their peers to be more happy, less sad, and less angry (Trentacosta, Izard, Mostow, & Fine, 2006). Finally, in an experimental study, Rueda, Posner, and Rothbart (2005) found that brief attention training (completing a computerized 45-minute video game five times over a 2- to 3-week period) increased preschoolers' visual–spatial skills and resulted in changes in brain activity that suggested maturation of the attention systems of the brain. In summary, good regulation of attention seems to be a precursor to adaptive school functioning.

Emotional Regulation

"Emotional regulation processes" refer to skills and strategies that serve to manage, modulate, inhibit, and enhance emotional arousal in a way that supports adaptive social and nonsocial responses (Calkins, 1997; Kopp, 1982, 1989; Thompson, 1994). Displays of affect and affect regulation are powerful mediators of interpersonal relationships and socioemotional adjustment, including behavioral self-control, in the first few years of life (Calkins, 1994; Cicchetti, Ganiban, & Barnett, 1991; Rothbart, 1989; Thompson, 1994). Children dramatically improve their ability to control their emotions during infancy and toddlerhood. For example, by the end of first year of life, infants become much more active and purposeful in their attempts to control affective arousal. They begin to employ organized sequences of motor behavior that enable them to reach, retreat, redirect, and self-soothe in a flexible manner that suggests they are responsive to environmental cues. Additionally, infants' signaling and redirection become explicitly social as they recognize that caregivers and others may behave in ways that will assist them in the regulation of affective states (Rothbart et al., 1992).

By toddlerhood, developments in language and mobility set the stage for more autonomous behavior across all domains of functioning. And although toddlers are not entirely capable of controlling their own affective states, they are capable of using specific strategies to attempt to manage their emotions (e.g., asking a parent for help or putting down a frustrating new toy to play with a familiar toy), albeit sometimes unsuccessfully (Calkins & Dedmon, 2000; Calkins, Gill, Johnson, & Smith, 1999).

The development of emotion regulation during early childhood is facilitated by functioning in a variety of nonemotional domains, including motor, language, cognition, and social development (Kopp, 1989, 1992). For example, increases in motor ability facilitate the use of strategies, such as withdrawal from a source of negative arousal. The emergence of language facilitates verbal expressions of distress, as well as private speech to guide behavior. And, increases in problem-solving skills enhance the range of alternative coping strategies a child may use in an emotionally evocative situation. In this way, the regulation of emotional reactivity in the service of adaptive functioning is linked in important ways to developments often viewed as independent of emotional functioning.

The research on emotion regulation demonstrates (1) individual differences in the use of particular emotion regulation behaviors that are observable by toddlerhood, (2) some behaviors that are more effective than others for reducing negative affect, (3) the use of particular emotion regulation behaviors that change over time, and (4) certain behaviors that affect the development of social competence. For example, Stifter, Spinrad, and Braungart-Rieker (1999) found that infants who could successfully regulate their emotions in response to frustration evidenced better compliance during toddlerhood. Eisenberg and colleagues (1993; Eisenberg, Fabes, Murphy, & Maszk, 1995; Eisenberg, Fabes, Nyman, Bernzweig, & Pinuelas, 1994) found that good emotion regulation skills are associated with peer competence in early childhood.

Deficits in emotion regulation may manifest in different ways. Although problems with emotion regulation may be broadly related to externalizing behavior problems characterized by aggression (Calkins, Gill, & Williford, 1999), Shipman, Schneider, and Brown (2004) hypothesized that they may differentially predict children who are prone to oppositional defiant disorder (ODD). More specifically, problems with undercontrolled emotion regulation may distinguish between children who display reactive aggression and those who display proactive aggression, which may in turn differentiate between behavioral outcomes characterized by ODD and early indicators of conduct disorder (CD) (Keenan & Shaw, 2003). In addition, the overcontrol of emotion may characterize children with internalizing behavior problems, such as anxiety and depression (Eisenberg et al., 2004). Thus, patterns of emotion regulation that children acquire early in development influence the nature of their subsequent psychological functioning in important ways (Fox & Calkins, 2003).

Impact on School Functioning

Considerable research on emotion regulation demonstrates that successful regulation of affect influences children's functioning in both social and nonsocial domains (Blair, Denham, Kochanoff, & Whipple, 2004; Calkins, 1994; Calkins et al., 1998; Cicchetti et al., 1991; Thompson, 1994). Eisenberg, Fabes, and colleagues in several studies have reported that individuals who are highly emotional in response to anger-inducing events and low in regulation are likely to be aggressive with others (Eisenberg et al., 1993, 1994; Fabes & Eisenberg, 1992). Similarly, other researchers have found that preschoolers who are high in negative emotionality and who use predominantly passive coping strategies (avoiding and denying emotions) are at risk for later behavior problems (Blair, Denham, et al., 2004).

We found in our own research that in children at low risk of developing persistent externalizing behavior problems, those who evidenced better emotion regulation at 2 years of age, and had mothers who were warm and responsive, were more liked by their classmates in kindergarten. In contrast, children with equally well-developed emotion regulation strategies, but with mothers who were not warm and responsive, were less well liked by their classmates in kindergarten (Blandon, Calkins, & Keane, 2009). These results provide further evidence that the emotional climate of mother–child interactions is important for children to use their emotion regulation strategies successfully.

In terms of early school success, Shields and colleagues (2001) found that pre-schoolers with good emotion regulation skills at the beginning of the school year were reported by their teachers to have better school functioning (acquired early reading, language, and math skills; adapted to routines; complied with rules; formed positive relationships with peers and teachers) at the end of the year. Blair (2002) proposed that inefficient emotion regulation physiologically inhibits the use of higher-order cognitive regulation. In support of this proposal, Trentacosta and Izard (2007) found that after they controlled for verbal ability, children who were reported by their teachers to be able to regulate their emotions successfully in kindergarten better attended to academic tasks and subsequently had higher academic achievement in the first grade. Additionally, they found that emotion knowledge in kindergarten was directly and positively associated with academic skills in first grade. In summary, emotion regulation appears to play a significant role in preparing children for school.

Behavioral Regulation

"Behavioral regulation" is the ability to manage or control one's own behavior, including compliance to adult demands and directives, and the ability to control impulsive responses, delay engagement in specific activities, and monitor one's own behavior (Kopp, 1982; Kuczynski & Kochanska, 1995). Increasingly, these kinds of demands are placed on children during early childhood. Consequently, the task for the child is to overcome impulsive reactions or to suspend desired activity to meet external demands. Importantly, earlier acquired biological, attentional, and emotional control processes are integral to the successful regulation of behavior. Compliance to external directives is often achieved in situations in which the child must cease or initiate an undesirable (from the child's point of view) activity, for instance, refraining from immediately calling out an answer to a question posed by a teacher and instead raising one's hand and waiting to be called upon, or not cheating on a difficult task when no one is looking (i.e., behavioral inhibition). The regulation of arousal is necessary to meet such demands; therefore, to the extent that children successfully achieve a level of control of biological, attentional, and emotional arousal, greater behavioral compliance is expected. Failures of behavioral self-regulation characterize profiles of behavior problems in early childhood. Clear evidence exists for a negative relation between the child's early success at behavioral regulation (compliance, control of impulsivity, and delay of gratification ability) and later externalizing problem behavior (Eisenberg et al., 1996, 2000).

Impact on School Functioning

Behavioral regulation is critical to the child's transition into the social and school environment. Importantly, these skills support the development of internally driven standards of behavior and conduct that the child will need to function independently in the school and peer domains. For example, "effortful control," a construct that Kochanska and others have identified as incorporating both attentional and behavioral demands, has also been implicated in the development of conscience and the internalization of standards of conduct (Eisenberg et al., 2004; Kochanska, Murray, & Coy, 1997; Kochanska et al., 2000). This suggests that the absence of such behavioral control skills may be implicated in behavioral outcomes characterized by a lack of empathy and conscience. Thus, children who have good behavioral control are more likely to feel responsible for acting in a way that is expected by their parents and teachers. In other research, parent ratings of impulsivity, inhibition control, and global self-control predicted parent ratings of later problem behavior and teacher ratings of children's social competence (Eisenberg et al., 1996). In another study, children who were observed to express high levels of behavioral dysregulation within the classroom (unable to sit quietly, running instead of walking, having a temper tantrum) were rated by their teachers as having lower general school readiness skills in terms of early knowledge of reading and math, understanding of routines, or making friends (Miller, Gouley, Seifer, Dickstein, & Shields, 2004). Other research indicates that providing teachers with a mental health consultation focused on increasing children's behavioral control within the classroom led to more positive classroom environments, greater teacher sensitivity, and better behavior management (Raver et al., 2008). This research implicates good behavioral regulation as a necessary element for school success.

Cognitive Regulation

"Cognitive regulation," often called "cognitive control" or "executive functioning," encompasses a number of cognitive factors, including "working memory" (the mental ability to hold and to manipulate information) and "inhibitory control" (the ability to resist the temptation to do something). "Executive functioning" involves the use of planfulness, control, reflection, competence, and independence when completing tasks (Paris & Newman, 1990). This more sophisticated level of self-regulation is supported by components of self-regulation developed earlier. In fact, Kuhl and Kraska (1993) argue that children's early school performance, which requires executive processes, is influenced by not only behavioral self-regulation but also attentional and emotional control. To the extent that children can utilize effective strategies for monitoring and maintaining attention, and that they are able to control frustration in the face of challenging cognitive tasks, they become more successful at completing such tasks.

Significant development in cognitive regulation occurs during preschool. For example, Zelazo and his associates (Zelazo & Boseovski, 2001; Zelazo, Müller, Frye, & Marcovitch, 2003) have shown marked increases from age 3 to 5 years in children's ability to switch between two incompatible classification rules. The ability to hold multiple stimuli and/or perspectives in mind also improves markedly during this time just before formal school entry. Still, preschoolers' cognitive and behavioral problem-solving activity is often characterized by failure to control attention and behavior, and to initiate, monitor, or otherwise control organizational and planning activities; and by inflexibility in their ability to alter representational perspectives or response alternatives to arrive at new solutions or use new rules when solving problems (cf. Isquith, Gioia, & Espy, 2004) because their executive functioning skills are still maturing.

Studies have linked executive functioning deficits in children to a range of early behavioral difficulties. For example, immature executive functioning is common in children with attention problems (Hinshaw, 1994; Nigg, Hinshaw, Carte, & Treuting, 1998), but executive function deficits have also been linked to conduct problems and learning style differences (Moffitt, 1993; Pennington & Ozonoff, 1996). Moreover, the frequently reported association between executive function and disruptive behavior is independent of IQ (Moffitt, 1993). Rutter (1987) proposes that executive functions mediate the development of psychopathology in children. Although the causal role of executive functioning deficits has not often been examined in longitudinal studies, several studies have found that early problems with inhibitory control are associated with later behavior problems (Nigg, Quamma, Greenberg, & Kusche, 1999; Riggs, Blair, & Greenberg, 2003).

Impact on School Functioning

Compelling indirect evidence indicates positive developmental trajectories, beginning with advanced executive function skills in toddlers. For example, Carlson, Mandell, and Williams (2004) found that early executive function predicts later "theory of mind" abilities—that is, the ability to attribute knowledge, desires, intents and other mental states to oneself and others, and the understanding that others may have different mental states than one's own (see also Hughes [1998] for a similar pattern in children between 3 and 4 years of age). In turn, advances in theory of mind are related to a number of positive outcomes, including improvements in cooperative interactions (Dunn, Brown, Slomkowski, Tesla, & Youngblade, 1991) and important antecedents to the understanding of cognitive states (Bartsch & Estes, 1996). Executive function abilities are heavily implicated in academic success (preschool: Alloway et al., 2005; Espy et al., 2004; elementary school: Bull & Scerif, 2001; Holmes & Adams, 2006; secondary school: Chinnappan & Lawson, 1996; St. Clair-Thompson & Gathercole, 2006). Additionally, Riggs, Jahromi, Razza, Dillworth-Bart, and Mueller (2006) provide a thorough review of the links between executive function skills and socioemotional development broadly defined, and they suggest several mechanisms for how executive functioning may alter socioemotional development. However, there has been surprisingly little research on whether executive function skills prior to school translate into school success. In the most recent research, Blair and Razza (2007) reported that inhibitory control and attention-shifting abilities in Head Start preschool children predicted their literacy and math scores in kindergarten. Similarly, McClelland and colleagues (2007) found that improvements in working memory, attention, and inhibitory control skills predicted improvements in early literacy and math skills during the preschool year. Thus, although more longitudinal research is needed to study the development and stability of executive function and cognitive control from infancy to the school years, it appears that the development of good early regulation of cognition fosters school success during the preschool, kindergarten, and early primary years.

Summary of Self-Regulatory Processes

This brief review of the self-regulatory processes that emerge and become functional during early development highlights the central role these processes play in many dimensions of emerging childhood competence. This review suggests that there may be expected trajectories of skills in the subdomains of self-regulation, and that patterns of regulatory deficits are related to patterns of adjustment versus maladjustment across many domains, including school readiness. Such a framework has implications for an understanding of both normative and compromised development, and clearly contributes to the identification of *mechanisms* of development that may explain optimal versus less than optimal outcomes.

We acknowledge that these discrete self-regulatory processes are likely to be so intertwined that once integration across levels occurs in support of more complex skills and behaviors, it is difficult to parse these complex behavioral responses into separate or independent types of control. Nevertheless, from a developmental point of view, it is useful to describe explicit types of control and how they emerge because this specification may provide insight into non-normative developments and problems that emerge as a result of deficits in specific components of self-regulation at particular points in development (Calkins, in press).

One hypothesis that we have been exploring (Howse et al., 2003; Leerkes, Paradise, O'Brien, Calkins, & Lange, 2008) is that *emotion control processes* moderate trajectories of development of other more sophisticated control processes. Our rationale for this hypothesis is derived from recent work in the more broadly construed area of self-regulation (Baumeister & Vohs, 2004), and from research in the area of attention development (Posner & Rothbart, 2007). First, at both neural and behavioral levels, emotion regulation processes recruit and integrate multiple psychological functions (attention, appraisal, affective experience, and motor responding) (Lewis & Stieben, 2004). Thus, it is clear that emotions have the capacity to organize and facilitate, or to disorganize and disrupt, other psychological processes (Cole, Martin, & Dennis, 2004; Gray, 2004), both "in the moment" and at the level of the emergence of these skills over the course of early development (Bell & Wolfe, 2004). Second, emotion control processes appear to emerge earlier in development than do cognitive control processes (Blair, 2002). Recent work by Blair and Razza (2007) provides support for such a conceptualization of self-regulation and for the importance of self-regulation in children's early academic skills. Specifically, they found that attentional regulation (effortful control) and cognitive regulation (attention shifting and inhibitory control) were moderately correlated with one another. Even so, measures of both in preschool uniquely predicted academic achievement in kindergarten. To the extent that children understand and control emotions successfully, they have a greater opportunity to attend to, assimilate, and process events in the world around them, thus enhancing both social and academic competence. Therefore, from both a behavioral and a neuroscience perspective, there appears to be support for the developmental model we have proposed.

The review of the research in this area demonstrates that the development of self-regulation is critical for school readiness. Accordingly, strategies that promote the development of self-regulation in young children should be incorporated as integral components of early childhood instruction. Next, we present recommendations for the incorporation of learning strategies that may foster the development of self-regulation within the preschool, kindergarten, and early primary grades (first through third) classrooms.

Translations to Early Childhood Curricula

Patterns of school achievement often begin early, with a high degree of continuity relative to later school success (Blair, 2001). Moreover, there are significant individual differences in self-regulation abilities that have an important impact on children's success as they enter the school domain. The beginning of formal schooling is a major developmental step requiring the acquisition of important skills, such as the ability to follow instructions, comply with rules, cooperate/communicate with peers, work independently, carry out self-care activities, learn basic academic knowledge, and meet teacher expectations (Belsky & Mackinnon, 1994). Research using a national sample of kindergarten teachers found that, on average, 16% of children evidenced many adjustment problems in their transition to kindergarten, with over one-third of teachers reporting that at least half of the children in their classes had several specific problems (Rimm-Kaufman et al., 2000). Interestingly, the majority of the problems that teachers identified were behaviors associated with a lack of self-regulatory abilities (i.e., difficulties in following directions, working independently, working in a group, interacting with peers).

Equally troubling is a report from a recent national study indicating that within the preschool classroom, children are being expelled three times more frequently than children in grades K–12 (Gilliam, 2005). The fact that expulsion rates were much lower when teachers had access to a mental health consultant (Gilliam, 2005) suggests that these children are being removed from the learning environment because of failures within the emotional and behavioral domains of self-regulation (e.g., because they cannot initiate self-restraint, they do not inhibit disruptive behaviors, such as grabbing toys, hitting or biting other children, arguing with teachers, breaking classroom rules). Given that prevention and intervention practices have the potential to be most beneficial if implemented when developmental trajectories are still malleable (Keenan & Shaw, 1994), the early childhood classroom presents as an environment that holds promise for encouraging self-regulation abilities in children and enhancing their success in later years (Blair & Diamond, 2008).

Researchers who study self-regulation have suggested various strategies for teachers to facilitate its development, such as increasing children's knowledge of emotions, coaching children on understanding and identifying their own emotions, and teaching children specific strategies for dealing with negative emotions (Blair, Peters, et al., 2004; Shields et al., 2001). Such strategy use is most effective when it occurs within the context of a positive teacher–student relationship to foster self-regulation within the classroom setting (Blair, Peters, et al., 2004; Shields et al., 2001). This recommendation coincides with clear evidence of the impact of primary caregivers in facilitating children's self-regulation. Across the domains of self-regulation, warm and responsive caregiving has been shown to enhance children's regulatory abilities. For instance, good parental scaffolding (parents who provided appropriate cognitive and emotional support, while also allowing children to be autonomous) was related to better self-regulation across several domains (attentional, cognitive, and behavioral) within the preschool classroom (Neitzel & Stright, 2003). In short, children whose mothers provided appropriate support during challenging tasks at home were better able to sustain their attention and effort on tasks, use self-talk to assist in problem solving, and comply with the rules of conduct with the classroom.

One implication of this finding is that children enter school with different caregiving experiences, so they come equipped with different abilities to handle the challenges they face in the classroom. Given this, it seems important that teachers consider strategies for helping parents assist their children at home. This is especially important in the primary grades, when children receive more homework and often require parents' assistance to improve their performance on assignments. The fostering of positive parent–teacher relationships during the early years is predictive of later academic achievement (Hawkins, Catalano, Kosterman, Abbott, & Hill, 1999). These results highlight the need for a close and positive parent–teacher relationship. Positive experiences between teachers and parents should begin early, during preschool, thus encouraging parents to be actively engaged with teachers during later years. Teachers can encourage parents to assist children at home with difficult tasks because appropriate assistance may help promote the development of self-regulation that allows the child to work more effectively within the classroom. A parent may be encouraged to provide emotional support to children, especially when the child may become frustrated in trying to solve a difficult problem. Strategies such as encouraging children for their effort ("You are working so hard on this really difficult problem"); suggesting distractions to manage frustration ("You have been working on this for a while. Why don't you take a short break or work on a different problem, and come back to this in a little while"); and knowing when to offer help ("Wow, you have done a lot of this all by yourself. Would you like me to help you on just this part?") may be effective in improving parent–child interactions that occur within the context of schoolwork.

This research calls for intervention programs that help to foster positive parent–child relationships in the school setting. Such programs have been found to have higher attendance and to increase positive parent–teacher relationships. Furthermore, they have also been found to be effective in both preschool and early primary grades (Reid, Webster-Stratton, & Hammond, 2007; Webster-Stratton, Reid, & Hammond, 2001). Additionally, children who received classroom intervention, and whose parents received parent training, evidenced greater improvement in their emotion regulation compared to those who did not receive treatment (Webster-Stratton et al., 2008).

In much the same way that caregiver practices can facilitate development of self-regulation in young children, the strategies that teachers use in the classroom strengthen self-regulatory skills when provided within the context of a supportive teacher–child relationship. In the early school years, a particularly effective student–teacher relationship is likely one that facilitates children's self-regulation in much the same way that warm and responsive parents support children's self-regulation (Pianta & Stuhlman, 2004). Research has shown that establishment of a warm and close student–teacher relationship at the beginning of preschool is associated with better emotion regulation (Shields et al., 2001), better social competence, and fewer problem behaviors (Mashburn et al., 2008) at the end of year. However, the student–teacher relationship requires the active engagement of *both* the teacher and the child. Given this requirement, it is easy to understand that teachers are less likely to develop close, positive, high-quality relationships with students who evidence significant behavior problems or difficulty with emotion regulation within the classroom (Coie & Koeppl, 1990; Graziano, Reavis, et al., 2007; Ladd, Birch, & Buhs, 1999). To the extent that teachers make concerted efforts to form positive, supportive relationships with the students (and their parents) who evidence significant self-regulatory failures in their classrooms, the children are more likely to develop appropriate classroom behaviors.

To promote the development of self-regulation during early childhood, we focus on strategies related to emotional, behavioral, and cognitive self-regulation because these are the domains in which children make the most significant strides during preschool, kindergarten, and the early primary grades. To illustrate how our model of self-regulation may be usefully applied to school readiness curricula, we take note of two programs whose core principles are consistent with our model. We examine Webster Stratton's Incredible Years teacher and child training curricula (Reid et al., 2007; Webster-Stratton et al., 2008), which promote self-regulation within the emotional and behavioral domains, and Bodrova and Leong's (2007) Tools of the Mind approach, which promotes cognitive control. We have selected these two programs specifically for the following reasons. Although neither program was developed solely as a self-regulation intervention, both programs use strategies that specifically address self-regulation within the classroom, targeting children ages 3–8, and they do so within the context of a supportive teacher–child relationship in the traditional classroom. Additionally both programs have been tested by recent, rigorous, experimental research within high-risk populations (low socioeconomic status [SES] communities) and have been shown to improve self-regulation skills effectively. These programs are readily accessible to teachers and administrators, and include books, websites, and formal training opportunities.

Incredible Years

Webster-Stratton's Incredible Years series, which includes parent, teacher, and child training programs, was originally developed to reduce conduct problems in children diagnosed with ODD or CD (Webster-Stratton & Reid, 2003). More recently, these programs have been adapted for preventive use with all children (Reid et al., 2007; Webster-Stratton et al., 2008). Although the primary purpose of these interventions is to decrease disruptive behavior, improvement in self-regulation serves as one of the primary mechanisms through which the strategies in these programs are effective. This is why many researchers who study self-regulation identify these programs as examples that use strategies to encourage adaptive development of self-regulatory abilities (e.g., Blair & Diamond, 2008; Denham & Burton, 2003; Pelco & Reed-Victor, 2007). Indeed, Webster-Stratton, in her most recent examinations of the effectiveness of her school-based programs, found that children's emotion regulation skills improved significantly (measured by both observation and parent report), and that children evidenced greater general school readiness skills when she compared classrooms that implemented the programs to those that did not (Reid et al., 2007; Webster-Stratton et al., 2008).

The Child Training component of Incredible Years focuses on training teachers to improve children's emotion regulation by providing a consistent and supportive classroom environment, and strategies that increase children's emotional knowledge, encourage appropriate expression of emotion, handle negative emotions, and promote positive self-talk. As an example, to handle negative emotion, Webster-Stratton encourages the use of the "turtle technique" (Schneider, 1974), which focuses on both controlling the physiological arousal associated with negative emotions and active problem solving to facilitate emotion regulation. Children are taught through teacher explanation, role plays, storybooks, and teacher modeling to pretend that they have a shell, like a turtle, and when something makes them angry they can go into the shell to calm down (to take deep breaths) and to think (use self-talk to say "I can relax," "I know how to control myself," "I can play with another toy"). A technique that is specifically for children who have problems controlling anger is use of an "anger thermometer." Child and teacher create an anger thermometer, which involves identifying triggers for angry behavior, and strategies teacher and child can use both to prevent an anger outburst and to serve as a visual reminder for the child. The technique includes having teacher and child determine a secret code phrase (e.g., "code orange," "red light") that both can use to indicate that the child is becoming too angry, and to signal the child to begin using regulation strategies to reduce negative emotionality (e.g., breathing techniques or imagery that the child has previously been taught). Children can look at their thermometers (that can be pasted on their desk or cubby hole) to remind themselves what steps to take to regulate their emotions.

The Teacher Training component of Webster-Stratton's program focuses on providing teachers with effective proactive classroom management techniques, including the use of classroom rules and routines, limit setting, positive reinforcement, incentives, and natural consequences for unwanted behavior to help children self-monitor behavior (Webster-Stratton et al., 2001). When teachers use these strategies in their classroom, children are better able to regulate their own behavior. For example, teachers are encouraged to use the "Give me five" signal to help children give their full attention. In this technique, each finger on the hand represents a specific behavior in which the child needs to engage. After children are taught, using a picture, what "Give me five" means, the teacher can simply raise his or her own open hand to get children's attention. This technique helps children to remember which behaviors to engage in (e.g., looking at the teacher with their hands in their laps) and which behaviors to inhibit (e.g., looking at and manipulating a toy).

Tools of the Mind

The Tools of the Mind program (Bodrova & Leong, 2007) uses Vygotskian theory (Kozulin, 1990) as a framework for teachers to provide cognitive strategies or "mental tools," or to enhance children's socioemotional and cognitive development, and academic learning within the classroom. The program provides appropriate strategies for children throughout early childhood (infancy through the early primary grade years). Many of the Tools of the Mind strategies that Bodrova and Leong (2007) encourage teachers to use in their classroom specifically facilitate children's self-regulation of cognition. Diamond, Barnett, Thomas, and Munro (2007) conducted an experimental study in which classrooms were randomly assigned to use either Tools of the Mind or another program. They found that children exposed to the Tools of the Mind program evidenced greater executive functioning skills compared to children in the control condition. Blair and Diamond (2008) encourage the use of this program to enhance children's cognitive control and, subsequently, to prevent school failure. They provide an excellent review of how many of the strategies in this program specifically facilitate cognitive control in children through executive function training. For example, the Tools of the Mind program transforms a common preschool activity, dramatic play, into one that actively exercises children's executive functioning skills. Here, a child develops a "play plan" with another classmate before they enter into the dramatic play area. During the actual play, children exercise several aspects of cognitive control, including working memory, by sticking to their play plan (e.g., playing "restaurant" and not "fireman"); inhibitory control, by staying within designated roles (e.g., being the "waiter" and not switching to become the "chef"); and cognitive flexibility, by dealing with changes that arise during play (e.g., because the "waiter" can only find eggs and orange juice play pieces, he or she brings breakfast instead of dinner).

An example of a Tools of the Mind strategy used in elementary grades involves two children working together on a writing assignment. One child is assigned the author role and writes a story, while the other child takes the role of the editor and monitors the writing (looking for mistakes, such as misspelled words). In this example the "editor" helps the "author" exercise cognitive control over the writing assignment in such a way that the child eventually is able to do it him- or herself (i.e., eventually the child can master both content and grammar, while completing a writing assignment). Many of the strategies in the Tools of the Mind program serve to increase children's abilities to persist in working through difficult tasks, to hold information in mind to complete multiple-step tasks, and to increase problem-solving skills, so that they have the mental flexibility to solve more difficult problems as they move into the primary grades.

Summary, Implications, and Future Directions

In this chapter, we have described a self-regulatory framework for understanding important developments across a range of skill domains (from the biological to the cognitive) that support emerging social and academic skills in young children. The evidence presented in this chapter clearly supports the development of self-regulation across domains related to early school success, as indexed by a range of important skills and behaviors. We note the important role played by teachers and caregivers in this developmental process, and we advocate the use of empirically validated programs in preschools and elementary schools that target specific self-regulatory skills and processes. In our view, self-regulatory behaviors are the most proximal indicator of a child's success or failure in a range of school-related social and academic tasks. To the extent that these "control" skills can be improved, children's learning, social lives, and mental health are enhanced.

It is important to recognize, though, that we have much to learn about how self-regulation develops. As developmentalists, our task is to understand the way in which *different* rudimentary control processes become integrated into more sophisticated functioning over time. For example, a putatively emotional task of early childhood, the management of frustration, may be parsed into many smaller challenges for the child, involving processes that are observable in different ways and across different levels of functioning (biological responses, attention skills, emotion control behaviors, thinking skills) from infancy through childhood. And many of these same component processes might also be involved in the successful negotiation of other childhood challenges that may not have an obvious emotion regulation demand, such as a math test, a soccer game, or a plea to a parent to attend a social event with friends. Understanding how these processes emerge individually and in concert over time is important to understanding the factors that may facilitate or disrupt their development.

Much of the research on self-regulation has been correlational in nature. Thus, more experimental research is needed. Izard and colleagues (2008) recently tested the effectiveness of an intervention that focuses exclusively on the development of emotion regulation. The Emotion-Based Prevention Program (EBP) teaches emotion knowledge and regulation of the most common and basic emotions (happiness, sadness, fear, anger, interest, and contempt). Children are encouraged to use language to express and to respond to their emotions, thereby facilitating control of emotions. Tests of specific interventions that are effective in altering basic control processes are needed to demonstrate the causal role of these processes in children's functioning. Finally, more work is needed to test the basic hypotheses that these control processes have an influence on children's mental health and social behaviors beyond the classroom environment.

Acknowledgment

The writing of this chapter was supported in part by a National Institute of Health Research Scientist Career Development Award (K02) to Susan D. Calkins (No. MH 74077).

References

Achenbach, T. M. (1991). *Manual for the Child Behavior Checklist/4–18 and 1991 profile*. Burlington: Department of Psychiatry, University of Vermont.

Alloway, T., Gathercole, S., Adams, A., Willis, C., Eaglen, R., & Lamont, E. (2005). Working memory and phonological awareness as predictors of progress towards early learning goals at school entry. *British Journal of Developmental Psychology, 23*, 417–426.

Barkley, R. A. (2004). Attention-deficit/hyperactivity disorder and self-regulation: Taking an evolutionary perspective on executive functioning. In R. F. Baumeister & K. D. Vohs (Eds.), *Handbook of self-regulation: Research, theory, and applications* (pp. 301–323). New York: Guilford Press.

Barkley, R. A., Shelton, T. L., Crosswait, C. R., Moorehouse, M., Fletcher, K., Barrett, S., et al. (2002). Preschool children with disruptive behavior: Three-year outcomes as a function of adaptive disability. *Development and Psychopathology, 14*, 45–67.

Bartsch, K., & Estes, D. (1996). Individual differences in children's developing theory of mind and implications for metacognition. *Learning and Individual Differences, 8*, 281–304.

Baumeister, R. F., & Vohs, K. D. (Eds.). (2004). *Handbook of self-regulation: Research, theory, and applications*. New York: Guilford Press.

Beauregard, M., Levesque, J., & Paquette, V. (2004). Neural basis of conscious and voluntary self-regulation of emotion. In M. Beauregard (Ed.), *Consciousness, emotional self-regulation and the brain* (pp. 163–194). Amsterdam: Benjamins.

Bell, M. A., & Wolfe, C. D. (2004). Emotion and cognition: An intricately bound developmental process. *Child Development, 75*, 366–370.

Belsky, J., & Mackinnon, C. (1994). Transition to school: Developmental trajectories and school experiences. *Early Education and Development, 5*, 106–119.

Bierman, K. L., Nix, R. L., Greenberg, M. T., Blair, C., & Domitrovich, C. E. (2008). Executive functions and school readiness intervention: Impact, moderation, and mediation in the Head Start REDI program. *Development and Psychopathology, 20*, 821–843.

Blair, C. (2001). The early identification of risk for grade retention among African American children at risk for school difficulty. *Applied Developmental Science, 5*, 37–50.

Blair, C. (2002). School readiness: Integrating cognition and emotion in a neurobiological conceptualization of children's functioning at school entry. *American Psychologist, 57*, 111–127.

Blair, C., & Diamond, A. (2008). Biological processes in prevention and intervention: The promotion of self-regulation as a means of preventing school failure. *Development and Psychopathology, 20*, 899–911.

Blair, C., Granger, D., & Razza, R. (2005). Cortisol reactivity is positively related to executive function in preschool children attending Head Start. *Child Development, 76*, 554–567.

Blair, C., Peters, R., & Granger, D. (2004). Physiological and neuropsychological correlates of approach/withdrawal tendencies in preschool: Further examination of the behavioral inhibition system/behavioral activation system scales for young children. *Developmental Psychobiology, 45,* 113–124.

Blair, C., & Razza, R. P. (2007). Relating effortful control, executive function, and false belief understanding to emerging math and literacy ability in kindergarten. *Child Development, 78,* 647–663.

Blair, K. A., Denham, S. A., Kochanoff, A., & Whipple, B. (2004). Playing it cool: Temperament, emotion regulation, and social behavior in preschoolers. *Journal of School Psychology, 42,* 419–443.

Blandon, A. Y., Calkins, S. D., & Keane, S. P. (2009). *Predicting emotional and social competence from toddler risk and maternal control.* Manuscript submitted for publication.

Bodrova, E., & Leong, D. J. (2007). *Tools of the Mind: The Vygotskian approach to early childhood education* (2nd ed.). Upper Saddle River, NJ: Prentice-Hall.

Bull, R., & Scerif, G. (2001). Executive functioning as a predictor of children's mathematics ability: Inhibition, switching, and working memory. *Developmental Neuropsychology, 19,* 273–293.

Calkins, S. D. (1994). Origins and outcomes of individual differences in emotional regulation. *Monographs of the Society for Research in Child Development, 59*(2), 53–72.

Calkins, S. D. (1997). Cardiac vagal tone indices of temperamental reactivity and behavioral regulation in young children. *Developmental Psychobiology, 31,* 125–135.

Calkins, S. D. (2007). The emergence of self-regulation: Biological and behavioral control mechanisms supporting toddler competencies. In C. A. Brownell & C. B. Kopp (Eds.), *Socioemotional development in the toddler years: Transitions and transformations* (pp. 261–284). New York: Guilford Press.

Calkins, S. D. (in press). Regulatory competence and early disruptive behavior problems: The role of physiological regulation. In S. Olson & A. Sameroff (Eds.), *Regulatory processes in the development of behavior problems: Biological, behavioral, and social–ecological interactions.* New York: Cambridge University Press.

Calkins, S. D., Blandon, A. Y., Williford, A. P., & Keane, S. P. (2007). Biological, behavioral and relational levels of resilience in the context of risk for early childhood behavior problems. *Development and Psychopathology, 19,* 675–700.

Calkins, S. D., & Dedmon, S. A. (2000). Physiological and behavioral regulation in two-year-old children with aggressive/destructive behavior problems. *Journal of Abnormal Child Psychology, 2,* 103–118.

Calkins, S. D., Dedmon, S. E., Gill, K. L., Lomax, L. E., & Johnson, L. M. (2002). Frustration in infancy: Implications for emotion regulation, physiological processes, and temperament. *Infancy, 3,* 175–197.

Calkins, S. D., & Fox, N. A. (2002). Self-regulatory processes in early personality development: A multilevel approach to the study of childhood social withdrawal and aggression. *Development and Psychopathology, 14,* 477–498.

Calkins, S. D., Gill, K., Johnson, M. C., & Smith, C. L. (1999). Emotional reactivity and emotional regulation strategies as predictors of social behavior with peers during toddlerhood. *Social Development, 8,* 310–334.

Calkins, S. D., Gill, K., & Williford, A. P. (1999). Externalizing problems in two-year-olds: Implications for patterns of social behavior and peers' responses to aggression. *Early Education and Development, 10,* 267–288.

Calkins, S. D., Graziano, P. A., & Keane, S. P. (2007). Cardiac vagal regulation differentiates among children at risk for behavior problems. *Biological Psychology, 74,* 144–153.

Calkins, S. D., & Keane, S. P. (2004). Cardiac vagal regulation across the preschool period:

Stability, continuity, and implications for childhood adjustment. *Developmental Psychobiology, 45,* 101–112.

Calkins, S. D., Smith, C. L., Gill, K. L., & Johnson, M. C. (1998). Maternal interactive style across contexts: Relations to emotional, behavioral and physiological regulation during toddlerhood. *Social Development, 7,* 350–369.

Carlson, S. M., Mandell, D. J., & Williams, L. (2004). Executive function and theory of mind: Stability and prediction from age 2 to 3. *Developmental Psychology, 40,* 1105–1122.

Chinnappan, M., & Lawson, M. J. (1996). The effects of training in the use of executive strategies in geometry problem solving. *Learning and Instruction, 6,* 1–17.

Cicchetti, D., Ganiban, J., & Barnett, D. (1991). Contributions from the study of high-risk populations to understanding the development of emotion regulation. In J. Garber & K. Dodge (Eds.), *The development of emotion regulation and dysregulation* (pp. 15–48). New York: Cambridge University Press.

Coie, J., & Koeppl, G. (1990). Adapting intervention to the problems to the problems of aggressive and disruptive rejected children. In S. Asher & J. Coie (Eds.), *Peer rejection in childhood* (pp. 309–337). New York: Cambridge University Press.

Cole, P. M., Martin, S. E., & Dennis, T. A. (2004). Emotion regulation as a scientific construct: Methodological challenges and directions for child development research. *Child Development, 75,* 317–333.

Denham, S. A., & Burton, R. (2003). *Social and emotional prevention and intervention programming for preschoolers.* New York: Kluwer Academic/Plenum Press.

Derryberry, D., & Rothbart, M. K. (1997). Reactive and effortful processes in the organization of temperament. *Development and Psychopathology, 9,* 633–652.

Diamond, A., Barnett, W. S., Thomas, J., & Munro, S. (2007). Preschool program improves cognitive control, *Science, 30,* 1387–1388.

Donzella, B., Gunnar, M. R., Krueger, W. K., & Alwin, J. (2000). Cortisol and vagal tone responses to competitive challenge in preschoolers: Associations with temperament. *Developmental Psychobiology, 37,* 209–220.

Dunn, J., Brown, J., Slomkowski, C., Tesla, C., & Youngblade, L. (1991). Young children's understanding of other people's feelings and beliefs: Individual differences and their antecedents. *Child Development, 62,* 1352–1366.

Eisenberg, N., Fabes, R. A., Bernzweig, J., Karbon, M., Poulin, R., & Hanish, L. (1993). The relations of emotionality and regulation to preschoolers' social skills and sociometric status. *Child Development, 64,* 1418–1438.

Eisenberg, N., Fabes, R. A., Karbon, M., Murphy, B. C., Wosinski, M., Polazzi, L., et al. (1996). The relations of children's dispositional prosocial behavior to emotionality, regulation, and social functioning. *Child Development, 67,* 974–992.

Eisenberg, N., Fabes, R. A., Murphy, B., & Maszk, P. (1995). The role of emotionality and regulation in children's social functioning: A longitudinal study. *Child Development, 66,* 1360–1384.

Eisenberg, N., Fabes, R. A., Nyman, M., Bernzweig, J., & Pinuelas, A. (1994). The relations of emotionality and regulation to children's anger-related reactions. *Child Development, 65,* 109–128.

Eisenberg, N., Guthrie, I. K., Fabes, R. A., Shepard, S., Losoya, S., Murphy, B. C., et al. (2000). Prediction of elementary school children's externalizing problem behaviors from attention and behavioral regulation and negative emotionality. *Child Development, 71,* 1367–1382.

Eisenberg, N., Spinrad, T. L., Fabes, R. A., Reiser, M., Cumberland, A., Shepard, S. A., et al. (2004). The relations of effortful control and impulsivity to children's resiliency and adjustment. *Child Development, 75,* 25–46.

Espy, K. A., McDiarmid, M. M., Cwik, M. F., Stalets, M. M., Hamby, A., & Senn, T. E. (2004).

The contribution of executive functions to emergent mathematic skills in preschool children. *Developmental Neuropsychology, 26,* 465–486.

Fabes, R. A., & Eisenberg, N. (1992). Young children's coping with interpersonal anger. *Child Development, 63,* 116–128.

Fox, N. A. (1989). Heart-rate variability and behavioral reactivity: Individual differences in autonomic patterning and their relation to infant and child temperament. In S. J. Reznick (Ed.), *Perspectives on behavioral inhibition* (pp. 177–196). Chicago: University of Chicago Press.

Fox, N. A. (1994). Dynamic cerebral processes underlying emotion regulation. *Monographs of the Society for Research in Child Development, 59*(2), 152–166.

Fox, N. A., & Calkins, S. D. (2003). The development of self-control of emotion: Intrinsic and extrinsic influences. *Motivation and Emotion, 27,* 7–26.

Fox, N. A., & Card, J. A. (1999). Psychophysiological measures in the study of attachment. In J. Cassidy & P. R. Shaver (Eds.), *Handbook of attachment: Theory, research, and clinical applications* (pp. 226–245). New York: Guilford Press.

Gilliam, W. S. (2005). *Prekindergarteners left behind: Expulsion rates in state prekindergarten systems.* New Haven, CT: Yale University Child Study Center. Retrieved April 21, 2008, from *http://childstudycenter.yale.edu/faculty/pdf/gilliam05.pdf.*

Gray, J. R. (2004). Integration of emotion and cognitive control. *Current Directions in Psychological Science, 13,* 46–48.

Graziano, P., Keane, S. P., & Calkins, S. D. (2007). Cardiac vagal regulation and early peer status. *Child Development, 78,* 264–278.

Graziano, P., Reavis, R., Keane, S. P., & Calkins, S. D. (2007). The role of emotion regulation in children's early academic success. *Journal of School Psychology, 45,* 3–19.

Hawkins, J. D., Catalano, R. F., Kosterman, R., Abbott, R., & Hill, K. G. (1999). Preventing adolescent health-risk behaviors by strengthening protection during childhood. *Archives of Pediatric Medicine, 153,* 226–234.

Hinshaw, S. P. (1994). *Attention deficits and hyperactivity in children: Vol. 29. Developmental clinical psychology and psychiatry.* Thousand Oaks, CA: Sage.

Hofheimer, J. A., Wood, B. R., Porges, S. W., Pearson, E., & Lawson, E. E. (1995). Respiratory sinus arrhythmia and social interaction patterns in preterm newborns. *Infant Behavior and Development, 18,* 233–245.

Holmes, J., & Adams, J. W. (2006). Working memory and children's mathematical skills: Implications for mathematical development and mathematics curricula. *Educational Psychology, 26,* 339–366.

Howse, R. B., Calkins, S. D., Anastopoulos, A. D., Keane, S. P., & Shelton, T. L. (2003). Regulatory contributors to children's kindergarten achievement. *Early Education and Development, 14,* 101–119.

Hughes, C. (1998). Finding your marbles: Does preschoolers' strategic behavior predict later understanding of mind? *Developmental Psychology, 34,* 1326–1339.

Isquith, P. K., Gioia, G. A., & Espy, K. A. (2004). Executive function in preschool children: Examination through everyday behavior. *Developmental Neuropsychology, 26,* 403–422.

Izard, C., King, K. A., Trentacosta, C. J., Morgan, J. K., Laurenceau, J., Krauthamer-Ewing, S. E., et al. (2008). Accelerating the development of emotion competence in Head Start children: Effects on adaptive and maladaptive behavior. *Development and Psychopathology, 20,* 369–397.

Keane, S. P., & Calkins, S. D. (2004). Predicting kindergarten peer social status from toddler and preschool problem behavior. *Journal of Abnormal Child Psychology, 32,* 409–423.

Keenan, K. (2000). Emotion dysregulation as a risk factor for child psychopathology. *Clinical Psychology: Science and Practice, 7,* 418–434.

Keenan, K., & Shaw, D. S. (1994). The development of coercive family processes: The interaction between aversive toddler behavior and parenting factors. In J. McCord (Ed.), *Coercion and punishment in long-term perspectives* (pp. 165–180). New York: Cambridge University Press.

Keenan, K., & Shaw, D. S. (2003). Starting at the beginning: Exploring the etiology of antisocial behavior in the first years of life. In B. B. Lahey, T. E. Moffitt, & A. Caspi (Eds.), *Causes of conduct disorder and juvenile delinquency* (pp. 153–181). New York: Guilford Press.

Kieras, J. E., Tobin, R. M., Graziano, W. G., & Rothbart, M. K. (2005). You can't always get what you want: Effortful control and children's responses to undesirable gifts. *Psychological Science, 16,* 391–396.

Kochanska, G., Murray, K., & Coy, K. C. (1997). Inhibitory control as a contributor to conscience in childhood: From toddler to early school age. *Child Development, 68,* 263–277.

Kochanska, G., Murray, K. T., & Harlan, E. T. (2000). Effortful control in early childhood: Continuity and change, antecedents, and implications for social development. *Developmental Psychology, 36,* 220–232.

Kopp, C. (1982). Antecedents of self-regulation: A developmental perspective. *Developmental Psychology, 18,* 199–214.

Kopp, C. (1989). Regulation of distress and negative emotions: A developmental view. *Developmental Psychology, 25,* 243–254.

Kopp, C. (1992). Emotional distress and control in young children. In N. Eisenberg & R. Fabes (Eds.), *Emotion and its regulation in early development* (pp. 41–56). San Francisco: Jossey-Bass.

Kozulin, A. (1990). *Vygotsky's psychology: A biography of ideas.* Cambridge, UK: Cambridge University Press.

Kuczynski, L., & Kochanska, G. (1995). Function and content of maternal demands: Developmental significance of early demands for competent action. *Child Development, 66,* 616–628.

Kuhl, J., & Kraska, K. (1993). Self-regulation: Psychometric properties of computer-aided instrument. *German Journal of Psychology, 17,* 11–24.

Ladd, G. W., Birch, S. H., & Buhs, E. S. (1999). Children's social and scholastic lives in kindergarten: Related spheres of influence? *Child Development, 70,* 1373–1400.

Leerkes, E., Paradise, M., O'Brien, M., Calkins, S. D., & Lange, G. (2008). Emotion and cognition processes in preschool children. *Merrill–Palmer Quarterly, 54,* 102–124.

Lewis, M. D., & Stieben, J. (2004). Emotion regulation in the brain: Conceptual issues and directions for developmental research. *Child Development, 75,* 371–376.

Mashburn, A. J., Pianta, R. C., Hamre, B. K., Downer, J. T., Barbarin, O. A., Bryant, D., et al. (2008). Measures of classroom quality in prekindergarten and children's development of academic, language, and social skills. *Child Development, 79,* 732–749.

McClelland, M. M., Cameron, C. E., Connor, C. M., Farris, C. L., Jewkes, A. M., & Morrison, F. J. (2007). Links between behavioral regulation and preschoolers' literacy, vocabulary, and math skills. *Developmental Psychology, 43,* 947–959.

Miller, A. L., Gouley, K. K., Seifer, R., Dickstein, S., & Shields, A. (2004). Emotions and behaviors in the head start classroom: Associations among observed dysregulation, social competence, and preschool adjustment. *Early Education and Development, 15,* 147–165.

Moffitt, T. E. (1993). The neuropsychology of conduct disorder. *Development and Psychopathology, 5,* 135–151.

Moore, G. A., & Calkins, S. D. (2004). Infants' vagal regulation in the still-face paradigm is related to dyadic coordination of mother–infant interaction. *Developmental Psychology, 40,* 1068–1080.

Morales, M., Mundy, P., Crowson, M. M., Neal, R. A., & Delgado, C. E. F. (2005). Individual differences in infant attention skills, joint attention, and emotion regulation behaviour. *International Journal of Behavioral Development, 29,* 259–263.

Neitzel, C., & Stright, A. D. (2003). Mothers' scaffolding of children's problem solving: Establishing a foundation of academic self-regulatory competence. *Journal of Family Psychology,* *17,* 147–159.

Nigg, J. T., Hinshaw, S. P., Carte, E. T., & Treuting, J. J. (1998). Neuropsychological correlates of childhood attention-deficit/hyperactivity disorder: Explainable by comorbid disruptive behavior or reading problems? *Journal of Abnormal Psychology, 107,* 468–480.

Nigg, J. T., & Huang-Pollock, C. L. (2003). An early-onset model of the role of executive functions and intelligence in conduct disorder/delinquency. In B. B. Lahey, T. E. Moffitt, & A. Caspi (Eds.), *Causes of conduct disorder and juvenile delinquency* (pp. 227–253). New York: Guilford Press.

Nigg, J. T., Quamma, J. P., Greenberg, M. T., & Kusche, C. A. (1999). A two-year longitudinal study of neuropsychological and cognitive performance in relation to behavioral problems and competencies in elementary school children. *Journal of Abnormal Child Psychology, 27,* 51–63.

Ochsner, K. N., & Gross, J. J. (2004). Thinking makes it so: A social cognitive neuroscience approach to emotion regulation. In R. F. Baumeister & K. D. Vohs (Eds.), *Handbook of self-regulation: Research, theory, and applications* (pp. 229–255). New York: Guilford Press.

Paris, S. G., & Newman, R. S. (1990). Developmental aspects of self-regulated learning. *Educational Psychologist, 25,* 87–102.

Pelco, L. E., & Reed-Victor, E. (2007). Self-regulation and learning-related social skills: Intervention ideas for elementary school students. *Preventing School Failure, 51*(3), 36–42.

Pennington, B. F., & Ozonoff, S. (1996). Executive functions and developmental psychopathology. *Journal of Child Psychology and Psychiatry, 37,* 51–87.

Pianta, R., & Stuhlman, M. (2004). Teacher–child relationships and children's success in the first years of school. *School Psychology Review, 33,* 444–458.

Porges, S. W. (1991). Vagal tone: An autonomic mediatory of affect. In J. A. Garber & K. A. Dodge (Eds.), *The development of affect regulation and dysregulation* (pp. 11–128). New York: Cambridge University Press.

Porges, S. W. (1996). Physiological regulation in high-risk infants: A model for assessment and potential intervention. *Development and Psychopathology, 8,* 43–58.

Porges, S. W., Doussard-Roosevelt, J. A., & Maita, A. K. (1994). Vagal tone and the physiological regulation of emotion. *Monographs of the Society for Research in Child Development, 59*(2), 167–186.

Porges, S. W., Doussard-Roosevelt, J. A., Portales, A. L., & Greenspan, S. I. (1996). Infant regulation of the vagal "brake" predicts child behavior problems: A psychobiological model of social behavior. *Developmental Psychobiology, 29,* 697–712.

Posner, M. I., & Rothbart, M. K. (1992). Attentional mechanisms and conscious experience. In D. A. Milner & M. D. Rugg (Eds.), *The neuropsychology of consciousness* (pp. 91–111). San Diego, CA: Academic Press.

Posner, M. I., & Rothbart, M. K. (1998). Summary and commentary: Developing attentional skills. In J. E. Richards (Ed.), *Cognitive neuroscience of attention: A developmental perspective* (pp. 317–323). Mahwah, NJ: Erlbaum.

Posner, M. I., & Rothbart, M. K. (2007). *Educating the human brain.* Washington, DC: American Psychological Association.

Raver, C. C., Jones, S. M., Li-Grining, C. P., Metzger, M., Champion, K. M., & Latriese, S. (2008). Improving preschool classroom processes: Preliminary findings from a randomized trial implemented in Head Start settings. *Early Childhood Research Quarterly, 23,* 10–26.

Raver, C. C., & Knitzer, J. (2002). *Ready to enter: What research tells policymakers about strategies to promote social and emotional school readiness among three- and four-year-olds.* New York: National Center for Children in Poverty.

Reid, M. J., Webster-Stratton, C., & Hammond, M. (2007). Enhancing a classroom social competence and problem-solving curriculum by offering parent training to families of moderate- to high-risk elementary school children. *Journal of Clinical Child and Adolescent Psychology, 36,* 605–620.

Repetti, R. L., Taylor, S. E., & Seeman, T. E. (2002). Risky families: Family social environments and the mental and physical health of offspring. *Psychological Bulletin, 128,* 330–366.

Richards, J. E., & Cameron, D. (1989). Infant heart-rate variability and behavioral developmental status. *Infant Behavior and Development, 12,* 45–58.

Riggs, N. R., Blair, C. B., & Greenberg, M. T. (2003). Concurrent and 2-year longitudinal relations between executive function and the behavior of 1st and 2nd grade children. *Child Neuropsychology, 9,* 267–276.

Riggs, N. R., Jahromi, L. B., Razza, R. P., Dillworth-Bart, J. E., & Mueller, U. (2006). Executive function and the promotion of social–emotional competence. *Journal of Applied Developmental Psychology, 27,* 300–309.

Rimm-Kaufman, S. E., Pianta, R. C., & Cox, M. J. (2000). Teachers' judgments of problems in the transition to kindergarten. *Early Childhood Research Quarterly, 15,* 147–166.

Rothbart, M. K. (1989). Temperament and development. In G. A. Kohnstamm, J. E. Bates, & M. K. Rothbart (Eds.), *Temperament in childhood* (pp. 187–247). Oxford, UK: Wiley.

Rothbart, M. K., & Bates, J. E. (1998). Temperament. In D. William & N. Eisenberg (Eds.), *Handbook of child psychology: Vol. 3. Social, emotional, and personality development* (5th ed., pp. 105–176). Hoboken, NJ: Wiley.

Rothbart, M. K., Ziaie, H., & O'Boyle, C. G. (1992). Self-regulation and emotion in infancy. In N. Eisenberg & R. A. Fabes (Eds.), *Emotion and its regulation in early development* (pp. 7–23). San Francisco: Jossey-Bass.

Rueda, M. R., Posner, M. I., & Rothbart, M. K. (2005). The development of executive attention: Contributions to the emergence of self-regulation. *Developmental Neuropsychology, 28,* 573–594.

Ruff, H. A., & Rothbart, M. K. (1996). *Attention in early development: Themes and variations.* New York: Oxford University Press.

Rutter, M. (1987). The role of cognition in child development and disorder. *British Journal of Medical Psychology, 60,* 1–16.

Schneider, M. (1974). Turtle technique in the classroom. *Teaching Exceptional Children, 7,* 22–24.

Sethi, A., Mischel, W., Aber, L. J., Shoda, Y., & Rodriguez, M. L. (2000). The role of strategic attention deployment in development of self-regulation: Predicting preschoolers' delay of gratification from mother–toddler interactions. *Developmental Psychology, 36,* 767–777.

Shields, A., Dickstein, S., Seifer, R., Giusti, L., Magee, K. D., & Spritz, B. (2001). Emotional competence and early school adjustment: A study of preschoolers at risk. *Early Education and Development, 12,* 73–96.

Shipman, K., Schneider, R., & Brown, A. (2004). Emotion dysregulation and psychopathology. In M. Beauregard (Ed.), *Consciousness, emotional self-regulation, and the brain* (pp. 61–85). Amsterdam: Benjamins.

Snow, K. L. (2006). Measuring school readiness: Conceptual and practical considerations. *Early Education and Development, 17,* 7–41.

St. Clair-Thompson, H. L., & Gathercole, S. E. (2006). Executive functions and achievements in school: Shifting, updating, inhibition, and working memory. *Quarterly Journal of Experimental Psychology, 59,* 745–759.

Stansbury, K., & Gunnar, M. R. (1994). Adrenocortical activity and emotion regulation. *Monographs of the Society for Research in Child Development, 59*(2), 108–134.

Stifter, C. A., & Fox, N. A. (1990). Infant reactivity: Physiological correlates of newborn and 5-month temperament. *Developmental Psychology, 26,* 582–588.

Stifter, C. A., Spinrad, T., & Braungart-Rieker, J. (1999). Toward a developmental model of child compliance: The role of emotion regulation. *Child Development, 70*, 21–32.

Suess, P. E., Porges, S. W., & Plude, D. J. (1994). Cardiac vagal tone and sustained attention in school-age children. *Psychophysiology, 31*, 17–22.

Thompson, R. A. (1994). Emotion regulation: A theme in search of definition. *Monographs of the Society for Research in Child Development, 59*(2), 25–52.

Trentacosta, C. J., & Izard, C. E. (2007). Kindergarten children's emotion competence as a predictor of their academic competence in first grade. *Emotion, 7*, 77–88.

Trentacosta, C. J., Izard, C. E., Mostow, A. J., & Fine, S. E. (2006). Children's emotional competence and attentional competence in early elementary school. *School Psychology Quarterly, 21*, 148–170.

Wachs, T. D. (1999). The what, why, and how of temperament: A piece of the action. In L. Balter & C. S. Tamis-LeMonda (Eds.), *Child psychology: A handbook of contemporary issues* (pp. 23–44). Philadelphia: Taylor & Francis.

Webster-Stratton, C., & Reid, M. J. (2003). The Incredible Years Parents, Teachers, and Children training series: A multifaceted treatment approach for young children with conduct problems. In A. E. Kazdin & J. R. Weisz (Eds.), *Evidence-based psychotherapies for children and adolescents* (pp. 224–240). New York: Guilford Press.

Webster-Stratton, C., Reid, M. J., & Hammond, M. (2001). Preventing conduct problems, promoting social competence: A parent and teacher training partnership in Head Start. *Journal of Clinical Child Psychology, 30*, 283–302.

Webster-Stratton, C., Reid, M. J., & Stoolmiller, M. (2008). Preventing conduct problems and improving school readiness: Evaluation of the Incredible Years teacher and child training programs in high-risk schools. *Journal of Child Psychology and Psychiatry, 49*, 471–488.

Williford, A. P., Calkins, S. D., & Keane, S. P. (2007). Predicting change in parenting stress across early childhood: Child and maternal factors. *Journal of Abnormal Child Psychology, 35*, 251–263.

Wilson, B. J., & Gottman, J. M. (1996). Attention—the shuttle between emotion and cognition: Risk, resiliency, and physiological bases. In M. E. Hetherington & E. A. Blechman (Eds.), *Stress, coping, and resiliency in children and families* (pp. 189–228). Hillsdale, NJ: Erlbaum.

Zelazo, P. D., & Boseovski, J. J. (2001). Video reminders in a representational change task: Memory for cues but not beliefs or statements. *Journal of Experimental Child Psychology, 78*, 107–129.

Zelazo, P. D., Müller, U., Frye, D., & Marcovitch, S. (2003). The development of executive function. *Monographs of the Society for Research in Child Development, 68*(3, Serial No. 274).

CHAPTER 10

Teaching Hearts and Minds in Early Childhood Classrooms

Curriculum for Social and Emotional Development

Janet E. Thompson
Kelly K. Twibell

Early childhood educators and primary grade teachers have long recognized the importance of young children's social and emotional capacities to their learning at school. Surveys of kindergarten teachers indicate that obstacles encountered by the children they teach include difficulty controlling emotions or behavior, problems with social skills, difficulty working independently (or in a group), problems with taking turns or sharing, and lack of enthusiasm or interest in learning (Lewit & Baker, 1995; Rimm-Kaufman, Pianta, & Cox, 2000). These social, emotional, and motivational characteristics are mentioned far more frequently by teachers than are problems with letter recognition and number or preliteracy skills, which are far more commonly the focus of current school readiness efforts. For children in more challenging circumstances, the importance of socioemotional capacities is even greater. In one study, Head Start teachers reported that their children exhibited signs of serious emotional distress, including depression and antisocial conduct, that impaired learning (Yoshikawa & Knitzer, 1997; see also Egger & Angold, 2006; Raver & Knitzer, 2002).

These reports from the field are complemented by the findings of developmental science, which indicate that cognitive growth is strongly influenced by a child's social preparation for group learning, self-regulatory capacities, and emotional maturity (for a review, see R. Thompson & Raikes, 2007). In Chapter 8, this volume, R. Thompson and Goodman have described some of the social, emotional, and motivational qualities relevant to early school success, including children's social and emotional understanding of others, initiative as learners, self-regulation, self-concept, group participation, cooperation and sense of responsibility, and interactions with peers and teachers. Research studies that they cite indicate that these social, emotional, and motivational characteristics are directly and indirectly linked to young children's preparation for school and success in academic achievement.

It is one thing to recognize the importance of socioemotional skills to early learning. It is a greater challenge to develop early childhood curriculum and program practices to foster the development of these skills. Our purpose in this chapter is to outline curriculum principles that can contribute to the growth of many of the capacities identified by Thompson and Goodman (Chapter 8, this volume). Our goal is to show how, through a well-designed early childhood curriculum, teachers can contribute both to the growth of children's cognitive skills and to their socioemotional preparation for school, and that there is no conflict with advancing these dual goals simultaneously. Indeed, we would argue that striving to enhance cognitive development, without attending to children's motivational, social, and emotional capacities, may be self-defeating, especially for children growing up in challenging environments.

Our discussion is based on our work on the socioemotional development section of the California Preschool Curriculum Framework, a resource to provide guidance for early childhood educators on strategies to foster school readiness in California preschoolers. As primary authors of this section, our goal was to help educators understand the formal and informal ways that young children's sense of themselves as learners, skills for social interaction, and relationships with others contribute to learning in preschool, and how these skills can be encouraged by teachers and caregivers. Although the approaches we describe are most often observed in the context of preschool programs, the design, planning, and interaction strategies are equally relevant and effective in kindergarten and primary grade classrooms.

We begin by considering general foundations for the kind of curriculum that can enhance children's social and emotional development during the preschool years. We then discuss three specific foundations of an early childhood classroom that can be used to promote social and emotional development: (1) the design of the classroom environment, (2) important elements of the program's daily routine, and (3) the child's interactions with teachers. While considering these, we highlight specific aspects of socioemotional growth and curricular practices that can encourage their development. The chapter closes with an expanded illustration of one constructivist curriculum approach that effectively addresses both socioemotional and cognitive skills development, followed by summary comments and observations.

Curriculum Foundations

The immediate goal of working to enhance socioemotional development within the preschool and primary grade context is to increase children's capacity to benefit from the curriculum content and learning opportunities in all domains of the educational program. Unlike most of the other domains, however, growth in socioemotional competence is not primarily an outcome of specific content taught through a program of organized, sequential lessons. Group activities designed specifically to emphasize empathy and cooperation are important, for example, but they augment and reinforce broader lessons that are implicit in how teachers interact with children throughout the day. In the same way, stories selected within the language arts and social studies curricular areas are excellent ways to weave prosocial content into children's experience, but prosocial motivation is best learned through example and gentle coaching in many social contexts.

Having an articulated curriculum framework is important, however, in providing a general orientation to the educational plan that guides the design of the classroom environment, routines and activities, and teacher–child interactions. All curricular approaches have strengths and weaknesses in terms of their impacts on children's cognitive and socioemotional growth. With respect to fostering socioemotional development, the following specific features provide a foundation for success.

The curricular design must be one that allows ample opportunity for practicing social interaction and relationship skills; provides support for the development of age-appropriate self-regulation skills; encourages curiosity and initiative; and gives each child a network of nurturing, dependable adults, capable of actively scaffolding their learning in a group setting. Key elements for the effective implementation of such a design include the following:

- An interesting, engaging, and varied environment, both indoors and outdoors, within which child-initiated play and exploration provide the primary context for learning.
- A classroom environment that enhances children's opportunities to make activity and learning choices independently.
- Daily program routines that provide children with a sense of security, predictability, and mastery of manageable transitions.
- Adult engagement as coexplorers with children.
- Verbal and active scaffolding of children's experience-based learning.
- Adult participation as coaches in social conflict-resolution situations.
- Facilitated collaboration in problem solving across all areas of the curriculum.
- Opportunities for children to function in responsible and cooperative roles within the classroom community.

In the pages that follow, we discuss these and other elements of a socioemotional curriculum for young children. An outline of our discussion is in Table 10.1.

TABLE 10.1. Strategies to Support Children's Socioemotional Development in Early Childhood Classrooms

Designing the physical environment	Planning daily routines and activities	Using teacher–child interactions
• Considering aesthetics • Designing learning areas • Using low shelving • Planning group meeting spaces • Providing for privacy • Reflecting the individual • Selecting appropriate play materials	• Providing predictability, with flexibility • Balancing active and quiet play • Balancing individual and group experiences • Planning transitions	• Providing consistent, nurturant support • Engaging in continuous attentive observation • Modeling behavior and attitudes • Narrating children's experiences • Supporting children's mastery orientation • Generalizing from specific rules to values • Building classroom community • Guiding and coaching children's behavior

Design of the Classroom Environment

The classroom environments that teachers design for young children set the tone for play and interaction. When educators are mindful of the aesthetics, organization, and function of each area in their classroom, challenging behavior is likely to decrease and prosocial behavior to increase. A program's vision for learning and philosophy of care, ideally based on theory, current research, and best practice, dictates how the space is conceptualized and designed. For example, if the curricular orientation is based on the view that children are competent directors of their own learning, educators develop environments that reflect children's emerging interests and provide easy access to meaningful play materials. Adult–child interactions build and expand on children's questions and comments. This broader vision creates synchrony among environment, routines, and teacher–child interactions.

As stated earlier, child-initiated, active learning experiences promote socioemotional development (Phyfe-Perkins & Shoemaker, 1986; Shonkoff & Phillips, 2000; Thompson, 2006). Therefore, educators must plan classroom environments that present opportunities for such child-initiated learning. Additionally, programs must incorporate knowledge of aesthetics and organization of space to encourage a sense of respect, responsibility, and community. Designated learning areas prescribe the nature of play, for example, and low shelving allows children and adults visual access to play and learning materials. Public and private spaces create an atmosphere of community and simultaneously acknowledge the presence of individuals. Materials can be challenging, yet developmentally appropriate. Each of these key elements of environmental design and its implications for socioemotional development is discussed below. More specifically, we discuss the aesthetics of the learning environment, the importance of designated learning areas and of low shelving to give children access to play and learning materials, the value of both large- and small-group spaces and activities, the importance of providing private places in an environment that reflects individual characteristics and backgrounds, and the importance of selecting appropriate play materials.

Aesthetics

A classroom is more than its walls, furniture, and toys. The visual landscape also has a significant influence on behavior. The colors, textures, and scale of items in the physical environment can do much to intensify or modulate children's energy (Bakley, 2001). Choosing soft, soothing hues for walls and furniture allows these items to fade into the background and, more importantly, bring children and their activity into focus (Hohmann & Weikart, 2002). By contrast, even an adult would find a room with brightly colored furniture and sharp lines distracting after a short period of time. Maintaining an appropriate level of stimulation in this manner facilitates children's self-regulation, so that they may actively engage with their peers and the materials made available to them.

Other elements of classroom aesthetics influence the socioemotional atmosphere of the classroom. Keeping furnishings child-size and draping fabric to visually lower the room's ceiling height creates an appropriate scale within which children can explore and, in so doing, enhances their sense of efficacy (Tegano, Moran, DeLong, Brickey, & Ramanssini, 1996). Additionally, the intentional use of art and other items that reflect children's home cultures does much to create familiarity and a sense of community. This home-like atmosphere shows respect for children's family culture, thus promoting warmth, security, and a positive self-concept. The attractive space that adults prepare for children publicizes expectations for its cooperative care: *We all play in and care for this beautiful place together.*

Designated Learning Areas

Within a classroom, children engage in a range of distinct play explorations. These activities vary in terms of their activity level, the degree of concentration they require, and the amount of social interaction they involve. An environment set up to support this wide range of social interaction choices provides a variety of well-defined and labeled learning areas of different sizes, with some meant to accommodate active group play and others to provide private spaces for quiet individual pursuits (Epstein, 2007; Ratcliff, 2001). The characteristics of each type of activity, as well as its popularity with a particular classroom of children, dictate the amount of space allotted for it. With a dynamic, emergent curriculum approach, this may change throughout the school year as children's interests evolve. By contrast, when teachers set up for all kinds of play using exclusively large, open areas, children may run through without pausing or wander from place to place without intentionality, and temperamentally more inhibited children may be intimidated and hesitant to join groups of peers.

Sensitive educators are also mindful of the possibilities for social learning in each classroom area. Dramatic play and block construction, characterized by lively collaboration and group decision making, tend to require more room than a book area or writing station. Such energetic activities can be disruptive to children focusing on quieter tasks. For this reason educators should place these active play zones in proximity to each other, and away from quiet areas (Harms, Clifford, & Cryer, 2005). This intentional arrangement of space leads to more purposeful engagement in play and can help children self-regulate, seeking out appropriately stimulating spaces as they learn to monitor their own internal needs. An "invitation" from the physical environment to engage periodically with just one or a small group of other children makes social demands more manageable for younger children.

Low Shelving

Low shelving provides children with visual access to their peers and a survey of opportunities for both individual and collaborative play (Hohmann & Weikart, 2002). Being able to scan visually the possibilities for materials to use in creative representation can lead to more creative problem solving (Gandini, 2004). A child may select learning areas based on interests, as well as important relationships. For example, after watching a small group of children explore insects in the science area, one child may approach the area for the chance to watch ants and dragonflies, but another child may elect to follow a close friend who has chosen to explore there. A visually accessible physical layout also facilitates children's assertions of their own initiative. Rather than waiting for an adult to be free to retrieve an object from a cabinet, children can decide what they need and independently collect the necessary materials. Finally, using low shelving also affords children of varying temperaments the opportunity to select play settings at their own pace. A slow-to-warm-up child can watch the classroom from a distance and enter social contexts that feel most comfortable.

Group Meeting Spaces

As we detail later, a well-balanced daily schedule includes group learning experiences, as well as time for individual exploration. To facilitate children's successful participation in small-group and large-group activities, teachers must skillfully prepare both the group meeting spaces and materials to be used. Well-designed group experiences can promote self-regulation, encourage behavioral and attentional control, facilitate group participation and commitment, build event knowledge, and support children's perspective-taking abilities. Poorly planned group times often undermine growth in these areas and can contribute to negative attitudes about the kinds of group-learning demands that children will confront as they enter formal school settings.

A clear, thoughtful vision for group experiences dictates the design of the environment and the selection of materials. Large-group experiences provide children with the opportunity to gather as a community to read stories, sing songs, and share conversation about ongoing classroom explorations. A large, open meeting space is most conducive toward helping children stay focused, socially constructive, and actively engaged. Within the designated space, teachers develop seating arrangements based on their vision for group participation. Forming a circle, for example, allows individuals a clear view of teachers and peers, enabling them to attend to and respond to verbal and nonverbal communication, as well as visual prompts (which may be especially effective in engaging beginning English language learners). Children can learn from the examples of peers (e.g., raising hands) and the teacher (e.g., a quiet voice).

The design of large-group settings can contribute significantly to children's self-regulatory skills as they learn to manage the distractions of adjacent peers, enticing toys, or their own impulses. Some educators choose to use carpet squares as a concrete reminder for children to maintain ample personal space and resist poking nearby children. Providing a small, quiet squeeze toy assists a child who needs something tactile to manipulate to maintain self-control. Preparing an area (e.g., "cool-down area") for children to self-regulate away from the group can be an additional support to meet individual needs. This space should be viewed, and used, as a positive alternative to group participation ("Sasha, it looks like you might want to wiggle. You can go to the cool-down area if you need a break"). If the group experiences are meaningful and reflective of children's interests, children will return to the group activity as their bodies and minds are ready to participate effectively.

Small-group activities present to children a focused opportunity for collaborative exploration or problem solving. To facilitate self-regulation and attentional control, educators should choose a space that is both comfortable and conducive to work, such as small tables or enclosed, carpeted spaces. Working in a consistent designated space builds children's knowledge of routines and enables them to recall and apply group rules and expectations, thus imparting a sense of belonging and control (Hohmann & Weikart, 2002).

The social experience of large-group and small-group participation is significantly influenced by group composition and size. To form well-balanced groups, teachers use their knowledge of individual interests, energy, temperament, developmental age, and emerging friendships. Some children participate more frequently when they are matched with children of the same age, whereas others may participate more actively with older peers. Some children may benefit from working with children who match their individual temperament. Maintaining group cohorts for a length of time—at least several months—encourages group cooperation and leads children to expand their self-awareness to include a sense of identity as members of a group. Younger children are likely to function more successfully in smaller groups than in larger groups because of the challenges of simultaneously maintaining interaction with many peers.

Finally, the preparation and use of materials in small- and large-group activities are important in developing skills for group participation. Books, songs, and curricular materials should be meaningfully selected and based on observations of children's ongoing explorations in the classroom and home culture and community. Older children, as they express a desire to exercise leadership, can distribute materials and demonstrate their use for younger children. A job list, with pictures of individual children, can help them anticipate and execute shared responsibilities. Additionally, all children can serve as models for each other, with adult attention to these opportunities (e.g., "I noticed Sofia is using the rhythm sticks to beat out a new pattern. Let's listen to Sofia's idea"). Visual prompts, such as props and picture cues, remind children of routines and expectations, and can facilitate self-regulation, attentional control, and event knowledge. Posting a picture of an ear can preface story time, for example, and remind children of behavioral expectations (e.g., listening).

Providing for Privacy

The sounds of actively engaged learning can be loud and at times overstimulating. Some children respond negatively by running around the classroom, unable to focus on making their own learning choices, or they may overtly cover their ears and shout, "Too loud!" In these and other situations, many children need "private" spaces (sometimes equipped with pillows or stuffed toys) they can self-select that are conducive to self-regulation by providing a respite from group participation (Bell, Carr, Denno, Johnson, & Phillips, 2004; Fields & Fields, 2006). Such spaces for seclusion are especially necessary in all-day contexts. When it appears that children are uninterested or unable to maintain focus during large- or small-group activities, suggesting an alternative low-energy activity can help them decide what they most need at the moment, which can increase a sense of personal control in an institutional setting where many choices are made for them.

Reflecting the Individual

Self-awareness and self-understanding are important elements of socioemotional development. A classroom is a community setting, but it should also reflect each individual. Including space for personal belongings, incorporating children's unique artwork, and providing documentation of individual learning experiences give children a sense of personal esteem, as well as ownership over the space. Having an individual storage unit (e.g., a "cubby") allows children the space to store personal items and important "works in progress." This can be reassuring to children when everything else in the classroom must be shared with others.

Seeing themselves and their work reflected positively in the environment influences children's self-concepts as their creations are proudly displayed. These displays also contribute to development of group initiative because children are reminded of previous investigations and inspired to take part in new explorations (Epstein, 2007). Finally, encouraging self-understanding incorporates elements of the child's cultural context (Bredenkamp & Copple, 1997; Epstein, 2007; Riley, San Juan, Klinkner, & Ramminger, 2008). Inviting families to loan items from home to enhance the classroom provides children with a sense of pride, as well as security and familiarity. Books in their home language, music from their culture, family photos, and even simple food containers all help children to feel comfortable and confident.

Selecting Appropriate Play Materials

Children need to be appropriately challenged. This means providing learning experiences that work at the level of a child's emerging abilities, while allowing practice of already-mastered skills. They should be stimulated to think but able to approach tasks with reasonable expectations of success. Open-ended materials are flexible enough to complement the skills of all children. These traditional childhood staples, such as blocks, art supplies, and sand with digging tools and containers, all may be manipulated in multiple ways. Because of the open format, a child with beginning skills is able to use the materials with the same expectations of success as a more experienced playmate, simply because of the differentiated explorations he or she self-selects. Open-ended, multipurpose play materials allow children to express their unique creativity, experience feelings of self-efficacy, and develop divergent thinking skills.

It is also appropriate to provide a variety of closed-ended activities, such as puzzles and matching games. Closed-ended activities often lead to one right answer or outcome. For the reasons mentioned previously, teachers should be careful to select activities that match children's emerging skills (Prescott, 1994). The positive support that children receive from adults while completing such challenging tasks can do much to promote their persistence and sense of competence.

Play materials should not only reflect emerging skills but also be selected with an awareness of emerging classroom interests (Bredenkamp & Copple, 1997). Adults who watch children at play and document evolving investigations capitalize on children's initiative. Curriculum that is meaningful to children and reflective of their play themes facilitates a positive sense of self as they see their ideas valued and implemented on a larger scale (Curtis & Carter, 1996). Children build social understanding when they are invested stakeholders in the learning environment and observe each other's individual strengths as they collaborate on classroom projects. Providing plenty of materials ensures that children are able to execute their own intentions for play (Epstein, 2007).

Educators can be intentional in their support of social skills and collaborative play by incorporating play materials that promote and encourage peer play (Epstein, 2007). Large wooden blocks, too difficult to carry alone, require the effort and cooperation of a pair of children. Purposefully planning a "birthday party" in the dramatic play area provokes discussion of friendship and inclusion. Working together to create a large bubble tunnel with a hula-hoop involves a shared goal and requires teamwork to achieve success. Just as children learn letters, speech sounds, and word-making skills through the use of letter-making tools, they learn effective peer interaction and problem solving through a planned social curriculum.

Effectively organizing toys influences children's behavior (Riley et al., 2008). Materials that are conceptually arranged and carefully labeled offer children a visual menu of potential opportunities for play. They see their options and can thoughtfully make their own activity choices. This intentional organization supports the child's developing autonomy and decision making.

Daily Routines and Activities

Just as the design of the physical environment of the classroom creates setting conditions that enable young children to function successfully with the social, self-regulatory, attentional, and other socioemotional demands of the curriculum, so also the design of the daily schedule accomplishes similar goals. Teachers in many respects enable young children to manage themselves and their relationships in the classroom through the skill with which they organize daily routines and activities predictably (so that they can be anticipated), signal and support transitions, and balance relatively active and relatively quiet play, and group and individual activities. In this section, we discuss the balance of predictability and flexibility in the daily routine, the importance of active and quiet play, the balance of individual and group activity, and the significance of attention to transitions.

Predictability, with Flexibility

A consistent daily routine facilitates children's trust in their learning environment and offers them a foundation for predictability and self-reliance (Bakley, 2001; Epstein, 2007). When children can anticipate what comes now, next, and later, they are able to regulate their expectations, energy, and activity. Furthermore, they become active participants within each daily routine because they are prepared to join in. Children's ability to make sense of and recall scheduled events may be strengthened by having at hand a picture schedule of the daily routine to help them anticipate important events (Bell et al., 2004). For example, educators may use this visual prompt to help a child self-regulate after a difficult separation from a parent or guardian ("First we play inside, then we go to large group. We have snack and play outside. Dad will come back at small-group time"). A child may also use the picture schedule to help another child remember expectations for behavior ("Feet stay on the ground. During outside time you can climb").

Although it is valuable to provide children with a predictable daily schedule, program needs warrant sensitivity and flexibility (Hohmann & Weikart, 2002). A rigid routine leaves little room to follow children's emerging interests and can work against self-regulation. A child who may require a few extra minutes to finish a project should be permitted extra time to complete the task because doing so respects the child's initiative and self-efficacy. On the other hand, adults decrease a child's ability to self-regulate actively when they regularly or unexpectedly change the order of daily activities. In these circumstances, adults may notice children responding to such varying routines with visible unease, off-task behavior, and general disruptiveness. To prevent such unnecessary negative reactions, educators should thoughtfully prepare children for any inconsistencies in routine: "Today we are going to the fire station before we eat snack. Usually we go on walks after snack, but today we are doing something different." Attentive teachers plan ahead to help children anticipate.

Balance of Active and Quiet Play

The quality of activity throughout the daily routine—high-energy versus low-energy or active versus quiet—can impact children's behavior (Bredenkamp & Copple, 1997). If children continuously engage in active play, such as outdoor time or interactive free play, they may become overly tired and overstimulated. Furthermore, their spent energy diminishes their ability to engage cognitively with the classroom environment. Similar behaviors may be displayed by children required to sit or lie still and participate in consecutive low-energy activities (e.g., a nap, quiet time, storybook reading). Because they are restless and off-task, children also fail to benefit from learning opportunities.

These negative outcomes of poor planning can be eliminated by intentionally alternating between active and quiet routines. The inherent balance in such a daily schedule encourages self-regulation as children are guided through appropriately varied levels of stimulation. This leads to positive behavior and enhances a child's ability to engage constructively with the learning environment and socialize with peers and teachers.

Balance of Individual and Group Experiences

Children need opportunities for both individual and large-group exploration, time alone and time together. Each of these routines offers children a different skill building experience (Epstein, 2007). For example, large-group experiences are an ideal setting in which to establish community and build shared knowledge. Children acquire turn-taking skills and active listening techniques as they participate in cooperative conversation. For these reasons, as well as others already discussed, group experiences should be incorporated into the schedule each day.

Attending to a group experience can, however, be somewhat difficult for young children. Preschoolers have a fairly short attention span, limited social skills, and in social situations must work hard to maintain self-control. To better match young children's limited abilities to self-regulate and to maintain attention, educators should keep group experiences brief, generally 10–15 minutes for younger preschoolers and 15–20 minutes for older preschoolers. This guideline may be adjusted, based on how well the group functions, and should be modified if children appear disengaged or uninterested in the activity. Ignoring a group's need for a transition can lead to more disruptive behavior and a general lack of cooperation. For example, the adult who insists on finishing a book during a large-group story time despite children's restless behavior may incite more problem behavior and, contrary to intent, work against cognitive learning objectives.

Individual explorations work in concert with children's need for autonomy, and permit older children appropriate venues for asserting their initiative. During play or choice time, they are free to select activities and carry out individual plans. Children may decide to work alone, in pairs, or in small groups while at play. A child's initiative as a learner is encouraged when educators provide sufficient time for in-depth experimentation and exploration. A recommended work session would be at least an hour in length (Hohmann & Weikart, 2002). This provision of a large, uninterrupted block of time also supports cognitive learning goals. For example, through repeated exposure, children are able to notice patterns, explore differences, and consider multiple mechanisms in the science area. They can form ideas about how something works, make a plan for testing their hypotheses, actively carry out their plans, and reflect on the outcome of their experiments. This process could not be completed as easily within a more limited time frame.

Meaningful adult–child interaction is also more likely when educators have time to observe and talk with children about their individual work. An adult's ability to interact with a child is maximized when there is enough time to slow down and connect daily with each individual child and his or her unique interests. Rather than bouncing between children or busying themselves with preparation for the next activity on the schedule, educators who provide children with substantial time for individual exploration afford themselves ample opportunity to watch and wonder along with children.

Transitions

Transitions in early childhood programs can be challenging for young children, and sometimes also for their teachers. Transitions require children to move from one activity to another as a group, and to shift from one settled activity to begin another. A transition can mean shifting from an active experience to a low-energy one. It may require group participation in multiple settings, such as cleanup of the classroom, or it may call on individual children to wait for a period of time (e.g., to wash their hands before snack). Such transitional circumstances can cause a typically positive classroom climate to unravel as activity and intensity levels increase. Children find it more difficult to maintain behavioral regulation during complex transitions.

Although transitions can involve unsettling change, educators can intentionally plan them in ways that maximize focus and encourage constructive involvement. Songs and visual prompts remind children of what is occurring, their responsibility during the changeover, and what they can do to help them self-regulate through the transition (Riley et al., 2008). Doing so enables young children to anticipate what is changing and how they can participate in the transition. This strategy is illustrated by an adult leading a group of children in singing a "cleanup song" as they pick up and reshelf toys and materials. Furthermore, teachers who use transitions to cue children about expectations for the upcoming activity guide children's behavior and promote competence in the behavioral change (Hohmann & Weikart, 2002). A brief, teacher-led stretching and relaxation exercise between outdoor play and small-group work exemplifies this kind of transition strategy. The calming activity helps children to regulate their bodies and prepares them for a more focused subsequent exploration.

Teacher–Child Interaction

The social environment of an early childhood program can also motivate children to take initiative to explore, experiment, and engage with peers and adults in ways that would not occur in a less supportive and interactive context. The social norms and expectations established for children's, as well as adults', behavior in the program shape the kinds of interactions that occur. In addition, the support and intentional coaching provided by adults as children learn to articulate their emotions, and express their impulses and desires, are key to children's mastery of these self-regulation capacities.

Children's healthy psychological growth occurs in the context of warm, supportive relationships with adults and peers (Thompson, 2006). In the school environment, teachers set the tone for learning—not only in the ways they knowledgeably design the physical environment but also in the ways they create a socioemotional environment that motivates children to participate; establishes mutual trust and respect; and teaches, both directly and indirectly, the social and emotional skills children will need for academic success. Children's interactions within the school environment are the most important determinants of what they learn there and how they feel about the learning process (Bowman, Donovan, & Burns, 2000).

The following general principles are meant to guide the educator's approach to interacting with children to maximize their socioemotional growth and to help children generalize their emerging competencies to other contexts. All are especially important when working with children who may not experience social and emotional support at home. The principles we discuss include the importance of consistent, nurturant adult support; the value of continuous, attentive observations of children's behavior; adult modeling of desirable behavior and attitudes; the caregiver's narration of experiences to provide a verbal structure for understanding; support of children's mastery orientation; the adult generalizing from specific rules to more general values; ideas for building classroom community; and strategies for guidance and coaching of children's behavior.

Consistent, Nurturant Support

Children grow and learn best within the context of relationships with those they trust to be there for them when needed (Shonkoff & Phillips, 2000). This is, of course, a core principle in the design of infant/toddler programs, but is often overlooked when administrators assign and schedule staff for preschool programs. It also sometimes takes a backseat to the demands of classroom management and daily routines. Preschoolers need a person at school who is consistently there to greet them in the morning, demonstrate a friendly, cooperative relationship with their primary family caregivers, and comfort them during times of sadness or upset. Also important to young children is to have someone special, who expresses delight in their accomplishments and notices when they may need help solving a problem.

Close relationships with their preschool teachers and caregivers contribute to young children's positive attitudes about school (Ladd, Birch, & Buhs, 1999). The warmth and security of particularly the teacher–child relationship predicts later school performance, social competence, and the ability to focus attention on a task (Pianta, Nimetz, & Bennett, 1997; Pianta & Stuhlman, 2004). Teachers who develop close relationships with the children in their care foster security and confidence that clearly carries over into the primary grades. Likewise, the quality of adult–child relationships motivates children toward cooperation and responsibility, key markers of their school readiness. Children are motivated to cooperate with adult requests and standards partly by their emotional attachments to those adults and their desire to maintain positive relationships with them (Kochanska, 2002).

Continuous Attentive Observation

Effective teaching is built on a foundation of good observational skills. Careful observation of behavior has always been a mainstay of clinical intervention with young children. It is also a basic element of most formal tools used for the assessment of child progress. Children are observed systematically to assess their achievement of specific skills and competencies, and these competencies include social and emotional skills, as well as cognitive–linguistic abilities. Ideally, the observations are used not only to meet reporting requirements but also to inform teaching content and practices.

In excellent early childhood programs, observation is also the core practice on which all others are based. The goal of attentively observing each child can be achieved in whatever ways the program's design most easily allows. In many team-teaching situations, it is possible for teachers to take turns sitting in the background to watch and listen to a particular child's activities for a few minutes, taking notes as needed to integrate observations into future planning. It is also possible to observe while engaged peripherally in activity with a child or group of children, especially when children are engaged in informal activity or play.

Evidence of a child's social and emotional maturity is sometimes more challenging to observe than are discrete skills in academic content areas. Does the child approach others with confidence and enter into group activity successfully, able to play a variety of roles in various social situations? Does the child initiate and sustain complex interactions with adults and children, using language effectively to assert opinions and ideas, identify and express feelings, and negotiate conflicts productively? Is the child able to request help and support when needed, but pursue solutions to some problems independently? Many of these important social and emotional indicators are not apparent during teacher-directed instruction, but require attentive observation during informal activity times by a skilled adult who knows the dynamics of the particular group and its participants. For teachers, the most helpful observations of children's socioemotional competencies occur in the course of their typical daily activities.

Teacher planning in a responsive environment incorporates these observations of children's interests, their existing levels of socioemotional functioning, and the areas in which there is the need to stimulate growth. Formal assessment tools that make room for brief notes are sufficient for some teachers, but others find it helpful to augment a checklist of skills with their own compilation of anecdotal notes or journal entries about individual children.

Modeling of Behavior and Attitudes

Watching how significant adult caregivers behave is the way young children from the earliest ages learn many of their social and emotional skills. Teachers often note how closely children's behavioral styles reflect those of their parents. The fact that children are so open to behavioral modeling by watching adults is an advantage for teachers, especially in the socioemotional domain. Because young children closely observe and imitate the behavioral examples of adults they care about, caregivers can intentionally model desired behavior for them.

Modeling positive social interactions (e.g., sharing, helping) is the most obvious example of how adults use this practice. The modeling of constructive emotional coping strategies (e.g., anger management) is less often observed in teachers, but it can be equally influential. Modeling is easiest to do as situations arise naturally during the course of the day. The simplest form is audible self-talk. A teacher who stumbles and spills a tray of colored beads can express her exasperation in a way that children can hear and understand (e.g., "Oh, no! I just sorted the beads, and now it looks like I'll have to do it all over again! It's so frustrating when that happens! Well, I guess I'll start with the green ones. It won't take too long"). The teacher is describing the situation and expressing her feelings about it (or at least a socially appropriate version of them). She continues by modeling a constructive course of action to remedy the situation. By that time, she will probably have plenty of child helpers picking up green beads. Of course, she can then continue the impromptu lesson by expressing gratitude to her helpers and commenting on how much faster the job goes when so many people work together on it.

This kind of teacher self-talk works well for modeling self-regulation skills, self-confidence (e.g., expressing assurance in being able to complete a difficult puzzle), and social and emotional understanding (e.g., "I used to be afraid when I climbed up high like this, but then I figured out that if I held onto the railing I wouldn't fall. Now being up here doesn't scare me anymore").

Modeling behavior and attitudes is often as straightforward as having authentic conversations with children, individually or in groups, during which teachers show interest and enthusiasm about what a child is saying. A teacher conveys engagement in the conversation by listening with full attention and making appropriate eye contact, just as he or she wants children to do when they interact with each other. The teacher shows excitement about making a discovery and is animated when reading aloud a funny new story. The dispositions toward learning that teachers convey in the presence of children are contagious. To model positive attitudes, coping strategies, and interaction skills is the single most effective way to transmit them to children (Bilmes, 2004).

Narration of Experience

Preschool children are interested in other people's thoughts and feelings, as well as their own. They wonder about the reasons for people's beliefs and emotions, and frequently ask about them (e.g., "Why are you crying?"). As they gain experience and sophistication, they begin to understand the mental and psychological reasons that people behave the way they do (R. Thompson, 2008). This social and emotional understanding is partial, at best, during the early years, and this capacity varies immensely among children of the same age. Part of this variation can be attributed to family culture, and whether emotions are discussed at home. Much of this variability, however, is because children do not yet have the language to label the emotions, motives, desires, and other mental states they feel or observe. Even if they know the terms for familiar emotions, such as happy, sad, angry, and excited, they may not routinely use them to describe their own feelings (Denham & Weissberg, 2004).

Teachers can help supply these emotion and mental words—particularly the more sophisticated ones—by narrating what they observe children expressing. They can also go further and link an emotion label with a probable cause, being careful to confirm with a preschool-age child whether their causal attributions are correct. This common practice among infant/toddler program caregivers is referred to as "reflective listening."

When used to describe a situation, action, or interaction and the feelings or attitudes of children engaged in it, the technique can help preschoolers sort out mental states and "fine-tune" their understandings.

Additionally, this running commentary can help children link the causes and consequences of behavior, which are challenging for young children to understand. It can also help to emphasize the difference between feelings and actions (Bilmes, 2004). Just because Sophia *really* wants the first turn with the new sand shovel does not mean that grabbing it from David must necessarily follow. Using language to describe these connections between cause and effect, emotion and action, deepens children's understanding of them and contributes to the growth of self-regulation skills. Teacher speech of this kind can further children's understanding that people are different in their characteristics, responses, and preferences (e.g., Liam laughs and thinks it is funny when his block tower is knocked down, but Meera cries and is upset and angry when the same thing happens to hers).

Finally, adults can verbalize general observations based on narration of specific experiences (e.g., "It looks like you are sad about your daddy leaving this morning. Sometimes it's hard for children to stay at school without their mommies or daddies"). Giving language to children's own experiences increases their emotional understanding (Denham, 1998). Moreover, teacher speech provides an avenue for young children to explore negative feelings with an adult and acquire greater insight into feelings that are otherwise confusing, anxious, or frightening to them.

Supporting Children's Mastery Orientation

Children vary significantly in their learning orientation: Some children are mastery-oriented, and others are performance-oriented (Dweck & Leggett, 1988). Children who focus on performing to elicit the approval of others are less likely to attempt challenging tasks and to follow their natural curiosity and interests. By contrast, children with a mastery orientation, who focus their efforts on increasing their ability, best predict high achievement, and this can be seen as early as the preschool years.

This mastery orientation can be strongly influenced by the kinds of interactions with adults that predominate in a child's life. Especially important are adults' reactions to children's achievement successes and failures (Stipek, Recchia, & McClintic, 1992). When teachers provide positive responses to children's hard work and express confidence in their ability to solve problems and achieve success, children become more confident themselves. The confidence that significant adults have in children and their respect for children's efforts affect children's orientation toward learning.

Early childhood educators at times express uncertainty about whether to praise children for what they do and how to express their valuation of children's efforts and accomplishments. Rather than encourage children's dependence on adult expressions of approval, they want to guide children toward intrinsic motivation, while simultaneously showing support for them and pleasure in their demonstrations of self-confidence. One way to accomplish this is for the teacher to focus his or her response on a child's specific effort or accomplishment, without making broad judgments of a child's worth based on the specific product or behavior. A statement that specifically describes the situation or activity and what a child did to achieve success serves multiple purposes. It contributes to the child's ability to remember the event in a way that emphasizes his or her positive role in it. It also describes the child's hard work, cooperation, or problem solving concretely, in a way that increases the child's ability to repeat a similar action in the future (e.g., "Everyone wanted to use the block ramps for their own cars but there were only two of them, so you figured out how to make the plain boards into ramps by propping them up with the small blocks. That made enough ramps for all of you!").

This kind of specific, descriptive feedback from a significant adult builds the adult–child relationship. It shows that the adult is attentive and engaged in, rather than merely supervising, the activity. It reinforces the role of the adult as a coexplorer with children. It contributes to both academic and socioemotional readiness goals.

Generalizing from Specific Rules to Values

Adults adapt their behavior to the expectations and norms of various settings, often without giving this behavior much conscious thought. When walking through a library, for example, most people generally lower their voices or stop talking to companions. Young children have already learned a variety of general rules that apply to their home lives (e.g., removing shoes upon entering the house, trying to be quiet while the baby is sleeping, or asking for permission before snacking on cookies). If asked why they perform these specific actions, children may be able to generalize about the principle behind the family rule. However, they are likely to see some of these regulations as simply adult rules that they are required to follow if they want to avoid "getting in trouble."

During the preschool years, children are beginning to develop the capacity to apply general moral values to specific situations (Thompson, Meyer, & McGinley, 2006). Teachers can help them strengthen this link by routinely moving beyond the statement of rules to include the guiding principle behind each rule. "Let's all take two steps backwards to make room in the circle for everyone" informs children of the immediate request. Adding "In our class we make sure that everyone is included" broadens that goal and states the general principle behind it. When children understand that rules and expectations are based on values and principles, they reach a new awareness about how their actions contribute to the welfare of themselves, others, and their surroundings.

Stating reasons for rules also shows respect for children as learners and as people with the capacity to understand and to make choices to act in prosocial ways. It contributes to their motivation to cooperate and to take responsibility for their actions. Once this pattern of interaction becomes established within adult–child interactions, it then generalizes to peer interactions as young children mature. They are more likely to identify and to verbalize a goal during cooperative play, and to figure out how to achieve it with their peers. Ideally, cooperation becomes not only a means for achieving a goal but also a goal in itself. Later in their development, they will be able to identify and to link their actions and goals to the broad principles their culture values.

Building Classroom Community

A sense of community is a wonderful achievement for a diverse group of children and adults in a learning setting. Rather than being an automatic outcome of spending a school year assigned to the same classroom, it is most often the result of teachers' intentional leadership. As with many other aspects of social learning, teachers set the tone with their own words and actions. Teachers who model friendly, respectful interactions with everyone in the group see their tone reflected in children's behavior toward one another (Epstein, 2007). To expand on this modeling, teachers can also draw children's attention to instances of cooperation and teamwork among themselves. When children enthusiastically retell what they have observed, it stays with them in the same manner as descriptive feedback, and it builds a pattern of similar behavior among peers.

Other intentional practices can strengthen and reinforce positive peer connections within a group. These include the practice of holding class meetings, either on a regular basis or when an event occurs that involves the larger group. At class meetings, adults and children can share information ("We have a new guinea pig who has joined our classroom. What shall we do to care for her well?"), make decisions or engage in formal voting ("What shall we name our guinea pig?"), brainstorm solutions to problems that arise ("Luke and Emma noticed today that people have been dropping small things that are not food into the guinea pig's cage"), and plan for a special occasion, often with an adult taking dictation from children ("Jorge's mom is a veterinarian, and she is visiting us tomorrow to help us learn more about guinea pigs. What questions would you like to ask her?"). An appropriate amount of large-group discussion can help to build cohesiveness and group identity.

Along with class meetings, educators can build camaraderie among children by encouraging brainstorming and problem solving in pairs or small groups. The teacher's attitude that the children can solve whatever issue they encounter in their work or play—with adult coaching, if necessary—builds children's trust in their own social competence and good judgment. Referring children to each other for assistance instead of to an adult also emphasizes their competence and strengthens peer connections (Epstein, 2007). Group brainstorming or decision making can also draw on the strengths of children who may be overlooked in other social situations.

An important part of developing social and emotional understanding is awareness of the ways that people differ from one another. In some contexts, this can lead to negative thoughts and attitudes about people who are different. To some extent, this is a necessary step in the process of identifying positively with one's own culture, gender, language, and other aspects of personal identity. When conversing, adults need to acknowledge young children's awareness of differences, while also expanding their understanding of these differences. In response to a child's skeptical comment about a classmate who "eats with sticks," a teacher could respond, "Yes, you've noticed that Sowon already knows how to eat with chopsticks. At her house, her family uses chopsticks at mealtimes. It can be tricky, and it takes a lot of practice. Would you like to ask her to help us learn how to do it?" Acknowledging, then showing interest and admiration or respectful curiosity when noticing a difference, provides children with a positive model of how to view the variations among people. Later, a sensitive teacher might find an opportunity to emphasize how the two children are alike to highlight connections between them.

Deliberately speaking in terms of "we" rather than "I" or "you" also models this sense of connection and community. Asking how can *we* solve this problem or find Tony's hat, or put away all these blocks, models a cooperative approach to the situation at hand. It subtly encourages identification with the cohort of fellow participants. It also resonates more comfortably with children whose home cultures are communally oriented. Affirming that people have characteristics, experiences, and goals in common is an important complement to the many differences young children are beginning to notice all around them. Rather than minimizing differences, adults can include similarities in discussions with children in the classroom community.

Guidance and Coaching of Children's Behavior

How should teachers respond when young children are not behaving effectively or are interfering with the behavior of others? Although an adult's natural impulse is to intervene directly to correct the child's behavior, teachers who see their role as guides in helping children develop their social and emotional competencies often use these occasions as learning opportunities. Their goals include not only stopping or redirecting the behavior in question but also helping children learn other, more productive ways to solve a problem, resolve a conflict, or get the help or attention they need.

These are "teachable moments" in the classroom. The effective teacher works alongside children as a coach or guide rather than direct the action from a position of control. In guidance, the teacher brings together all the other interaction strategies discussed thus far. A teacher approaches the child with whom he or she has already established a trusting relationship, then may share what he or she has observed, asking for clarification or offering his or her own interpretation. "I've noticed that you've been standing here at the edge of the block area for a long time. It looks like you might want to help our other friends build. (pauses to allow for response) Would you like me to walk over with you to ask how you could help work on the project with them?" The teacher can then proceed to support, model for, and coach the hesitant child through the process of entering peer-group play.

This example illustrates how an educator who knows the group well can use this knowledge to assess a situation and determine how to effectively help a child learn and practice a particular social skill. The teacher can name the emotions the hesitant child may be experiencing, and model possible approaches the child can use to enter a group. He or she can remain in the area to provide security and support, then give verbal feedback by recounting the episode with the child, at an appropriate time, to reinforce and generalize the learning. If the classroom already feels like a familiar community to the child, then the task will be easier.

Interpersonal conflict resolution is often a more complex situation, but one to which the same general interaction guidelines apply: observe, name emotions, narrate what occurs, help children generate and choose ideas for resolving the conflict, and provide descriptive feedback later to help children evaluate and generalize their own effective actions to other situations. A pattern of successful, guided experiences reinforces for children the sense that their classroom is a supportive community within which they can take initiative to try new social behaviors and develop new social skills safely.

As children gain more experience and skill, adults can gradually move from the center to the periphery of problem solving and conflict resolution. During whole-group times, books, puppet stories, and discussions can introduce emotion language, portray characters that face and resolve social dilemmas, and provide practice in perspective taking. Children can often draw analogies between stories about familiar characters, and choices and situations they themselves face.

In all of these activities, the focus is on guidance and coaching rather than control and punishment. Many guidance strategies require considerably more adult time and skill than would assigning blame and meting out consequences. Exerting firm external control often works well to achieve the short-term goal of maintaining classroom order. It can also show children how much more smoothly things can work when everyone follows the same rules. Using this approach exclusively, however, does not contribute to moral internalization (Grusec & Goodnow, 1994), nor does it teach children how to take an active role in social problem solving. When children hear adults describe the steps they took to resolve a conflict, include a peer in play, or take initiative in cleaning up the art area without prompting, their sense of pride and self-efficacy as responsible members of the classroom community grows. Adults acknowledge and appreciate their prosocial behavior, but the children, with coaching as needed, are responsible for that behavior.

Socioemotional Learning in a Constructivist Classroom

The soundness of a constructivist, active learning approach to early education has been well established over the past two decades (Bredekamp & Copple, 1997). In many of their required criteria for high-quality ratings, evaluation tools designed to assess the quality of early childhood program environments include measures of the availability of opportunities and materials for children to explore freely "for a substantial portion of the day" (Harms, Clifford, & Cryer, 2005). A token daily period designated as "choice time," or an orchestrated rotation among teacher-prepared classroom centers, does not achieve the purposes of this guideline concerning the importance of children's self-determined active play and exploration.

In addition to facilitating cognitive goals, this emphasis on the child's ability to choose freely and pursue interests and activities has substantial socioemotional implications. Children who choose what to do and when to do it are demonstrating an awareness of personal preferences and are acting on their own initiative in learning. They are translating thoughts and ideas into actions and experiments. In this way, they begin to solidify a set of self-perceptions about their characteristics and abilities as learners, as well as a sense of self-efficacy in the learning environment. Their overall level of self-awareness as learners increases, especially as observant adults help them give voice to and reflect on their discoveries.

A programmatic approach based on choice within a thoughtfully planned environment also addresses the motivational aspects of learning that are crucial to later school success. Children who are encouraged to take initiative in planning their own activities become increasingly confident in doing so. They practice making well-reasoned choices and come to feel that their ideas are worthwhile. When their own curiosity drives their pursuits, engagement is generally fuller and their efforts to solve problems are more persistent (California Department of Education, 2008). A "why?" question more often leads to a "let's find out" response. When children's investigations lead them down a variety of possible paths, they discover that learning involves the ongoing modification of their initial assumptions about how the world works. Their understanding of concepts deepens rather than stopping as soon as a single right answer to a problem or question is presented.

This crucial motivational element of children's socioemotional readiness to benefit from a formal kindergarten or primary education environment is variously labeled "initiative in learning," "dispositions toward learning," or "approaches to learning." It is now included in most states' standards for early childhood education programs and is incorporated into assessments of child progress in a variety of widely used assessment tools (e.g., California Department of Education, 2008). In an ideal world, these motivational foundations for learning would be nurtured from infancy within every child's home environment. We cannot assume, however, that all children enter school with the eagerness to pursue knowledge and the confidence in their own abilities that we would wish for them. Through participation in early childhood programs designed to support children in mastering new skills and concepts through their own explorations, educators can stimulate their active involvement in the learning process.

The foundation for an eager, confident attitude toward school can be built through this intentional pursuit of *engaged learning* (Helm & Katz, 2001). We most often employ this core constructivist idea as a framework for understanding children's mastery of cognitive concepts through free and active experimentation with *objects*. Piaget's familiar "little scientist" image of the child has been an important reminder to early childhood educators that children master concepts most effectively by discovering and refining them in the course of active exploration. Less frequent references, though, are made to the importance Piaget, in his original writings, placed on building a cooperative "sociomoral" atmosphere in the classroom (DeVries, Zan, Hildebrandt, Edmiaston, & Sales, 2002). This atmosphere, characterized by adult–child relationships of mutual cooperation and respect, is essential to sustaining the child's motivation to be an active learner rather than a passive recipient of information. Attention to socioemotional, as well as physical, components of program design can enhance learning in all developmental domains.

A sophisticated example of constructivist-inspired early education that incorporates strong socioemotional components can be observed in the Reggio Emilia schools of northern Italy (Edwards, Gandini, & Forman, 1993). In this approach to curriculum, children are encouraged to engage with a wide range of experiences, materials, and people in their environment. Teachers observe the children's activity closely and converse with them at length about it. Then they facilitate further exploration of children's interests by providing additional materials, access to knowledgeable community resource people, and opportunities for collaboration in the subsequent study. Projects are typically pursued by groups of peers, and teachers are engaged in the process as "coexplorers" as they help children actively construct their own knowledge. Teachers do not hesitate to challenge children's theories, and vigorous discussion and questioning are integral parts of every investigation, whether the topic is the construction of buildings or the physiology of jumping. The Reggio Emilia approach nicely reflects an orientation toward engaged learning.

As the designers of the Reggio schools readily acknowledge, much of their approach to curriculum for young children is specific to their cultural context. Elements that are fundamental to their schools' culture include vigorous dialogue and debate, work in the context of collaborative groups, the valuing of strong interdependent relationships, an emphasis on creative expression and symbolic representation, and the strengthening of children's sense of place and relationship to the broader community (Edwards et al., 1993). Because this project-based approach has been translated into early childhood programs in other parts of the world, some of its specific elements have been modified and adapted to reflect local values, resources, and norms.

Regardless of these minor modifications, however, the heart of this "project approach" to curriculum is that it gives children the opportunity to "initiate, investigate, and follow through on their interests" (Helm & Katz, 2001, p. 5). This opportunity to pursue their own interests in depth over a period of time allows a full investigation that stimulates children's engaged learning. Repeated, satisfying experiences of engaged learning lead to the kind of curious, confident disposition that serves children well throughout their schooling.

The distinctive indicators of engaged learning, as defined by Jones, Valdez, Norakowski, and Rasmussen (1994), are that the learners "are responsible for their own learning; they take charge and are self-regulated. They define learning goals and problems that are meaningful to them ... and they evaluate how well they have achieved the goal(s)." This definition makes it clear that in addition to enhancing initiative in learning, an inquiry-based curriculum also contributes to several other key areas of socioemotional growth. A choice-based constructivist program provides children with opportunities to learn and practice social interaction skills with familiar adults and peers. This is the means by which children become able to cooperate in planning, coordinating, and sustaining complex interactions with others.

Play with peers demands a high level of social and emotional understanding, as well as self-regulation skills. In a constructivist classroom, children spend considerable time engaged with peers. They share ideas, challenge each other's thinking, and develop perspective-taking skills as they observe and express a range of emotions, and learn to identify and respond with caring to the needs of others. As this child-initiated play and exploration with peers becomes more complex, children must employ more sophisticated turn-taking and negotiating skills to maintain their collaboration. A key element of this process involves learning how to negotiate and to resolve the inevitable social conflicts that arise during group play and investigation. This process of conflict resolution becomes part of the socioemotional curriculum for young children (DeVries et al., 2002). Active adult support and coaching facilitate this as children and adults work as partners within the learning community.

Concluding Thoughts

When knowledgeable educators design learning environments that meet young children's needs for movement and flexibility, soft and private spaces, choice among activities and play partners, a manageable noise level, and appropriately interesting and challenging materials, play and instructional times will more typically be harmonious and productive. When they plan a daily schedule that reflects reasonable expectations for children's attentional and behavioral control, ability to handle transitions, and need for a balance between active and quieter times, negative and challenging behaviors will decrease. When teachers further guide and coach young children's developing social and emotional skills by modeling desirable conduct, work to develop a sense of classroom community and individual responsibility to the group, and provide a cognitive structure of socioemotional understanding through the narration of experience and articulation of values and goals, children grow socially, as well as cognitively.

Building social and emotional competence requires the continuous engagement of both teachers and children. Educators design learning environments and employ program-planning strategies that guide children toward making positive choices. Their responsive interaction styles and guidance techniques support children's ongoing reflection about themselves and about the social world. They challenge children's understandings and prompt them to stretch their socioemotional skills within a supportive learning community.

This intentionality does not mean employing a formal checklist of criteria for a classroom's environment, interactions, and activities. Rather, it means absorbing the guiding principles behind the practices and incorporating them into everyday interactions with children. The adult's image of the child guides the adult's work (Gandini, 2004). The image of the child as an active learner, who continuously builds and revises understanding in all domains, including the social and the emotional, means that educators will continuously be addressing socioemotional development, no matter what the formal content focus of the moment may be. Success in learning in a group setting will require from children continuously expanding self-awareness, competence in self-regulation, social and emotional understanding, and initiative. It will draw on children's abilities to engage in more complex interactions with adults and peers, and to sustain productive relationships with them over extended periods of time. When early learning environments provide the elements that children need to become socially competent and emotionally mature, they will be setting the stage for children's success in every developmental domain.

References

Bakley, S. (2001). Through the lens of sensory integration: A different way of analyzing challenging behavior. *Young Children, 56,* 70–76.

Bell, S. H., Carr, V., Denno, D., Johnson, L. J., & Phillips, L. R. (2004). *Challenging behaviors in early childhood settings: Creating a place for all children.* Baltimore: Brookes.

Bilmes, J. (2004). *Beyond behavior management.* St. Paul, MN: Redleaf Press.

Bowman, B. T., Donovan, M. S., & Burns, M. S. (Eds.). (2000). *Eager to learn: Educating our preschoolers.* Washington, DC: National Academy Press.

Bredekamp, S., & Copple, C. (Eds.). (1997). *Developmentally appropriate practice in early childhood programs.* Washington, DC: National Association for the Education of Young Children.

California Department of Education. (2008). *California preschool learning foundations: Vol. 1. Social–emotional development, language and literacy, English-language development, mathematics.* Sacramento: Author.

Curtis, D., & Carter, M. (1996). *Reflecting children's lives: A handbook for planning child-centered curriculum.* Saint Paul, MN: Redleaf Press.

Denham, S. A. (1998). *Emotional development in young children.* New York: Guilford Press.

Denham, S. A., & Weissberg, R. P. (2004). Social–emotional learning in early childhood: What we know and where to go from here? In E. Chesebrough, P. King, T. P. Gullotta, & M. Bloom (Eds.), *A blueprint for the promotion of prosocial behavior in early childhood* (pp. 13–50). New York: Kluwer Academic/Plenum Press.

DeVries, R., Zan, B., Hildebrandt, C., Edmiaston, R., & Sales, C. (2002). What is constructivist education?: Definition and principles of teaching. In *Developing constructivist early childhood curriculum* (pp. 35–52). New York: Teachers College Press.

Dweck, C. S., & Leggett, E. L. (1988). A social-cognitive approach to motivation and personality. *Psychological Review, 95,* 256–273.

Edwards, C., Gandini, L., & Forman, G. (Eds.). (1993). *The hundred languages of children: The Reggio Emilia approach to early childhood education.* Norwood, NJ: Ablex.

Egger, H. L., & Angold, A. (2006). Common emotional and behavioral disorders in preschool children: Presentation, nosology, and epidemiology. *Journal of Child Psychology and Psychiatry, 47,* 313–337.

Epstein, A. (2007). *The intentional teacher: Choosing the best strategies for young children's learning.* Washington, DC: National Association for the Education of Young Children.

Fields, M. V., & Fields, D. (2006). *Constructive guidance and discipline* (4th ed.). Upper Saddle River, NJ: Pearson.

Gandini, L. (2004). Foundations of the Reggio Emilia approach. In J. Hendrick (Ed.), *Next steps toward teaching the Reggio way* (2nd ed., pp. 13–26). Upper Saddle River, NJ: Pearson.

Grusec, J., & Goodnow, J. (1994). Impact of parental discipline methods on the child's internalization of values: A reconceptualization of current points of view. *Developmental Psychology, 30,* 4–19.

Harms, T., Clifford, R. M., & Cryer, D. (2005). *Early Childhood Environment Rating Scale: Revised Edition.* New York: Teachers College Press.

Helm, J. H., & Katz, L. G. (2001). *Young investigators: The Project Approach in the early years.* New York: Teachers College Press.

Hohmann, M., & Weikart, D. P. (2002). *Educating young children* (2nd ed.). Ypsilianti, MI: High/Scope Press.

Jones, B., Valdez, G., Norakowski, J., & Rasmussen, C. (1994). *Designing learning and technology for educational reform.* Oakbrook, IL: North Central Regional Educational Laboratory.

Kochanska, G. (2002). Committed compliance, moral self, and internalization: A mediated model. *Developmental Psychology, 38,* 339–351.

Ladd, G. W., Birch, S. H., & Buhs, E. S. (1999). Children's social and scholastic lives in kindergarten: Related spheres of influence? *Child Development, 70,* 1373–1400.

Lewit, E. M., & Baker, L. S. (1995). School readiness. *The Future of Children, 5,* 128–139.

Phyfe-Perkins, E., & Shoemaker, J. (1986). Indoor play environments: Research and design implications. In G. Fein & M. Rivkin (Eds.), *The young child at play: Reviews of research* (Vol. 4, pp. 177–193). Washington, DC: National Association for the Education of Young Children.

Pianta, R. C., Nimetz, S. L., & Bennett, E. (1997). Mother–child relationships, teacher–child relationships, and school outcomes in preschool and kindergarten. *Early Childhood Research Quarterly, 12,* 263–280.

Pianta, R. C., & Stuhlman, M. W. (2004). Conceptualizing risk in relational terms: Associations among the quality of child–adult relationships prior to school entry and children's developmental outcomes in first grade. *Educational and Child Psychology, 21,* 32–45.

Prescott, E. (1994). The physical environment: A powerful regulator of experience. *Child Care Information Exchange, 100,* 9–15.

Ratcliff, N. (2001). Use the environment to prevent discipline problems and support learning. *Young Children, 56,* 84–88.

Raver, C., & Knitzer, J. (2002). *Ready to enter: What research tells policymakers about strategies to promote social and emotional readiness among three- and four-year-old children.* New York: National Center for Children in Poverty.

Riley, D., San Juan, R. R., Klinkner, J., & Ramminger, A. (2008). *Social and emotional development: Connecting science and practice in early childhood settings.* St. Paul, MN: Redleaf Press.

Rimm-Kaufman, S. E., Pianta, R. B., & Cox, M. J. (2000). Teachers' judgments of problems in the transition to kindergarten. *Early Childhood Research Quarterly, 15,* 147–166.

Shonkoff, J. P., & Phillips, D. A. (Eds.). (2000). *From neurons to neighborhoods: The science of early childhood development.* Washington, DC: National Academy Press.

Stipek, D., Recchia, S., & McClintic, S. (1992). Self-evaluation in young children. *Monographs of the Society for Research in Child Development, 57*(Serial No. 226).

Tegano, D., Moran, J., DeLong, A., Brickey, J., & Ramanssini, K. (1996). Designing classroom spaces: Making the most of time. *Early Childhood Education Journal, 23,* 135–141.

Thompson, R. A. (2006). The development of the person: Social understanding, relationships, self, conscience. In W. Damon & R. M. Lerner (Series Eds.) & N. Eisenberg (Vol. Ed.), *Handbook of child psychology: Vol. 3. Social, emotional, and personality development* (6th ed., pp. 24–98). New York: Wiley.

Thompson, R. A. (2008). The psychologist in the baby. *Zero to Three Journal, 28*(5), 5–12.

Thompson, R. A., Meyer, S., & McGinley, M. (2006). Understanding values in relationship: The development of conscience. In M. Killen & J. Smetana (Eds.), *Handbook of moral development* (pp. 267–297). Mahwah, NJ: Erlbaum.

Thompson, R. A., & Raikes, H. A. (2007). The social and emotional foundations of school readiness. In D. F. Perry, R. F. Kaufmann, & J. Knitzer (Eds.), *Social and emotional health in early childhood: Building bridges between services and systems* (pp. 13–35). Baltimore: Brookes.

Yoshikawa, H., & Knitzer, J. (1997). *Lessons from the field: Head Start mental health strategies to meet changing needs.* New York: National Center for Children in Poverty.

CHAPTER 11

Supporting Peer Relationships in Early Education

Kathleen Cranley Gallagher
Patricia R. Sylvester

The Sunshine School teachers were looking forward to a good day. All 18 children had arrived, put their things away, and moved into the room to play before it was time for group activities. Gabby and Yosef were stamping red circles on yellow paper. Chatting with one another at a table, Ethan and Rasheda were making one long string of beads. Standing in the window with a clipboard, Travis was keeping track of passing red cars.

Rasheda had again arranged chairs into an airplane for her trip to Rome. Children always wanted to play with Rasheda. She typically had many play ideas and included other children in her play. This morning, she'd already drawn Allegra, Julian, Dylan, and Heather into her airplane. Dylan and Julian were in their seats when Heather said, "I want to sit in the big chair today."

"No, you sit right here," Rasheda answered Heather. "That's the captain's chair and I'm the captain." Heather moved, but there were tears in her eyes.

Crashing noises soon emanated from the block area, where Anthony and Justin had been building a castle. Now Anthony and Justin were glaring at each other over a pile of blocks.

Across the room, Miles was working the cat-and-kittens puzzle when Chrissy sat down next to him. She took the train puzzle off the shelf and pushed it in front of Miles. "You work the train puzzle. That's a boy puzzle. I'll work the kitty cat puzzle; it's a girl puzzle," she said, taking the puzzle away from him.

Miles reached over and took the puzzle back, bellowing, "Hey, I was doing that one."

In dramatic play, Lydia had been watching Isabella, Luis, and Marjory set up their store. Picking up a doll and a shopping bag, she approached them. "My baby's hungry. Do you have any baby food in your store?" Lydia asked.

"Yes, we do," said Marjory, "but we're not selling it to you." Then Isabella explained why, "Your baby is brown and we don't sell food for brown babies." Lydia looked from one girl to the other, not knowing what to do.

Another school day was under way.

Mornings like this one at the Sunshine School are common in early education class-rooms. Children face the challenge of entering peer play, accessing classroom materials and equipment, and making and keeping friends, all the while negotiating an ever-changing social and cultural environment. In classrooms, children often rely on teachers to help them meet these challenges, to learn positive ways to solve problems and resolve disputes, and to develop appropriate social skills. Thus, positive teacher–child relation-ships may offer many children the secure base and the guidance necessary for social success.

In the years following a child's third birthday, a remarkable constellation of emer-gent abilities and skills support the development of peer relationships (Gallagher, Dadis-man, Farmer, Huss, & Hutchins, 2007). In nature's elegant manner, children master language in these years, facilitating their ability to communicate needs and desires with peers. Simultaneously, the child's preferences and sense of self develop. The child's "the-ory of mind," or ability to understand that thinking and thoughts are a distinct part of the self, develops in the fourth and fifth years, when the child begins to realize that oth-ers also have a sense of self and can perceive and think differently than he or she thinks. With improving memory and ability to categorize, children begin to be able to follow rules in play and to structure play experiences with peers. Improved motor abilities in these years increases independence from adult care, facilitating children's reliance on peers for company. As they move into the elementary years, communication, cognitive, and emotional maturity enable children to understand others' needs and goals, and they begin to shape their own behavior to fit that of their peers. From age 3 years, when many children enter group programs, to age 8 years, children's interest slowly shifts from the adults who care for them to the children who surround them daily. The processes of this elegant dance are complex, and children's successes and struggles are influenced by mul-tiple factors, including their own characteristics, families, peers, teachers, and schools.

During preschool and primary grades, peers relationships and friendships grow in importance. The harmonious peer interactions and satisfying friendships that emerge in this period have often been associated with a host of other developmental competencies. For example, children who play well with others and have at least one close friend have been found to adjust better during the transition to school, to achieve academically, and to exhibit better mental health (Ladd, Birch, & Buhs, 1999; Ladd & Price, 1987) than do their less socially competent peers.

Our purpose in this chapter is to review aspects of children's classroom-based peer relationships and to suggest ways teachers can support children's social and academic development by applying knowledge gleaned from developmental literature. With this in mind, we begin by examining classroom-based peer relationships among typically developing children ages 3–8 years. We first examine the meaning and role of children's friendships. Usually thought of as mutual, "dyadic" (two person) relationships (Mendel-son, Aboud, & Lanthier, 1994), preschoolers' friendships tend to be based on common activities, whereas friendships of children in the early grades are based on more abstract characteristics, such as shared interests, loyalty, and spending time together (Hartup & Abecassis, 2004). We then consider children's peer groups, including the role of play in children's development and the hierarchical nature of peer groups. Problems in early peer relationships, such as bullying and social isolation, are also considered in these sec-tions. Next, we examine various influences (external to the classroom) on children's peer relationships, including children's family, home culture, abilities, and gender. Finally, we discuss classroom processes that facilitate positive peer relationships. In this section, we suggest specific ways that teachers and schools can support positive peer interactions and relationships. To begin, we present four theoretical perspectives, discussed briefly below, as a framework for understanding young children's classroom-based peer relationships and the classroom practices expected to facilitate the development of positive peer relationships.

Theoretical Perspectives on Children's Peer Relationships

Over the years, several perspectives have been employed to study and support children's development of peer relationships. Because we believe that practice is best informed by an integration of perspectives, we present the following four as guides: social learning, social information processing, social networking, and ecological perspectives.

In social learning theory (Bandura, 1977), adults function as environmental experts, modeling appropriate behaviors and structuring the environment in ways that encourage appropriate behaviors in children. Peers may also serve as models from whom children learn. Whereas observing a peer's success in a difficult situation may encourage children to try similar strategies, seeing a peer's failure may discourage children from following a similar plan. Social learning theories have figured prominently in how educators socialize and support children in developing relationship skills, including those with peers. For example, curricular approaches based on social learning theories (e.g., Developing Understanding of Self and Others [DUSO]) often use animal "models" for peer interaction and friendship, and employ built-in reward systems that reinforce positive peer behavior. The social learning approach is important to consider because it has guided proactive (direct play skills instruction) and emergent (pointing out peers' successful strategies) classroom strategies.

The social information-processing approach (Crick & Dodge, 1994) proposes that children process social experiences in much the same way they process cognitive ones. Using memories, rules, and existing knowledge and schemas, children interpret cues, set goals, and select and carry out a response. When children interpret social cues accurately, set appropriate goals, and employ prosocial responses, they tend to get along well with peers. However, when children are biased toward perceiving social cues as hostile and responding with hostility, they experience more conflict in their peer relationships. The role of the adult, from a social information-processing perspective, is to help the child to interpret social cues accurately, set goals, and respond appropriately.

Social network perspectives acknowledge that children's friendships are nested in larger peer groups. Dyadic friendships are a part of groups that share certain characteristics. Originally applied solely to adolescent peer relationships (Cairns, Leung, Buchanan, & Cairns, 1995), researchers have found that younger children also develop relationships within social networks (Gest, Farmer, Cairns, & Xie, 2003; Lee, Howes, & Chamberlain, 2007). Younger children may structure their groups around interests, such as sports or arts. In groups that share characteristics and interests, children construct social ideas and impose order in their play by establishing smaller, more manageable subgroups.

An ecological perspective (Bronfenbrenner & Morris, 1998) suggests that children develop as participants in an elaborate concert in which their own characteristics interact with those of other people and contexts over time. Development is the result of increasingly complex interaction between the child and his or her environments. Environments in which the child actively participates, such as home and school, influence development more than do contexts in which participation is indirect, such as a parent's workplace or government agencies. In an ecological approach, the "village" supports the child's development, with the adults, especially parents and teachers, serving as protectors and facilitators, and providing supportive relationships in children's daily interactions. Ecological theory incorporates the diverse perspectives used to study children's peer relationships.

Each of these theoretical perspectives describes different roles for adults who support children's classroom peer interactions. In social learning theory, the adult is a model and guide for socialized behavior, and structures the child's environment. The social information-processing approach emphasizes the adult's role in helping children to interpret social cues and choose appropriate responses. According to a social network perspective, adults help children connect with peers who have similar interests or complementary dispositions. Finally, in the ecological systems perspective, the adult is the social "mentor," who sensitively guides children's interactions and experiences in different contexts.

Which perspective is most useful for teachers in early education? In fact, contemporary teachers need tools from each of these approaches, or a "basket of tricks," to support the social needs of young students. Children come to school with experience with relationships, some of which may be with peers. However, the classroom teacher is the cultural guide and mentor who supports children's success with peers (Gallagher et al., 2007). In establishing the classroom social climate, the teacher's initial role is that of a skilled observer. The teacher observes friendship qualities that promote or interfere with each friend's optimal development. He or she observes children at work and play in the classroom, on the playground, and in the lunchroom. Aware of characteristics that support or hurt children's social success, the teacher notes social hierarchies and behaviors of individual children that support or interfere with their acceptance and inclusion among peers. Impressively, the skilled teacher in early education does this while teaching reading, writing, mathematics, science, and social studies.

Friendships

Who would choose to live, even if possessed with all other things, without friends?
—ARISTOTLE

Friendships play a critical role in children's development. Children ages 3–8 years are beginning to learn what it means to have and to be a friend. Research suggests that friendships, distinct from other peer relationships, may provide benefits for children's social and academic development in school (Ladd et al., 1999; Ladd, Herald, & Andrews, 2006; Ladd & Price, 1987). Friendships can provide support in times of stress, teach social skills that may be difficult to learn in a group, help to prevent loneliness, and protect a child from the negative effects of bullying and victimization. It is likely their reciprocal nature that makes friendships beneficial to children's development. In fact, research has often measured friendship in terms of children's joint endorsement of the other as being a "friend." Having a friend can buffer the effects of shyness in the transition to school (Ladd et al., 1999) and provide a safe space in which children learn and practice new social skills (Vaughn, Colvin, & Azria, 2001). Because friends engage in more lengthy play sessions with each other (Tremblay, Strain, Hendrickson, & Shores, 1981), friends may benefit more from the social and cognitive gains associated with extended play. Within the context of friendships, children can safely experiment with social interactions, learn social rules and expectations, and develop an appreciation of the benefits and demands of reciprocal relationships.

Some children appear to develop friendships easily. Children who regulate their behavior and emotions, along with those who are predisposed to approach novel situations comfortably, build relationships with peers competently (Sanson, Hemphill, & Smart, 2004a). These children are more likely to identify their peers' emotions accurately and to demonstrate better cooperative play skills than those who are less able to manage their own emotions and behaviors (Fantuzzo, Sekino, & Cohen, 2004; Spinrad et al., 2004). Children who organize play activities, share equipment and materials, and notice and compliment peer efforts are more likely to have friends in the classroom (Tremblay et al., 1981). These children are also more likely to respond to other children's play initiations and to initiate play in equal proportions.

Some children have difficulty developing friendships, due at least in part to their temperamental characteristics (Eisenberg et al., 2001, 2003; Smart & Sanson, 2001). For example, children with poorer self-regulation, and those prone to express negative emotion easily, often have difficulty making good choices in social interactions and may withdraw from peers when emotional demands are high. Children who are prone to fearfulness, or shyness, are less likely to seek peer companionship and may also withdraw from social situations. Difficulty sustaining attention may lead some children to move between activities, without engaging with peers. For these children, and for others who struggle with friendship, teachers support and facilitate peer interactions in the face of social challenges.

Studies of friendship in early education have focused primarily on "reciprocal dyads," or children who mutually identify each other as a friend. Younger children play more in dyads and small groups, gradually building up to large-group play. Children tend to choose friends who share their interests and interaction style, who are "like them," a tendency known as "homophily." Although groups of friends are common among older children and adolescents, less is known about friendship groups among young children. However, we know that children play more with peers who share certain characteristics, such as academic achievement (Estell, Farmer, Cairns, & Cairns, 2002) and aggression (Estell, Cairns, Farmer, & Cairns, 2002; Farver, 1996). Even in preschool, "popular" children, or those most nominated by their peers as well liked, are more likely to play with other popular children (Ladd, 1983).

Play in Peer Groups

Whether with friends, other peers, or alone, children enjoy playing and do so at every opportunity (Rogers & Sawyers, 1992). Developmental science distinguishes between forms and levels of participation in children's play. Smilansky and Shefatya (1990) described four basic forms of play: functional or exploratory, constructive, dramatic, and games with rules. Children explore their physical environments and the objects in it during functional play. Constructive play leads to creation, perhaps a block structure or a drawing. In dramatic play, children imitate, pretend, and reexamine their own experiences. Games with rules, from board games to baseball, demand compliance with predetermined rules and procedures. Pellegrini (1987) added a fifth form, rough-and-tumble play, which increases in frequency over the early education years (Pellegrini, 2002).

Parten (1932) described six levels of children's social participation in play. The lowest levels—unoccupied, onlooker, and solitary play—are nonsocial, whereas parallel, associative, and cooperative levels of play involve more than one child. Whereas the unoccupied child seems neither to play nor to watch others, the onlooker watches, and may even talk with children who are playing, but does not enter the ongoing play. The child engaged in solitary play pays little regard to the activities of children playing nearby. In parallel play, the child plays next to other children, engaging in similar activities, whereas in associative play, a loosely organized group of children share common activities and interests. Children's cooperative play, the highest form of play, is marked by mutually determined, clearly defined roles and rules.

Over the early education years, children progress from primarily nonsocial levels of play to predominantly social ones; however, it is not unusual for children to play alone. During free play, preschoolers frequently engage in solitary constructive play, and kindergarten-age children play alone more often than in groups (Rubin, Watson, & Jambor, 1978). During the preschool years, children's abilities to sustain play sequences, take turns, and agree on rules (Watson, Nixon, Wilson, & Capage, 1999) support their increasing engagement in dramatic play and games with rules (Goncu, Patt, & Kouba, 2002; Pellegrini & Perlmutter, 1989).

Social play requires gaining acceptance into ongoing group play. Of the children who are initially excluded from the group, only half manage to gain entrance (Corsaro, 1981). Children who successfully join ongoing play often use a sequence of play behaviors that appear to facilitate entry (Robinson, Anderson, Porter, Hart, & Wouden-Miller, 2003), They first engage in parallel play nearby, observing the group's play. By engaging in similar play nearby and talking with group members about their activities, children ease into the group's ongoing play and are accepted (Puttallaz & Gottman, 1981; Rubin, Bukowski, & Parker, 2006). Once admitted to group play, children's abilities to communicate clearly, appropriately, and saliently (Levin & Rubin, 1983); to negotiate the content and direction of play (Howes & Wishard, 2004); and to maintain emotional equanimity (Eisenberg, Fabes, Guthrie, & Reiser, 2000) are important to remaining in the group.

Sustaining peer-group play demands a wide range of social, emotional, and cognitive skills (Halberstadt, Denham, & Dunsmore, 2001). Children must often wait for a turn, go along with the plans of others, and share equipment and materials. Temperament (Sanson, Hemphill, & Smart, 2004b) and self-regulation (Bronson, 2000) influence children's ability to engage in and sustain play with peers. Children who are wary of new or challenging situations have fewer peer interactions (Kagan, Reznick, Clarke, Snidman, & Garcia-Coll, 1984) and play alone more frequently (Parker-Cohen & Bell, 1988) than do less wary peers (Parker-Cohen & Bell, 1988; Skarpness & Carson, 1986). Children who effectively regulate their emotions and behavior are preferred playmates

(Eisenberg et al., 1997), possibly because they more effectively negotiate disputes (Eisenberg, Fabes, Nyman, Bernzweig, & Pinuelas, 1994) and are easier to get along with (Cumberland-Li, Eisenberg, & Reiser, 2004). Thus, children who are less wary and better regulated may have more opportunities to practice play.

Status in Peer Groups

Children, like adolescents and adults, want to be accepted and respected by those they identify as "peers." However, human nature and history seem to dictate that competition, hierarchy, and meeting goals are important for how we demonstrate competence in our culture. Children's peer culture, and the negotiation of acceptance and dominance, emerges in the contexts of play and school activities (Hawley, 1999, 2002).

Within larger peer groups, some children are well liked, others are disliked, and most children fall somewhere in between. Children may be leaders or followers; they may wield power or be submissive. In summary, there is much inequality within groups of children. Based on their classroom observations, Strayer and Trudel (1984) described children's social interactions as "clear status hierarchies" (p. 283). Although peer interactions were generally reciprocal and friendly, occasionally a more dominant child's behavior elicited the playmate's submission. In the classroom pecking order, each child held sway over those below him or her. Among 3-year-olds, dominance relationships, often established by aggression, were readily observable. By age 5, dominance required fewer demonstrations of physical prowess because children appeared to have a tacit understanding of their own and other children's social positions.

Sociometric ratings have been used in research to examine children's social status among peers. Researchers ask children to name (nominate) the peers they like and dislike, or like–dislike as play partners. "Popular" children are liked by many children and disliked by few. "Rejected" children are more disliked than liked; and "neglected" children, ignored by peers, are neither liked nor disliked. Most children fall somewhere in the average range, receiving a balance of "liked" and "disliked" ratings. Socially dominant, well-liked children are typically friendly, cooperative, and helpful (Coie, Dodge, & Kupersmidt, 1990). They communicate clearly by sharing ideas and responding relevantly to others' communications (Black & Hazen, 1990; Hazen & Black, 1989). Despite a tendency to use aggressive tactics, dominant preschoolers are often well-liked by their peers (Hawley, 2002, 2003) and are more adept at accessing favorite activities and materials (Hawley, 1999). However, preschoolers dislike children who try verbally to manipulate access to play and peer relationships (Crick, Casas, & Mosher, 1997). Whereas younger children sometimes are well-liked despite their disruptive, antisocial behaviors on the playground, older children, especially girls, seem to prefer more prosocial playmates (Hart, DeWolf, Wozniak, & Burts, 1992). Though children may tolerate aggression when trying to resolve disputes (Price & Dodge, 1989), by the early elementary grades, most children are intolerant of children who exhibit antisocial, coercive behaviors (Coie & Dodge, 1983; Hart et al., 1992).

Peer rejection is not confined to children who behave in aggressive, antisocial ways. Distinct from shy, socially reticent children who join peer activities in familiar settings (Rubin, 1982), socially withdrawn children are solitary despite familiar settings and people (Rubin, Burgess, & Coplan, 2004). Socially withdrawn children are often targets of peer rejection in preschool that continues into elementary school (Rubin, Hymel, & Mills, 1989).

Bullying is yet another manifestation of difficulty among peers. Although most children experience conflict with their peers at times (Willoughby, Kupersmidt, & Bryant, 2001), bullies persistently abuse the power they hold over other children (Rigby, 2004), using physical and verbal aggression toward their victims (Crick, Casas, & Ku, 1999; Crick et al., 1997; Kochenderfer & Ladd, 1996). Bullies often vent their angry, impulsive behaviors on victims who are physically weak, timid, anxious, and friendless (Ladd et al., 2006). Though bullying is relatively common in early education settings; research suggests that it is less likely to occur in classrooms and playgrounds where adults monitor children's activities and intervene (Rigby, 2004).

Cooperative children are generally better liked than are their argumentative, confrontational peers (Denham, McKinley, Couchard, & Holt, 1990; Ladd & Price, 1987), but learning to get along with peers takes time and experience (Rubin, Burgess, Dwyer, & Hastings, 2003). For children who have not sufficiently internalized "lessons of grace and courtesy" (Standing, 1984, p. 215), having prosocial, ready responses may be challenging. In novel social situations, children make decisions about others' intents and respond accordingly. When children misinterpret peers' actions or remarks and vent their negative feelings (Denham et al., 2003; Smith, 2001) or respond angrily, they are less likely to be accepted among their peers (Hubbard & Dearing, 2004; Yoon, Hughes, Cavell, & Thompson, 2000). However, even children who are prone to negative emotions are liked by peers when they regulate their attention and behavior (Eisenberg et al., 2000). Peer acceptance and status are most assured for children who remain calm when things don't go their way (Eisenberg et al., 2005), refrain from impulsive actions (Eisenberg, Champion, & Ma, 2004), respond sympathetically to others (Valiente et al., 2004), and are generally more agreeable (Cumberland-Li et al., 2004).

Influences on Peer Relationships

As children begin school, they bring personal characteristics, attitudes, and behaviors that can affect their abilities to build peer relationships. Outside of school, many things influence children's readiness to engage in successful relationships with peers. These influences include parents, culture, disability, and gender. Each of these influences on children's peer relationships is discussed briefly below.

Parents

Research suggests that parents who have positive relationships with their children more frequently scaffold children's burgeoning social relationships. Warm, nurturing parenting, marked by sensitivity and responsiveness to children's needs, supports prosocial development (McDowell & Parke, 2000; Olsen et al., 2002). For example, children learn constructive coping strategies from parents who comfort them when they are upset (Eisenberg & Fabes, 1994). When mothers use prosocial, group-oriented strategies to help their children join ongoing play (Finnie & Russell, 1998) or suggest prosocial solutions to problems with peers (Parke et al., 2004), children are likely to use similar behaviors during subsequent peer interactions.

When parents organize and sensitively supervise children's play, they provide a safe setting for development of positive peer relationships. Frequent opportunities for organized, regularly occurring peer play allow children to practice and hone skills (Chen, Fein, Killen, & Tam, 2001; Rubin et al., 2003), get along better with peers at school (Ladd & Hart, 1992), and communicate better with playmates (Lieberman, 1977). During play, children sometimes require adult assistance to resolve disputes and other problems, for example, when parents or playmates encourage the use of prosocial behaviors during peer play by inviting "give-and-take through their use of reasoning and guidance" (Crockenberg & Lourie, 1996, p. 498), sharing decision making about play content and direction, and cooperating with children's ideas (see Russell, Pettit, & Mize, 1998). However, children benefit most when adults withdraw their assistance as children become more skilled with peers (Lollis, Ross, & Tate, 1992).

Children's interactions and relationships with their parents also influence their status with peers. The warm, nurturing parental care that underlies secure attachments is linked to positive peer relationships (Sroufe, 1997), such that sensitive, responsive parent–child interaction is associated with greater peer acceptance (Harrist, Pettit, Dodge, & Bates, 1994; McDowell & Parke, 2000). For example, children whose parents comfort them when they are hurt or upset cope more constructively with their own anger (Eisenberg & Fabes, 1994). On the other hand, intrusive, overcontrolling, or distant parents undermine children's peer competence, leading to poorer peer acceptance and status (Finnegan, Hodges, & Perry, 1998; McDowell & Parke, 2000). When parents explicitly teach prosocial behavior, coach children regarding peers' seemingly hostile interactions, and encourage a "resilient, bounce-back attitude" (Mize & Pettit, 1997, p. 316), children fare better with their peers. Unfortunately, parents' harsh discipline of their children's antisocial behavior or ignoring such behaviors (Coplan, Hastings, Lagace-Sequin, & Moulton, 2002; Dodge, Pettit, & Bates, 1994) leads children to engage in similar behaviors with their peers (McDowell & Parke, 2000; Mize & Pettit, 1997).

Home Culture

Cultural differences have been noted in parents' socialization of their children's play and peer relationships (Goncu et al., 2002) As one example, Korean American parents view play primarily as amusement, and encourage an academic focus and provide fewer opportunities for peer pretend play. European American parents more commonly encourage pretend play and see it as a context for learning. Thus, European American children spend more of their free-play time in make-believe play than do their Korean American peers (Farver, Kim, & Lee, 1995; Farver & Shin, 1997). In play, as in most things because experience is important to success, Korean American children may need school to provide the play opportunities that are important to early friendships and positive peer relationships.

Children's cultural background may also be associated with the composition of their peer groups. In a study of ethnically diverse kindergartners and third-graders, Howes and Wu (1990) found no association between children's social status and ethnicity; in fact, positive relationships flourished in the diverse classroom context. However, third-graders were more likely than kindergartners to form cross-group friendships and to have positive cross-group interactions. Cross-ethnic relationships developed over the elementary school years, and girls' social networks were more diverse than those of boys. These cultural differences may underlie some of the social skills that children bring to their early school experiences, thus possibly influencing children's abilities to get along in the peer culture (Lee et al., 2007).

Another study suggests that not all cross-cultural experiences are positive for all children. Aboud, Mendelson, and Purdy's (2003) found that white children rated white classmates more highly than black classmates and were more likely to exclude black children from their interactions. Black children in this study did not make similar discriminations. The discrepancies between these findings lead to questions concerning how parents' and teachers' attitudes and practices with respect to cross-group peer relationships may influence children's social relationships at school.

Disability

Children with disabilities often face additional challenges as they negotiate the classroom social environment. For example, children with attention-deficit/hyperactivity disorder (ADHD) can experience a wide range of "social problems" in the classroom (see Stormont, 2001), and children with learning disabilities and mild cognitive delays are often less pursued as playmates than are nondisabled classmates (Diamond, LeFurgy, & Blass, 1993; Guralnick, 1999). Furthermore, research suggests that children with disabilities are less likely to have a friend in the early education classroom (Buysse, Goldman, West, & Hollingsworth, 2008). Children with disabilities, in particular those with language disabilities or pervasive developmental disorders (e.g., autism), struggle to develop intimate friend relationships (Guralnick, Hammond, Connor, & Neville, 2006). However, similar to their typically developing peers, children's social skills ultimately determine how well they are liked by peers (Siperstain & Leffert, 1997). Thus, regular, inclusive peer interactions have been found to offer children with disabilities a context for developing and practicing important social skills (Roeyers, 1996). It is important to remember that children with disabilities reap the same benefits of friendship, such as more positive self-esteem and less loneliness, as their peers without disabilities (Bauminger, Shulman, & Agam, 2004).

Gender

Overheard:

"Girls rule, boys drool."—BRIDGET, age 4

"I tried to be friends with a girl once, but it didn't work out."—JACK, age 8

Gender earns its consideration in peer relationships in this chapter for reasons that are clear to anyone who has observed children on a playground. Young children, beginning in the preschool years, prefer same-sex playmates and engage in gender-specific play styles with their group of peers (Fabes, Shepard, Guthrie, & Martin, 1997; Gorman-Smith & Loeber, 2005). Two perspectives of this phenomenon have been considered. In the first, developmental scientists have viewed the social worlds of boys and girls as "separate cultures," both in their activities and their ongoing social relationships (Maccoby, 1990). In general, girls are more intimate than boys with their friends. Girls' peer play is more verbal, and more time is spent negotiating play members' needs. Boys are more activity-focused with their friends, and their friendships are more stable. Their peer play is more physical and intense. Parents and teachers alike rate girls as more socially competent than boys.

The second perspective, an extension of this "two cultures" idea, elaborates on the advantages and risks that participation in these separate, gendered peer cultures affords. For example, girls' emphasis on intimate, exclusive friendships may not only provide support in times of stress but also appears to be associated with girls' susceptibility to anxiety and depression. Boys may benefit from large social networks in their active group play, but may become more aggressive and less socially competent over time as a result of boy-only play (Rose & Rudolph, 2006). Within same-sex peer groups, children identify and reinforce same-sex activities and play (Roopnarine, 1984), and the more children play in same-sex groups, the more they manifest the stereotyped attitudes and behaviors of their sex (Fabes, Martin, & Hanish, 2004).

What are the sources of gender differences in peer relationships? Subtle sex differences in behavior are seen from infancy (Prior, Smart, & Sanson, 2001). For example, baby boys are perceived as slightly more active and difficult to engage, whereas baby girls are easier to comfort. These differences increase over the course of development, such that children progressively spend most of their free time in elementary school with same-sex playmates (Maccoby, 1990). Explanations regarding the source of these gender differences are controversial, but some researchers concur (Brooks-Gunn & Warren, 1989; Leaper, 2002) that gender's contribution to children's behavior can largely be attributed to socialization and culture. Parents and teachers may treat boys and girls differently, or similar treatment may be related to different outcomes for boys and girls. For example, in one study, mothers' coaching on peer relationships supported girls' social competence, but not that of boys (Pettit, Brown, Mize, & Lindsey, 1998).

Evidence suggests some biological sources for these gendered social differences (Prior et al., 2001); however, family attitudes and processes play a strong socializing role (Fagot, Leinbach, & O'Boyle, 1992; Mize & Pettit, 1997). It is no coincidence that children's gender-typed play and social relationships increase soon after school entry. School settings traditionally reinforce gender types and stereotypes. Older urban schools often still bear the signs "Girls" on one entrance and "Boys" on the other, even though separate entrances may no longer be used. The sexes are often separated for activities and organizational reasons.

Practices that promote gender-balanced school settings for children are supported by developmental science. For example, children who participate in primarily same-sex play groups demonstrate more gender-typed play over time (Fabes et al., 2004). Participation in gender-typed play and activities is subsequently associated with more anxiety and depression among girls, and more aggression among boys. More "androgynous," or gender-balanced, play activities are preferable for children's long-term social development, and girls' and boys' play and groups offer different benefits for children's development (Lee et al., 2007; Rose & Rudolph, 2006; Underwood, 2007). Because gender-typed social relationships are so culturally bound and reinforced, schools and teachers need to take an active role to reduce the negative effects of gendered relationships over time, while recognizing the supportive role that some gendered groups provide.

Classroom Processes

Teachers can use myriad strategies to support positive peer relationships in their classrooms (Gallagher et al., 2007). We can think about these strategies as being either proactive or emergent. "Proactive strategies" involve environmental and curricular design, behavior guidelines and expectations, and the classroom's emotional climate. Proactive strategies arise from the value systems of schools and teachers as they are enacted in the classroom. Research suggests that classroom design, structure, and climate influence children's adjustment and performance in school. "Emergent strategies" are responses to ongoing classroom events and interactions. From these dynamic situations come opportunities for teachers to support children's learning about social interactions, peer relationships, and friendships. Using emergent strategies, teachers can model appropriate behaviors and attitudes, and help children cope constructively in the face of difficult peer interactions. Unfortunately, teachers sometimes react reflexively to conflict situations, missing opportunities to model, support, and teach healthy conflict resolution. When this happens, teachers sometimes discipline children publicly or vent emotion, albeit unintentionally, in ways that may damage peer relationships. In busy, demanding classrooms, teachers can easily miss opportunities to support children's peer interactions, and they may inadvertently ignore or minimize situations of peer conflict.

Supporting positive peer relationships in early childhood classrooms requires a wide repertoire of proactive and emergent strategies. In the following section, we discuss some ways that teachers can support children's developing social skills during busy school days. First, we examine proactive strategies for supporting social development. Then, we consider emergent strategies that teachers can use to capitalize on teachable moments.

Proactive Strategies

Adults influence how children develop friendships, and teachers can assist children in developing friendships and acquiring long-term, friendship-building competencies. First and foremost, the classroom must be welcoming and inclusive for children of all ethnicities, languages, cultures, families, and abilities. Evidence from developmental science suggests several strategies that help teachers create a classroom climate with an "ethos of friendship" (Joseph & Strain, 2003). Displaying photographs of children's families, and artifacts from their home life, signals each child's value to the classroom community. Exhibits of children's artwork instead of commercial decorations adds to children's sense of belonging (Katz, 1990). When children feel comfortable and accepted at school, they engage more fully in classroom interactions (Ladd & Kochenderfer, 1996). Classroom activities can focus on collaborative rather than competitive interaction, engender positive relationships, help children learn to cooperate, and provide opportunities for mutual success. Although the recent focus on academic accountability may discourage play in the schools (Kagan & Carroll, 2004), the National Association for the Education of Young Children (Bredekamp & Copple, 1997) continues to endorse classroom support for peer play. When teachers encourage children to select their activities from well-organized, clearly defined options and let them set their own pace rather moving at teacher-determined intervals, children initiate and engage in higher-quality peer interactions (Moore, Goltsman, & Iacofano, 1987).

The physical environment of the classroom offers opportunities for proactive support of positive peer interactions. Early in the 20th century, Montessori (1964) discussed the importance of preparing the environment. More recently, Reggio Emilio classroom environments have been described as an extra teacher (Gandini, 1995). Careful planning of the physical and socioemotional environments of the classroom can provide the foundation for the emotional security that children need to interact confidently with peers (Bowlby, 1969; Shonkoff & Phillips, 2000). The physical environment should help children stay safe, get their work done, and interact productively. Needless to say, placement of furniture and equipment should allow a teacher to see all areas of the classroom, provide easy access to materials, and encourage children to move about the classroom freely and safely. However, the classroom arrangement can also be arranged to facilitate children's peer relationships. For example, placing tables or desks in groups allows cooperative learning that supports not only positive peer interactions (Madden & Slavin, 1983; Manning & Lucking, 1993), but also academic achievement (Walters, 2000).

Activity centers encourage the appropriate, responsible choices that have been associated with long-term benefits to children's social development (Schweinhart & Weikart, 1997). Children's interactions vary among centers (Smilansky & Shefatya, 1990) such that whereas some centers (e.g., dramatic play and block building) lend themselves to cooperative play, others may encourage parallel play. Centers should be structured in ways that invite children to talk, share, and cooperate with one another while using the materials. For example, when centers are filled with open-ended materials that support children's creativity (e.g., paper, crayons, books, and dress-up clothes) and teachers limit their intervention, children engage more in associative and cooperative peer play (Kontos, Burchinal, Howes, Wisseh, & Galinsky, 2002). Particularly important for shy children, quiet places provide an escape from the classroom's busy-ness and opportunities for children to refuel after intense social interactions (Frost, Wortham, & Reifel, 2005).

Although preparing the environment is an excellent beginning, prosocial behavior must often be explicitly taught in early education (Eisenberg, Fabes, & Spinrad, 2006). Establishing a classroom community that provides a secure base for children's explorations also necessitates establishing clear rules and expectations (Stormont, Lewis, & Becker, 2005). For the classroom to function harmoniously, teachers must establish clear behavioral expectations and encourage compliance. Because school may be a child's first experience with formal rules, it is important that rules be taught, modeled, and rehearsed. Children need opportunities to role-play examples of rules and appropriate behavior. Even with ample opportunities for practice, children inevitably forget rules, run down hallways, use very loud voices, and spill paint. On these occasions, gentle, consistent reminders support children walking rather than running and using indoor voices, and cleaning up messes (Grisham-Brown, Hemmeter, & Pretti-Frontczak, 2005; Katz & McClellan, 1997).

Many social skills curricula have been developed for early childhood classrooms (Hemmeter, Ostrosky, & Fox, 2006). The lessons, stories, and activities in these programs have been designed to reduce social problems proactively and increase prosocial behaviors. In a review of eight comprehensive curricula, Joseph and Strain (2003) argued that many of the curricula were unlikely to reproduce previously reported results. However, from their analysis, they described two curricula, Second Step and Promoting

Alternative Thinking Strategies (PATHS), as "promising" (p. 232). Each curriculum is self-contained, designed to be delivered by classroom teachers, without additional training. Second Step (Committee for Children, 1989) is a program for early elementary schoolchildren. With two lessons each week, children engage in discussions and follow-up role plays. According to the Joseph and Strain (2003) review, teachers can expect less physical and verbal aggression, accompanied by increasing prosocial behaviors. The second program, PATHS (Kusche & Greenberg, 1994), provides short, developmentally appropriate lessons that focus on emotion knowledge, self-control, and social skills, and take place three times each week. Again, teachers can anticipate more prosocial and fewer antisocial behaviors among their children. In each of these programs, children identify emotions, examine perspectives of others, and develop positive solutions to problems.

Raising Healthy Children (RHC; Catalano et al., 2003), another school-based program, is designed to prevent behavior problems. This three-faceted program includes separate workshops for teachers and parents, along with summer camps for students referred by teachers or parents based on academic or behavioral problems. Students participating in the RHC program increased their commitment to school and their social competence compared to nonparticipants. This program reflects the teaching pyramid approach to supporting children's social and emotional development (Hemmeter et al., 2006), emphasizing the importance of building positive relationships with children and their families, and teaching socioemotional skills in the context of a supportive classroom community.

Possibly the most important proactive strategy is establishing a positive relationship with each child. Research asserts the importance of teacher–child relationships to children's well-being throughout the school years. In one study, children with close relationships with their kindergarten teachers also developed better relationships with their first-grade teaches (Pianta, Steinberg, & Rollins, 1995). Children with closer relationships with their teachers participate more fully in peer activities, behave in more prosocial ways, have more reciprocated friendships (Ladd et al., 1999), and are more confident in new situations (Birch & Ladd, 1998). Nurturing classroom environments set the stage for positive peer interactions and provide time, space, and materials for children's play.

Establishing positive relationships with easygoing children likely presents little difficulty for most teachers (Birch & Ladd, 1998), but close teacher–child relationships appear to be particularly beneficial for children who are vulnerable to problems with peers. For example, kindergartners with problem behaviors who had close teacher–child relationships exhibited fewer of behavior problems in first- and third-grades, even as peers with less serious problem behaviors had increased problems when their relationships with teachers were less close (Silver, Measelle, Armstrong, & Essex, 2005). In an intervention focused on enhancing teacher–child relationship quality, researchers used "floor time" as an opportunity for young children to spend quality time with their teachers (Denham & Burton, 1996). Teachers used floor time to observe and to interact with each child, responding to the child's individual interests and needs. The enhanced relationships resulted in fewer displays of negative emotions, more interactions with peers, and greater classroom involvement. Thus, whereas it may take extra effort to establish close, positive relationships with some children, such relationships are definitely worthwhile.

Finally, children learn as much from what teachers do as what they say. The classroom is built on a climate of friendship in which adults in the setting interact not only with the children but also with each other in ways that are respectful and friendly. Adults can model greetings and social initiation, and reinforce children's attempts to do the same. We believe a key aspect of modeling these strategies is that the adult is authentic and not "modeling" as show; children are very sensitive to the authenticity of adult interactions and likely notice when adults role-play solely for their benefit.

Emergent Strategies

The need arises for emergent strategies when children have difficulty joining or sustaining peer play. Traditionally, teachers have often taught children entering peer groups to ask, "Can I play?" However, research suggests that successful strategies are more subtle. When teachers notice a child having difficulty entering a group at play, they can coach the child to observe and to play next to the group, and encourage him or her to talk about what is going on during the play scenario and to talk with members of the group, thereby scaffolding the child's entrance to the group's play. To help the children in her classroom join ongoing play, Vivian Paley (1992) decided to establish a new rule: "You can't say you can't play." This policy demands that all children be accepted into ongoing play. Using Paley's ideas in an intervention, Harrist and Bradley (2003) found that kindergartners whose teachers read stories about peer play inclusion, followed by discussions and children's role play, reported more positive sentiments about classmates than did children who had not participated in these activities. Teachers may also need to act as playmates for novice players, inviting them to play, encouraging them to make choices about play content and directions, and suggesting that they invite other children to join them. Once play is established, teachers can withdraw their support.

Disputes and disagreements among children provide opportunities for teachers to talk about emotions, scaffold negotiation, and encourage children to resolve problems. Giving each child an opportunity to be heard and to understand another's ideas and needs, finding mutually agreeable solutions, and putting those solutions into action affirms each child's value to the classroom community, teaches prosocial problem-solving skills, and encourages children to take their new skills into other situations. Children's disputes often arise over access to popular materials. Such disputes can easily be resolved by helping a child explain that he or she would like to use the puzzle next, or join the group at the sand table when someone leaves. It may even mean posting a list at popular activities, so that each child is certain to have a turn. In addition to supporting the desired classroom climate, learning to wait and to stay with a task are both important for school success (Kusche & Greenberg, 1994).

Few types of school settings actively support nongendered play and relationships. These settings are more commonly found in preschool than in elementary classrooms, and they include some Montessori and Reggio Emilio programs. Miletta (2005) describes processes in which teachers respond to children's struggles with peer relationships and social/moral development in the classroom, without resorting to didactic teaching and reciting truisms about peers or friendships. The community is proactive in the design of the educational setting, ensuring that spaces draw parents, staff, teachers, and children alike into the community of engagement. Learning emerges as a function of community interaction and active sharing of experience on the part of the teachers. Dilemmas serve as teachable moments. Teachers take considerable time to allow "manners," or social/moral conduct, to occur. Manners are not taught as a separate topic, with the advantage of puppets and stories, but are embedded into the daily routines. Teachers come to know what manners children need to learn by careful observation and thoughtful planning of authentic activities and experiences.

Implementing an emergent approach for supporting children's development of peer relationships is important but possibly more challenging for teachers than practicing proactive strategies whose effectiveness is well-documented in the literature. Very little research has examined how teachers support peer interactions in the context of ongoing problem solving. Teachers can begin to see children's social challenges as opportunities to teach and to model respect. By viewing conflict as opportunity, teachers support struggling children and communicate that all individuals in the classroom are valued.

Summary

Children do not enter peer relationships as blank slates. They bring their own unique compilation of characteristics that influence, and are influenced by, their social interactions. Children's relationships with peers emerge as they engage in daily processes with children and adults. Their temperaments, abilities, and developmental statuses all contribute to how these interactions transpire. Additionally, a child's gender, family culture, and community provide a context for the directions in which these interactions occur. The scenario presented at the opening of the chapter presented interactions common to peer relations in early education settings. Thus, supporting a child's peer relationships in school can appear to be a complex, if not daunting, task.

Consistent with social learning, social information processing, social network perspectives, and proactive and emergent strategies provide a means for teachers to organize their support of children's social development. Teachers can, and should, set individual social goals for children, much as they set goals for reading and mathematics achievement. By actively teaching social skills, teachers help children find a place in the classroom (Berk, 2003). Using books and stories to open discussions and engender role play about manners and consideration of others is an important way to help children. Over time, teachers must also be certain that each child is included in class discussions and activities. Teachers can bring children together in small-group activities, encourage prosocial interactions, and share their own positive ideas about each child's contribution. By teaching positive ways for children to settle disputes and resolve differences, teachers help children grow and learn. Rather than teaching children to say, "I'm sorry," teachers may encourage children to offer some form of restitution, be it a tissue, a hug, or simply staying with the upset child until he or she feels better. This practice serves not only to stop the aggression in the short term but also makes it clear that bullying will not be tolerated. When teachers proactively model and teach positive social skills, while refusing to allow antisocial behaviors, they guide children toward social understanding and equity.

From an ecological perspective, it takes a village to raise a child. Families, schools, and communities can support the development of healthy peer relationships. Schools can limit class sizes and provide classrooms with support personnel, allowing the teacher to take time to work through children's social challenges. Schools can also provide sufficiently well-trained personnel to be with children on the playground for support and supervision in handling social problems and preventing bullying. School districts can make sure that sufficient time is allotted for children's peer interactions, encouraging use of centers and play in early education classrooms and scheduling regular, frequent recess opportunities for children's social growth. Communities need citizens who value and interact well with diverse peers in a variety of settings. Schools and classrooms are places where children can, and should, learn to engage in and benefit from high-quality relationship values and skills.

References

Aboud, F. E., Mendelson, M. J., & Purdy, K. T. (2003). Cross-race peer relations and friendship quality. *International Journal of Behavioral Development, 27,* 165–173.

Bandura, A. (1977). *Social learning theory.* Oxford, UK: Prentice-Hall.

Bauminger, N., Shulman, C., & Agam, G. (2004). The link between perceptions of self and of social relationships in high-functioning children with autism. *Journal of Developmental and Physical Disabilities, 16*(2), 193–214.

Bennett, A., & Dervensky, J. (1995). The medieval kingdom topology: Peer relations in kindergarten children. *Psychology in the Schools, 32,* 130–141.

Berk, L. E. (2003). *Child development* (6th ed.). Boston: Allyn & Bacon.

Birch, S. H., & Ladd, G. W. (1998). Children's interpersonal behaviors and the teacher–child relationship. *Developmental Psychology, 34*(5), 934–946.

Black, B., & Hazen, N. (1990). Social status and patters of communication in acquainted and unacquainted preschool children. *Developmental Psychology, 26,* 379–387.

Bowlby, J. (1969). *Attachment and loss: Vol. 1. Attachment.* New York: Basic Books.

Bredekamp, S., & Copple, C. (1997). *Developmentally appropriate practice in early childhood programs* (rev. ed.). Washington, DC: National Association for the Education of Young Children.

Bronfenbrenner, U., & Morris, P. (1998). The ecology of developmental processes. In R. M. Lerner (Ed.), *Theoretical models of human development* (5th ed., Vol. 1, pp. 993–1028). New York: Wiley.

Bronson, M. B. (2000). *Self-regulation in early childhood: Nature and nurture.* New York: Guilford Press.

Brooks-Gunn, J., & Warren, M. (1989). Biological and social contributions to negative affect in young adolescent girls. *Child Development, 60,* 467–482.

Buysse, V., Goldman, B. D., West, T., & Hollingsworth, H. (2008). Friendships in early childhood: Implications for early education and intervention. In W. H. Brown, S. L. Odom, & S. R. McConnell (Eds.), *Social competence of young children: Risk, disability, and intervention* (pp. 77–97). Baltimore: Brookes.

Cairns, R. B., Leung, M. C., Buchanan, C., & Cairns, B. D. (1995). Friendships and social networks in childhood and adolescence: Fluidity, reliability, and interrelations. *Child Development, 66,* 1330–1345.

Catalano, R. F., Mazza, J. J., Harachi, T. W., Abbott, R. D., Haggerty, K. P., & Fleming, C. B. (2003). Raising healthy children through enhancing social development in elementary school: Results after 1.5 years. *Journal of School Psychology, 41,* 143–164.

Chen, D. W., Fein, G. G., Killen, M., & Tam, H. P. (2001). Peer conflicts of preschool children: Issues, resolution, incidence, and age-related patterns. *Early Education and Development, 12,* 523–544.

Coie, J. D., & Dodge, K. A. (1983). Continuities and changes in children's social status: A five-year longitudinal study. *Merrill–Palmer Quarterly, 29,* 261–282.

Coie, J. D., Dodge, K. A., & Kupersmidt, J. B. (1990). Peer group behavior and social status. In

S. R. Asher & J. D. Coie (Eds.), *Peer rejection in childhood* (pp. 17–59). New York: Cambridge University.

Committee for Children. (1989). *Second Step violence prevention program.* Seattle, WA: Author.

Coplan, R. J., Hastings, P. D., Lagace-Sequin, D. G., & Moulton, C. E. (2002). Authoritative and authoritarian mothers' parenting goals, attributions, and emotions across different childrearing contexts. *Parenting: Science and Practice, 2,* 1–26.

Corsaro, W. A. (1981). Friendship in the nursery school: Social organization in a peer environment. In S. R. Asher & J. Gottman (Eds.), *The development of children's friendships* (pp. 207–241). New York: Cambridge University Press.

Crick, N. R., Casas, J. F., & Ku, H.-C. (1999). Relational and physical forms of peer victimization in preschool. *Developmental Psychology, 35,* 376–385.

Crick, N. R., Casas, J. F., & Mosher, M. (1997). Relational and overt aggression in preschool. *Developmental Psychology, 33,* 579–588.

Crick, N. R., & Dodge, K. A. (1994). A review and reformulation of social information-processing mechanisms in children's social adjustment. *Psychological Bulletin, 115*(1), 74–101.

Crockenberg, S., & Lourie, A. (1996). Parents' conflict strategies with children and children's conflict strategies with peers. *Merrill–Palmer Quarterly, 42,* 495–518.

Cumberland-Li, A., Eisenberg, N., & Reiser, M. (2004). Relations of young children's agreeableness and resiliency to effortful control and impulsivity. *Social Development, 13*(2), 193–212.

Denham, S. A., & Burton, R. (1996). A social–emotional intervention for at-risk 4-year-olds. *Journal of School Psychology, 34*(3), 225–245.

Denham, S. A., McKinley, M., Couchard, E. A., & Holt, R. (1990). Emotional and behavioral predictors of preschool peer ratings. *Child Development, 61,* 1145–1152.

Diamond, A., LeFurgy, W., & Blass, S. (1993). Attitudes of typical preschool children toward their peers with disabilities: A year-long study in four integrated classrooms. *Journal of Genetic Psychology, 154,* 215–222.

Dodge, K. A., Pettit, G. S., & Bates, J. E. (1994). Socialization mediators of the relation between socioeconomic status and child conduct problems. *Child Development, 65,* 649–665.

Eisenberg, N., Champion, C., & Ma, Y. (2004). Emotion-related regulation: An emerging construct. *Merrill–Palmer Quarterly, 50*(3), 236–259.

Eisenberg, N., Cumberland, A., Spinrad, T. L., Fabes, R., Shepard, S. A., Reiser, M., et al. (2001). The relations of regulation and emotionality to children's externalizing and internalizing problem behavior. *Child Development, 72*(4), 1112–1134.

Eisenberg, N., & Fabes, R. (1994). Mothers' reactions to children's negative emotions: Relations to children's temperament and anger behavior. *Merrill–Palmer Quarterly, 40,* 138–156.

Eisenberg, N., Fabes, R., Guthrie, I. K., & Reiser, M. (2000). Dispositional emotionality and regulation: Their role in predicting quality of social functioning. *Journal of Personality and Social Psychology, 78*(1), 136–157.

Eisenberg, N., Fabes, R., Nyman, M., Bernzweig, J., & Pinuelas, A. (1994). The relations of emotionality and regulation to children's anger-related reactions. *Child Development, 65,* 109–128.

Eisenberg, N., Fabes, R., & Spinrad, T. L. (2006). Prosocial development. In W. Damon & R. Lerner (Eds.), *Handbook of child psychology* (Vol. 3, pp. 646–718). Hoboken, NJ: Wiley.

Eisenberg, N., Guthrie, I. K., Fabes, R., Reiser, M., Murphy, B., Holgren, R., et al. (1997). The relations of regulation and emotionality to resiliency and competent social functioning in elementary school children. *Child Development, 68*(2), 295–311.

Eisenberg, N., Sadovsky, A., Spinrad, T. L., Fabes, R., Losoya, S., Valiente, C., et al. (2005). The relations of problem behavior status to children's negative emotionality, effortful control, and impulsivity: Concurrent relations and prediction of change. *Developmental Psychology, 41*(1), 193–211.

Eisenberg, N., Valiente, C., Fabes, R., Smith, C. L., Reiser, M., Shepard, S. A., et al. (2003). The relations of effortful control and ego control to children's resiliency and social functioning. *Developmental Psychology, 39*(4), 761–116.

Estell, D. B., Cairns, R. B., Farmer, T. W., & Cairns, B. L. (2002). Aggression in inner-city early elementary classrooms: Individual and peer-group configurations. *Merrill–Palmer Quarterly, 48*(1), 52–76.

Estell, D. B., Farmer, T. W., Cairns, R. B., & Cairns, B. L. (2002). Social relations and academic achievement in inner-city early elementary classrooms. *International Journal of Behavioral Development, 26*(6), 518–528.

Fabes, R. A., Martin, C. L., & Hanish, L. D. (2004). The next 50 years: Considering gender as a context for understanding young children's peer relationships. *Merrill–Palmer Quarterly, 50*, 260–273.

Fabes, R. A., Shepard, S. A., Guthrie, I. K., & Martin, C. L. (1997). Roles of temperamental arousal and gender-segregated play in young children's social adjustment. *Developmental Psychology, 33*(4), 693–702.

Fagot, B. I., Leinbach, M. D., & O'Boyle, C. (1992). Gender labeling, gender stereotyping, and parenting behaviors. *Developmental Psychology, 28*(2), 225–230.

Fantuzzo, J., Sekino, Y., & Cohen, H. L. (2004). An examination of the contributions of interactive peer play to salient classroom competencies of urban Head Start children. *Psychology in the Schools, 41*(3), 323–336.

Farver, J. A. (1996). Aggressive behavior in preschoolers' social networks: Do birds of a feather flock together? *Early Childhood Research Quarterly, 11*(3), 333–350.

Farver, J. A., Kim, Y., & Lee, Y. (1995). Cultural differences in Korean- and Anglo-American preschooler's social interaction and play behavior. *Child Development, 66*, 1089–1099.

Farver, J. A., & Shin, L. (1997). Social pretend play in Korean- and Anglo-American preschoolers. *Child Development, 68*, 544–556.

Finnegan, R. A., Hodges, E. V. E., & Perry, D. G. (1998). Victimization by peers: Association with children's reports of mother–child interaction. *Journal of Personality and Social Psychology, 75*, 1076–1086.

Finnie, V., & Russell, A. (1998). Preschool children's social status and their mothers' behavior and knowledge in the supervisory role. *Developmental Psychology, 24*, 789–801.

Frost, J., Wortham, S., & Reifel, S. (2005). *Play and child development.* Upper Saddle River, NJ: Merrill/Prentice-Hall.

Gallagher, K., Dadisman, K., Farmer, T. W., Huss, L., & Hutchins, B. C. (2007). Social dynamics of early childhood classrooms. In O. Saracho & B. Spodek (Eds.), *Contemporary perspectives on social learning in early childhood education* (pp. 17–48). Charlotte, NC: Information Age.

Gandini, L. (1995). Educational and caring spaces. In C. Edwards, L. Gandini, & G. Forman (Eds.), *The hundred languages of children: The Reggio Emilia approach to early childhood education* (pp. 135–149). Norwood, NJ: Ablex.

Gest, S. D., Farmer, T. W., Cairns, B. D., & Xie, H. (2003). Identifying children's peer social networks in school classrooms: Links between peer reports and observed interactions. *Social Development, 12*, 513–529.

Goncu, A., Patt, M. B., & Kouba, E. (2002). Understanding young children's pretend play in context. In P. K. Smith & C. H. Hart (Eds.), *Blackwell handbook of childhood social development* (pp. 418–437). Malden, MA: Blackwell.

Gorman-Smith, D., & Loeber, R. (2005). Are developmental pathways in disruptive behaviors the same for girls and boys? *Journal of Child and Family Studies, 14*(1), 15–27.

Grisham-Brown, J., Hemmeter, M. L., & Pretti-Frontczak, K. (2005). *Blended practices for teaching young children in inclusive settings.* Baltimore: Brookes.

Guralnick, M. J. (1999). Family and child influences on the peer-related social competence of young children with developmental delays. *Mental Retardation and Developmental Disabilities Research Reviews, 5,* 21–29.

Guralnick, M. J., Hammond, M. A., Connor, R. T., & Neville, B. (2006). Stability, change, and correlates of the peer relationships of young children with mild developmental delays. *Child Development, 77*(2), 312–324.

Halberstadt, A. G., Denham, S. A., & Dunsmore, J. C. (2001). Affective social competence. *Social Development, 10*(1), 79–117.

Harrist, A., Pettit, G. S., Dodge, K. A., & Bates, J. E. (1994). Dyadic synchrony in mother–child interaction: Relation with children's subsequent kindergarten adjustment. *Family Relations, 43,* 417–424.

Harrist, A. W., & Bradley, K. D. (2003). "You can't say you can't play": Intervening in the process of social exclusion in the kindergarten classroom. *Early Childhood Research Quarterly, 18,* 185–205.

Hart, C. H., DeWolf, K. M., Wozniak, P., & Burts, D. C. (1992). Maternal and parental disciplinary styles: Relations with preschoolers' playground behavioral orientation and peer status. *Child Development, 63,* 879–892.

Hartup, W. W., & Abecassis, M. (2004). Friends and enemies. In P. K. Smith & C. H. Hart (Eds.), *Blackwell handbook of childhood social development* (pp. 285–306). Malden, MA: Blackwell.

Hawley, P. H. (1999). The ontogenesis of social dominance: A strategy-based evolutionary perspective. *Developmental Review, 19,* 97–132.

Hawley, P. H. (2002). Social dominance and prosocial and coercive strategies of resource control in preschoolers. *International Journal of Behavioral Development, 26,* 167–176.

Hawley, P. H. (2003). Strategies of control, aggression, and morality in preschoolers: An evolutionary perspective. *Journal of Experimental Child Psychology, 85,* 213–235.

Hazen, N., & Black, B. (1989). Preschool communication skills: The role of social status and interactional context. *Child Development, 60,* 867–876.

Hemmeter, M. L., Ostrosky, M., & Fox, L. (2006). Social and emotional foundations for early learning: A conceptual model for intervention. *School Psychology Review, 35*(4), 583–601.

Howes, C., & Wishard, A. G. (2004). Revisiting shared meaning: Looking through the lens of culture and linking shared pretend play through proto narrative development to emergent literacy. In E. Zigler, D. G. Singer, & S. J. Bishop-Josef (Eds.), *Children's play: The roots of literacy* (pp. 143–158). Washington, DC: Zero to Three.

Howes, C., & Wu, F. (1990). Peer interactions and friendships in an ethnically diverse school setting. *Child Development, 61,* 537–541.

Hubbard, J. A., & Dearing, K. F. (2004). Children's understanding and regulation of emotion in the context of their peer relations. In J. B. Kupersmidt & K. A. Dodge (Eds.), *Children's peer relations: From development to intervention* (pp. 81–99). New York: Wiley.

Joseph, G. E., & Strain, P. S. (2003). Comprehensive evidence-based social–emotional curricula for young children: An analysis of efficacious adoption potential. *Topics in Early Childhood Special Education, 23*(2), 65–76.

Joseph, G. E., & Strain, P. S. (2003). *You've got to have friends.* Nashville, TN: Center of the Social and Emotional Foundations for Early Learning, Vanderbilt University.

Kagan, J., Reznick, J. S., Clarke, C., Snidman, N., & Garcia-Coll, C. (1984). Behavioral inhibition to the unfamiliar. *Child Development, 55,* 2215–2225.

Kagan, S. L., & Carroll, J. (2004). *Alignment in early care and education: A pilot study.* New York: National Center for Children and Families.

Katz, L. F. (1990). Impressions of Reggio Emilia preschools. *Young Children, 45*(6), 4–10.

Katz, L. F., & McClellan, D. E. (1997). *Fostering children's social competence: The teacher's role.* Washington, DC: National Association for the Education of Young Children.

Kochenderfer, B. J., & Ladd, G. W. (1996). Peer victimization: Cause or consequence of school adjustment? *Child Development, 67,* 1305–1317.

Kontos, S., Burchinal, M. R., Howes, C., Wisseh, S., & Galinsky, E. (2002). An eco-behavioral approach to examining the contextual effects of early childhood classrooms. *Early Childhood Research Quarterly, 17,* 239–258.

Kusche, C. A., & Greenberg, M. T. (1994). *The PATHS curriculum.* Seattle, WA: Developmental Research and Programs.

Ladd, G. W. (1983). Social networks of popular, average, and rejected children in school settings. *Merrill–Palmer Quarterly, 29,* 283–307.

Ladd, G. W., Birch, S. H., & Buhs, E. S. (1999). Children's social and scholastic lives in kindergarten: Related spheres of influence? *Child Development, 70*(6), 1373–1400.

Ladd, G. W., & Hart, C. H. (1992). Creating informal play opportunities: Are parents' and preschoolers' initiations related to children's competence with peers? *Developmental Psychology, 28,* 1179–1187.

Ladd, G. W., Herald, S. L., & Andrews, R. K. (2006). Young children's peer relations and social competence. In B. Spodek & O. Saracho (Eds.), *Handbook of research on the education of young children* (pp. 23–54). Mahwah, NJ: Erlbaum.

Ladd, G. W., & Kochenderfer, B. J. (1996). Linkages between friendship and adjustment during early school transitions. In W. Bukowski, A. F. Newcomb, & W. W. Hartup (Eds.), *The company they keep: Friendships in childhood and adolescence* (pp. 322–345). New York: Cambridge University Press.

Ladd, G. W., & Price, J. M. (1987). Predicting children's social and school adjustment following the transition from preschool to kindergarten. *Child Development, 58,* 1168–1189.

Leaper, C. (2002). Parenting girls and boys. In M. H. Bornstein (Ed.), *Handbook of parenting: Vol. 1. Children and parenting* (2nd ed., pp. 189–225). Mahwah, NJ: Erlbaum.

Lee, L., Howes, C., & Chamberlain, B. (2007). Ethnic heterogeneity of social networks and cross-ethnic friendships of elementary school boys and girls. *Merrill–Palmer Quarterly, 53*(3), 325–346.

Levin, E., & Rubin, K. H. (1983). Getting others to do what you want them to do: The development of children's requestive strategies. In K. Nelson (Ed.), *Child language* (Vol. 4, pp. 157–186). Hillsdale, NJ: Erlbaum.

Lieberman, A. F. (1977). Preschoolers' competence with peers: Relations with attachment and peer experience. *Child Development, 70,* 202–213.

Lollis, S. P., Ross, H. S., & Tate, E. (1992). Parents' regulation of children's peer interactions: Direct influence. In R. D. Parke & G. W. Ladd (Eds.), *Family–peer relationships: Modes of linkage* (pp. 255–294). Hillsdale, NJ: Erlbaum.

Maccoby, E., E. (1990). Gender and relationships: A developmental account. *American Psychologist, 45*(4), 513–520.

Madden, N. A., & Slavin, R. E. (1983). Cooperative learning and social acceptance of mainstreamed academically handicapped students. *Journal of Special Education, 17,* 171–182.

Manning, M. L., & Lucking, R. (1993). Cooperative learning and multicultural classrooms. *Clearning House, 67*(1), 12–16.

McDowell, D. J., & Parke, R. D. (2000). Differential knowledge of display rules for positive and negative emotions: Influence for parents, influence on peers. *Social Development, 9,* 415–432.

Mendelson, M. J., Aboud, F. E., & Lanthier, R. P. (1994). Personality predictors of friendship and popularity in kindergarten. *Journal of Applied Developmental Psychology, 15,* 113–135.

Miletta, A. (2005). Managing dilemmas: Uncovering moral and intellectual dimensions of life in a Reggio Emilia classroom. In J. Koch & B.J. Irby (Eds.), *Gender and schooling in the early years* (pp. 79–97). Charlotte, NC: Information Age.

Mize, J., & Pettit, G. S. (1997). Mothers' social coaching, mother–child relationship style, and children's peer competence: Is the medium the message? *Child Development, 68,* 312–332.

Montessori, M. (1964). *The Montessori method.* New York: Schocken.

Moore, R., Goltsman, S., & Iacofano, D. (1987). *Play for all guidelines: Planning, design, and management of outdoor play settings for all children.* Berkeley, CA: MIG Communications.

Olsen, S. F., Yang, C., Hart, C. H., Robinson, C. C., Wu, P., Nelson, D. A., et al. (2002). Maternal psychological control and preschool children's behavioral outcomes in China, Russia, and the United States. In B. K. Barber (Ed.), *Intrusive parenting: How psychological control affects children and adolescents* (pp. 235–262). Washington, DC: American Psychological Association.

Paley, V. G. (1992). *You can't say you can't play.* Cambridge, MA: Harvard University Press.

Parke, R. D., Simpkins, S. D., McDowell, D. J., Kim, M., Killian, C., Dennis, J., et al. (2004). Relative contributions of families and peers to children's social development. In P. K. Smith & C. H. Hart (Eds.), *Blackwell handbook of childhood social development* (pp. 156–177). Malden, MA: Blackwell.

Parker-Cohen, N. Y., & Bell, R. Q. (1988). The relationship between temperament and social adjustment to peers. *Early Childhood Research Quarterly, 3,* 179–192.

Parten, M. B. (1932). Social participation among preschool children. *Journal of Abnormal and Social Psychology, 27,* 243–269.

Pellegrini, A. D. (1987). Rough-and-tumble play: Developmental and educational significance. *Educational Psychologist, 22*(1), 23–43.

Pellegrini, A. D. (2002). Rough-and-tumble play from childhood through adolescence: Development and possible functions. In P. K. Smith & C. H. Hart (Eds.), *Blackwell handbook of childhood social development* (pp. 438–453). Malden, MA: Blackwell.

Pellegrini, A. D., & Perlmutter, J. C. (1989). Classroom contextual effects on children's play. *Developmental Psychology, 25,* 289–296.

Pettit, G. S., Brown, E. G., Mize, J., & Lindsey, E. (1998). Mothers' and fathers' socializing behaviors in three contexts: Links with children's peer competence. *Merrill–Palmer Quarterly, 44,* 173–193.

Phyfe-Perkins, E., & Shoemaker, J. (1986). Indoor play environments: Research and design implications. In G. G. Fein & M. Rivkin (Eds.), *The young child at play: Reviews of research* (Vol. 4, pp. 177–193). Washington, DC: National Association for the Education of Young Children.

Pianta, R., Steinberg, M. S., & Rollins, K. B. (1995). The first two years of school: Teacher–child relationships and deflections in children's classroom adjustment. *Development and Psychopathology, 7,* 295–312.

Price, J. M., & Dodge, K. A. (1989). Reactive and proactive aggression in childhood: Relations to peer status and social context dimensions. *Journal of Abnormal Child Psychology, 17,* 455–471.

Prior, M., Smart, D., & Sanson, A. (2001). Longitudinal predictors of behavioural adjustment in pre-adolescent children. *Australian and New Zealand Journal of Psychiatry, 35*(3), 297–307.

Puttallaz, M., & Gottman, J. (1981). An interactional model of children's entry into peer groups. *Child Development, 52*(3), 986–994.

Rigby, K. (2004). Bullying in childhood. In P. K. Smith & C. H. Hart (Eds.), *Blackwell handbook of childhood social development* (pp. 549–568). Malden, MA: Blackwell.

Robinson, C. C., Anderson, G. T., Porter, C. L., Hart, C. H., & Wouden-Miller, M. (2003). Sequential transition patterns of preschoolers' social interactions during child-initiated play: Is parallel-aware play a bidirectional bridge to other play states? *Early Childhood Research Quarterly, 18*, 3–21.

Roeyers, H. (1996). The influence of nonhandicapped peers on the social interactions of children with a pervasive developmental disorder. *Journal of Autism and Developmental Disorders, 26*, 303–320.

Rogers, C. S., & Sawyers, J. K. (1992). *Play in the lives of children.* Washington, DC: National Association for the Education of Young Children.

Roopnarine, J. L. (1984). Sex-typed socialization in mixed-age preschool classrooms. *Child Development, 55*(3), 1078–1084.

Rose, A. J., & Rudolph, K. D. (2006). A review of sex differences in peer relationship processes: Potential trade-offs for the emotional and behavioral development of girls and boys. *Psychological Bulletin, 132*(1), 98–131.

Rubin, K. H. (1982). Non-social play in preschoolers: Necessary evil? *Child Development, 53*, 651–657.

Rubin, K. H., Bukowski, W., & Parker, J. G. (2006). Peer interactions, relationships, and groups. In N. Eisenberg (Ed.), *Handbook of child psychology* (Vol. 3, pp. 571–645). Hoboken, NJ: Wiley.

Rubin, K. H., Burgess, K. B., & Coplan, R. J. (2004). Social withdrawal and shyness. In P. K. Smith & C. H. Hart (Eds.), *Blackwell handbook of child social development* (pp. 329–352). Malden, MA: Blackwell.

Rubin, K. H., Burgess, K. B., Dwyer, K. M., & Hastings, P. P. (2003). Predicting preschoolers' externalizing behaviors from toddler temperament, conflict, and maternal negativity. *Developmental Psychology, 39*, 164–176.

Rubin, K. H., Hymel, S., & Mills, R. (1989). Sociability and social withdrawal in childhood: Stability and outcomes. *Journal of Personality, 57*, 238–255.

Rubin, K. H., Watson, K., & Jambor, T. (1978). Free play behavior in pre-school and kindergarten children. *Child Development, 49*, 534–536.

Russell, A., Pettit, G. S., & Mize, J. (1998). Horizontal qualities in parent–child relationships: Parallels with and possible consequences for children's peer interactions. *Developmental Review, 18*, 313–352.

Sanson, A., Hemphill, S. A., & Smart, D. (2004a). Connections between temperament and social development: A review. *Social Development, 13*(1), 142–170.

Sanson, A., Hemphill, S. A., & Smart, D. (2004b). Temperament and social development. In P. K. Smith & C. H. Hart (Eds.), *Blackwell handbook of childhood social development* (pp. 97–116). Malden, MA: Blackwell.

Schweinhart, L. J., & Weikart, D. P. (1997). The High/Scope preschool curriculum comparison study through age 23. *Early Childhood Research Quarterly, 12*, 117–143.

Shonkoff, J. P., & Phillips, D. A. (2000). *From neurons to neighborhoods: The science of early childhood development.*Washington, DC: National Academy Press.

Silver, R. B., Measelle, J. R., Armstrong, J. M., & Essex, M. J. (2005). Trajectories of classroom externalizing behavior: Contributions of child characteristics, family characteristics, and teacher–child relationship during the school transition. *Journal of School Psychology, 43*, 39–60.

Siperstain, G. N., & Leffert, J. S. (1997). Comparison of socially accepted and rejected children with mental retardation. *American Journal on Mental Retardation, 101*, 339–351.

Skarpness, L. R., & Carson, D. K. (1986). Temperament, communicative competence and psychological adjustment of kindergarten children. *Psychological Review, 59*, 1299–1306.

Smart, D., & Sanson, A. (2001). Children's social competence: The role of temperament and behaviour, and their "fit" with parents' expectations. *Family Matters, 59*, 10–15.

Smilansky, S., & Shefatya, L. (1990). *Facilitating play: A medium for promoting cognitive, socio-emotional and academic development in young children*. Silver Spring, MD: Psychosocial and Educational Publishers.

Smith, M. (2001). Social and emotional competencies: Contributions of young African-American children's peer acceptance. *Early Education and Development, 12*(1), 49–72.

Spinrad, T. L., Eisenberg, N., Harris, E., Hanish, L., Fabes, R., Kupanoff, K., et al. (2004). The relation of children's everyday nonsocial peer play behavior to their emotionality, regulation, and social functioning. *Child Development, 40*(1), 67–80.

Sroufe, L. A. (1997). *Emotional development: The organization of emotional life in the early years*. Cambridge, UK: Cambridge University Press.

Standing, E. M. (1984). *Maria Montessori: Her life and work*. New York: Penguin.

Stormont, M. (2001). Social outcomes of children with AD/HD: Contribution factors and implications for practice. *Psychology in the Schools, 38*(6), 521–531.

Stormont, M., Lewis, T. J., & Becker, R. (2005). Positive behavior support systems: Applying key features in preschool settings. *Teaching Exceptional Children, 37*(6), 42–49.

Strayer, F. F., & Trudel, M. (1984). Developmental changes in the nature and function of social dominance among young children. *Ethnology and Sociobiology, 5*, 279–295.

Tremblay, A., Strain, P. S., Hendrickson, J. M., & Shores, R. E. (1981). Social interactions of normal preschool children: Using normative data for subject and target selection. *Behavior Modification, 5*(2), 237–253.

Underwood, M. K. (2007). Gender and children's friendships: Do girls' and boys' friendships constitute different peer cultures, and what are the trade-offs for development? *Merrill–Palmer Quarterly, 53*(3), 319–324.

Valiente, C., Eisenberg, N., Fabes, R., Shepard, S. A., Cumberland, A., & Losoya, S. (2004). Prediction of children's empathy-related responding from their effortful control and parents' expressivity. *Developmental Psychology, 40*(6), 911–926.

Vaughn, B. E., Colvin, T. N., & Azria, M. R. (2001). Dyadic analyses of friendship in a sample of preschool-age children attending Head Start: Correspondence between measures and implications for social competence. *Child Development, 72*(3), 862–878.

Walters, L. S. (2000). Putting cooperative learning to the test. *Harvard Education Letter, 16*(3), 1–6.

Watson, A. C., Nixon, C. L., Wilson, A., & Capage, L. (1999). Social interaction skills and theory of mind in young children. *Developmental Psychology, 35*, 386–391.

Willoughby, M., Kupersmidt, J. B., & Bryant, D. (2001). Overt and covert dimensions of antisocial behavior in early childhood. *Journal of Abnormal Child Psychology, 29*, 177–187.

Yoon, J. S., Hughes, J. N., Cavell, T. A., & Thompson, B. (2000). Social cognitive differences between aggressive-rejected and aggressive-nonrejected children. *Journal of School Psychology, 38*, 551–570.

CHAPTER 12

Promoting Social Acceptance and Respect for Cultural Diversity in Young Children

Learning from Developmental Research

Oscar A. Barbarin
Erica Odom

Jamal stands expressionless and alone, facing the wall in the time-out corner. He has been sent there often by the teacher, who complains out loud that he is nothing but trouble and does not know how the play nicely like the other children. As one of the few African Americans in a predominantly white preschool Jamal often finds himself singled out by his teacher for punishment and made to sit by himself during recess, while the other children play. His classmates often point him out to classroom visitors: "That's Jamal, ... he's bad."

Meanwhile, on the other side of the Atlantic Ocean, a similar process of stigmatization is taking place as a child is singled out by peers for ridicule and social exclusion because of her ethnicity.

Two German girls in the kindervelt gossip together about Sibel, a Turkish immigrant girl who dresses differently and brings food from home that one of the German girls describes as "nasty." One whispers to the other that Sibel won't be invited with the other children to her birthday party, and that Sibel is "dumb" and "stinky."

Despite a rich body of evidence to the contrary, many adults remain skeptical that preschool children are capable of true prejudice or discrimination, unless they are explicitly taught them. For these skeptics, it may be all too easy to minimize the incidents described here as innocent child's play or innocuous comments that have no long-term impact on Jamal or Sibel. At worst, the sentiments captured in calling Jamal "bad" or Sibel "stinky" may be dismissed as simply offensive or ill-mannered. Moreover, the skeptics would argue that children can't appreciate the impact of scapegoating, especially in the case of Jamal, where it is instigated and reinforced by the teacher. However, the Jamal and Sibel vignettes suggest that young children do form prejudiced attitudes and are capable of discriminatory behavior. Even without the encouragement and facilitation of adults, negative views about those outside of one's identity group are more common among young children than negative views about those perceived as similar or part of one's identity group (Ramsey & Myers, 1990). As these vignettes illustrate, subtle forms of stigmatization and intolerance occur early in life, in the form of disparaging comments, excluding others from play, and negative evaluations of groups who are different. Even if Jamal's and Sibel's experiences are unusual, they underscore need for vigilance and assiduous efforts to counter negative attitudes and to foster prosocial behavior in early childhood settings. How, then, do we prepare children to embrace life in a multicultural world in which differences are respected and getting along with those who are different is valued? We could begin by reframing these early manifestations of social nonacceptance and aversion to difference as points of intervention by sensitive adults. Although challenging, the situations illustrated in these vignettes point out opportunities that occur in the natural course of events within early education settings to counter the processes of social stigmatization, and to influence how children form views about and interact with those who are different.

Efforts to form prosocial attitudes or to redirect discriminatory behavior are more likely to succeed if they are informed by an understanding of the developmental processes that give rise to stigma, social exclusion, and devaluing of difference on the one hand, and prosocial responses of social acceptance and respect for diversity on the other (Perkins & Mebert, 2005). We begin this chapter by defining "social acceptance and respect for diversity" (SARD), and discussing its importance for society. We then offer a way of thinking about how the attitudes, dispositions, and behaviors that make up SARD form by situating them within the broader context of children's cognitive and social development. We conclude the chapter with a discussion of the role of adult caregivers in promoting SARD and recommendations for ways teachers might support young children's positive attitudes and behaviors toward others, and encourage children to value the diversity of the people around them.

Defining SARD

SARD is used here to refer specifically to *cross-ethnic comity and social harmony in interethnic group relationships, which arise from an attitude of tolerance*. SARD can be said to exist when there is an absence of discrimination, stereotyping, stigmatizing, and social exclusion of one group by another, and when the tensions that inevitably arise in the relationships between ethnic group members are resolved amicably, without resort to coercion or aggression. SARD combines two constructs based on slightly different philosophical stances in how one group of individuals relates to groups that are different. "Social acceptance" is as an openness to and sympathy for the beliefs and practices of others, even if they conflict with one's own. It implies tolerance, moral relativism, and commitment to the right of individuals and groups to be different, even if those differences are a source of personal discomfort. Social acceptance, at a minimum, implies affective neutrality toward and allowance of differences or variation, without disparagement of or the expectation that others ought to change to fit in. "Respect for diversity" goes a step further along the dimension of acceptance of and comfort with difference. It involves a proactive and positive evaluation of human differences. It implies placing a premium on and seeing benefit in that which is different. Far from a threat, a source of conflict, or an obstacle to be overcome, diversity is construed as "the spice" that adds variety and makes life interesting. Thus, difference is not simply to be accepted; it is to be actively embraced because it has intrinsic value. In this way, respect for diversity is not simply acquiescence to or reluctant acceptance of that which is foreign. It values and sees difference as positive.

The constructs of "social acceptance" and "respect for diversity" are not synonymous. Whereas social acceptance is affectively neutral, respect for diversity is affectively positive. Embracing diversity opens children up to people, experiences, and approaches to life that they may never have conceived. In this way, their lives may be enriched. These two constructs have different goals and are based in different philosophical frameworks. The notion of social acceptance suggests the ability to respond favorably to difference, while remaining passive in the face of challenges to currently held ideals. Respect for diversity in its purest form suggests a more proactive stance that not only includes acceptance but also embraces differences. Social acceptance suggests that one respects the beliefs of another. It requires that one put his or her own beliefs aside and use perspective-taking skills. Respect of diversity is more action oriented. Respecting diversity indicates that an individual is interested in other ideas and ways of knowing, and is open to incorporating them into his or her ways of interacting. In social acceptance, diversity possesses a neutral valence, whereas respect for diversity attaches a strongly positive valence to difference. The imperative of social acceptance is to do no harm; that of respect for diversity is to savor and to seek out variation.

Importance of SARD

Around the world and across the centuries, peaceful coexistence in communities has been disrupted by the pestilence of religious and ethnic strife. The downward spiral of intolerance often has proceeded from competition for scarce resources and suspicion to social denigration, discrimination, and exclusion. These have sometimes erupted in the form of mass murder, full-scale warfare, and genocide, resulting in social upheaval from which communities find it difficult to recover. Thus ethnic, cultural, religious, and other forms of intolerance impose a high cost on societies in the form of psychological and physical risks that give rise to human misery and make life unbearable. In light of these costs, efforts to nurture social acceptance and respect for diversity become essential for maintaining social order.

Schools play a role in preparing children for adulthood by not only developing knowledge and skills for economic productivity but also promoting civic engagement and shaping views of their social world that contribute to social comity. Schools, along with families, nurture personal identity and cultivate the ability to establish relationships with others. Schools are also settings in which children experience diversity close-up, often for the first time. Although neighborhoods are largely segregated on the basis of social class and discriminatory housing policies, many school districts are ethnically, culturally, and religiously diverse. In the United States and elsewhere around the globe, publicly supported schools have become the meeting place, the point of intersection, for diverse groups that otherwise might have few opportunities to interact with one another.

The need to consider SARD is compelling as our schools confront serving increasingly diverse student bodies. Public education is at the vortex of a demographic tidal wave that will increase the ethnic diversity of student enrollment. Early childhood programs already reflect this expected expansion of diversity. The U.S. Bureau of the Census indicates that, today, 45% of children younger than age 5 are ethnic minorities. In fact, the increase in diversity among young children is largely due to a growing Hispanic population. Hispanic children younger than age 5 represented 70% of the growth in the U.S. child population in 2005 (U.S. Bureau of the Census, 2005). As the American racial landscape expands, it is expected that early childhood classrooms will continue to reflect a greater diversity of children from differing racial and ethnic backgrounds. A National Center for Education Statistics (2007) report showed that 42% of public school students were racial or ethnic minorities in 2003, up markedly from 22% in 1972. Many U.S. schools have enrolled successive waves of immigrant children from Asia, Africa, and Latin America. Some school districts have over 50 languages represented among the first languages spoken by their students, many of whom arrive at the school doors with a tenuous hold on the English language. In addition, federal legislation has put into place deliberate policies to include children with special educational or physical needs in classrooms with typically developing children. The systemic forces giving rise to and reinforcing intolerance are complex, and the difficulty of combating and neutralizing them should not be underestimated. Teachers need to be able to help students negotiate their responses to others who have different abilities or are culturally different. The promotion of SARD in these settings does not happen automatically. Discontinuity in cultural practices and social backgrounds among students requires that children acquire new skills for social discourse and develop relationships with children who are not entirely like themselves. These qualities do not occur simply by placing diverse people together. Instead, they require active cultivation and thoughtful intervention. Consequently, early childhood educators must become active participants in creating environments that lay the groundwork for children to respond with respect and acceptance to peers who are different in any number of ways. Early education classrooms offer a unique social context in which to observe the developmental processes that give rise to acceptance of others and respect for diversity. For this reason, early childhood education occupies an important niche, a setting that contributes uniquely to the social development of children and, as a result, has the potential to help children bridge demographic and cultural divides, and contribute to a more socially cohesive society.

Establishing a foundation in children of cross-ethnic comity and intergroup cooperation is an important contribution that early childhood education can make toward improving the quality of life of all people. Efforts of educators to promote cross-cultural acceptance and to engender respect for diversity are more likely to be successful if they are informed by insights about the evolution of intolerance and how respect for diversity develop over time. In the next section we situate SARD within prosocial development and identify the network of related processes that support it. By actively nurturing social acceptance and valuing diversity, schools have the potential to help children gain confidence and competence in negotiating the diverse settings that schools are becoming. The consequences of intolerance can be measured not only in human suffering and loss of social cohesion but also in economic stagnation, derailment of social progress, and a diversion of human energy from solving many of the pressing economic, health, environmental, and social problems that affect the well-being of all.

SARD as a Component of Prosocial Development

Although the theoretical foundations of the early development of SARD are present in several distinct intellectual traditions, such as multicultural education, early childhood education, and liberation education, we find that they are most compellingly conceptualized within the intellectual traditions of moral or prosocial development. Accordingly, both social acceptance and respect for diversity may be construed as constructs that fit within a larger class of prosocial behaviors. The term *prosocial behavior* has been used to refer to "voluntary behavior intended to benefit another," and it includes "acts motivated by concern for others or by internalized values and goals" (Eisenberg, Fabes, & Spinrad, 2006, p. 682). Included in the class of prosocial behaviors, along with SARD, are other-conscious behaviors intended to benefit others. As a domain, prosocial behavior requires an ability to transcend narrow self-interest and to value the perspectives of others. This implies an ability to see the world as others see it. It involves a range of behaviors and attitudes, including empathy, caring, sharing, generosity, and sympathy. In other words, because social acceptance and respect for diversity have parallels with many other behaviors grouped under the rubric of prosocial behavior, it is possible to draw inferences from this body of theory and empirical work as a starting point in understanding SARD. More specifically, by positioning SARD conceptually within the broader class of prosocial behaviors, it is possible to benefit from an extensive body of theory and empirical work to understand the developmental processes that give rise to SARD.

Figure 12.1 shows where SARD fits within the broader framework of cognitive and social development. It suggests that development of SARD rests on a foundation of prosocial behaviors and attitudes about differences, which in turn arise from the developing capacity for social perspective taking, discrimination, and social identity.

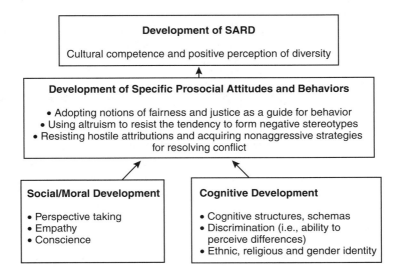

FIGURE 12.1. Dimensions in development of social acceptance and respect for diversity (SARD).

In the neo-Piagetian view of development, children's knowledge and understanding of the world is organized around several central conceptual structures (Case & Okamoto, 1996). Early on, children develop the ability to perceive differences among people, objects, and their physical world, and in time form a stable personal identity (e.g., with respect to ethnicity and gender) and learn to make distinctions between themselves and others using categories and schemas. The content of these structures forms the basis of narratives in which children attach value to the differences they perceive and shape how they respond to others in their world. The content of these narratives is influenced by an emergent capacity for perspective taking and empathy (an ability to read and to respond to the emotional states of others), and by the evolution of prosocial attitudes, such as fairness, justice, and equity, and prosocial behaviors, such as altruism and generosity. Figure 12.1 suggests that SARD arises from a combination of factors: children's personal identities; their capacity to detect and their tendency to evaluate differences; their ability to take the perspective of and be empathic with others; and altruism and an emergent sense of justice and fairness that they can apply in deciding how to act. The ability to detect or notice difference is fundamental to SARD. By the preschool period, children are well aware of differences attributable to gender, skin color, ethnicity, race, language, and physical ability. At the outset we should note that discrimination and perception of differences are not inherently wrong and, to the contrary, may be ethologically adaptive, especially in risky environments. Similarity and familiarity may be linked to a higher probability of nurturance and safety, just as difference and unfamiliarity may be associated with the higher probability of harm, such as from predators (Bugental & Grusec, 2006). In this way, recognizing difference is part of a biologically driven developmental pathway that may be linked to species survival. When the ability to detect differences is combined with the growing personal identity, interesting consequences emerge. Children show a decided preference for the familiar, for characteristics associated with self and the persons they care about, especially family (Bugental & Grusec, 2006). As a result, preschool-age children have more positive views of their own group and more negative views of other groups. "Ingroup" refers to groups the child sees as similar to the self, related, and to which he or she identifies as belonging. "Outgroups" are those groups with which the child does not identify or claim membership. It is at this stage that children have the greatest potential for discrimination against others because they are mired in ethnocentrism and a strong preference for the ingroup over the outgroup (Aboud, 2003; Katz, 2003).

Fortunately, this extreme ethnocentricism and ego-centered preference for the ingroup over the outgroup wanes as the child matures and gains experience and familiarity with those who are different (Aboud & Levy, 2000; Cameron, Rutland, & Brown, 2007). The possibility of facilitating the demise of ethnocentrism by providing positive experiences with diversity highlights a valuable aspect of participation in early childhood programs. In these settings, the link between strong group identity in very young children and intolerance of those who are different can pose significant problems for adult caretakers, including parents and teachers. Should adult caretakers nurture and encourage in young children a strong identification with their own ethnic, racial, national, or religious group if it means that children will develop negative views of those who are different? Viewing one's owns group as favorable does not immediately have to trigger avoidance and dislike of groups that are different (Aboud, 2003). Ideally, it should be possible to nurture children's attachment to or preference for familiar groups and at the same time provide social experiences that promote acceptance and the value of diversity. With these points in mind, the factors identified in Figure 12.1 can be thought of as entry points for efforts to nurture SARD in young children.

Cultural competence can play a role in neutralizing to tendency toward stereotypical schemas and stigmatization of those who are different. Identity formation provides an alternative set of forces that, under optimal conditions, operate favorably on SARD. In the development of prosocial attitudes and behaviors, conscience, altruism, and empathy contribute to the foundation of moral development and social awareness that supports and sustains SARD. On the negative side, aggression, particularly aggression that flows from hostile attributional biases in the absence of prosocial conflict management, can have a negative effect on SARD.

Ontogeny of Prosocial Behavior

The principles extracted from research on prosocial development can be used to theorize about the developmental progression of SARD, as established through social relationships and within the social context. It is possible to focus on individual differences in prosocial behavior and emphasize the role of "constitution." In this view individuals are born with temperaments that predispose them to prosocial behavior. Another more compelling view focuses on individual–environment interactions. In this view, the social context, including social relationships and experience, plays a determinative role in the development and expression of prosocial behavior. Take altruism and helping others as an example. The likelihood of an individual coming to the aid of another in distress or in need of assistance depends on the attributes of the person in distress, the visibility or public nature of helping, the helper's prior history as a recipient of help, and the cost to the individual of helping another (Hamburg & Hamburg, 2004). Accordingly, positive social relations and responsive, caring attention from adults may be especially important in the evolution of prosocial behavior. The role of secure attachments has received a great deal of attention as a contributor to the development of prosocial behavior (Steelman, Assel, Swank, Smith, & Landry, 2002). For example, in infancy, a parent's sensitivity of response to a child's emotions is integral to the development of prosocial behaviors. The security and trust formed in this most basic relationship may determine whether a child will be open and trusting or apprehensive and wary in future social relationships. Children who have stronger and more secure attachments to warm, responsive adult caretakers early in life are more likely to exhibit prosocial behavior later (Maccoby, 1992; Steelman et al., 2002). By inference, children who are securely attached to adult caregivers may be more likely to exhibit SARD. In this sense, SARD might be viewed as reciprocity or imitative behavior in response to caring attention the child has received from others. However, it is unlikely that secure attachments by themselves guarantee the development of SARD. As toddlers, children's developing empathy and concern for others provide a less egoistic and more firm foundation on which to build attitudes of social acceptance and respect for diversity. In toddlerhood, prosocial behavior is initially motivated by concern for self and personal distress (Charlesworth, 1991). Self-oriented hedonism as a motivation for prosocial behavior is manifested in compliance with social norms mostly to gain rewards, to avoid punishment, and to avoid the personal distress one experiences when someone else is injured or in distress (Zahn-Waxler, Radke-Yarrow, Wagner, & Chapman, 1992).

Motivations for prosocial behavior change with age. True empathetic responses require an ability to distinguish the needs of the self from the needs of others, to understand and decode the emotions of others, and to evaluate behaviors against some moral code (Kochanska & Aksan, 2004; Zahn-Waxler et al., 1992). For young children, empathy and altruism often emerge out of self interest. Young children frequently base what adults call "moral decisions" on the need to reduce discomfort and avoid punishment. Promotion of personal welfare of self and the need to adapt to peers' standards are high on the list of motivations for young children's moral motivations. In contrast, older children are more likely to base decisions in moral dilemmas on conceptions of justice and individual rights (Eisenberg et al., 2006). As competencies related to perspective taking, empathy, and conscience develop, it is expected that children's capacity to resist stigma, and exhibit social acceptance and respect for diversity improves. Beyond early and middle childhood, children begin to internalize abstract norms, become self-reflective, and may come to view help, social acceptance, and respect for diversity as good in their own right, as rewards in themselves (Kochanska & Thompson, 1997; Miller, Eisenberg, Fabes, & Shell, 1996). These developmental changes in the motivations for prosocial behavior parallel and perhaps are driven by the social-cognitive development (Eisenberg et al., 2006; McKown, 2005). Later in middle childhood, children have a more firmly established conscience and morality that have been honed through the exercise of perspective taking (Miller et al., 1996). This refined conscience, and sense of justice and fairness, provides a more durable and resilient basis for social acceptance and respect for diversity than what existed in early childhood.

Implications of Research for Promoting SARD

Adult–child relationships represent an especially important contextual factor to be considered in children's development of SARD. If we extended the results of studies on prosocial development and applied them to SARD, we would propose a discernible developmental progression from infancy to adolescence. In infancy, representations of secure attachment as an internalized state are associated with later prosocial attitudes and behaviors. As children mature, executive functions are strengthened, become more sophisticated, and exert greater control over behavior. As part of this maturing of executive function, the capacity for perspective taking arises and serves to support more altruistic behaviors, including social acceptance and respect for diversity. However, as alluded to in the prior section, development does not occur linearly or within a vacuum. Children's notions of social acceptance and respect for diversity are influenced by experiences within close relationships.

Figure 12.2 is a model of our current understanding of the potential contributions of teachers and parents to the development of SARD in children. Family members, as the first teachers, instill in children the basic notions about social relationships and attitudes about other social groups. They often accomplish this through indirect means, such as fairytales, myths, and other stories (Parke & Buriel, 2006). Even when familial boundaries are extended to other social institutions that provide cultural and spiritual supports, children are more likely to be exposed to people and beliefs that replicate those of their family than to diverse peoples and beliefs that challenge their views of what is typical and normal. The early childhood program may offer many children their first encounter with a diverse world. In this way, early educational settings, especially

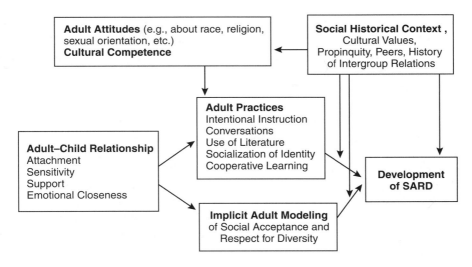

FIGURE 12.2. Parent and teacher influences on the development of social acceptance and respect for diversity.

in nonprivate schools, often serve as an initial exposure to the public forum, a proving ground wherein convictions about the universality of family beliefs, practices, routines, and rituals meet their first challenge (Friendly, 2007).

High levels of sensitivity, relaxed firmness, and mutual negotiation of conflict characterize high-quality adult–child relationships and may facilitate reciprocity within the teacher–child dyad. Adults who reason, demonstrate warmth, provide guidance, reinforce behavior with positive incentives, model prosocial behavior, and give the child a chance to perform prosocial behaviors are more likely to engender altruism in children (Chase-Lansdale, Wakschlag, & Brooks-Gunn, 1995; Kochanska & Aksan, 2004; Maccoby, 1992; Steelman et al., 2002). Moreover, when parents are emotionally supportive and responsive, children are more likely to adopt patterns of behavior that reflect a concern for others' well-being and to engage in helping behaviors toward others, even when no direct enforcement is evident (Chase-Lansdale et al., 1995; Eisenberg et al., 2006). As a result, strong attachments, social support, emotional closeness, and adult sensitivity and responsiveness to children's needs are linked to children's self-control and the ability to resolve conflicts without aggression (Hamburg & Hamburg, 2004).

To the extent that teachers are esteemed and liked by children, their behaviors and attitudes are more likely to be emulated by their students. In this way, adult practices and modeling shape and encourage SARD. Teachers' indirect modeling of prosocial behavior and attitudes, and their direct efforts to foster SARD are likely to be moderated by historical context, children's previous experiences with diverse populations, and values to which children have been exposed regarding identity, race and religion, and sexual orientation. To the extent that teachers project open-minded attitudes, judge experiences with diverse populations as positive, and hold values that favor acceptance of difference, the classroom environment in which children are taught can be a positive spawning ground for SARD. In this way, educators in early childhood settings play a special role in children's lives and can help to develop and strengthen children's SARD.

Teachers have the opportunity to impart prosocial skills that aid children in conflict management through conversations, modeling, and specialized curricula. In classroom play, teachers who focus children's judgments of one another based on internal dispositions and motives rather than external attributes support prosocial behaviors (Derman-Sparks, 1992; Miller & Pedro, 2006). Also, in classrooms where teachers encourage empathy, there tends to be increased helpfulness, cooperativeness, concern for others, and decreased aggression among children (Hamburg & Hamburg, 2004). On the other hand, in classrooms where teachers endorse biased beliefs, a child is more sensitive to perceptions of bias and likely to feel less valued as a member of the classroom, particularly if the child is a member of a stigmatized group (Brown & Bigler, 2005; Miller & Pedro, 2006). Teachers, similar to parents, must display sensitivity and respond in ways indicating that all children (regardless of color, heritage, socioeconomic status, or physical ability) have equal access to resources and equal responsibility to their peers, if they expect children in the classroom to emulate social acceptance and respect for diversity (Miller & Pedro, 2006).

SARD in the Early Childhood Classroom

There are a number of developmental dimensions identified in Figure 12.1 that might be targeted in efforts to facilitate development of SARD. Development of social identities and social awareness is an important starting point for nurturing SARD. Fostering positive ethnic and gender identity, noting differences in others, and developing the ability to take the perspective of others are not sufficient *in se* for the development of SARD. To attain high levels of SARD, teachers and adults need to focus on the meaning that students attached to social differences and to nurture children's perspective taking and view of what they have in common with those who are different. Next, promoting social attitudes and behaviors, such as altruism and nonaggressive conflict management, along with promoting notions of fairness, equity, and justice, are essential to create positive narratives that support SARD. Finally, the cultural competence inherent in SARD is an outcome of children's positive experiences with diversity and their abilities to negotiate differences. All of these things may be easier said than done.

Creating a social environment that leads to greater understanding and appreciation of diversity requires teachers themselves be open to the benefits and advantages inherent in diversity. To do this teachers need to cultivate an understanding of the life experiences of the families of children in their classrooms and the communities to which the families belong. In classrooms teachers can work to strengthen children's personal identities (a primary step toward SARD). Young children who feel positive about themselves are more likely to develop ease in engaging those who are different (Dowling, 2000; Miller & Pedro, 2006). Children's acceptance or rejection of comments during play can be used as a springboard for discussion. For example, if a child is being teased about his or her weight, teachers may bring in posters of famous people of different sizes and engage children in conversations about the importance of body size versus personality characteristics, such as kindness. In doing this, a primary goal for promoting SARD is to enhance social awareness while maintaining the personal well-being of all children.

In classrooms of teachers who encourage social acceptance and respect for diversity, children share ideas and form friendships across the boundaries of the ingroup and the outgroup. The literature on cooperative learning and respectful classrooms suggests that SARD may be enhanced by reducing perceived dissimilarity or anxiety about differences through mixed-group settings. Play groups that comprise boys and girls, children from different ethnic and cultural backgrounds, and children with different physical abilities are more favorable settings and are likely to foster SARD. It has been shown that ingroup favoritism and outgroup prejudice are correlated with homogenous settings, but not as strongly in heterogeneous settings (Aboud, 2003). Well-designed programs strengthen the development of SARD by increasing "cognitive dissonance" (contradictions) of stigmatizing beliefs or stereotypes (e.g., by getting children to behave in nonstigmatizing ways). For example, dramatic play areas may help to counter stereotypes by providing examples of men and women doing different jobs. Adults can join in play groups and act out roles that help to counter stereotypes, including a man caring for a baby or a woman doing construction work. In addition, reading texts that focus on familiar social and ethical issues to children may provide opportunities for increasing the overlap between how ingroups and outgroups are perceived.

Educators and researchers have developed typologies of classrooms that indicate the level at which diversity is celebrated through curriculum and practice. Some early childhood programs are classified as having a European American, culture-centered or difference-denial approach to education. In these programs, children are taught that people are all the same, and neither curriculum nor teacher practices acknowledge the cultural heritage of children, experiences of racism, or the impact of dominant culture on developmental outcomes for children (Derman-Sparks, 1992). Multicultural education classrooms represent the first step toward recognition of the diverse cultural contexts in which children are raised. A major goal of multicultural education is to reform schools, so that students of diverse racial, ethnic, gender, and social groups experience educational equality. Multicultural programs often fall short of their goals by representing a tourist approach to education. Activities about culture are presented as manageable, discrete educational moments; however, the lessons are often disconnected from the overall cultural context from which they are derived. As a result, activities may misrepresent, trivialize, and stereotype the diversity that exists within individuals of the culture being explored (Derman-Sparks, 1992). For example, cutting out pictures of shamrocks and leprechauns on St. Patrick's Day does not teach children about the culture of Irish people or why the holiday came into existence. Developmentally appropriate concepts related to culture should be a part of the everyday environment in early childhood classrooms, particularly when they represent the culture of a child in the classroom or a celebrated experience of that community (Derman-Sparks, 1992). Finally, multicultural programs often do not integrate content about diversity across other subject areas (Derman-Sparks, 1992). One center activity dedicated to coloring shamrocks green is not enough to promote reflective thinking in children. When children experience adjunctive content about cultural diversity that is not weaved into the content of the entire programmatic agenda, cognitive processes may not be reliably changed, leading children to develop a superficial understanding of and respect for diverse groups.

In the literature, multicultural curricula are often distinguished from the antibias approach. Antibias programs are also committed to the educational equality of diverse children, but they tend to be more comprehensive in nature by addressing cultural diversity, gender differences, and differences in physical ability (Derman-Sparks & the ABC Task Force, 1989). An antibias curriculum may be adapted to take into account the cultural makeup of the classroom and individual variations in children's ability. Adults in the antibias classroom are committed to thoughtful and responsive answers to children's questions about difference. Teachers must also commit themselves to a lifelong reflection process about the historical impact of discrimination in society, about how their own biases are acted out, about how to adapt their teaching style effectively for children, and about how to engage comfortably in cultural conflict resolution (Derman-Sparks, 1993; McKown, 2005). Antibias education openly raises issues of privilege, injustice, and oppression with young children (Derman-Sparks & ABC Task Force, 1989; McKown, 2005). Antibias ideas permeate curriculum and the classroom environment (toys, books, language, art materials, and center options), events, stories, and interactions grounded in a developmental approach (Derman-Sparks, 1993). Antibias education rests on the premise that adults will commit to individual exploration about discrimination and bias, and to teach children openly to explore differences, challenge negative stereotypes, and develop the confidence to become activists in the face of discrimination (Derman-Sparks, 1993).

Summary

The research on children's progression of moral and prosocial development provides a rich base of knowledge on which to draw inferences about SARD. This body of work has pointed to the important role of parents and teachers, secure attachments, children's evolving ability to detect differences, the critical role of emotional arousal and response, the shift of the basis of prosocial motivation from egoistic behaviors, and the development of a range of social-cognitive competencies, such as empathy, social comparisons, conscience, and altruism. Scholarly discourse on the impact of parent and teacher practices on children's social development flourishes, but SARD is rarely treated as a developmental outcome of interest. Whereas respect for diversity and social acceptance represents a focus on positive desirable outcomes, much of the research and scholarly discourse has concentrated on the negative and obverse side of the social acceptance–diversity coin. This side includes xenophobia, chauvinism, intolerance, bigotry, bias, prejudice, discrimination, and injustice. Much more scholarly attention has been paid to the origins and effects of intolerance; relatively little attention has been paid to the conditions that give rise to SARD.

As a body, the research on the ways that parents and teachers influence the social development of preschool children can be described as rigorous, and its theories as robust. However, the discourse takes place largely in developmental science and is usually presented under the rubric of adult socialization of child outcomes (e.g., attachment, social learning, and moral development (Kohlberg, 1984) and moral socialization theories (Hoffman, 1979). A major limitation within this literature is that the conclusions are too often based on observations of European American families from advantaged backgrounds. Possibly for this reason, discussion of how parents and teachers affect the promotion of social acceptance and respect for diversity rarely surfaces in scholarly discourse. In contrast, a group of researchers is exploring issues of social identity that have implications for SARD (e.g., see Coard, Foy-Watson, Zimmer, & Wallace, 2007; Hughes et al., 2006). This developing work focuses on cross-racial friendships, parental racial socialization of children of color, children's beliefs about stereotypes, and coping with racial discrimination. Even with the current limitations in SARD research, the theoretical principles and empirical findings of the socialization research provide a robust foundation for speculating how social acceptance and respect for diversity develop.

The current emphasis in the United States on school readiness offers an opportunity to bring attention to SARD by conceptualizing and positioning it as a core component of social competence. Given the national interest in school readiness, a case could be made about the need to prepare children for school experiences with ethnically, religiously, and economically diverse students. Current concerns about social competence as a critical preschool outcome, surprisingly, does not include respect for diversity and social acceptance. Notions of social competence could be expanded to incorporate respect for diversity and social acceptance in the discourse about the social skills needed for success in school. In the next section we highlight strategies for promoting SARD in early childhood educational settings through classroom management, the physical environment, and modeling of acceptable behaviors.

Strategies for Promoting SARD in the Classroom

Aiding children in the development of social acceptance and respect for diversity should be a primary goal of any classroom that espouses developmentally appropriate practices. Promotion of SARD involves development of social categories and schemas, especially schemas of personal identity, and the ability to make discriminations, such as ingroup–outgroup distinctions. Moreover, it is dependent on the development of social awareness and evolving capacities for perspective taking, empathy, and altruism, in the sense of justice. Table 12.1 recapitulates and summarizes many of the strategies teachers can use to foster SARD. The likelihood of successful efforts to foster SARD increases with the overall quality of the classroom climate and of adult–child interactions. Accordingly, strategies that generally improve the overall quality of the program can also contribute to the development of SARD.

For examples, teachers need a well-rounded knowledge of the major domains of development (i.e., physical, cognitive, language, social, and emotional) and an understanding of the appropriate milestones for the age groups. Teachers must also actively acknowledge that children's overall development is embedded within myriad sociocultural contexts (Bronfenbrenner & Morris, 1998). Even in a racially homogenous classroom, children may differ based on cultural, religious, and economic factors. The ecology of the family and features of community contexts may be influential in the expression of social and emotional developmental differences for children in the classroom setting. A child's angry outbursts during tasks that require sharing of limited resources (i.e., crayons during a writing activity) may be linked to his or her experiences in an overcrowded household or in witnessing violence in the community. Research has consistently shown that protective factors for prosocial development include secure, warm adult attachments; economic stability; and safe neighborhood environments (Chase-Lansdale et al., 1995). Given that SARD falls under the rubric of prosocial development, it is expected that environments lacking stability or granting minimal access to infrastructure that support family life, or environments that are unsafe, put children at risk for social and emotional difficulties. Thus, finding out about a child's family history, behavior at home,

TABLE 12.1. List of Teacher Interventions to Promote SARD

Promote altruism, empathy, tolerance, fairness, and prosocial behavior.

- Develop the expectation that children will be accountable for their own behaviors, and treat other with kindness and respect.
- Employ strategies in teaching children that promote altruism:
  - Use reason.
  - Demonstrate warmth.
  - Provide guidance.
  - Reinforce behavior with positive incentives.
  - Give children opportunities to engage in prosocial behaviors such as helpfulness, cooperativeness, concern for others.
- Organize class so that all children have equal access to resources.
- Encourage, model, and practice empathic responding to the discomfort, injury, and hurt of others.
- Model open-minded attitudes, judging experiences with diverse populations as positive, and project values that favor acceptance of difference.
- Lead discussions that help children interpret differences in the context of similarities.
- Focus children's judgments of one another on internal dispositions and motives rather than external attributes.
- Increase dissonance of stigmatizing beliefs or stereotypes—for example, by getting children to behave in nonstigmatizing ways by enacting dramatic play that counters stereotypes by providing examples of men and women doing different jobs (a man caring for a baby or a woman as a construction worker).
- Respond thoughtfully and with sincerity to children's questions about difference.
- Openly raise issues of injustice. Help children to gain a compassionate understanding of how different families live by talking about poverty, hunger, wants versus needs, and overconsumption.

Prevent or correct stigma, social rejection, and aggression.

- Act immediately to stop peer interactions that are disrespectful of physical or cultural differences. Use a firm tone, address the child's behavior and not the child's personality (i.e., "Those words you used made Leo sad. It hurt his feelings when you said that his skin looks dirty" rather than "Good boys and girls don't call one another names"), and openly talk about feelings.
- Directly confront all hints of racism, sexism, xenophobia, homophobia, religious intolerance, national chauvinism, and discrimination of all types.
- Use children's acceptance or rejection during play as a springboard for discussion.
- Help children alter the negative attributional biases that undergird aggression.
- Coach children to use nonaggressive strategies for problem solving and conflict resolution.

Create positive experiences of diversity.

- Encourage children to share ideas and form friendships across the boundaries of the ingroup and the outgroup. Use cooperative learning gender-mixed play groups to reduce perceived dissimilarity or anxiety about differences through mixed-group settings.
- Cultivate an understanding of the social contexts of children's families and communities through exchanges, visits, and reaching out to their families.

Introduce topics of diversity into the curriculum.

- Encourage children's active learning about the lives of others. Expand children's exposure to the practices and beliefs of diverse peoples, and especially those that challenge their views of what are typical and normal.
- Infuse dramatic play areas with culturally distinct items.
- Provide positive experiences with diversity to strengthen children's abilities to negotiate differences.
- Read texts that focus on social and ethical issues that are familiar to children and provide reveal overlap between how the ingroup and the outgroup are perceived.
- Talk about local and national events (i.e., political rallies, the history of voting rights, the effects of natural disasters on families).
- Use the life and legacy of Martin Luther King, Jr. as a starting point to talk about issues of race, discrimination, civil rights, and nonviolence throughout the school year.
- Use literature such as fairy tales, myths, and other stories to promote altruism, empathy, and tolerance indirectly.
- Use conversations, modeling, and specialized curricula to impart prosocial skills that aid children in conflict management.

and neighborhood environment may be critical for assessing behavior in the classroom. Teacher home visits, scheduled early in the academic year, may provide informative clues about how to handle a child's behavior in the classroom and awareness of and sensitivity to the family culture. Likewise, although the recommendations that follow are intended to help teachers promote SARD, practice must be tailored to the social and demographic characteristics, and past experiences of the students in a classroom. Teachers who are responsive to individual variation in children's development promote equity in learning and provide opportunities for all children to be successful.

Classroom Management

A classroom environment that supports SARD is well organized and visually appealing. Organized classrooms are staffed with sufficient teacher–child ratios, which vary depending on the age of the children, group size, the inclusion of children with special needs, the time of day, and other factors. However, teacher staffing patterns should allow adult supervision of children at all times. Teachers should be available to support conflict management among peers and to guide conversational learning opportunities within center activities. Importantly, in a tolerant and respectful classroom, diversity of students should be reflected in the diversity of staff. As children build ideas of self-image and self-esteem, adult figures who are leaders in the classroom or in the school setting help children to create positive ideas about the opportunity and potential to be successful.

Organized classrooms also allow for choice in center activities, yet across centers, teachers may strategically distribute children to promote peer interactions that support SARD. Knowing and recording the social and emotional individual differences of the children in one's classroom can advance the development SARD. For example, a child who is more verbally advanced and expresses notions of equity and fairness may be paired with a child who is less advanced during certain times of the day, or in an activity that requires sharing of limited resources and cooperation (Aboud & Fenwick, 1999; Spears-Brown & Bigler, 2005).

Finally, teachers with well-organized classrooms implement routines, particularly during transitions, that minimize opportunities for conflict. For example, having preschool children quietly form a straight line may not be realistic or developmentally appropriate. A more creative way of having children move orderly as a group from one location to another would be to have them hop like bunnies, move like a snake, or float like balloons. Helping children prepare for naptime is another important transition. Having children do quiet activities, such as reading, prior to a nap; speaking in a soft voice and dimming the lights; playing gentle music; or having children "wiggle their sillies out" may help them to relax. Children feel more secure when they can anticipate what will happen next. Inconsistency of routines may create an environment of frustration for teachers and misbehavior by children (Chesebrough, King, Gullotta, & Bloom, 2004).

Physical Environment and Materials

Social acceptance and respect for diversity may also be enhanced by physical materials in the classroom. Environmental print on classroom walls should reflect children of various ethnic backgrounds, wearing the traditional attire of their culture. Teachers may also ask children to bring in pictures of themselves and their families at special family or cultural events (family reunions, christenings, quince celebrations, New Year's events, etc.) and place them in frames around the classroom. Environmental print helps to expose children to visual differences, yet, guided by teachers, must give rise to conversations about being respectful of differences. Alongside the family pictures, teachers can have children write about the celebration and any unique features (e.g., family members' attire, the food they ate, or the person in the picture) and what these mean to family members.

Classrooms that support SARD have a variety of supplies that reflect attention to issues of diversity. Culturally tolerant and respectful classrooms may incorporate music from genres that reflect the cultural heritage of children in the classroom. Teachers may also introduce new genres of music, and talk about the history and cultural significance for the country in which the song originated. Another popular classroom supply is skin-colored crayons, clay, and construction paper. Again, the use of these materials should be guided by a teacher who is well read and can deal with and teach social acceptance and respect for diversity. In a guided activity using skin-toned crayons, teachers may ask children to talk about differences in colors that represent each child's own skin tone, while having them trace their hands. Within this activity, teachers should also lead a discussion about children's similarities in spite of their differences—how children are responsible members of the same classroom, how each child is accountable for his or her own behaviors, and how each child is a kind and respectful person (Chesebrough et al., 2004). Dramatic play areas can also be infused with culturally distinct items. Culturally sensitive guidance is again required when using props that, at first glance, might be construed as racially insensitive. A popular dramatic play scenario includes items from a Chinese restaurant—including chopsticks, carryout boxes, lanterns, and menus with Chinese text. In a classroom that promotes social acceptance and respect for diversity, an integration of learning and cultural sensitivity is required. For instance, along the same lines as this theme, teachers could invite a parent who speaks Chinese and knows Chinese customs as a special guest to talk about his or her heritage. Simple words, such as *please* or *thank you* in Chinese, can be taught, so that children can incorporate knowledge about a new language into their play. Finally, books in different languages and that represent children from different cultures can be part of a rotating book collection in the classroom. Young children who are immigrants, and who speak a primary language other than English, appreciate seeing familiar words and pictures. Books that have themes representative of unique cultural traditions help to validate racial-minority children as integral members of the classroom. Children, with the aid of teachers, can also use books as a segue to making new friendships.

Modeling Acceptable Behavior

SARD in a preschool classroom is most readily evident in the way children are taught to behave toward one another. Through interactions with adults and with other children, the teacher is one of the child's primary models of respectful behavior. Children are keen observers of the teacher's interactions and often imitate the behaviors he or she has observed through play. Adults provide models of how to greet others, how to share enthusiastically in others' accomplishments, how to empathize with others' disappointments, and how to resolve conflicts. Therefore, it is important to create an environment of warmth, with firm limits on behaviors that are acceptable in the classroom, in the hallways, and on the playground. An effective way of instituting classroom rules that guide respectful interactions is to have children nominate rules that they think are important. Children are more likely to abide by classroom rules when they feel empowered. Once rules are established, teachers must be consistent in rule enforcement, with clear consequences for misbehavior.

As children try to establish their own identities, conflict is an inevitable part of any early childhood classroom. Specifically, peer interactions that are disrespectful of physical or cultural differences must be stopped immediately. Teachers must be ready to use a firm tone, address the child's behavior and not the child's personality (i.e., "Those words you used made Leo sad. It hurt his feelings when you said that his skin looks dirty" rather than "Good boys and girls don't call one another names"), and openly talk about feelings, using developmentally appropriate language. Helping children manage conflict, anger, and frustration is a challenge, particularly in preschool classrooms. However, a teacher seeking to effectively promote SARD is observant, distinguishing between frustration and intentional aggression, and helping children recognize the motivation for their behavior (Chesebrough et al., 2004). Creating opportunities for leadership and community building may help to create a sense of connectedness among children in a classroom and reduce negative interactions. For example, giving children chores (i.e., serving snack to others, picking the book for large-group time, helping with laundry, or assisting in cleanup activities) that serve to keep the classroom orderly may help to infuse a sense of responsibility for self and others.

Finally, teachers who espouse virtues of social acceptance and respect for diversity should openly raise issues of injustice with young children (Derman-Sparks & the ABC Task Force, 1989). Talking about poverty, hunger, wants versus needs, and overconsumption can help children to gain a compassionate understanding of how different families live. The life and legacy of Martin Luther King, Jr. can also be a starting point in talking about issues of race, discrimination, civil rights, and nonviolence throughout the school year, even in early childhood classrooms. Talking about local and national events (i.e., political rallies, the history of voting rights, the effects of natural disasters on families) can also enlighten children about events in the world around them. Adults in a tolerant and respectful classroom must be committed to thoughtful and responsive answers to children's questions about differences, and encourage children's active learning about the lives of others.

Teachers themselves must also commit to a lifelong reflection process about the historical impact of discrimination in society, how their own biases are acted out in the classroom, how effectively to adapt their teaching style for children, and how to engage in culturally responsive teaching and conflict resolution (Derman-Sparks, 1993). Teachers may also benefit from familiarizing themselves with literature and curricula that address issues of social acceptance and respect for diversity. Many websites and books contain examples of classroom activities that may be adapted for different ages and grade levels. Finally, teachers within a school can encourage the adoption of social acceptance and diversity schoolwide through book clubs, strategy sessions, and teacher–parent outreach initiatives.

References

Aboud, F. (2003). The formation of in-group favoritism and out-group prejudice in young children: Are they distinct attitudes? *Developmental Psychology, 39*(1), 48–60.

Aboud, F., & Fenwick, V. (1999). Exploring and evaluating school-based interventions to reduce prejudice. *Journal of Social Issues, 55*(4), 767–785.

Aboud, F., & Levy, S. R. (2000). Interventions to reduce prejudice and discrimination in children and adolescents. In S. Oskamp (Ed.), *Reducing prejudice and discrimination* (pp. 269–293). Hillsdale, NJ: Erlbaum.

Bronfenbrenner, U., & Morris, P. A. (1998). The ecology of developmental processes. In W. Damon & R. M. Lerner (Eds.), *Handbook of child psychology: Vol. 1: Theoretical models of human development* (5th ed., pp. 993–1028). New York: Wiley.

Brown, C., & Bigler, R. (2005). Children's perceptions of discrimination: A developmental model. *Child Development, 76*(3), 533–553.

Bugental, J., & Grusec, D. (2006). Socialization processes. In N. Eisenberg & W. Damon (Eds.), *Handbook of child psychology: Vol. 3. Social, emotional, and personality development* (6th ed., pp. 646–718). New York: Wiley.

Cameron, L., Rutland, A., & Brown, R. (2007). Promoting children's positive inter-group attitudes towards stigmatized groups: Extended contact and multiple classification skills training. *International Journal of Behavioral Development, 31*(5), 454–466.

Case, R., & Okamoto, Y. (1996). The role of Central Conceptual Structures in the development of Children's Thought. *Monographs of the Society for Research in Child Development, 61*(1–2, Serial No. 265).

Charlesworth, W. (1991). The development of the sense of justice. *American Behavioral Scientist, 34*, 350–370.

Chase-Lansdale, P., Wakschlag, L., & Brooks-Gunn, J. (1995). A psychological perspective on the development of caring in children and youth: The role of the family. *Journal of Adolescence, 18*(5), 515–556.

Chesebrough, E., King, P., Gullotta, T., & Bloom, M. (2004). *A blueprint for the promotion of prosocial behavior in early childhood.* New York: Springer.

Coard, S., Foy-Watson, S., Zimmer, C., & Wallace, A. (2007). Considering culturally relevant parenting practices in intervention development and adaptation: A randomized control trial of the Black Parenting Strengths and Strategies (BPSS) Program. *Counseling Psychologist, 35*, 797–820.

Derman-Sparks, L. (1992). Reaching potentials through antibias, multicultural curriculum. In S. Bredekamp & T. J. Rosengrant (Eds.), *Reaching potentials* (Vol. 1, pp. 114–128). Washington, DC: National Association for the Education of Young Children.

Derman-Sparks, L. (1993). Empowering children to create a caring culture in a world of differences. *Childhood Education, 70*(2), 66–72.

Derman-Sparks, L., & the ABC Task Force. (1989). *Anti-bias curriculum: Tools for empowering young children.* Washington, DC: National Association for the Education of Young Children.

Dowling, M. (2000). *Young children's personal, social, and emotional development.* Thousand Oaks, CA: Sage.

Eisenberg, N., Fabes, R., & Spinrad, T. (2006). *Pro-social development.* In N. Eisenberg & W. Damon (Eds.), *Handbook of child psychology: Vol. 3. Social, emotional, and personality development* (6th ed., pp. 646–718). New York: Wiley.

Friendly, M. (2007). How ECEC programmes contribute to social inclusion in diverse societies. *Early Childhood Matters, 108*, 11–14.

Hamburg, D. A., & Hamburg, B. A. (2004). Development of pro-social behavior. In *Learn-*

ing to live together: Preventing hatred and violence in child and adolescent development (pp. 64–82). Oxford, UK: Oxford University Press.

Hoffman, M. (1979). Development of moral thought, feeling, and behavior. *American Psychologist, 34*(10), 958–966.

Hughes, D., Rodriguez, J., Smith, E., Johnson, D., Stevenson, H., & Spicer, P. (2006). Parents' ethnic–racial socialization practices: A review of research and directions for future study. *Developmental Psychology, 42*(5), 747–770.

Katz, P. A. (2003). Racists or tolerant multiculturalists? How do they begin? *American Psychologist, 58*, 897–909.

Kochanska, G., & Aksan, N. (2004). Conscience in childhood: Past, present, and future. *Merrill–Palmer Quarterly, 50*, 299–310.

Kochanska, G., & Thompson, R. (1997). The emergence and development of conscience in toddlerhood and early childhood. In J. Grusec & L. Kucynski (Eds.), *Parenting and children's internalization of values: A handbook of contemporary theory attachment* (pp. 53–75). New York: Wiley.

Kohlberg, L. (1984). *The psychology of moral development.* New York: Harper & Row.

Maccoby, E. E. (1992). The role of parents in the socialization of children: An historical overview. *Developmental Psychology, 28*, 1006–1017.

McKown, C. (2005). Applying ecological theory to advance the science and practice of school-based prejudice reduction interventions. *Educational Psychologist, 40*(3), 177–189.

Miller, P. A., Eisenberg, N., Fabes, R. A., & Shell, R. (1996). Relations of moral reasoning and vicarious emotion to young children's pro-social behavior toward peers and adults. *Developmental Psychology, 32*, 210–219.

Miller, R., & Pedro, K. (2006). Caring respectful classroom environments. *Early Childhood Education Journal, 33*(5), 293–299.

National Center for Education Statistics. (2007). *The condition of education 2007* (NCES 2007-064). Washington, DC: U.S. Government Printing Office.

Parke, R. D., & Buriel, R. (2006). Socialization in the family: Ethnic and ecological perspectives. In W. Damon & R. M. Lerner (Eds.) & N. Eisenberg (Vol. Ed.), *The handbook of child psychology* (Vol. 3, pp. 429–504). New York: Wiley.

Perkins, D. M., & Mebert, C. J. (2005). Efficacy of multicultural education for preschool children: A domain specific approach. *Journal of Cross-Cultural Psychology, 36*(4), 497–512.

Ramsey, P. G., & Myers, L. C. (1990). Salience of race in young children's cognitive, affective, and behavioral responses to social environments. *Journal of Applied Developmental Psychology, 11*(1), 49–67.

Spears-Brown, C., & Bigler, R. (2005). Children's perceptions of discrimination: A developmental model. *Child Development, 76*(3), 533–553.

Steelman, L., Assel, M., Swank, P. R., Smith, K. E., & Landry, S. H. (2002). Early maternal warm responsiveness as a predictor of child social skills: Direct and indirect paths of influence over time. *Journal of Applied Developmental Psychology, 23*(2), 135–156.

U.S. Bureau of the Census. (2005). *Current Population Reports, P23–209, 65+ in the United States.* Washington, DC: U.S. Government Printing Office.

Zahn-Waxler, C., Radke-Yarrow, M., Wagner, E., & Chapman, M. (1992). Development of concern for others. *Developmental Psychology, 28*, 126–136.

PART IV

LANGUAGE AND LITERACY

Language and literacy are at the heart of children's learning. From the earliest days of their lives through the most advanced education, children gain knowledge of their world and open doors into learning through their language and literacy skills. In this section the authors examine in depth how children come to develop language and literacy, beginning with an examination of their social environments, and moving to their educational settings.

Gordon Wells (Chapter 13) provides detailed insights into the ways all children develop into competent members of their community, beginning in infancy, as children and parents engage in interactions that develop the foundation for language. Children's entry into literacy also begins in the home as they are exposed to environmental print and have their parents read to them. Wells discusses the importance of parent talk with children and how this dialogue contributes to children's development of not only language but also an understanding of how written language works. He addresses ways that schools can encourage reading motivation, and how children can gain from interactions with peers in joint writing activities. He provides detailed descriptions of ways one can create classrooms in which reading, writing, and talking are valued. He includes a description of the role of the teacher as researcher, noting the value of this role for obtaining information about children and especially the value of modeling the processes of inquiry for children.

In Chapter 14, Barbara Hanna Wasik and Beth Anne Newman provide a developmental framework for the development of language and literacy, noting the roots for literacy that occur during the child's earliest years through conversations with parents. They then describe the widely recognized early literacy skills associated with preschool and those associated with kindergarten through third grade (K–3) education. Noting that these early literacy skills are frequently discussed as two separate sets of skills, these authors provide a model for viewing early literacy skills across the prekindergarten through third grade (P–3) span, bringing into consideration those skills identified nationally. They then present a set of strategies that teachers across the P–3 range can use effectively to encourage language and literacy development.

In Chapter 15, David K. Dickinson, Catherine Darrow, Sara M. Ngo, and Linda A. D'Souza provide an in-depth analysis of teacher–child conversations. First, they address research from a large set of studies indicating that through intentional teacher interactions, positive changes can be brought about in children's syntactic development, vocabulary, narrative abilities, and story understanding. Then, drawing on recent professional development research for teachers that focuses on language and literacy, they describe two different approaches. In the first approach, teachers were provided explicit information on what to do as they read to children, including a set of book reading strategies to be implemented with the same book on different occasions. In the second approach, teachers were told how they were doing as they interacted with children. Using data from these studies, the authors make recommendations for conducting teachers' professional development aimed at fostering children's language and literacy.

Steve Amendum and Jill Fitzgerald (Chapter 16) provide research-based insights on the reading development of young English language learners, and encourage teachers to help these young children development their full English reading potential. They begin by describing the changing demographics of our country, with increasing numbers of children raised in homes where English is not the first language. Next, they describe results from a research study that illustrates one way of facilitating cognitive development in reading, and they draw conclusions from this research for classroom reading instruction. From this research, they identify the following critical features of English reading instruction practices: having teachers understand the English language learners' developmental reading trajectories; identifying the English language learners' English developmental reading level on that trajectory; and knowing the critical reading processes for that level, then intensely teaching those features.

Before children arrive at school, their parents have been the most significant contributors to their language and literacy development. Oscar A. Barbarin and Nikki Aikens (Chapter 17), provide educators with detailed evidence on the relation between specific parental practices and children's language and literacy outcomes. They describe two kinds of parental practices. First are child-focused strategies, such as reading to children, conversations, didactic instruction, and enrichment. Second are more implicit, environment-focused strategies that include creating advantageous home conditions for children's development. Next, they place parental practices within a social context, helping the reader understand why certain practices are more prevalent or acceptable than others. They conclude with recommendations for how parents can support their children's literacy, language, and academic development, including ways to integrate parental practices into daily routines and facilitate parental involvement in children's education.

In summary, these chapters take us from an understanding of the early roots of language and literacy to ways of facilitating children's mastery of these skills, at home and in the classroom. These authors help us appreciate the complexity of making changes both in the classroom and within homes, while also providing compelling evidence for why we need to continue to direct our resources to these two settings, and the relationships within these settings that provide the support that children need to become competent readers.

CHAPTER 13

The Social Context
of Language and Literacy Development

Gordon Wells

As educators, we have long paid attention to the social context in which children learn and develop. But to many, the phrase "social context" may suggest no more than the societal setting in which events occur—in this case, the various surroundings at home, at school, and in the community in which children learn to talk, read, and write. In recent years, however, a much more radical understanding of the importance of the social context of development has emerged as the result of a convergence of theoretical and empirical research in a variety of disciplines. According to this new understanding of social context, human infants are not only influenced by the social context in which they develop, but also their very development as humans is dependent on opportunities to participate with others, notably parents, family members, peers, and teachers, in the activities that constitute the culture in which they are growing up. Thus, children's development is as much a social as an individual achievement. Therefore, in this chapter I attempt to explain current thinking about the relationship between individual development, and societal and interpersonal practices, then explore the implications of this new understanding for how best to assist children in their learning of language and literacy.

This revolution in thinking about human development has many and varied roots, ranging from mounting dissatisfaction with the limited explanatory power of behaviorists' stimulus–response association theory of learning to neuropsychologists' rapid advances in understanding the functioning of the human brain, and from Piaget's work on cognitive development to anthropological studies of technologically less developed cultures. The question at the heart of all these very different lines of research is: How do all human infants, no matter where they are born, in a few short years become socially competent members of the particular community in which they grow up?

The Development of Shared Intentionality

Initially, the newborn human is totally dependent on others, particularly the mother, not only for nourishment and bodily welfare but also for access to the material environment. Babies have very limited ability to change their position to interact with the world around them, and it is their caregivers who control what they can see, hear, and touch when they are not feeding or sleeping. In the earliest stage, infants look at what is in view and act on objects within range by trying to grasp and put them in their mouths. Piaget described this as the beginning of the *sensorimotor stage of cognitive development*. But some of the time is spent in face-to-face contact with the mother or other caregiver and, in this context, the infant begins to engage in deliberate mutual gazing and some behavioral imitation, such as tongue protrusion. Trevarthen (1979) refers to this form of joint attention to each other as the establishment of "primary intersubjectivity," in which both caregiver and infant know that they are attending to each other. By about the eighth month, there develops the stage of "secondary intersubjectivity," when, by following the other's direction of gaze or pointing, mother and infant are able to achieve joint attention to some person or object that is of mutual interest.

At this stage, the mother frequently signals her awareness of the infant's interest by bringing the object within the infant's reach and/or naming the object and making some comment about it. By doing so, the mother treats the object of attention as having meaning, as well as material form. For example, an infant shows an interest in the spoon that is used to feed her, and her mother hands her the "tool" and at the same time names it. Then, in due course, the infant takes over the use of the word *spoon* to call attention to, or ask for, the spoon, and this signing coordinates the mother's and the infant's actions with respect to the spoon and the uses to which it may be put.

Equally important in such events is the affective dimension of the joint activity (Immordino-Yang & Damasio, 2007). As has been argued by a variety of scholars, the motivation for the early emergence of joint attention and shared intentional actions grows out of the infant's emotional bond with his or her caregiver and, subsequently, with close family members and friends. It is the satisfaction the infant experiences in these events (as does the adult) that sustains joint engagement in repeated episodes and creates the intersubjectivity that is both the prerequisite for, and the intended outcome of, their object-oriented communicative interaction (Bruner, 1983). The development of intersubjectivity of attention and action is, in fact, the earliest form of dialogue. It demands the active and collaborative participation of both infant and caregiver, as each attempts to achieve what Rommetveit calls "attunement to the attunement of the other" (1992, p. 20).

Learning Language through Using Language

I suspect that nobody remembers how he or she learned to talk, yet this is probably the most important learning that anyone ever undertakes. There are two likely reasons for its forgetability. The first is that personal (autobiographical) memory is to a large extent dependent on occasions of recall in conversation with others (Middleton & Edwards, 1990), which cannot happen until the child has already gained considerable mastery of language. But equally important is that neither child nor parent is conscious of the learning-and-teaching that occurs in everyday interaction, the context in which language learning occurs. Unlike much later learning, in which learning often precedes use, children learn language by using it to the best of their current ability to take part in ongoing activity.

Clearly, infants are innately predisposed to engage in meaningful interaction with others, as described earlier; they are also innately equipped to discover the organizational patterns of the language of whatever community into which they are born. This may be because they are born with a "language acquisition device," which contains knowledge of the underlying principles on which all languages are based (Chomsky, 1965), though this view is by no means universally accepted. However, there *is* strong evidence that the ease and speed with which infants learn is related to the extent to which parents and other family members engage in conversation with them, in which they build on infants' expressed interest and adjust their speech to the child's current level of comprehension (Wells, 1985). The following example illustrates some of these features of caregiver–child interaction.

Mark (age about 20 months) and his mother are looking out of the window onto the garden, where he can see some birds. In this and all extracts, the following transcription conventions apply: [ ] enclose interpretations and contextual information; < > enclose segments where the transcription is in doubt; * indicates an unintelligible word; CAPS indicate a segment spoken with emphasis; underline indicates segments spoken simultaneously; . (a period) marks an approximately 1-second pause; — indicates a false start or an interruption.

MARK: öa [Look-at-that] . jubs [birds], Mummy

MOTHER: Mm

MARK: Jubs

MOTHER: What are they doing?

MARK: Jubs bread [Birds eating bread]

MOTHER: Oh look! They're eating the berries, aren't they?

MARK: Yeh

MOTHER: That's their food . they have berries for dinner

MARK: Oh

This conversation is very typical of those in families in which beginning language learners have responsive interactants. There are several features worth noting. First, it is Mark who starts the conversation by drawing attention to something that interests him. His actual utterance starts with a sequence of sounds that, to an outsider, might have been totally unintelligible, but his mother makes a good guess (based on having heard this string of sounds before) and responds by showing interest, followed by an invitation to Mark to say more about the birds. Finally, she adds some further information about the birds and links it to eating dinner, which is something that she knows Mark will understand.

Unfortunately, not all adults have the time or the intuitive understanding to engage in such a contingently responsive manner. Some adults, for example, adopt a more instructional approach, although this is unlikely to have a positive effect and may even discourage the child from initiating interaction (Brown, 1973). There are, of course, other ways in which adults adjust their speech to ensure their child's full comprehension, but space does not permit a fuller discussion of them (see Cross, 1977).

Much information about the similarities and differences between children in the course of early language development emerged from the Bristol Study of Language at Home and at School (Wells, 1985, 1986). This study involved a representative sample of 128 children, whose naturally occurring conversations were randomly sampled by means of a "bugging" device worn by the child for a complete day, once every 3 months over 2½ years. One-half of the children were first recorded at 15 months, and the other half at 39 months. Half of the younger group subsequently was regularly observed at school until age 10.

One of the main findings, subsequently confirmed by others, was that, by and large, rapidly developing children experience both a greater amount of interaction with adults and a greater proportion of conversational episodes in which the adults respond to and extend the children's initiations. As a result, it is difficult to determine whether it is the quality of adult–child interaction or the sheer quantity that is facilitative of children's language development. The answer seems to be that whereas quantity is certainly beneficial, there are additional benefits for the child when adults also respond to his or her contributions in ways that extend—or help the child to extend—the topic in which he or she is interested (Barnes, Gutfreund, Satterly, & Wells, 1983).

Several important consequences can be attributed to this "contingently responsive" kind of interaction. First, the child who is treated as an interesting conversational partner, and whose contributions are taken up and extended by his or her interlocutor, is likely to gain greater confidence in his or her own ability to contribute to collaborative meaning making and, second, he or she is likely to become more knowledgeable about the topics that are discussed. A further important result is that the child is also likely to acquire a larger vocabulary, which, as Hart and Risley (1999) found, is a significant predictor of later academic success in school.

Of course, much of the talk in which very young children engage at home is concerned with routine matters, such as feeding, dressing, cleaning, and monitoring the child's activity to avoid accidents. However, what is routine to the adult may not be so to the child. As we discovered from our longitudinal recordings, from quite an early age, children are keen to "help" their parents in tasks around the home and, as they take part or merely observe, many things interest or puzzle them. Typically, around the age of 2½–3, this interest leads to a spate of questions about the *how* and *why* of what is going on, which, if answered, considerably extend the child's language and his or her understanding of the world. Here are two examples in which a mother supports and extends her child's interest.

In the first example, Elizabeth (age 4 years), who is helping with the housecleaning, watches with interest as her mother shovels wood ash from the fireplace into a bucket:

ELIZABETH: What are you doing that for?

MOTHER: I'm gathering it up and putting it outside so that Daddy can put it on the garden

ELIZABETH: Why does he have to put it on the garden?

MOTHER: To make the compost right

ELIZABETH: Does that make the garden grow?

MOTHER: Yes

ELIZABETH: Why does it?

MOTHER: You know how I tell you that you have to eat different things like eggs and cabbage and rice pudding to make you grow into a big girl?

ELIZABETH: Yes

MOTHER: Well, plants need different foods too . and ash is one of the things that's good for them

In the second example, James (age 3½ years) has been playing alone in the garden; as he reenters the house, his mother tries to get him to take off his muddy shoes. However, at that moment, he sees a bird outside, which interests him more than changing his shoes, and his mother takes the opportunity to share his interest.

MOTHER: There we are . there, one slipper on

JAMES: I can see a bird

MOTHER: A what, love?

JAMES: See a bird

MOTHER: (whispering) Is there? Outside?

JAMES: (pointing and whispering) Yes . see
(both continue to speak very softly)

MOTHER: Is he eating anything?

JAMES: No

MOTHER: Where? Oh yes, he's getting—do you know what he's doing?

JAMES: No

MOTHER: He's going to the—the paper sack to try to pick out some pieces—Oh, he's got some food there . and I expect he'll pick out some pieces of thread from the sack to go and make his nest under the roof, James . Wait a minute and I'll—

[James now wants to go out to see more closely but at that moment the bird flies away.]

JAMES: That bird's gone

In both these examples, the mother willingly responds to the child's interest and provides information to explain the significance of what the child is seeing or hearing, even when, as in the second example, this interrupts the mother's plan. Both cases show how the child's participation in the activity with the adult ensures that there is intersubjectivity of attention to what interests the child, and this enables the mother to provide relevant information. The talk that occurs on these occasions thus plays a particularly important role in helping children to attend to and understand the world around them in terms of the culture's ways of "making sense" of it. For, as Halliday (1993) emphasizes, "Language has the power to shape our consciousness; and it does so for each human child, by providing the theory that he or she uses to interpret and manipulate their environment" (p. 107).

Not all caregivers take up these opportunities, however, as Hasan (2002) found in her investigation of mother–child talk in Australia. Some mothers she studied typically behaved like those in the examples quoted earlier, whereas others rarely did so. In the following example of a missed opportunity, Karen is helping her mother to wash and dry the dishes they have been using and asks where to put the pot she has dried.

MOTHER: Put it up on the stove and leave it there

KAREN: Why?

MOTHER: 'cause

KAREN: That's where it goes?

MOTHER: Yeah

Clearly, this is a routine situation in which nothing of importance is at issue. Nevertheless, what is significant about this and similar examples quoted by Hasan (2002) is that the mother apparently does not perceive Karen's "Why?" as needing any explanation by way of response. Indeed, her unwillingness to consider alternative possibilities is reinforced by her uninformative retort, " 'cause." The result is that when such opportunities are habitually ignored, the message indirectly conveyed to children is that reasons and explanations are of little importance: The world is the way it is, and there is no point in asking questions.

Hasan (2002) explains the significance of these two patterns of maternal behavior in terms of the longer-term consequences of the contrasting "mental habits" that children develop as a result of their differing interactional experiences:

> Children have a massive experience of certain specific ways of saying and meaning, which are characterised by a particular semantic direction. Participation in this discourse shapes the children's consciousness, orients them to taking certain ways of being, doing and saying as legitimate and reasonable; in short, it defines the contours of reality and provides a map for navigating that reality. There is consistent and strong evidence that, at this early stage of three and a half to four years, the children belonging to these two groups have established different ways of learning, different ways of solving problems, different forms of consciousness, or mental disposition. ... Through this mediation, the mother's culture becomes the growing child's map of reality, thus ensuring its own continuance. (p. 120)

Hasan (2002) deliberately picked her sample of mother–child pairs to give equal representation to middle- and working-class families to test Bernstein's (1971, 1975) theory that the persistence of class-related differential educational achievement is not the result of differential intelligence but of class-related differences in the ways in which language is used in children's homes. Simply put, he argued that although all have access to the same language, adults of different social classes tend to adopt characteristically different ways of using language, different orientations to meaning, according to their involvement in material and symbolic production either as laborers, as directors, or as creators; these differences then carry over to the ways in which they talk with their children, thereby differentially preparing the children for the ways in which they will be expected to use language in the context of formal education.

Hasan's (2002) findings seemed to confirm Bernstein's (1971, 1975) theory. However, she was at pains to point out that these observed differences in mothers' ways of using language are not irrevocable. As children later participate in contexts beyond the home—in school or in out-of-school activities—they may encounter different ways of saying and meaning, from which they may appropriate different orientations to meaning. This is a very important qualification because, as I discuss below, one of the major hurdles that lower-class children face on entry to school is the low expectations that teachers frequently have about their language and intelligence, based on their unfamiliarity with the ways in which they are expected to use language in the classroom. If teachers then set lower expectations for such children's progress, they unintentionally contribute to the perpetuation of the class-based inequality of educational achievement (Heath, 1983; Michaels, 1981).

Whatever their home environment, however, all children successfully learn to talk before they begin their formal education. This is not to deny the very considerable differences between children's rates of language development, but unless they are physically or mentally impaired, by 5 years of age, all children are able to engage in spoken interaction with their caregivers about matters of shared importance. This is a very remarkable achievement, and one that would not be possible without the active contribution of their caregivers.

In the Bristol Study a comparison was made between all 128 children at the age of 3½ years. Whereas some children were already functioning in advance of the average 5-year-old, others were still at the average level of a 2-year-old. Nevertheless, by the age of 5, all had mastered the basic grammar of English and had a vocabulary of several thousand words. Furthermore, it is worth pointing out that when the children's scores on a scale of language development were correlated with their scores on a scale of family background, the relationship was found to be statistically nonsignificant. Whereas the extremely high and extremely low scorers on the language scale (12 in total) were found to be from the high and low ends, respectively, on the scale of family background, the distribution of the remaining 116 children showed no evidence of a relationship between the two variables (Wells, 1985).

Children's Entry into Literacy

Although provision for the learning of literacy is often seen as being the responsibility of the school, in highly literate societies, such as those of North America, Europe, China, and Japan, there can be few children who have not already discovered some of the functions of written texts in their preschool years. In fact, the vast majority are already in the stage of "emergent literacy" when they first go to school, for they have come to recognize important signs, such as McDonald's Golden Arches, or traffic signs, such as STOP; they probably also have looked at magazines or been involved in using *TV Guide* to choose their favorite programs (Hall, 1987; Teale & Sulzby, 1986). What is important about these first encounters with written language at home is that they typically occur in the context of social interaction and as part of some larger, purposeful activity.

For a substantial proportion of children, being read to is probably their preferred introduction to written language. Many parents include reading a story as part of the bedtime ritual; they may also choose to share a picture storybook or an illustrated magazine at other times, when the child is upset or bored. In fact, some adults start reading to their child in the first weeks after birth—or even before birth! The value of this practice in preparing children to succeed in their formal education is now well established. For example, one of the most striking findings from the Bristol Study of Language Development is that the frequency with which children were read to during the preschool years strongly predicted not only their knowledge of literacy on entry to school but also their overall academic achievement 5 years later, at age 10 (Wells, 1986).

The benefits of being read to are many. First, from listening to stories read aloud, children become familiar with the cadences of written language and the generic structure of stories and other types of text. They also increase their vocabularies in domains that are rarely the subject of everyday talk. And, equally important, they learn that books are a source of interest and enjoyment that can introduce them to real, as well as imaginary, objects, places, and events that they do not encounter in their immediate environment. In all these ways, the practice of reading to children in the early years enlarges their experience in ways that prepare them to make the most of the instruction they will receive in school.

Listening to a story or nonfiction book is only part of this valuable practice, however. Much of the benefit—as well as the child's enjoyment—comes from the talk that accompanies the sharing of the book. Discussing the characters and their actions, predicting what is likely to happen next, clarifying the meaning of particular words and phrases—all these kinds of talk help the child to make connections between the meanings and language forms of the text and his or her actual experiences, including the use of language in other, familiar contexts. As the child gets older, talk about the text typically also begins to include attention to the written representation itself—the visual appearance of interesting words, and the forms of the letters and their correspondence to the sounds of speech. Described technically as "phonemic awareness," the knowledge about the relationship between spoken and written language that a child gains in this way is certainly an important aspect of becoming literate; indeed, it is argued by some to be a prerequisite for learning to read and write.

However, research has shown that there are differences in the ways in which parents talk with their children about the books they read together (Dale, Crain-Thoreson, Notari-Syverson, & Cole, 1996). Some parents, unfortunately, seem to think that they should quiz their children about the "facts" of the story or deliberately teach the letter names and sounds. But when the adult is willing to follow the child's lead, the talk frequently takes the form of a more open-ended exploration of what the child finds interesting in the story and, in this way, as in other activities, helps the adult to provide the sort of information that the child wants or needs (Tizard & Hughes, 1984).

Here is one of my favorite examples of a shared story reading. It was recorded when David was 3 years old. At his mother's invitation, David has chosen the picture storybook *The Giant Jam Sandwich* (Lord & Burroway, 1975), which obviously has been read to him before, and he sits next to his mother on the sofa so that he can see the book as she reads.

DAVID: The Giant Sandwich

    [4-second pause]

MOTHER: Who's this here on the first page?

DAVID: The wasps

MOTHER: The wasps are coming [Turns the page] . here's some more, look . [Reads]
    One hot summer in Itching Down
    Four million wasps flew into town.

DAVID: I don't like wasps … flying into town.

MOTHER: Why's that?

DAVID: Because they sting me.

MOTHER: Do they?

DAVID: Mm . I don't like them.

MOTHER: They won't sting you . but four million would be rather a lot, wouldn't
    it? . they'd get rather in the way.

    [Reads the following two pages and they talk about them]

As his mother turns to the next page, David looks intently at the illustration, which
shows three male inhabitants of Itching Down, each attempting in his own way to get
rid of the wasps, the first with an aerosol, the second with a butterfly net, and the third
with a fly swatter.

DAVID: Is that a spray to shoo them away? is that a spray to shoo them away?

MOTHER: Yes, it's probably some sort of insecticide . to get rid of them . . and
    what's that net for, do you think? [referring to a butterfly net in the picture]

DAVID: It's for catching them with

MOTHER: It doesn't seem to be much good though, does it?

DAVID: No . they come out the holes.

MOTHER: [laughs] The holes are too big, aren't they? . and what about this man?
    what's he got?

DAVID: He's—what's he got?

MOTHER: What's that?

DAVID: A note . what does the note say?

MOTHER: A note on a stick, is it? is that what you think?

DAVID: Actually it's a sound

MOTHER: A what?

DAVID: A sound
What's it called on the—on the stick? what is it? what's that man got?

MOTHER: Well you know, um—

DAVID: Yes . . sign

MOTHER: You think it's a sign? . yes it looks very like a sign with writing, doesn't
    it?

DAVID: Yes

MOTHER: But it isn't . it's like Mummy's—um—fish slice [slotted spatula].

DAVID: What is it?

MOTHER: It's a swatter . he's going to hit the wasp with it

DAVID: How d'you hit wasps with . otters?

MOTHER: Swatters? [checking] . well, they're made of plastic usually—

DAVID: Yes

MOTHER: And they—you bang them down . see if you can squash the wasp . . looks
    very angry [referring to the man with the swatter]
[5-second pause]

DAVID: Is he hurt?

MOTHER: It looks as if he might be . he's making a funny face

DAVID: Why he making a funny face? . is that man—is that man shouting
them to go away?

MOTHER: Think so, he's got his mouth open, so he could be shouting
[5-second pause as David continues to explore the picture]

MOTHER: Anyway—

DAVID: Yes

MOTHER: [Reads] They called a meeting in the village hall
And Mayor Muddlenut asked them all,
"What can we do?" And they said, "Good question,"
But nobody had a good suggestion.
Then Bap the baker leaped to his feet
And cried, "What do wasps like best . to—

DAVID: [completing the line]				—eat

MOTHER: Strawberry—

DAVID: [completing] —jam.

MOTHER: If we made a giant sandwich—

DAVID: Yes

MOTHER: We could trap them in it

There are a number of significant features about this episode. First, there is the
pace. The interaction is very relaxed, and several long pauses occur while David looks
at the pictures or thinks about how to complete what he has started to say. Notice, too,
how the mother takes time to explore features in which David shows interest. Particularly striking is David's interest in the man who is attempting to use the fly swatter.
He apparently mistakes the object for a notice, a sign telling the wasps to go away
and, as the mother agrees, the swatter in the picture does look like a sign with writing
on it, as the representation of the holes arranged in lines is similar to letters or words
on a page. Clearly, David has already come to understand that one of the important
functions of written language is to convey information or instructions. Finally, there
is the collaborative nature of the event, particularly apparent in David's completion of
several lines of the text. Not only is this an enjoyable experience for both mother and
child, but it also contributes to David's growing understanding of how written language works.

Somewhat comparable opportunities for learning can also occur in relation to the creation of written texts in the course of daily life. Tizard and Hughes (1984) cite the following example in their report of a longitudinal study of 4-year-old girls at home and at nursery school.

Pauline and her mother are discussing the items they still need to buy from the local grocery store. A neighbor (Irene) has just offered to buy some of the items, and Pauline's mother starts to cross off from her shopping list the items Irene is going to buy for them:

MOTHER: We've only got that little bit of shopping to get now [shows Pauline the list].

PAULINE: Mummy? can I have one of them drinks? can I?

MOTHER: Get some more drink?

PAULINE: Yeah . can write it down on there [points to where she wants it written on the list] up here

MOTHER: I'll get you some when I go tomorrow

PAULINE: Aw! [disappointed]

MOTHER: All right? 'cause I'm not getting it today . . haven't got Daddy's money yet

PAULINE: I've got no money [She seems to have misheard her mother at this point. Her mother corrects her.]

MOTHER: No, I haven't got enough to get my shopping—all of it.

PAULINE: Not all of it?

MOTHER: Irene's just taken five pounds . she'll bring some change back . if she's got some, she'll bring some change back . it's not enough to get all that, is it? [points to the shopping list]

PAULINE: No.
[A few minutes later, Pauline asks to look at the list again.]

PAULINE: Mum, let's have a look! [Mother shows child the list] do it again

MOTHER: We gotta get rice, tea, braising steak, cheese, pickle, carrots, fish, chicken, bread, eggs, bacon, beefburgers, beans . . oh, Irene's gone to get them [she crosses off beans] . . peas, ham, corned beef

PAULINE: And what's that? [points to a word on the list]

MOTHER: That's lemon drink [crosses off lemon drink] she's just gone down to get that one, see?

Commenting on this episode, Tizard and Hughes (1984) point out that although the mother reported that she was using the occasion to teach Pauline to count, Pauline was also learning about shopping and the function of a shopping list in planning and organizing this activity. They then continue:

What may be less obvious is that Pauline was also acquiring some important knowledge about the nature of written language. It is often suggested that working-class children do not have much experience of their parents engaging in "literate" activities; yet a shopping list provides an extremely vivid demonstration of the way in which written language may be used within a meaningful human activity. The power of the written word lies in its ability to link up different contexts in space or time, and here it is doing precisely that—forming a link between the home, where the decisions and choices are made, and the shop, where they are carried out. (pp. 75–76)

In the home environment, then, fortunate children experience an extended "apprenticeship" into literacy as they engage with literate family members in joint activities in which written texts play an instrumental role. In these activities, the adults' aim is not to teach their children to read and write *per se*, but to assist them to contribute to the activity to the extent of children's current capability, while managing those parts that are beyond them.

However, before starting to consider how schooling might build on the development of language and literacy that has already taken place in the preschool years, it may be helpful to expand on the overall theory of development to which I alluded in the preceding sections.

A Sociocultural Theory of Learning and Development

The ideas presented so far are to a large extent based on ideas first proposed by Vygotsky in the early 1930s. Because of political repression, however, Vygotsky's writings did not become known in the Soviet Union until the 1950s, and in English translation some two decades later. In some important respects, Vygotsky and Piaget held similar views about children's intellectual development, notably, about the active and constructive nature of children's understanding of the world. However, they differed on three important points. First, whereas Piaget believed that children's early development resulted mainly from their action on the material world, Vygotsky saw development as resulting from children's participation in social activities. Second, while Piaget sought universal characteristics of development, Vygotsky recognized the importance of children's specific social and cultural environments in the ways they develop. And third, whereas Piaget treated language development as depending on prior cognitive development, Vygotsky saw language as the principal mediator of social as well as intellectual development.

Over the last quarter of a century, Vygotsky's (1978, 1987) theory of learning and development has gradually been recognized as providing the most helpful basis for rethinking the principles on which early education should be based, so here I emphasize three of its key features.

Vygotsky distinguished between biologically given functions and those functions that depend for their development on the young child becoming a member of a particular culture through participation in activities that are central to that culture. Biologically given functions include orientation to other humans, particularly the principal caregiver, and their intentional actions; action-guided perception of the material environment; and memory for significant experiences that are regularly repeated. These functions do not involve conscious awareness, so they cannot be deliberately invoked. Equally important, they are private in the sense that, although socially embedded, they are only meaningful to the infant in relation to his or her own experiences.

"Higher" mental functions, as Vygotsky referred to them, are dependent on *meanings* that are socially shared. These begin to be "appropriated"—taken over from others—during the latter part of the first year and beyond, as infants and caregivers establish agreement ("intersubjectivity") about aspects of their shared world that are of mutual interest. And once the procedures for creating mutuality of interest are in place, the infant begins to initiate, as well as to respond to, invitations to explore the shared environment. But for the infant to understand the cultural meaning of these shared foci of attention, he or she needs to learn the language in which those meanings are encoded. How this happens can be clearly seen in the examples cited earlier, as the mother shapes her contributions to the young child's developing comprehension. Any particular example is, of course, somewhat trivial. But, cumulatively, occurring many times a day, such events provide the meaningful material out of which the 1- or 2-year-old gradually constructs his or her individual model of the language system by means of which meanings are shared between members of a culture.

Language learning was, in fact, one of the first examples that Vygotsky proposed as an instance of adult and child working together in the "zone of proximal development" (ZPD). More generally, he characterized the ZPD as the means whereby what a child can do today with help, he or she will be able to do tomorrow alone, and on this basis Vygotsky proposed the following principle:

> In the process of development, children begin to use the same forms of behavior in relation to themselves that others initially used in relation to them. Children master the social forms of behavior and transfer these forms to themselves. (1981, p. 157)

Thus, through the process of appropriation, children construct their own versions of the systems of communication (actional, gestural, intonational, verbal—and, subsequently, mathematical, scientific, and artistic) that have enabled knowledge constructed in the past to be available for use and improvement in the present. Nevertheless, it is important to emphasize that appropriating skills and knowledge originally developed by others does not mean simply copying them. Whether in early childhood or in adulthood, appropriation necessarily involves transformation, as each individual always makes sense of new information in the light of his or her previous experience and current concerns.

However, this does not imply that all knowledge remains idiosyncratic, which would render shared understanding impossible to achieve, since, over time, individual understandings tend to converge as a result of the calibration and negotiation of meaning that is an essential aspect of engaging in activities jointly with others. It is for this reason that Vygotsky emphasized the importance of goal-directed joint activity. For as Franklin (1996) puts it, "Knowledge is constructed (and reconstructed) in the discourse between people doing things together."

In summary, because all higher mental functions and the knowledge that they mediate are appropriated from other members of the culture in which children are growing up, it is clear that children's significant others play a critical role in their early development by making these cultural resources available and assisting children in making them their own. This we saw in the preceding examples of caregiver–child interaction at home in the preschool years, but the potential value of adult assistance remains equally true of children's learning and development in the time they spend at school.

Making the Transition from Home to School

Fifty years ago, the majority of children started school at the age of 5 or 6 years, varying from country to country depending on the laws concerning the age at which school attendance became mandatory. Prior to school entry, children spent their days at home in the company of their mothers and their siblings. Now, with greater equality for women in the workplace, as well as the need, in many cases, for both mothers and fathers to work to enable the family to survive economically, these norms no longer hold. Today, children may start spending time in some organized setting outside the home from a few months of age onwards. Not all of these settings are "schools"; they range from nurseries to playgroups, day care, or preschool classes. But what they have in common is that the child-to-adult ratio is considerably greater than in the home, and that the adult personnel are salaried workers rather than family caregivers. These conditions are less than optimal for young children. Much depends, therefore, on how these adults understand their role in meeting the developmental needs—physical, emotional, and intellectual—of the children in their care.

As has been emphasized, as well as a safe and interesting environment, the young child needs opportunities for sustained interaction with an adult who is willing and able to respond to the child's interests and to help him or her to build on and extend them by constructing meaning together through talk and shared activity. All too often, however, adults in preschool settings are too concerned to carry out their own agenda for the group of children for whom they are responsible to be able to give sustained attention to individual children.

In a study of playgroups and nurseries in Britain, carried out as part of the Preschool Research Project directed by Jerome Bruner in the 1970s, Wood, McMahon, and Cranstoun (1980) found that most adults working in day care or preschool settings did not see their primary role as that of teacher, and they were generally unwilling to engage in set periods of formal instruction. Instead, they typically gave priority to large-group management, and when they did interact with one child, or a small number of children, they tended to direct the interaction by asking questions and voicing their own ideas about the topic rather than making their talk responsive to the children's contributions.

Clearly, there is a considerable difference between this kind of talk and the sort of activity-oriented interaction that aims, in Vygotsky's terms, to provide assistance in children's ZPDs. Ideally, this is what children experience with their caregivers at home and, although necessarily modified in the light of the different conditions, it is also most beneficial for them in preschool institutions. Indeed, with the additional opportunity to take part in shared activities and to socialize with similar-age peers, such institutions have the potential to be excellent environments for children's all-around development in the early years, provided that the adults arrange for, and take up, opportunities to extend individual children's interests and problem-solving strategies.

Significantly, the importance of this kind of interaction was understood by the preschool personnel observed by Wood and colleagues (1980) when these adults subsequently saw or heard recordings of their own behavior. Recognizing the limitations their style of interaction imposed on children's development, many explored ways to become more contingently responsive. For example, they found that if they avoided areas of high management, such as the painting corner, sat down more frequently for a considerable time in one place, and encouraged one or two children to join them in an activity, they were able to engage in sustained interaction, supporting and guiding the children to think and talk about what they were doing. In addition, they discovered that in getting to know individual children better by spending more time in focused activities with them, and observing how they approached activities and attempted to solve problems they encountered, they were also better able to provide helpful support and to gear their instruction to each child's current level of competence (Wood et al., 1980).

From Home to School

Whether or not they have attended some form of preschool institution, in many countries all children are required to enter the first year of elementary education at around age 5 or 6. Typically, classes are larger than in preschool and, from this point on, there is a mandated curriculum that has to be followed. Increasingly, too, there are regular state- or nationally mandated tests of achievement. All these factors put considerable pressure on teachers to attempt to ensure that all children proceed at the same pace, even though there is ample evidence that, at any one age, children are not all at the same developmental stage, and they do not all develop at the same rate. To these challenges facing the teacher must be added the inclusion in many classes of children who are in the process of learning the language of instruction, and others who have various kinds of disability. It is not surprising, therefore, that the opportunities for learning are less than optimal for almost all children.

In the Bristol Study of Language Development, which was carried out when the pressures just enumerated were less severe, we conducted a comparison of children's interactional experiences just before and just as they entered school. For the 32 children whom we followed from home into school, we randomly selected seven 5-minute samples from audiorecordings in the children's homes a few weeks before they started school. We also made a comparable videorecoding during their first few weeks in school and selected seven 5-minute samples on a similar basis. We then coded the recorded samples of interaction in terms of their linguistic characteristics and of their supportiveness of the children's linguistic and intellectual development. A summary of the results is presented in Table 13.1.

Table 13.1 indicates that there were some significant differences between the two settings, home and school, in the amount of speech produced by the children and addressed to them by their caregivers or teachers and, more specifically, in the characteristics of the children's and adults' contributions. As can be seen, when interacting with an adult, children talked significantly less in the classroom than at home. At school, of course, many of the adult's utterances were addressed to the whole class or to a group that included the child being observed, so the overall imbalance between the amount of speech by the adult and by the child is understandable. Nevertheless, when the children did have an opportunity to speak in the classroom, their speech was both semantically less varied and syntactically less complex than at home. Particularly significant was the much-reduced frequency with which they initiated interaction, either to make a request or to ask a question; furthermore, on inspection, their questions at school were found to be mainly about what they were supposed to do rather than about things that puzzled them. This difference in the degree to which the children were

TABLE 13.1. Children's Experience of Language Use at Home and at School

Feature of language use	Home	School
Absolute values		
No. of child utterances to an adult	122.0*	45.0*
No. of adult utterances to the child	153.0	129.0
No. of child speaking turns per conversation	4.1*	2.5*
No. of different types of meaning expressed by child	15.5*	7.9*
No. of grammatical constituents per child utterance	3.1*	2.4*
Proportions (child)	(Percent)	(Percent)
Initiates conversation	63.6*	23.0*
Questions	12.7*	4.0*
Requests	14.3*	10.4*
Elliptical utterances; fragments	29.4*	49.4*
References to nonpresent events	9.1*	6.4*
Proportions (adult)	(Percent)	(Percent)
Questions	14.3*	20.2*
Display questions	2.1*	14.2*
Requests	22.5*	34.1*
Extends child's meaning	33.5*	17.1*
Develops adult's meaning	19.1*	38.6*

Note. Figures are averaged over all 32 children in the study. From Wells (1986, p. 86).

actively involved in the exploration of matters in which they were personally interested was fairly directly related to the ways in which the adults in the two settings typically engaged with them.

Limiting the data to just those conversations in which the adult was interacting with the child being observed, all adult utterances were coded as to whether and in what way they built on what had been said in the immediately preceding conversation. In both settings, utterances that incorporated matter contributed in previous speaking turns accounted for about 50% of the total. However, in a comparison between those adult utterances that picked up and extended matter contributed by the child ("extending" utterances) and those that developed matter previously introduced by the adult ("developing" utterances), a very significant difference was found. Whereas, at home, twice as many adult utterances were extending rather than developing, the ratio was reversed in the classroom, with teachers developing matter introduced by themselves twice as often as they extended matter contributed by the children.

These findings are particularly ironic, in that almost half of the 32 children being studied lived in predominantly lower-class areas and attended schools that were charged with providing a "language enrichment program," since it was a widely held belief that children from lower-class homes entered school with a less advanced mastery of English than their middle-class peers. However, for *every* child in this sample, the language experience at school was significantly impoverished compared with that at home. Moreover, whereas few, if any, studies similarly compare home and school, other studies of language in the classroom provide ample evidence that confirms the limited nature of most children's opportunities to use and extend their language ability to the full extent in the elementary years at school (Cazden, 1988; Galton, Hargreaves, Comber, & Wall, 1999; Nystrand, 1997; Tizard & Hughes, 1984).

In light of the arguments developed in the first part of this chapter, and particularly those concerning the central role of language in children's intellectual, social, and emotional development, as explained by Vygotsky and other sociocultural scholars and researchers (Bruner, 1996; Hicks, 1995; Mercer, 1995; Wells & Claxton, 2002), these findings point to one of the most troubling aspects of most education in the elementary years (and beyond). And, unfortunately, the situation has recently deteriorated still further as a result of the growing emphasis on ensuring that children perform well on the mandated standardized tests. Indeed, in some schools on California's central coast, there is practically no "exploratory talk" (Barnes, 1976) at all, as teachers are obliged to teach to an imposed program in which their every utterance is prescribed and no deviations are permitted.

At the same time, however, there *are* classrooms and schools in which serious attempts are being made to create more challenging and supportive environments for learning and development, where teachers recognize the critical importance of activities in which literacy plays a functional role, and of dialogue as the medium for learning and teaching. These form the basis for the concluding sections of this chapter. But before turning to them, it is important to consider how literacy fits into the overall picture.

The Centrality of Literacy

First, I should be clear why I believe it is important for all young people to become literate. Written language is first and foremost a form of external memory. It allows us to preserve information—ideas, plans, reports, and instructions—in a permanent form that can be accessed at different times and places by the self, as well as others, without it having to be committed to individuals' biological memories. Over the course of history, it has enabled kings and governments to keep track of people's assets and to tax them accordingly, to promulgate laws, and to administer public services. In more recent times, enhanced by visual media, such as graphs, diagrams, and photography, written language has provided the means for cumulative development of science and technology, as a medium for broadcasting news and for political debate, and most recently, with the advent of the Internet, for greatly enhanced communication worldwide for a wide variety of purposes. It is therefore no exaggeration to say that contemporary societies could not survive without a literate population, and individual members are at a disadvantage if they cannot participate in the various transactions mediated by written text. These in themselves are good reasons for making literacy learning a key part of any school curriculum.

However, an equally good reason is what literacy provides by way of enhancement of each individual's unique development. Quite apart from the role of written texts in making available the knowledge accumulated in the different academic disciplines that provides the foundation for school learning and access to higher education, books, magazines, Internet webpages, art media, and instruction manuals allow each of us to develop interests and acquire expertise in areas of our own choosing and to share our interests with others. But perhaps most importantly, being able to write to communicate with ourselves, as well as with others, provides a means of reflective self-development that is unequalled in power and versatility by any other means. And this in turn makes each of us better able to contribute to the society to which we belong. Thus, there is every reason to emphasize literacy in children's development.

What is significant about the various kinds of literacy referred to here is that they are all functional in the various spheres of contemporary life in which they are found. When people read or write and use other literate modes of communication, they do so for some purpose, and that purpose determines their choice of genre and style. People rarely read or write to engage in the activity for its own sake. It seems clear, therefore, that this should be the first guiding principle in planning the activities by means of which we hope to enable young people to become literate. In other words, we should assume that the best way to help them learn to read and write is by providing occasions for them to engage in reading and writing for some genuine purpose. As Vygotsky wrote, "Teaching should be organized in such a way that reading and writing are necessary for something. ... Writing should be incorporated into a task that is relevant and necessary for life" (1978, pp. 117–118). As he fully understood, without the motivation created by purposes of their own, children fail to develop the drive to learn to read and write and, as a result, they have considerable difficulty in mastering the knowledge, skills, and dispositions that enable them to become purposeful, fluent, and critical readers and writers. For this reason, literacy should not be treated as a separate, self-contained "subject" in the curriculum but as a communication "toolkit" that can be used, as appropriate, in theme-based studies of various kinds.

Earlier, I presented two examples of how children begin to learn about the functions and values of literacy in the home environment. The first illustrated how sharing a story can be an enjoyable experience in its own right, while, at the same time, developing the disposition to interact actively with what is read to enlarge one's understanding of possible worlds beyond one's firsthand experience. The second illustrated the practical utility of reading and writing in organizing everyday activities, such as buying needed food and drink. There are many more examples of how children begin to learn about the functions and forms of literate activities in family life (Taylor, 1998).

What I emphasized in presenting these examples was the way in which the mothers interacted with their children about the text they were reading or writing together. Rather than focus on the form—letter–sound relationships—they focused on how the children made sense of the text in terms of their interests and concerns; instead of imposing their own understanding and values with respect to the text in question, the mothers supported the children's own quest for understanding (DeBruin-Parecki, 1999). This is the second guiding principle for organizing literacy instruction in school.

In certain fundamental respects, then, learning to read and write is similar to learning the spoken form of language. But this does not imply that we should ignore the very real differences between the two modes of language use. Writing is a second-order form of language in that it uses patterns of visual symbols to represent the meanings that are expressed in speech. In alphabetic languages, such as English and other European languages, the written code fairly directly represents the sounds of the spoken word, so, at least initially, emphasis needs to be given to mastering the letter–sound correspondences that aid in decoding when reading, and in spelling when writing. These are essential skills and, for many children, learning them may require systematic instruction and practice. But unless learning these skills is set in the context of reading and writing for purposes that are meaningful to the learner, there is a danger that children will become adept at coding and decoding instructional material but will either have difficulty in bringing these skills to bear when attempting to read and write autonomously or will become so bored with what for them are purposeless activities that they never discover the value to themselves of being able to read and write (Gallas, 2003).

The third guiding principle follows from the first two: No large group of children, such as make up a typical elementary school class, can be taught effectively by having everyone carry out the same program of activities in unison. Instruction needs to be differentiated according to individual interests and strengths, as well as needs for assistance. In other words, instructional planning should be as concerned to work with each child in his or her ZPD as to ensure that externally required curriculum standards are met. Although this principle applies at any age, it is particularly important in the early years.

The work of Marie Clay (2005) offers a particularly well-thought-out and principled approach to helping children to master the "basics" of print literacy, in which the sequence of instruction is tailored to the particular needs of individual children. In the United States, her approach has become known through its application in Reading Recovery, but the principles involved should not be thought of as applying only in remedial contexts. Using both children's own writing and a wide selection of short, illustrated books as the basis for talk about texts and how to make meaning with them, Clay's approach can be adapted to suit the range of needs for assistance across the early grades.

Of particularly significance in Clay's work is her emphasis on treating spoken and written language as complementary. Because fluent reading and writing are normally carried out individually and in silence, the mental processes involved cannot be inferred by a preliterate child in the same way that they can for processes involved in material activities, such as cooking, cleaning, or doing the laundry. It is essential, therefore, that a teacher or some other adult talk with the child about how texts work while actually engaged in reading or writing. Encouraging children to write as best they can is particularly helpful because, even more than reading, writing draws attention to the decisions that have to be made in order to represent the meanings that the child first composes in speech in the sequential construction of the written text.

Another good way to have adults read and write with children is to encourage students to choose a book to take home to share with family members. In my son's K–1 class, the teacher had two large collections of appealing books, with some of them in languages other than English for the English language learners. The children were encouraged to choose two books to take home: the first would be one that they would read to a family member, and the other, more difficult, would be one that they would ask someone to read to them. Parents were encouraged to talk with the children about the books they chose in the ways I described earlier. This scheme proved to be very popular with children and parents alike, and was soon used in other schools in the district. It also inspired quite a number of parents to come to the classroom to continue the book sharing there (Wells & Hart-Hewins, 1990).

Reading and Writing with Peers

So far, the emphasis has been on tailoring instruction to the different needs of individuals. But the differences between children's degree of understanding about how written language works can be turned into an asset when children help each other and share what they know. One way of doing so is seen in the following example.

In Karla Poremba's kindergarten class (Richgels, Poremba, & McGee, 1996), children often find a new text on display as they enter the classroom in the morning, and they are encouraged to make time to take a careful look at it. Poremba selects texts, such as a poem, a recipe, or a story, that relate to what the children are doing in class and uses them for shared reading with the whole class. However, before she reads the text, Poremba engages the children in an activity that she calls "What can you show us?" She invites individual children to come and point to something they know about the text.

One day in early October, the children found the following letter from Uncle Wally (one of the large dolls in the book corner):

> Dear Kindergarteners,
>   It is fall!
>   Fall is apple time.
>   We picked an apple
>   On a tree.
>   Yum! Yum!
> Love,
>   Uncle Wally.

Poremba had drawn an apple over each occurrence of the word *apple* and a tree over the word *tree*, and the first child called attention to these words. Next, Nathan pointed to the *K* in *Kindergarteners*, then to the *KP* written on his name collar, so that other teachers could identify him as a child in Karla Poremba's class. He did not know the name of the letter, but other children were able to inform him. Once the *K* in the long word at the beginning of the letter had been located, Erin called out "Kindergarteners." Jason then went to the easel and, pointing to the words, read "Dear Kindergarteners."

After Jason, with help from others, had read some individual words, then the phrase "on a tree," Eric offered what he knew, associating individual letters with classmates' names: "The *Y* for Freddy (pointing to the *Y* in *Yum* . . and he has an *F* (pointing to the *F* in *fall*) . . and an *I* for Ian (pointing to the *I* in *It*) . . There's an *E* for me (pointing to the end of *tree*)." Next, Elise told what she thought the letter was about: "They got in an apple tree." Finally, Kaitlynn returned to the letter *K*, which she identified in the middle of *picked*, and as the first letter in her name.

In these exchanges, each child is recognized for what he or she knows and can do; at the same time, there is an opportunity for collaboration as one child builds on what another has contributed. Between them, the children draw attention to many aspects of the written code, and the teacher is able to see what sort of individual assistance to give to each child.

The next example involves a different kind of talk about a text, which occurred in a class of 8-year-old students, many of whom were still mastering English as their second language. Here, a group of five Portuguese Canadian children were working collaboratively to create a text to share with the rest of the class. The task the teacher had set was to base what they wrote on the research they had been doing on dinosaurs, and they embarked on the task with enthusiasm. In the following extract, we see them not only generating an amusing "story" but also helping each other with all aspects of the writing process. The transcript below contains a small number of extracts from a conversation that remained focused on the task for about 40 minutes.

TANYA: Think of the title . . Dinosaur Time.

TONY: Back in the dinosaur time?
[Children sit in silence thinking for a while.]

TANYA: Dinosaur school?

TONY AND BARB: (simultaneously) Yeah
[The group agrees eagerly; several children laugh.]

BARB: It will be fun then

TONY: How do you spell *dinosaur*?
[Several children look around the classroom to find the word displayed.]

Having fairly quickly decided to write about "Dinosaur schools," they begin to negotiate the opening of their text. The exact location of dinosaur schools is discussed over the next several turns, and they decide that the inside of volcanoes is a suitable location. Together they generate the first sentence, and Tony begins to write.

TONY: Baby—(as he writes)

MANY: Baby dinosaurs . dinosaurs (group members chime in)

TANYA: Hm you put dinosaur . . DinoSAURS (emphasizing the plural form)

TONY: I can't do anything now (refers to erasing)

EERIC: What did he do wrong? dinosaur school?

TANYA: Dinosaurs, he must put dinoSAURS (again emphasizing the plural) like
        thousands of them, more than one

TONY: So, so that's what the school is

TANYA: A school with one kid? (laughs)

BARB: Dinosaur school, school of one kid

TANYA: Baby dinosaurs must go to school inside a volcano (laughs) . . once every 5
        years, a fire alarm will go on as an eruption.

BARB: Ya, that's funny (everyone laughs)

Tony continues to write down what the group has composed, while the others monitor and comment on what he is writing.

TONY: (reading as he writes) Baby dinosaurs schools are in—are in volcanoes

TANYA: WERE in

EERIC: Were in—

TANYA: They are not right now, are dinosaurs living right now? WERE (repeating
        as Tony writes)
[Tony continues to write, vocalizing each word as he writes it]

TONY: —were in volcanoes, in a volcano

TANYA: In volcano . S (emphasizing plural)

TONY: V O K—V O K (invents spelling) . . V O K—K A

EERIC: Tony, I think you've got it wrong . . it's V O L—volcanoes

TONY: (continuing to vocalize as he writes) Every 500 years—'

EERIC: I know ***** (his utterance is unclear but seems to be raising an objection)

TONY: OK

TANYA: Yeah, 5 years because they won't be alive in 500 years

EERIC: Yes, they would

TANYA: But they wouldn't be babies anymore

TONY: (agreeing) Yeah

BARB: They'll be 5

EERIC: So they'll be in grade 6 **

TANYA: They are in grade 6 . . they'll be in school, they'll be teenagers, not babies anymore

TONY: I made a mistake

BARB: Who cares?

TANYA: They'll . . they'll be in high school

These extracts, which involve only the first few lines of the students' final text, show very clearly the complexity of the challenge facing novice writers. First there is the search for what to write. Here the decision was assisted somewhat by the teacher's specification of the general topic, and by the knowledge that the rest of the class was the intended audience. But even when children have decided on the general idea—which occurred fairly early in this writing episode—writers have to generate specific detail and ensure that there is coherence in the emerging structure of meaning. Then there is the problem of "wording"—the choice of both appropriate words and the correct morphological structure for their role in the context of the sentence. Finally, children must grapple with the conventions of spelling and punctuation as the spoken version of the text is encoded in graphological form. Not surprisingly, managing all these levels simultaneously can seem an overwhelming task, particularly when the physical formation of the letters is still also very time consuming.

For this group of writers, all of whom were still mastering English as their second language, there were obvious benefits in undertaking this task collaboratively. Not only were they able to draw on the diverse range of relevant expertise that was distributed among the group members but together they were also able to overcome the problems of short-term memory involved in retaining the intended meaning that they had composed while dealing with the difficulties of accurately representing the text on the page. And, most important, their shared commitment to the task sustained their motivation to continue.

Here is the text that they had produced at the end of the 40-minute activity. Probably because of its witty inventiveness, the class judged it to be the best produced by any group.

DINOSAURS SCHOOL ...

Baby DINOSAURS Schools were in VOCKANOS.

Every 5 Years The Fire Drial would Go On as an ERUPTION

THEY WriHT About People. THE Paper was 10 mters long. And
The Pencil is 5 mters long. There Close is poka Doted. And THERE
Poget is about THE Fugter. THE Librery is called Home read stone.
And The books or made of saled. Rock. THEY live in haya rock.
THERE Brians or as small as marbells. THERE LUnCH is Brontobrgers.
THERE TOYS ARE all With batreries, THERE HOUES is MADE OF Pebulls.
by Tony, Tanya, Barbara, Margaret and Eric.

This practice of writing collaboratively is also helpful for older students, particularly for second language learners or students with learning difficulties, who lack confidence in their ability to compose extended texts on their own. Not only does the social nature of the enterprise increase students' interest in and enjoyment of the task but also students who might be reluctant to review and revise their own texts when writing individually are more willing to do so when their contributions are challenged by peers whose opinion they value. Of course, the ultimate aim is that they take responsibility for the texts they produce in solo mode, but for many students, the support of collaborative peers is an excellent way to help them to reach this stage.

Creating a Classroom Where Reading, Writing, and Talking Are Valued

As I emphasized earlier, speaking, listening, reading, and writing are—or should be—modes of communication about matters that are of personal and social significance to the persons involved. In Vygotskian terms, they mediate various forms of joint activity. Spoken and written interactions are thus the principal means of "thinking together" (Mercer, 2002), and, as the various genres of communication are appropriated from participation in dialogue with others, they become the means for individual thinking in the dialogue of "inner speech" (Vygotsky, 1987) and reflective writing.

These may seem to be rather advanced forms of language use for children in the early years, but this need not be the case. Under appropriate conditions, even first-graders are able to talk constructively about matters they think are important, as Gallas (1995) found when her children engaged in "science talks." Similarly, when they write with and for each other instead of for the teacher, children are able to use the emerging text as a means of thinking together, as seen in the case of the authors of "Dinosaurs School." But whether in speech or writing, for sustained dialogue to develop, certain conditions must be met:

- The topic must be of interest to the participants.
- Individual students must have relevant ideas, opinions, or experiences that they want to share.
- Others must be willing to listen or to read attentively and critically.
- The teacher must share control and the right to evaluate with students.

Over a period of almost 10 years, I worked with a group of elementary teachers to explore ways to create these conditions in regular classrooms in Metro Toronto. As the title of our project, Developing Inquiring Communities in Education (DICEP), suggests, we believed that the best way to proceed would be to approach the curriculum through theme-based inquiries, in which children worked in self-chosen groups on aspects of the theme that particularly interested them.

Vygotskian theory was one source of inspiration for our work; another was the educational philosophy of Dewey (1966). Of one thing Dewey was quite sure: For students to engage with a topic, it must be of interest to them. But it must also be one that poses problems or raises doubts that motivate students to explore further. This led Dewey to place great emphasis on inquiry, both as the motivation for engaging in, and as the organizing principle for, the selection of learning activities. These, he believed, should grow out of firsthand experience and be largely determined by the students themselves, with the teacher acting more as facilitator than as director. Although more recent writers in this tradition have placed less emphasis on individual choice of topic for inquiry, they agree with Dewey in emphasizing that the key characteristic of investigatory activities should be that they take as their object significant and often problematic features of the students' experience and environment, and have as their intended outcome growth in the students' understanding, which is taken to mean not simply factual knowledge but knowledge growing out of, and oriented to, socially relevant and productive action.

Vygotsky, on the other hand, while agreeing on the importance of interest and the motivational value of inquiry, placed much greater emphasis on collaborative group investigation. This was in part because he saw the social group, in this case, the classroom community, as the source from which the individual appropriated the language-mediated practices that are the foundation of higher mental functions. But equally important was the much more active role he attributed to the teacher in selecting the topics for students' inquiries, and in providing guidance as students engaged in the problem solving to which these inquiries were intended to give rise. It was in such situations, he believed, that the teacher was able to work most effectively with students in their ZPDs (Vygotsky, 1987).

However, for both Dewey and Vygotsky, despite their different emphases, one of the most important functions of inquiry was to generate occasions for purposeful dialogue. When students pursue investigations, they develop ideas and acquire information that they want to share and debate; at the same time, the problems they encounter call for the joint consideration of alternative possible solutions. In these circumstances, students have reason to learn the skills necessary for using reference materials, taking notes, and engaging in productive dialogue. Over time, they also develop the disposition to approach problem solving of all kinds in this way, which will be of value both to them in the future and to the larger society of which they are becoming members.

Over the years of the project, we constructed a general model of "dialogic inquiry," which we found helpful as a tool for thinking about the key components of a theme-based curriculum unit (see Figure 13.1). The overall aim is to engage children in collaborative knowledge building through action, talk, and use of written text. Key is the choice of theme and the way it is launched. The theme should allow multiple approaches, which both enable connections to be made to curricular guidelines and suggest a variety of student inquiries. Students choose possible topics of interest that they wish to investigate and form small groups around these topics. In their groups, students engage in three components: research to gather relevant evidence; interpretation of the evidence in the light of their questions (these two components are repeated as necessary until the group members consider they have made answers to the questions or changed their questions in light of the evidence they have collected); and presentation of the results of their investigation to the whole class, either orally or through poster presentations. Each component involves the students in practical investigation (experiment, observation, survey, etc.), as well as library research; dialogue in planning and carrying out investigations; interpretation of the evidence and preparation for presentation; written notes in a log or journal; and, where appropriate, the creation of a written report. However, the final component, reflection, is equally important. In a whole-class discussion, students consider the relationships between the different groups' results, exploring discrepancies and alternative interpretations, and decide what they now understand about the theme, and what further questions have arisen as a result. At the same time, they also discuss the processes in which they have engaged and consider ways in which they could improve in the future (Wells, 2001, 2002).

The preceding description of the model is obviously very schematic and should not be taken as a blueprint to be followed in a mechanical manner. What is important is the identification of the key components and the relationships among them. A further point to note is that some themes may well develop into subthemes corresponding to curricular subjects. For example, a theme on Monarch butterflies might include a subtheme on the mathematics of the measurement of distance, time, and speed; another on the metamorphosis of caterpillars into butterflies; and yet another on color in relation to painting pictures of the butterflies' wings (Gamberg, Kwak, Hutchings, & Altheim, 1988; Harste, 1994).

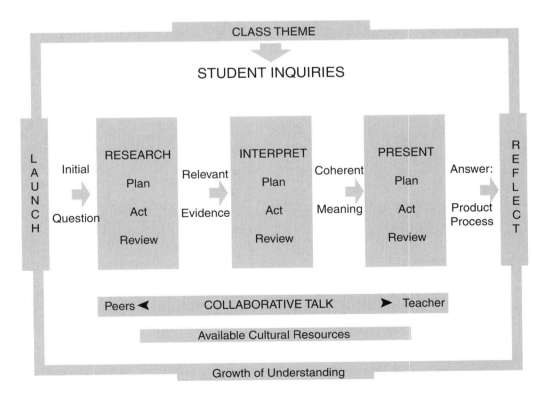

FIGURE 13.1. Model of dialogic inquiry.

The value of the model to us, as teachers, is that it gives a central place to the students' questions, allowing students to bring their interests, skills, and knowledge to bear in genuine inquiry and the dialogue that this requires, while pushing them "to go beyond themselves" (Vygotsky, 1987) in developing new interests, skills, and understanding and in making connections between the new information and what they already know. At the same time, the overarching theme enables students to benefit from each others' newfound expertise and to learn about relationships among the different questions they have addressed (Brown & Campione, 1994). Finally, working together in this way creates a classroom ethos of inquiry, collaboration, and dialogue that encourages students to learn with and from each other. All this can be achieved while still meeting curriculum standards, as Donoahue (2003) explains in her detailed account of how such a theme-based unit was developed in relation to the curriculum standards on "sound."

The Teacher's Roles

Teachers of young children have many roles to play: maintaining productive relationships with parents; monitoring children's physical health and emotional well-being; promoting positive social relationships, self-discipline, and concern for others; amassing or borrowing additional resources for the units they plan to teach, including building a classroom library; and many more. Here, I focus on the teacher's roles in relation to the curriculum and children's academic progress.

I have found it helpful to think of the teacher's role as operating at two levels (see Figure 13.2). At the first level, the teacher is responsible for choosing themes that both incorporate learning goals from the grade-level curriculum standards and take into account children's interests and out-of-school experiences, then for devising a range of activities through which the chosen theme can be explored. To a considerable degree, this role concerns planning and organization to provide the conditions in which his or her charges can learn new knowledge and skills and develop self-confidence as inquirers, and problem posers and solvers. This role also includes presenting new information and procedures through exposition by the teacher or other experts, either in person or through their writings, and the use of various forms of direct instruction when appropriate.

At the level of individual students or small groups, however, the teacher has the rather different role of supporter and guide as he or she works with the children in their ZPDs. In this role, the teacher acts as respondent to the students' implicit, as well as explicit, requests for help. There are many forms in which help can be given, such as prompting; inviting the child to talk about what he or she is trying to do, and what strategies he or she has available that may be useful; asking specific questions that may help the child to see what to do next; drawing attention to some aspect of the task that he or she seems to have ignored; and so on. There is also a place for direct instruction, but now not broadcast to the class as a whole but, instead, in what might be termed "just-in-time teaching" to enable a child to proceed successfully. The important point about such scaffolding is that the aim is to enable the child to manage the task without help in the future. This has been called the "handover principle," the aim of which is to foster children's confidence and autonomy, and to wean them away from dependence on the teacher or other props.

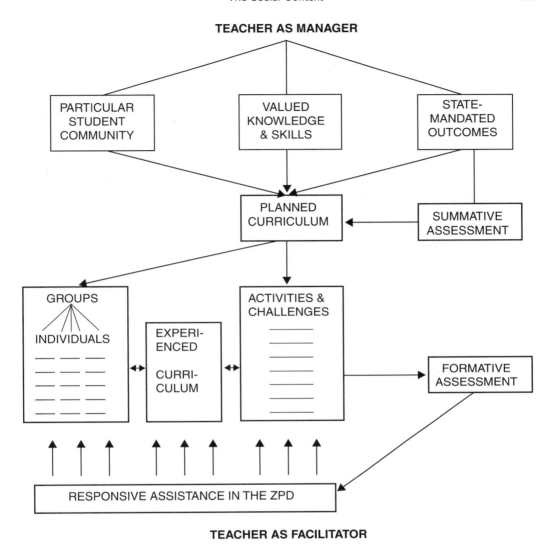

FIGURE 13.2. The teacher's roles.

Cutting across these two levels is the activity of assessment. This is an essential aspect of effective teaching at each of the two levels. At the facilitation level, formative assessment should be ongoing, as this is how the teacher adjusts the assistance he or she provides when interacting with individual students or groups. This form of assessment requires no formal instruments; rather, it is achieved by observing what students are doing and saying to monitor what and how well they are understanding (or misunderstanding); this enables the teacher to make appropriate adjustments to the task conditions in the moment, as well as decisions about whether to intervene when individuals or groups encounter difficulties and, if so, the best way to do so (Drummond, 1997). As far as maximizing children's progress is concerned, this kind of formative assessment is much more useful than summative assessment (Black, Harrison, Lee, & Marshall, 2003).

At the managerial level, some form of summative assessment is also important to find out whether the learning opportunities that were planned and put into effect in collaboration with the students effectively achieved the intended outcomes. However, what was planned is rarely enacted as originally anticipated because the enactment is a joint process that is affected by all manner of factors, and particularly by the students' uptake of the opportunities made available and by their contributions to ongoing activities. In this sense, the curriculum is always emerging from moment to moment and is inevitably experienced differently by individual participants. For this reason, summative assessment should not be thought of as an evaluation of the students alone; the teacher's part in keeping the ship afloat and attempting to navigate it should also be evaluated. Similarly, the students should also be involved in the summative evaluation of what was helpful to them and what was not.

There is one further role that teachers who adopt this sort of approach to teaching are increasingly taking on, and that is the role of "teacher-researcher." Even when teachers are already reflective about their own classroom practice, there are several excellent reasons for taking this additional step. First, if they systematically document the two kinds of assessment discussed earlier, they already have useful data to answer a variety of questions about the degree of match between their intentions and their practice. It is then worthwhile, having reflected on the results of this first level of investigation, to decide what changes they wish to make and to collect further evidence to test the success of their attempts. This process can be even more illuminating and rewarding if teachers work together in a group, as did the DICEP group, to share their findings and their ideas for further improvement. Not only do members provide mutual support and encouragement but when they tackle a common issue, their findings are also likely to carry more weight and to be more useful to other teachers. And when they embark on preparing to present their work at conferences and to publish it for other teachers, the opportunity for collaborative knowledge building that the group provides is a further benefit (Wells, 2001).

But there is a further reason to become a teacher-researcher: both to experience firsthand and to model for students the same processes of inquiry that, it has been suggested, should be central to the way one organizes students' learning. As the DICEP teachers found, it is a natural next step to include the students as coinvestigators about the work they are doing together (see *Networks* 6(1) for accounts of their joint projects).

In the current climate, where standardized test results are treated as the major goal of learning and teaching, many other equally important goals of education are downplayed or completely ignored. These include nontested subjects, such as the arts; making connections across disciplines; providing opportunities for imagination and creativity to flourish; and the development of dispositions for collaboration, inquiry, and self-directed learning and mastery of self-chosen skills and topics of interest. As the DICEP teachers found, all of these goals have a place when learning and teaching are organized around theme-based curricular units approached through collaborative inquiry. Adopting this approach leads to the development of a classroom that functions as a community, and participating in a community enhances the development of the skills, knowledge, and understanding on the part of all its members.

The same argument also holds for teachers who want the best for their students. The struggle to meet the demands of the educational bureaucracy, while creating the sort of community just described, can easily become overwhelming when a teacher undertakes it alone. However, when a group of like-minded teachers form their own community of inquiry, they not only benefit from the sharing of successful strategies in the choice of themes, activities, materials, and forms of assessment, but they also provide mutual support and a sense of collective achievement. As group members who collect evidence of what is effective in their particular shared situation, they may also begin to influence their colleagues and administrators in deciding how to balance the various demands faced by the school and the district. Although they cannot significantly change those demands, an inquiring community of educators is better able to make good decisions than a collection of individuals, each making their decisions alone.

Conclusion

In opening this chapter, I rejected the notion that human beings live their lives as solitary individuals surrounded and influenced by a "social context." On the contrary, I have argued that all of us live our lives in constant interaction with others—close family members, friends, neighbors, colleagues, and even casual acquaintances—in which the outcomes of our jointly undertaken activities bring about our mutual transformation, as well as transformations of our shared environment. Infancy and childhood are the periods of most rapid and consequential transformation because it is during these periods that the individual is apprenticed into the local culture; its historically developed ways of acting, thinking, and valuing; and forms the dispositions that will strongly influence how he or she will take up opportunities for further development throughout his or her life.

Understood in this way, the parts played by significant others—parents, caregivers, teachers—in the child's early life are key to his or her future and, less directly, to that of all the people with whom he or she will interact. How they engage with the child in the activities they undertake together not only facilitates—or impedes—his or her active and interested participation but also models what activities are worth undertaking and how they should be approached. In particular, the ways in which child and adult talk about what they are doing together enable the young child both to appropriate the resources of the spoken language and, in the process, to take over the cultural knowledge encoded in that language.

Cultures and families differ in the ways in which they make sense of experience and in their images of the ideal course and end point of development, and these differences affect the ways in which parents interact with their children. Clearly, the resulting differences in children's early experiences must be taken into account by those who plan and organize the learning experiences that are made available in day care and school settings. But in the increasingly global environment in which all cultures are now involved, there is a need for all children to develop the dispositions and knowledgeable skills to become resilient, adaptable, and resourceful learners, who are able to be interdependent as well as independent agents, to take the lead as well as to follow, and to selectively draw upon and extend the knowledge that they inherit from previous generations in order to contribute to solving the problems that they will undoubtedly encounter in their lives beyond school.

The best way to assist children in their development, I have suggested, is by approaching learning and teaching through dialogic inquiry, in which spoken and written language, together with action and reflection, provide the principal mediational means. Since the appropriate themes, and the manner in which they are approached, need to be different for children of different ages and different previous experiences, there can be no single blueprint that is universally applicable. For this reason, I have recommended that teachers, too, engage in dialogic inquiry with their colleagues to create and improve learning opportunities that are most appropriate for the children in their care.

Almost a century ago, Dewey put forward similar arguments in *Democracy and Education*:

> In directing the activities of the young, society determines its own future. ... Since the young at a given time will at some later date compose the society of that period, the latter's nature will largely turn upon the direction children's activities were given at an earlier period. (1966, p. 41)

In the intervening years, the world has changed in ways that make the future for today's children more uncertain and more challenging than it was when Dewey wrote these words. Therefore, it is all the more important that the activities we design for their education enable children to meet those challenges with relevant knowledge and the disposition to use it in collaboration with others with a concern for the interests of others as well as themselves, and for the well-being of the planet on which we all live.

References

Barnes, D. (1976). *From communication to curriculum*. Harmondsworth, UK: Penguin.

Barnes, S., Gutfreund, M., Satterly, D., & Wells, G. (1983). Characteristics of adult speech which predict children's language development. *Journal of Child Language, 10*(1), 65–84.

Bernstein, B. (1971). *Class, codes and control: Vol. I. Theoretical studies towards a sociology of language*. London: Routledge & Kegan Paul.

Bernstein, B. (1975). *Class, codes and control: Vol. 3. Towards a theory of educational transmissions*. London: Routledge & Kegan Paul.

Black, P., Harrison, C., Lee, C., & Marshall, B. (2003). *Assessment for learning: Putting it into practice*. Maidenhead, UK: Open University Press.

Brown, A. L., & Campione, J. C. (1994). Guided discovery in a community of learners. In K. McGilly (Ed.), *Integrating cognitive theory and classroom practice: Classroom lessons* (pp. 229–270). Cambridge, MA: MIT Press/Bradford Books.

Brown, R. (1973). *A first language: The early stages*. London: Allen & Unwin.

Bruner, J. S. (1983). *Child's talk*. New York: Norton.

Bruner, J. S. (1996). *The culture of education*. Cambridge, MA: Harvard University Press.

Cazden, C. (1988). *Classroom discourse: The language of teaching and learning*. Portsmouth, NH: Heinemann.

Chomsky, N. A. (1965). *Aspects of the theory of syntax*. Cambridge, MA: MIT Press.

Clay, M. (2005). *Literacy lessons: Designed for individuals: Part One: Why? when? and how?* Portsmouth, NH: Heinemann.

Cross, T. G. (1977). Mothers speech adjustments: The contribution of selecterd child listener variables. In C. E. Snow & C. Ferguson (Eds.), *Talking to children: Language input and acquisition*. Cambridge, UK: Cambridge University Press.

Dale, P. S., Crain-Thoreson, C., Notari-Syverson, A., & Cole, K. (1996). Parent–child book reading as an intervention technique for young children with language delays. *Topics in Early Childhood Special Education, 16*(2), 213–235.

DeBruin-Parecki, A. (1999). *Assessing adult/child storybook reading practices* (CIERA Reports). Ann Arbor: Center for the Improvement of Early Reading Achievement, University of Michigan School of Education.

Dewey, J. (1966). *Democracy and education.* New York: Free Press.

Donoahue, Z. (2003). Science teaching and learning: Teachers and children plan together. *Networks, 6*(1). Retrieved January 24, 2009, from *http://journals.library.wisc.edu/index.php/networks.*

Drummond, M. J. (1997). *Learning to see.* Portland, ME: Stenhouse.

Franklin, U. (1996). Introduction. *Towards an ecology of knowledge.* Toronto: University of Toronto.

Gallas, K. (1995). *Talking their way into science: Hearing children's questions and theories, responding with curricula.* New York: Teachers College Press.

Gallas, K. (2003). *Imagination and literacy: A teacher's search for the heart of learning.* New York: Teachers College Press.

Galton, M., Hargreaves, L., Comber, C., & Wall, D. (1999). *Inside the primary classroom: 20 years on.* London: Routledge.

Gamberg, R., Kwak, W., Hutchings, M., & Altheim, J. (1988). *Learning and loving it: Theme studies in the classroom.* Portsmouth, NH: Heinemann.

Hall, N. (1987). *The emergence of literacy.* Portsmouth, NH: Heinemann.

Halliday, M. A. K. (1993). Towards a language-based theory of learning. *Linguistics and Education, 5,* 93–116.

Harste, J. (1994). Literacy as curricular conversations about knowledge, inquiry and morality. In M. R. Ruddell & R. B. Ruddell (Eds.), *Theoretical models and processes of reading.* Newark, DE: International Reading Association.

Hart, B., & Risley, T. R. (1999). *The social world of children learning to talk.* Baltimore: Brookes.

Hasan, R. (2002). Semiotic mediation and mental development in pluralistic societies: Some implications for tomorrow's schooling. In G. Wells & G. Claxton (Eds.), *Learning for life in the 21st century: Sociocultural perspectives on the future of education* (pp. 112–126). Oxford, UK: Blackwell.

Heath, S. B. (1983). *Ways with words.* Cambridge, UK: Cambridge University Press.

Hicks, D. (1995). Discourse, learning, and teaching. *Review of Research in Education, 21,* 49–95.

Immordino-Yang, M. H., & Damasio, A. (2007). We feel, therefore we learn: The relevance of affective and social neuroscience to education. *Mind, Brain, and Education, 1*(1), 3–10.

Lord, J. V., & Burroway, J. (1975). *The giant jam sandwich.* Boston: Houghton Mifflin.

Mercer, N. (1995). *The guided construction of knowledge–talk amongst teachers and learners.* Clevedon, UK: Multilingual Matters.

Mercer, N. (2002). Developing dialogues. In G. Wells & G. Claxton (Eds.), *Learning for life in the 21st century: Sociocultural perspectives on the future of education* (pp. 141–153). Oxford, UK: Blackwell.

Michaels, S. (1981). "Sharing time": Children's narrative styles and differential access to literacy. *Language in Society, 10,* 423–442.

Middleton, D., & Edwards, D. (Eds.). (1990). *Collective remembering.* London: Sage.

Nystrand, M. (1997). *Opening dialogue: Understanding the dynamics of language and learning in the English classroom.* New York: Teachers College Press.

Richgels, D. J., Poremba, K. J., & McGee, L. M. (1996). Kindergartners talk about print: Phonemic awareness in meaningful contexts. *Reading Teacher, 49,* 632–642.

Rommetviet, R. (1992). Outlines of a dialogically based social-cognitive approach to human cognition and communication. In A. H. Wold (Ed.), *The dialogic alternative: Toward a theory of language and mind* (pp. 9–44). Oslo: Scandinavian University Press.

Taylor, D. (1998). *Family literacy: Young children learning to read and write.* Portsmouth, NH: Heinemann.

Teale, W. H., & Sulzby, E. (Eds.). (1986). *Emergent literacy: Writing and reading.* Norwood, NJ: Ablex.

Tizard, B., & Hughes, M. (1984). *Young children learning: Talking and thinking at home and at school.* London: Fontana.

Trevarthen, C. (1979). Communication and cooperation in early infancy: A description of primary intersubjectivity. In M. Bullowa (Ed.), *Before speech: The beginning of interpersonal communication.* Cambridge, UK: Cambridge University Press.

Vygotsky, L. S. (1978). *Mind in society: The development of higher psychological processes.* Cambridge, MA: Harvard University Press.

Vygotsky, L. S. (1981). The genesis of higher mental functions. In J. V. Wertsch (Ed.), *The concept of activity in Soviet psychology* (pp. 144–188). Armonk, NY: Sharpe.

Vygotsky, L. S. (1987). Thinking and speech. In R. W. Rieber & A. S. Carton (Eds.), *The collected works of L. S. Vygotsky: Vol. 1. Problems of general psychology* (pp. 39–285). New York: Plenum Press.

Wells, G. (1985). *Language development in the pre-school years.* Cambridge, UK: Cambridge University Press.

Wells, G. (1986). *The meaning makers: Children learning language and using language to learn.* Portsmouth, NH: Heinemann.

Wells, G. (Ed.). (2001). *Action, talk, and text: Learning and teaching through inquiry.* New York: Teachers College Press.

Wells, G. (2002). Learning and teaching for understanding: The key role of collaborative knowledge building. In J. Brophy (Ed.), *Social constructivist teaching: Affordances and constraints* (pp. 1–41). Oxford, UK: Elsevier/JAI.

Wells, G., & Claxton, E. (Eds.). (2002). *Learning for life in the 21st century: Sociocultural perspectives on the future of education.* Oxford, UK: Blackwell.

Wells, J., & Hart-Hewins, L. (1990). *Real books for reading: Learning to read with children's literature.* Portsmouth, NH: Heinemann.

Wood, D., McMahon, L., & Cranstoun, Y. (1980). *Working with under fives.* London: Grant McIntyre.

CHAPTER 14

Teaching and Learning to Read

Barbara Hanna Wasik
Beth Anne Newman

In our society, learning through reading is essential for gaining access to all segments of our society, and the advantages conveyed by competent reading go to the heart of why reading is among the most important educational accomplishments every child can attain. Teaching and learning to read do not happen automatically and are more complex than they appear. As a consequence of difficulty on both sides of the teaching–learning equation, many children in our society do not achieve adequate reading skills. Over one-third of children assessed in fourth and eighth grade fail to read at grade level, and the majority of these children will face a lifetime of low academic attainment, as well as fewer social and financial accomplishments. The distressing data on the number of children who do not develop into competent readers (National Assessment of Educational Progress, 2007) have set off alarms among the ranks of educators and policymakers. This concern has contributed to the widespread attention to reading and the systemic changes that have been brought about to increase substantially the amount of time devoted to reading instruction in primary schools.

National efforts to understand and address problems with reading achievement have brought attention to many reading-related processes, including how curriculum and instruction relate to reading, and how children's characteristics interact with reading mastery. As a result we have seen the development and implementation of a variety of approaches to reading instruction with differing theoretical assumptions and pedagogical methods, each with its own advocates arguing that their approach offers solutions for helping children master reading skills. Support for alternative ways of promoting reading is a topic of intensive debate, so much so that the term "reading wars" has entered our vocabulary to describe discordant views on how children should be taught to read.

Nevertheless, we also see a consensus emerging on the specific skills that serve as the foundation for reading competency (National Early Literacy Panel, 2004; National Institute of Child Health and Human Development [NICHD], 2000; Snow, Burns, &

Griffin, 1998). One of the most significant areas of agreement on development of reading is that a foundation for literacy is laid long before school entrance, beginning in the child's home and in preschool settings. Moreover, we have made considerable progress in identifying the specific components of early literacy that, when mastered, help to ensure that children become strong readers.

In this chapter, we review the scientific knowledge on how reading proficiency is acquired during the period from ages 3 to 8. This period is often identified as most critical. However, important accomplishments also occur prior to age 3. We first summarize these very early roots of literacy. Second, we review the precursory skills developed in preschool that provide the foundation for reading in the primary grades. Third, we identify literacy skills that are considered essential for children in kindergarten to third grade (K–3). Fourth, we propose a model of early literacy skills across both preschool and the primary grades as a framework to ensure that all critical literacy skills are part of the scope of instruction for children from preschool to grade three (P–3). Fifth, we discuss classroom and child variables that influence literacy and reading skills. Finally, we present strategies that promote mastery of literacy skills, specifically, teaching strategies that promote the acquisition of literacy skills for all children.

Early Roots of Literacy

During much of the last century we expected that children would learn to read when they entered school, and we entrusted teachers with this responsibility. We now know that children's ability to learn to read has its roots in infancy and is developed throughout the preschool years. The dominant current view, sometimes labeled "emergent literacy," is that literacy comprises a range of skills that develop along a continuum that begins early in a child's life. Substantial "root work" (Sparling, 2004, p. 45) takes place prior to a child ever reading the first word as the biological, cognitive, and social preconditions surface. Fusaro and Nelson (Chapter 4, this volume) have provided a lucid account of the neurobiological development that occurs during this period and have explained how this development is related to competent reading. Although there is no consensus on the exact chronological or mental age that children must reach before they are ready to read, they must achieve developmental milestones to learn to read (Snow et al., 1998). Many factors, such as maternal health, nutrition, stress, and temperament, can affect the overall development of an infant, and in turn have a later impact on literacy (Snow et al., 1998). In the following section we focus on language acquisition and preliteracy behaviors that have particular importance for later reading.

"Phonological development," a refinement of the capacity to discriminate and interpret different sounds, is foundational and a component of emergent literacy. Phonological development begins at birth, with the infant's ability to discriminate the sound of human language. While infants are heard to babble and to make nonspeech sounds, their perceptual abilities are becoming attuned to the sounds used by speakers of their native tongue. Around 12 months of age, children typically speak their first words and demonstrate increased comprehension of words. From this point on, children's vocabulary rapidly increases at a rate of seven new words per day. Children's grammatical development also begins early in life and becomes increasingly linguistically sophisticated. Children younger than 2 years of age are sensitive to the syntax of the English language, and as they mature their sentences become longer and increasingly more complex (Snow et al., 1998)

Concurrent with the acquisition of language, the developing motor skills of young children also relate to the preliteracy behaviors associated with emergent literacy. Schickedanz (1999) describes four types of developmental accomplishments for children from birth to age 3. These include book-handling behaviors, looking and recognizing behaviors, story-reading behaviors, and picture and story comprehension. Though these four categories of developmentally appropriate behaviors for children from birth to age 3 are not exhaustive, they help us to recognize the importance of book behaviors in children's progression along the path to literacy.

Book-handling behaviors emerge late in the first year of life, when children begin purposely to grasp and manipulate objects, and books become part of their exploration. Eight- to 12-month-old infants eventually move from grabbing and mouthing a book's cover to turning the pages of the book (Snow et al., 1998). Early on, children also begin looking at and paying attention to pictures in a book by pointing or laughing at a favorite picture. As young as age 12 months, children also demonstrate story-reading behaviors through their verbal interactions with books and their increased understanding of the meaning of print. For instance, young children babble in imitation of reading and run their fingers along the words of a page. As their speech becomes more intelligible, young children also demonstrate picture and story comprehension by talking about the story or imitating an action from the book (Snow et al., 1998).

Though there has been interest in how literacy skills in the preschool years relate to later reading, examinations of the potential skills, knowledge, and attitudes that are precursors to more formal reading and writing skills have traditionally focused on the correlates of reading among preschoolers (Lonigan, 2004; Missall et al., 2008; Whitehurst & Lonigan, 1998). Little empirical research addresses the earliest signs of literacy from infancy to 3 years of age. The few studies conducted with young children have demonstrated that, along with IQ, early language skills, such as expressive vocabulary, are strongly predictive of reading (Snow et al., 1998).

One noteworthy study that does address literacy development during the very early years outlined the developmental course of literacy skills from infancy through the age of 8. The pathway to reading progressed from expressive vocabulary skills at 1 year of age, through inflectional morphology in early preschool, to phonological awareness components, such as alliteration and rhyme, at the preschool and kindergarten years, and finally to reading words before and after school begins. Because this study involved a small sample of Finnish children, applicability of the findings to English-speaking children may be limited. Nevertheless, the research suggests that reading at age 8 is related to phonological abilities at a very young age (Silvén, Poskiparta, Niemi, & Voeten, 2007).

Given the close relationship between language and literacy, we review next the home literacy environment and parent–child relationships, both of which play a very prominent role in children's early language development. The now classic work of Hart and Risley (1995) documented the importance of parent–child verbal interaction patterns and found very large differences in the language development of 3-year-olds from middle-class and low-income families. The significant differences in language and literacy skills were attributable to the tremendous differences in the families' amount and kind of talk. The quantity of words spoken to the child was a major distinction between the groups. Children from higher-income families were exposed to a much larger vocabulary than were children from families at moderate- to low-income levels. Parents from the highest income group addressed their children with utterances 2.5 times more per hour, and used 3.5 times more words in their utterances per hour compared to the families with the lowest income. Parents who talked more with their children also had many more positive and encouraging verbal interactions with their children (Hart & Risley, 1995). Though language skills are highly influenced by the quality of parent–child interaction, verbal input alone is not sufficient during these early years (Landry & Smith, 2006). Rather, the quality of speech input provided gives children the kind of rich stimulation they need to develop their language skills. Specific features of a parent's speech input, such as word expansion, questioning, and rich and varied vocabulary, significantly influence a child's language and literacy skills (Landry & Smith, 2006; Snow, 1986).

Perhaps the most important aspect of the home literacy environment is shared book reading between parent and child (Bowman, Donovan, & Burns, 2001; Sénéchal, Cornell, & Broda, 1995). Wells (1985), in examining the daily speech of 24-month-old children, found that 5% of their daily speech occurred in the context of story time. Shared book reading and exposure to print also promotes vocabulary development (Bowman et al., 2001; Sénéchal et al., 1995). Furthermore, a positive relation exists between joint reading and children's own reading performance (Hood, Conlon, & Andrews, 2008). A modest relation occurs between the frequency of parent–child reading and children's language skills, letter knowledge and phonological processing, and reading achievement (Bus, van IJzendoorn, & Pellegrini, 1995). These effects are larger for younger children, suggesting that the association between adult–child reading and children's later skills is most significant when children are developing emergent literacy skills (Hood et al., 2008).

Most studies also show, on the one hand, a consistently strong relationship between parent–child reading and children's language skills, usually measured by receptive language (Burgess, Hecht, & Lonigan, 2002; Hood et al., 2008; Sénéchal & LeFevre, 2002; Sénéchal, LeFevre, Thomas, & Daley, 1998). On the other hand, the relation between parent–child reading and preliteracy skills, such as phonological awareness and letter knowledge, are mixed (Hood et al., 2008).

Researchers have also examined the role of formal parent teaching and children's literacy development. Although this line of research is rather limited, formal letter-based activities are predictive of preschoolers' emerging literacy skills (Hood et al., 2008). In addition, children read earlier and have more advanced letter knowledge and emergent word identification skills when parents formally teach them letters and writing skills (Haney & Hill, 2004; Hood et al., 2008). Formal parent teaching is related to children's literacy and language outcomes, though this relation is mediated by word identification skills (Hood et al., 2008).

More teaching during parent–child reading, however, is not consistently associated with advanced language skills. Some evidence exists that formal teaching of letter sounds is associated with advanced vocabulary (Haney & Hill, 2004), but this relation is not found after researchers account for the unique variance due to grade level, phonological awareness, and emergent literacy and parent education (Sénéchal & LeFevre, 2002). Instead, the relation between parental teaching and vocabulary is mediated by letter–word identification (Hood et al., 2008; Sénéchal & LeFevre, 2002).

Along with home literacy practices, the emotional quality of the parent–child relationship is predictive of children's literacy skills. Mothers who are warm, responsive, and sensitive to their children during infancy are more likely to have higher-performing children in school (Dodici, Draper, & Peterson, 2003) because positive parent–child relationships offer an instructional benefit to young children (Pianta, 2004). The socioemotional quality during parent–child reading has been correlated with children's vocabulary development and subsequent reading comprehension (de Jong & Leseman, 2001). In addition, within a supportive and secure relationship, children have more opportunities to interact with print (Bus & van IJzendoorn, 1997), and are more attentive to and more likely to follow the directions of an adult with whom they have a positive relationship (Pianta, 2004). In Part III of this volume, on social and emotional development, the authors provide more detail on the relationships between positive parent–child relationships and children's literacy and language development.

In summary, we have reported in this section the strong support for the role of the home environment and positive parent–child interactions on language and early literacy development in the first 3 years of life. We turn in the next section to early literacy skills at the preschool level. These preschool skills are essential to discussions of teaching and learning, for just as the skills of children from infancy to age 3 are predictive of later performance, so do the skills of preschoolers predict performance in kindergarten and beyond.

Preschool Precursory Skills

The early roots of literacy, which include strong language development and an understanding and interest in books and print, are followed by the growth of precursor skills during the preschool years that enable the child to master reading in the primary grades. Previously, most attention to the components of reading focused on the primary grades (NICHD, 2000; Snow et al., 1998). Only more recently has the significance of the preschool period in the development of early literacy skills been recognized (Bowman et al., 2001; National Early Reading Panel, 2008; Whitehurst & Lonigan, 1998). Furthermore, a convergence of opinion has emerged relative to the preliteracy skills that are essential for children to develop during the preschool years. These preliteracy skills, based on numerous studies and conclusions of national groups, include the following: oral language (vocabulary, expressive language, and listening comprehension), concepts of print, phonological awareness, and alphabet knowledge. A more recently acknowledged essential skill for reading is content knowledge.

"Oral language" is a predictor of reading ability and encompasses a range of skills. It refers to receptive skills, such as the ability to comprehend vocabulary, along with expressive abilities in putting words together to form grammatically appropriate phrases and sentences, and combining words together in meaningfully ways (Landry & Smith, 2006). A child with "concepts of print" is skilled in the structure, function, and conventions of print. For example, a child understands that print moves from left to right, knows that print carries a message, and grasps how books are organized, including the beginning and end of a book, and the title, author, print, and pictures (Wasik, 2007b).

Young children are also beginning to understand that letters provide the code to reading as they develop phonological awareness and alphabetic knowledge. "Phonological awareness" is the knowledge that words are made of individual sounds that can be recognized, identified, and manipulated. Phonological skills include rhyming, alliteration, blending sounds into words, and segmenting words into syllables and sounds. Also, for skilled reading to develop, children need alphabetic knowledge. They must be able to recognize and identify letters of the alphabet, and develop an understanding that sounds are represented by letters, and that letters can be combined to form words. These two skills are crucial in later decoding and reading comprehension.

Even young children need content knowledge and vocabulary skills to gain meaning from text. Information about their world, from knowledge about social communities (firefighters, doctors) to science (plants and animals), influences children's ability to listen with comprehension and later to read with comprehension. Children with well-developed reading abilities are able to acquire content knowledge in an array of different domains in school and throughout their lifetime, but children who struggle to read are less likely to read than their more skilled peers; consequently, they have less exposure to content knowledge gained through books (Lonigan, 2006).

As evidence of the recognition of the preschool skills described here, these skills are listed as part of the national Early Reading First program, and have been included as the essential skills in other federally funded efforts (i.e., Even Start Family Literacy Program and Head Start; see *www.fpg.unc.edu/~literacy*). Evidence of how widely these preliteracy skills are influencing the field is seen not only in their acceptance by educators but also in the numerous curricula designed to provide materials and strategies that address these skills for young children.

One effort that is especially pertinent to this section on preschool children is the work of the National Early Literacy Panel (2008), which investigated emerging literacy abilities at the preschool level that are predictive of later reading, writing, and spelling outcomes. This large-scale effort used a meta-analysis of 300 correlational studies that related early literacy skills from birth to kindergarten to subsequent formal reading skill (e.g., decoding, reading comprehension, or spelling). To interpret a relation between variables as moderate or strong, the National Early Literacy Panel stipulated that, at a minimum, three studies were needed in which the correlation between the early literacy skill and later reading outcome was greater than .30. From a range of predictor variables, several skills consistently showed a moderate to strong relationship across separate analyses for decoding and reading comprehension. Alphabetic knowledge and phonological awareness were found to have strong relations with both decoding and reading comprehension. Concepts of print, name writing, and invented spelling all had moderate to strong association with decoding and reading comprehension. Rapid automatic naming of letters or digits and rapid automatic naming of objects and colors showed a moderate relationship with decoding and reading comprehension. Phonological short-term memory was moderately related to reading comprehension but had a weak relationship to decoding; and a global rating of oral language had a weak association with decoding and reading comprehension. In addition, understanding of the use of syntax, listening comprehension, and definitional vocabulary were better predictors of decoding and comprehension than were measures of expressive or receptive vocabulary. The strength of the relation between variables was not affected by the age at which either a predictor variable or a reading outcome was measured (National Early Literacy Panel, 2008). In another examination of preschool data, Lonigan (2006) reviewed four studies investigating the relation of oral language to code-related skills (i.e., alphabetic knowledge, print concepts, and phonological awareness) and comprehension among preschoolers. He concluded that phonological processing, especially phonological awareness, in addition to alphabetic knowledge and concepts of print, is predictive of early reading abilities when assessed in preschool and kindergarten. During preschool, code-related skills and oral language are correlated, but code-related skills have a stronger relation to decoding than do oral language skills. However, code-related skills and oral language skills both predict reading comprehension (Lonigan, 2006).

This research at the preschool level continues to support the proposition that the groundwork for learning to read begins long before a child enters kindergarten. Taken together, these findings demonstrated that phonological processing skills, such as phonological awareness and alphabet knowledge, are strong determinants of reading acquisition. These emergent skills and knowledge that children gain prior to entering kindergarten are not end points important unto themselves; rather, they serve as a critical base upon which to build reading skills.

It is helpful to recall that only recently have there been widespread calls for educators of young children to focus specifically and intentionally on early literacy skills. For many years, teaching early reading skills to children at the preschool level was frequently viewed as developmentally inappropriate and, indeed, this view remains a significant one in the field. Yet when faced with the large numbers of children who enter school without a strong foundation for learning in kindergarten and first grade, the large numbers of children who continually have difficulties in reading by third grade, and the long-term adverse outcomes for those with low reading skills, we must examine all our preliteracy theories and interventions designed to help preschool children build the foundation for later reading.

The importance of reading-related skills at the preschool level takes on urgency in light of research that shows reading-related skills remain stable from preschool to kindergarten and through elementary school (Spira, Bracken, & Fischel, 2005; Storch & Whitehurst, 2002). Children who enter school with stronger early literacy skills tend to perform better academically and are more likely to master reading skills. Yet the children who enter kindergarten without a strong foundation in these emergent literacy skills are expected to profit from the same instruction in conventional reading skills as do their more advanced peers. These children cannot benefit from the same instruction because they do not bring to the learning situation the same foundational emergent literacy skills (Lonigan, 2006). These findings have implications for educators who strive to ensure that all children learn to read. In the following section we identify the skills that have gained considerable credibility as the foundation for reading programs for kindergarten through third grade. Then we propose a model that integrates the skills identified for preschoolers with those for children in kindergarten through grade 3.

Kindergarten–Grade 3 Essential Literacy Skills

Interest in reading instruction during the time between kindergarten and third grade has been the focus of literally thousands of studies and has generated groups of individuals who believe strongly in one instructional or curricular approach over another (Dickinson & Neuman, 2006; Neuman & Dickinson, 2001; Snow et al., 1998). We have seen convergence recently in identifying the following literacy skills as essential components for learning to read: phonemic awareness, phonics, fluency, vocabulary, and compre-hension (e.g., Put Reading First; NICHD, 2000). Just as instructional strategies and curricular materials have been developed to address important early literacy skills at the preschool level, so too have numerous materials been developed to address these five skills identified for children between ages 5 and 8. These skills also make up the essen-tial focus of the national Reading First programs, as well as other national efforts that address the reading skills of children in kindergarten and the primary grades. Next, we discuss briefly these five skills and how they are related to reading.

To become a skilled reader, children must develop word recognition and decoding skills. Phonemic awareness, phonics, and fluency all play integral roles in these tasks. "Phonemic awareness," the ability to hear and manipulate phonemes, sets the stage for phonics, the process of blending together sounds and letters. Early deficits in phonemic awareness and phonics have been documented as having a cumulative adverse effect and can result in a reading disability (Lyon, 1995). Children who start school with weakness in these areas tend to fall further behind as they move through the primary grades (Con-nor, Morrison, & Slominski, 2006).

Once phonemic awareness and phonics are well established, children can recognize and pronounce words quickly and accurately, and reading becomes fluent. Fluent read-ing tends to emerge between first and third grades, when decoding skills become auto-matic for the child (Kuhn & Stahl, 2003). Fluency is important because of its positive relation with reading comprehension. Fluent readers are considered to have made the transition from learning to read to reading to learn.

Vocabulary, along with oral language, provides the groundwork for reading com-prehension (National Institute of Child Health and Human Development, Early Child Care Research Network, 2005; Whitehurst & Lonigan, 1998). A larger vocabulary makes it easier for a reader to make sense of the written word. There is also evidence that vocabulary is associated with decoding, along with strong support that vocabulary has a longitudinal and predictive role for reading comprehension, the ultimate goal of reading (Ouellette, 2006). A measure of skilled comprehension is the ability to answer not only literal questions but also inferential ones after reading a text (Cain, Oakhill, & Bryant, 2004).

The importance of mastering these skills early in one's school years cannot be over-emphasized. As noted earlier, researchers have demonstrated a cumulative reading tra-jectory, whereby children with initially better skills become increasingly better readers in comparison to peers with poorer skills (Leppänen, Niemi, Aunola, & Nurmi, 2004). Children without these skills, especially those from low-income families, are more likely to have difficulty learning to read, and, in general, their performance is below that of their peers throughout school (Entwisle & Alexander, 1988). These early-established trajectories are difficult to change. Even when poor readers make gains in reading, they are still likely to develop a negative attitude toward reading (Juel, 1988) and spend sig-nificantly less time practicing reading than do strong readers (Allington, 1994).

These two sets of skills identified for the preschool level (oral language, alpha-betic knowledge, concepts of print, and phonological awareness) and for kindergarten through third grade (vocabulary, comprehension, phonemic awareness, phonics, and fluency) have validity, in that the first set of skills is generally learned earlier, and the second set is generally learned later. However, the separation into two sets tends to make more difficult the conceptualization of ways to bridge the instructional needs of children across the early education years. The two sets tend to send an implicit message that all children will have mastered the first set prior to entering kindergarten. Yet children enter kindergarten with a dramatic range in skills, from not being able to label alphabet letters or numbers to demonstrating early reading competency. Teachers of these children are better served by viewing the entire spectrum of early literacy skills to be addressed, thus providing support for attending to the needs of children who enter without these skills. In the following section we discuss the importance of bridging this gap between preschool and early elementary school.

A Integrative Model for Early Literacy Skills across the Early Education Spectrum

Though prekindergarten is not on the same education continuum as the K–12 system, many educators have called for aligning the two systems (Reynolds, Magnuson, & Ou, 2006; Takanishi & Kauerz, 2008). In particular are the calls to integrate preschool with kindergarten through third grade. Calls for alignment frequently identify the need to align standards and to implement similar expectations for teacher training. Some educators call for alignment of instructional supports and learning opportunities. Few writers, however, have articulated the kinds of alignment that would pull together a comprehensive set of early literacy skills. If we align across this age span the essential skills to becoming competent readers, and if we align effective instructional strategies across these ages, we may realize considerable gains for children.

Though research has shown that prekindergarten programs produce positive short-term gains for young children, these positive effects sometimes diminish over time as children progress through the primary grades (Kauerz, 2006). It is reasonable to ask whether this might be attributable in part to the discrepancies in what is taught or what is omitted at each level. A connected and seamless learning experience for children ages 3–8 can help to sustain the gains children make prior to kindergarten. By bridging the experiences of preschool and elementary, the foundational skills that are first taught can be sustained and further built upon as children progress through school (Bogard & Takanishi, 2005; Kauerz, 2006).

One of the potential obstacles to providing a seamless educational experience for children ages 3–8 relates to the segmentation of the precursor skills for reading into two groups—the early literacy skills that are emphasized and taught in preschool, and those identified as critical by state standards for kindergarten through third grade. In Figure 14.1, we have placed all these early literacy skills on a continuum that shows the overlap of skills across the different age groups, and ordered them based on research across the age span. Of note, we have expanded considerably the age range of many skills. We have shown vocabulary and comprehension across the entire spectrum. Though vocabulary is generally listed as a distinct skill beginning in kindergarten, and grouped under oral language before this time, we believe it should be distinguished across the age span given the now extensive documentation of the importance of vocabulary development in young children. Also, adding comprehension in the earlier years highlights its importance in both oral language and print. Problems with comprehension are just as serious and should be identified just as rigorously in pre–K as in K–3. More focus on comprehension during the preschool years will help teachers determine whether children have difficulties in receptive language, limited vocabularies, or insufficient content knowledge

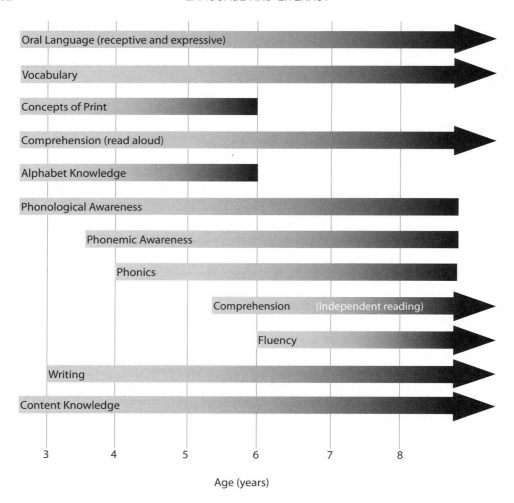

FIGURE 14.1. Language and literacy skill development.

to understand what is said, or read, to them. Remaining attentive to comprehension is also critical when addressing the needs of English language learners. We added writing. Although the benefits of adding writing skills to reading mastery are supported by research, their contribution to reading development is often overlooked (Aram & Biron, 2004; Hammill, 2004). The addition of writing is also important because as children's reading and writing skills emerge, the skills mutually reinforce each other and become progressively more organized and entwined (Dickinson & McCabe, 2001).

For kindergarten children, a distinction between the sets of early literacy skills can have unfortunate consequences because teachers may expect that children will have mastered earlier skills by the time of kindergarten, and they may not see the need to provide instruction in these foundation skills. Teachers need to remain cognizant of the earlier skills, especially alphabetic knowledge and phonological awareness because these skills are not fully mastered by many children at the time of kindergarten entrance, and this needs to be addressed before children can move forward with more complex skills development, such as phonemic awareness and phonics. By identifying the skills for P–3 as part of the overall set of literacy skills, teachers have a more integrated and comprehensive set of literacy skills to guide their instruction.

Conceiving these skills as a continuum is likely to help teachers within both the preschool and the K–3 systems because it provides an understanding of individual differences in children's skills development across this age span. Given the wide range in children's skills, with some children reading in kindergarten and some not reading until second grade or later, teachers can benefit by a comprehensive view of early reading skills and ways to differentiate instructions.

As we move toward an integration of instructional practices across the early education years, this model is an important step in creating high-quality, coordinated learning experiences for children ages 3–8. Though the literature recognizes the value of preschool education for later reading, the crossover between the literacy skills addressed in preschool programs and those in K–3 have not often been addressed. It is understandable why the field first focused on the two distinct groups of children, before beginning to consider the linkages across literacy and language skills for these children. This situation most likely exists because of the historical separation of preschool education from K–3 education and the concerns with extending downward instructional strategies and standards that might not be developmentally appropriate, and because the emphasis on the importance of skills during the preschool years for later reading is relatively recent. We are seeing, however, more attention to these skills as interest in an integrated P–3 initiative gains support.

This integrative model for early literacy skills helps to conceptualize how we can address literacy and language for children ages 3–8. It also helps educators determine the competencies of children across this set of skills, and tailor instruction for the needs of each child. This list alerts teachers at the kindergarten level and above to remain vigilant to the presence or absence of precursor skills, such as letter knowledge and phonological awareness, that are essential for children to progress to higher skills levels. During preservice education programs, teachers can benefit by developing an intensive understanding of all the emergent literacy skills. Also, from this perspective, researchers can examine the development of literacy and reading across a longer time period. In light of the continuum, curriculum designers at the kindergarten level and above may be motivated to produce materials that address the needs of children who require instruction on fundamental skills that in the past they may have been assumed to know.

Numerous variables in the classroom influence both teaching and learning. In the next section, we address the influence of variables within the classroom on children's literacy and language. As part of this presentation, we describe a second major factor for integrating and linking educational programs for P–3, namely, implementing effective teaching strategies that span this age range. We know that transition activities improve social and academic outcomes for children entering kindergarten, especially those children at risk (LoCasale-Crouch, Mashburn, Downer, & Pianta, 2008). As such, when teachers use similar teaching strategies, children have a more consistent educational experience, and there may be less need for educators to focus on transitions between the preschool and primary grades. Indeed, with information that shows transitions can be disruptive for children and families, working to reduce transitions can help children continue to progress rather than spend time and energy learning to respond to different conditions. Information shared among teachers of preschoolers and older children would also have common sets of information related to children's literacy and language.

Influences on the Teaching and Learning Process

In addition to the value in recognizing the common literacy and language skills across the P–3 span, educators also benefits by recognizing common classroom and child characteristics, and teaching characteristics that promote learning. Certainly instructional strategies and classroom environments need to vary for children of different ages (Bowman et al., 2001), but many commonalities exist for children ages 3–8. In this section, we examine both the classroom environment and child characteristics as significant contributors to children's mastery of reading. We follow this section with a set of teaching strategies that are relevant and effective across this age span.

Classroom Environment

Though we know that individual children may vary in response to the same environmental conditions and may need individualized educational plans, we also know that certain environments provide a set of strong antecedent conditions that can prompt engagement and learning on the part of children. In the chapters on social and emotional development in Part III of this handbook, authors have identified numerous ways to set up a classroom to facilitate positive and appropriate classroom behaviors, and to foster social and emotional development. Many of these same recommendations for promoting positive classroom behaviors and social and emotional development are also fundamental procedures to have in place for the development of reading skills. To begin with, classrooms should be warm and welcoming, offer spaces for groups of different sizes, include a wide range of materials appropriate for children at varying levels of achievement, provide materials that children can select on their own, and include quiet spaces for reading. Careful thought should be given to the amount of materials in the classroom and how they are arranged. Both impact children's learning. Books placed in close physical proximity to children and within their line of vision, for example, enhance children's access to books (Neuman, 1999). The proximity of certain learning centers to each other, such as the housekeeping area and a grocery story area, can enhance children's oral language as they incorporate both settings into their play.

Classrooms rules, routines, and schedules are important for creating a climate that facilitates learning. Children should be socialized into the routines and rules, and provided clear schedules. Students spend time more productively, on-task, and in engaging, academic activities when teachers take the time to organize and orient them to the instructional activities, explain the purposes of the activities, and provide the steps students can follow to complete the tasks successfully (Cameron, Connor, Morrison, & Jewkes, 2008). The influence of classroom organization on a specific literacy skill, first-grade word reading, has recently been demonstrated. Cameron and colleagues (2008) compared the word-reading skills among first-grade students in different classrooms. Students in classrooms in which teachers devoted more time to organization at the start of the school year, and decreased the amount of time in organizational activities throughout the school year, showed stronger word-reading skills at the end of the school year compared to students in less organized classrooms. Effective teachers instructed students on the objectives and steps of tasks and classroom systems. In less organized classrooms, the time devoted to organizational activities did not decline over the year. In addition, classroom organization predicted students' word-reading skills growth after controlling for language arts instruction. These results provide evidence that teachers need not only to provide and follow a schedule, implement rules, and help children to follow them, but also to explain to children the purpose and objectives of activities and daily routines (Cameron et al., 2008).

In addition to the structural variables in a classroom, teacher–child relationships and interactions are also critical for academic performance. The emotional dimensions of the relationship between teacher and child support language and literacy development. The frequency and quality of teacher–child conversations have been documented as facilitating children's learning (Dickinson, St. Pierre, & Pettengill, 2004). Children demonstrate higher engagement and greater academic competence when enrolled in emotionally supportive classrooms (Pianta, La Paro, Payne, Cox, & Bradley, 2002; Rimm-Kaufman, La Paro, Downer, & Pianta, 2005).

Hamre and Pianta (2005) demonstrated ways in which classroom structural and emotional processes can enhance a child's development by following the progress of at-risk kindergarten students who received strong instructional and emotional support in the first grade. Children were identified as being at risk based on demographic characteristics and teacher report of behavioral, attention, academic, and social problems. At-risk students who were placed in supportive first-grade classrooms had achievement scores and student–teacher relationships equal to those of their low-risk peers. At-risk students in less supportive classrooms displayed lower levels of achievement and were more likely to develop poor relationships with their teachers. The classrooms that altered the trajectory for the at-risk students were characterized as positive and well managed, with a sensitive teacher who engaged in frequent literacy instruction, gave students evaluative feedback, encouraged children to engage in conversations and expand on their ideas, and promoted a child's responsibility. These findings underscore the moderating role that classroom processes can play in children's academic and relational adjustment (Hamre & Pianta, 2005).

Child Characteristics

As we observed earlier, wide ranges exist in the literacy skills of children entering kindergarten. When the child enters preschool or kindergarten, his or her early literacy knowledge and skills at that point will be significant in predicting how well the child benefits from the classroom setting and the instruction. From considerable evidence over time, we know that among children in poverty, children of color, children with preschool hearing impairments and language impairments, and those whose parents had trouble learning to read are more likely to enter school reading at a lower level than their peers (e.g., Harlaar, Hayiou-Thomas, Dale, & Plomin, 2008; Snow et al., 1998). Lower IQ, slower processing speed, and poor working memory also place children at risk for reading difficulties (Tiu, Thompson, & Lewis, 2003).

Children whose primary language is not English are also at risk for reading difficulties. On a positive note, accumulating evidence indicates that language and reading proficiency in a child's native language are strong predictors of their ultimate English reading performance (Guglielmi, 2008; Slavin & Cheung, 2003). Of increasing concern, however, are the very large numbers of children from immigrant families whose parents have low literacy skills themselves and are therefore unable to support their children's literacy acquisition at home (García & Gonzáles, 2006). Though much work remains to be done to understand how an English language learner balances two languages while learning to read, and how they are supported at home (Gerber & Durgunoglu, 2006), researchers are providing information on effective instructional practices. For example, in Chapter 16, this volume, Amendum and Fitzgerald have described learning characteristics of English language learners that need to be considered when instructing these children. As one example of how teachers may need to individualize instruction for these children, the authors noted that Latino students need additional support to gain English phonological awareness skills early on, and that this focus during the first few months in an all-English classroom might be central to their development of more advanced literacy skills.

Behaviors related to deficits in executive functioning are also significant risk factors for reading failure (Morgan, Farkas, Tufis, & Sperling, 2008). Behavioral regulation is linked with higher levels of academic achievement (McClelland et al., 2007). In particular, attention and inhibitory control are important for early academic skills and success. Prosocial behaviors, such as compliance with the teacher requests and cooperation with peers, are key elements that influence children's success in school (Rimm-Kaufman, Pianta, & Cox, 2000).

Behavioral engagement is also a strong predictor of school success and is considered to mediate the relationship between instruction and school outcomes (Greenwood, 1996). The time that children spend reading, silently or aloud, and writing has been positively related to grades and test scores. In contrast, time spent engaging in disruptive and inattentive behaviors is negatively associated with children's academic achievement (Finn, Pannozzo, & Voelkl, 1995). A longitudinal effect has also been demonstrated; task engagement in first grade is a strong predictor of reading skill in the third grade (Morgan, Farkas, Tufis, & Sperling, 2008). Going beyond general attentional behavior, the proportion of time students are actively, successfully, and productively engaged can maximize their learning (Gettinger & Seibert, 2002).

Motivation is also correlated with literacy and reading skills, and there is evidence that this relationship may be bidirectional (Morgan & Fuchs, 2007). As noted earlier, young children who are good readers tend to read more often; therefore, they become stronger readers. Children who struggle to read, however, are less motivated to read; therefore, they do not spend time practicing their reading. This difference between strong and weak readers is important because frequent reading practice is crucial for enhancing a child's word recognition, vocabulary, fluency, reading comprehension, and content knowledge (Morgan, Fuchs, Compton, Cordray, & Fuchs, 2008).

Beyond what we have identified briefly here, an extremely large body of research documents the need for differentiation of early literacy skills development and reading instruction for many children. Consequently, educators need to be sensitive to the varying needs, prior knowledge, and skills of the young children in their classroom. Teachers are urged to modify and reshape their instructional approaches to individualize learning experiences for students. In the following section we review strategies for educators that specifically focus on ways to individualize learning for students.

Instructional Strategies across the P–3 Continuum

In this section we discuss a set of instructional strategies that has been documented as supporting children's learning in the classroom. The first four strategies include techniques related to teacher–child interactions: (1) scaffolding; (2) instructional conversations; (3) activities before, during, and after book reading; and (4) extended teaching. The following three strategies are more structural in nature and relate to how the teacher sets up classroom time: (5) instructional time, (6) grouping strategies, and (7) instructional delivery. The last two strategies include (8) screening and assessing children's performance and (9) monitoring progress over time.

Scaffolding

We have placed scaffolding first because we believe this teaching strategy embodies the most appropriate process for helping children develop into competent readers. At its most fundamental level, scaffolding calls for an adult to facilitate learning by providing the structure for a child to move from an existing skill level to a more advanced, sophisticated level. Scaffolding explicitly calls for knowledge of an individual child's current skill level and provision of the kinds of prompts, guides, and structure to help him or her move forward. This strategy is pertinent regardless of the skill one is helping the child to master. It is used in acquisition of early literacy skills when, for example, an adult may prompt a child to look at a picture on a page, touch a picture of a ball on a book page, or say the word *ball*. It is used when a child has more complex skills, providing the supports the child need to sound out parts of a word or identify the beginning, middle, and end of a story, or retell a story. We believe that scaffolding underscores all the instructional strategies we describe next in this section, and that teacher competence in scaffolding may be the most important skill for teachers to master.

Instructional Conversations

We now have considerable documentation that promotion of oral language is highly related to children's mastery of preliteracy skills. As important as this component is, research has demonstrated that children are not being exposed to high-quality or high-intensity oral language environments. Teachers do use oral language to communicate knowledge, to give directions, to engage children, to determine what children know, and to gauge comprehension. Nevertheless, a wide gap exists between documented quality teaching practices and actual classroom practices. As a result, many children do not participate in meaningful dialogue with teachers. In Figure 14.2, we provide the results from a study illustrating that for nearly three-quarters of a preschool day, teachers are not interacting with their students (Ritchie, Howes, Kraft-Sayre, & Weise, 2001; Winton & Buysse, 2005). The remaining part of the day, teachers are interacting with children, but only 8% of this time is spent in elaborated interactions. Levels of this kind cannot provide the language-rich environments needed by so many children if they are to master the foundational skills for reading. Nor does it provide the interactive teacher–child relationship known to be so important to literacy and reading outcomes. Illustrating this point, Gormley and Ruhl (2005) demonstrated a positive relation between teacher talk and children's expressive vocabulary, syntax, and storytelling.

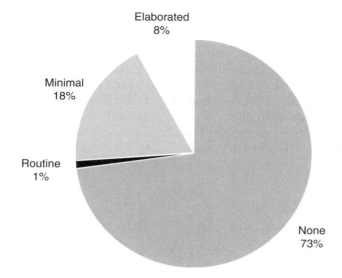

FIGURE 14.2. Percent of time observed for teacher–child interactions across the day.

Conversations before, during, and after Reading

We recommend a framework for teaching that has been used by educators for many years, namely, going beyond reading to elaborate on the books through conversations and activities with children before, during, and after reading (Wasik, 2007b). These strategies are used to increase motivation, promote comprehension, and develop advanced book concepts. As an example, before reading a book, the adult introduces the book, perhaps asking the child to look at the cover and say what the book's subject might be. Or the teacher might say, "What do you remember about this book?" While reading with a child, the teacher might encourage conversation by talking about the characters, events, and setting: "The lion is frowning. How do you think he is feeling?" or "Oh, no! What is going to happen to the mouse?" Both during and after reading, the teacher can make effective use of *Wh-* questions. An example for *The Lion and the Mouse* might include "What happened to the lion in the story?" Asking children to retell all or part of the story, providing props, or providing art or music activities that relate to the book all can enhance comprehension, build vocabulary, and increase children's motivation for reading.

Extended Teaching

To gain the most instructional time in school, children need learning opportunities throughout the day, not just during times of more formal instruction. Teachers should take advantage of every opportunity and activity throughout the day to engage children in conversations. "Extended teaching" is intentional teaching that can occur during transitions, arrival and departure, snack time, circle time, and outdoor play. These routine times during the day become part of the total instructional time. Extended teaching is similar to "teachable moments" but goes considerably beyond watching for occasions that might be excellent teaching times to determine all those occasions when one can further children's knowledge and skills. Teachers integrate lessons from the school day into unstructured learning time throughout the day, not just when special materials are being used or taught. Through teacher–child interactions, teachers first establish the kinds of positive relationships that are important for children's learning and, second, they foster language while also individualizing each child's learning during these conversations. Through these conversations, teachers can help children master vocabulary, learn about environmental print and learn content knowledge, and become more confident in speaking and using language, first in words and simple sentences, then in more sophisticated dialogue.

Grouping Strategies

Almost all educational standards for both preschool and early primary grades call for teachers to provide large-group, small-group, and individual instruction. Though such calls have come without as much evidence as we need of the match between groups of different sizes and the kinds of content that are addressed, or the individual needs of children, we know that differentiating the size of the group in many preschool classrooms is often not done. A recent time-sampling study of six state-funded prekindergarten programs illustrates that students spend little time, only 6%, in small groups. A majority of a child's time was spent in free-choice center activities, whole-group activities, and routines, with meals accounting for 14% of the time. Furthermore, even in small groups or during free play, good opportunities for one-on-one exchanges, teacher–child interactions, occurred on average less than 3% of the time (Ritchie et al., 2001; Winton & Buysse, 2005).

Use of small groups has also been shown to benefit developing readers (Denti, 2004; Purcell & Rosemary, 2008). Some experts suggest that students benefit from small groups more than from one-on-one tutoring (Foorman & Torgesen, 2001). Strong evidence indicates that instructional groups of three to five students are just as effective as one-on-one instruction. For instance, using homogeneous small groups, Juel and Minden-Cupp (2000) compared word recognition instruction among four classrooms. They found that the more time students with lower requisite skills spent in homogeneous reading groups, the more they improved. The students in classrooms with the most differentiated word recognition instruction scored highest on word recognition outcome measures overall, and the lowest performing students in that classroom outperformed the lower performing students from less differentiated instructional classrooms. In addition, intensive phonics instruction was beneficial for children with lower levels of literacy skills. Once these children were able to read independently, however, they benefited from instruction, similar to their high performing peers (Juel & Minden-Cupp, 2000).

Theoretical and practical reasons explain why whole- or large-group instructional configurations may not support the needs of a child (Powell, Burchinal, File, & Kontos, 2008). In a small-group setting, a teacher can tailor instruction to meet the individual needs of students in the group. The teacher can use the student's zone of proximal development to guide or to scaffold instruction, providing individual assistance when the student is frustrated or lacks the sufficient skills for mastery. In addition, teachers are more able to match the task with the learner and control the difficulty of materials.

Furthermore, to intensify and to individualize instruction, small-group interventions are more practical than working one-on-one with each student.

In small groups, teachers can help to facilitate a student's behavioral engagement with the task, which, as we discussed previously, is a strong predictor of success. Compared to larger groups, children are more engaged during small-group configurations. Some experts have speculated that small groups are more beneficial because the teacher can help to keep the child on-task and focused on the academic activity (Downer, Rimm-Kaufman, & Pianta, 2007). In one study, 4-year-olds were more passively engaged during large-group configurations compared to all other groupings (Powell et al., 2008). With preschool children, pairs may be an ideal way to group children. When working with children in pairs, preschool teachers are able to provide highly individualized instruction within a group size that may be more appropriate and manageable for younger children (Wasik, 2007a).

Instructional Time

Whereas small groups increase a child's engagement and promote more teacher–child interactions, increasing instructional time, another well-supported strategy, is associated with academic achievement and has been examined by numerous researchers. Harn, Linan-Thompson, and Roberts (2008) investigated whether the amount of instructional time affected the reading outcomes for struggling first-grade readers. Students in the less intensive intervention received 30 minutes of instruction for 25 weeks, whereas students in the more intensive intervention received 60 minutes of instruction for 24 weeks. Those who received more instructional time performed significantly better on all reading outcome measures, except comprehension, compared to students who received the less intensive intervention (Harn et al., 2008). Findings such as these call for arranging schedules to ensure that students are provided with sufficient opportunities throughout the day for focused learning. Many educators have recognized the importance of instructional time, as demonstrated by the move toward having longer periods of the day in grades 1 through 3 devoted to literacy activities.

Instructional Delivery

How to teach literacy and reading has been an intensely debated issue within the professional literature. Supporters of explicit instruction argue for more systematic and direct teaching, whereas those in favor of whole-language approaches support teaching children through more indirect and incidental activities. Unlike incidental learning, which "relies on seizing the moment to bring up" a topic (Phillips, Clancy-Menchetti, & Lonigan, 2008, p. 8), explicit instruction is intentional and topics are generally introduced to a child in a specific sequence. Another difference includes the goals of instruction. Whole-language approaches attempt to make children eager to read and excited about books, and to act like readers and authors, whereas direct instructional delivery focuses on teaching students the skills necessary to become skilled readers and writers (Ashby & Rayner, 2006).

Although some children may benefit from a balanced instructional approach, there is convincing evidence in favor of direct and explicit instruction, particularly for children who lack the foundational skills of reading (Foorman & Torgesen, 2001; NICHD,

2000; Venn & Jahn, 2003). We cannot assume that sparking children's interests in reading will be sufficient to make all children become skilled readers (Ashby & Rayner, 2006). Rather, to ensure that beginning reading skills are mastered and retained, many children require direct, explicit instruction and practice in areas such as phonemic awareness, letter–sound correspondence, and word blending (Casey & Howe, 2002). Children also benefit from reading connected text and practicing fluency, guided practice and explicit instruction in words that do not conform to spelling conventions, and other advanced word recognition skills (Casey & Howe, 2002).

Ongoing Assessment and Monitoring

Though instructional delivery, group size, and instructional time are all factors to consider in literacy and reading instruction, a child's entry skills and knowledge influence the effectiveness of these various instructional practices. Instead of assuming that instructional practices will be equally effective for all learners, the effectiveness of any particular instructional practice depends on skills of the student (Connor et al., 2006; Morrison & Connor, 2002). Instructional strategies that help one student may be ineffective when applied to another student with a different skills level. Thus, efforts to delineate and look for universal, quality instructional environments, though of benefit for many children, need to be balanced by determination of the needs of individual children to create individualized learning that matches students' needs.

At this time, many educational systems are moving toward an instructional approach, referred to as "response to intervention." Within this approach, teachers begin with their standard protocol and, as the class progresses, they begin to identify children who are not learning from this approach, or not learning at optimal levels. Modifications are then made for these children. We believe that a teacher beginning with a new class may start with a standard approach for all children but may also need early screening and monitoring to move quickly when children are not benefiting. Once the teacher has identified children who are not benefiting from the regular procedures, and these identifications should be made early, he or she needs to modify content or strategies for the child. When the teacher has children with more serious needs, he or she may seek input from school resource personnel on ways to meet the child's instructional needs.

To determine the appropriate instructional strategy, teachers can monitor student progress and engage in ongoing assessment. Through frequent assessments of children's progress and skills, the teacher can determine whether children need differentiated and intensified instruction. Curriculum-based measurement (CBM), originally a special education technique that has expanded to general education, is a useful tool for gathering student data to evaluate the effects of instructional programs and to adjust interventions when data show poor outcome. CBM includes short, standardized and validated tests in the basic skills of reading, spelling, math, and writing. When teachers use CBM to write data-based goals, monitor the effects of the intervention, and make adjustments accordingly, children's academic outcomes improve (Menzies, Mahdavi, & Lewis, 2008).

For younger children, normative assessments may require more flexibility and be combined with teacher reports and other data to inform decision making. Early childhood is an extremely variable period, with sporadic and highly individual growth and development. It may be difficult to apply uniform decision rules or standards to determine whether intensive instruction is needed.

In summary, to ensure that all children are gaining the literacy skills they need to become competent readers, educators need to ensure that children are being taught with materials and instruction that match their skills levels. Scaffolding techniques should be an integral part of all instructional processes. Classrooms should be rich in oral language opportunities; instructional conversations between teacher and child should take place in both formal and informal activities. The structure of the classroom day, including grouping strategies and instructional time, should facilitate children's learning. Children who enter school performing more poorly than their peers need explicit and intensive instruction. To ensure that instruction is individualized, and that children are progressing, assessments need to be an integral part of the school environment, tailored to be both developmentally appropriate and able to inform instruction.

Conclusion

In this chapter, we first illustrated early literacy for three time periods, birth to age 3, ages 3–5 (preschool), and ages 5–8 (or K–3), identifying critical environmental supports, including parent–child and teacher–child interactions. We then reviewed the sets of literacy skills most often associated with the preschool years and K–3. Next, we presented an integrated model of early literacy skills for children across the age span from 3 to 8, incorporating both sets of skills and other early literacy skills. This model provides educators, researchers, and policymakers with an expanded view of early literacy skills, one that should facilitate more individualized and integrated instruction for young children. We have also outlined strategies that build children's literacy skills to reverse the low reading levels in the primary grades and to help bring all children to a level of reading competence that ensures reading enjoyment and the ability to use reading in lifelong pursuits.

Children in our contemporary society enter both preschool and kindergarten with vastly different competencies regarding their language and early literacy skills. Our task is to provide the educational strategies and procedures that support the needs of children as they move along the path toward reading competency. No single strategy, curriculum, or approach meets the needs of every child. Our job is to find those that do work for each child.

References

Allington, R. (1994). What's special about special programs for children who find learning to read difficult? *Journal of Reading Behavior, 26*(1), 95–115.

Aram, D., & Biron, S. (2004). Joint storybook reading and joint writing interventions among low SES preschoolers: Differential contributions to early literacy. *Early Childhood Research Quarterly, 19*(4), 588–610.

Ashby, J., & Rayner, K. (2006). Literacy development: Insights from research on skilled reading. In D. Dickinson & S. B. Neuman (Eds.), *Handbook of early literacy research* (Vol. 2, pp. 52–63), New York: Guilford Press.

Bogard, K., & Takanishi, R. (2005). PK–3: An aligned and coordinated approach to education for children 3 to 8 years old. *SRCD Social Policy Report, 29*(3), 3–23.

Bowman, B. T., Donovan, M. S., & Burns, M. S. (Eds.). (2001). *Educating our preschoolers.* Washington, DC: National Academy Press.

Burgess, S. R., Hecht, S. A., & Lonigan, C. J. (2002). Relations of the home literacy environment (HLE) to the development of reading related abilities: A one year longitudinal study. *Reading Research Quarterly, 37,* 408–426.

Bus, A. G., & van IJzendoorn, M. H. (1997). Affective dimensions of mother–infant picture book reading. *Journal of School Psychology, 35*(1), 47–60.

Bus, A. G., van IJzendoorn, M. H., & Pellegrini, A. D. (1995). Joint book reading makes success in learning to read: A meta-analysis of intergenerational transmission of literacy. *Review of Educational Research, 65,* 1–21.

Cain, K., Oakhill, J., & Bryant, P. E. (2004). Children's reading comprehension ability: Concurrent prediction by working memory, verbal ability, and component skills. *Journal of Educational Psychology, 96,* 31–42.

Cameron, C., Connor, C., Morrison, F., & Jewkes, A. (2008). Effects of classroom organization on letter word reading in first grade. *Journal of School Psychology, 46,* 176–193.

Casey, A., & Howe, K. (2002). Best practices in early literacy skills. In A. Thomas & J. Grimes (Eds.), *Best practices in school psychology* (Vol. 4, pp. 721–735). Bethesda, MD: National Association of School Psychologists.

Connor, M., Morrison, F., & Slominski, L. (2006). Preschool instruction and children's emergent growth. *Journal of Educational Psychology, 98*(4), 665–689.

de Jong, P. F., & Leseman, P. P. (2001). Lasting effects of home literacy on reading achievement in school. *Journal of School Psychology, 39,* 389–414.

Denti, L. (2004). Introduction: Pointing the way: Teaching reading to struggling readers at the secondary level. *Reading and Writing Quarterly, 20*(2), 109–112.

Dickinson, D., & McCabe, A. (2001). Bringing it all together: The multiple origins, skills, and environmental supports of early literacy. *Learning Disabilities Research and Practice, 16*(4), 186–202.

Dickinson, D., St. Pierre, R., & Pettengill, J. (2004). High-quality classrooms: A key ingredient to family literacy programs' support for children's literacy. In B. H. Wasik (Ed.), *Handbook of family literacy* (pp. 137–154). Mahwah, NJ: Erlbaum.

Dickinson, D. K., & Neuman, S. (Eds.). (2006). *Handbook of early literacy research* (Vol. 2). New York: Guilford Press.

Dodici, B. J., Draper, D. C., & Peterson, C. A. (2003). Early parent–child interactions and early literacy development. *Topics in Early Childhood Special Education, 23*(3), 124–136.

Downer, J. T., Rimm-Kaufman, S. E., & Pianta, R. C. (2007). How do classroom conditions and children's risk for school problems contribute to children's behavioral engagement in learning? *School Psychology Review, 36*(3), 413–432.

Entwisle, D. R., & Alexander, K. L. (1988). Factors affecting achievement test scores and marks of black and white first graders. *Elementary School Journal, 88*(5), 449–471.

Finn, J. D., Pannozzo, G. M., & Voelkl, K. E. (1995). Disruptive and inattentive–withdrawn behavior and achievement among fourth graders. *Elementary School Journal, 95*(5), 421–434.

Foorman, B. R., & Torgesen, J. (2001). Critical elements of classroom and small-group instruction promotes reading success in all children. *Learning Disabilities Research and Practice, 16*(4), 203–212.

García, E. E., & Gonzáles, D. M. (2006, July). *Pre-K and Latinos: The foundation for America's future.* Washington, DC: Pre-K Now.

Gerber, M., & Durgunoglu, A. Y. (2006). Reading risk and intervention for young English learners: Evidence from longitudinal intervention research: Introduction to special series. *Learning Disabilities Research and Practice, 19,* 199–201.

Gettinger, M., & Seibert, J. K. (2002). Best practices in increasing learning time. In A. Thomas & J. Grimes (Eds.), *Best practices in school psychology* (Vol. 4, pp. 773–787). Bethesda, MD: National Association of School Psychologists.

Gormley, S., & Ruhl, K. (2005). Dialogic shared storybook reading: An instructional technique for use with young students in inclusive settings. *Reading and Writing Quarterly, 21*, 307–313.

Greenwood, C. R. (1996). The case for performance-based instructional models. *School Psychology Quarterly, 11*(4), 283–296.

Guglielmi, S. (2008). Native language proficiency, English literacy, academic achievement, and occupational attainment in limited-English-proficient students: A latent growth modeling perspective. *Journal of Educational Psychology, 100*(2), 322–342.

Hammill, D. D. (2004). What we know about the correlates of reading. *Exceptional Children, 70*(4), 453–468.

Hamre, B. K., & Pianta, R. C. (2005). Can instructional and emotional support in the first grade classroom make a difference for children at risk of school failure? *Child Development, 76*(5), 949–967.

Haney, M., & Hill, J. (2004). Relationship between parent teaching activities and emergent literacy in preschool children. *Early Child Development and Care, 17*, 215–228.

Hargrave, A., & Sénéchal, M. (2000). A book reading intervention with preschool children who have limited vocabulary: The benefits of regular reading and dialogic reading. *Early Childhood Research Quarterly, 15*(1), 75–90.

Harlaar, N., Hayiou-Thomas, M., Dale, P., & Plomin, R. (2008). Why do preschool language abilities correlate with later reading?: A twin study. *Journal of Speech, Language, and Hearing Research, 51*(3), 688–705.

Harn, B., Linan-Thompson, S., & Roberts, G. (2008). Intensifying instruction: Does additional instructional time make a difference for the most at-risk first graders? *Journal of Learning Disabilities, 41*(2), 115–125.

Hart, B., & Risley, T. R. (1995). *Meaningful differences in the everyday experience of young American children.* Baltimore: Brookes.

Herman, G. (1998). *The lion and the mouse.* New York: Random House.

Hood, M., Conlon, E., & Andrews, G. (2008). Preschool home literacy practices and children's literacy development: A longitudinal analysis. *Journal of Educational Psychology, 100*(2), 252–271.

Howes, C., Burchinal, M., Pianta, R., Bryant, D., Early, D., Clifford, R., et al. (2008). Ready to learn?: Children's pre-academic achievement in pre-kindergarten programs. *Early Childhood Research Quarterly, 23*, 27–50.

Juel, C. (1988). Learning to read and write: A longitudinal study of 54 children from first through fourth grades. *Journal of Educational Psychology, 80*(4), 437–447.

Juel, C., & Minden-Cupp, C. (2000). Learning to read words: Linguistic units and instructional strategies. *Reading Research Quarterly, 35*(4), 458–492.

Kauerz, K. (2006, January). *Ladders of learning: Fighting fade-out by advancing PK–3 alignment* (Issue Brief No. 2). Washington, DC: New America Foundation Education Policy Program.

Kuhn, M., & Stahl, S. (2003). Fluency: A review of developmental and remedial practices. *Journal of Educational Psychology, 95*(1), 3–21.

Landry, S. H., & Smith, K. E. (2006). Parents' support of children's language provides support for later reading competence. In R. K. Wagner, A. E. Muse, & K. R. Tannenbaum (Eds.), *Vocabulary acquisition: Implications for reading comprehension* (pp. 32–51). New York: Guilford Press.

Leppänen, U., Niemi, P., Aunola, K., & Nurmi, J. E. (2004). Development of reading skills among preschool and primary school pupils. *Reading Research Quarterly, 39*(1), 72–93.

LoCasale-Crouch, J., Mashburn, A., Downer, J., & Pianta, R. (2008). Pre-kindergarten teachers' use of transition practices and children's adjustment to kindergarten. *Childhood Research Quarterly, 23*(1), 124–139.

Lonigan, C. (2006). Development, assessment, and promotion of preliteracy skills. *Early Education and Development, 17*(1), 91–114.

Lonigan, C. J. (2004). Emergent literacy skills and family literacy. In B. H. Wasik (Ed.), *Handbook of family literacy* (pp. 57–81). Mahwah, NJ: Erlbaum.

Lyon, G. R. (1995). Toward a definition of dyslexia. *Annals of Dyslexia, 45,* 3–27.

McClelland, M. M., Cameron, C. E., Connor, C. M., Farris, C. L., Jewkes, A. M., & Morrison, F. J. (2007). Links between behavioral regulation and preschoolers' literacy, vocabulary, and math skills. *Developmental Psychology, 43*(4), 947–959.

Menzies, H., Mahdavi, J., & Lewis, J. (2008). Early intervention in reading: From research to practice. *Remedial and Special Education, 29*(2), 67–77.

Missall, K., Reschly, A., Betts, J., McConnell, S., Heistad, D., Pickart, M., et al. (2008). Examination of the predictive validity of preschool early literacy skills. *School Psychology Review, 36*(3), 433–452.

Morgan, P. L., Farkas, G., Tufis, P. A., & Sperling, R. A. (2008). Are reading and behavior problems risk factors for each other? *Journal of Learning Disabilities, 41*(5), 417–436.

Morgan, P. L., & Fuchs, D. (2007). Is there a bi-directional relationship between children's reading skills and reading motivation? *Exceptional Children, 73*(2), 165–183.

Morgan, P. L., Fuchs, D., Compton, D. L., Cordray, D. S., & Fuchs, L. S. (2008). Does early reading failure decrease children's reading motivation? *Journal of Learning Disabilities, 41*(5), 387–404.

Morrison, F., & Connor, C. (2002). Understanding schooling effects on early literacy: A working research strategy. *Journal of School Psychology, 40*(6), 493–500.

National Assessment of Educational Progress. (2007). *The nation's report card: Reading 2007* (NCES Publication No. 2007496). Washington, DC: U.S. Government Printing Office.

National Early Literacy Panel. (2008). *Developing early literacy: Report of the National Early Literacy Panel.* Washington, DC: National Institute for Literacy.

National Institute of Child Health and Human Development (NICHD). (2000). *Report of the National Reading Panel: Teaching children to read: An evidence-based assessment of the scientific research literature on reading and its implications for reading instruction* (NIH Publication No. 00-4769). Washington, DC: U.S. Government Printing Office.

National Institute of Child Health and Human Development, Early Child Care Research Network. (2005). Pathways to reading: The role of oral language in the transition to reading. *Developmental Psychology, 41*(2), 428–442.

Neuman, S. B. (1999). Books make a difference: A study of access to literacy. *Reading Research Quarterly, 34*(3), 286–311.

Neuman, S. B. & Dickinson, D. K. (Eds.). (2001). *Handbook of early literacy research.* New York: Guilford Press.

Ouellette, G. P. (2006). What's meaning got to do with it: The role of vocabulary in word reading and reading comprehension. *Journal of Educational Psychology, 98*(3), 554–566.

Phillips, B., Clancy-Menchetti, J., & Lonigan, C. (2008). Successful phonological awareness instruction with preschool children: Lessons from the classroom. *Topics in Early Childhood Special Education, 28*(1), 3–17.

Pianta, R. (2004). Relationships among children and adults and family literacy. In B. H. Wasik (Ed.), *Handbook of family literacy* (pp. 175–191). Mahwah, NJ: Erlbaum.

Pianta, R. C., La Paro, K. M., Payne, C., Cox, M. J., & Bradley, R. (2002). The relation of kindergarten classroom environment to teacher, family, and school characteristics and child outcomes. *Elementary School Journal, 102*(3), 225–238.

Powell, D., Burchinal, M., File, N., & Kontos, S. (2008). An eco-behavioral analysis of children's engagement in urban public school preschool classrooms. *Early Childhood Research Quarterly, 23*(1), 108–123.

Purcell, T., & Rosemary, C. A. (2008). Differentiating instruction in the preschool classroom: Bridging emergent literacy instruction and developmentally appropriate practice. In L. Justice & C. Vukelich (Eds.), *Achieving excellence in preschool literacy instruction* (pp. 221–241). New York: Guilford Press.

Reynolds, A. J., Magnuson, K., & Ou, S. (2006). *PK-3 education: Programs and practices that work in children's first decade.* New York: Foundation for Child Development.

Rimm-Kaufman, S. E., La Paro, K. M., Downer, J. T., & Pianta, R. C. (2005). The contribution of classroom setting and quality of instruction to children's behavior in kindergarten classrooms. *Elementary School Journal, 105*(4), 377–394.

Rimm-Kaufman, S. E., Pianta, R. C., & Cox, M. J. (2000). Teachers' judgments of problems in the transition to kindergarten. *Early Childhood Research Quarterly, 15*(2), 147–166.

Ritchie, S., Howes, C., Kraft-Sayre, M., & Weise, B. (2001) Emerging academic snapshot. Unpublished manuscript, University of California at Los Angeles. Retrieved from *www. fpg.unc.edu/~ncedl/pages/measures_0103.cfm*

Schickedanz, J. A. (1999). *Much more than the ABCs: The early stages of reading and writing.* Washington, DC: National Association for the Education of Young Children.

Sénéchal, M., Cornell, E. H., & Broda, L. S. (1995). Age-related differences in the organization of parent–infant interactions during picture-book reading. *Early Childhood Research Quarterly, 10,* 317–337.

Sénéchal, M., & LeFevre, J. (2002). Parental involvement in the development of children's reading skill: A 5-year longitudinal study. *Child Development, 73,* 445–460.

Sénéchal, M., LeFevre, J., Thomas, E. M., & Daley, K. E. (1998). Differential effects of home literacy experiences on the development of oral and written language. *Reading Research Quarterly, 33,* 96–116.

Silvén, M., Poskiparta, E., Niemi, P., & Voeten, M. (2007). Precursors of reading skill from infancy to first grade in Finnish: Continuity and change in a highly inflected language. *Journal of Educational Psychology, 99*(3), 516–531.

Slavin, R., & Cheung, A. (2003). Synthesis of research on language of reading instruction for English language learners. *Review of Educational Research, 75,* 247–284.

Snow, C., Burns, S., & Griffin, P. (Eds.). (1998). *Preventing reading difficulties in young children.* Washington, DC: National Academy Press.

Snow, C. E. (1986). Conversations with children. In P. Fletcher & M. Carman (Eds.), *Language acquisition* (2nd ed., pp. 69–89). New York: Cambridge University Press.

Sparling, J. (2004). Earliest literacy: From birth to age 3. In B. H. Wasik (Ed.), *Handbook of family literacy* (pp. 45–56). Mahwah, NJ: Erlbaum.

Spira, E. G., Bracken, S. S., & Fischel, J. E. (2005). Predicting improvement after first grade reading difficulties: The effects of oral language, emergent literacy, and behavior skills. *Developmental Psychology, 41*(1), 225–234.

Storch, S. A., & Whitehurst, G. J. (2002). Oral language and code-related precursors to reading: Evidence from a longitudinal structural model. *Developmental Psychology, 38*(6), 934–947.

Takanishi, R., & Kauerz, K. (2008). PK inclusion: Getting serious about a P–16 education system. *Phi Delta Kappan, 89,* 480–487.

Tiu, R. D., Thompson, L. A., & Lewis, B. (2003). The role of IQ in a component model for reading. *Journal of Learning Disabilities, 36*(5), 424–436.

Venn, E. E., & Jahn, M. D. (2003). *Teaching and learning in a pre-kindergarten program.* Newark, NJ: International Reading Association.

Wasik, B. H. (2007a). *Extended teaching: Growing Literacy Curriculum*. Chapel Hill, NC: Partners for Literacy.

Wasik, B. H. (2007b). *Interactive book reading: Growing literacy curriculum*. Chapel Hill, NC: Partners for Literacy.

Wells, G. (1985). *Language development in the preschool years*. New York: Cambridge University Press.

Whitehurst, G., & Lonigan, C. (1998). Child development and emergent literacy. *Child Development, 69*(3), 848–872.

Winton, P., & Buysse, V. (2005). How is the Pre K day spent? *Early Developments, 9*(1), 22–27.

CHAPTER 15

Changing Classroom Conversations

Narrowing the Gap between Potential and Reality

David K. Dickinson
Catherine Darrow
Sarah M. Ngo
Lisa A. D'Souza

Research reported in other chapters in this volume makes evident that preschool-age children have remarkable intellectual and linguistic abilities. Indeed, their capacities for learning are greater than have been recognized by many curriculum planners and preschool teachers. Regrettably, the predictable reality for most children who attend preschool programs for low-income families is that the level of intellectual and linguistic stimulation provided falls far short of optimal learning environments that might narrow the gap between children's learning potential and the benefits they derive from preschool.

In this chapter we first review research that highlights the potential power of fostering learning among young children. We then describe the reality of preschool classrooms and the extent to which they typically fail to take advantage of children's potential for learning. We then discuss two distinct projects designed to help teachers overcome these challenges. In each case we gave background information about language and literacy development to teachers. In addition, the first approach gave teachers explicit information about *what to do* as they read to children, and the second approach emphasized telling teachers *how they were doing* as they sought to change their behaviors. We close by considering what we have learned from our successes and failures.

The Power of Tapping Children's Potential for Learning

Parents have long known that children are remarkably adept at learning language, and research has demonstrated that children acquire sophisticated language skills by the time they enter kindergarten. Strong language skills are critical to children's abilities to navigate the social world and make substantial contributions to their reading abilities (Dickinson, McCabe, & Essex, 2006; Dickinson & Porche, 2009). In addition, children's conceptual understanding of the world is deeply dependent upon their language skills and ability to use language to develop concepts and to gain new information (Chouinard, 2007; Nelson, 1996). Children's emergent understanding of profound aspects of their world, such as time, personal history and identity, and number, all have been linked to the growing language competencies that children display during the years between birth and school entry. Evidence of the importance of language to other areas of cognitive and academic functioning is especially strong with respect to literacy. For example, several studies have found that children with stronger language skills at age 3 (Early Child Care Research Network, 2005; Hart & Risley, 1995; Walker, Greenwood, Hart, & Carta, 1994), age 4 (Storch & Whitehurst, 2002), and when in kindergarten (Dickinson & Porche, 2009; Spira, Bracken, & Fischel, 2005; Tabors, Roach, & Snow, 2001) demonstrate improved reading in middle elementary grades.

This increasingly heightened awareness of the role of language as a driving force of intellectual development runs counter to Piagetian views of the child as a solitary scientist, who builds concepts of the world through observation and individual experimentation. Many early childhood educators were trained to view the world through the lens of Piaget's theories, and curricula have been based on these views. However, in classrooms based on cognitive science, the quality of the conversations between teachers and children moves to center stage, along with the children's active investigations, as a major force driving intellectual development. Teacher's comments, the information they communicate verbally, their responses to children's comments and questions, and the questions they ask are all of central importance. The ability of teachers to draw children into sustained conversations that stretch children's linguistic and conceptual abilities, and to teach vocabulary that fosters conceptual growth become equally if not more important than the activities they provide.

Early intervention studies have demonstrated positive results for an increased focus on teachers' communications with students, and observational studies have found that natural variation in teachers' language use is related to differences in children's language skills. Variation among classrooms in the quality of support for language learning has been found to affect children's syntactic development (Huttenlocher, Vasilyeva, Cymerman, & Levine, 2002), vocabulary, narrative abilities, and story understanding (Dickinson, 2001; Dickinson & Porche, 2009; Dickinson & Smith, 1994). The quality of teacher–child interactions in preschool classrooms is not restricted to supporting language skills. Variation in children's experiences with teachers in classrooms also relates to growth in mathematical knowledge (Klibanoff, Levine, Huttenlocher, Vasilyeva, & Hedges, 2006), letter knowledge, decoding and phonemic awareness (Connor, Morrison, & Slominski, 2006; Tabors et al., 2001), and later reading comprehension (Dickinson & Porche, 2009). Clearly, the quality of interaction between teachers and young children is of considerable importance to children's later academic success.

The most detailed information about routine behaviors in preschool classrooms that are related to enhanced learning comes from a longitudinal study in which researchers collected information about 3- to 5-year-old children's home and classroom experiences and followed them into school (Dickinson & Tabors, 2001). Four-year-old children and their teachers were audiotaped for a full day. Analyses of these conversations have revealed features of classroom interactions associated with children's later language and literacy skills in kindergarten and grade 4, even after taking into account the children's language skills at age 3, their parents' educations and income, and the amount of literacy support children received in preschool (Dickinson & Porche, 2009). Children displayed stronger vocabulary knowledge, reading comprehension, and decoding ability as 4-year-olds when they were in classrooms with the following traits:

- During free-play times, teachers talked more with children, and these conversations included more sophisticated words (these factors were closely related; that is, more talk with teachers resulted in children's use of more interesting words).
- During free play, the amount of teacher talk with children was relatively less than the amount of child talk; more talking by children was better.
- During free-play conversations, teachers extended topics by asking children to clarify their thoughts.
- During group meeting times, teachers held children accountable for being involved by making quick, nonpunitive efforts to focus them (e.g., calling their names).
- During book reading, teachers engaged children in talk to analyze the story and discuss the meaning of words.

This set of desirable features of conversations has guided our subsequent research, some of which we describe later. We have sought to determine how common these kinds of supportive strategies are in classrooms and to increase their frequency through different means.

Researchers have documented with increasing emphasis the fact that classrooms with early language skills can foster learning, but these studies hinge on comparing variations in the quality of naturally occurring support from one classroom to the next. What this approach does not tell us is the extent to which children receive optimal support for learning and truly realize their capacities for learning. These studies may be telling us that mediocre support for learning is better than very weak support; thus, researchers may be underestimating the full extent to which classrooms might be able to support early learning. To know whether typical classrooms actually provide environments that optimize children's learning capacities, we need to look in detail at the conversations occurring in classrooms to see how often the kinds of interactions that foster learning actually take place.

The Reality of Preschool Classroom Support for Learning

Although preschool teachers can create exciting explorations of topics that fascinate children, often teachers who serve low-income children in publicly funded programs have limited education, are poorly paid and, as a result, lead lives that are stressed by the burdens of poverty. They lack the time to plan and the financial resources to supplement their classroom curricula. When these factors converge with long-standing beliefs about appropriate models of caring for children and curricula that do not provide systematic guidance for developing knowledge and skills, the result often has been classrooms lacking in intellectual vitality. Support for this claim comes from a study of 238 classrooms across six states that used the Classroom Assessment Scoring System (CLASS; Pianta, La Paro, & Hamre, 2008), a tool that rates the quality of classrooms. Researchers found that classroom quality was lower when over 60% of children were from low-income homes and the teacher had limited education (Pianta et al., 2005).

Classrooms seem to be especially weak in their support for intellectual development. Data supporting this proposition were collected between 1998 and 1999 in 150 classrooms that served low-income children. These classrooms provided data used for the norming sample for the Early Language and Literacy Classroom Observation toolkit (ELLCO; Smith & Dickinson, 2002). One tool in this toolkit is the Classroom Observation Rating Scale. It has two anchored rating scales: (1) General Classroom Environment (GCE), which describes aspects of classrooms related to organization, management and support for children's emotional well-being; and (2) Language, Literacy, and Curriculum (LLC), which describes the curriculum and support for language, literacy, and informal assessment. A score of 3 is considered evidence of basic support. On average, classrooms received a score of 2.79 on the LLC scale and 3.33 on the GCE scale. More telling was an analysis that identified classrooms as weak (i.e., below 2.50), basic (2.51–3.50), or strong (3.51 and above). On the GCE scale, only 11.3% were weak, 48.1% were basic, and 40.6% were strong. The LLC results were a mirror image, with 43.6% at the weak level, 43.6% at the basic level, and only 12.8% at the strong level. Clearly, preschool teachers tend to be better at creating emotionally supportive, well-managed classrooms than classrooms that are vibrant with learning opportunities that take full advantage of children's potential.

The quality of teacher–child exchanges is the engine that drives conceptual learning in strong preschools. Such conversations model sophisticated language and support learning of concepts and vocabulary. Unfortunately, data collected in 240 classrooms rated by CLASS revealed that ratings for Instructional Support, which includes conceptual learning and modeling of language, were barely adequate, falling between poor and average. In contrast, scores for classroom management and emotional support were on the high end of average. Once again we see evidence that teachers know how to focus on creating well-organized, pleasant classrooms but fall short when it comes to fostering learning. More fine-grained examinations of classrooms provide a more concrete depiction of what is and what is not happening when teachers and children converse. The microscopic approach reveals shortcomings in classroom discourse with striking clarity.

Observations of classrooms that serve low-income children are not encouraging. In the mid-1990s, teachers were observed in 61 Head Start classrooms for an average of 16- to 30-second intervals during free play and mealtimes (Dickinson, McCabe, & Clark-Chiarelli, 2004). These observations revealed that teachers engaged children in conversations that stayed on and developed a single topic less than 19% of the time during meals and only 14% of the time during free play. An example of an "extended topic" is a conversation about the family's new cat, a discussion of a project done earlier in the day, or talk about new clothes a child is wearing. To code something as "extended," we required that the same topic be sustained for at least 20 seconds. During the observations that we did, teachers almost never made explicit efforts to teach vocabulary (1% or less of the intervals). "Teaching" vocabulary could be as simple as the following:

CHILD: Its eyes was open.

TEACHER: Oh, its eyes were open so it was awake.

Here we see the teacher both modeling correct grammar and giving a quick lesson on the meaning of the word *awake*.

About one-fourth of the time teachers engaged children in the kind of cognitively enriching conversations that are likely to foster development of language skills associated with literacy development—talk about academic content, the meanings of words, past or future events, children's personal preferences, or problem-solving discussion (see Table 15.1) (Dickinson, St. Pierre, & Pettengill, 2004). To determine the rate of such interaction to which teachers might aspire, we looked at teachers who were at the 75th percentile in our distributions—those who were relatively strong compared to others—to determine what is possible for teachers to achieve. These teachers sustained topics of talk 22% of the time during free play and 29% of the time during meals, and the top teacher engaged in such conversations 38% of the time during centers activity and an amazing 63% of the time during meals. Vocabulary-focused talk was still rare for the teacher at the 75th percentile, but the top teacher engaged in such talk during 9% of the free-play intervals and 13% of the time during meals.

Recently we observed four Head Start teachers over 3 days in two free-play settings and again found low frequencies of high-quality conversations. During the 30 minutes, when one teacher was interacting one-on-one or with small groups, she discussed words or taught new information only five times (i.e., one utterance every 6 minutes). She engaged in extended sequences of topically related talk with a cognitive or instructional goal only four times. The other teachers displayed similar disappointing patterns of conversation (Dickinson, Darrow, & Tinubu, 2008). What is most disappointing is that these teachers had been participants in a group professional development session that focused specifically on engaging children in good conversations during free-play times.

These limitations in the intellectual depth of teacher–child conversations are neither new nor are they restricted to the United States. Over 20 years ago, Tizard and Hughes

TABLE 15.1. Conversational Content during 30-Second Intervals in Two Settings in Head Start Classrooms in the Late 1990s

	Mean	SD	Maximum	75%ile	25%ile	Minimum
Developed topic						
Free play	.14	.10	.38	.22	.06	0
Mealtime	.19	.17	.63	.29	0	0
New vocabulary						
Free play	.01	.02	.09	.03	0	0
Mealtime	.009	.03	.13	0	0	0
Cognitively enriched talk[a]						
Free play	.27	.16	.66	.36	.18	0
Mealtime	.34	.21	.80	.50	.17	0

Note. Entries are percent of intervals observed.
[a]Includes talk about language, mathematics, and general knowledge, and about future and past events, pretending, and personal preferences and feelings.

(1984) examined children in homes and classrooms, and found the richness of language in classrooms to be limited, especially for children from working-class backgrounds. In the early 1990s, researchers (Layzer, Goodson, & Moss, 1993) spent a week observing in 116 classrooms around the United States and found that in 20% of the classrooms, one-half or more of the children had no opportunities for individual attention from an adult during an entire day. A study that examined language practices in university-affiliated preschool classrooms found that when teachers and children were in close proximity (3 feet apart or less), 81% of the time teachers did not talk to children they were near (Wilcox-Herzog & Kontos, 1998).

On the one hand, these persistent findings should alert those seeking to introduce change to the fact that powerful forces are at work, resulting in the limited quality of teacher–child interactions. On the other hand, the observation that some teachers are able to provide much better support than others suggests that given the constraints of classroom life, it is possible to provide children with a much richer language learning environment than typically is found. But knowing that it is possible to provide rich opportunities to learn is only a start. The next challenge is to identify ways to help teachers come closer to optimizing the supports they provide children. Here we describe two such efforts and use our findings to consider the challenges we face and to suggest possible responses.

Can We More Fully Optimize Children's Potential?

No doubt there are many ways to increase the level of support teachers provide for children's conceptual and linguistic development. We are just beginning to understand the features of professional development that result in enduring changes in practice. Two elements that seem to be important are explicit guidance regarding desired strategies and feedback to enable teachers to know whether they are implementing the desired strategies. To date, researchers have examined interventions that provide both guidance and feedback about performance. There is some evidence that group experiences that introduce broad principles, link them to practical classroom strategies, and build onsite support have effects on practice that translate into enhanced learning (Dickinson & Brady, 2005; Dickinson & Caswell, 2007). There also is evidence of beneficial effects on teaching and learning by having onsite coaches (Wasik & Bond, 2001; Wasik, Bond, & Hindman, 2006), as well as distant coaches, who examine video and provide feedback and tips (Pianta, Mashburn, Downer, Hamre, & Justice, 2008). What researchers have not done is to see whether these ingredients of guidance and feedback may be provided in other ways that are more efficient yet still effective, and whether change can occur by emphasizing one element and not the other. In the two studies discussed, we emphasize one ingredient in particular in an effort to see whether we can support change in a more efficient manner. In both cases, other important ingredients are always active and hard to control—teachers' engagement in the intervention, and principals' and supervisors' external support for the endeavor.

The first approach examined the impact of providing explicit guidance or telling teachers <u>what to do</u>; one vehicle for communicating this information was written guidance, which some might call "scripts," to display desired behaviors while reading and discussing books. The guidance came from a curriculum that was about to be published at the time, Opening the World of Learning (OWL; Schickedanz & Dickinson, 2005).[1] The second approach focused on conversations during centers time, so it was not possible to provide detailed guidance by telling teachers how to the read and discuss a book. Instead, this intervention focused on telling teachers <u>how they were doing</u> as they sought to make clearly specified changes.

Telling Teachers What to Do: Using Curriculum to Change Practice

A long-standing approach to improving instruction and ensuring consistency is to adopt and use a good curriculum. Although it is common in elementary school, requiring use of a curriculum is relatively new in preschool, as indicated by the fact that curriculum use only became a feature of accreditation standards of the National Association for the Education of Young Children (NAEYC; 2005) in its recently revised standards. Use of a curriculum may be especially important in preschool because many states lack certification requirements for early childhood educators; therefore, many early childhood teachers do not hold college degrees (Snow, Burns, & Griffin, 1998). Also, the high attrition of teachers in many preschool programs means that desired practices may not be sustained even if they are put into place (Dickinson & Brady, 2005). Evidence supporting the assertion that use of a strong literacy-based curriculum is important comes from a study of 370 classrooms in which researchers found stronger growth associated with curriculum use (Landry, Swank, Smith, Assel, & Gunnewig, 2006). We provided in our study a limited amount of professional development, designed to give teachers some understanding of *why* we were asking them to make changes and guiding them in the use of a well-structured, detailed curriculum that instructed them about *what to do* as they read books. No coaching was supplied.

The study took place at an early childhood learning center within an elementary school. This public school serves a diverse, low-income community in a large urban area that includes a large student population of English language learners and students qualifying for special education services. The early learning center contained six classrooms and children ages 3–6 years, with a staff of one principal, six day teachers, five afternoon teachers, multiple paraprofessionals, and an administrative assistant.

We provided the preschool teachers with curriculum materials for two units from OWL (Schickedanz & Dickinson, 2005). Teachers were given 10 picture books (e.g., *Peter's Chair, Snowy Day* and *Whistle for Willie* by Ezra Jack Keats) and guidelines for how to read them, which included reading the books four times within 2 weeks using strategies that varied across the four readings. The guidelines provided teachers with before-, during-, and after-reading prompts and questions for each book. A key feature of the curriculum was that each book was to be read four times and include integrated reading, vocabulary, and comprehension learning goals for each reading. For the first and second readings of a book, guidance is conveyed by a page-by-page model script of how to define words and what questions to pose. For the third reading, the guidance identifies which words and phrases to highlight, and for the fourth reading, general guidance is given for organizing the activity.

Teachers participated in two training sessions prior to the intervention, each of which lasted about 1½ hours. One session introduced strategies for reading books in the same manner as in the curriculum using books from two of the six units. Teachers were told to read each book four times and employ strategies that varied according to how many times they had read the book. Teachers also observed Schickedanz, an author of the curriculum, model reading in the classrooms of the teachers. After this modeling, the teachers discussed with the author what they observed. Briefly, the recommended reading strategies are as follows.

Reading One: Teach Vocabulary, Support Initial Comprehension

- Provide for children an overall sense of the story.
- Encourage interest and enjoyment by reading smoothly and with some variety in pace, pitch, and volume.
- Respond briefly to appropriate questions, but do not pose questions or engage in extended back-and-forth exchanges.
- Introduce the book quickly.
- Select vocabulary and teach its meaning. Use different strategies to make the meanings of words clear, including brief definitions, pointing to pictures, and regulating tone of voice, expression, and gestures.
- Help children to understand the story by telling key pieces of information and modeling the thinking process required to understand the story.
- Ask one or two thought-provoking questions at the end.

Reading Two: Discuss and Deepen Understanding

- Engage children in reconstructing the story.
- Introduce the book quickly, encouraging children to recall key details (title, characters).
- Read the story, encouraging children to recall what is happening and explaining why characters do what they do. If children do not have answers, supply them and keep the reading moving.
- Address key vocabulary from Reading One by asking children to explain what words mean and defining words for them.
- Ask follow-up questions that encourage deeper thinking about the story.

Reading Three: Engage Children in Use of Vocabulary, Recall, and Display of Understanding

- Ask children to join you in rereading the story.
- Read the story and encourage the children to chime in, completing words and phrases that they can recall.
- Ask brief questions to prompt for key aspects of comprehension (e.g., character motivation).
- Encourage children to produce key vocabulary words taught in the first two readings. Pause and, if necessary, give hints to help children recall the words. Do not scold or force recall if children can't produce them.
- Pose one or two questions that encourage deeper thinking about the story.

Reading Four: Display Recall and Vocabulary Knowledge

- Engage children in retelling the story. When possible, given the book, give children roles of different characters to play. Help children say the words their characters said.
- When role playing is not appropriate, use strategies from Reading Three.
- Especially encourage children to use the key vocabulary.
- In a follow-up discussion, encourage deeper thinking about the story. Emphasize links between the story and children's lives.

After the two initial training sessions, teachers received curricular materials to guide their reading. On the third day, Dickinson led a session about the quality of conversations during mealtimes. This training included discussion of the value of having conversations and included video clips of a teacher having a conversation with a student during mealtime. Teachers were given a handout with guidelines for having conversations with children, and ideas about topics to help generate conversations. In two additional meetings that took place between the trainer and the teachers, the teachers shared their problems and successes in adopting recommended strategies for reading books and having mealtime conversations. During these sessions, issues such as teacher concerns about favoritism arose when mealtime conversations were addressed (e.g., "If I sit with some children, then is it fair to the others?").[2] Teachers also voiced management concerns, such as, "If I sit with the children, then it's too hard to be sure everyone gets what they need, and things might get out of hand." During book reading discussions some teachers expressed reservation about being asked to insert comments into the story; others were skeptical about the value of rereading books so often. During these sessions, teachers also received feedback in the form of comments about general patterns that the trainer observed and additional guidance for book reading and mealtime conversations. Feedback was not tailored to individual teachers.

Data

Five teachers were observed and their interactions coded using a systematic time sampling system (Dickinson & Fanelli, 2005) before and after the intervention. Interrater reliability was achieved prior to data collection (Cohen's kappa of .80 or better). After watching classroom interaction for 30 seconds, the observer stopped for 30 seconds, to record interactions seen in a previous interval. Interactions of particular interest were those found by prior work to be associated with enhanced learning (e.g., efforts to teach words, analysis of the meaning of stories, sustained topics of conversation) (Dickinson & McCabe, 2001; Dickinson & Porche, 2009; Dickinson & Smith, 1994; Hoff & Naigles, 2002). Prior to the intervention, each teacher was observed reading books on two occasions (5–13 30-second intervals, 97 total intervals), and during mealtimes once (three teachers) or twice (two teachers) (total intervals = 62). In addition, two researchers attended and recorded training sessions and interviewed all five teachers about their book reading practices. At the conclusion of the study, each teacher was again observed reading books to children, with one teacher being observed once, two teachers observed three times, and one teacher observed on five occasions (total intervals = 153). Teachers were again observed during mealtimes, with three teachers observed once, one teacher observed twice, and one teacher observed five times (total intervals = 68). In addition, teachers were again interviewed regarding their book reading. Three case study teachers were interviewed two additional times, and their participation in training sessions was examined in a review of field notes and videotapes of the sessions.

Finally, research assistants gave children ($N = 47$) pre- and posttests using the standardized Peabody Picture Vocabulary Test (PPVT; Dunn & Dunn, 1997), a measure of syntax comprehension (Huttenlocher et al., 2002) and vocabulary production. There were 20 pictures for the syntax measure. Children were shown two pictures and asked to point to the one that the research assistant described. Sentences included complex syntax (e.g., "The lamp broke because it fell off the table"). For the word production task, children were asked to guess the word the experimenter was thinking. Target words were those taught in the book, and the cues provided the proper syntactic frame and were relevant to the story. For example, the cue to elicit the word *crib* or *cradle* was "The kind of bed that a baby sleeps in is called a ... "

Results

Teachers made substantial changes in how they read and discussed books. As shown in Figure 15.1, teachers greatly reduced the time they spent either reading without discussing the book or organizing the group, and increased the frequency of discussions that engaged children in talk about the meaning of words. Evidence that teachers were using some of the specific recommended strategies was obtained by a comparison of strategies used during the first two readings, in which the curriculum asks teachers to tell or to discuss with children the information about words, characters, and plot, and the last two readings, in which children are encouraged to chime in with responses to questions addressed in prior readings. As shown in Figure 15.2, much more chiming in was noted in the latter two readings, consistent with the recommended approach. Qualitative data made clear the role of the curriculum in teachers' adoption of these strategies. One teacher was observed with the curricular materials on her lap while reading. Other teachers complained that the materials were not always provided far enough in advance to allow them sufficient time to prepare, suggesting that they, in fact, were using them. When case study teachers were interviewed, one stressed how much he had come to

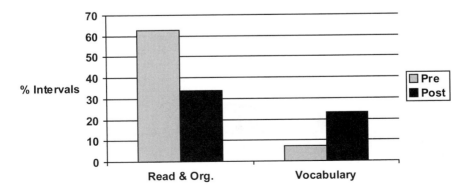

FIGURE 15.1. Changes in use of teaching strategies and reduction in noninstructional talk.

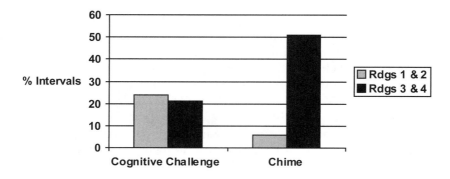

FIGURE 15.2. Differentiating strategies according to children's prior exposure to a book.

realize the value of reading books several times, and of changing how books were read across these multiple readings. He stated that he planned to continue using the recommended strategies because he believed he could see differences in his children's vocabulary knowledge and general language skills.

Implementing changes in patterns of conversation during mealtimes proved to be more challenging than making changes during book reading. One teacher, concerned about management matters, was reluctant to sit with one group for a period of time; another teacher, who had no aide during mealtimes, tended to be busy distributing food and handling behavior issues. Despite these challenges, there were substantial changes in teachers' practices after the intervention (see Figure 15.3), with half as many of the 30-second intervals that we observed being devoted to oversight and management (70 vs. 35%) and far more intervals including talk about personal events (4 vs. 28%) and discussion of cognitively enriching topics (0 vs. 18%). This shift in the content of conversations was accompanied by structural changes. At the end of the project, teachers were much more likely to stay engaged in discussions of a single topic, with sustained topic conversations increasing from 4% of the intervals at the beginning of the project to 32% at the end. These changes suggest that the adjustments we observed were the result of teachers having educational goals for mealtimes. It is not possible to prescribe how

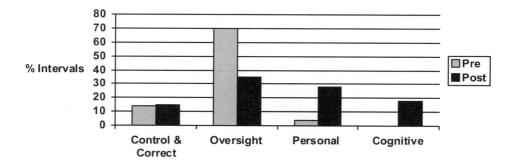

FIGURE 15.3. Changes in topics of mealtime conversations from managerial to interpersonal and instructional foci.

one should engage in a particular conversation during a meal; therefore, this increase in ability to engage in sustained-topic conversations likely indicates that teachers had internalized some understanding of the recommended instructional methods.

Data collected before the project and at the end indicate that teachers' perceptions that children were making language gains during the 2-month intervention were accurate. There were no pre- to postmeasurement changes in PPVT scores, a standardized test that is insensitive to short-term interventions, but there were significant changes in children's comprehension of complex syntax ($t = 21.59$, $p < .001$) and in their ability to produce vocabulary that was included in the stories ($t = 13.21$, $p < .001$).

Conclusion

The observational data strongly indicate that teachers were able to adopt new instructional strategies that have been found to help children use their language-learning capacities. At the beginning of the project, book reading time either involved straight reading of books or managerial talk. Books were rarely read a second time, but when they were, teachers gave no thought to making changes in how the book was presented. In effect, books were used to extend a theme by being about a current topic, but teachers did not give much thought to how the book would be read, or to specific words or ideas they could teach using the book. Our evidence suggests that *telling* teachers what to teach as they read and providing careful written curriculum-based guidance can lead to rapid and substantial changes in how they read books. Furthermore, telling teachers how to engage children during mealtimes, such as the engagement implemented in the context of this language-focused intervention, also appeared to help teachers adopt higher-level strategies.

To be optimally effective it is likely that such changes among teachers require strong leadership. In this case, the principal was an advocate for the intervention, which is why the project was possible, but was too busy to remain engaged during its delivery. This lack of sustained support limited the level of engagement of at least one, and maybe more, of the five teachers. Case studies also revealed that the impact of idiosyncratic personal factors likely impeded adoption of any intervention. One teacher found the book *Whistle for Willie* to be difficult to use because whistling in her culture is not appropriate behavior, especially indoors. Another teacher, resentful of the time and effort required, felt that she was already overworked and lacked the planning time needed to prepare.

This targeted study suggests that written guidance and a list of recommended strategies taught during a group training can help teachers dramatically change practices, and that these changes can result in enhanced learning.

Telling Teachers What They Did: Using Feedback to Foster Change

An alternative to telling teachers *what* to do using written guidance from a well-designed curriculum is to bring about change by helping teachers set goals and become aware of how they relate to children. Rather than telling teachers *what to say*, coaches might tell them *what they were saying* as they related to children. This suggestion is based on the fact that it is extremely difficult to be aware of the details of what one is saying in the midst of teaching. Language is used as a tool to accomplish things, but we tend not to attend to the tool; rather, we attend to the effect it has on the world. Prior work by Wasik and colleagues (Wasik & Bond, 2001; Wasik et al., 2006) has demonstrated that teachers can make substantial changes in teaching behaviors that result in enhanced learning, but their approach requires skilled people who are capable of delivering professional development and, of more concern, extensive onsite follow-up coaching. Whereas Wasik and her colleagues' findings are encouraging, their approach requires that skilled coaches be available to visit classrooms. Because this is not possible in many places, an alternative is to develop ways to coach teachers from a distance. Recently this has been done effectively by an intervention in which teachers were videotaped as they taught, and coaches in a distant location provided feedback on their performance (Pianta, Mashburn, et al., 2008). The distant coaching was linked to a curriculum and to the CLASS (Pianta, La Paro, et al., 2008), and the teachers had access to video models of effective practice. The current study adopted a somewhat similar but less comprehensive and technologically sophisticated method for coaching teachers who are distant from those who support changes in practice.

This intervention was delivered to three teachers of varying backgrounds and professional experience in two different schools in rural Tennessee. This professional development effort involved three teachers who varied in their level of commitment to the project. Two were experienced teachers, interested in improving, and the third was willing but stressed by life pressures (i.e., completing a Master's degree, caring for a sick husband). The principals of the two schools were informed of the project but offered no support. All teachers had taught in early childhood settings for at least 6 years. Ms. Darcy, a 25-year veteran, had extensive experience in teaching first grade; her involvement with this study was during her first year of teaching preschool. Ms. Thomas and Ms. Jefferson had taught preschool for 4 and 3 years, respectively. Ms. Darcy received Master's level training in early childhood education, whereas Ms. Thomas was completing her final semester of a Master's program at the time of the intervention. Ms. Jefferson received her Bachelor's degree and certificate in elementary and early childhood education. The children came from rural, low-income, primarily white families.

The Intervention

The trainer provided a half-day of professional development onsite in late February, similar to that provided in the first study—an overview of the importance of language and strategies for supporting language learning. Distance coaching was then provided by phone until the next half-day professional development session in late March. Coaching continued until a series of culminating discussions and reflections with each of the three teachers in early May. Researchers captured full days of video data prior to the initial training session, at the midpoint of the study, and again during the final week of school in May. All video was transcribed and coded for instructional moves, and codes were verified.

The first professional development (PROFESSIONAL DEVELOPMENT) session introduced teachers to the importance of fostering language development and explored two basic strategies: (1) increasing the length and depth of conversations and (2) broadening the variety of words used and providing needed information about word meanings. At the end of the PROFESSIONAL DEVELOPMENT session, each teacher decided which of these two goals she wanted to focus on during centers time and when working with small groups. This narrowing of focus was chosen to reduce the burden. Teachers also indicated whether they wanted to focus more on their language when interacting one-to-one with children as opposed to groups. The teachers audiotaped themselves during centers time for 1 day, and two teachers sent digital recording via e-mail, whereas the third teacher mailed the tape. These tapings lasted 5 minutes or less because longer sessions could not be sent through the school's Internet system, and were difficult to transcribe and analyze in a timely manner. After the taping was done, and before the tape was sent to the researchers at Vanderbilt, each teacher filled out a reflection form, in which she indicated how the session had gone and the extent to which she felt she had made the kinds of changes she had identified as being of interest. The purpose was to obtain the teacher's perspective, but, more importantly, to encourage her to reflect on her patterns of language use.

The tape was transcribed at Vanderbilt into a format that could be analyzed with automatic transcript analysis system, Systematic Analysis of Language Transcripts (SALT; Language Analysis Lab, 2006). It was analyzed for features, including the number of words used by the teacher and the children, then length of utterances of teachers and children, and the variety of words used. The transcript and analyses of the transcript were sent back to the teacher that included information such as the total number of words she and the child used, the length of her turns and those of the child, and the variety of different words she used. The lead investigator also read the transcript and noted issues worthy of discussion. In a phone conversation, the lead researcher and the teacher then discussed the transcriptions and the data that had been sent. They discussed the extent to which the teacher met her established goals and restated or revised goals for the next session. This cycle was repeated twice before the next PROFESSIONAL DEVELOPMENT session, and two to three times again after the second half-day of PROFESSIONAL DEVELOPMENT in late March.

Data

We studied the impact of the intervention by analyzing transcripts made from videotapes of teachers during centers and small-group times prior to, during, and near the end of the intervention. Thus, for each teacher, we transcribed and coded transcripts that gave us a glimpse of their teaching before, during, and at the end of the project in two instructional contexts. We coded for (1) intentional teaching of information and words or linking to the curriculum (TIWL); (2) asking thought-provoking questions or making statements of an inquiring nature (TPQS); and (3) extended interactions with a cognitive–enriching focus. These were teacher–child exchanges of five or more turns that remained on one topic and contained either a thought-provoking question or a connection to curriculum-based words and information (COG-EXT). The following transcription from center time in Ms. Darcy's classroom, captured at midsemester, provides examples of these instructional moves:

ADULT: Have you ever been to an aquarium [TPQS]?

BOY: Uh uh.

ADULT: Come over here and sit down beside me, and let's you and I look at this book.

ADULT: You know what an aquarium is?

ADULT: What do you think an aquarium is [TPQS]?

BOY: I don't know.

ADULT: It's kind of like a zoo for animals that live in the ocean [TIWL].

ADULT: What's that?

BOY: A shark!

ADULT: A shark.

ADULT: So this book's gonna have some sharks and things in it.

ADULT: Want to look at it with me?

ADULT: This is where I went on my spring break.

ADULT: That's a puffer fish [TIWL].

ADULT: Have you ever seen a puffer fish [COG-EXT]?

Analysis of the talk generated by these three preschool teachers provides an informative yet disappointing picture of classroom conversations directed by teachers and involving children.

Results

Each teacher was coached with respect to the goal she chose, engaging in more sustained conversations when children played a greater role, or using more varied vocabulary in a more intentional manner. Whereas Ms. Darcy and Ms. Thomas chose to work on extending their interactions, Ms. Jefferson chose vocabulary support. Our analyses of teachers' conversations revealed stylistic variation among teachers in the amount of teacher and child speech (see Tables 15.2, 15.3, and 15.4). In small-group time, a teacher-led instructional activity, Ms. Darcy varied between 114 to 135 words per minute (see Table 15.2). In contrast, Ms. Thomas ranged from 70 to 90 wpm, and Ms. Jefferson, from 51 to 78 wpm (see Tables 15.3 and 15.4, respectively). The inverse is the amount of talking done by the children, who contributed as little as 4.4 wpm (in Ms. Darcy's first session) to as many as 44 wpm (in Ms. Jefferson's first session). Between-teacher variability in the amount of speech by teachers also was evident in centers time, with Ms. Darcy again being the most voluble teacher. When confronted with the overwhelming imbalance between how much she talked as opposed to the children, Ms. Darcy was appalled and

TABLE 15.2. Patterns of Language Use in Ms. Darcy's Classroom in Two Settings at Three Points in Time

	Small group			Centers		
	Time 1 (13:00)	Time 2 (15:28)	Time 3 (12:00)	Time 1 (18:00)	Time 2 (19:42)	Time 3 (18:00)
Teacher words per minute	129.38	113.53	135.17	94.94	101.98	114.28
Teacher mean turn length	56.07	21.13	17.98	13.74	13.92	16.2
Child words per minute	4.38	16.1	20.17	19.44	25.03	17.56
Child % one-word utterances	72.41	45.56	44.12	51.11	32.26	25.69

TABLE 15.3. Patterns of Language Use in Ms. Thomas's Classroom in Two Settings at Three Points in Time

	Small group			Centers		
	Time 1 (18:22)	Time 2 (14:15)	Time 3 (20:07)	Time 1 (19:08)	Time 2 (17:02)	Time 3 (18:00)
Teacher words per minute	69.53	89.75	84.36	61.72	74.38	64.56
Teacher mean turn length	9.66	27.21	23.25	13.42	15.84	16.60
Child words per minute	23.68	6.11	9.05	17.51	16.91	8.28
Child % one-word utterances	47.89	77.55	44.59	38.38	38.2	50.0

sought to make changes. She commented that she had been about to see a laryngologist about her throat and voice, but when she saw how much she was talking, she realized that if she just talked less, then her voice would be better.

Our data suggest that in small groups Ms. Darcy was successful in curbing her rate of speaking midway through the intervention, but she did not sustain the changes. More encouraging were patterns in the children's data as they displayed increased participation, rising from 4.4 to 16.1 to 20.2 wpm in small-group activities. In contrast to her speech during small-group activities, no changes were apparent in Ms. Darcy's conversations during centers time. In addition, no systematic changes were apparent in Ms. Thomas's data; Ms. Jefferson's data revealed a dramatic decline in the amount of child contributions to the conversation between the middle and the end of the intervention. Thus, there is some indication of positive and possibly educationally meaningful change in one of the three teachers, Ms. Darcy, when talk is viewed through the microscopic lens of the SALT analyses.

A second lens for viewing change was provided by our coding of content of the conversations during centers time. The content codes revealed that the types of interactions we valued were infrequent but rates of use varied. At the start of the intervention, Ms. Jefferson was the teacher who most often sought to teach words and make connections to the curriculum (TIWL), with just below 4% of her talk devoted to such high-level connections (see Figure 15.4). In contrast, Ms. Thomas rarely made such connections (1.2% of her talk). It is somewhat encouraging that, at some point, all three teachers demonstrated increased use of this strategy. Both Ms. Darcy and Ms. Thomas showed a spike in frequency midway, followed by a drop-off at the end of the year. The decline at the final time point might have been related to the fact that final data collection

TABLE 15.4. Patterns of Language Use in Ms. Jefferson's Classroom in Two Settings at Three Points in Time

	Small group			Centers		
	Time 1 (5:42)	Time 2 (10:05)	Time 3 (9:02)	Time 1 (19:00)	Time 2 (6:14)	Time 3 (12:34)
Teacher words per minute	77.54	50.68	72.20	66.53	70.91	68.28
Teacher mean turn length	13.0	9.46	21.70	10.23	8.34	12.42
Child words per minute	44.21	30.15	10.87	29.0	39.14	22.20
Child % one-word utterances	35.0	26.76	34.48	48.0	15.15	30.23

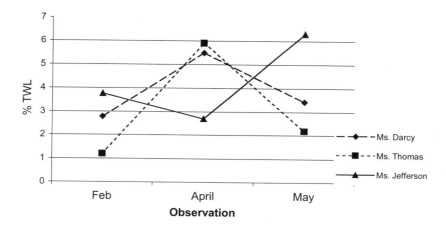

FIGURE 15.4. Frequency of efforts to teach words and information or to make connections to the curriculum during centers time in three classrooms.

occurred during the last 2 weeks of the school year, and one day of data collection was truncated by an early dismissal, brought by the danger of approaching storms capable of spawning tornadoes. Ms. Jefferson showed the largest increase from the first to the third measurement, moving from 3.77 to 6.30%.

An even less common strategy was to pose thought-provoking questions (TPQS). Initially, the teachers rarely used any statements to extend children's thinking, but at the midpoint of the intervention, over 16% of Ms. Darcy's utterances were of this type, only to decline sharply at the final observation (see Figure 15.5). This pattern mirrored her rate of talking and children's participation. As was the case in the SALT measures, the other two teachers showed no improvements in use of this strategy. A more hopeful result came from our identification of the rate of higher-level instructional turns, in which the teacher engaged children in a sustained conversation with a cognitive emphasis (COG-EXT). Teachers received this code if they produced at least five successive turns that contained thought-provoking questions, the teaching of words and informa-

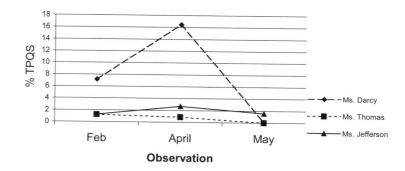

FIGURE 15.5. Frequency of efforts to ask thought-provoking questions or make instructional comments during centers time in three classrooms.

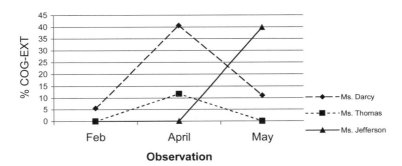

FIGURE 15.6. Frequency of extended conversation with a cognitive focus during centers time in three classrooms.

tion, and other cognitively enriched language. All teachers started quite low in this category but showed some improvement. Ms. Darcy and Ms. Thomas demonstrated improvement midway through the treatment and experienced a considerable drop-off at the end of the year (see Figure 15.6). Ms. Jefferson displayed a dramatic increase in frequency of cognitive extensions at the final stage of the intervention, with almost 40% of her conversation comprising higher-level extension of children's thinking.

Conclusion

The data collected from these three preschool teachers revealed the variability among teachers and the generally low frequency of intellectually engaging conversations in many preschool classrooms. The aim of the coaching and feedback systems in this intervention was to increase teachers' awareness of the relationship between the complexity and the intent of their talk and children's language development. Telephone conversations between the lead investigator and the teachers, and the teacher's comments during the final interview, provided evidence that Ms. Jefferson and Ms. Darcy were invested in trying to change, but Ms. Thomas was less fully invested. Quantitative analyses indicated growth for all three teachers, but, with the exception of changes in child participation noted in Ms. Darcy's room, changes in teacher's strategies were not sustained for more than one observation.

There are several possible explanations for these rather disappointing results. First, the intervention may have started too late in the year or was not sustained long enough, or the final data collection may have occurred so close to the end of the year that teachers were tired and could not sustain the changes they had displayed earlier. Second, the intervention was conducted by someone external to the system, and no individual within the system was tracking the effectiveness of the intervention. Any changes that teachers made were solely because they wanted to put forth extra effort. Third, all three teachers were learning to use a new, time-consuming curriculum, and they may have had scant energy to focus on changing the details of how they relate to children. Finally, these kinds of changes in the nuances of how one relates to children during centers time are extremely difficult to achieve. The type of feedback and coaching used in this intervention might be more effective if it were embedded within a more systemic initiative in which external personnel transcribe and analyze data, with feedback given by people internal to the system, with established relationships with teachers.

Implications for Practice

These two efforts to help teachers change how they relate to children met with varying degrees of success. The first endeavor, which attempted to alter teachers' instructional reading practices using a structured curriculum, had clear effects on teachers in two contexts and on children's learning; the second endeavor, which required teachers to set goals and presented to them information about their communication patterns, appeared to have some impact on teacher practice, but it was not clear that teachers were able to sustain the changes.

Knowledge about Language and Literacy

Prior professional development efforts have found that building teacher knowledge is related to improved instruction (Dickinson & Caswell, 2007; Taylor, Pearson, Peterson, & Rodgriguez, 2004; Wasik et al., 2006). Both of these projects provided some background information, but time spent building teachers' general knowledge was limited. In each case the background information, conveyed in roughly 2 hours of professional development time, was intimately linked to introduction of instructional strategies. Our data suggest that providing background information may be helpful, but other factors may be more powerful in determining the ultimate impact of the intervention.

Degree of Specification of Guidance

Every effective professional development intervention of which we are aware has some means to introduce teachers to effective strategies, but the specificity of guidance varies greatly. For example, a relatively nonprescriptive approach is to have teachers meet in study groups to discuss readings and to consider suggested methods (Dickinson & Caswell, 2007; Taylor et al., 2004). A moderately prescriptive approach was taken by Wasik and her colleagues (Wasik & Bond, 2001; Wasik et al., 2006), who introduced teachers to specific strategies for book reading and conversing with children. This level of specified guidance is comparable to the approach we took with teachers in our first intervention with respect to mealtime and in the entire second intervention. The most specific approach was the curriculum-based intervention we used in relation to book reading in the first study because we told teachers the kinds of strategies they should use for each reading of each book, the words on which they should focus, and the specific questions to ask. In the training, these approaches were modeled in live classroom settings.

It is noteworthy that the strongest evidence of changes in practice came with respect to book reading, the activity that was most highly specified. These changes came despite the fact that when asked to alter existing practices, some teachers were not convinced of the appropriateness of the novel methods they were asked to adopt. None of the five teachers expressed annoyance at the prescriptive nature of the materials, though some found the preparation too time consuming and believed that the number of readings of each book was excessive. Their general acceptance of the approach may partly have been because they were told that the curriculum materials only provided suggestions; they were encouraged to make the readings their own, using methods consistent with the examples given.

In both studies we also sought to get teachers to adopt new strategies in less predictable settings, mealtimes and centers. For each setting, we gave examples of the kinds of interactions they might employ. For mealtimes it was possible to provide relatively clear guidance because those conversations often were about children's past or future experiences; thus, the teachers had a limited range of strategies to employ. Also, during mealtimes there were no other competing instructional agendas. A teacher might be concerned about nutrition, manners, and behavior, but the pedagogical focus could be relatively consistently placed on engaging in effective conversations. Centers time, the focus of the second intervention, is a far more challenging context. We sought to suggest effective strategies but had only limited precision because of the complexity of centers time. During this period, teachers have managerial responsibilities and move from one setting to the next. In each setting children are engaged in different activities in distinct instructional situations. For example, helping a child with a malfunctioning computer is very different from reading a book, playing house, or building a tower. In our professional development sessions we only were able to suggest broad, general-purpose strategies, such as extending conversations, listening to and responding to children, and using varied vocabulary. These methods were illustrated in specific contexts, but teachers did not have opportunities to discuss or practice context-specific strategies. Thus, the relatively limited success in changing centers time conversations may reflect both the managerial complexity of that setting and the limited specificity of the guidance and associated practice with recommended strategies.

Feedback and Ongoing Support

Our two interventions varied in the nature of the information teachers had about their adoption of the recommended strategies. The first project included no coaching, but there were ways that teachers could get a general sense of their success in adopting recommended strategies. There were two group sessions in which teachers discussed their efforts and saw a videotape of effective practice. Although they were not given feedback by a coach regarding their success, the specificity of the curricular materials for book reading enabled teachers to know whether they were using recommended strategies. Thus, reflective teachers could have used group feedback and the written material to get a sense of their own success in adopting the recommended strategies, but they were not given individualized information to arrive at a determination of their own effectiveness.

In the second approach, teachers were given very concrete, specific feedback. We were unsure about the level of detail that they would find to be useful. Our data provided a microscopic view of interactions (e.g., spoken wpm, the ratio of new words to total words), a level of detail that we doubted would be useful to teachers. From the rich details provided by the SALT analyses, we gave teachers a few pieces of information that, we hypothesized, described aspects of their interactions that they might notice and change (amount of their talk, amount of child talk, number of sustained conversations, explicit efforts to teach words). We also sent the teachers transcripts of the conversations they had recorded and sent to us. In our coaching conversations by phone, teachers tended to focus on the transcripts rather than on the quantitative data. They varied in their ability to engage in reflective analyses of their teaching. All wanted to re-create the context of the day and had problems thinking in detail about the specific interactions represented by the transcripts. Ms. Jefferson and Ms. Darcy did manage to engage in some focused reflection on the interactions captured by the audiotaping, but Ms. Thomas was primarily interested in knowing "how she did" and offered few thoughts of her own. In the final interview, the first two teachers specifically noted that they especially liked seeing the transcripts, and said that they would like to have that kind of information in the future.

We conclude that those providing interventions need to identify different ways to enable teachers to know "how they are doing." We anticipate that teachers might be helped to reflect on their performance if they are provided with clearly delineated criteria and concrete data about exactly what they did in the form of transcripts or videotapes of themselves. Such strategies have recently been employed in successful interventions that use coaching and provide feedback on adults' (teachers or parents) effectiveness in adopting recommended strategies (Landry, Smith, & Swank, 2006; Pianta, Mashburn, et al., 2008).

Teacher Motivation

Our interventions varied in the extent to which teachers viewed the project as important to their program and its leadership. In the first effort, the principal was present at initial meetings, and was in the building and aware of teachers' efforts. Teachers in that case varied in their enthusiasm, but all showed significant change. In contrast, the second effort was not connected to any broader initiatives, and no one at a supervisory level within the school district was explicitly supportive of teachers' efforts. The limited institutional support might have been partially responsible for Ms. Thomas's low level of engagement in the effort. Ms. Darcy and Ms. Jefferson were energized by the opportunity to have support for professional growth, but Ms. Thomas had limited time and energy to devote to it as she completed a Master's program and cared for an ill husband. Thus, motivational factors are important and are the result of intrinsic factors, such as a desire for professional development and enthusiasm for enhancing children's learning opportunities as well as extrinsic factors, such as supervisor support for the effort.

Our findings suggest that changes in practice are likely to vary by instructional context, with changes most quickly accomplished and possibly best sustained for instructional contexts in which a written curriculum provides guidance (e.g., book reading). Teachers are likely to understand and implement changes in less well-defined settings (e.g., centers time) when provided general guiding principles in the context of professional development, but changing practices in such contexts may be a more difficult proposition. Models of effective practice and specific feedback about performance also are likely to be beneficial. These conclusions are consistent with results of our studies and the findings of a large professional development study that examined changes in practice that resulted when teachers could see models of effective practice and were provided feedback from coaches (Pianta, Mashburn, et al., 2008).

Further evidence of the potential value of providing all three key elements—a strong written curriculum, professional development and ongoing, onsite coaching—comes from a secondary analysis of data from eight Early Reading First programs that used OWL (Wilson, Morse, & Dickinson, 2008). Analysis of results of multiple years of data for over 2,000 children revealed growth of language skills relative to national norms, with the amount of growth increasing across the years. In the first year, when programs made limited use of the curriculum, the effect of the programs on receptive vocabulary was 0.16, but in years 2–4 it was 0.35–0.36. In the four programs that used assessments other than the PPVT (e.g., expressive vocabulary, comprehension), stronger changes in effect sizes were observed (year 1 = 0.48, year 2 = 0.74, year 3 = 0.93). These increasing effect sizes suggest that programs consistently increased the fidelity of implementation, and that these improvements resulted in improved learning. The potential importance of a written curriculum to ensure consistent effects is indicated by the consistency of results across all eight programs. However, it may also be that this consistency of effects reflects the influence of the high levels of coaching support available in all sites.

We conclude by noting that this volume gives testimony to the enormous amount of research that has gone into understanding children's capacities and in developing approaches that place them in richly supportive learning settings. Far less work has gone into determining how we can help teachers in standard classrooms begin to adopt methods that maximize children's capacity to learn. Our experience suggests that the most difficult challenges are related to helping teachers learn to pose thought-provoking questions and to build on children's chance observations by asking questions and making comments that lead to deeper, sustained thinking about complex issues and concepts. These profound challenges can be addressed only through interventions that combine curriculum with professional development and coaching that includes specific feedback about specific teaching behaviors. Furthermore, we anticipate that these ingredients must be accompanied by strong and sustained institutional support.

Acknowledgments

The research reported in this chapter was supported by university awards from the Lynch School of Education at Boston College and the Peabody College of Education at Vanderbilt University. We thank the teachers in Boston and Tennessee for their participation in these efforts. This chapter was written with support to David K. Dickinson and Catherine Darrow from the Institute of Education Sciences, U.S. Department of Education (Grant No. 4-26-130-2011).

Notes

1. Dickinson is a coauthor of OWL; therefore, he has a financial interest in it.
2. These are not verbatim quotations; rather, they are compiled statements reflecting concerns that were voiced.

References

Chouinard, M. M. (2007). Children's questions: A mechanism for cognitive development. *Monographs of the Society for Research in Child Development, 72*(1).

Connor, C. M., Morrison, F. J., & Slominski, L. (2006). Preschool instruction and children's emergent literacy growth. *Journal of Educational Psychology, 98*(4), 665–689.

Dickinson, D. K. (2001). Putting the pieces together: The impact of preschool on children's language and literacy development in kindergarten. In D. K. Dickinson & P. O. Tabors

(Eds.), *Beginning literacy with language: Young children learning at home and school* (pp. 257–287). Baltimore: Brookes.

Dickinson, D. K., & Brady, J. (2005). Toward effective support for language and literacy through professional development. In M. Zaslow & I. Martinez-Beck (Eds.), *Critical issues in early childhood professional development* (pp. 141–170). Baltimore: Brookes.

Dickinson, D. K., & Caswell, L. (2007). Building support for language and early literacy in preschool classrooms through in-service professional development: Effects of the Literacy Environment Enrichment Program (LEEP). *Early Childhood Research Quarterly, 22,* 243–260.

Dickinson, D. K., Darrow, C. L., & Tinubu, T. A. (2008). Conversations in preschool: Toward cognitively enriching and responsive discourse. *Early Education and Development, 19*(3), 396–429.

Dickinson, D. K., & Fanelli, S. (2005). *Teacher–child discourse analysis (TCDA).* Unpublished manuscript, Newton, MA.

Dickinson, D. K., & McCabe, A. (2001). Bringing it all together: The multiple origins, skills and environmental supports of early literacy. *Learning Disabilities Research and Practice, 16*(4), 186–202.

Dickinson, D. K., McCabe, A., & Clark-Chiarelli, N. (2004). Preschool-based prevention of reading disability: Realities versus possibilities. In C. A. Stone, E. R. Silliman, B. J. Ehren, & K. Apel (Eds.), *Handbook of language and literacy: Development and disorders* (pp. 209–227). New York: Guilford Press.

Dickinson, D. K., McCabe, A., & Essex, M. J. (2006). A window of opportunity we must open to all: The case for preschool with high-quality support for language and literacy. In D. K. Dickinson & S. B. Neuman (Eds.), *Handbook of early literacy research* (Vol. II, pp. 11–28). New York: Guilford Press.

Dickinson, D. K., & Porche, M. (2009). *The relationship between teacher–child conversations with low-income four-year olds and grade four language and literacy development.* Manuscript submitted for publication.

Dickinson, D. K., & Smith, M. W. (1994). Long-term effects of preschool teachers' book readings on low-income children's vocabulary and story comprehension. *Reading Research Quarterly, 29*(2), 104–122.

Dickinson, D. K., St. Pierre, R., & Pettengill, J. (2004). High quality classrooms: A key ingredient to family literacy programs. In B. Wasik (Ed.), *Handbook of family literacy* (pp. 137–154). Mahwah, NJ: Erlbaum.

Dickinson, D. K., & Tabors, P. O. (Eds.). (2001). *Beginning literacy with language: Young children learning at home and school.* Baltimore: Brookes.

Dunn, L. M., & Dunn, L. M. (1997). *Peabody Picture Vocabulary Test—Third Edition.* Circle Pines, MN: American Guidance Service.

Early Child Care Research Network. (2005). Pathways to reading: The role of oral language in the transition to reading. *Developmental Psychology, 41,* 428–442.

Hart, B., & Risley, T. R. (1995). *Meaningful differences in the everyday lives of American children.* Baltimore: Brookes.

Hoff, E., & Naigles, L. (2002). How children use input in acquiring a lexicon. *Child Development, 73,* 418–433.

Huttenlocher, J., Vasilyeva, M., Cymerman, E., & Levine, S. (2002). Language input and child syntax. *Cognitive Psychology, 45*(3), 337–374.

Klibanoff, R. S., Levine, S. C., Huttenlocher, J., Vasilyeva, M., & Hedges, L. V. (2006). Preschool children's mathematical knowledge: The effect of teacher "math talk" *Developmental Psychology, 42*(1), 59–69.

Landry, S. H., Smith, K. E., & Swank, P. R. (2006). Responsive parenting: Establishing early foundations for social, communication, and independent problem solving skills. *Developmental Psychology, 42*(4), 627–642.

Landry, S. H., Swank, P. R., Smith, K. E., Assel, M. A., & Gunnewig, S. B. (2006). Enhancing early literacy skills for preschool children: Bringing a professional development model to scale. *Journal of Learning Disabilities, 39*(4), 306–324.

Language Analysis Lab. (2006). *Systematic Analysis of Language Transcripts* (Windows Research Version 9). Madison: Waisman Research Center, University of Wisconsin.

Layzer, J. I., Goodson, B. D., & Moss, M. (1993). *Life in preschool* (Vol. 1). Cambridge, MA: Abt Associated.

National Association for the Education of Young Children. (2005). *New NAEYC Early Childhood Program Standards.* Retrieved March 9, 2008, from *naeyc.org/academy/standards*

Nelson, K. (1996). *Language in cognitive development: The emergence of the mediated mind.* New York: Cambridge University Press.

Pianta, R., Howes, C., Burchinal, M., Bryant, D., Clifford, R., Early, D., et al. (2005). Features of pre-kindergarten programs, classrooms, and teachers: Do they predict observed classroom quality and child–teacher interactions? *Applied Developmental Science, 9*(3), 144–159.

Pianta, R. C., La Paro, K. M., & Hamre, B. K. (2008). *Classroom Assessment Scoring System™: Manual K–3.* Baltimore: Brookes.

Pianta, R. C., Mashburn, A. J., Downer, J. T., Hamre, B. K., & Justice, L. (2008). Effects of Web-mediated professional development resources on teacher–child interactions in pre-kindergarten classrooms. *Early Childhood Research Quarterly, 23*(4), 431–451.

Schickedanz, J., & Dickinson, D. K. (2005). *Opening the World of Learning: A comprehensive literacy program.* Parsippany, NJ: Pearson Early Learning.

Smith, M. W., & Dickinson, D. K. (2002). *Early language and literacy classroom observation (ELLCO) toolkit, research edition.* Baltimore: Brookes.

Snow, C. E., Burns, M. S., & Griffin, P. (Eds.). (1998). *Preventing reading difficulties in young children.* Washington, DC: National Research Council, National Academy Press.

Spira, E. G., Bracken, S. S., & Fischel, J. E. (2005). Predicting improvement after first-grade reading difficulties: The effects of oral language, emergent literacy, and behavior skills. *Developmental Psychology, 41*(1), 225–234.

Storch, S. A., & Whitehurst, G. J. (2002). Oral language and code-related precursors to reading: Evidence from a longitudinal structural model. *Developmental Psychology, 38,* 934–947.

Tabors, P. O., Roach, K. A., & Snow, C. E. (2001). Home language and literacy environment: Final results. In D. K. Dickinson & P. O. Tabors (Eds.), *Beginning literacy with language: Young children learning at home and school* (pp. 111–138). Baltimore: Brookes.

Taylor, B. M., Pearson, P. D., Peterson, D. S., & Rodgriguez, M. C. (2004). The CIERA school change framework: An evidence-based approach to professional development and school reading improvement. *Reading Research Quarterly, 40*(1), 40–69.

Tizard, B., & Hughes, M. (1984). *Young children learning.* Cambridge, MA: Harvard University Press.

Walker, D., Greenwood, C., Hart, B., & Carta, J. (1994). Prediction of school outcomes based on early language production and socioeconomic factors. *Child Development, 65,* 606–621.

Wasik, B. A., & Bond, M. A. (2001). Beyond the pages of a book: Interactive book reading and language development in preschool classrooms. *Journal of Educational Psychology, 93*(2), 243–250.

Wasik, B. A., Bond, M. A., & Hindman, A. (2006). The effects of a language and literacy intervention on Head Start children and teachers. *Journal of Educational Psychology, 98*(1), 63–74.

Wilcox-Herzog, A., & Kontos, S. (1998). The nature of teacher talk in early childhood classrooms and its relationship to children's play with objects and peers. *Journal of Genetic Psychology, 159*(1), 30–44.

Wilson, S. J., Morse, A. B., & Dickinson, D. K. (2008). *Examining the effectiveness of OWL as used in ERF projects: Report of project results.* Nashville, TN: Center for Evaluation Research and Methodology, Vanderbilt University.

CHAPTER 16

Young Latino Children's English Reading Development

Insights for Classroom Teachers

Steve Amendum
Jill Fitzgerald

What should we do? Thirty-five percent of the students in our district are multilingual learners. Most of our teachers have received very little formal training or professional development on working with multilingual learners. Each of five elementary schools in our district has one bilingual Spanish–English kindergarten classroom, but no other bilingual education program exists. Our school has an English-as-a-second-language (ESL) classroom, but the ESL teacher is only able to see students once a week, in a group, for about 50 minutes each time. Some of our English language learners (ELLs)[1] have had no prior schooling, whereas others have excelled in their homeland schools, and read and write well in their native language. How can we teach so that our ELLs succeed in school? How can we help them to read and write well? Can we, or even should we, start reading and writing instruction right away? Can research help us to know what to do?

Do these issues sound familiar? For educators, such questions are common across the United States, as well as in other countries around the world. Often literacy instruction is at the heart of ELLs' learning, in part because reading and writing can be instruments of content-area academic success. Our purpose in this chapter is to offer research-based insights into ELLs' cognitive English reading development and to encourage teachers to work in ways that unleash the ELL's full English reading potential. The chapter is organized into four parts. First, we present the nationwide backdrop for young Latino children's English reading, and we consider issues related to their early reading development. Specifically, we examine the following issues: the potential role of orality in Latino children's English reading development; what their early English reading trajectory might hypothetically be; and the importance of learning more about that trajectory.

Second, we report a study (Fitzgerald, Amendum, & Guthrie, 2008) of young Latino students' English reading growth that demonstrates cognitive development in reading in all-English settings. Third, we draw conclusions and discuss implications of the study findings, especially with regard to classroom reading instruction. Finally, we provide guiding principles and illustrative classroom practices that emanate from the study findings.

As a preface to our chapter, we want to say that although the classroom context of our study is English-only settings, and although we reference ELLs throughout the chapter, we fully endorse the potential benefits provided to ELLs through bilingual education and bilingual reading.

A Nationwide Backdrop and Issues Related to Young Latino Students' Early English Reading Development

Nationwide Backdrop

The numbers of ELLs attending schools in the United States have increased dramatically over the years. For instance, across the United States between the 1990–1991 and 2000–2001 school years, the percentage of ELLs increased by 105% (Kindler, 2002). In 2000, Latino students represented 17% of nationwide K–12 enrollments, and Latino school enrollment may increase by 25% by the year 2025 (ERIC Clearinghouse on Urban Education, 2001). Forty-three percent of all teachers have at least one ELL in their class (Zehler et al., 2003). Notably, most ELLs spend all or most of their school day in regular, all-English classrooms (General Accounting Office, 2001; Thomas & Collier, 2002).

Reading education for ELLs has recently gained prominent attention (August & Shanahan, 2006; Slavin & Cheung, 2005). Evidence suggests a significant gap between ELLs' reading achievement and that of their monolingual native-English-speaking peers. For example, on the most recent National Assessment of Educational Progress (NAEP) reading assessments Latino students' average performance was substantially lower than that of Caucasians of European heritage (U.S. Department of Education National Center for Education Statistics, 2005).

The Potential Role of Orality in Young Latino Children's English Reading

Learning to read in a new language introduces a range of complications and challenges for both students and teachers. Although practitioners and the general public tend to believe that oral language factors play significant roles in learning to read in English, the exact role of oral native and/or oral English proficiency in English-reading growth is not completely clear (Lesaux & Geva, 2006). To our knowledge, no comprehensive formal theories guide understandings about relationships connecting oral native and/ or oral English language abilities and English reading (cf. Cummins, 1986; Fitzgerald, 2003; Mitchell & Myles, 2004). At the same time, some limited evidence suggests that global English language oral proficiency is not related to young ELLs' English reading achievement (Durgunoglu, Nagy, & Hancin-Bhatt, 1993; Quiroga, Lemos-Bitton, Mostafapour, Abbott, & Berninger, 2002). However, most second-language theorists suggest that oral proficiency takes on increasing importance as children become more expert in lower-level sound processes and word recognition, and as they begin to read at higher reading levels (Cummins, 1986; Nation, 2001; Proctor, Carlo, August, & Snow, 2005). In particular, meaning vocabulary knowledge in the new language is generally considered to be of critical importance for ELLs' English reading comprehension (Proctor et al., 2005).

The picture that arises from collective current wisdom on the relationship of orality in new or native language to ELLs' English reading is a complicated one. At the lower reading levels, ability to recognize English words in reading may supercede English oral proficiency in importance, and as English reading level increases, the importance of specific oral language factors may tend to grow (Proctor et al., 2005).

Hypothetically, What Might Latino Children's English Reading Trajectory Look Like?

Is there a theory that leads to inferences about what Latino children's English reading development might be? Again, we know of no formal theory about young, beginning ELLs' English reading to guide us (Fitzgerald, 2003; Mitchell & Myles, 2004). Lacking such a theory, it might be useful though to examine monolingual early reading developmental theory. Chall (1996) and Clay (2001) have elaborated similar, and widely accepted, outlooks on early monolingual reading development. Fitzgerald and Shanahan (2000) also presented a developmental sequence for both reading and writing, building on Chall and Clay's work.

A key finding from research on the development of reading is that critical features of learning about reading vary from one phase to another (Adams, 1990). The earliest phase of learning to read has been called Literacy Roots (Chall, 1996; Fitzgerald & Shanahan, 2000). One of the most critical kinds of knowledge developed during Literacy Roots is phonological awareness, or the ability to hear and manipulate words as words, chunks or parts of words, and sounds in words (Adams, 1990; Siegel, 2003; Tumner & Nesdale, 1985). Phonological awareness has been established as having paramount importance for progress in early monolingual reading (Adams, 1990; Siegel, 2003).

A second period of monolingual early reading development is called Initial Reading by Chall (1996). Two of Clay's (2001) progressions in acts of processing appear most prominent in the Initial Reading period—"proficient beginners negotiating more transitions," and "proficient readers/writers using subsystems to support each other." Both Chall and Clay refer to the complex interplay of literacy subprocesses or subsystems in early reading. Two critical features of the Initial Reading phase are expansion of sound awareness (phonological awareness) and an increased focus on letters, and associating letters with parts of spoken words. During Initial Reading children are acquiring grapheme awareness and learning orthographic and morphological patterns in words. They begin to develop strategies for selecting textual cues to read words (Clay, 2002; Schwartz, 1997).

A third phase of beginning reading is Confirmation, Fluency, and Ungluing from Print (Chall, 1996; Fitzgerald & Shanahan, 2000). During the third phase, the learner consolidates what he or she learned earlier, and aspects of reading become more fluent or automatic. The critical ability in the Confirmation and Fluency phase is procedural—smoothly integrating strategies and processes. With smooth integration, what the learner knows becomes internalized and less intentional.

Another way to hypothesize what young Latino students' English reading trajectory might look like is to consider the early reading trajectory for native Spanish speakers reading in Spanish. Perhaps Latino children's English reading development might parallel native Spanish reading development. But here, again, we know of no comprehensive theory for learning to read in Spanish. However, limited evidence suggests that at least some of the early reading processes are the same in Spanish and in English reading. For instance, we know that for English monolinguals, phonological processing ability is a significant predictor of later reading success. The same relationship has been found for native Spanish speakers reading in Spanish (Bravo-Valdivieso, 1995; Carillo, 1994; Defior & Tudela, 1994; González & García, 1995; González & Valle, 2000). Similarly, word recognition processes in Spanish are significant predictors of later reading success, just as they are for monolingual native-English-speaking children (Bravo-Valdivieso, 1995; Lindsey, Manis, & Bailey, 2003; Signorini, 1997). Finally, some evidence suggests strong positive correlations between phonological awareness abilities in Spanish and English (English, Leafstedt, Gerber, & Villaruz, 2001). Taken collectively, prior evidence suggests at least some cross-language developmental parallels in the early phases of learning to read.

What does past evidence tell us about young Latino children's early English reading trajectory? The answer is, "It's not clear." Some researchers have examined ELLs' reading *achievement*—a global outcome. A few studies have revealed mixed results when comparing ELLs' English reading *achievement* development with that of their monolingual native-English-speaking peers. Some researchers who have focused on children in kindergarten through second grade have documented how, across one school year, ELLs can accomplish gains in reading achievement similar to those of their monolingual native-English-speaking peers (Araujo, 2002; Fitzgerald & Noblit, 1999, 2000; Hutchinson, Whiteley, Smith, & Connors, 2003; Lesaux & Siegel, 2003; Manis, Lindsey, & Bailey, 2004; Muter & Dietholm, 2001; Weber & Longhi-Chirlin, 2001). However, others have documented a lag in the reading achievement of some young Latino ELLs in English immersion classrooms (Fitzgerald & Noblit, 1999; Hutchinson et al., 2003; Neufeld & Fitzgerald, 2001). In another well-known study, Thomas and Collier (1997) revealed that long-range English reading achievement for students in all-English settings took on an inverted U shape.

Whereas some researchers have focused on English reading *achievement*, a very few others have examined ELLs' reading *subprocesses* development (e.g., phonemic awareness, phonics knowledge, and word recognition). Most of these were case studies of individual kindergarten through second-grade learners followed for 1 year or less. The following subprocesses have been studied: Word recognition strategies, phonological awareness assessed in literacy contexts, phonics knowledge, comprehension, writing, and spelling (Araujo, 2002; Fitzgerald & Noblit, 1999, 2000; Geva, Yaghoud-Zadeh, & Schuster, 2000; Hutchinson et al., 2003; Lesaux & Siegel, 2003; Manis et al., 2004; Muter & Dietholm, 2001; Neufeld & Fitzgerald, 2001; Weber & Longhi-Chirlin, 2001). Findings from the studies suggest that ELLs' and monolingual learners' English reading subprocesses develop similarly.

In short, for young Latino ELLs beginning to read in English, with the exception of phonological awareness, the role of other specific (e.g., meaning, vocabulary, comprehension) or global (overall oral ability) proficiencies in oral English, although important, may perhaps temporarily rank relatively low in importance. Lacking a well-elaborated theory of young ELLs' early reading development, one might hypothesize that under optimal instructional conditions, the developmental pattern might parallel the three periods known for monolingual English speakers—Literacy Roots; Initial Reading; and Confirmation, Fluency, and Ungluing from Print. Limited evidence from prior research examining *achievement* is unclear about the extent to which the trajectories might run in parallel, but the few existing studies of reading subprocesses suggest that similarities in trajectories might be possible.

Why Do We Need to Learn More?

An elaborated understanding of English reading development for young ELLs, especially as compared to their monolingual peers, is important because it could inform teachers' instructional decisions. If the development revealed that certain subprocesses of reading (e.g., phonological awareness, phonics knowledge, word recognition) tended typically to develop at particular periods, then teachers might especially emphasize those subprocesses during certain phases of instruction—as a developmental "booster." Moreover, studying ELLs' English reading developmental progression in the most common instructional setting in the United States—English immersion—is critical because policy implications for types of instructional situations for ELLs are hotly debated.

A Study of Young Latino Students' English Reading Growth

We asked the following questions:

1. Is the pattern of Latino ELLs' English reading growth (for instructional reading level, word- and sound-level understandings of reading, comprehension, and fluency) across 2 years the same as that for monolingual native-English-speaking peers?
2. If the pattern of reading growth is the same for ELLs and monolingual native-English-speaking students, does one group outperform the other group?

We conducted a 2-year study that would allow us to compare young Latino ELLs' reading growth with that of their monolingual native-English-speaking peers. We collected reading assessment data at two schools in two different districts. Two cohorts of children were followed during the 2 years. In one cohort, children who began school in first grade were followed into second grade. In the other cohort, children who began school in second grade were followed into third grade. Reading assessments were done at the beginning, middle, and end of each of the 2 years, with all children receiving the same set of assessments.

Schools and Students in Our Study

Eden and Hatterson Elementary Schools were located in different school districts. Eden was located in a moderate-size city, whereas Hatterson was located in the largest city in the state. Across all grade levels in the first year of the study, each school served approximately 600 students. Each school had a diverse student body. At Eden, 46% of students were African American, 32% were Latino, 19% were Caucasian of European heritage, and 3% were other ethnicities. At Hatterson, 76% were African American, 22% were Latino, and 2% were Caucasian of European heritage. At Eden, 82% of the students received subsidized lunch, whereas at Hatterson 91% received subsidized lunch. Each school met state Department of Public Instruction and federal definitions of high-poverty, low-performing schools during the years of the study.

A subset of 122 students was randomly selected from both schools (73 at Hatterson and 49 at Eden), except that, to the extent possible, all Latino ELLs were included. Across both schools, there were 66 children in the first- to second-grade cohort, and 56 children in the second- to third-grade cohort. Seventy children were females, and 52 were males. Almost 82% (81.9%) of the children received subsidized lunch. Across both schools, ethnicities were 34.43% African American, 9.02% Caucasian of European heritage, 54.92% Latino, and 1.64% multiple ethnicities.

Sixty-seven students were Latino children learning English, and 55 were monolingual native English speakers. Of the 67 Latino students, 23 were born outside the United States, and the length of time they had been in the country ranged from 1 to 7 years, with an average of 2.29 years. All students were in all-English classrooms, and all reading instruction for all students was done in English. The Latino students received no native language instruction. At the time of Latino students' entry into school, officials administered tests to determine their English abilities. At Eden they administered the Woodcock–Munoz Language Survey (Woodcock & Munoz-Sandoval, 2001), and at Hatterson they administered the IDEA Proficiency Tests (Dalton, Tighe, & Ballard, 1991). At Eden, Latino participants' scores ranged from 1 (non-English speaker) to 5 (fluent English speaker), with a mean of 2.06 (limited English speaker). At Hatterson, Latino participants' scores ranged from 1 (non-English speaker) to 6 (fluent English speaker), with an average of 3.95 (limited English speaker). The Latino and monolingual native-English-speaking students did not significantly differ on a marker typically used to represent socioeconomic status—85.07% ($N = 67$) of the Latino students and 78.18% ($N = 55$) of the monolingual native-English-speaking students received subsidized lunch.

What Reading Assessment Data Were Collected from Students?

Four individual reading assessments were administered to students in a different order each time to account for any effect of a particular assessment in a certain administration position: (1) Oral Reading of Successively Difficult Passages (Bader & Weisendanger, 1994; Barr, Blachowicz, Katz, & Kaufman, 2002; Clay, 2002); (2) Basic Sight Vocabulary (Barr et al., 2002); (3) Hearing Sounds in Words (Clay, 2002; Johnston, 1992); and (4) Phonics Knowledge (adapted from Shefelbine, 1995). The assessments were selected for three reasons: (1) to assess critical features of early reading development supported by prior research, (2) to ensure use of assessments that have been widely used in practice and in prior research, and (3) most importantly, to represent authentic assessments that are typically used in school settings.

In the following paragraphs we provide procedural information about how each reading assessment was administered and detail the reading variables that were created for statistical analysis. Reliability estimates were obtained for each variable for faithfulness of test administration and to determine the extent to which another individual could reliably obtain the same score as the examiner. All reliability estimates were adequate, ranging from .83 to 1.00.

For *Oral Reading of Successively Difficult Passages* (Bader & Weisendanger, 1994; Barr et al., 2002; Clay, 2002), as students read aloud increasingly difficult graded texts from the Bader Reading and Language Inventory (Bader & Weisendanger, 1994), the examiner recorded miscues on a separate copy of the passage (Barr et al., 2002; Clay, 2002). Using Clay's (2002) method, the examiner determined each student's "instructional reading level" score, which was the highest level at which the student read with at least 90% word recognition accuracy. Then, for the instructional reading level passage, the examiner asked the comprehension questions listed in the Bader Reading and Language Inventory (Bader & Weisendanger, 1994). In addition, during the instructional reading level passage, the examiner timed each student's reading for 1 minute, marking a line after the last word read during the minute. From the Oral Reading of Successively Difficult Passages assessment, three variables were created for analysis—Instructional Reading Level, Comprehension, and Fluency. Comprehension was the percentage of correctly answered comprehension questions from the instructional level passage. Fluency was the number of words read correctly in 1 minute.

For the *Basic Sight Vocabulary* (Barr et al., 2002) assessment, students were asked to look at lists of words (total = 220) and say them aloud. Lists were arranged in order of difficulty. If a student missed more than two words on a list, then a less difficult list (or lists) was read. A word was scored as correct if the student pronounced it correctly in 3 seconds or less. From the Basic Sight Vocabulary assessment, one variable was created for statistical analysis—Reading Words in Isolation, which was the percentage of words read correctly across all lists (including unread words on lower lists, which assumes that if students can read more difficult lists, they can also read easier lists).

For the *Hearing Sounds in Words* (Clay, 2002; Johnston, 1992) assessment, the examiner slowly read a lengthy sentence containing 37 sounds. Students wrote letters for any sounds. A response was correct if there was a letter written for a sound in a word regardless of whether the letter was correct. From Hearing Sounds in Words, one variable was created for statistical analysis—Phonological Awareness, which is the percentage of sounds (37) for which students supplied a representation.

For *Phonics Knowledge* (adapted from Shefelbine, 1995), as students looked at letters and letter combinations on lists, the examiner prompted with statements such as "Look at these letters, and tell me how they sound" and "Tell me the long sounds of these letters." Items included consonants, consonant digraphs, long and short vowels, consonant blends, r-controlled vowels, and common phonograms (e.g., *ad, ame*). One variable was created for statistical analysis—Phonics Knowledge, which was the percentage of items answered correctly.

What Did We Learn from Our Analyses?

To address our two research questions, four statistical analyses were run, one each for the following dependent variables: Instructional Reading Level; word- and sound-level understandings (ability to Read Words in Isolation, Phonological Awareness, and Phonics Knowledge as a set); Comprehension; and Fluency. For each analysis, Latino ELLs' growth was compared to that of their monolingual native-English-speaking peers.

Instructional Reading Level

For our questions involving Instructional Reading Level, the pattern of growth for first- and second-grade Latino ELLs at each grade level was similar to that of their monolingual native-English-speaking peers, and, on average, there was no statistically significant difference between Latino students' performance and that of their monolingual native-English speaking peers. It is helpful to examine the patterns in Figure 16.1, which shows Instructional Reading Level means across the six time points by language status and grade cohort. Notice that there is a similar pattern of growth and similar achievement levels for both language status groups within each grade. Even though the Latino students' growth was, practically speaking, lower than that of their peers over the 2 years, it was not statistically significant. For the cohort that began in first grade, Latino ELLs' average Instructional Reading Level at the beginning of Year 1 was 0.05 (a very early reading level), while the corresponding score for monolingual native-English-speaking students was 0.10 (also a very early reading level). For the cohort that began in second grade, the Latino ELLs' average Instructional Reading Level at the beginning of Year 1 was 1.29 (about a late first-grade level), whereas the corresponding score for monolingual native-English-speaking students was 1.86 (a middle to late second-grade level). At the end of Year 2, the first-into-second-grade students' respective scores were 2.67 and 3.35, and the second/third grade scores were 4.37 and 5.46, respectively. On average, both groups of students in both grades showed remarkable progress.

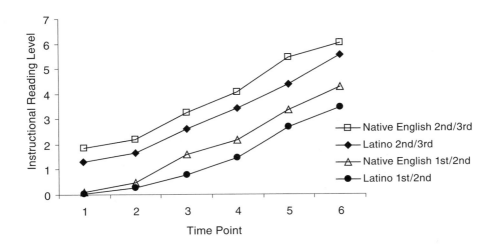

FIGURE 16.1. Average Instructional Reading Level scores across six time points for Latino ELLs and monolingual native English speakers by grade cohort (first/second, second/third) across all six time points. A score of 0 indicated that a student did not pass even the lowest reading passage; 0.25 indicated approximately a preprimer level, which, for typically developing students, is achieved around the beginning of first grade; 0.50 indicated approximately a primer level, achieved by typically developing students around the middle of first grade; 1.00 indicated approximately end-of-first-grade level; 2.00 indicated approximately second-grade level; and so on.

Word and Sound Level Outcomes

For word- and sound-level understandings (ability to Read Words in Isolation, Phonological Awareness, and Phonics Knowledge as a set), Latino ELLs exhibited a different growth pattern for Phonological Awareness than did their monolingual native-English-speaking peers. Because there were not statistically significant differences for the different language status groups by grade cohort across the six time points, both grade cohorts (first/second, and second/third) are grouped together for Phonological Awareness in Figure 16.2, which shows that Latino students began Year 1 at a much lower level (70.18%, SD = 36.04) of Phonological Awareness than their peers (90.35%, SD = 14.70) and witnessed a steep learning curve over the course of Year 1. By the end of Year 2, their Phonological Awareness was equivalent to that of their peers and reasonably highly developed: 97.38% (SD = 10.72) and 98.60% (SD = 5.84), respectively.

For Reading Words in Isolation and Phonics Knowledge, Figure 16.2 shows that monolingual native-English-speaking children on average outperformed Latino children continuously over time by a slim margin, although both groups were scoring quite well on average by the end of Year 2. Because there were not statistically significant differences for the language status groups by grade cohort across the six time points, both grade cohorts (first/second, and second/third) are grouped together for Reading Words in Isolation in Figure 16.2. The Latino ELLs began Year 1 with an average Reading Words in Isolation score of 30.20% (SD = 33.21), whereas the monolingual native English speakers began Year 1 with an average Reading Words in Isolation score of 35.61% (SD = 31.09). Both language status groups made approximately linear growth across the 2 years, and the Latino ELLs ended Year 2 with an average Reading Words in Isolation score of 85.41% (SD = 25.52), whereas the monolingual native English speakers ended Year 2 with an average Reading Words in Isolation score of 93.10% (SD = 20.14). Even though the Latino students' average Reading Words in Isolation scores at each time point appear to be slightly lower than those of their monolingual counterparts, the differences were not statistically significant.

Also, because there were no statistically significant differences for the different language status groups by grade cohort across the six time points, both grade cohorts (first/second, and second/third) are grouped together for Phonics Knowledge in Figure 16.2. The Latino ELLs began Year 1 with an average Phonics Knowledge score of 46.62% (SD = 29.73), whereas the monolingual native English speakers began Year 1 with an average Phonics Knowledge score of 55.63% (SD = 22.22). Both language status groups made approximately linear growth across the 2 years, and the Latino ELLs ended Year 2 with an average Phonics Knowledge score of 89.85% (SD = 16.14), whereas the monolingual native English speakers ended Year 2 with an average Phonics Knowledge score of 94.14% (SD = 10.76). Even though the Latino students' average Phonics Knowledge scores appear to be slightly lower at each time point than those of their monolingual counterparts, the differences were not statistically significant.

Comprehension and Fluency

Because students' reading levels were so low at the beginning of first grade, it was not possible to assess their comprehension or fluency well. Consequently, only Year 2 was included in the Comprehension and Fluency analyses. In addition, because there were

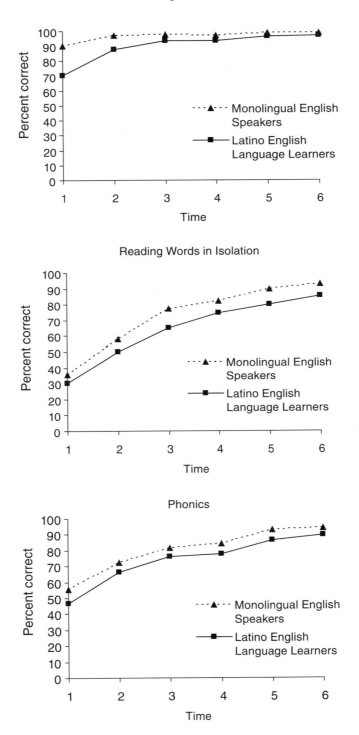

FIGURE 16.2. Average Reading Words in Isolation, Phonological Awareness, and Phonics Knowledge scores for Latino ELLs and monolingual native English speakers across all six time points.

no statistically significant differences for the different language status groups by grade cohort across the six time points, both grade cohorts (first/second, and second/third) are grouped together in Figure 16.3. For Comprehension and Fluency, the pattern of growth was the same for Latino ELLs and monolingual native-English-speaking students, and on average, one group did not outperform the other. Figure 16.3 shows Comprehension and Fluency average scores across Year 2 (three time points) for the two language status groups. For Comprehension, the pattern of growth appears similar for the Latino ELLs and the monolingual native English speakers. Latino ELLs began Year 2 with an average Comprehension score of 78.01% (SD = 26.76) and ended Year 2 with an average Comprehension score of 63.51% (SD = 33.71). Similarly, monolingual native English speakers began Year 2 with an average Comprehension score of 78.20% (SD = 30.35) and ended Year 2 with an average Comprehension score of 66.32% (SD = 33.64). An important note is that comprehension levels appear to decline in Figure 16.3. The average scores shown are unadjusted averages. "Unadjusted" means that the average scores

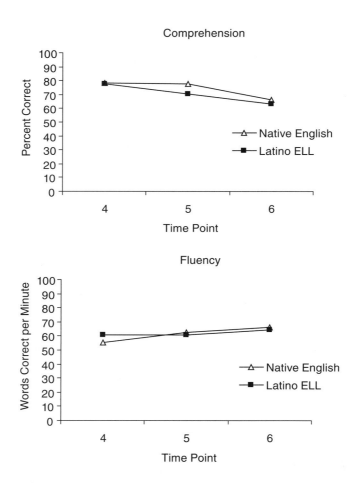

FIGURE 16.3. Unadjusted average Comprehension and Fluency scores for Latino ELLs and monolingual native English speakers across three time points in Year 2.

do not take into account students' increasing Instructional Reading Level scores across the three time points. As expected, when students read increasingly difficult passages, sometimes above grade-level expectations, Comprehension scores were lower than they might have been, on average, with grade-level material.

For Fluency, the pattern of growth appears similar for the Latino ELLs and the monolingual native English speakers, with average scores increasing slightly across Year 2. Latino ELLs began Year 2 with an average Fluency score of 60.62 words per minute (wpm) (*SD* = 25.60) and ended Year 2 with an average Fluency score of 64.55 wpm (*SD* = 24.58). Similarly, monolingual native English speakers began Year 2 with an average Fluency score of 55.48 wpm (*SD* = 23.41) and ended Year 2 with an average Fluency score of 66.30 wpm (*SD* = 25.42).

Study Conclusions and Implications for Classroom Reading Instruction for ELLs

In this section, we first summarize the main conclusions for the research questions, then discuss possible implications of each of the conclusions in order. We then suggest specific implications of the findings for classroom reading instruction for Latino ELLs.

Main Conclusions

1. The *pattern* of Instructional Reading Level growth for first- and second-grade Latino ELLs was similar to that of their monolingual native-English-speaking peers and, on average, there was no significant difference between the two groups' performance.

2. Latino ELLs exhibited a different Phonological Awareness growth pattern than did their monolingual native-English-speaking peers. Latino students began Year 1 at a much lower level of Phonological Awareness than their peers and witnessed a steep learning curve over the course of the Year 1. By the end of Year 2, their Phonological Awareness was equivalent to that of their native-English-speaking peers. For Reading Words in Isolation and Phonics Knowledge, the growth pattern was similar, but monolingual native-English-speaking children, on average, outperformed Latino children continuously over time by a slim margin, although both groups were scoring quite well, on average, by the end of Year 2.

3. For Comprehension and Fluency, the pattern of growth was the same for Latino ELLs and monolingual native-English-speaking students, and, on average, one group did not outperform the other.

Implications for the Pattern of Instructional Reading Level Growth

The similar Instructional Reading Level growth patterns across the 2 years suggest that the two language status groups of students were on similar overall reading level trajectories (see Figure 16.1). The result provides new evidence, and its implications are significant for the field. It is important to note, on average, both groups ended Year 2 with excellent Instructional Reading Levels that were, on average, 2 years above their grade level. Because the Instructional Reading Level variable was based principally on word recognition accuracy in context, such an achievement suggests the Latino students had learned word recognition strategies in context exceptionally well.

Remarkably, on average, the Latino students' Instructional Reading Level performance was not *statistically* lower than that of their monolingual native-English-speaking peers. The finding corroborates limited prior research accomplished over shorter periods of time that documented kindergarten through second-grade ELLs' ability to attain reading achievement levels similar to those of monolingual native-English-speaking students (Araujo, 2002; Fitzgerald & Noblit, 1999, 2000; Hutchinson et al., 2003; Lesaux & Siegel, 2003; Manis et al., 2004; Muter & Dietholm, 2001; Weber & Longhi-Chirlin, 2001). However, whether such an upward trajectory may be sustained for periods longer than 2 years is not clear. Thomas and Collier's (1997) study of ELLs' performance on standardized academic tests over time implies that our students' English immersion circumstances may impact their ability to continually advance their reading performance.

Although there was not a *statistically* significant difference, it is important to point out that, in *practical* terms, there was a steady gap between the average scores of monolingual native-English-speaking students and the Latino ELLs. This average Instructional Reading Level language status difference occurred at each point in time and did not lessen over time (see Figure 16.1). From a practical perspective, for Latino children to close this achievement gap at some time period, their trajectory must accelerate and differ from that of their monolingual native-English-speaking peers (Lesaux & Geva, 2006; Thomas & Collier, 1997). Results from prior research with monolingual native-English-speaking children suggest that, over time, students with higher reading achievement make rapid progress, whereas those with lower reading achievement make slower progress, a phenomenon referred to as the Matthew effect, with the "rich getting richer" and the "poor getting poorer" (Stanovich, 1986). Given the practical significance of the demonstrated steady achievement gap, we could become discouraged if growth trajectories similar to the ones in the reported study remain constant in subsequent years.

Implications for Growth Patterns of Word- and Sound-Level Abilities

Differences in Phonological Awareness growth patterns for Latino ELLs compared to their monolingual native-English-speaking peers suggest that whereas the Latino ELLs began Year 1 at a significant disadvantage in English phonological awareness, they quickly attained phonological understandings equal to those of their counterparts, ending Year 2 at the same high knowledge level as their peers (see Figure 16.2). It is quite startling that the Latino children's English phonological knowledge could increase so rapidly. This rapid increase foretells positively for the Latino children's future reading development because prior research with monolingual native-English-speaking students suggests that early development of phonological awareness is vital to future reading achievement (National Institute of Child Health and Development, 2000; Snow, Burns, & Griffin, 1998). Also, documentation of the dissimilar Phonological Awareness trajectories may be notable because prior investigators have suggested that phonological awareness may develop similarly for ELLs and for monolingual native English speakers (cf. Fitzgerald & Noblit, 1999, 2000; Geva et al., 2000; Lesaux & Siegel, 2003; Manis et al., 2004; Muter & Dietholm, 2001).

At the same time, however, developmental trajectories for Reading Words in Isolation and Phonics Knowledge were similar for Latino ELLs and monolingual native English speakers, with the latter, on average, consistently outscoring the Latino children by a slight margin at each time point (see Figure 16.2). The result parallels a few previous findings about word recognition, again, accomplished in a shorter time frame (Araujo, 2002; Fitzgerald & Noblit, 1999, 2000; Geva et al., 2000; Hutchinson et al., 2003; Lesaux & Siegel, 2003; Manis et al., 2004; Weber & Longhi-Chirlin, 2001). Although both groups in this study performed extremely well on both measures by the end of Year 2—on average achieving 85–96% correct—again, the steady achievement gap between the two groups may be troubling.

Implications for Growth Patterns for Comprehension and Fluency

The lack of significant differences between the two language status groups for Comprehension, or differences in growth pattern for Comprehension, is another interesting result. The Comprehension result upholds findings from studies suggesting that when measured at one time point or over a short time period, young Latino ELLs' comprehension may be similar to that of their monolingual native-English-speaking peers (Fitzgerald & Noblit, 2000; Hutchinson et al., 2003; Lesaux & Siegel, 2003; Manis et al., 2004; Weber & Longhi-Chirlin, 2001). Our result is different from a recent conclusion of the National Literacy Panel (August & Shanahan, 2006). They concluded that language-minority students infrequently approach the same levels of comprehension aptitude as native English speakers. Reasons for the differences in results are not immediately evident.

Both language status groups' Comprehension, on average, was quite good—in the mid-60% to high 70% correct range (see Figure 16.3). Strong comprehension is not unexpected for students reading primary grades material (if they are able to read most of the words) because primary grades passages characteristically do not involve difficult or complex concepts. The Latino ELLs, on average, did not experience difficulty with understanding the material, at least compared to their monolingual native-English-speaking counterparts. The finding is important because it suggests that when young Latino ELLs read material in which they recognize most of the words, they comprehend quite well.

Similarly, the lack of significant differences between the two language status groups for Fluency, or for growth pattern for Fluency, is noteworthy. It seems a remarkable achievement that Latino ELLs' fluency, on average, was comparable to that of their monolingual native-English-speaking peers. The range of Fluency scores (approximately 55 to 66 wpm; see Figure 16.3) is comparable to fluency averages for typically developing monolingual English-speaking first- and second-graders. Barr and colleagues (2002) reported first-grade average fluency as 30–70 wpm, and second grade mean fluency as 50–100 wpm (citing Hasbrouck & Tindal, 1992; Morris, 1999; Pinnell et al., 1995).

It is important to note that, on average, at least as measured in our study, the Latino ELLs' oral English was far less than fluent. The similar Fluency trajectories of both language status groups could not be explained by the argument that the ELLs' oral English levels were similar to those of their monolingual native-English-speaking counterparts.

Implications for Classroom Reading Instruction for ELLs

First, we address an implication of the similar Instructional Reading Level trajectories for Latino ELLs and monolingual native-English-speaking students. We find ourselves in the atypical situation of weighing the practical group average differences in

Instructional Reading Level over the nonstatistically significant result. We also take into account the significant language status group difference in Phonological Awareness, and the persistent practical gap in the other two sound- and word-level subprocesses (Reading Words in Isolation and Phonics Knowledge) favoring the monolingual native-English-speaking students. It is difficult to disregard a steady disparity between the Latino ELLs and the monolingual native-English-speaking students across 2 years. As we weigh the practical difference, in combination with the similar growth pattern, we question whether certain forms of instruction might enhance the Latino ELLs' reading growth trajectory. Latino ELLs may benefit each year from more intense English reading instruction that exposes them to more English print more quickly, and conceivably provides more recurrent experience in sound- and word-level subprocesses. One option might be to provide a supplemental reading specialist who can provide individual or small-group reading instruction for ELLs. Most teachers and researchers would likely argue, though, that any supplemental English reading instruction should be done within the context of the language needs and the English developmental reading level of individual students.

Second, the steep Phonological Awareness learning curve for Latino ELLs during Year 1 suggests that teachers might be especially responsive to the need to support their Latino students in acquiring English phonological awareness early on. Extra attention to helping students expand their phonological awareness understandings during the first few months in all-English classrooms might be central.

Third, the lack of significant differences between the language status groups for Comprehension or Fluency in the context of differences for sound- and word-level reading abilities is not surprising if we consider the possibility that the established pattern of early reading development for monolingual native-English-speaking students may hold true for ELLs. These results suggest that classroom instructional strategies for both Comprehension and Fluency that benefit monolingual native-English-speaking students may likely also benefit Latino ELLs.

Guiding Principles for Classroom Instruction and Illustrations of Classroom Practice

In this section, based on the implications from our reported study, we first propose four guiding principles for classroom reading instruction with Latino ELLs. Second, we present two illustrations of classroom practices that incorporate the guiding principles for classroom reading instruction. In addition, there are many excellent resources on reading instruction with ELLs, two of which are Fitzgerald and Graves (2004) and Peregoy and Boyle (2004).

Guiding Principles for Classroom Instruction

The guiding principles we present for working with Latino ELLs are intended to support teachers and school personnel as they make instructional decisions about reading for Latino ELLs. We firmly believe that instructional decisions for each individual child are best made by knowledgeable teachers, with the support of informed school personnel.

1. Provide Sound Reading Instruction

First, our results suggest that when Latino ELLs in English immersion classrooms have the same instructional opportunities as their peers, as did the students in our study, they can, on average, make similar progress in Instructional Reading Level, Comprehension, and Fluency. Based on the similar developmental trajectories, our first guiding principle is the following: Provide English reading instruction from the beginning, with the same sound reading instruction practices used with monolingual native-English-speaking students (August & Shanahan, 2006). A corollary to the guideline is that it may not be necessary to wait for an "optimum" level of oral English proficiency before beginning English reading instruction.

2. Modulate Instruction

Two important ideas from our study inform our second guiding principle. First, there was a different Phonological Awareness growth pattern for Latino ELLs compared to their monolingual native-English-speaking peers. Second, although there wasn't a significant difference between Latino students' average Instructional Reading Levels, Reading Words in Isolation, and Phonics Knowledge and that of their peers, a practical gap did exist. The two results suggest the need for modulated instruction that might raise Latino students' levels to be more commensurate with those of their peers. Our second guiding principle is the following: Modulate, modulate, modulate the sound reading instruction practices you would use with monolingual native-English-speaking students for the individual reading and language needs of new language learners.

A potentially critical feature of modulating English reading instruction practices is that teachers understand their ELLs' developmental reading trajectories, locate ELLs' English developmental reading level on that trajectory, know the critical reading process and/or subprocess features for that level, and intensely teach *those* features. For example, our results for sound- and word-level reading subprocesses suggest that Latino students might benefit from particularly intense instruction in those subprocesses at particular moments in time—specifically, in Phonological Awareness at the beginning of first grade. Assuming that ELLs' developmental patterns might parallel the three periods known for monolingual English speakers—Literacy Roots; Initial Reading; and Confirmation, Fluency, and Ungluing from Print (Chall, 1996)—we likely find many beginning Latino ELLs in the Initial Reading stage, where the critical instructional features are expansion of sound awareness, and increased focus on letters and associating letters with parts of spoken words.

Illustrations of Classroom Practice

Next, we provide two illustrations of classroom reading instruction activities for Latino ELLs based on our two guiding principles. We provide a common format for both illustrations. First, we give a summary description of the activity. Then we list the guiding principle to which the activity is specifically related, explaining why the particular activity is likely to be beneficial for young Latino ELLs. We then provide the reading instructional purposes for the activity. Next, we provide the setting for our illustration.

The activity is then shown through a scenario or description, and finally, we provide possible adaptations for the activity.

Activity: Picture Sorting and Sound Spelling

Description. Picture sorting is an activity that develops English phonological awareness, vocabulary meaning, and sound-to-letter correspondence. A teacher names picture cards with a student, then coaches him or her to sort the cards into piles by initial sound, saying the name of each card while emphasizing the initial sound. Then, the teacher guides the student to write the names of the picture cards using sound spellings into separate columns based on initial sound (e.g., a student may write *BOT* for the word *boat*).

Guiding Principles for Instruction. Picture sorting and sound spelling are particularly related to our second guiding principle—modulating for ELLs the sound reading instruction practices used with monolingual native-English-speaking students. In reading the illustration, notice how Mr. Washington addresses the second guiding principle by intensifying his instruction in word- and sound-level reading subprocesses, repeatedly focusing his two ELLs' attention on the initial sounds from the picture cards. In addition, picture sorting and sound spelling also address the first guiding principle—providing English reading instruction from the beginning with the same sound reading instruction practices used with monolingual native-English-speaking students. Mr. Washington starts instruction with his ELLs at the beginning of the year and uses a sound instructional strategy that he might use with monolingual English speakers. Moreover, Mr. Washington does not wait for an "optimum" level of oral English proficiency, and he provides English reading instruction and English reading opportunities before his ELLs are fully proficient in oral English.

Reading Instruction Purposes. The purposes of picture sorting and phonetic spelling are primarily to develop students' phonological understandings and phonics knowledge. The picture sorting task supports students' English phonological awareness, whereas the phonetic spelling task adds phonics knowledge abilities through writing. The picture sorting and phonetic spelling activity typically would be used with Latino ELLs who are new to learning English.

Setting in Our Illustration. Our picture sorting and phonetic spelling activity takes place in an urban, third-grade classroom with African American or Latino students. All students in the classroom are instructed in English throughout the entire day. Approximately 45% of the students are Latino, and about half of those Latino students are ELLs. The teacher, Mr. Washington, is an African American, monolingual native English speaker with 4 years of teaching experience. For this picture sorting and phonetic spelling activity, Mr. Washington has chosen two Latino ELLs who are new to the school and just learning to speak English.

Reading Activity. Mr. Washington begins the picture sorting and phonetic spelling activity with two students at a table in the back of the classroom, while the rest of the class reads independently. The two students, Isabel and Elena, have been working with

Mr. Washington three times per week on this activity as they begin to learn English. Each student has her own identical set of picture cards, recording sheet, and pencil. Mr. Washington has chosen two focal sounds—/ĭ/, because the letter *i* has a different sound in Spanish, and /ŏ/ as a contrasting sound. Mr. Washington has a set of picture cards as well and begins by supporting the students as they name each picture card.

MR. WASHINGTON: All right! Let's begin like we always do and go through the picture cards and say what they are. What's this one? *(Holds up a picture of an insect.)*

ISABEL: Bug.

MR. WASHINGTON: Yes, Isabel. It is a bug. But there's also another word for bugs that have six legs. Do you know what it is?

ELENA: Spider.

MR. WASHINGTON: Good guess, Elena. But this is a picture of an insect. Can you both say *insect* with me?

ALL: Insect.

MR. WASHINGTON: Good! An insect is like a bug. Now what is this picture? *(Holds up the picture of an ox.)*

ELENA: A cow!

MR. WASHINGTON: Very good guess. It's kind of like a cow, but it's different. Look closer and see if you know what it is. *(Both girls shrug their shoulders.)* It's called an ox. Can you say *ox* with me?

ALL: Ox. *(Mr. Washington follows the same process with Isabel and Elena for the remaining four pictures he has selected—olive, ostrich, igloo, and ink.)*

MR. WASHINGTON: OK, let's begin like always and sort these pictures into two groups. One group will have the /ŏ/ sound, and the other group will have the /ĭ/ sound. Let's do one together. How about this one? *(Holds up the picture of the ox.)* Would this go with /ŏ/ or /ĭ/?

ISABEL: /ŏ/

MR. WASHINGTON: Yes, very good, Isabel. Let's say it together and listen for that /ŏ/ sound.

ALL: Ooooooooooox.

MR. WASHINGTON: Great! Now see if you can do the others on your own. *(Coaches Isabel and Elena through sorting the other picture cards into piles based on initial sounds, encouraging them to work as independently as possible. Next, he prepares to move Isabel and Elena to the phonetic spelling task.)* Great job sorting those pictures! Now let's take our paper and pencils and write down the names of the pictures. Look on your paper and you'll see two columns like always. At the top of the left side is the letter *o*, which makes the /ŏ/ sound. On the right side is the letter *i*, which makes the /ĭ/ sound. Let's look at what you have. Which pictures have the /ŏ/ sound?

ELENA: Ox.

ISABEL: Ostrich.

MR. WASHINGTON: Great! Let's start with *ox*. Which side will we write *ox* on? *(Isabel points to the column for /ŏ/.)* Good! Lets write *ox*. What do you hear first?

ELENA: /ŏ/

MR. WASHINGTON: Yes! What would we write for /ŏ/? *(Both Isabel and Elena glance at the column header and write o underneath.)* Great! What comes next?

ISABEL: /ks/

MR. WASHINGTON: Very good! How do we write /ks/? *(Next to the o Isabel writes ks to spell oks. Elena glances over at Isabel's writing and writes the same thing).* Excellent job listening for those sounds! I'll show you one thing. In English, we can also make the /ks/ sound with one letter—*x*. So you can spell *ox* like this. *(Mr. Washington writes the conventional spelling ox so Isabel and Elena can see it, though he does not yet expect Isabel and Elena to change their spellings. Then, Mr. Washington, Isabel, and Elena work through the rest of the words using phonetic spellings, while categorizing their words into the two target sounds.)*

Adaptations. Picture sorting and sound spelling can be adapted to address individual student needs. For young emergent readers who are just learning English, just the picture sorting task may be appropriate. For students who are more advanced in their English reading abilities, target sounds for picture sorts might be final sounds, medial vowel sounds, and/or closer contrasting sounds, such as /ĕ/ and /ĭ/. Also, picture cards can be replaced with word cards as students begin to read independently. Word cards may also be sorted by target sounds that could have multiple spellings. For instance, words with the /ō/ sound could be represented with the spellings *o* (as in *go*), *ow* (as in *low*), *oa* (as in *boat*), or *o_e* (as in *rode*).

Activity: Small-Group Guided Reading

Description. Guided reading (Fountas & Pinnell, 1996, 1999, 2001) is a small-group reading activity in which the teacher "guides" students through a text by providing needed support for comprehension, word identification, or meaning vocabulary. Guided reading lessons frequently follow a structured format (e.g., Stauffer, 1969) that varies depending on students' developmental levels. The guided reading lesson's small-group setting allows a teacher to attend better to students' individual reading instruction needs.

Guiding Principles for Instruction. Small-group guided reading is particularly founded on our first guiding principle—providing English reading instruction with the same sound reading instruction practices used with monolingual native-English-speaking students. Small-group guided reading is a well-known, common model of reading instruction, often used with monolingual native English speakers, designed to address students' individual reading needs (Fountas & Pinnell, 1996, 1999). Mrs. Allen creates small heterogeneous groups that support the reading development of both ELLs and monolingual native English speakers. Furthermore, Mrs. Allen addresses the first guiding principle and does not wait for an "optimum" level of oral English proficiency, and provides exposure to new English meaning vocabulary, opportunities for practicing fluency, and occasions to develop comprehension abilities through reading and discussion prior to full oral English proficiency. In addition, Mrs. Allen addresses the second guiding principle—modulating the sound reading instruction practices used with monolingual native-English-speaking students for the individual reading and language needs of new language learners. She provides extra, direct, intense English reading instruction focused on English sound- and word-level reading subprocesses (e.g., reading sight words, phonological awareness, and phonics knowledge), while focusing on key sight words (e.g., *my*) and decoding strategies (e.g., using phonics knowledge).

Reading Instruction Purposes. The purposes of guided reading vary widely depending on the developmental levels of the students within a particular guided reading group. For our illustration, Mrs. Allen is working with a small group of students on multiple beginning reading skills and concepts about English print (Clay, 2002), paying particular attention to students' grasp of key sight words and word identification strategies.

Setting in Our Illustration. Our guided reading lesson takes place in an English-only K–1 classroom with students who are European American, African American, and Latino. Approximately one-third of the students are Latino ELLs. All students in the classroom are instructed in English throughout the entire day. The teacher, Mrs. Allen, is a monolingual native English speaker with 16 years of teaching experience. For this guided reading lesson group, Mrs. Allen has chosen five beginning readers—three monolingual native English speakers and two Latino ELLs. Both Latino ELLs are still learning English but have good conversational English abilities.

Reading Activity. Mrs. Allen begins her guided reading lesson by calling the five students to a quiet table in the back of the classroom, while the other students work independently in learning centers. The children gather at the table, each with his or her own copy of the book *In the Mirror* (Cowley, 1998). The patterned book shows a little girl examining herself in the mirror on each page, with the patterned text "See my _____."

MRS. ALLEN: Hello, boys and girls. Let's take a look at the book we are going to read today. This book is called *In the Mirror*. Everyone, look at the words on the front of your book. Get your fingers ready, and let's point to the words and read the title.

ALL: In the Mirror.

MRS. ALLEN: Let's look at the pictures and see what's happening. First, everyone turn and point to the front of your book. *(The students all turn their books and lay them flat, pointing to the front cover.)* Great! Who or what do you see on the front?

CATALINA: A girl.

ABBY: A bird.

BRETT: A mirror.

MRS. ALLEN: Very good! I see a girl and a bird, too. That kind of bird is called a parrot. It looks like they're playing in front of the mirror. Let's open the book and look at the pictures on each page. *(Leads the five students through each page of the book, viewing the pictures and discussing what might be happening. During the discussion she implants key vocabulary the students will need to read the book, such as* fingers, toes, tongue, nose, elbow, *and* knee.*)*

MRS. ALLEN: Now, everyone, close your books and put them down for a minute. I want you to look up here on my whiteboard. There are two important sight words we will need to know when we read this book. Let's look at the first one. *(Prints the word* See *on the whiteboard.)* Does anyone know this word?

JUAN: Sofia!

MRS. ALLEN: Good guess, Juan. Your sister's name is Sofia, and her name starts with *S,* too. *(Points to the* S *at the beginning of* see.*)* OK, let's look at this word. What sound is at the beginning?

BRETT: *S*

MRS. ALLEN: Good, Brett. That's the letter name, but what sound does it make?

SEVERAL STUDENTS: /sssss/

MRS. ALLEN: Great! Now these two *e*'s that you see together make one sound. They say their own name! So, these two *e*'s say /ē/. Let's blend these together. All together now.

ALL: /s/ - /ē/, /s/ - /ē/, see!

MRS. ALLEN: Great! Everyone get it? You know, see? With your eyes? *(Holds her hands around her eyes like binoculars and says, "I see* Juan.*" She asks all the students to mimic her and do the same.)* Excellent! All right, what is this word again *(pointing to* see)?

ALL: *See!*

MRS. ALLEN: Great. Let's look at this next word. Does anyone know this word? I'll give you a hint. It's on our word wall!

CATALINA: *My!*

MRS. ALLEN: Great, Catalina! How did you know that word was *my?*

CATALINA: Because it starts with /m/.

MRS. ALLEN: Very good, Catalina. Let's all look at this word and say /m/ when I put my finger under the first sound. Ready? *(Points to the first sound in* my.*)*

ALL: /mmmmmm/

MRS. ALLEN: And what's the word?

ALL: *my!*

MRS. ALLEN: Very good! Let's read these two words together because they will make an important pattern in our story. *(Points to* See *and* my *in succession as the students read the two words chorally.)* OK, open your books to the first page. What do we call this page?

ALL: Title page!!

MRS. ALLEN: Very good! Everyone turn to the first page. Get your finger ready and let's read together.

ALL: See my ...

JUAN: Fingers!

MRS. ALLEN: Very good! How did you know it said *fingers?*

JUAN: I look at the picture.

MRS. ALLEN: That's a very good strategy, Juan! It does look like she sees her fingers in the mirror in the picture. How else could you have known that word was *fingers?*

TIERRA: It starts with *F.*

MRS. ALLEN: Very good, Tierra. And what sound does that make?

TIERRA: /f/

MRS. ALLEN: Right! Everyone put your finger under the *f* and say /f/. Now let's read that whole page again.

ALL: See my fingers. *(Mrs. Allen leads the students through the rest of the text in the same way, examining key words and supporting students to use multiple strategies, such as using pictures or phonics knowledge to read unfamiliar words.)*

Adaptations. Guided reading can be adapted for a wide variety of instructional purposes. Further direct instruction in English concepts and vocabulary in print can be incorporated once the text is written. For example, target English letters, sounds, or words could be searched for in the text. In addition, guided reading can be used for intensive one-on-one instruction to introduce new language learners to introduce to English, while providing support through illustrations.

Closure

In this chapter we have presented a nationwide backdrop for young Latino children's English reading and have considered issues related to their early reading development, reported a study of young Latino students' English reading growth, presented implications of the study findings with regard to classroom reading instruction for multilingual learners, and, finally, have presented guiding principles and illustrative classroom practices originating from our study findings. As greater numbers of classroom teachers work with ELLs on a daily basis, it becomes increasingly important for teachers to expand their understanding of ELLs' English reading development and consequent classroom reading instruction to meet the instructional needs of increasing numbers of students.

The developmental research evidence presented in this chapter has potential classroom instruction application. A deeper understanding of English reading development for young ELLs, especially compared to their monolingual peers, is important because it could inform teachers' daily classroom reading instruction. Our hope is that the consequent implications, guiding principles, and classroom illustrations we present may have an impact on how teachers conceptualize ELLs' cognitive English reading development and, subsequently, impact the classroom English reading instruction that teachers provide.

Note

1. As a matter of principle, we generally prefer to write out the full term "English language learner" to avoid diminishing people to acronyms. However, editorial constraints require that we use the acronym in our chapter.

References

Adams, M. J. (1990). *Beginning to read: Thinking and learning about print.* Cambridge, MA: MIT Press.

Araujo, L. (2002). The literacy development of kindergarten English-language learners. *Journal of Research in Childhood Education, 16,* 232–247.

August, D., & Shanahan, T. (Eds.). (2006). *Developing literacy in second-language learners: Report of the National Literacy Panel on Language-Minority Children and Youth.* Mahwah, NJ: Erlbaum.

Bader, L. A., & Weisendanger, K. (1994). *Bader Reading and Language Inventory* (2nd ed.). New York: Merrill.

Barr, R., Blachowicz, C. L. Z., Katz, K., & Kaufman, B. (2002). *Reading diagnosis for teachers: An instructional approach* (4th ed.). Boston: Allyn & Bacon.

Bravo-Valdivieso, L. (1995). A four-year follow-up study of low socioeconomic status, Latin American children with reading difficulties. *International Journal of Disability, Development, and Education, 42,* 189–202.

Carillo, M. (1994). Development of phonological awareness and reading acquisition: A study in Spanish language. *Reading and Writing: An Interdisciplinary Journal, 6,* 279–298.

Chall, J. S. (1996). *Stages of reading development* (2nd ed.). Fort Worth, TX: Harcourt Brace.

Clay, M. M. (2001). *Change over time in children's literacy development.* Portsmouth, NH: Heinemann.

Clay, M. M. (2002). *An observation survey of early literacy achievement* (2nd ed.). Portsmouth, NH: Heinemann.

Cowley, J. (1998). *In the mirror.* Bothell, WA: Wright Group.

Cummins, J. (1986). Wanted: A theoretical framework for relating language proficiency to academic achievement among bilingual students. In C. Rivera (Ed.), *Language proficiency and academic achievement* (pp. 2–19). Clevedon, UK: Multilingual Matters.

Dalton, E. G., Tighe, P. L., & Ballard, W. S. (1991). *IPTI: Oral: IDEA Oral Language Proficiency Test, English.* Brea, CA: Educational IDEAS, Inc.

Defior, S., & Tudela, P. (1994). Effect of phonological training on reading and writing acquisition. *Reading and Writing: An Interdisciplinary Journal, 6,* 299–320.

Durgunoglu, A. Y., Nagy, W. E., & Hancin-Bhatt, B. J. (1993). Cross-language transfer of phonological awareness. *Journal of Educational Psychology, 85,* 453–465.

English, J. P., Leafstedt, J., Gerber, M., & Villaruz, J. (2001, April). *Individual differences in phonological skills for Spanish speaking kindergartners learning English: Relationship between English and Spanish phonological measures.* Paper presented at the annual meeting of the American Educational Research Association, Seattle, WA.

ERIC Clearinghouse on Urban Education. (2001). *Latinos in education: Early childhood, elementary, secondary, undergraduate, graduate.* Washington, DC: The White House Initiative on Educational Excellence for Hispanic Americans. (ERIC Document Reproduction Service No. ED449288)

Fitzgerald, J. (2003). Multilingual reading theory. *Reading Research Quarterly, 38,* 118–122.

Fitzgerald, J., Amendum, S., & Guthrie, K. (2008). Young Latino students' English-reading growth in all-English classrooms. *Journal of Literacy Research, 40,* 59–94.

Fitzgerald, J., & Graves, M. F. (2004). *Scaffolded reading experiences for English-language learners.* Norwood, MA: Christopher-Gordon.

Fitzgerald, J., & Noblit, G. (1999). About hopes, aspirations, and uncertainty: First-grade English-language learners' emergent reading. *Journal of Language Research, 31,* 133–182.

Fitzgerald, J., & Noblit, G. (2000). Balance in the making: Learning to read in an ethnically diverse first-grade classroom. *Journal of Educational Psychology, 92,* 1–20.

Fitzgerald, J., & Shanahan, T. (2000). Reading and writing relations and their development. *Educational Psychologist, 35,* 39–50.

Fountas, I. C., & Pinnell, G. S. (1996). *Guided reading: Good first teaching for all children.* Portsmouth, NH: Heinemann.

Fountas, I. C., & Pinnell, G. S. (1999). *Matching books to readers: Using leveled books in guided reading, K–3.* Portsmouth, NH: Heinemann.

Fountas, I. C., & Pinnell, G. S. (2001). *Guiding readers and writers, grades 3–6: Teaching comprehension, genre, and content literacy.* Portsmouth, NH: Heinemann.

General Accounting Office. (2001). *Meeting the needs of students with limited English proficiency.* Washington, DC: Author.

Geva, E., Yaghoud-Zadeh, Z., & Schuster, B. (2000). Understanding individual differences in word recognition skills of ESL children. *Annals of Dyslexia, 50,* 123–154.

González, J. E. J., & García, C. R. H. (1995). Effects of word linguistic properties on phonological awareness in Spanish children. *Journal of Educational Psychology, 87,* 193–201.

González, J. E. J., & Valle, I. H. (2000). Word identification and reading disorders in the Spanish language. *Journal of Learning Disabilities, 33,* 44–60.

Hasbrouck, J. E., & Tindal, G. (1992). Curriculum-based oral reading fluency norms for students in grades 2–5. *Teaching Exceptional Children, 24*(3), 41–44.

Hutchinson, J. M., Whiteley, H. E., Smith, C. D., & Connors, L. (2003). The developmental progression of comprehension-related skills in children learning EAL. *Journal of Research in Reading, 26,* 19–23.

Johnston, P. H. (1992). *Constructive evaluation of literate activity.* New York: Longman.

Kindler, A. E. (2002). *Survey of the states of limited English proficient students and available education programs and services 2000–2001 summary report.* Retrieved February 22, 2006, from *www.ncela.gwu.edu*

Lesaux, N. K., & Geva, E. (2006). Synthesis: Development of literacy in language-minority students. In D. August & T. Shanahan (Eds.), *Developing literacy in second-language learners: Report of the National Literacy Panel on Language-Minority Children and Youth* (pp. 53–74). Mahwah, NJ: Erlbaum.

Lesaux, N. K., & Siegel, L. S. (2003). The development of reading in children who speak English as a second language. *Developmental Psychology, 39,* 1005–1019.

Lindsey, K. A., Manis, F. R., & Bailey, C. E. (2003). Predictions of first-grade reading in Spanish-speaking English-language learners. *Journal of Educational Psychology, 95*(3), 482–494.

Manis, F. R., Lindsey, K. A., & Bailey, C. E. (2004). Development of reading in grades K–2 in

Spanish-speaking English-language learners. *Learning Disabilities Research and Practice, 19*, 214–224.

Mitchell, R., & Myles, F. (2004). *Second language learning theories* (2nd ed.). London: Arnold.

Morris, D. (1999). The role of clinical training in the teaching of reading. In D. E. Evensen & P. B. Mosenthal (Eds.), *Advances in reading/language research* (Vol. 6, pp. 69–100). Greenwich, CT: JAI Press.

Muter, V., & Dietholm, K. (2001). The contribution of phonological skills and letter knowledge to early reading development in a multilingual population. *Language Learning, 51*, 187–219.

Nation, I. S. P. (2001). *Learning vocabulary in another language*. Cambridge, UK: Cambridge University Press.

National Institute of Child Health and Development. (2000). *Report of the National Reading Panel: Teaching children to read: An evidence-based assessment of the scientific research literature of reading and its implications for reading instruction: Reports of the subgroups*. Washington DC: Author.

Neufeld, P., & Fitzgerald, J. (2001). Early English reading development: Latino English learners in the "low" reading group. *Research in the Teaching of English, 36*, 64–109.

Peregoy, S. F., & Boyle, O. F. (2004). English learners reading English: What we know, what we need to know. In R. D. Robinson, M. C. McKenna, & J. M. Wedman (Eds.), *Issues and trends in literacy education* (pp. 103–118). Boston: Pearson Education.

Pinnell, G. S., Pikulski, J., Wixon, K., Campbell, J. R., Gough, P. B., & Beatty, A. S. (1995). *Listening to children read aloud: Data from the NEAP Integrated Reading Performance of Grade 4*. Washington, DC: U.S. Government Printing Office.

Proctor, C. P., Carlo, M., August, D., & Snow, C. E. (2005). Native Spanish-speaking children reading in English: Toward a model of comprehension. *Journal of Educational Psychology, 97*, 246–256.

Quiroga, T., Lemos-Bitton, Z., Mostafapour, E., Abbott, R., & Berninger, V. W. (2002). Phonological awareness and beginning reading in Spanish-speaking ESL first graders: Research into practice. *Journal of School Psychology, 40*, 85–111.

Schwartz, R. M. (1997). Self-monitoring in beginning reading. *Reading Teacher, 51*, 40–48.

Shefelbine, J. (1995). *Learning and using phonics in beginning reading* (Scholastic Literacy Research Paper No. 10). Jefferson City, MO: Scholastic.

Siegel, L. S. (2003). Basic cognitive processes and reading disabilities. In H. L. Swanson, K. R. Harris, & S. Graham (Eds.), *Handbook of learning disabilities* (pp. 158–181). New York: Guilford Press.

Signorini, A. (1997). Word reading in Spanish: A comparison between skilled and less skilled beginning readers. *Applied Psycholinguistics, 18*, 319–344.

Slavin, R. E., & Cheung, A. (2005). A synthesis of research on language of reading instruction for English language learners. *Review of Educational Research, 75*, 247–284.

Snow, C. E., Burns, M. S., & Griffin, P. (Eds.). (1998). *Preventing reading difficulties in young children: A report of the National Research Council*. Washington, DC: National Academy Press.

Stanovich, K. E. (1986). Matthew effects in reading: Some consequences of individual differences in the acquisition of literacy. *Reading Research Quarterly, 21*, 360–407.

Stauffer, R. (1969). *Directing reading maturity as a cognitive process*. New York: Harper & Row.

Thomas, W. P., & Collier, V. P. (1997, December). *School effectiveness for language minority students*. National Clearinghouse for Bilingual Education (NCBE) Resource Collection Series, No. 9.

Thomas, W. P., & Collier, V. P. (2002). *A national study of school effectiveness for language minority students' long term academic achievement, final report: Project 1.1.* Santa Cruz: University of California, Center for Research on Education, Diversity, and Excellence.

Tumner, W. E., & Nesdale, A. R. (1985). Phonemic segmentation skill and beginning reading. *Journal of Educational Psychology, 77,* 417–427.

U.S. Department of Education National Center for Education Statistics. (2005). *National assessment of educational progress: The nation's report card.* Retrieved April 6, 2007, from *nationsreportcard.gov/reading_math_grade12_2005/s0412*

Weber, R. M., & Longhi-Chirlin, T. (2001). Beginning in English: The growth of linguistic and literate abilities in Spanish-speaking first graders. *Reading Research and Instruction, 41,* 19–50.

Woodcock, R. W., & Munoz-Sandoval, A. F. (2001). *Woodcock–Munoz Language Survey Normative Update, English Form.* Itasca, IL: Riverside.

Zehler, A., Fleischman, H., Hopstock, P., Stephenson, T., Pendzick, M., & Sapru, S. (2003). *Descriptive study of services to LEP students and LEP students with disabilities* (Vol. 1A: Research report). Retrieved January 15, 2004, from *www.devassoc.com/devassoc/vol_1_text.pdf*

CHAPTER 17

Supporting Parental Practices in the Language and Literacy Development of Young Children

Oscar A. Barbarin
Nikki Aikens

Research leaves little doubt about the critical role of families in preparing children for school. The influence of a strong learning foundation during the 0–5 years, or the lack thereof, is still evident by the time children depart from secondary education (Jencks & Phillips, 1998). A child's life at home presents multiple opportunities for enhancing literacy, language, and academic skills, but many of these opportunities may go unrecognized by families. Even when parents recognize the importance of their role, without support they may lack confidence in their own abilities to help their children develop early skills because, for example, of limitation in their own education or English proficiency. Early childhood educators can be especially helpful by encouraging families to identify and to take advantage of opportunities to promote children's development by highlighting specific activities parents can do, and by enlisting parents as collaborators in the teaching of young children.

This chapter is intended to be a resource to early childhood programs and educators in conceptualizing and designing efforts for parents to help their children prepare academically for school. It describes specific parental practices and provides evidence of their association with children's language and literacy outcomes, discusses social context factors that may influence the adoption of these practices, and makes recommendations to support parents in utilizing strategies that promote children's learning and development. The first section of this chapter describes several commonly used parental practices, both child- and environment-focused, and reviews evidence of their effectiveness in promoting children's readiness for school. Demonstrated effectiveness, however, is no guarantee that a practice will be adopted by families. Parents reinforce the skills that they value in children. What they value is evidenced in their attitudes and beliefs, for example, about what is important for school readiness. The second part of the chapter addresses the sociocultural contexts that gives rise to diverse patterns of parental practices and beliefs related to school readiness. In this section we argue that families' use of practices can be understood within the context of worldviews, life conditions, and parental views of the skills children need to be successful at school. A recent discernible shift on the part of parents, from an almost exclusive focus on social competence to inclusion of cognitive skills as a condition for school readiness, augurs well for a greater emphasis in parental practices on promoting cognitive skills. In the final section, we recommend ways of supporting and promoting parental practices to foster children's language, literacy, and academic development.

Parental Practices

Types of Parental Practices

Many different parental practices have been associated with the development of early language skills and acquisition of knowledge required for competent reading (Sénéchal & LeFevre, 2002; Whitehurst & Lonigan, 2002). These parental practices can be categorized as either child-focused or environment-focused. Child-focused strategies often involve parental interventions that target the child, including strategies such as (1) reading and exposure to books; (2) conversations, storytelling, and activities or games that stimulate language development; (3) intentional teaching or didactic instruction; and (4) enrichment activities. Joint reading and exposing children to books are commonly used strategies that begin early in life. Conversations and dialogic interaction are often embedded in family routines and include expanding children's knowledge of words and stimulating their use of gradually more complex syntax. Intentional teaching is didactic in nature, usually involves direct instruction, and most often focuses on imparting nominal knowledge and memorization of facts, such as names for body parts, letters, and numbers; the sounds associated with letters; as well as writing letters and words. Enrichment practices are intended to expand the horizons of the channel beyond what the family can provide and often involve a range of experiences and activities that take the child outside of the home to acquire musical, artistic, or athletic skills, and to visit educational settings, such as museums or artistic performances.

Whereas child-focused practices are direct and explicit in their attempt to enhance children's skills, environment-focused practices are often implicit with respect to improving children's competence, motivation, or engagement with school. Environment-focused practices represent efforts to create conditions in the home or school that are auspicious for children's learning and development. In this way, their impact on children's development of competence is indirect and they do not specifically target the child. Most often, environment-focused strategies are intended to create a setting that generally sustains academic motivation and values achievement. These practices include creation of a home climate that encourages learning (Beals, DeTemple, & Dickinson, 1994; Neuman, 1999; Sénéchal & LeFevre, 2002; Whitehurst & Lonigan, 1998). In addition, environment-focused strategies include parental involvement in the child's school and development of an open, trustful, mutually supportive and collaborative relationship with school staff. The most important aspect, and perhaps the active ingredient of environment-focused practices that is shared to an extent with child-focused strategies, is to convey values and instill attitudes that the family considers helpful to the child's adaptation to the school milieu and to life. In the next sections we review evidence that illustrates the importance of child- and environment-focused parental practices for the development of children's language and literacy skills.

Child-Focused Strategies

Reading and Exposure to Books

Research on early reading indicates that environments that are rich in print materials are associated with enhanced reading development (Neuman, 1999). For young children, an especially important aspect of exposure to print also comes in the form of joint reading with parents. The most common, and perhaps the most important form of family support for early literacy development, is shared book reading between children and family members (Dickinson & DeTemple, 1998; Neuman, 1999). The influence of book reading experiences on early language and literacy skills is widely documented (Bus, 2002; Bus, van IJzendoorn, & Pellegrini, 1995; Lee & Burkam, 2002; Sénéchal & LeFevre, 2001; Sénéchal, LeFevre, Hudson, & Lawson, 1996), including among low-income children. Recent research using nationally representative samples of preschool-age children in Head Start (Administration for Children and Families, 2003), and infants and toddlers enrolled in Early Head Start (Raikes et al., 2006) demonstrates links between joint book reading frequency and low-income children's scores on literacy measures. Several early literacy skills relate to being read to regularly, including letter recognition (Beals et al., 1994; Toomey & Sloane, 1994), oral language skills (Sénéchal, LeFevre, Thomas, & Daley, 1998; Whitehurst & Lonigan, 1998, 2002), vocabulary and word knowledge (Evans, Shaw, & Bell, 2000; Toomey & Sloane, 1994; Whitehurst & Lonigan, 1998, 2002), knowledge of concepts about print and written language (Clay, 1979; Dickinson & DeTemple, 1998; Evans et al., 2000; Toomey & Sloane, 1994; Whitehurst & Lonigan, 1998, 2002), and knowledge of how books convey meaning (Toomey & Sloane, 1994). Exposure to books reinforces for children the link between spoken words and print (Rush, 1999). It provides greater opportunity to acquire increased vocabulary and knowledge about print. Moreover, frequent reading experiences are likely to promote the value of literacy and improve the reading strategies used by children independently (Chiarelli, 1994), particularly joint reading experiences that are coupled with positive emotional interactions between parent and child (Baker, Mackler, Sonnenschein, & Serpell, 2001). A direct link between shared book reading and phonological processing skills has not been found, however (Whitehurst & Lonigan, 1998).

Though there is little doubt that storybook reading is a powerful strategy for promoting reading success, it is most effective when parents extend the meaning of the text through conversation and discussion by providing children opportunities to ask and answer questions. In fact, work by Whitehurst and colleagues (Whitehurst, Arnold, et al., 1994; Whitehurst, Epstein, et al., 1994; Whitehurst et al., 1988; Whitehurst & Lonigan, 1998, 2002) suggests that "dialogic reading," a method of storybook reading in which the adult provides opportunities for the child to talk and to engage with the story by asking questions and listening actively, promotes children's language use and development.

Exposure to books as a construct includes possession of or access to and use of printed materials. It includes the varied strategies that parents use to make books available for children, acquiring them for the home by either purchasing or borrowing, or by visiting libraries. In research, exposure is often indexed by the number of books a child possesses. However, when family material resources are limited, how well a family takes advantage of public sources, such as libraries, may be critical. Thus, the regularity with which the child visits the library can also be a useful indicator of exposure to books. There is evidence that library visits are correlated with vocabulary development when the effects of children's print exposure are controlled (Sénéchal et al., 1996). Similarly, the number of books a child possesses is related to vocabulary development (Sénéchal et al., 1996).

Conversations with the Child

Opportunities to stimulate children's language development arise in conversations that take place between the child and his or her family during many mundane activities and in commonly occurring settings, such as meals, bedtimes, and traveling from one place to another (Beals et al., 1994; Jordan, Snow, & Porche, 2000). In fact, the vocabulary- and discourse-level skills that are crucial to literacy development are promoted by adults in settings such as book reading and other routine events in which family members share experiences, explain events, and discuss opinions (Beals et al., 1994). Language-stimulating practices include encouraging children to ask and to answer questions during joint reading and writing activities, and guided television watching (Marvin & Mirenda, 1993). These practices may also take the form of encouraging verbal descriptions of nonshared experiences, recalling shared experiences, explaining events, and discussing opinions. Also important are adult responses to children's queries in these conversations, and efforts to explain events and to elaborate verbally on children's experiences.

These practices lead to fortuitous consequences with respect to expanding children's vocabulary, listening, and language skills (Whitehurst & Lonigan, 1998). These parental practices also deepen children's understanding of the meaning of words, ideas, narratives, and the world around them (Beals et al., 1994; Jordan et al., 2000; Rush, 1999). They can also engender a motivation for and love of reading. Moreover, parents who engage in behaviors that increase the types and number of words to which their children are exposed provide very important opportunities for growth in language and reading skills. In fact, mothers who use more complex and diverse sentences and words in daily conversations have children with greater expressive language skills and better scores on vocabulary- and literacy-oriented tasks in kindergarten (Britto & Brooks-Gunn, 2001) and second grade (Weizman & Snow, 2001). Hart and Risley's work (1995) also demonstrates links between the frequency and complexity of mothers' speech and young children's vocabulary development. In fact, the quantity, variety, and complexity of parental discourse with young children is predictive of the variety and quality of children's language, memory, and early literacy skills (Haden Ornstein, Eckerman, & Didow, 2001; Hart & Risley, 1992, 1995; Minami, 2001; Pratt, Kerig, Cowan, & Cowan, 1988; Whitehurst, Arnold, et al., 1994). Such experiences also allow children the opportunity to understand the function of language (Rush, 1999). Conversely, lack of language stimulation of sufficient quality and quantity in early life may account for deficient vocabulary development and poor reading achievement observed in later life (Rush, 1999).

"Dialogic practices" refer to a class of practices, such as explaining and elaborating, that involve narrative exchange between the parent and child covering cause–effect relations, present or future events, or connections between events and ideas in ways that help children understand and draw conclusions (Powell, 2004; Tabors, Beals, & Weizman, 2001). Dialogic practices include strategies such as offering explanations, elaboration, and responding sensitively to difficulty, and providing emotional support in learning situations. These practices include a related set of strategies that have been labeled as scaffolding, elaboration, open-ended questioning, and supportive communication. At the core of dialogic practices are developmentally sensitive and supportive responses from adults that help children to stretch beyond their present skills and understanding, but not so far as to cause frustration (Plumert & Nichols-Whitehead, 1996). Key to the impact of these practices is the ability of parents to follow the child's focus of attention, to comment on his or her activity, and to expand on the theme of their child's conversation or play (Murray & Hornbaker, 1997). This requires a child-centered rather than adult-directed perspective in which adult actions arise in response to signals from the child during mundane activities or joint reading (Lonigan, 1994). Strategies such as asking questions or commenting on new information have the effect of directing attention to critical features of a problem in a way that leads the child to a solution (Haden et al., 2001). Dialogic practices in the context of storybook reading have been linked to children's language use and development (Whitehurst & Lonigan, 1998).

Intentional Teaching Practices

"Intentional teaching practices" typically involve explicit attempts to inculcate early language and literacy skills with strategies such as familiarizing children with the alphabet and the sounds associated with letters, or teaching children how to write letters and words. Direct teaching can occur naturally as part of family routines and games, for example, through finger play with infants and toddlers or pointing out letters and words with preschoolers in home and community environments (Sénéchal & LeFevre, 2002). Sénéchal and LeFevre (2002) propose that literacy-related experiences within the home can be defined as either formal or informal, citing "informal activities" as those for which the primary purpose is the general message contained in the text rather than the text itself (i.e., storybook reading). "Formal activities" are defined as those in which parent and child focus explicitly on the print (i.e., talking about letters, providing name and sounds of specific letters).

Compared to informal activities, much less is known about the influence of parents' formal, intentional teaching of early literacy skills. However, parents vary greatly in their beliefs about whether they should formally teach reading-related skills to their children (Sénéchal & LeFevre, 2002). Research by Anderson (1995) suggests that parents who value providing more structured, formal literacy activities also have children with stronger early literacy skills. Furthermore, Sénéchal and colleagues (1996, 1998) found that formal and informal activities are related to different language and literacy skills. Their investigations suggest that informal experiences such as storybook reading are related to the development of receptive language skills (i.e., vocabulary and listening comprehension), whereas formal teaching activities are related to the development of literacy skills such as print concepts, alphabetic knowledge, invented spelling, and decoding simple consonant–vowel–consonant words. Whitehurst and Lonigan (1998) also found that teaching activities are related to children's letter naming, sound recognition, and phonological processing skills.

Others have found that parents' use of intentional teaching strategies is associated with children's knowledge of letters and print conventions, phonological processing, receptive vocabulary, inventive spelling, and the enhanced ability to decode simple consonant–vowel–consonant words (Evans et al., 2000; Marvin & Mirenda, 1993). In fact, a study of 66 Canadian children by Evans and colleagues (2000) indicates that activities such as letter-sound practice are most predictive of children's knowledge of letter names, letter sounds, and phonological sensitivity, even outweighing the importance of storybook exposure to these oral language and early literacy skills. Relationships between intentional efforts to teach children how to write words and the ability to identify letters and their sounds have also been found (Haney & Hill, 2004).

Enrichment Strategies

On some occasions, parents look outside of the family for resources to expand the family's efforts to promote development of its children. Parents provide extrafamilial enrichment experiences to extend children's knowledge, artistic talents, or athletic skills beyond what the family can provide. Parents may employ enrichment strategies that involve efforts to provide learning opportunities by exposing children to new information and experiences. Enrichment practices are based on the premise of intensely cultivating children's skills by enrolling them in classes or clubs, or placing them in settings where they are likely to acquire new and specific skills, such as dancing or playing chess, or a musical instrument. Enrichment practices may be academic or social in nature and include trips to museums or libraries and attendance at a dramatic or musical performances, or storybook reading time at the library. Employing enrichment strategies often entails costs related to materials, transportation, and entrance and participation fees. Consequently, the use of enrichment strategies is highly correlated with socioeconomic status (SES) and access to financial resources (Lee & Burkam, 2002). Although enrichment practices, such child participation in the performing and creative arts, are more likely to occur among the affluent, these practices do seem to be associated with children's reading achievement at the beginning of kindergarten after researchers control for race, social class, and household demographics (Lee & Burkam, 2002).

Summary

We have reviewed parents' child-focused practices that ostensibly have a direct effect on enhancing literacy, language, and academic skills, and preparing children for school. Specifically, parents read to, talk to, teach, and provide enrichment activities for their children. These child-focused practices are not the only ways that families influence language and literacy development, and readiness for school. Parents also sculpt and act on the child's environment in ways that promote these skills. For example, families contribute to reading and academic development indirectly through the general climate of literacy in the home, transmission of beliefs and values, household routines, or the quality of home–school collaboration. In the next section we focus on parental practices that have an indirect effect on children's skills through their influence on the child's social milieux, specifically, the home environment and the school.

Practices Affecting the Home and School Environments

Home-Focused Strategies

Valuing learning is an important but often overlooked contribution that families make to children's reading development. Through the attitudes that parents espouse, the priorities they set, the behaviors in which they engage, the choices they make about how to allocate financial resources and time, and the ways they relate to educational institutions, parents convey to children powerful messages about education and impart to them the value of academic effort, education, and learning (Eccles, 1983). By purchasing print materials, taking pleasure in reading themselves, and encouraging children's use of books, parents transmit the value they attach to literacy. Parents also demonstrate value for learning and literacy through the expectations they hold for children's academic success and participation in schooling. Parental attitudes and expectations that convey a valuing of books, literacy, and learning motivate children to read (Snow, Burns, & Griffin, 1998). For example, work using the Early Childhood Longitudinal Study—Kindergarten cohort (ECLS-K; Lee & Burkam, 2002) draws relations between children's fall kindergarten reading performance and parent's educational expectations.

A literacy-rich environment characterized by the ready availability of print materials and writing utensils, and adults who use them as a part of daily routines, and create opportunities for children to use these materials, contributes significantly to the development of reading (Jordan et al., 2000; Marvin & Mirenda, 1993; Sénéchal & LeFevre, 2001). These environmental factors are important because they not only promote a child's interest in reading but also the development of language skills related to reading achievement. Children with early exposure to literacy-rich environments are especially likely to have positive early reading outcomes (Marvin & Mirenda, 1993; Sénéchal & LeFevre, 2001). Evidence using a nationally representative sample of kindergartners from the ECLS-K suggests that the number of books and records, CDs, and tapes in the home is positively related to children's reading scores upon school entry (Denton, West, & Walston, 2002; Lee & Burkam, 2002).

In addition to the literacy-rich environment that parents create, children's literacy and language skills may also be influenced by parents' environment-focused practices. Parental literacy and language practices are probably best understood within a larger context of parental strategies to socialize and prepare children for lives that their parents imagine for them. To accomplish this broad goal, parents employ a wide range of practices, many of which interact with and influence their specific practices to promote literacy and language. For example, families may impact children's literacy, language, and academic development indirectly through the use of *selective experiences*, in which parents direct children toward some activities and away from others through the information they share with their children and the social relationships they facilitate for them. For example, parents often *monitor the quality of the environments* in which they place their children. To the extent that parents exercise control, they select propitious environments, such as safe neighborhoods, schools that set high expectations and provide sound instruction, and peer groups that share academic and prosocial values. Through conversations, especially *interpretive comments* on events or people, parents convey values, attitudes, knowledge, and problem-solving skills. Through observing *parents as models* of persistence in striving toward their goals in the face of obstacles, children acquire a strong inclination to achieve. Provision of a *social identity* is another means through which parents influence literacy and language development. For example, through specific instruction and reliance on non-English language for daily life, parents may support the child's use of a language other than English, thereby keeping a child connected to the parents' cultural heritage.

School-Focused Practices

Active family involvement in the school is often considered an important way that parents can have a positive effect on children's academic performance. Frequent contact with school staff can often help families understand school expectations and acquire knowledge about ways to reinforce at home the learning that takes place at school. Family involvement in school activities (e.g., parent–teacher conferences, helping in the classroom) is associated with child language outcomes as early as preschool (Marcon, 1999). Among a sample of low-income kindergarten through fifth-grade children, such activities were associated with positive literacy outcomes (Dearing, Kreider, Simpkins, & Weiss, 2006). However, notions of what constitutes effective involvement should not be construed too narrowly. Accordingly, definitions of family involvement, which are based exclusively on the amount of time that family members spend in the school itself through frequent visits, fundraising, parent–teacher organization (PTO) involvement, chaperoning school events, class field trips, or volunteering in the classroom, are too limited and fail to capture the full range of strategies parents may employ to affect child academic outcomes. Family involvement can occur at a variety of levels, even when sustained presence at the school is not possible. Christenson and Sheridan (2001) present a fuller vision of family involvement that gives priority to the quality of the home–school relationship as a core feature. "Effective parental involvement" refers to family practices that go beyond volunteerism to include open communication, ability to resolve conflicts or disagreements, and true collaboration built on mutual respect between family and school staff (Comer & Haynes, 1991). For example, developing an open, trustful relationship with school staff is an important way that parents promote the academic engagement of their children (Christenson & Sheridan, 2001). Communication and maintaining positive relationships between home and school convey very powerful messages to the child about the importance of schooling, and that the home and the school work in unison to foster the child's school success. Through understanding, buttressed by effective communication, families form a viable working arrangement that serves their children well (Epstein & Dauber, 1991; Marcon, 1999).

Summary

The importance of parental practices, whether focused on the child, the home, or the school, is well documented and supported by empirical research (Marvin & Mirenda, 1993; Nye, Turner, & Schwartz, 2006; Purcell-Gates, 1996; Sénéchal & LeFevre, 2001). This evidence is compelling, especially for the effects of child-focused intentional teaching practices on early literacy skills (Evans et al., 2000; Sénéchal & LeFevre, 2002; Sénéchal et al., 1998; Whitehurst & Lonigan, 1998). Although the evidence for strategies focused on the environment is less compelling, it is nevertheless strong enough to warrant attention to strengthening the use of home- and school-focused strategies by families as a way of impacting children's language, literacy, and academic outcomes. If family practices are as important for children's skills as the research suggests, it seems reasonable to engage in efforts to promote the use of the strategies by families to enhance children's literacy in academic performance. The success of efforts to increase particular practices will depend in part on the understanding of why families are inclined or disinclined to use them.

The Social Context of Parental Practices

In this section we consider the social processes that influence the prevalence of parental practices. The social context includes widely held beliefs about what children should learn prior to school entry and who is responsible for teaching these skills. Because socioeconomic and ethnic niches are associated with differential access to resources and differential threats or life stress that may lead diverse families to prioritize different sets of skills, we focus on the social conditions of race/ethnicity and social class associated with language and literacy development.

On the question of what children should learn, a surprising unanimity exists among parents about the importance of nominal knowledge for readiness. "Nominal knowledge," such as colors, letters and numbers, and the ability to name common objects and parts of the body, is widely considered by parents to be important (Barbarin et al., in press). In fact, irrespective of income level, parents more often cite nominal knowledge than all other abilities and knowledge as critical for school readiness. This emphasis on nominal knowledge represents a shift in attitudes from earlier research by West, Jausken, and Collins (1993), who noted that parents' views of readiness most often emphasize the social dimensions of early school adjustment, such as the ability to wait one's turn and follow directions, the motivation to learn, the ability to resolve conflicts without resorting to aggression, and the ability to use words to communicate needs and wants.

Although parents' values and beliefs about readiness now have a discernible academic tilt, their beliefs do not yet reflect the importance of viewing higher-order cognitive skills as foundational to academic readiness. These higher-order cognitive or inferential skills may take the form of representational language and higher-level reasoning processes. These inferential skills have been shown to be especially important to literacy and language maturation (see Snow et al., 1998). Inferential skills in readiness involve understanding words, ideas, and narrative progression (Beals et al., 1994; Jordan et al., 2000; Rush, 1999). In a study of parents of children in a state-sponsored prekindergarten, few parents identified inferential skills as important for school readiness (Barbarin et al., in press). Thus, even though most recent data on parental attitudes reflect a greater emphasis on academic or cognitive skills than in the past, few parents verbalize the growing concern about the value of inferential reasoning skills over rote learning.

This omission is important to note because parental beliefs and values about school readiness are not trivial. They have a fairly consistent relationship to children's academic competencies. For example, Barbarin and colleagues (in press) found that parents' readiness beliefs about the importance of autonomous behavior, social skills, nominal knowledge, and inferential thinking corresponded with the outcomes their children attained in those domains. This finding suggests that children are more likely to acquire skills that their parents value. In addition to expressing their values, parents may reinforce children's attempts to master the valued skills. In this way, parental practices constitute a putative link between beliefs and child outcomes. Parents' emphasis on inferential skills is related not only to children's vocabulary and problem solving but also to "phonemic awareness" (i.e., recognition of the correspondence between sounds and letters). It is possible that parents who value inferential skills involve themselves more actively and frequently in a range of literacy-related activities that provide children opportunities to make letter–sound connections. These results suggest that when parents' views of readiness emphasize higher-order cognitive skills, children are more likely to master these skills successfully. The failure to include inferential thinking among the essential skills for school readiness is likely to be reflected in a more limited role given to dialogic interactions and exploratory conversations with children around books and other aspects of their lives.

Now we turn to a discussion of ethnic and social class differences observed in the prevalence of parental practices and the factors offered as explanations for those differences. Race/ethnicity and social class are associated with a constellation of parents' socialization goals and beliefs about the skills children need and the persons best equipped to impart them (Gallimore & Goldenberg, 1993; Lareau, 2000). Among low SES and ethnic/minority families, beliefs that are widely held even outside their groups combine with beliefs that arise out of their unique social milieux and experiences. For example, a few of the beliefs attributed to low SES and to ethnic/minority families include the following:

1. Knowing how to behave, having concrete information, and memorizing letters, numbers and the spelling of one's name are the best and primary preparation needed for school.
2. Children learn best from direct instruction and not through exploration and discovery.
3. The optimal learning environment is one in which children are quiet, passive, and orderly, so that knowledge can be "poured in."
4. Conversation means a monologue in which adults talk, and children listen and only respond to direct questions.
5. The criterion for successful learning is that a child gives the correct answer, using a single correct method to arrive at that answer.
6. Parents lack sufficient knowledge; therefore, they should cede to teachers the responsibility for children's learning.

What is the evidence for these assertions, and how might they be related to parental practices? SES differences have been observed in parental skills, involvement, beliefs, and practices (Baker, Serpell, & Sonnenschein, 1995; Evans, 2004; Lee & Burkam, 2002; Whitehurst & Lonigan, 1998). At the most basic level, family practices related to talking and reading to young children vary widely by race/ethnicity and SES (Hart & Risley, 1992, 1995; Lee & Burkam, 2002; Rothstein, 2004; Whitehurst & Lonigan, 2002). It is widely acknowledged that poorer children have less exposure and access to literacy materials and to home experiences that promote reading acquisition (Neuman,

1999). Low SES influences children's development not only directly, through limitations in materials, experiences, and services that parents are able to purchase for their children (Yeung, Linver, & Brooks-Gunn, 2002), but also indirectly, through its impact on parenting practices (Conger, Rueter, & Conger, 2000; Linver, Brooks-Gunn, & Kohen, 2002; McLoyd, 1998; Mistry, Vandewater, Huston, & McLoyd, 2002; Yeung et al., 2002). Striking social class differences have been observed in parents' beliefs about parental involvement in children's education. Several researchers have observed that low-SES and working-class parents consider education to be the specialized domain of teachers and the school, and not the domain for parental activity (Entwisle & Alexander, 1993; Lareau, 2000). As a result, these parents may be less likely to be involved in the school and in providing some literacy-related experiences for the child. In addition, some practices and sets of beliefs may be more possible to maintain and enact in sociocultural niches characterized by material sufficiency, physical safety, highly educated parents, and discretionary time to invest in interactions with children. In fact, lower-class parents, in particular, perceive themselves as less able to intervene or to make positive contributions to their children's school readiness (Marcon, 1999).

Emerging work with low-income, immigrant families has investigated the ways in which parental involvement in the school and engagement in the child's learning are shaped by cultural beliefs, social class, and language barriers (Hyslop, 2001; Li, 2003; Sampson, 2003). Explanations of these differences must begin with the observation that parental practices do not arise out of a vacuum. Immigrant parents may feel handicapped by their lack of proficiency with the English language. This leads to estrangement, which is made even worse by their limited knowledge of how American schools and instruction are organized (Fuligni & Yoshikawa, 2003). Moreover, they may be unaware of practices and activities in which they can engage to prepare their children for school (Li, 2003, 2006a).

Practices can also be shaped by cultural inclinations and traditions, as well as the exigencies and constraints of the material conditions under which families live. Specifically we argue that sociocultural conditions shape families' beliefs about their children and the strategies they adopt to reach those goals. Consistent with this view, Gee (2001) has argued that literacy itself is a culture-bound and context-sensitive phenomenon because language is both instrumental and tied to personal and cultural identity. Similarly, Gadsden (2004) suggests that parents' goals for their children, and the strategies of literacy and language development they use, arise out of social and cultural contexts. Moreover, definitions of what comprises competence vary from one social and cultural context to another (Keller, 2003). Parental beliefs, feelings, and knowledge about desired child outcomes shape the behaviors they use to produce those outcomes (Benasich & Brooks-Gunn, 1996). With regard to parental practices, just as attitudes about what children ought to learn vary by cultural group, so do the socializing behaviors associated with those attitudes (Bus, 2002). For example, Gallimore and Goldenberg (1993) observed that Latino parents emphasized correct performance of reading related tasks (i.e., writing or naming letters correctly) rather than a focus on the meaning of the text with their kindergarten children. Similar observations have been made by scholars of other groups, such as Asian immigrant parents (Chao, 1996; Li, 2002, 2006a, 2006b). Such behavior may result from cultural values around parental authority, conformity, and correctness as the hallmark of knowledge acquisition (Harry, 1992; Kotchick & Forehand, 2002).

In addition, in the United States and elsewhere, differential vulnerability to racial discrimination and its attendant distress has given rise to parental practices that clearly affect child development (Williams, 1999). The adverse effects of inequality in employment, housing, and education impact health, emotional well-being, and academic performance, and each of these affects the day-to-day lives of families of color (Williams, Neighbors, & Jackson, 2003). In addition, many ethnic/minority families in the United States experience emotional distress associated with financial instability, a factor that undoubtedly affects patterns of parenting behavior (McLoyd, 1990). Together, the forces of discrimination and inequality shape experiences within sociocultural niches formed by the intersection of ethnicity and economic status, and give rise to distinctive coping strategies, worldviews, aspirations, and beliefs about how life should be lived (Barbarin, 2002). Ethnic/minority parents are more likely to have to deal with issues of race, racial discrimination, and low family resources, which may complicate involvement in the child's school and make more difficult the formation of close, collaborative relationships with school staff. In short, although a variety of practices and beliefs within the home potentially contribute to fluency in recognizing and recalling letters and words, to enhance the ability to manipulate speech sounds, and to facilitate the formation of informal hypotheses about letters and words, familial abilities to engage in such activities, utilize these activities, and understand the meaning of those behaviors may vary considerably based on socioeconomic and cultural factors (Purcell-Gates, 1996). "Cognitive–linguistic abilities ... [are] linked in this way to a child's everyday experiences which [are] embedded in the cultural practices or 'scripts' of his or her family and society" (National Research Council, 2000, p. 68).

Supporting Parental Involvement and Promoting a Positive Relationship with the School

In this section we discuss approaches for engaging parents in the use of effective strategies to promote literacy, language, and academic development. These approaches, of course, must begin by acknowledging the influence of context and addressing parental beliefs that help to determine practices that parents will find acceptable and actually employ. We then offer recommendations about the content, methods, and settings for supporting the development and use of practices that foster parental involvement and nurture a positive home–school relationship. Specifically, we offer ideas about the content of the messages that teachers might give parents about ways to foster their children's literacy, language, and academic development. We briefly discuss methods that teachers can use to support adoption of the effective parental practices. We also identify a variety of settings in which supportive interventions may be offered.

Content of Supportive Efforts

There are many ideas that we might cover regarding the efforts of school staff to support parental practices and involvement in their children's literacy, language, and academic development. To facilitate decisions about what to include, and not to include, we recommend that priority be given to content designed to (1) identify overlooked opportunities for integrating effective parental practices into daily routines; (2) clarify the role and expectations of schools, how they are organized, and how they operate; and (3) increase access to and use of literacy materials.

Integrating Parental Practices into Daily Routines

If these effective practices are to be adopted by parents, supportive efforts should identify ways to integrate the desired parental practices into the routines of family life. Accordingly, efforts to support parental involvement should also identify opportunities to use these practices at home. Teachers can encourage parents to think about using settings, activities, and occasions that are already built into their daily routines. For example, parents can be encouraged to engage in conversations with the child during mealtimes, transitional times between activities, before bed, or while watching television. Parents can have the child recall the events of the day (e.g., what the child did at school), or discuss upcoming or past events or people in the child's or parents' life. Parents can also be encouraged to explain events thoroughly, including, for example, how things work, how others might feel, and why things are done a certain way. Especially important is that parents respond contingently to the child's speech and ask questions that expand on the child's vocabulary and require more than a yes–no response. During daily interactions, parents can also point out new words or letters in the environment. All of these activities help to build children's language skills (Beals et al., 1994; Jordan et al., 2000; Marvin & Mirenda, 1993; Sénéchal & LeFevre, 2002; Whitehurst & Lonigan, 1998). It is especially good to encourage language-stimulating practices in families, grouped here under the rubric of "dialogic reading." Based on the research we have reviewed here, dialogic practices have proven to be very effective. Workshops that are based on these practices help parents to utilize questions and queries in dialogue during joint book reading with their children. These practices are more likely to be implemented when integrated into the activities in which families normally engage.

As children mature, other important functions must be incorporated in the parental role. Parents, for example, may need to act as their child's advocate and take a more active role in helping the child to navigate the school environment, by learning about the school and its resources. Instead of direct teaching, parents may model reading as a leisure activity and writing as a way to acquire important information. For parents with limited English proficiency, talking and reading to the child in their native language may serve as an opportunity to engender motivation to read and help the child learn the parent's native language.

Informing Parents about School Organization, Expectations, and Operation

Providing parents with information about practices is important, but it is not enough. To effectively promote their children's learning, parents also need information about how the school operates, its staff regulations and expectations. Parents who have this information gain a better idea of what to expect and how to work with the school effectively. This information is a *sine qua non* for collaboration. In other words, a close working relationship with the school depends on knowledge of the school's organization and how it operates. Schools and teachers can help by *providing general information* about how the school is organized to orient new families to the teaching and administrative staff, so that parents know who to contact for specific needs. Also important is sharing with families the expectations of school personnel about the effort, performance, behavior, and outcomes for each child. But expectations are not a one-way street. The school should also sponsor conversations with families about what they expect of the schools. Information that is most valuable to parents is centered around how well the child is meeting academic expectations. Parents often lack information about progress the child is making in specific areas. Schools can enhance parental involvement by communicating children's progress specifically, through school-sponsored celebratory events that focus on childrens' specific skills.

Expanding Access to Quality Literacy Materials

Early childhood education and literacy has received a great deal of emphasis in terms of desired outcomes. Though many children come to school with vast knowledge of and interests in books, this is not true for all children. Schools can play an important role in leveling the playing field for families whose experiences with literacy materials may not be extensive. In addition to sharing effective parental practices and the benefits to children, schools can support parental involvement by providing information on appropriate books and reading materials that might interest the child. For example, teachers can send books home for children to share with parents to reinforce what happens at school. They can develop *a list of suggested books* that parents can use as a basis for purchasing books or borrowing them from the library. To facilitate use of these booklists, schools can also organize book fairs and encourage the use of lending libraries.

Although efforts to support parental involvement may be clear, the best methods for conveying this are not always apparent. In the next section we suggest methods that teachers might use to strengthen the home–school relationship and to reinforce parental practices that promote literacy, language, and academic development.

Methods for Promoting Parental Practices

Meeting the challenge of conveying information and promoting growth in parents' use of effective practices requires creativity in the use of multiple methods. The formats for parent support may include traditional workshops, discussion groups, ongoing parent cafés, and ad hoc conversations when the parent picks up the child, or even handouts sent home with children. A variety of pedagogical techniques may be used, including traditional didactic methods, such as readings and lectures or seminar discussions. The most effective methods and best practices involve skills building techniques that use principles of modeling in which parents talk about a specific practice, are given an opportunity to employ the practice, and are observed and given feedback about their performance. In this effort to encourage parental involvement, however, staff must respect diverse families and perspectives, and encourage behaviors that allow the greatest number of families to engage successfully in their children's early language, literacy, and academic development. This is particularly the case for families that, for whatever reason, may be the least likely to be involved with the school or the child's learning.

Parents can use multiple resources and information available on the Web that foster the early skills of their children. Schools can help parents by informing families and even providing access to websites, such as *www.walearning.com*, which contains information developed by Dr. Angela Notari-Syverson and colleagues under a grant from the U.S. Department of Education. These materials include activities that can be used at home or in a variety of places in the community to promote children's language and literacy skills. With the variety of strategies we described earlier, such as workshops, regular contact, and providing access to resource materials, schools can play a very important role in helping parents who want to be involved with their children. By taking these steps, schools can build on family efforts and ultimately increase the possibility of their own success.

Settings for Promoting Parental Involvement

There are a multitude of occasions and settings through which school districts and teachers can reach parents to support parental practices that nurture the development of children's competence. These settings are limited only by imagination and include home visits, parent–teacher conferences, parent workshops, discussion groups, telephone contacts, ad hoc meetings when parent picks up a child, celebratory and performance events at school, broadcast e-mails or phone calls, handouts sent home with the child, and, in some cases, public service announcements on radio and television.

During home visits, which are often made by prekindergarten and kindergarten teachers, teachers can share information with parents about the importance of reading and talking with children, as well as other strategies that parents can use. Home visits can be used to share information about the school and its academic expectations or to model the specific strategies a parent might use with the child. Typically, parent–teacher conferences are held once or twice a year. This is an optimal time to convey information about what parents can do to support the learning activities that are taking place in the classroom. However, teachers and school programs can also use other occasions, such as child performance nights or academic celebrations, to share generic information that might otherwise be conveyed in parent–teacher conferences.

Parenting groups or workshops are often offered as a way to provide parents more intensive and sequenced instruction about ways to help their children develop literacy and academic skills. Parent workshops are also an excellent way to help parents to focus on their own developmental needs and on goals for their children. One example of this approach is the PAS (Promoting Academic Success of Boys of Color) curriculum, developed at the Frank Porter Graham Child Development Institute (see *www.fpg. unc.edu/~pas*). This curriculum focuses on helping parents to develop specific strategies associated with favorable outcomes for children. The program promotes parents' skills around partnering with schools, talking and having fun with the child, and reading and using mathematics with children. By engaging in these behaviors, parents foster the development of early skills that augur well for the children's long-term achievement in school. These workshops are less effective if they are limited to didactic instructional monologues and more effective when they involve active participation either through discussion or learning activities. In some cases it is effective to pair a mini-workshop with a social purpose. Serving food, offering child care, and including fun activities are effective ways to engage parents over time in learning about ways to help their children.

Conclusion

The importance of the role of parents in the education of their children is indisputable. We have reviewed research demonstrating that parental practices are associated with desired outcomes in literacy and language. There is also evidence, not reviewed here, that these practices can also impact the development of mathematical skills. Research suggests that child-focused strategies have the strongest and most direct effects on children's language literacy outcomes. Intentional instruction by parents is highly effective during the early childhood years but may have more limited usefulness after first grade, when the child is mastering basic skills for reading. Thereafter, it is likely that the effects of environment-focused strategies become more evident and salient relative to children's motivation, effort, persistence, and school engagement.

Considerable evidence also suggests that families of the most vulnerable children are using child-focused strategies less frequently than might be optimal. The challenge for early childhood educators is how to disseminate information to parents about what helps their children, and how to expand on the arsenal of strategies parents have available to help their children succeed at school. Therefore, the biggest challenge is how to reach and to involve parents who have the greatest need but for whom use of effective strategies is lowest.

Part of the answer to this puzzle is an appreciation of the contexts of all families. Effective support for school involvement means understanding the difficulties and challenges that families face, and it requires an appreciation of the culture and values that drive parents' understanding of what children need and how they learn. Teachers and schools can promote positive relationships with parents and positive outcomes for children by showing respect for home–school differences in perspectives and empowering parents as advocates for and teachers of their children. This means that knowledge of specific practices must be translated and adapted to fit the contexts in which they are to be applied. An important lesson in this regard is reflected in the comments of a dental school dean when asked to sort out the competing claims of toothbrush manufacturers about the superiority of their products. What did he recommend as the best toothbrush to buy? His cryptic but wise response was: "Without question, the best toothbrush to buy is the one you will use (often)." The wisdom of this response lies in the insight that no tool or in our case, no strategy can be effective if it is not used. The more effective strategies are the ones that parents use with regularity. If a strategy is used consistently and with a sense of purpose, even if not optimally applied, it is more likely to have an intended effect than a perfectly conceived strategy that is never used. Therefore, the challenge here is to apply our understanding of families' sociocultural contexts to frame ideas, and to modify practices so that they fit into the rhythm and contexts of the lives of parents who, we hope, will employ them. To strengthen motivation, parents can be provided information about how implementation of these parental practices benefit children's development. If this is done systematically, then parents will be more likely to use them for the benefit of their children. To be successful, schools must initiate collaboration under the assumption that families are motivated to provide what their children need. By working closely and respectfully with families, schools amplify their own efforts. In this way, the child wins, the school is more successful, and parents receive needed support in fulfilling their educational role with their children. Efforts on the part of early childhood programs and teachers to cultivate and support parental involvement in this way are likely to pay handsome dividends for children.

References

Administration for Children and Families. (2003). *Head Start FACES (2000): A whole child perspective on program performance—fourth progress report*. Washington, DC: Author.

Anderson, J. (1995). How parents' perceptions of literacy acquisition relate to their children's emergent literacy knowledge. *Reading Horizons, 35*, 209–228.

Baker, L., Mackler, K., Sonnenschein, S., & Serpell, R. (2001). Parents' interactions with their first-grade children during storybook reading and relations with subsequent home reading activity and reading achievement. *Journal of School Psychology, 39*(5), 415–438.

Baker, L., Serpell, R., & Sonnenschein, S. (1995). Opportunities for literacy learning in homes of urban preschoolers. In L. M. Morrow (Ed.), *Family Literacy: Connections in schools and communities* (pp. 236–252). New Brunswick, NJ: International Reading Association.

Barbarin, O. A. (2002). Culture and ethnicity in social, emotional and academic development. *Kauffman Early Education Exchange, 1*, 45–61.

Barbarin, O. A., Frome, P., Early, D., Clifford, R., Bryant, D., Burchinal, M., et al. (in press). School readiness: The perspectives of families of children enrolled in public sponsored pre-K programs. *Early Education and Development*.

Beals, D. E., DeTemple, J. M., & Dickinson, D. K. (1994). Talking and listening that support early literacy development of children from low-income families. In D. K. Dickinson (Ed.), *Bridges to literacy: Children, families, and schools* (pp. 19–40). Malden, MA: Blackwell.

Benasich, A. A., & Brooks-Gunn, J. (1996). Maternal attitudes and knowledge of child-rearing: Associations with family and child outcomes. *Child Development, 67*, 1186–1205.

Britto, P. R., & Brooks-Gunn, J. (2001). The role of family literacy environments in promoting young children's emerging literacy skills: Concluding comments. *New Directions for Child and Adolescent Development, 92*, 91–99.

Bus, A. G. (2002). Joint caregiver–child storybook reading: A route to literacy development. In S. B. Neuman & D. K. Dickinson (Eds.), *Handbook of early literacy research* (Vol. 1, pp. 179–191). New York: Guilford Press.

Bus, A. G., van IJzendoorn, M. H., & Pellegrini, A. D. (1995). Joint book reading makes for success in learning to read: A meta-analysis of intergenerational transmission of literacy. *Review of Educational Research, 65*, 1–21.

Chao, R. K. (1996). Chinese and European American mothers' beliefs about the role of parenting in children's school success. *Journal of Cross-Cultural Psychology, 27*(4), 403–423.

Chiarelli, P.A. (1994). Early intervention strategies for family literacy. In N. J. Ellsworth & C. N. Hedley (Eds.), *Literacy: A redefinition* (pp. 233–246). Hillsdale, NJ: Erlbaum.

Christenson, S. L., & Sheridan, S. M. (2001). *Schools and families: Creating essential connections for learning*. New York: Guilford Press.

Clay, M. M. (1979). *Reading: Patterning of complex behavior* (2nd ed.). Auckland, New Zealand: Heinemann.

Comer, J. P., & Haynes, N. M. (1991). Parent involvement in schools: An ecological approach. *Elementary School Journal, 91*, 271–278

Conger, K. J., Rueter, M. A., & Conger, R. D. (2000). The role of economic pressure in the lives of parents and their adolescents: The family stress model. In L. J. Crockett & R. K. Silbereisen (Eds.), *Negotiating adolescence in times of social change* (pp. 201–223). New York: Cambridge University Press.

Dearing, E., Kreider, H., Simpkins, S., & Weiss, H. B. (2006). Family involvement in school and low-income children's literacy performance: Longitudinal associations between and within families. *Journal of Educational Psychology, 98,* 653–664.

Denton, K., West, J., & Walston, J. (2003). *Reading–young children's achievement and classroom experiences* (NCES 2003-070). Washington, DC: U.S. Department of Education.

Dickinson, D. K., & DeTemple, J. (1998). Putting parents in the picture: Maternal reports of preschool literacy as a prediction of early reading. *Early Childhood Research Quarterly, 13*(2), 241–261.

Eccles, J. (1983). Expectancies, values, and academic behaviors. In J. T. Spence (Ed.), *Achievement and achievement motivations* (pp. 75–146). San Francisco: Freeman.

Entwisle, D. R., & Alexander, K. L. (1993). Entry into school: The beginning school transition and educational stratification in the United States. *Annual Review of Sociology, 19,* 401–423.

Epstein, J. L., & Dauber, S. L. (1991). School programs and teacher practices of parent involvement in inner-city elementary and middle schools. *Elementary School Journal, 91*(3), 289–306.

Evans, G. W. (2004). The environment of childhood poverty. *American Psychologist, 59*(2), 77–92.

Evans, M., Shaw, D., & Bell, M. (2000). Home literacy activities and their influence on early literacy skills. *Canadian Journal of Experimental Psychology, 54*(2), 65–75.

Fuligni, A., & Yoshikawa, H. (2003). Socioeconomic resources, parenting, and child development among immigrant families. In M. H. Borstein & R. H. Bradley (Eds.), *Socioeconomic status, parenting, and child development* (pp. 107–124). Mahwah, NJ: Erlbaum.

Gadsden, V. L. (2004). Family literacy and culture. In B. H. Wasik (Ed.), *Handbook of family literacy* (pp. 401–425). New York: Erlbaum.

Gallimore, R., & Goldenberg, C. (1993). Activity settings of early literacy: Home and school factors in children's emergent literacy. In E. A. Forman & N. Minick (Eds.), *Contexts for learning: Sociocultural dynamics in children's development* (pp. 315–335). London: Oxford University Press.

Gee, J. G. (2001). A sociocultural perspective on early literacy development. In S. B. Neuman & D. K. Dickinson (Eds.), *Handbook of early literacy research* (Vol. 1, pp. 30–42). New York: Guilford Press.

Haden, C. A., Ornstein, P. A., Eckerman, C. O., & Didow, S. M. (2001). Mother–child conversational interactions as events unfold: Linkages to subsequent remembering. *Child Development, 72*(4), 1016–1031.

Haney, M. H., & Hill, J. (2004). Relationships between parent-teaching activities and emergent literacy in preschool children. *Early Child Development and Care, 17*(3), 215–228.

Harry, B. (1992). *Cultural diversity, families, and the special education system: Communication and empowerment.* New York: Teachers College Press.

Hart, B., & Risley, T. (1995). *Meaningful differences in the everyday experiences of young American children.* Baltimore: Brookes.

Hart, B., & Risley, T. R. (1992). American parenting of language-learning children: Persisting differences in family–child interactions observed in natural home environments. *Developmental Psychology, 28,* 1096–1105.

Hyslop, N. (2001). Hispanic parental involvement in home literacy. *ERIC Digest, D158* (ED 446340).

Jencks, C., & Phillips, M. (1998). *The black–white test score gap.* Washington, DC: Brookings Institute.

Jordan, G. E., Snow, C. E., & Porche, M. V. (2000). Project EASE: The effect of a family literacy project on kindergarten students' early literacy skills. *Reading Research Quarterly, 35*(4), 524–546.

Keller, H. (2003). Socialization for competence: Cultural models of infancy. *Human Development, 46,* 288–311.

Kotchick, B. A., & Forehand, R. (2002). Putting parenting in perspective: A discussion of the contextual factors that shape parenting practices. *Journal of Child and Family Studies, 11*(30), 255–269.

Lareau, A. (2000). *Home advantage: Social class and parental intervention in elementary education* (rev. ed.). New York: Rowman & Littlefield.

Lee, V. E., & Burkam, D. T. (2002). *Inequality at the starting gate: Social background differences in achievement as children begin school.* Washington, DC: Economic Policy Institute.

Li, G. (2002). *"East is east, west is west?": Home literacy, culture, and schooling.* New York: Peter Lang.

Li, G. (2003). Literacy, culture, and politics of schooling: Counter narratives of a Chinese-Canadian family. *Anthropology and Education Quarterly, 34*(2), 184–206.

Li, G. (2006a). *Culturally contested pedagogy: Battles of literacy and schooling between mainstream teachers and Asian immigrant parents.* Albany: State University of New York Press.

Li, G. (2006b). What do parents think?: Middle class Chinese immigrant parents' perspectives on literacy learning, homework, and school-home communication. *School Community Journal, 16*(2), 25–44.

Linver, M. R., Brooks-Gunn, J., & Kohen, D. E. (2002). Family processes as pathways from income to young children's development. *Developmental Psychology, 38*(5), 719–734.

Lonigan, C. (1994). Reading to preschoolers exposed: Is the emperor really naked? *Developmental Review, 14*(3), 303–323.

Marcon, R. A. (1999). Positive relationships between parent school involvement and public school inner-city preschoolers' development and academic performance. *School Psychology Review, 28*(3), 395–412.

Marvin, C., & Mirenda, P. (1993). Home literacy experiences of preschoolers enrolled in Head Start and special education programs. *Journal of Early Intervention, 17*(4), 351–367.

McLoyd, V. C. (1990). The impact of economic hardship on black families and children: Psychological distress, parenting, and socioemotional development. *Child Development, 61,* 311–346.

McLoyd, V. C. (1998). Socioeconomic disadvantage and child development. *American Psychologist, 53*(2), 185–204.

Minami, M. (2001). Maternal styles of narrative elicitation and the development of children's narrative skill: A study of parental scaffolding. *Narrative Inquiry, 11*(1), 55–80.

Mistry, R., Vandewater, E., Huston, A., & McLoyd, V. C. (2002). Economic well-being and children's social adjustment: The role of family process in an ethnically diverse low-income sample. *Child Development, 73,* 935–951.

Murray, A. D., & Hornbaker, A. V. (1997). Maternal directive and facilitative interaction styles: Associations with language and cognitive development of low risk and high risk toddlers. *Development and Psychopathology, 9,* 507–516.

National Research Council. (2000). *From neurons to neighborhoods: The science of early childhood development.* Washington, DC: National Academy of Sciences Press.

Neuman, S. B. (1999). Books make a difference: A study of access to literacy. *Reading Research Quarterly, 34*(3), 286–311.

Nye, C., Turner, H., & Schwartz, J. (2006). *Approaches to parent involvement for improving the academic performance of elementary school age children.* London: Campbell Collaboration. Retrieved from *www.campbell-collaboration.org/doc-pdf/nye_pi_review.pdf*

Plumert, J. M., & Nichols-Whitehead, P. (1996). Parental scaffolding of young children's spatial communication. *Developmental Psychology, 32*(3), 523–532.

Powell, D. (2004). Parenting and parent education. In B. H. Wasik (Ed.), *Handbook of family literacy* (pp. 157–173). Mahwah, NJ: Erlbaum.

Pratt, M. W., Kerig, P., Cowan, P. A., & Cowan, C. P. (1988). Mothers and fathers teaching 3-year-olds: Authoritative parenting and adult scaffolding of young children's learning. *Developmental Psychology, 24*(6), 832–839.

Purcell-Gates, V. (1996). Stories, coupons, and the *TV Guide*: Relationships between home literacy experiences and emergent literacy knowledge. *Reading Research Quarterly, 31,* 406–428.

Raikes, H., Pan, B. A., Luze, G., Tamis-LeMonda, C. S., Brooks-Gunn, J., Constantine, J., et al. (2006). Mother–child bookreading in low-income families: Correlates and outcomes during the first three years of life. *Child Development, 77*(4), 924–953.

Rothstein, R. (2004). *Class and schools: Using social, economic, and educational reform to close the black–white achievement gap.* Washington, DC: Economic Policy Institute.

Rush, K. L. (1999). Caregiver–child interactions and early literacy development of preschool children from low-income environments. *Topics in Early Childhood Special Education, 19*(1), 3–14.

Sampson, W. A. (2003). *Poor Latino families and school preparation: Are they doing the right things?* Lanham, MD: Scarecrow Press.

Sénéchal, M., & LeFevre, J. (2001). Storybook reading and parent teaching: Links to language and literacy development. In P. R. Britto & J. Brooks-Gunn (Eds.), *New directions in child development: The role of family literacy environments in promoting young children's emergent literacy skills* (pp. 39–52). San Francisco: Jossey-Bass.

Sénéchal, M., & LeFevre, J. (2002). Parental involvement in the development of children's reading skill: A five-year longitudinal study. *Child Development, 73*(2), 445–460.

Sénéchal, M., LeFevre, J. A., Hudson, E., & Lawson, E. P. (1996). Knowledge of storybooks as a predictor of young children's vocabulary. *Journal of Educational Psychology, 88,* 520–536.

Sénéchal, M., LeFevre, J. A., Thomas, E., & Daley, K. (1998). Differential effects of home literacy experiences on the development of oral and written language. *Reading Research Quarterly, 32,* 96–116.

Snow, C. E., Burns, M. S., & Griffin, P. (Eds.). (1998). *Preventing reading difficulties in young children.* Washington, DC: National Academy Press.

Tabors, P. O., Beals, D. E., & Weizman, Z. (2001). "You know what oxygen is?": Learning new words at home. In D. K. Dickinson & P. O. Tabors (Eds.), *Beginning literacy with language: Young children learning at home and school* (pp. 93–110). Baltimore: Brookes.

Toomey, D., & Sloane, J. (1994). Fostering children's early literacy development through parent involvement: A five-year program. In D. K. Dickinson (Ed.), *Bridges to literacy: Children, families, and schools* (pp. 129–149). Malden, MA: Blackwell.

Weizman, Z., & Snow, C. E. (2001). Lexical input as related to children's vocabulary acquisition: Effects of sophisticated exposure and support for meaning. *Developmental Psychology, 37*(2), 265–279.

West, J., Jausken, E. G., & Collins, M. (1993). *Readiness for kindergarten: Parent and teacher beliefs* (NCES Publication No. 93257). Washington, DC: U.S. Department of Education, Office of Research and Improvement.

Whitehurst, G. J., Arnold, D. S., Epstein, J. N., Angell, A. L., Smith, M., & Fischel, J. E. (1994). A picture book reading intervention in day care and home for children from low-income families. *Developmental Psychology, 30,* 678–689.

Whitehurst, G. J., Epstein, J. N., Angell, A. C., Payne, A. C., Crone, D. A., & Fischel, J. E. (1994). Outcomes of an emergent literacy intervention in Head Start. *Journal of Educational Psychology, 86,* 542–555.

Whitehurst, G. J., Falco, F., Lonigan, C. J., Fischel, J. E., DeBaryshe, B. D., Valdez-Menchaca,

M. C., et al. (1988). Accelerating language development through picture-book reading. *Developmental Psychology, 24,* 552–558.

Whitehurst, G. J., & Lonigan, C. J. (1998). Child development and emergent literacy. *Child Development, 68,* 848–872.

Whitehurst, G. J., & Lonigan, C. J. (2002). Emergent literacy: Development from pre-readers to readers. In S. B. Neuman & D. K. Dickinson (Eds.), *Handbook of early literacy research* (Vol. 1, pp. 11–29). New York: Guilford Press.

Williams, D. R. (1999). Race, SES, and health: The added effects of racism and discrimination. *Annals of the New York Academy of Sciences, 896,* 173–188.

Williams, D. R., Neighbors, H. W., & Jackson, J. S. (2003). Racial/ethnic discrimination and health: Findings from community studies. *American Journal of Public Health, 93*(2), 200–208.

Yeung, W. J., Linver, M. R., & Brooks-Gunn, J. (2002). How money matters for young children's development: Parental investment and family processes. *Child Development, 73*(6), 1861–1879.

PART V

MATHEMATICS AND SCIENCE

Although math and science education are considered important in early childhood, progress in integrating math and science into early childhood programs has been very slow, particularly when compared to the advances made in early childhood literacy. In early childhood education much more attention has been paid to the development of curricula, pedagogical approaches, and teacher professional development for literacy than for math and science. This imbalance is also reflected in large differences in the amount of time devoted to math or science instruction in early childhood. As a consequence far greater progress has been made in literacy development than in math or science.

The chapters in Part V make specific recommendations for enriching the content and creative approaches to teaching math and science to make children's experiences more engaging and the curricula more effective. As a group the chapters present information on a range of topics that include number sense, positional representation of numbers, the significance of zero, spatial reasoning, problem solving, and conceptual changes that are necessary for, and that occur as consequence of children's mastery of number and science concepts. In addition, the chapters illustrate pedagogical techniques that can be used to facilitate children's learning.

Herbert P. Ginsburg (Chapter 18) describes the obstacles that account for the minimalist treatment of math in early education. Drawing on existing and tested curricula, his chapter is chock full of advice about what might be included in and how to implement mathematics curriculum in early childhood. His recommendations are consistent with those of the National Council of Teachers of Mathematics (NCTM), which identifies numbers and operations, shapes and space, measurement, and patterns as topics to be covered in math education. More importantly, Ginsburg emphasizes that early mathematics education fundamentally is about helping children to think mathematically, to take a mathematical view of their experiences in the world. In other words, early childhood math should enhance children's abilities to use mathematics to understand and describe the world around them with greater and greater precision. He points out that mathematics for 3- to 5-year-olds is heavily dependent on language. It requires children to understand and to master spatial concepts (e.g., over, under, and behind) and numerical concepts (e.g., ordinal numbers), and measurement concepts (e.g., more and less, big and small). As children's skills in mathematics increase, they become able to use mathematics to describe their world more precisely and to model problems mathematically with greater accuracy. With respect to instruction, Ginsburg emphasizes the importance of careful observation, scaffolding, and close interactions with the child.

An important aspect of thinking mathematically is to develop a sense for numbers. The concept of the number line has often been adapted in education to convey to children the difficult concept of the linear nature of numbers, which in turn undergirds their ability to estimate accurately the magnitude of numbers. This issue is taken up in Chapter 19 by Robert S. Siegler, who uses information-processing theory to conceptualize approaches for improving children's number sense. He describes a very simple but powerful method for strengthening children's number sense that involves playing with number board games. In some ways, this approach reinforces the notion of early childhood educators that children can learn through play.

Maria G. Bartolini Bussi and Mara Boni discuss several topics in Chapter 20 that are often conceptually difficult for children, namely, the positional representation of numbers and the conceptual significance of zero. They demonstrate how the use of artifacts, such as the abacus, the pescaline, and zero + 1, can facilitate children's understanding of how position is used to represent large numbers.

Like Ginsburg, Beth Casey, in Chapter 21, reflects on what should be taught and how it should be taught. She also builds on insights provided by Piagetian theory to propose specific approaches to instruction. In keeping with the integrative focus of this handbook, Casey places her discussion of the theory, pedagogy, and curriculum within the context of the instructional divide between early childhood and K–12 education. She concludes that the dichotomy between developmentally appropriate practice and structured curriculum-based instruction is a false one, and that these approaches can be compatible. She underscores this point with an illustration of how practices described as developmentally appropriate can complement and be integrated with direct instruction.

Rossana Falcade and Paola Strozzi address in Chapter 22 the question of spatial reasoning and representation in young children. They present a pedagogical technique that gives children experiences in representing space. Specifically, the chapter describes a straightforward but pedagogically rich task (the village task) and how it can be used with young children. In their example, the authors demonstrate the importance of teacher observation of child performance and how fledgling abilities can be used to enhance student understanding and skills growth. Much can be learned from the rich descriptions of teacher–child interactions.

The use of mathematics by children in problem solving is taken up by Erik De Corte, Lieven Verschaffel, and Fien Depaepe in Chapter 23. They illustrate an approach that relies on close collaboration between university-based researchers and elementary school educators to improve students' mathematical reasoning in everyday problem solving. They describe an intriguing method they use to teach children to solve real-world problems with specific strategies. Children apply the problem-solving principles by working cooperatively in groups with other children who may be in different classrooms, and even in a different country. The authors provide striking observations about the elements of classroom climate or culture that need to be introduced to make the teaching of mathematics more effective. These innovations depend on close collaboration between researchers and teachers, greater autonomy and responsibility for students, and very active participation by students in the process of teaching and learning. Like Casey (Chapter 21), they illustrate how direct instruction can be combined fruitfully with project-oriented exploration and discovery that is student-driven and directed. The teacher moves back and forth in a delicate balancing act between facilitator and conveyer of direct instruction. Importantly, they emphasize moving away from a focus on a single, correct response or method toward recognizing the value of multiple approaches and strategies. Learning through active student engagement, challenging students to solve real problems, and utilizing cooperative discussions all contribute to the development of higher-order thinking skills that are central to mastery of problem solving.

Chapter 24 by Stella Vosniadou takes up the issue of science education. A central theme is the need to promote underlying conceptual change in children and the critical role of the errors children make as they learn new concepts. These errors provide a unique window onto children's thinking that can inform teachers about the conceptual shifts that children need to make if they are to understand and master scientific information. The author adopts a position that may be quite startling to many in science education. She argues that a major problem is that science education of young children attempts to cover too many different topics. She makes specific suggestions about how to narrow the scope of science education to educate children more effectively. Her recommendations, if followed, have the potential to transform dramatically the science curriculum in early education.

Mark Enfield and Dwight Rogers take on directly the challenge of teacher professional development in Chapter 25. They raise several issues and problems in how we currently prepare teachers of math and science. The authors identify characteristics of effective professional development programs and attribute an important role to communities of practice, or professional learning communities, in which teachers take the lead in investigating and solving problems in teaching through reading, reflection, planning, and implementation of change. At the heart of their proposed approach to professional development is the requirement that educational programs view and treat teachers as active partners in setting the learning agenda and implementing a plan of study.

CHAPTER 18

Early Mathematics Education and How to Do It

Herbert P. Ginsburg

In this chapter I answer some basic questions about mathematics education for little children, 3, 4, and 5 years of age. Some of the questions are both fundamental and frequently asked, such as "Can little children really learn mathematics?" Others may not have occurred to you, such as "What is the role of language in early mathematics?" But even if you have not asked the questions I try to answer, I hope that by the end of this chapter you will agree that the questions are important and that the answers are informative.

Perhaps the first question is how, I, the author, know what questions to raise and how to answer them. Or, as one child asked me after I had interviewed her about her mathematics knowledge for about 40 minutes, "Who are you?" By academic training, I am a developmental psychologist who has been particularly concerned with "cognitive development," that is, how the mind grows from birth and beyond. I have done some basic research into young children's mathematical thinking—a topic I address at greater length below. But more importantly for this chapter, I have spent the past 15 years working on early mathematics education. I have developed methods for assessing what children know about mathematics, programs to teach them mathematics, and methods to help teachers and parents understand early mathematics. In the course of this work, I have spent many hours in preschool and kindergarten classrooms in both low-income and wealthy neighborhoods. As a result, I have acquired some insight into what teachers, parents, and the public at large see as the fundamental issues.

The next question refers to the appropriate audience for this chapter. I know that readers are not likely to be researchers interested in every last detail of cognitive research or mathematics activities. The editors of this volume say that readers are likely to be preservice teachers and their instructors in community and 4-year colleges. But I take a more expansive view. I hope that readers include practicing teachers and their supervisors, as well as school administrators, policymakers, and parents. In any event, I try to present the answers in a clear and nontechnical way that will be useful for all who work with and care about young children. Here are the questions and answers.

Why Should We Care about Early Mathematics Education?

Over the past decade, there has been increasing interest in early childhood mathematics education (ECME) among political figures, some early childhood educators, and parents. One reason is that as early as preschool (Miller & Parades, 1996) and first grade (Mullis et al., 2000), American children's mathematics performance is lower than that of children in East Asian countries, such as Japan, Korea, and Singapore. The result is actually more complex than it is usually made out to be: Middle- and higher-income American children do very well on the average in international comparisons; low-income children do not, thus bringing down the rating for the country as a whole (Berliner, 2006). Indeed, this points out a persistent problem in American education. Low-income American children, who comprise a shocking 39% of the child population (National Center for Children in Poverty, 2006), consistently score lower in mathematics than do their more advantaged peers (Arnold & Doctoroff, 2003).

The poor performance of low-income students at all levels of American education should arouse outrage. Maria Montessori, the famous early childhood educator who worked in the early 1900s with children in the slums of Rome, put it like this: "Ah, before such dense and willful disregard of the life which is growing within these children, we should hide our heads in shame and cover our guilty faces with our hands!" (Montessori, 1964, p. 27). And the very rational philosopher Alfred North Whitehead, who, with Bertrand Russell, wrote one of the seminal books on the foundations of mathematics, said, "When one considers ... the importance of this question of the education of a nation's young, the broken lives, the defeated hopes, the national failures, which result from the frivolous inertia with which it is treated, it is difficult to restrain within oneself a savage rage" (Whitehead, 1929, p. 14). So the first reason to care is that our school system is a shameful national failure that breaks lives, particularly those of the poor.

Another reason to care is that there is some evidence that early childhood education can indeed give young children a "head start," a foundation for later academic success (Reynolds & Ou, 2003), in at least the first few grades of school (Gormley, 2007) and perhaps even beyond (Ludwig & Phillips, 2007). Responding to this argument, many states and local education authorities are beginning to stress the importance of ECME. Head Start is beginning to strengthen its early mathematics programs, and states such as New Jersey and Texas are implementing ECME on a wide scale for low-income children. At the same time, we should not entertain unrealistic expectations from these efforts. Unless we improve the failing K–12 schools that low-income children typically attend (Lee & Burkam, 2002), the initial gains from early childhood education are likely to dissipate over time (Brooks-Gunn, 2003) and, in any event, children's later school experience will not be as productive as it could be. So put early education in perspective: It will not solve all the problems of American education, and it does not absolve us from attempting comprehensive education reform, from kindergarten through high school.

A third reason to care about ECME is seldom cited. It is that if you visit child care centers, preschools, and kindergartens, then you will find—and this is my personal observation—that young children are often bored or wild because they don't have enough to do that is interesting and challenging. As I show later, young children are spontaneously interested in mathematical questions. If this is true, then we should care about ECME because it can help children to satisfy their intellectual curiosity and engage in an enjoyable and challenging activity. I know that adults who have suffered through the dreary mathematics education that is all too common in the school system, from the elementary grades through college, will find this hard to believe. But it's true: We should care about teaching early mathematics not only as preparation for the future but also because it can provide young children with rich and engaging intellectual stimulation while they are in preschool or kindergarten. As John Dewey (1938) put it, "What, then, is the true meaning of preparation in the educational scheme? In the first place, it means that a person, young or old, gets out of his present experience all that there is in it for him at the time in which he has it" (p. 49). So we should care about early education because we are outraged about how badly our schools serve children, particularly the poor, because early education can help children do better once they get to school, and because it can stimulate children's naturally active minds.

Why Are Adults Often Reluctant to Consider ECME?

Although there are some good reasons for implementing programs of ECME, many adults—teachers and others—are reluctant to do so. This is the very large elephant in the room that needs to be addressed directly. To put it bluntly, in the United States, there is widespread fear and loathing of mathematics. The problem is primarily emotional. Many early childhood teachers fear or dislike teaching mathematics. One of my students very honestly said, "My previous history as a poor math student makes me fear teaching math to young children in the future, that being partially my reason for choosing early childhood education." Another early childhood education student reported, "Many teachers do not like to teach math. In my last student teaching placement, my supervising teacher told me to take over the math lessons for the class." My students' sentiments and experiences are typical, I think, of the general population of early childhood educators.

There is also an intellectual reason for early childhood educators' avoidance of mathematics instruction. For many years the dominant ethos of the field as a whole was that ECME is bad for children: They are not ready for it, and it produces hurried, anxious children. In other words, it would make mathematics as loathsome for little children as it is for their teachers. Of course, if done badly, ECME is likely to have the negative effects described. But done well, ECME does not have to be "developmentally inappropriate." Below I discuss research showing that the older early childhood ideology—still championed by many in the field—is misguided.

But the main point here is that many are reluctant to implement early mathematics because they are afraid of it. What to do? I tell my students that if they really want to help the children, they have to get over the fear. I also tell them that it can be done, and that they can indeed eventually enjoy teaching mathematics to young children. Experience shows that this is true.

Can Little Children Learn Mathematics?

The admonition to my students is based on the assumption that children can learn something as abstract as early mathematics. Is that really true? The overwhelming body of research over the past 25 years or so suggests that, contrary to much popular opinion, young children can learn mathematics, concrete *and* abstract (Baroody, Lai, & Mix, 2006; Clements & Serama, 2007; Ginsburg, Cannon, Eisenband, & Pappas, 2006). And what's more, they often enjoy it, too (Ginsburg, 2006). Let me explain.

From birth to age 5, young children develop an "everyday mathematics"—informal mathematical ideas and skills about numbers, shapes, space, patterns, and other mathematical topics. In their ordinary physical and social environments, children can see that this plate of five cookies has *more* than this plate of three cookies. They may not know that here there are three and that there are five there, but they do know which plate has more. They have a harder time knowing which is *less*, but the idea of *more* is fundamental. At age 3 or 4, children know that "adding makes more" (Brush, 1978), even though they may not be able to figure out exactly what the total is. They can easily distinguish between a circle and a square, although they may not know the words for these shapes. They can locate objects in space (Newcombe & Huttenlocher, 2000), remembering, for example, that something fell *under* the couch on the *right* side, even if, again, they do not know the words for these concepts. Mostly, young children develop everyday mathematics on their own, although sometimes parents do attempt to teach the counting words and the names of common shapes, and may reinforce children's spontaneous attempts to deal with mathematical issues (Saxe, Guberman, & Gearhart, 1987). But, in general, parents and educators fail to appreciate the extent of young children's mathematical knowledge. Indeed, psychologists were largely unaware of its existence for many years, despite Vygotsky's (1978) famous dictum that "children have their own preschool arithmetic, which only myopic psychologists could ignore" (p. 84).

There are many "laboratory" studies that make these points by presenting specially designed problems to which children are asked to respond. For example, you can show a young child four randomly arranged dots on the right and eight on the left, and ask him or her to point to the side having more. Alfred Binet (1969) did this with his own children in the early 1900s. But even more convincing than studies in which the adult determines the problem to be solved are cases in which the child chooses to engage in mathematical activities without adult intervention.

One area of interest has been early counting. Young children spontaneously count out loud (Saxe et al., 1987; Walkerdine, 1988), and children as young as age 3 sometimes even say numbers as high as 10 (Durkin, Shire, Riem, Crowther, & Rutter, 1986). This past weekend, my 5-year-old granddaughter, in the summer before entering kindergarten, attempted to count to 100 (I did not ask her to!). After making a mistake and being corrected, Rachel insisted on starting again each time from 1, and did indeed eventually get to 100 (skipping a number here and there). Court (1920) reported that her 5-year-old child was interested in learning to count by fives. Indeed, children at this age enjoy counting up to relatively large numbers, like 100 (Irwin & Burgham, 1992). In brief, it appears that young children have an everyday interest in various aspects of counting.

They are interested in adding, too. Anderson (1993, p. 28) reports that at 3 years of age her daughter was spontaneously interested in the composition of numbers. She wanted to know, "What's another way [apart from holding up one hand] to make five [fingers]?" She then attempted to hold up four fingers and one more, as well as other combinations. At age 5, Anderson's daughter created addition problems, asking, "Two and three, how many's that?" (p. 28). Court (1920) reported that her son displayed interest in creating addition problems. He brought his mother three blocks, asked whether she wanted four, then brought her another block.

Several studies indicate that differences and changes in magnitude may be another topic of interest to young children. Corsaro (1985) notes that children are vitally concerned with growing both bigger and older, and Isaacs (1930) reports that children "sometimes discussed eagerly, 'Who is the tallest?' with a keen sense of rivalry" (p. 41). Walkerdine (1988) shows that the words *a lot* and *a little* are used in consuming food and drink, and *big* often refers to the child's growth.

Isaacs (1930) found that 4- and 5-year-old children show a spontaneous interest in perspective. Thus, the children were discussing how the garden would look to a person in an airplane. A 5-year-old said that the man in the airplane would "see some little specks moving about," and other children agreed that he would see "only the tops of heads" (p. 115).

Our own research (Ginsburg, Pappas, & Seo, 2001) shows that during free play, young children frequently get involved in exploring shapes and patterns (e.g., when they decide to make squares out of the triangular-shape blocks), are concerned with "relative magnitude (e.g., "My tower is bigger than yours"), and deal with number (e.g., "I think I need three more blocks").

Now all of this makes a lot of sense when you think about it. Young children obviously don't normally do *formal* mathematics in the sense of what is taught in school. (An unfortunate exception occurs when overzealous parents force children to do the kind of boring written worksheets that are widely available in stores such as Wal-Mart or Borders.) But how can children, or anyone else, get around in life without knowing about more and less, over and under, many and few, and the shape that characterizes this animal as opposed to that? Informal mathematical thinking is so fundamental a feature of our minds that we are often oblivious to it, as is the proverbial fish to the water in which it swims. Hence, when asked to observe carefully and report on whether their children engage in activities like these, parents or teachers usually tell me, with some surprise, that the answer is "yes," but that they never thought of these kinds of behavior as mathematical. Yet they are.

How Powerful Is Children's Mathematics?

I hope I have convinced you that in their everyday lives young children do things that can legitimately be considered to involve mathematics, even if informally. But how powerful is this everyday mathematics?

Modern research has shown that children's minds are complex; their thinking is not necessarily "concrete." From an early age, they seem to understand some abstractions involving numbers (e.g., that the order of counting a group of objects does not matter, so long as you count each object once and only once) (Gelman & Gallistel, 1986), and are even concerned to know the "largest number" (Gelman, 1980), clearly a very abstract mathematical issue. They do not simply remember isolated "addition facts" but can instead spontaneously develop, without adult help (Groen & Resnick, 1977), various general methods or "strategies" for figuring them out, such as counting on from the larger number (Baroody & Wilkins, 1999). Thus, given the problem "How much are three apples and two apples?", many 4- or 5-year-old children can get the sum by counting, "*three*, four, and five." Children can easily do problems like these when they involve concrete objects placed right in front of them, but they can also solve similar mental problems involving imaginary apples.

At the same time, children display certain kinds of mathematical ineptitude, for example, when they have difficulty understanding that a set of seven objects spread out in a long line is the same number as a set of seven objects arranged in a shorter line. This is a quite remarkable thing to see: You can ask the children to count each group, and although they say that there are seven objects in both cases, they argue that one line of objects has more because it is longer than the other (Piaget, 1952). Another example involves shapes. Children easily say that a figure with three equal straight sides is a triangle. But shown an extremely elongated, non-right-angle "skinny" figure with three sides, children often refuse to believe that it is a triangle (Clements, 1999). At the same time, they can easily see that the long, skinny, three-sided shape is obviously not a square or a circle or a rectangle.

Children's thinking may be complex and hard to decipher, but it is not merely simple, concrete, or trivial. When you work with young children and try to take their thinking seriously and follow where it leads, you often encounter wonderful and indeed beautiful surprises, such as 4- and 5-year-olds trying to count by twos or to reproduce complex musical patterns evidenced in clapping rhythms, or predict what happens when you keep taking away one object from a group of 10 ("Now you have nine, now you have eight ... now you have *none*!), or to build a castle that has symmetrical towers (each with two turrets) on the east, west, north, and south sides. I believe that these kinds of everyday, very informal intellectual explorations are more genuinely mathematical than what often passes for mathematics in school. Figuring out what is the largest number is clearly more exciting and profound than solving page after page of dreary problems in a textbook.

Usually we have little insight into the complexity, abstraction, and relative power of children's mathematical thinking. Children's mathematics is a kind of hidden world that adults have to learn to see. And obtaining this insight is one of the joys of cognitive psychology, and the kind of child study that teachers need to learn to do.

How can teachers learn more about children's mathematical thinking? There are several things they can do. They can read about it: There are several accessible papers and books on young children's mathematics (e.g., Copley, 1999). But more importantly, they can spend time carefully observing their students. If possible, they should make videos of children playing with blocks or engaging in pretend play in the dress-up area. They should then discuss these videos with other teachers from *a mathematical point of view*. Usually, teachers tend to see social interaction among children, and that is certainly important for them to see. But if they also look from another perspective, the mathematical, they will be very surprised at what the children are doing. One example is the mathematical thinking that occurs when children read ordinary storybooks (Ginsburg & Seo, 2000). You cannot read about *The Three Bears* or almost any other children's book (or even Shakespeare's sonnets) without encountering and understanding basic mathematical ideas (Ginsburg & Seo, 1999).

What Is the Role of Language in Children's Mathematical Thinking?

This may not be a question you are likely to have asked, but it is a good issue to think about. What are the relations between everyday mathematics and language? Usually we think of language as one thing and mathematics as something quite different. Often teachers enjoy teaching literacy, but as we have seen, they don't want to teach mathematics. Yet the two are more closely linked than you might suppose.

Many types of language are vital for mathematics learning. One is simply mathematical vocabulary. The words *more* and *another* are among the first that toddlers learn (Bloom, 1970). Indeed, young children's early language comprises many words that refer to quantity, shape, location, and the like, such as *one, only one, the most, round, straight, in front of, behind, underneath, big, bigger,* and *biggest*. Now you do not usually think of these words as mathematical, but they are: They refer to fundamental concepts that mathematics formalizes and clarifies. This is another demonstration of the point that mathematical ideas are so basic, familiar, and pervasive that we usually are unaware of them. Mathematical ideas, and the words associated with them, are seen as aspects of general cognitive (intellectual) development; indeed, test items relating to these concepts and words have long been used on tests of "intelligence" (Binet & Simon, 1916). Another way of putting it is that our basic intelligence is at least partly mathematical.

An even more important function of language is to express and justify mathematical thinking. One of the important goals of mathematics education is communication: the ability to make one's thoughts public so that they can be examined; to talk with others about mathematical ideas; and to justify one's conclusions (to oneself as well as to others). Therefore, children need to learn to say, "I think this is a circle because it is round. This one is not a circle because the sides are straight." Or "I think that this picture has more cats than this one because there are three extra cats over here." This kind of language is not simply a list of vocabulary words, although the words are certainly needed. It is instead a way to express reasoning and to justify mathematical arguments (and other kinds, too). Mathematical language of this type is the language of thought and rationality, and begins to develop in children as young as 4 or 5 years of age (Pappas, Ginsburg, & Jiang, 2003). It should be a prime focus of early mathematics education. Indeed, this kind of language is vital in virtually all areas of learning.

Do Low-Income Children Have These Abilities?

As they do in many other areas, low-income preschool children generally perform more poorly on simple mathematical tasks than their more privileged peers (Denton & West, 2002). If you look at any set of educational statistics, you will find that low-income children do worse on the average than other children. Of course, this statement is about *groups* of children and does not refer to every single one of them. Many *individual* low-income children do very well. Yet if there is a single replicable fact about American education, it is that low-income children's school achievement is relatively low, and more importantly, lower than it could and should be.

Yet test scores that are the "gold standard" of conventional educational research are crude and may underestimate or fail to reveal children's competence. A closer look at low-income children's mathematical abilities reveals a complex and interesting situation. First, cognitive-developmental research shows that although low-income children's *performance* on informal addition and subtraction problems usually lags behind that of middle-income children, the two groups often employ similar *strategies* to solve problems (Ginsburg & Pappas, 2004; Ginsburg & Russell, 1981). For example, both groups may add by counting on from the larger number (e.g., "Four and three are seven because I go '*four*, then five, six, seven'"). It's not that the low-income children are clueless; it's that they often don't implement reasonable strategies as accurately as do middle-income children. There are several possible explanations for why low-income children may perform more poorly on tests of mathematics, even they employ similar strategies. First, they may be less well socialized for schooling or test taking. For example, they may not have as much practice as the middle-income children in testing situations of this type or understand the task instructions on the test as well. Second, although lower-income children exhibit difficulty with *verbal* addition and subtraction problems, they perform as well as middle-income children on *nonverbal* forms of these tasks (Jordan, Huttenlocher, & Levine, 1994). Third, naturalistic observation shows that low- and middle-income children exhibit few if any differences in the everyday mathematics they spontaneously employ in free play (Ginsburg et al., 2001). The low-income children traffic in pattern and shape, quantity differences, and number in the same ways, and as frequently, as do middle-income children.

Yes, the test scores are real and tell us something important. Low-income children's school achievement is not what it should be. At the same time, cognitive research shows that these children do not lack fundamental mathematical understanding, and they could do a lot better.

Observing these children can be heartbreaking. I have seen so many low-income, minority children in New York preschools who show a lively mathematical intelligence (if you know how to look for it), yet I know that it often goes unnoticed, and that they probably will struggle in the failing schools they are likely to attend. The bottom line is that we need to do far better in teaching and helping them to develop their everyday skills.

How Can We Help Them?

The first thing to do is to focus on mathematics education. Many preschool educators don't. Graham, Nash, and Paul (1997) observed that mathematics was not a salient topic of discussion, not even opportunistically or spontaneously, in two preschool programs with a reputation for high overall quality. When mathematics was discussed, the conversation lasted less than a minute, primarily centering on very basic concepts, such as age, numeral recognition, and names of shapes. Interestingly, these teachers reported that they believe mathematics is important and said that they engage in mathematical discussions with their children. Observing 20 preschool classrooms, Brown (2005) rarely saw teachers encourage children's exploration of mathematical ideas or suggest challenges. Brown also found that teachers who rated mathematics as important did not necessarily teach it frequently. In short, mathematics seems to be seriously overlooked in preschool classrooms, even when teachers say it is important and that they teach it.

This corresponds with my informal observations: At workshops, many teachers tell me that they don't need to learn about implementing mathematics education because they are already doing it. But when I observe in their classrooms, I find that they are not doing much of anything I consider to be mathematics education. They have a very limited view: Teach children how to count, and teach them the names of a few basic shapes, and that's quite enough, as Graham and colleagues (1997) observe. We need to do more and to do it much better. We need to implement a serious *program* of mathematics education. This has several features, including both mathematics content and the means for helping children learn it.

What Is the Mathematics in Early Mathematics Education?

The first thing to understand is that ECME does not involve only memorized or very simple material, such as counting to 10 or 20 and learning the names of the common shapes. Drawing on cognitive research like that I described earlier, the leading professional organizations in the field recommend that early mathematics instruction cover the "big ideas" of mathematics in areas such as number and operations, geometry (shape and space), measurement, and "algebra" (particularly pattern) (National Association for the Education of Young Children and National Council of Teachers of Mathematics, 2002; National Council of Teachers of Mathematics, 2000). The research-based expectation is that ECME should involve more challenging topics than those usually taught.

Does This Imply a "Push-Down" Curriculum?

Do the new recommendations mean that we should impose on young children the activities designed for higher grades? Not at all. That would be as much a disaster for young children as it often is for the children in the higher grades! The proposal is not to give young children textbooks, worksheets, and all the deadly drills that too often characterize (unsuccessful) elementary mathematics education. Rather, the goal is to engage children in "big ideas."

What Are Big Ideas?

Here is an example of a set of related big ideas concerning just one of the key topics identified by NCTM: *number.* Suppose you want to find out how many things are in a group of objects you see on a table in front of you—a haphazard arrangement including a red block; a small, stuffed dog; and a penny. Of course, you have to know the counting words to get an answer. The first 10 or so counting numbers need to be memorized—they make no sense in themselves. But assume that you know them pretty well. You can count much higher than 3. Now your job is not to recite the counting words you have memorized but to determine the number of objects in this collection. The mathematical ideas underlying "enumeration"—determining a set's numerical value—are complex, and among them are the following: One is that any kind of elements in a set can be counted. You can count nickels and cats, big things and small things. You can even count fantastical ideas, like red unicorns, existing only in your head. Counting is an enormously powerful tool that can be applied to any discrete real or imagined object.

A second idea is that each number word, "One, two, three, ... " must be associated once, and only once, with each object in the set. You point at the red block and say "one," at the dog and say "two," and at the penny and say "three." You can't say both "one" and "two" when referring to the red block, even though you describe it with two words, *red* and *block*. You cannot skip an object in the set. Each counting word must be in one-to-one correspondence with each element of the set.

A third idea is that the final number in the sequence, "three," does not refer to the penny alone. You first pointed to the block and said "one." It's true: there is one block. Then you pointed to the dog and said "two." But it's not true that there are two dogs. The two indicates that you have already counted two items, not that the second item, the dog, is itself two. Similarly, even though you say "three" while pointing to the penny, the number word describes not that individual object but the whole group of objects—how many there are all together. You could have started your count with the penny, in which case it would have been "one," not "three." Indeed, *any* of the objects in the group could have been "one," "two," or "three," but the group as a whole has three objects, whatever the order in which they are counted. The final counting word indicates the number of objects in the set as a whole—the total quantity, the cardinal value.

Notice that enumeration entails a very strange and distinctive use of language. In ordinary speech, we call an object a *block* or a *dog* or a *penny* because that is its name. You cannot legitimately call a *penny* a *red block*. But when we enumerate, the last number name we say refers not to the last individual object counted but to a very abstract property of the set as a whole. When, upon finishing the enumeration, we point to the penny and say "three," we do not mean that "three" is the name for the penny, but that it is a property of all the things we have enumerated as a collection. This is sometimes referred to as "cardinality." Cardinality and one-to-one correspondence are what I mean by big mathematical ideas—in this case, fundamental ideas underlying the counting of objects ("enumeration"). This is not the kind of mathematics that early childhood teachers usually teach. Nor is it the trivial mathematics of the drill sheets. It is a more genuine mathematics than either of these, and children can benefit greatly from learning about it under teachers' guidance.

What Else Does Early Mathematics Involve?

Probably you would not ask this question either, but it is important to consider. Mathematics involves not only the content—the big ideas—but also ways of *thinking*. Take again the example of number. Thinking about it involves reasoning about number (if 2 and 3 are five, then 3 and 2 must be the same number) (Baroody, 1985), making inferences (if we add something other than 0 to 3, the sum must be bigger than 3) (Baroody, 1992), developing a mental number line (100 is much further away from 2 than is 20) (Case & Okamoto, 1996), and inducing patterns from examples ("What comes after 11, 13, 15?") (Jordan, Kaplan, Olah, & Locuniak, 2006). Children spontaneously engage in thinking of this type. We need to help them do it better and more deeply.

Children also need to "mathematize"—to conceive of problems in explicitly mathematical terms. They need to understand that the action of combining one bear with two others can be meaningfully interpreted in terms of the mathematical *principles* of addition and the *symbolism* 1 + 2. One of the functions of mathematics education is to help children to advance *beyond* their informal, intuitive mathematics—what Vygotsky (1986) called "everyday knowledge." In Vygotsky's view, the goal is to help children develop, over a period of years, a meaningful, powerful, symbolic, and organized "scientific" knowledge—in this case, the formal concepts, procedures, and symbolism of mathematics.

How Can We Help Children to Learn Big Ideas and to Think Mathematically?

To teach children the "big ideas" and to think mathematically, we must consider five essential ingredients of mathematics education: the environment, play, teachable moments, projects, and the curriculum. Each of these elements is necessary but not sufficient by itself for effective early math education.

The Environment

The preschool classroom or child care center should contain a rich variety of objects and materials—such as blocks, water table, and puzzles—that can set the stage for mathematics learning. Some of these materials have proven to be valuable tools over the course of many years. In the 1850s, Froebel introduced a system of guided instruction centered on various "gifts," including blocks, variations of which have since been used widely all around the world to help young children learn basic mathematics, especially geometry (Brosterman, 1997). Modern electronic toys and computers can be useful too, but don't neglect simple objects, such as beads, blocks, puzzles, books, and more books. One thing you can do, then, is to make sure that your preschool or child care settings contain the things they ought to contain. To check, you can use the Early Childhood Environment Rating Scale (ECERS; Harms, Clifford, & Cryer, 1998), which primarily provides a rating of the quality of the preschool physical environment. Unfortunately, the ECERS has sometimes shown that preschools and day care centers are furnished in a disgracefully spartan fashion with minimal materials. Once, after working in a preschool, I managed to obtain for the children a large supply of good storybooks. When I returned one day to visit, I learned that the director had locked them in a cabinet because she thought the children might damage them. Of course, little children damage things. The director's job was to help them, to the extent possible, learn not to cause damage. But children must have easy access to things with which to work and play. The crucial factor is not what the environment makes possible, but what children actually *do* in it. We don't want children sitting in desks all day while the classroom gets a good ECERS score for an abundance of materials to which the children have restricted access. Although essential, providing a stimulating physical environment is only the first step.

Play

The second important component is play, which is beneficial for young and old alike (Singer, Golinkoff, & Hirsh-Pasek, 2006). Children have a good time when they play; it can help them learn to interact with others and to develop self-regulation; it stimulates cognitive development; and we know that children do indeed learn a good deal of everyday mathematics on their own in the course of free play (Seo & Ginsburg, 2004).

What is there not to like about play? But what many people—including teachers—fail to see is the complexity of mathematical activity involved in it. Here is an example taken from videotaped observations of children's everyday, unscripted behavior in a day care center. Jessica brings a book to a table where Matthew and Ralph are sitting side by side. Jessica and Ralph are 5, and Matthew is 4. All are from low-income families and attend a publicly supported child care center in New York City. Jessica sits around the corner of the table from Matthew and Ralph. She pretends that she is the teacher, and that the lesson is reading; Matthew and Ralph pretend that they are students. She opens the book, picks it up, holds it in her right hand, and tries to show a page to Matthew and Ralph. Before she can say anything, Ralph says to her, "You can't read it like that. You can't see it" (Ginsburg & Seo, 2000).

Ralph's comment reveals at least two important kinds of thinking. First, he is able to engage in "perspective taking." He considers Jessica's orientation in relation to the book. He notices that, from her point of view, the book is held at a bad angle and is more or less upside down. Second, he knows that it is very hard to read pages from such a perspective. Jessica is responsive to the feedback: She adjusts the orientation of the book so that all three of them can see it. "I can see," Ralph says. "Me too," Matthew says.

This shows how everyday mathematics—understanding something about orientation, perspective, and angle—is not only part of play but also a basic component of good "preliteracy." Children need to learn that reading requires viewing the book in the right orientation at a reasonable angle!

Next, as Matthew stands close to Ralph to see the book, Ralph seems annoyed and says to him, "Sit down, Matthew." Matthew returns to his seat. But from there, he cannot clearly see the pictures on the book. He moves his chair closer to Ralph's, saying, "Let me get a little bit far." "Little closer," Ralph corrects him. "Little closer, I mean," Matthew says.

This episode shows that as they prepare themselves for the story, Matthew and Ralph spontaneously deal with the idea of "relative distance." They do not want to be too close to each other, but both want to see the book. So they sit side by side, not too close, yet not too far from the book. Furthermore, they attempt to use the proper language to express these mathematical ideas. Matthew clearly has the idea of moving closer for a better view. He expresses this idea in terms of what an adult would consider an odd construction, "Let me get a little bit far." Apparently, he means that he wants to be "a little bit far" from the book as opposed to "a lot far." Although this makes perfect sense, Ralph corrects him, essentially pointing out that in this situation confersation usually refers to greater closeness rather than lesser distance. So children try to express mathematical ideas in words and sometimes learn from each other the desired conventional language.

Jessica then "reads" the book to Matthew and Ralph by making up a story based on the pictures. She comments on a picture of pumpkins on the page: *That's a lot.* Matthew wonders how much is *a lot.* He stretches out his arms and asks her, "A lot like this bunch?" Jessica nods her head, indicating agreement. He stretches his arms farther apart and asks her if that also indicates *a lot,* saying, "How about this?" Jessica nods again. Matthew stretches his arms even farther apart and asks, "How about this?" Jessica nods affirmatively yet a third time, indicating that all of the arm gestures indicate *a lot.*

Matthew seems to be trying to get a handle on what *a lot* means. I think that in doing this he is struggling with a big mathematical idea. He asks whether different "amounts" all indicate *a lot*. It's like saying, "Is 25 a big number? And 35? And 43, too?" To do this, he has to distinguish among different "relative magnitudes"; he has to know that one arm span is larger than another, and that the next is larger still. He is dealing with a kind of ordered series. Furthermore, Mathew attempts to represent an abstract idea—"a lot of pumpkins"—by stretching apart his arms. He enacts the idea with his body.

Jessica continues telling the story: "Put the masks back into that toy box. ... And then you can take it back out." Matthew repeats, "Take it back out!" So now the children have shifted from ideas about magnitude to the issue of *location*: put things "into" the box and take things "out of" the box.

The children go on to discuss the degree to which a pumpkin was "this tiny scary." My claim is that understanding a story—almost any story!—requires comprehending mathematical ideas of magnitude, location, quantity, and the like. And all this learning and intellectual activity occurred spontaneously in the course of free play (although it was almost certainly based on the model of a teacher who read to them).

So what is the moral of this story? Sure, learning and thinking (and much else) take place during play. But also it is important for teachers to learn to observe play carefully and to interpret it deeply. Understanding children's everyday play helps to provide insight into their competence, which otherwise might go unnoticed. Once I observed a young boy and a group of girls who persisted in counting out 100 beads during free play (Ginsburg, 2006). Toward the very end, some of the girls started to fight over the beads and minor pandemonium broke out—very minor. That is when the teacher came over to discipline the children. She saw them fighting; she missed the great adventure of counting the beads. Had she observed the counting and understood what was happening, she would have had a different view of the children's abilities and how to stimulate their learning. They were not simply misbehaving; they had expended serious effort and concentration for a long period of time on a significant mathematical task.

In brief, play in a rich environment provides valuable opportunities to explore and to undertake activities that can be surprisingly sophisticated from a mathematical point of view and at the same time involve fun, social learning, and other kinds of learning, as in the book reading example. But play is not enough. Play does not by itself prepare children for school, and it usually does not help children to "mathematize"—to interpret their experiences in explicitly mathematical form and understand the relations between the two.

The Teachable Moment

The third component is the "teachable moment," a form of adult guidance that enjoys widespread acceptance in the preschool world. The teachable moment involves the teacher's careful observation of children's play and other activities to identify the spontaneously emerging situation that can be exploited to promote learning. The Creative Curriculum program (Dodge, Colker, & Heroman, 2002), extremely popular in the United States, relies heavily on use of the teachable moment.

No doubt, the teachable moment, accurately perceived and suitably addressed, can provide a superb learning experience for the child (Copley, Jones, & Dighe, 2007). Suppose that the teacher observed the children reading and tried help Matthew learn more about "a lot," perhaps by engaging him in an activity specifically designed to help children learn about quantity. That would have been a wonderful exploitation of a splendid teachable moment.

But there is good reason to believe that, in practice, the teachable moment is not an effective educational method. As in the example of the beads, most early childhood teachers do not often engage in the careful observation necessary to perceive and interpret such moments (Lee, 2004). During free play, teachers spend very little time with children (Seo & Ginsburg, 2004) or tend only to manage their behavior (Kontos, 1999) as opposed to tending to their learning. Teachers do not appear to be sufficiently knowledgeable to see the opportunity for teaching a range of mathematical concepts in everyday situations (Moseley, 2005). First, it is very hard to interpret children's everyday behavior. I often have the benefit of a videotape to help me do it. Even then, I have to watch it over and over to come up with a reasonable interpretation. And creating cognitive interpretations of behavior is a key part of my profession. For the teachable moment to succeed, you not only have to interpret well—on the fly—but also you have to come up with an appropriate mathematical activity for the individual child. Now, even if you could do all this, how could you possibly respond to the haphazard occurrences of teachable moments in a group of 20 or so young children? Exploiting the teachable moment is an impossible demand to place on teachers, many of whom are not interested in teaching mathematics in the first place. When it works, use of teachable moments can be highly effective. However, under most circumstances, relying on the teachable moment as the primary basis for mathematics education is not a viable educational strategy.

Projects

A fourth component involves "projects" (Edwards, Gandini, & Forman, 1993; Helm & Katz, 2000), extensive teacher-initiated and -guided explorations of complex topics related to the everyday world. For example, the teacher can engage the children in figuring out how to create a map of the classroom. On the first day, the teacher might start out by showing the children different aspects of the room, like the water table in the corner and the blocks near the rectangular table. A discussion of the location and position of major objects in the room can present an interesting challenge. The teacher can ask the children to describe in words where the puzzles are stored, and where the bathroom is located. This blending of language and mathematics should be a theme running through all mathematics activities. The discussion of position and location can eventually lead to a kind of hide-and-go-seek. The teacher can show a child where something in the room is hidden and ask her to tell another child its location so that it can be found. The hider's first reaction might be to take the other child to the correct location. That is against the rules of the game. You have to "tell," that is, use the symbolism of language to describe the situation. The task is thus both "concrete" (there is a real object hidden) and "abstract," in that the concepts and language of position and location must be the tools for solving the problem. The hider might then say, "I hid it over there," as she points. Again, this is not fair. No pointing is allowed, except through the symbolic means of language. Prohibited from pointing, she might say, "It's where the teacher hid it." That's too egocentric and also doesn't count. Eventually, she has to use her (mathematical) words, saying perhaps, "It's *behind* the water table, *under* the chair that is *next* to the block area."

After this kind of background experience, the teacher can introduce a variation on the problem, namely, to use a map to "tell" where an object is hidden. Now the teacher puts a large piece of paper on the floor and asks the children to imagine that it is their classroom. Suppose the door is over there and the windows are here. Where would the table be located? And how do we show a table on a map? Do we draw a picture of the table with legs? Should the table on the map be bigger or smaller than the block area, as pictured on the map? This kind of activity, which, of course, extends over a period of days, can be very challenging for children because it involves ideas of representation, perspective, scale, approximation, and projection of three dimensions onto two. Eventually, it can lead children to make their own maps of the room, and even of their homes.

This kind of project can have very practical application and appeal (Worsley, Beneke, & Helm, 2003). A project can help children to learn that making sense of real-life problems can be stimulating and enjoyable. Yet, although projects can be enormously effective, the danger is that they may turn into a "a grab bag of any mathematics-related experiences that seem to relate to a theme" (National Association for the Education of Young Children and National Council of Teachers of Mathematics, 2002, p. 10). You may do maps one week and explore the economics of the lemonade stand the next. But where does that lead you and the children? Projects may be useful if guided by a larger plan (Helm & Beneke, 2003), namely, a *curriculum*, which is the fifth component of ECME.

Curriculum

A *curriculum* can be characterized as "a written instructional blueprint and set of materials for guiding students' acquisition of certain culturally valued concepts, procedures, intellectual dispositions, and ways of reasoning" (Clements, 2007, p. 36). A curriculum offers a carefully planned sequence of activities for the teaching of mathematics. The sequence should be based on knowledge of children's "learning trajectories" (Clements, Sarama, & DiBiase, 2004), that is, the progression in which they normally learn and can be taught mathematical concepts. Note that a curriculum is not necessarily a textbook. It very well may be a textbook for older children, but not for the younger children with whom we are concerned. Also the quality of curricula may vary: They may be good or bad or in between. Using just any curriculum will not do. You have to find a good one for your needs.

Here is an example from a curriculum that I have been involved in developing—Big Math for Little Kids (BMLK; Ginsburg, Greenes, & Balfanz, 2003). BMLK involves a sequence of mathematical topics, arranged in six units, to be covered over the course of the year. For example, the first unit, *Number*, involves topics such as *counting words* (1's and 10's); *enumeration* (finding out how many in a collection); *comparing sets* (more, less, and same); *reading, writing, and representing numbers*; and *ordinal numbers* (first, second, third …). The next five units cover *Shape* (two- and three-dimensional, and symmetry); *Pattern and Logic* (identifying, creating, and extending patterns and using deductive logic); *Measurement* (using nonstandard and standard units to compare and order dimensions such as length or weight); and *Operations on Number* (comparing, adding, subtracting, and representing numbers and operations). The last and fairly short unit, *Space*, involves *positions and locations* (e.g., right and left, forward and backward); *directions* (e.g., using a verbal statement to find a hidden object); and *maps* (reading them).

I present this detail to show that the content of the curriculum is extensive and arranged in a particular sequence. The order of the large topics—Number, Shape, Pattern and Logic, and the rest—to some extent derives from mathematical considerations. For example, you have to do the number basics before you can do operations on number. But the order of the larger topics is to some extent arbitrary or a matter of convenience. For example, we could have done *Pattern* before or after *Space*. But within a "unit"—a large mathematical topic—the dominating principle of organization is the sequence in which children normally learn the various concepts—the "developmental trajectory." Thus, BMLK introduces "enumeration"—figuring out how many—before concrete addition. And it introduces recognizing shapes before analyzing them.

The curriculum not only specifies the order of major units but it also lays out a planning chart for the various activities within a unit. Indeed the planning chart (one is shown in Figure 18.1) is the operational definition of a curriculum. The chart assumes 32 weeks of instruction. In many preschools and child care centers, the first 3 or 4 weeks are often devoted to introducing weepy children to the structure and culture of the classroom. It's not a good time to do mathematics. So Week 1 of the program may not happen until the first week of October. Then, in December, there are many celebrations and holidays that dominate classrooms activities, so mathematics instruction does not occur then either. Given all these considerations, we estimated that about 32 weeks of instruction are possible between September and June.

The planning chart designates that an activity called Count, Clap, and Stomp is to take place during the first 3 weeks of instruction. Show Me is also scheduled for Week 1, and My Number Book is scheduled for Week 5. The chart indicates that a storybook (*Henrietta Sees Numbers*) is a component of Activity 3; that a take-home activity is associated with Activity 6, Find the Match; and that an assessment is associated with Activity 9, Number Match. The Number unit concludes with Animal Parade and A Fishy Game during Week 9. The gray area of the chart, extending from Week 8 to the end of the year, indicates that these activities are to be practiced for the rest of the year—not necessarily every day, but frequently. Thus, Numbers with Pizzazz is essentially a counting word activity in which children may learn to count to, say, 20 by Week 7, but, given repeated practice over the remaining months, to 100 by the year's end. Practice makes perfect. Repetition is crucial and, of course, the trick is to make it interesting, not dreary. The order of activities is intended to follow children's learning trajectory. Thus, the children begin with the counting words, then investigate how many are in small sets by "subitizing" ("seeing" number without counting) and enumerating before they go on to think about cardinality in more explicit ways and learn relevant symbols for number. The next topic in the sequence involves ordinal numbers (first, second, third ...), which are extraordinarily difficult for children at this age.

Each activity has several features, illustrated by Activity 3 in Figure 18.2. The first thing to note is that this material is intended for the teacher. The children never see a textbook. The teacher's guide indicates the overall purpose of the activity, describes a time line for doing it, and suggests an optimal group size for different "tasks" (subactivities). In this case, the activity involves a storybook and various materials that the teacher should prepare beforehand. The description of each task is clear enough, I hope, and provides general guidelines for what to do. Sometimes there is a "script" (indicated in

Planning Chart

The planning chart will help you organize and schedule the activities in this unit. It shows a recommended sequence of activities. The chart also shows a recommended time frame of nine weeks for the entire unit and how the unit fits into a 32-week Big Math curriculum. To follow the schedule, plan to dedicate at least 30 minutes a day to working on math. Suggested pacing, included with each activity, will further describe the duration and the repetition of an activity. You may adapt this time frame and sequence to suit your school calendar and the needs of the children in your class.

For each activity, an X indicates the week in which the activity is introduced. Additional Xs indicate that the activity should be continued in those weeks. Shading to the right of an X indicates that the activity is linked to Continuing Assessment and should be repeated regularly throughout the school year.

What Are Numbers?

No.	Activity	Pg.	1	2	3	4	5	6	7	8	9	10	11	12	13	14	15	16	17	18	19	20	21	22	23	24	25	26	27	28	29	30	31	32
1	Count, Clap, and Stomp	1	X	X	X	X	X																											
2	Show Me	2	X																															
3	Henrietta Sees Numbers	4	X	X																														
4	Bag It!	6		X	X	X																												
5	Did I Make a Mistake?	8			X	X																												
6	Find the Match	9				X	X																											
7	My Number Book	11				X																												
8	What Comes Next?	13				X	X																											
9	Number Match	15					X	X																										
10	Numbers With Pizzazz!	20					X	X																										
11	Let's Line Up!	22					X																											
12	If You're Happy and You Know It	24					X																											
13	Animal Parade	26						X	X																									
14	Tell a Story	28						X																										
15	A Fishy Game	29						X	X																									

Key

📖 The Unit Storybook is introduced.

🏠 The Take-Home Game may be sent home after completing this activity.

✓ This activity may be used for Focused Assessment.

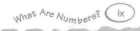

FIGURE 18.1. BMLK planning chart. From Ginsburg, Greenes, and Balfanz (2003). Copyright 2003 by Pearson Education. Reprinted by permission.

419

Henrietta Sees Numbers

See numbers of objects without counting

Suggested Pacing

Over a two-week period, allow several days to complete this activity and repeat Tasks 1–3 as time permits.

Group Size

Tasks 1 and 4: Whole class

Tasks 2 and 3: Small group

Language of Mathematics

count from 1 to 5

count to tell how many

1, 2, 3, 4, 5

Things You'll Need

☐ Crayons

☐ Stickers (optional)

☐ 4-by-6-inch index cards, 15 in all

☐ Classroom storybook *Henrietta Sees Numbers*

☐ Take-Home Storybooks of the same title, one for each child

Field-Test Note

One field-test teacher said, "To connect the activity to the theme of the month in our classroom, I used theme-related stickers to make the cards. I laminated the cards before putting them in my math center for children to use on their own."

ABOUT THE ACTIVITY

In Brief

Shown pictures of small sets of objects, children learn first to "see" the correct number without counting and then to check their answers by counting.

Activity Goals

• Recognize one to five objects in a set without counting.

• Count to verify the number "seen."

Skills Children Need at the Start

• Count one to five objects.

• Count from 1 to 5 aloud.

GETTING READY

Preparing the Materials Make three different sets of number cards for the numbers 1 to 5. Make the cards as shown below using stickers, cutout pictures, or drawings.

• Set of different object cards

• Set of same-but-different cards (showing objects that differ from one another only by color or size)

• Set of dot cards

Setting Up For Tasks 2 and 3, seat a small group of three or four children at a table. Place the three sets of number cards on the table.

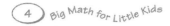

FIGURE 18.2. BMLK Activity 3. From Ginsburg, Greenes, and Balfanz (2003). Copyright 2003 by Pearson Education. Reprinted by permission.

LET'S GO!

Task 1 Read the classroom storybook *Henrietta Sees Numbers* to the whole class. Point out the importance of counting to verify the number of objects "seen."

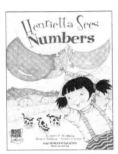

Task 2 Show the card with three objects from the different object card set to the group of children. Say, **When I look at this card, I see three objects. I can see three objects quickly, without counting them.** Explain that it is important to learn to "see" how many objects there are in a group and that counting can always be used to check the number. Children take turns "seeing," as quickly as possible, the number of objects on all the sets of cards that show the numbers 1 to 3. After deciding on the number "seen," each child checks the answer by carefully pointing to and counting the objects or dots on the card.

Task 3 Repeat Task 2 but increase the number to 5. Introduce cards with one to five objects or dots in random order and frequently ask children to check their answers by pointing to and counting the pictured objects.

Task 4 After children have heard the story *Henrietta Sees Numbers* several times, distribute the Take-Home Storybooks. Read the story with the children once again and have them fill in the blanks in the incomplete sentences on pages 12–14. Then have children color their storybooks. Children can take their completed storybooks home to share with their families.

MORE TO DO

Distribute five index cards and crayons or stickers to each child. Have the children paste stickers or draw objects, from one to five, on the fronts of the cards and record the numerals on the backs. Give children templates for forming the numbers or you may record the numbers yourself. Pairs of children can then play "See the Number." One child holds up a card and a friend tries to see the number of objects as quickly as possible. The friend checks by counting and then reads the number on the back of the card.

What Are Numbers? 5

FIGURE 18.2. *(cont.)*

421

bold font). It is intended only as suggested wording; teachers we worked with in preparing the materials wanted it. But the description of each task makes clear that the teacher has a good deal of freedom in how to implement it. We are not interested in promoting robot-like teaching. These, then, are some features of a curriculum. Clearly, it involves much more than letting children play or seizing on the teachable moment. No curriculum comes with an ironclad guarantee to work. To succeed, a curriculum needs to be high quality and implemented well. Neither of these is guaranteed.

How Rigidly Should I Follow the Sequence?

You should follow the sequence of major units and the sequence of activities within the units. The sequence was based on a rationale, I hope, a sound one. It is true that some aspects of a sequence could be changed, as I indicated earlier, but one reason for sticking with the sequence is that it allows you to exchange information with other teachers doing the same activities and also to attend workshops following the same sequence. Within a unit, you should also follow the sequence, but you have freedom to adjust the timing of the various activities and tasks according to the children's needs.

How Often Should I Do Math Activities?

BMLK recommends that you do at least one activity every day of the week for at least 20 minutes each day (perhaps a little less at the beginning of the year, when children are adjusting to school). Even if you teach only a half-day, you should be able find at least the 20 minutes. In my experience, once teachers become comfortable with a curriculum, they have no trouble finding time to teach it; indeed, they do math activities for much more than the 20 minutes.

Aren't Some of These Activities Too Hard for Little Children?

Of course, some of the activities will be too hard for some children, and actually they should be—at least at first. Why teach the children something they already know? But in general, given good instruction, young children can learn to do these activities. Cognitive research tells us that they can, and field-testing has shown that they can. Remember, you need to raise your expectations about what little children can do. Solving genuinely challenging problems promotes children's self-esteem more effectively than does unmotivated but well-intentioned praise (Stipek, 1998). (Another way of saying this is that meeting a challenge is better than being told you are smart.) Many teachers beginning to implement BMLK think it is too hard. By the end of the year, some tend to think it is too easy.

What If Children Don't Seem to Get It?

Despite the best planning and teaching, some children don't seem to understand what is taught. Of course, you should try different ways of reaching those children. But alternative teaching may not work either. What to do? In BMLK, we preach "relaxed patience." This is the recognition that some children, who at first do not seem to be learning, later show surprising mastery of the subject. The implication for teachers is to be patient and serene. Don't expect children to "get it" immediately. With practice and patience on your part, they are likely to learn eventually.

Isn't It Bad to Introduce the Reading and Writing of Numerals and Other Mathematical Symbols?

It could be bad, like anything else, but it does not have to be, if it is done the right way. The *meaningless* use of written symbols is the problem, not the symbols themselves. Stated differently, it is not helpful to use abstract number (or other) symbols that do not refer to something that is real or drawn from the child's experience, something that the child can see, hear, touch or imagine. In my experience, most 4-year-olds want to learn to read and write numbers. BMLK introduces symbolism in a meaningful context. For example, the child *sees* that there are three stars, counts the stars to check, and only *then* writes 3 to describe what he or she found. There is no problem in introducing the symbolism. If, by contrast, we introduce the written symbols *only* in the context of tracing numbers endlessly in a workbook, then there is a big problem.

Doesn't a Sequenced Curriculum Force Children to Learn, and Isn't That Bad?

A good curriculum should provide *opportunities* for children to learn. These opportunities should be field-tested—as was BMLK—to determine whether they are appropriate and challenging, and capture children's interest. The issue of forcing children to learn is at the heart of debates about education. John Dewey described the situation well in "The Child and the Curriculum" (Dewey, 1976), which should be required reading for everyone in early childhood education. He argues that we often face educational extremes. One involves basing everything on children's interests ("Let them play"), and the other entails domination by the adult regardless of children's interests ("Learn what I tell you to learn"). What's needed instead, Dewey argues, is the middle ground, in which the adult provides "guidance" designed to promote and advance the child's interests and abilities. "Guidance is not external imposition. *It is freeing the life-process for its own most adequate fulfillment*" (p. 281). The ideal curriculum, then, is one that provides thoughtful but firm guidance. It's just like good parenting. And like good parenting, it does not always produce immediate (or long-term) success!

Shouldn't Mathematics Be Integrated into Other Activities?

No, not necessarily. It can be, such as when teachers extend BMLK lessons on ordinality to the everyday activity of lining up, but it does not have to be. Insisting on integration assumes that mathematics needs to be sugar coated to appeal to young children (and perhaps for teachers as well). But we have seen that it can be an interesting and exciting subject of study in its own right. What could be more fascinating in a young child's eyes than the identity of the largest number (Gelman, 1980)? Also, excessive reliance on integration with other subjects precludes, or at least limits, the extent to which mathematics activities can be presented in an orderly sequence. Adults who fear introducing mathematics as such to young children may be reacting more to their own unfortunate encounters with the subject than to any appreciation of young children's interests and capabilities.

How Can You Possibly Use a Curriculum with a Diverse Group of Children?

There is very large intellectual variation among preschoolers. Four-year-olds differ enormously in their emotional maturity, their language, and their mathematical skills. Moreover, some preschool classrooms combine 4- and 5-year-olds, or 3- and 4-year-olds. Then again, it is becoming increasingly common in the United States to have children speaking several different languages in the same classroom. Doesn't all this make use of a curriculum impossible? What happens if you are teaching counting and a 3-year-old does not seem to get it? Do you just ignore him?

These are difficult and serious questions. The first step in an answer is to put the questions in perspective. These are perennial problems regardless of the age of the students or the subject being taught. Any system of organized group education is faced with the problem of meeting the diverse needs of students, and the language issue is common at all levels as well. In my graduate courses, the students have varied interests, backgrounds, and languages. I often feel that there is no way my course can be effective for all students. A pessimistic way to view the situation is to say that any organized form of group education must fail. It is impossible to meet the needs of all students at the same time. I think that's true. At the same time, organized group education provides many advantages, such as the opportunity for children to learn from peers and to see that others fail as well.

ECME is no different. It cannot meet the needs of all children, and it often must fail. Teachers must do their best, and what is best depends on the individual teachers. Many BMLK teachers break the class up into smaller groups, roughly according to perceived developmental level, and try to teach the groups separately, each according its needs. The teachers try to work with some children on an individual basis, as necessary.

The alternative to using a curriculum seems overwhelming. Suppose that you, as a teacher, do not have any planned organization for your students and instead try to improvise productive learning experiences for each of 20 children on an individual basis. I think that is basically impossible, and will lead to chaos and poor education for most of them. Diversity among children is an argument *for* some kind of organization, not *against* it. So, in some sense, a curriculum is bound to fail on at least some occasions, but not using a curriculum leads to even more extensive failure.

Is It Realistic to Implement a Program of ECME?

We certainly need to try. In this chapter, I have tried to make a convincing case for early childhood mathematics education. It can provide a sound foundation for later success in school, and it can satisfy young children's intellectual interests. It involves much more than mere memorization; it deals with big ideas and important types of thinking and language, and it can be both challenging and enjoyable. Research has shown that young children are capable of learning mathematics, and that doing so is developmentally appropriate and perhaps even salutary for emotional development. Many effective mathematics education materials are available, as are strategies to promote learning, from play to intentional teaching. So ECME is useful; it is important. Children can learn from it, and it can be taught—in a developmentally appropriate way. So we certainly ought to try to implement it.

At the same time, we have to be realistic and recognize the obstacles we face. One is that we do not yet have a teaching workforce prepared to teach early mathematics. We need to undertake the massive task of providing that preparation at both preservice and inservice levels. A second obstacle is that the entire enterprise requires considerable resources—money. It takes money to make preschool available to all those who need it or are eligible for it. New York State used to have a policy of universal preschool, which was rendered less than universal because there was inadequate budget for it. Head Start is a wonderful idea, but it is not fully funded, so that many who are eligible for it cannot attend. It takes money to pay teachers adequately. It takes money to buy curricula. And, perhaps most importantly, it takes money to make available intensive professional development over a period of years for large numbers of teachers. The final question, which I cannot answer, is this: *Do we have the political will to provide the resources?*

References

Anderson, A. (1993). Wondering—one child's questions and mathematics learning. *Canadian Children, 18*(2), 26–30.

Arnold, D. H., & Doctoroff, G. L. (2003). The early education of socioeconomically disadvantaged children. *Annual Review of Psychology, 54,* 517–545.

Baroody, A. J. (1985). Mastery of basic number combinations: Internalization of relationships or facts? *Journal for Research in Mathematics Education, 16,* 83–98.

Baroody, A. J. (1992). The development of preschoolers' counting skills and principles. In J. Bideaud, C. Meljac, & J. P. Fischer (Eds.), *Pathways to number: Children's developing numerical abilities* (pp. 99–126). Hillsdale, NJ: Erlbaum.

Baroody, A. J., Lai, M., & Mix, K. S. (2006). The development of young children's early number and operation sense and its implications for early childhood education. In B. Spodek & O. Saracho (Eds.), *Handbook of research on the education of young children* (Vol. 2, pp. 187–221). Mahwah, NJ: Erlbaum.

Baroody, A. J., & Wilkins, J. L. M. (1999). The development of informal counting, number, and arithmetic skills and concepts. In J. V. Copley (Ed.), *Mathematics in the early years* (pp. 48–65). Reston, VA: National Council of Teachers of Mathematics.

Berliner, D. C. (2006). Our impoverished view of educational research. *Teachers College Record, 108*(6), 949–995.

Binet, A. (1969). The perception of lengths and numbers. In R. H. Pollack & M. W. Brenner (Eds.), *Experimental psychology of Alfred Binet* (pp. 79–92). New York: Springer.

Binet, A., & Simon, T. (1916). *The development of intelligence in children.* Baltimore: Williams & Wilkins.

Bloom, L. (1970). *Language development: Form and function in emerging grammars.* Cambridge, MA: MIT Press.

Brooks-Gunn, J. (2003). Do you believe in magic?: What we can expect from early childhood intervention programs. *Social Policy Report: Society for Research in Child Development, 17*(1), 3–14.

Brosterman, N. (1997). *Inventing kindergarten.* New York: Abrams.

Brown, E. T. (2005). The influence of teachers' efficacy and beliefs regarding mathematics instruction in the early childhood classroom. *Journal of Early Childhood Teacher Education, 26,* 239–257.

Brush, L. R. (1978). Preschool children's knowledge of addition and subtraction. *Journal for Research in Mathematics Education, 9,* 44–54.

Case, R., & Okamoto, Y. (1996). The role of central conceptual structures in the development of children's thought. *Monographs of the Society for Research in Child Development, 61*(1–2, Serial No. 246).

Clements, D. H. (1999). Geometric and spatial thinking in young children. In J. V. Copley (Ed.), *Mathematics in the early years* (pp. 66–79). Reston, VA: National Council of Teachers of Mathematics.

Clements, D. H. (2007). Curriculum research: Toward a framework for "research-based curricula." *Journal for Research in Mathematics Education, 38*(1), 35–70.

Clements, D. H., & Sarama, J. (2007). Early childhood mathematics learning. In F. K. Lester (Ed.), *Second handbook of research on mathematics teaching and learning* (pp. 461–555). Charlotte, NC: Information Age.

Clements, D. H., Sarama, T., & DiBiase, A.-M. (2004). *Engaging young children in mathematics: Standards for early childhood mathematics education.* Mahwah, NJ: Erlbaum.

Copley, J. V. (Ed.). (1999). *Mathematics in the early years.* Reston, VA: National Council of Teachers of Mathematics.

Copley, J. V., Jones, C., & Dighe, J. (2007). *Mathematics: The Creative Curriculum approach.* Washington, DC: Teaching Strategies.

Corsaro, W. A. (1985). *Friendship and peer culture in the early years.* Norwood, NJ: Ablex.

Court, S. R. A. (1920). Numbers, time, and space in the first five years of a child's life. *Pedagogical Seminary, 27,* 71–89.

Denton, K., & West, J. (2002). *Children's reading and mathematics achievement in kindergarten and first grade.* Washington, DC: National Center for Education Statistics.

Dewey, J. (1938). *Experience and education.* New York: Collier Books.

Dewey, J. (1976). The child and the curriculum. In J. A. Boydston (Ed.), *John Dewey: The middle works, 1899–1924: Volume 2. 1902–1903* (pp. 273–291). Carbondale: Southern Illinois University Press.

Dodge, D. T., Colker, L., & Heroman, C. (2002). *The creative curriculum for preschool* (4th ed.). Washington, DC: Teaching Strategies.

Durkin, K., Shire, B., Riem, R., Crowther, R. D., & Rutter, D. R. (1986). The social and linguistic context of early number word use. *British Journal of Developmental Psychology, 4,* 269–288.

Edwards, C., Gandini, L., & Forman, G. (Eds.). (1993). *The hundred languages of children: The Reggio Emilia approach to early childhood education.* Norwood, NJ: Ablex.

Gelman, R. (1980). What young children know about numbers. *Educational Psychologist, 15,* 54–68.

Gelman, R., & Gallistel, C. R. (1986). *The child's understanding of number.* Cambridge, MA: Harvard University Press.

Ginsburg, H. P. (2006). Mathematical play and playful mathematics: A guide for early education. In D. Singer, R. M. Golinkoff, & K. Hirsh-Pasek (Eds.), *Play = learning: How play motivates and enhances children's cognitive and social–emotional growth* (pp. 145–165). New York: Oxford University Press.

Ginsburg, H. P., Cannon, J., Eisenband, J. G., & Pappas, S. (2006). Mathematical thinking and learning. In K. McCartney & D. Phillips (Eds.), *Handbook of early child development* (pp. 208–229). Oxford, UK: Blackwell.

Ginsburg, H. P., Greenes, C., & Balfanz, R. (2003). *Big math for little kids.* Parsippany, NJ: Dale Seymour.

Ginsburg, H. P., & Pappas, S. (2004). SES, ethnic, and gender differences in young children's informal addition and subtraction: A clinical interview investigation. *Journal of Applied Developmental Psychology, 25,* 171–192.

Ginsburg, H. P., Pappas, S., & Seo, K.-H. (2001). Everyday mathematical knowledge: Asking young children what is developmentally appropriate. In S. L. Golbeck (Ed.), *Psychological perspectives on early childhood education: Reframing dilemmas in research and practice* (pp. 181–219). Mahwah, NJ: Erlbaum.

Ginsburg, H. P., & Russell, R. L. (1981). Social class and racial influences on early mathematical thinking. *Monographs of the Society for Research in Child Development, 46*(6, Serial No. 193).

Ginsburg, H. P., & Seo, K.-H. (1999). The mathematics in children's thinking. *Mathematical Thinking and Learning, 1*(2), 113–129.

Ginsburg, H. P., & Seo, K.-H. (2000). Preschoolers' math reading. *Teaching Children Mathematics, 7*(4), 226–229.

Gormley, W. T. (2007). Early childhood care and education: Lessons and puzzles. *Journal of Policy Analysis and Management, 26*(3), 633–671.

Graham, T. A., Nash, C., & Paul, K. (1997). Young children's exposure to mathematics: The child care context. *Early Childhood Education Journal, 25*(1), 31–38.

Groen, G., & Resnick, L. B. (1977). Can preschool children invent addition algorithms? *Journal of Educational Psychology, 69*, 645–652.

Harms, T., Clifford, R. M., & Cryer, D. (1998). *Early Childhood Environment Rating Scale—Revised.* New York: Teachers College Press.

Helm, J. H., & Beneke, S. (2003). *The power of projects: Meeting contemporary challenges in early childhood classrooms—strategies and solutions.* New York: Teachers College Press.

Helm, J. H., & Katz, L. G. (2000). *Young investigators: The project approach in the early years.* New York: Teachers College Press.

Irwin, K., & Burgham, D. (1992). Big numbers and small children. *New Zealand Mathematics Magazine, 29*(1), 9–19.

Isaacs, S. (1930). *Intellectual growth in young children.* London: Routledge & Kegan Paul.

Jordan, N. C., Huttenlocher, L., & Levine, S. C. (1994). Assessing early arithmetic abilities: Effects of verbal and nonverbal response types on the calculation performance of middle- and low-income children. *Learning and Individual Differences, 6*, 413–432.

Jordan, N. C., Kaplan, D., Olah, L. N., & Locuniak, M. N. (2006). Number sense growth in kindergarten: A longitudinal investigation of children at risk for mathematics difficulties. *Child Development, 77*(1), 153–175.

Kontos, S. (1999). Preschool teachers' talk, roles, and activity settings during free play. *Early Childhood Research Quarterly, 14*(3), 363–382.

Lee, J. (2004). Correlations between kindergarten teachers' attitudes toward mathematics and teaching practice. *Journal of Early Childhood Teacher Education, 25*(2), 173–184.

Lee, V. E., & Burkam, D. T. (2002). *Inequality at the starting gate: Social background differences in achievement as children begin school.* Washington, DC: Economic Policy Institute.

Ludwig, J., & Phillips, D. (2007). The benefits and costs of Head Start. *Social Policy Report, 21*(3), 3–18.

Miller, K. F., & Parades, D. R. (1996). On the shoulders of giants: Cultural tools and mathematical development. In R. J. Sternberg & T. Ben-Zeev (Eds.), *The nature of mathematical thinking* (pp. 83–117). Mahwah, NJ: Erlbaum.

Montessori, M. (1964). *The Montessori method* (A. E. George, Trans.). New York: Schocken.

Moseley, B. (2005). Pre-service early childhood educators' perceptions of math-mediated language. *Early Education and Development, 16*(3), 385–396.

Mullis, I. V. S., Martin, M. O., Gonzalez, D. L., Gregory, K. D., Garden, R. A., & O'Connor, K. M. (2000). *TIMSS 1999 International Mathematics Report: Findings from IEA's repeat of the Third International Mathematics and Science Study at the eighth grade.* Boston: International Study Center, Boston College.

National Association for the Education of Young Children and National Council of Teachers of

Mathematics. (2002). Position statement: Early childhood mathematics: Promoting good beginnings. Retrieved from *www.naeyc.org/about/positions/psmath.asp*

National Center for Children in Poverty. (2006). *Basic facts about low-income children: Birth to age 18.* New York: Author.

National Council of Teachers of Mathematics. (2000). *Principles and standards for school mathematics.* Reston, VA: Author.

Newcombe, N. S., & Huttenlocher, J. (2000). *Making space: The development of spatial representation and reasoning.* Cambridge, MA: MIT Press.

Pappas, S., Ginsburg, H. P., & Jiang, M. (2003). SES differences in young children's metacognition in the context of mathematical problem solving. *Cognitive Development, 18*(3), 431–450.

Piaget, J. (1952). *The child's conception of number* (C. Gattegno & F. M. Hodgson, Trans.). London: Routledge & Kegan Paul.

Reynolds, A. J., & Ou, S.-R. (2003). Promoting resilience through early childhood intervention. In S. S. Luthar (Ed.), *Resilience and vulnerability: Adaptation in the context of childhood adversities* (pp. 436–459). New York: Cambridge University Press.

Saxe, G. B., Guberman, S. R., & Gearhart, M. (1987). Social processes in early number development. *Monographs of the Society for Research in Child Development, 52*(2, Serial No. 216).

Seo, K.-H., & Ginsburg, H. P. (2004). What is developmentally appropriate in early childhood mathematics education?: Lessons from new research. In D. H. Clements, J. Sarama, & A.-M. DiBiase (Eds.), *Engaging young children in mathematics: Standards for early childhood mathematics education* (pp. 91–104). Hillsdale, NJ: Erlbaum.

Singer, D., Golinkoff, R. M., & Hirsh-Pasek, K. (Eds.). (2006). *Play = learning: How play motivates and enhances children's cognitive and social–emotional growth.* New York: Oxford University Press.

Stipek, D. (1998). *Motivation to learn: From theory to practice* (3rd ed.). Boston: Allyn & Bacon.

Vygotsky, L. S. (1978). *Mind in society: The development of higher psychological processes.* Cambridge, MA: Harvard University Press.

Vygotsky, L. S. (1986). *Thought and language* (A. Kozulin, Trans.). Cambridge, MA: MIT Press.

Walkerdine, V. (1988). *The mastery of reason: Cognitive development and the production of rationality.* London: Routledge.

Whitehead, A. N. (1929). *The aims of education.* New York: Macmillan.

Worsley, M., Beneke, S., & Helm, J. H. (2003). The Pizza Project: Planning and integrating math standards in project work. *Young Children, 58*(1), 44–49.

CHAPTER 19

Improving Preschoolers' Number Sense Using Information-Processing Theory

Robert S. Siegler

Immanuel Kant, Albert Einstein, John Dewey, Kurt Lewin, and Leon Festinger are among the notable thinkers who have been credited with the saying, "There's nothing so practical as a good theory" (Google Search, August 2007). There is good reason why so many of the greats have come to this conclusion. If theories accurately explain the phenomena that they seek to explain, then they should guide us toward useful applications. This generalization is not always true—some major scientific theories have not had important practical applications, at least in the short run—but it does seem to be true more often than not.

For psychologists who study children's thinking, education is the key area for testing the practical usefulness of our theories. Thus, if these theories accurately explain how children develop increasingly effective ways of thinking, then they should suggest ways of improving the education that we provide. In particular, the theoretical analyses should suggest means of identifying strengths that teachers can build on, weaknesses that need to be remedied, and experiences that will be especially beneficial in promoting cognitive growth. Moreover, such theoretical analyses should point to reasons why some children's understanding progresses more slowly than that of their peers, and to instructive experiences that can help these children catch up.

This chapter examines how information-processing theory can be applied to one important educational problem: how to improve the number sense of preschoolers from low-income families, so that they enter school on an even footing with peers from middle-income families. I first provide background information regarding why this educational problem is so important, and then briefly examine how other developmental theories, in particular Piagetian and sociocultural theory, have proved useful in improving the mathematical understanding of preschoolers from low-income backgrounds. Finally, I examine at greater length a promising new program, based on information-processing theory, and the results that it is yielding.

Background

Children vary greatly in the mathematical knowledge they bring to school. These differences in initial mathematical knowledge appear to have large, long-term consequences. An analysis of six large, long-term longitudinal studies indicated that proficiency in mathematics at the beginning of kindergarten is strongly predictive of mathematics achievement test scores years later in elementary and middle school (Duncan et al., 2007). Another study indicated that very early mathematics knowledge is predictive of math achievement even in high school (Stevenson & Newman, 1986). These findings are consistent with the usual finding that initial knowledge is positively related to learning (Bransford, Brown, & Cocking, 1999), but the relations in math are unusually strong and persistent. For example, in the same six longitudinal studies reviewed by Duncan et al. (2007), the relation between early and later mathematical knowledge was considerably stronger than the relation between early and later reading proficiency, attention, or self-control.

Given the strong and persistent relation between early and later mathematical proficiency, it is especially unfortunate that preschoolers and kindergartners from low-income families enter school with far less numerical knowledge than peers from more affluent families. Substantial differences in the numerical proficiency of preschoolers and kindergartners from different socioeconomic backgrounds have been demonstrated on a wide range of foundational tasks: reciting the counting string, counting sets of objects, counting up or down from a given number other than 1, recognizing written numerals, adding, subtracting, and comparing numerical magnitudes (Ginsburg & Russell, 1981; Griffin, Case, & Siegler, 1994; Jordan, Huttenlocher, & Levine, 1992; Jordan, Kaplan, Olah, & Locuniak, 2006; Jordan, Levine, & Huttenlocher, 1994; Saxe, Guberman, & Gearhart, 1987; Starkey, Klein, & Wakeley, 2004; Stipek & Ryan, 1997). The early differences in numerical proficiency tend to become even more pronounced as children progress through school (Alexander & Entwisle, 1988; Geary, 1994, 2006). Even when children from disadvantaged backgrounds make as much progress as children from advantaged backgrounds within a school year, they still start behind and stay behind (Stipek & Ryan, 1997).

This difference between the mathematical knowledge of children from low-income and middle-income backgrounds is directly attributable to differences in environmental support for mathematics learning. Parents in middle-income families report providing their children with a broader range of numerical activities and engaging in these activities more frequently than do parents in low-income families (Clements & Sarama, 2007; Starkey et al., 2004). Parents who engage in more numerical activities generally have children with greater mathematical knowledge (Blevins-Knabe & Musun-Miller, 1996).

Mothers in low-income families tend to believe that the primary responsibility for providing instruction in math belongs to preschool teachers (Holloway, Rambaud, Fuller, & Eggers-Pierola, 1995; Tudge & Doucet, 2004). However, observations of home and preschool activities, as well as the self-reports of preschool teachers and the parents of preschoolers, are strikingly consistent in finding that neither the home nor the school environment provides children with much specifically mathematical activity (Plewis, Mooney, & Creeser, 1990; Starkey & Klein, 2000; Tudge & Doucet, 2004). This is the case with both low- and middle-income families, but it is even more the case with low-income families. For example, in a carefully conducted observational study of children's exposure to mathematical activities in their own homes, other people's homes, and child care centers, most children from working-class backgrounds, both African American and European American, were observed engaging in mathematical play or mathematical lessons in 0 of 180 observations (Tudge & Doucet, 2004). As Tudge and Doucet commented (2004, p. 36), "If it is indeed correct that working-class parents look to preschool settings to provide children with mathematics experiences ... our data suggest that they are mistaken—we found no evidence that children are more likely to be engaged in mathematical activities ... in formal childcare centers than at home."

Thus, it seems vitally important to create programs that help parents and teachers at preschools and child care centers to provide stimulating mathematical activities to young children, especially those from low-income backgrounds. Doing so may improve the foundation of mathematical knowledge with which children begin school, thus helping them learn from the instruction they subsequently receive. Moreover, reducing or eliminating the early differences between the mathematical knowledge of children from lower- and middle-income families may prevent those differences from growing into larger, less tractable, later ones.

A number of researchers have responded to this challenge by creating preschool programs that utilize insights from theories of cognitive development to improve low-income preschoolers' mathematical understanding. Several of the programs appear to be very effective. Two of these, one based on neo-Piagetian theory and the other based on sociocultural theory, are described briefly in the next section. Then, I describe at greater length a program based on information-processing theory that has been found to be particularly effective in promoting number sense, a key component of mathematical understanding. The fact that all of these programs are effective is heartening. It indicates that we do not have to reach consensus on the optimal theory of cognitive development for theory-based programs to improve children's learning. Instead, a variety of theoretical perspectives may help low-income preschoolers improve their mathematical understanding.

A Program Based on Neo-Piagetian Theory

Robbie Case's neo-Piagetian theory provided the theoretical basis for Griffin's (2004) Number Worlds curriculum. This theory is intended to preserve the broad, integrative character of Piagetian theory, while also incorporating contributions from information processing and sociocultural theories, such as analyses of domain-specific knowledge and of the surrounding culture.

A particularly important part of the foundation for Number Worlds is Case and Okamoto's (1996) construct of the "central conceptual structure." Such structures are defined as networks of concepts and relations that play a crucial role in organizing children's thinking about a particular domain. Thus, central conceptual structures provide a unifying framework that allows children to think about many topics in a content domain in similar ways. At a given age, all central conceptual structures share certain features, based on overall structural limits of the cognitive system at that age, but each conceptual structure also reflects the particulars of the domain to which it applies.

The central conceptual structures in each domain change with maturation and general experience, so that there is a typical central conceptual structure in each domain at age 6 years, a different one at 8 years, and so on.

Case and Okamoto (1996) hypothesized that for young children, there are three particularly important central conceptual structures: one for narratives, another for space, and still another for numbers. The theoretical foundation of the Number Worlds curriculum was provided by the numerical central conceptual structure for 6- to 8-year-olds. Case and Okamoto hypothesized that at this age, the predominant numerical central conceptual structure is the mental number line. To be specific, children are hypothesized to organize their thinking about whole numbers in terms of a line, in which individual numbers are ordered from right to left and linked by "next," "greater than," and "less than" relations. This structure allows children to make sense of varied numerical problems, such as which number is larger, which of two sets of coins is worth more, which of two girls is older, and so on.

Although most children acquire this structure around the time that they enter school, some children, particularly those from low-income minority backgrounds, do not. Number Worlds was developed to help these children acquire the central conceptual structure. The Number Worlds approach is based on five theoretical principles, all reflecting Case's theory: (1) Build on children's current knowledge; (2) follow the natural developmental progression in deciding on the sequence of instructional goals; (3) teach computational skills, as well as conceptual understanding; (4) provide ample opportunities for hands-on exploration and problem solving; and (5) provide children with experience in the ways numbers are represented and discussed in the wider society.

Number Worlds has produced impressive progress in preschoolers from low-income backgrounds. In an experimental test, the curriculum produced greater gains in conceptual understanding of numbers and number sense, as well as in computation, than those produced by a control curriculum (Griffin, 2002). Following participation in Number Worlds, low-income children from the United States performed as well as the mean of children from China and Japan on a test of computational skills administered at the end of first grade (Griffin & Case, 1997). The children who participated in Number Worlds also kept pace with more advantaged peers over the first few grades. Moreover, teachers reported gains in teaching other subjects after they were instructed in the theoretical principles on which Number Worlds is based (Griffin, 2004). Thus, this theory-based program produces impressive gains in the mathematical understanding of young children from low-income backgrounds.

A Program Based on Sociocultural Theory

Klein, Starkey, and Ramirez (2002) based their Pre-K Mathematics curriculum on sociocultural theory. Consistent with the views of the founding father of this theory, Lev Vygotsky, Pre-K Mathematics embodies the perspective that early mathematical knowledge develops in social settings, with concrete materials that children can manipulate. Scaffolding provided by more expert individuals and discussions about mathematics with teachers and peers are hypothesized to play key roles within sociocultural theory and are given prominent places in Pre-K Mathematics. In addition, the curriculum reflects specific results from experiments performed within the sociocultural tradition, such as Radziszewska and Rogoff's (1991) finding that people who have thoroughly mastered a content area are better able to lead the child to construct more advanced understanding than are peers or the child alone. Consistent with both sociocultural and neo-Piagetian theories, Pre-K Mathematics is organized so that the ordering of its lessons matches the typical developmental sequence in which children typically master the skills being taught.

Pre-K Mathematics includes 27 small-group activities; in all of them, children work with concrete materials. Among the topics included are counting, number sense, arithmetic reasoning, spatial sense, geometric reasoning, measurement, and logical relations. In recognition of the fact that preschoolers already differ greatly in their numerical knowledge, the curriculum includes downward extensions of these activities (for students whose knowledge lags behind that of most peers) and upward extensions (for students whose knowledge is advanced). New activities are introduced weekly from October to May, and children engage in each activity twice. Consistent with the sociocultural approach, children learn the activities in small groups of four to six children and are encouraged to discuss them with classmates and the teacher. Also consistent with sociocultural theory, teachers are provided 2 weeks of workshop activities, one before the school year and one midway through it, so that they can develop the necessary expertise in scaffolding the children's learning. The curriculum also includes a home component, in which parents learn how to help their children learn mathematical concepts and procedures; the parents also are given materials to help their children learn math at home.

Starkey and colleagues (2004) compared the learning of children from low-income and middle-income families who went through this program with that of peers who attended the same preschools the previous year but did not go through the program. Participating in the program significantly increased the mathematical knowledge of children from less affluent and more affluent backgrounds who progressed through it. However, the children from low-income families made even larger gains than did peers from middle-income backgrounds. By the end of the year, the mathematical knowledge of children from low-income backgrounds who participated in the Pre-K Mathematics program was equivalent to that of children from middle-income backgrounds who had not participated in it. Thus, the program allowed these children to start formal schooling with their mathematical knowledge on an equal footing with that of children from more privileged backgrounds.

A Program Based on Information-Processing Theory

The information-processing approach to development is characterized by precise analyses of the tasks that people need to perform, and of the mental representations and processes that they use to perform those tasks. Geetha Ramani, and I have used this theory to develop a program using board games to improve children's number sense. Information-processing theory is helpful in this regard because it explains how change occurs, both in terms of the experiences that lead to learning and in the way those experiences produce the desired representations and processes. This section offers a full discussion of the theory underlying the program, describes how the theory is applied in the program, and present the results when the program is used.

Theoretical Background

There is general agreement among researchers and educators that number sense is an important part of mathematical development and an important goal of mathematics instruction (e.g., National Research Council, 2001). Helping children achieve a good sense of number is more difficult than it sounds, however. One reason is that there is little agreement on what number sense is. Like a Supreme Court justice's famous comment about pornography, it's hard to define number sense, but it is easy to recognize it when we see it. This lack of a clear definition has contributed to difficulties in knowing how to study number sense and how to help children acquire it.

An information-processing analysis (Siegler & Booth, 2005) suggested that "number sense" can be defined as the ability to approximate numerical magnitudes. The approximations can involve the numerical magnitude of specific dimensions of objects, events, or sets (e.g., "About how long is this line?" or "About how many times have you been to New York?" or "About how many people were at the play?"), or they can involve the results of numerical operations ("About how much is 24 × 94?"). This definition emphasizes that number sense is about numerical *magnitudes*—being able to choose numbers whose magnitudes are close to the correct ones. The question then becomes how to measure children's ability to approximate numerical magnitudes, and how to help students do so more successfully.

The process of estimation is inherently related to number sense, in that both involve approximating magnitudes. The two are not identical: Some estimation tasks can be performed through stereotyped procedures, such as rounding to the nearest 10, without any deeper sense of the magnitudes that the estimates should yield. When executed through means other than these routine procedures, however, accurate estimation, like number sense, involves the ability to approximate numerical magnitudes.

This reasoning suggests that estimation tasks are a promising place to look for ways of studying number sense. Estimation tasks involving number lines have proved particularly useful in this regard. As shown in Figure 19.1, these number line estimation tasks involve presenting lines with a number at each end (e.g., 0 and 100) and no other numbers or marks in between, and asking participants to locate a third number on the line (e.g., "Where does 74 go?"). Then a new blank line is presented, and participants are asked to locate a different number on that line. The series of numbers continues until participants have estimated numbers from all parts of the numerical range.

The number line task has several important advantages for measuring children's sense of numerical magnitudes. It can be used with any type of number—large or small, positive or negative, integer or fraction, and so forth. It transparently reflects the ratio characteristics of the number system. For example, just as 80 is twice as large as 40, so the estimated location of 80 should be twice as far from 0 as the estimated location of 40. It is nonroutine; neither parents nor teachers typically instruct children in how to do

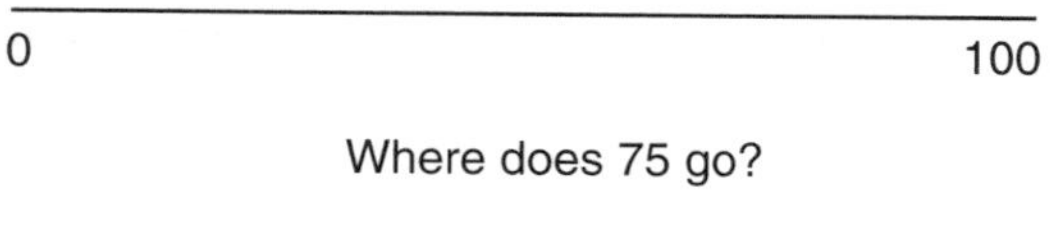

0   100

Where does 75 go?

FIGURE 19.1. The number line estimation task.

number line estimation, so children's sense of the magnitudes of the numbers is reflected directly in their estimates.

On the number line task, estimates should increase linearly with the size of the number, as in the equation $y = x$. Although this relation might seem obvious, children do not seem to understand it for a surprisingly long time. Many preschoolers, particularly those from low-income backgrounds, do not even know the rank order of the magnitudes of the numbers from 1 to 10 (Ramani & Siegler, 2008). Somewhat older children know the rank order of the numbers' magnitudes but still fail to understand that equal differences between numbers mean that the magnitudes of the numbers also must be equally discrepant. Instead, they use a logarithmic representation of numerical magnitudes, in which estimates of magnitudes at the low end of the scale are further apart than estimates at the high end for any given difference between numbers. Thus, as shown in Figure 19.2, the large majority of kindergartners, and about half of first-graders, think that on a 0–100 number line, the magnitudes of 12 and 20 are much more discrepant than the magnitudes of 72 and 80. Not until second grade do the number line estimates of most children indicate understanding that these differences are equal.

A similar change occurs on 0–1,000 number lines between second and fourth grades. Second-graders' estimates of numerical magnitudes in that range increase much more rapidly at the low end of the scale than at the upper end (the logarithmic pattern). In contrast, fourth-graders' and older children's estimates increase at a constant rate throughout the scale and accurately reflect relations among the numbers' magnitudes (the linear pattern) (Booth & Siegler, 2006; Opfer & Siegler, 2007; Siegler & Opfer, 2003).

Deviations from a linear representation of numerical magnitudes have serious consequences for number sense and estimation skills. Without a linear representation of numerical magnitudes, children's number sense and estimates are distorted, not just on the number line task but on other tasks as well. Children will think that the magnitudes represented by small numbers are more different than they are and that the magnitudes represented by large numbers are less different than they are. Consistent with this perspective, children's performance undergoes the same type of changes from nonlinear to linear estimation patterns on at least two other estimation tasks: numerosity estimation

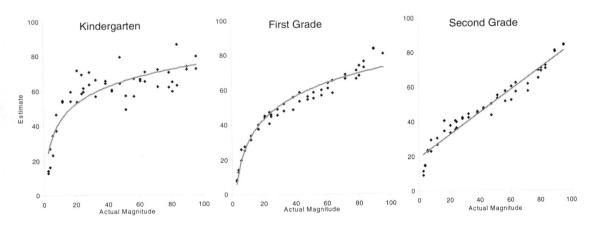

FIGURE 19.2. Kindergartners', first-graders', and second-graders' median estimates on 0–100 number lines. Data from Siegler and Booth (2004).

("Generate about N dots on a computer screen") and measurement estimation ("Draw a line about N zips long," after a very short length called a "zip" has been shown) (Booth & Siegler, 2006). Consistent individual differences are also present on these tasks, with most children within each grade from kindergarten through fourth grade either producing linear estimation patterns on number line, numerosity, and measurement estimation tasks or not producing such patterns on any of the three tasks (Booth & Siegler, 2006). Perhaps most striking, linearity of estimates on all three tasks correlates positively—and strongly—with scores on standardized math achievement tests (Booth & Siegler, 2006; Siegler & Booth, 2004).

These findings led us to ask: How do children form a linear representation of numerical magnitudes in the first place? Counting experience during the preschool period certainly contributes. However, such experience appears insufficient to create linear representations of the numbers' magnitudes. Children often can count perfectly in a numerical range more than a year before they generate linear representations of numerical magnitudes in that range (Schaeffer, Eggleston, & Scott, 1974).

If counting experience is insufficient to yield linear numerical magnitude representations, what experiences with numbers might contribute? One common activity that seems ideally designed for helping children generate linear representations is playing linear, numerical board games, that is, board games with linearly arranged, consecutively numbered, equal-size spaces (e.g., Chutes and Ladders). As noted by Siegler and Booth (2004), such board games provide multiple cues to both the order of numbers and the numbers' magnitudes. In such games, the greater the number in a square, the greater (1) the distance that the child has moved the token, (2) the number of discrete moves the child has made, (3) the number of number names the child has spoken, (4) the number of number names the child has heard, and (5) the amount of time since the game began. The linear relations between numerical magnitudes and these visual–spatial, kinesthetic, auditory, and temporal cues provide a broadly based, multimodal foundation for a linear representation of numerical magnitudes.

Both of the preschool curricula just described, as well as other promising intervention programs (e.g., Arnold, Fisher, Doctoroff, & Dobb, 2002; Clements & Sarama, 2007), utilize number board games as part of instructional interventions designed to improve the numerical knowledge of preschoolers from low-income backgrounds. However, all of these interventions include a wide range of numerical activities, not only board games but also simple arithmetic problems, monetary activities, number-related projects, number-related songs, and number-related books and computer games. This leaves unclear whether linear numerical board games should be included in future interventions because the effectiveness of the prior interventions may be due to features other than the number board games. Thus, although such games have been previously utilized within effective educational programs for low-income children, the causal contribution of the games to improvements in the children's numerical knowledge was unknown until recently.

Does Playing Numerical Board Games Improve Low-Income Preschoolers' Number Sense?

To determine whether playing linear number board games per se helps preschoolers from low-income backgrounds estimate more accurately and gain number sense, Ramani and

Siegler (2008) randomly assigned 58 four-year-olds to play either a number board game or a color board game. The children attended Head Start or child care centers that served impoverished populations. The sample was 58% African American and 42% European American.

As shown in Figure 19.3, the number boards and the color boards were identical in almost all respects. Both were 52 cm long and 24 cm high. Both had "The Great Race" written across the top. Both included 10 horizontally arranged, different-colored squares of equal size, with the word "Start" at the left end and the word "End" at the right end. The only difference was that the board used in the number version of the game had the numbers 1–10 listed consecutively from left to right in the squares, whereas the board in the color version of the game did not. Associated with the board games were spinners that determined how far the child or experimenter would move the token on each move. The spinner used by children who played the number board game had a "1" section and a "2" section, used by children in the color board condition had colors that matched the ones in the squares on the board. Children in both conditions chose a rabbit or a bear token, which they moved to mark their progress on the board.

At the beginning of each session, the experimenter told the child that in The Great Race, players take turns spinning the spinner, and that whoever reaches the end first wins. Children in the number board condition were told that, on each turn, they would move their token the number of spaces indicated on the spinner. Children in the color board condition were told that, on each turn, they would move their token to the nearest square with the same color as the one to which the spinner pointed. The experimenter also told the child to say the number (color) spun and the numbers (colors) on the spaces through which they moved. Thus, if a child in the number board group whose token was on a 3 then spun a 2, he or she would say "4, 5" when moving the token. Children in the color board group who spun a "blue" would say "red, blue."

If a child erred or could not name the numbers or colors, the experimenter correctly named them, then had the child repeat the names while moving the token. One common error involved children not naming the numbers in the spaces as they moved their tokens, and instead counting the number of spaces they were to move their tokens forward. If such children spun a 2, they would say "1, 2" as they moved their token, instead of saying the numbers in the spaces (e.g., "5, 6"). If children made this error, the experimenter would first remind them to name the numbers in the spaces as they moved. If children could not do so, the experimenter would point to and name the numbers in the spaces, then have the children repeat them as he or she pointed to the spaces.

Over the four sessions, each lasting about 15 minutes, the preschoolers played the number game or the color game about 20 times, with each game lasting 2–4 minutes. At the beginning of Session 1 and at the end of Session 4, children were presented the 0–10 number line estimation task as a pretest and posttest. This provided a measure of whether the children's sense of the numerical magnitudes of integers in that range increased as a result of playing the number board game.

The results indicated that playing the numerical version of the board game led to dramatic improvement in low-income preschool children's number line estimates (Figure 19.4). Before playing the number board game, the best-fitting linear function accounted for an average of 15% of the variance in individual children's number line estimates. After playing the game, the best-fitting linear function accounted for an average of 61%

Number Board Game

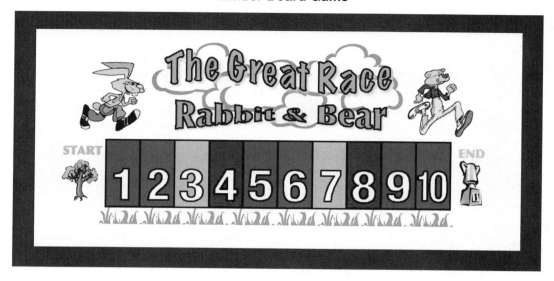

Color Board Game

FIGURE 19.3. The number board game (top) and the color board game (bottom).

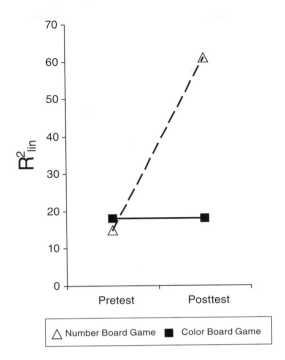

FIGURE 19.4. Mean percentage of variance in individual children's pretest and posttest estimates accounted for by the best-fitting linear function. Data from Ramani and Siegler (2008).

of the variance in the individual children's estimates. This was as high as the percentage of variance accounted for by the best-fitting linear function (60%) among same-age peers from middle-income backgrounds who did not play the game. In contrast, playing the color board game did not affect the low-income children's number line estimates.

The accuracy of the children's estimates, defined as the deviation of the estimates from the correct locations, confirmed these findings. Playing the number board game produced more accurate estimates; playing the color board version did not. Thus, playing the number board game for four 15- to 20-minute sessions over a 2-week period produced substantial improvements in low-income children's number line estimation.

Do the Benefits of Playing Number Board Games Generalize?

The second study in the series (Ramani & Siegler, 2008) was larger and more ambitious. It was designed to examine the generality of the benefits of playing the number board game, in terms of both the range of numerical knowledge that the children acquired and the stability of the knowledge over time. It had four specific goals.

The most basic goal of the study was to replicate Ramani and Siegler's (2008) findings with a larger sample of low-income children from Head Start programs. This seemed critical because the Siegler and Ramani study was the first to demonstrate a causal role of number board games in improving the numerical knowledge of young children. Too many promising educational interventions have failed to replicate initial results with new samples; it was crucial to make sure that this was not the case with the number board games.

The second goal of Ramani and Siegler (2008) was to examine the generality of the benefits of playing the number board game across varied numerical skills. In addition to the number line task examined in the earlier study, three additional measures of numerical knowledge were included. One was a numerical magnitude comparison task, in which participants were asked, "Which number is bigger: N or M?" The other two tasks were counting (from 1 to 10) and numeral identification (identifying randomly ordered printed numerals between 1 and 10). Playing the number board game required children to count and to read those numerals; therefore, it was expected to lead to improvements in these skills as well as on the two tasks believed to reflect representations of numerical magnitudes.

A third goal of the study was to examine stability of learning over time. If playing the number board game produces a general increase in understanding of numerical magnitudes, gains in number line estimation and numerical magnitude comparison should be stable over time. If playing the game produces enduring gains in counting and number identification skills, then gains in proficiency on those tasks should also continue. We tested these predictions by presenting all four tasks not only immediately after the final game playing session but also 9 weeks later.

A fourth goal was to determine whether different subgroups of children—ones who are older or younger, African American or European American, or above average or below average in initial knowledge—derive similar benefits from playing the number board game. Older children might be expected to learn more because they generally learn mathematical tasks more quickly than do younger children (Geary, 2006). However, younger children might learn more in this particular case because they started from a lower level and thus had more to learn, and because the new experience with the board games increased their total experience with numbers by a larger percentage. Yet another possibility was that these two influences would be equally strong, so that younger and older children would benefit equally. The same type of arguments could be made to hypothesize that children with more initial knowledge would learn more, that children with less initial knowledge would learn more, or that learning would be comparable for more and less knowledgeable children.

In this experiment, 124 children (mean age 4 years, 9 months), all of whom attended Head Start classrooms, played either the number board game or the color board game in four 15- to 20-minute sessions over a 2-week period. Nine weeks after the fourth session, these children, in a follow-up session, received the same four tasks as on the pretest and posttest. Slightly more than half of the children (52%) were African American; almost all of the rest (42%) were European American. The criteria for participating in Head Start meant that all of the families were extremely poor; for example, the income limit for a family of three in 2005–2006, the year in which the study was run, was $16,600.

In the pretest, posttest, and follow-up, children were presented four tasks in random order. On the *number line task*, the procedure was the same as that followed in the Siegler and Ramani (2008) study described earlier. On the *counting task*, children were asked to count from 1 through 10. Counting was coded as correct up to the point of the first error (e.g., a child who counted "1, 2, 3, 4, 5, 6, 7, 9, 10" received a score of 7). On the *numeral identification task*, children were presented 10 randomly ordered cards, one at a time, each with a numeral from 1 to 10 on it. On each trial, the experimenter held up a card and asked the child to identify the numeral. Finally, on the *numerical magnitude comparison* task, children were presented a 20-page booklet, each page of which displayed two numbers between 1 and 9 inclusive, side by side; the children's task was to choose the bigger number. Half of the children within each condition were presented a given number pair, with the larger number on the left; for the other half, the larger number was on the right.

Number Line Estimation

As in the previous study, accuracy of number line estimation increased significantly from pretest to posttest, and from pretest to follow-up, among children who played the numerical board game. In contrast, there was no change in the accuracy of estimates of children who played the color board game.

Linearity of number line estimation was the measure that most directly corresponded to the hypothetical construct of a linear representation of numerical magnitude. As shown in Figure 19.5a, among children who played the number board game, the mean percentage of variance in individual children's estimates that was accounted for by the best-fitting linear function increased substantially from the pretest to the posttest and the follow-up. In contrast, among children who played the color board game, linearity was unchanged across the pretest, posttest, and follow-up.

Number Identification

Playing the number board game also led to improvements in the low-income preschoolers' ability to identify numbers (Figure 19.5b). Children who played the number board game improved, from a mean of 70% correct identifications of the 10 numbers on the pretest to 82% correct identifications on the posttest, and to 87% correct identifications on the follow-up. In contrast, accuracy of numeral identification of children who played the color board game was essentially unchanged: 61% correct on the pretest; 63% correct on the posttest; and 66% correct on the follow-up.

Numerical Magnitude Comparison

Playing the numerical board game also improved the low-income preschoolers' accuracy in comparing the magnitudes of numbers. Among children who played the number board game, the percentage of correct identifications of the larger number on the magnitude comparison task increased from 73% on the pretest to 85% on the posttest, and from 73% on the pretest to 83% on the follow-up (Figure 19.5c). In contrast (as also shown in Figure 19.5c), there was no change over sessions in magnitude comparison accuracy for the children who played the color board game (68% correct on the pretest, 70% correct on the posttest, and 70% correct on the follow-up).

Counting

Like skills at number line estimation, numeral identification, and numerical magnitude comparison, the counting proficiency of children playing the number board game

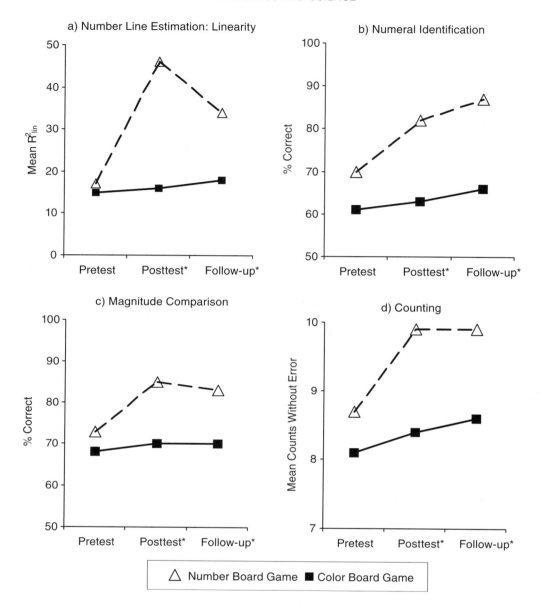

FIGURE 19.5. Differences in pretest, posttest, and follow-up performance between children who played the number board game and children who played the color board game. Data from Ramani and Siegler (2008).

improved (Figure 19.5d). Children in the number board game condition improved on average from 8.7 counts before the first error on the pretest to a virtually perfect 9.9 counts without an error on both the posttest and the follow-up. In contrast, there was little improvement in children's counting after playing the color board game: 8.1 counts without an error on the pretest, 8.4 counts without an error on the posttest, and 8.6 counts without an error on the follow-up.

Generality across Populations

To examine the range of children who benefited from playing the number board game, we contrasted the gains of older and younger children, of children who started with above-average or below-average knowledge (within this sample), and of African American or European American children. Learning was comparable across groups on all four tasks, as measured from both pretest to posttest and pretest to follow-up. Not surprisingly, the older preschool children exhibited greater initial knowledge than their younger peers on all four numerical tasks. However, the differences on the pretest neither grew nor shrank following exposure to the number board games (Figure 19.6). Thus, the learning of older and younger preschoolers was comparable.

Almost the same pattern emerged for children who started with above-average and below-average knowledge, relative to the children in this sample (Figure 19.7). On three of the four tasks, learning was similar in both groups. The one exception was the counting task, in which the children who started with below-average knowledge made greater progress because children with above-average knowledge scored almost perfectly on the pretest, as well as on the posttest and follow-up. With this one exception, playing the number board game increased numerical knowledge of children with above- and below-average initial knowledge by comparable amounts.

African American and European American children in this low-income sample also showed comparable learning on the four tasks (Figure 19.8). On three of the four tasks, there never were any differences between them. The only exception was that European American children showed somewhat greater linearity on the number line task at all three times of measurement. However, on all four tasks, the amount of learning from pretest to posttest to follow-up was comparable for African American and European American children.

Is Playing Board Games in the Everyday Environment Related to Numerical Knowledge?

It seems likely that both individual and socioeconomic differences in the numerical knowledge that children bring to school arise in large part from differences in informal numerical experiences in the preschool years. The results from the studies described earlier suggest that board game play might be particularly influential. To test this hypothesis, we obtained data about home experiences with board games, card games, and video games of preschoolers from lower-income families (the same ones as in Ramani & Siegler, 2008, Experiment 1) and from same-age peers from middle-income families. The main hypotheses were that children from middle-income backgrounds would have

(text continues on page 447)

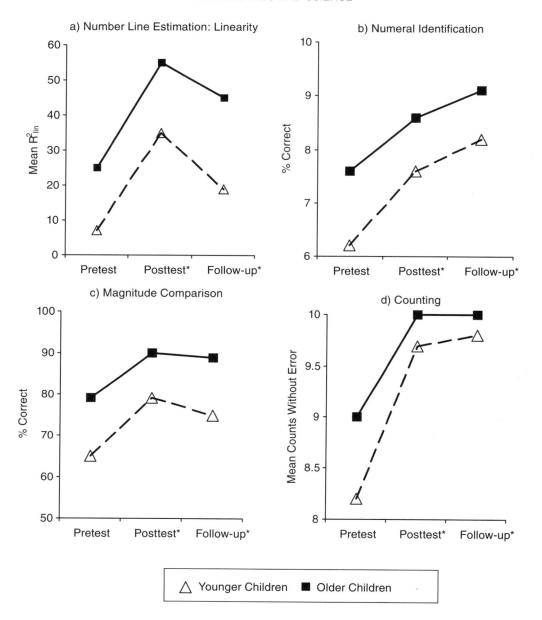

FIGURE 19.6. Pretest, posttest, and follow-up performance of younger and older children who played the number board game.

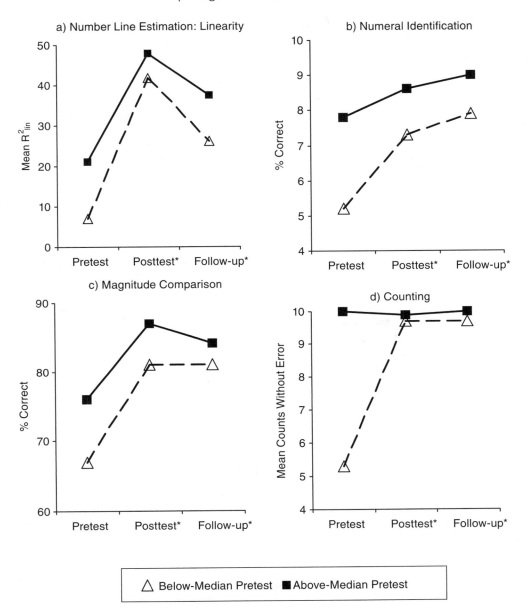

FIGURE 19.7. Pretest, posttest, and follow-up performance of more knowledgeable and less knowledgeable children who played the number board game.

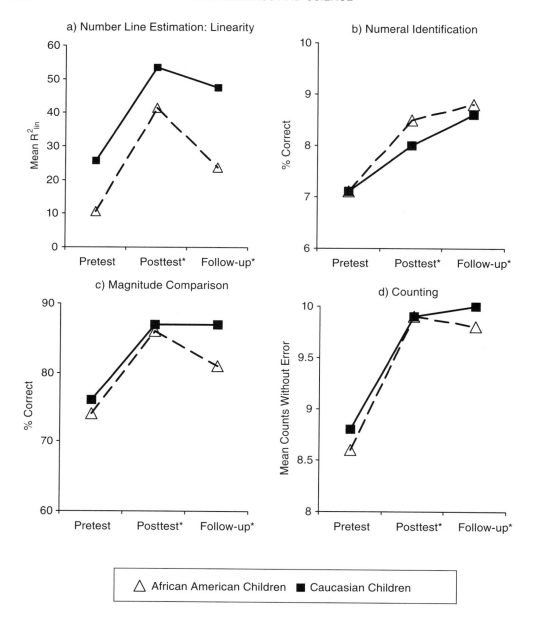

FIGURE 19.8. Pretest, posttest, and follow-up performance of African American and European American children.

greater experience than children from low-income backgrounds with board games, and that amount of experience playing board games would correlate positively with numerical knowledge.

A few prior studies have examined whether informal numerical experiences in general differ for preschoolers from middle-class and working-class backgrounds. However, the studies have yielded inconsistent results. In one study, mothers from middle-class and working-class families reported having similar numbers of number-relevant games, such as dominoes, in their homes (Saxe et al., 1987). However, in two other studies, parents in middle-income families reported providing their children with a broader range of numerical activities, and engaging in these activities more frequently, than did parents in low-income families (Clements & Sarama, 2007; Starkey et al., 2004). Similarly, some observational studies indicate that in the preschool context, children from high-, middle-, and low-income backgrounds engage in similar amounts of math-related play, such as counting toys, comparing the sizes of objects, and arranging objects into patterns (Ginsburg, Inoue, & Seo, 1999; Seo & Ginsburg, 2004). However, a very carefully executed time-sampling observational study in the home context found that middle-income parents and their preschoolers engage in a greater number of specifically numerical activities than do parents and preschoolers in low-income families (Tudge & Doucet, 2004). No published studies appear to have examined either children's exposure to specific types of games (e.g., board games, video games, card games) or the relation of such game-playing experience to children's numerical knowledge.

Given that playing the number board game in the lab increased preschoolers' numerical proficiency, it seemed useful to determine whether the board game experience of children from low- and middle-income backgrounds differs in ways that parallel the discrepancy in their numerical knowledge, and whether children's board game experience at home is related to their numerical knowledge. To determine whether these effects were unique to board games or reflected the more general family environment, we conducted parallel analyses of experience with card games and video games.

It seemed quite plausible that playing card games might enhance early numerical knowledge. For example, in the card game War, the player with the higher card wins the other player's card. For cards from 2 to 10, children can determine the winner by identifying the numerals on the pair of cards and comparing their magnitudes, two of the basic numerical skills measured in Ramani and Siegler (2008). It also seemed possible, but less likely, that playing video games would promote preschoolers' numerical knowledge. Some video games are designed to teach young children counting, arithmetic, and other number skills, but they are a small percentage of all such games and are not among the most popular games.

To address these questions, we asked 145 preschoolers (mean age 4 years, 9 months) a set of questions regarding their experiences playing board games, card games, and video games in their own homes and in the homes of friends and relatives. One subset of 30 children was recruited from a predominately middle-class, university-run preschool; the other subset of 115 children was from low-income backgrounds and had earlier participated in Experiment 1 of Ramani and Siegler (2008). All children were asked whether they ever played board games, card games, and video games at their own homes or at those of other family members or friends. If children responded "yes" to any of those questions, they were asked whether they played that type of game *all the time*, *sometimes*, or *hardly ever* and also were asked to name each board game, card game, and video game they had played outside of preschool.

As expected, a higher percentage of children from middle-income backgrounds reported having played at least one board game at home or at the homes of friends or relatives. To be specific, 80% of the middle-class children reported playing one or more board games outside of preschool, whereas 47% of the Head Start children did. Similarly, a higher percentage of children from middle-income families compared to Head Start children reported having played one or more card games at their homes or at friends' or relatives' homes (87% vs. 61%). A difference in the opposite direction was found for video games; 66% of the children from low-income backgrounds reported playing video games at home or at a friend's or relative's home, but only 30% of the children from middle-income backgrounds did. This last finding argued against the possibility that the first two differences reflect middle-income children being more willing to report playing games or better remembering their game-playing experience. Why would there be such differences in reporting standards or memory for board games and card games, but differences in the opposite direction for video games?

Table 19.1 lists the percentages of children from low- and middle-income backgrounds who reported playing the most common games in each of the three categories. Children from wealthier and poorer backgrounds most often reported playing the same specific board games and card games outside of school, although their amount of experience with them differed. The situation differed somewhat for the video games because children named a far greater variety of them (65) than board games or card games. This necessitated dividing the video games into three main genres: action/adventure, educational, and sports. As can be seen in Table 19.1, the absolute percentages for all three genres of video games were higher for children from low-income backgrounds, though the difference was smaller for educational games than for the other two types of games.

To determine whether low-income preschoolers' number knowledge was related to their game-playing activities outside of school, we correlated their pretest performance in Experiment 1 of Ramani and Siegler (2008) with their experience playing different types of games in the home environment. As shown in Table 19.2, the number of board games that the Head Start children named was positively correlated with measures of numerical knowledge on all four tasks. In contrast, the numbers of card games and video games that children named were only correlated with one task apiece.

One number board game, Chutes and Ladders, was named by a fairly high percentage of preschoolers (17%). Because we hypothesized that linear number board games like this one are especially important for gaining numerical knowledge, we tested whether children who reported playing this game had greater numerical knowledge than those who did not report playing it. Whether children reported having played Chutes and Ladders proved to be significantly correlated with numerical knowledge on three of the four tasks. This provided one more piece of evidence that playing numerical board games in the everyday environment contributes to young children's numerical knowledge.

Summary of Findings from Numerical Board Game Studies

These experiments examined whether experience playing linear number board games is (1) a source of social class and individual differences in young children's numerical

TABLE 19.1. Percentage of Children Who Reported Playing Specific Board Games and Card Games, and Types of Video Games

Game	Description	Percentage of children who named games	
		Head Start	Middle income
Board games			
Candyland	Players move tokens along winding path with colored spaces. First to reach the end wins.	29	63
Chutes and Ladders	Players move tokens along linearly ordered squares numbered from 1 to 100. First to reach Square 100 wins.	17	37
Checkers	Players move tokens diagonally on spaces of a checkerboard to capture opponent's pieces by jumping over them. First to eliminate opponent's pieces wins.	9	10
Card games			
Go Fish	Players ask other players for card to form pairs with their own cards. First to make pairs with all their cards wins.	30	37
Uno	Players place a card that matches the suit or rank of the current top card on top of the pile. First to use all cards wins.	9	33
Old Maid	Players choose cards from opponents and make pairs with own cards. Player with Old Maid card at end of game loses.	11	20
Memory	Cards are placed face down. Players choose cards to find matches. Player with the most matches wins.	8	10
Video games			
Action/adventure	Games with exploration and interaction with game characters (e.g., Super Mario Brothers, Donkey Kong, Sonic)	38	13
Education	Games marketed for educational value (e.g., Dora the Explorer video game focuses on solving puzzles and problems)	22	17
Sports	Sports games (e.g., football, baseball, car racing)	17	3

Note. Data from Ramani and Siegler (2008).

TABLE 19.2. Correlations between the Number of Board Games, Card Games, and Video Games That Head Start Children Reported Having Played Outside of Preschool and Their Performance on the Number Knowledge Tasks on the Pretest

Number knowledge tasks	Numeral identification	Magnitude comparison	Counting	Number line linearity
Board games	.25**	.26**	.20*	.38***
Card games	.13	.28**	.11	.18
Video games	.07	.02	.00	.21*

Note. Data from Ramani and Siegler (2008).
$*p < .05$; $**p < .01$; $***p < .001$.

knowledge and (2) a potential means for reducing those differences. The results supported both hypotheses. Children from low-income backgrounds reported only half as much experience playing board games as same-age peers from middle-income backgrounds; indeed, the majority of children in the low-income sample reported never having played a board game at home or at the homes of friends or relatives. The amount of board game experience they reported was positively correlated with their numerical knowledge. Most convincing, playing a linear number board game with children from low-income backgrounds for four 15- to 20-minute sessions led to large, broad-based, stable gains in the children's numerical knowledge.

Would teaching other numerical skills, such as counting and numeral identification, have had as large, positive effects as playing the number board game? Results of a previous study suggest that other activities are useful, but perhaps not as useful as playing the board games. For example, Malofeeva, Day, Saco, Young, and Ciancio (2004) presented instruction, practice, and feedback with counting and numeral identification to children at Head Start centers. That intervention led to improvements in counting and numeral identification, but not to improvement on tasks that assessed understanding of numerical magnitudes, including numerical magnitude comparison. This is not to deny the value of practice with counting and numeral identification, but rather to note that the value of playing number board games seems to extend to a broader range of numerical skills. A recent study of our own supported this conclusion (Siegler & Ramani, in press). That study specifically compared the effects of playing the number board game with the effects of receiving practice for equal amounts of time with counting as high as possible, counting objects, and recognizing numerals. Playing the number board game produced greater gains on all measures.

The benefits of playing The Great Race are not only important in themselves but they also seem likely to increase children's ability to acquire further numerical information. Consider how each of the skills is likely to facilitate learning of arithmetic, the main focus of math instruction in the first few years of elementary school. Counting skills are necessary for executing many arithmetic strategies, such as adding by counting from 1 (the sum strategy) and adding by counting on from the larger addend (the min strategy). Consistent with this interpretation, individual differences in first-graders' counting skill have been found to correlate positively with individual differences in their arithmetic proficiency (Geary, Bow-Thomas, & Yao, 1992). Automaticity in numeral identification reduces working memory load, which also is correlated with skill in solving arithmetic problems (Geary, 2006). Linearity of number line estimation correlates substantially with first-graders' arithmetic proficiency (Booth, 2005) and with kindergartners' through fourth-graders' math achievement test scores (which themselves are in large part measures of arithmetic proficiency) (Booth & Siegler, 2006; Siegler & Booth, 2004).

This analysis suggests that playing number board games should later help preschoolers from low-income backgrounds learn arithmetic, not only because it improves counting and numeral recognition but also because it enhances understanding of numerical magnitudes. Results from a very recent study (Siegler & Ramani, in press) support this prediction. Preschoolers from low-income backgrounds who played the number board game for four 15-minute sessions and were then provided practice in learning arithmetic problems showed greater learning of the arithmetic problems than peers who were given practice in alternative numerical activities (counting to 10, counting objects, and numeral identification) before being given the practice in learning the arithmetic problems.

Not all games that could plausibly promote numerical knowledge actually do so. Some card and video games include numerical content, but among the children examined by Ramani and Siegler (2008), playing such games was largely unrelated to numerical knowledge. This is consistent with the previous finding that when kindergartners from families with low incomes were given educational video games to play in their classrooms and at home, their mathematics abilities did not improve relative to those of peers who were not given the games (Din & Calao, 2001). One likely reason is that even though computer and video games are often marketed as promoting mathematics and problem-solving skills, many of these games only explore numerical concepts at superficial levels (Sarama & Clements, 2002). Well-designed computer-based games, especially if they are combined with relevant classroom activities and materials, can have large beneficial effects; they can offer children ways to develop skills and draw connections among concepts (Sarama, 2004; Sarama & Clements, 2002). However, this may not be true of the video games that young children typically play. Incorporation of cognitive-developmental theories and data into the design process may lead to construction of new computer-based games that are more effective than the ones that are commonly played at present.

Number board games, such as The Great Race, are promising candidates for broad adoption in Head Start centers, child care centers, and individual homes. They cost little or nothing; anyone with a pencil and large piece of cardboard or even paper can create a board. No special skills are required for parents or teachers or teachers' aides at child care and Head Start centers to play such games with children. An additional advantage is that children enjoy playing these games, based both on our observations and on the enduring popularity in diverse societies of games such as Chutes and Ladders and its first cousin Snakes and Ladders, a game played in India since the second century B.C.E.

There is also no reason to believe that the present version of The Great Race cannot be improved. Many features of the intervention were based on hunches and guesses rather than on empirical research. One such feature is amount of game-playing experience. The decision to have children play the game in four sessions was arbitrary. Varying the number of sessions would indicate whether children could derive greater benefits from playing the game for more sessions or, conversely, whether the same benefits could be realized in fewer sessions.

Related issues include whether the game produces comparable learning if played in small groups, whether it produces comparable gains if played by teachers' aides in Head Start programs and child care centers, and whether playing the game in an interactive DVD format produces as much learning as playing it with an adult or a more knowledgeable child. Addressing these issues should increase theoretical understanding of numerical development, and also indicate ways to reduce or eliminate the gap in mathematical knowledge with which children from different backgrounds typically enter school.

Conclusions

Taken together, these studies indicate that cognitive-developmental theories provide a foundation for interventions that improve the mathematical knowledge of preschoolers from low-income backgrounds. The theories differ in the types of interventions they suggest, but the effectiveness of all of them indicates that each has something useful to offer. Indeed, although each intervention was inspired primarily by a specific theory, all three interventions combine insights from all three theories. For example, all three interventions were influenced by the neo-Piagetian insight that activities should be presented in the order of the typical developmental progression. All three interventions also were influenced by sociocultural theory's emphasis on the importance of guided participation, scaffolding, and social interaction around culturally meaningful practices. All three interventions were also influenced by information-processing theory's insight that careful task analyses of component skills are necessary to build a general competence or conceptual structure.

When applying theories to practical problems, combining multiple theoretical perspectives is more the rule than the exception. This is as it should be. In education and other applied contexts, the clean distinctions that are crucial to theoretical precision are less important than the fundamental goal of producing the most effective application possible. Integrating lessons from multiple developmental theories, and multiple practical applications of the theories, should lead to even more effective educational applications in the future.

Acknowledgments

This research was supported by U.S. Department of Education Grant Nos. R305H020060 and R305H050035. We would like to thank the Allegheny Intermediate Unit Head Start classrooms and the Carnegie Mellon Children's School for their participation in this research. Special appreciation is also extended to Mary Wolfson and Jenna Zonneveld for their assistance with data collection and coding.

References

Alexander, K. L., & Entwisle, D. R. (1988). Achievement in the first 2 years of school: Patterns and processes. *Monographs of the Society for Research in Child Development, 53*(2, Serial No. 157).

Arnold, D. H., Fisher, P. H., Doctoroff, G. L., & Dobb, J. (2002). Accelerating math development in Head Start classrooms. *Journal of Educational Psychology, 92,* 762–770.

Blevins-Knabe, B., & Musun-Miller, L. (1996). Number use at home by children and their parents and its relationship to early mathematical performance. *Early Development and Parenting, 5,* 35–45.

Booth, J. L. (2005). *The importance of an accurate understanding of numerical magnitudes.* Unpublished doctoral dissertation, Carnegie Mellon University, Pittsburgh, PA.

Booth, J. L., & Siegler, R. S. (2006). Developmental and individual differences in pure numerical estimation. *Developmental Psychology, 41,* 189–201.

Bransford, J. D., Brown, A. L., & Cocking, R. R. (Eds.). (1999). *How people learn: Brain, mind, experience, and school.* Washington, DC: National Academy Press.

Case, R., & Okamoto, Y. (1996). The role of central conceptual structures in the development of children's thought. *Monographs of the Society for Research in Child Development, 61*(1–2, Serial No. 265).

Clements, D. H., & Sarama, J. (2007). Effects of a preschool mathematics curriculum: Summative research on the Building Blocks Project. *Journal for Research in Mathematics Education, 38,* 136–163.

Din, F. S., & Calao, J. (2001). The effects of playing educational video games on kindergarten achievement. *Child Study Journal, 31,* 95–102.

Duncan, G. J., Dowsett, C. J., Claessens, A., Magnuson, K., Huston, A. C., Klebanov, P., et al. (2007). School readiness and later achievement. *Developmental Psychology, 43,* 1428–1446.

Geary, D. C. (1994). *Children's mathematics development: Research and practical applications.* Washington, DC: American Psychological Association.

Geary, D. C. (2006). Development of mathematical understanding. In W. Damon & R. M. Lerner (Series Eds.) & D. Kuhn & R. S. Siegler (Vol. Eds.), *Handbook of child psychology: Volume 2. Cognition, perception, and language* (6th ed., pp. 777–810). Hoboken, NJ: Wiley.

Geary, D. C., Bow-Thomas, C. C., & Yao, Y. (1992). Counting knowledge and skill in cognitive addition: A comparison of normal and mathematically disabled children. *Journal of Experimental Child Psychology, 54,* 372–391.

Ginsburg, H. P., Inoue, N., & Seo, K. (1999). Young children doing mathematics: Observations of everyday mathematics. In J. Copley (Ed.), *Mathematics in the early years* (pp. 88–100). Washington, DC: National Association for the Education of Young Children.

Ginsburg, H. P., & Russell, R. L. (1981). Social class and racial influences on early mathematical thinking. *Monographs of the Society for Research in Child Development, 46*(6, Serial No. 69).

Griffin, S. (2002). The development of math competence in the preschool and early school years: Cognitive foundations and instructional strategies. In J. Royer (Ed.), *Mathematical cognition* (pp. 1–32). Greenwich, CT: Information Age.

Griffin, S. (2004). Number Worlds: A research-based mathematics program for young children. In D. H. Clements & J. Sarama (Eds.), *Engaging young children in mathematics: Standards for early mathematics education* (pp. 325–342). Mahwah, NJ: Erlbaum.

Griffin, S., & Case, R. (1997). Re-thinking the primary school math curriculum: An approach based on cognitive science. *Issues in Education, 3,* 1–49.

Griffin, S., Case, R., & Siegler, R. S. (1994). Rightstart: Providing the central conceptual prerequisites for first formal learning of arithmetic to students at risk for school failure. In K. McGilly (Ed.), *Classroom lessons: Integrating cognitive theory and classroom practice* (pp. 25–49). Cambridge, MA: MIT Press.

Holloway, S. D., Rambaud, M. F., Fuller, B., & Eggers-Pierola, C. (1995). What is "appropriate practice" at home and in child care?: Low-income mothers' views on preparing their children for school. *Early Childhood Research Quarterly, 10,* 451–473.

Jordan, N. C., Huttenlocher, J., & Levine, S. C. (1992). Differential calculation abilities in young children from middle- and low-income families. *Developmental Psychology, 28,* 644–653.

Jordan, N. C., Kaplan, D., Olah, L. N., & Locuniak, M. N. (2006). Number sense growth in kindergarten: A longitudinal investigation of children at risk for mathematics difficulties. *Child Development, 77,* 153–175.

Jordan, N. C., Levine, S. C., & Huttenlocher, J. (1994). Development of calculation abilities in middle- and low-income children after formal instruction in school. *Journal of Applied Developmental Psychology, 15,* 223–240.

Klein, A., Starkey, P., & Ramirez, A. (2002). *Pre-K Mathematics curriculum.* Glendale, IL: Scott Foresman.

Malofeeva, E., Day, J., Saco, X., Young, L., & Ciancio, D. (2004). Construction and evaluation of a number sense test with Head Start children. *Journal of Education Psychology, 96,* 648–659.

National Research Council. (2001). *Adding it up: Helping children learn mathematics.* Washington, DC: National Academy of Science Press.

Opfer, J., & Siegler, R. S. (2007). Representational change and children's numerical estimation. *Cognitive Psychology, 55,* 169–195.

Plewis, I., Mooney, A., & Creeser, R. (1990). Time on educational activities at home and education progress in infant school. *British Journal of Educational Psychology, 60*, 330–337.

Radziszewska, B., & Rogoff, B. (1991). Children's guided participation in planning imaginary errands with skilled adult or peer partners. *Developmental Psychology, 27*, 381–389.

Ramani, G. B., & Siegler, R. S. (2008). Promoting broad and stable improvements in low-income children's numerical knowledge through playing number board games. *Child Development, 79*, 375–394.

Sarama, J. (2004). Technology in early childhood mathematics: Building Blocks as an innovative technology-based curriculum. In D. H. Clements & J. Sarama (Eds.), *Engaging young children in mathematics: Standards for early mathematics education* (pp. 361–375). Mahwah, NJ: Erlbaum.

Sarama, J., & Clements, D. H. (2002). Learning and teaching with computers in early childhood education. In O. N. Saracho & B. Spodek (Eds.), *Contemporary perspectives in early childhood education* (pp. 171–219). Greenwich, CT: Information Age.

Saxe, G. B., Guberman, S. R., & Gearhart, M. (1987). Social processes in early number development. *Monographs of the Society for Research in Child Development, 52*(2, Serial No. 216).

Schaeffer, B., Eggleston, V. H., & Scott, J. L. (1974). Number development in young children. *Cognitive Psychology, 6*, 357–379.

Seo, K., & Ginsburg, H. P. (2004). What is developmentally appropriate in early childhood mathematics education?: Lessons from new research. In D. H. Clements & J. Sarama (Eds.), *Engaging young children in mathematics: Standards for early mathematics education* (pp. 91–104). Mahwah, NJ: Erlbaum.

Siegler, R. S., & Booth, J. L. (2004). Development of numerical estimation in young children. *Child Development, 75*, 428–444.

Siegler, R. S., & Booth, J. L. (2005). Development of numerical estimation: A review. In J. I. D. Campbell (Ed.), *Handbook of mathematical cognition* (pp. 197–212). New York: Psychology Press.

Siegler, R. S., & Opfer, J. (2003). The development of numerical estimation: Evidence for multiple representations of numerical quantity. *Psychological Science, 14*, 237–243.

Siegler, R. S., & Ramani, G. B. (in press). Playing linear number board games—but not circular ones—improves low-income preschoolers' numerical understanding. *Journal of Educational Psychology*.

Starkey, P., & Klein, A. (2000). Fostering parental support for children's mathematical development: An intervention with Head Start families. *Early Education and Development, 11*, 659–680.

Starkey, P., Klein, A., & Wakeley, A. (2004). Enhancing young children's mathematical knowledge through a pre-kindergarten mathematics intervention. *Early Childhood Research Quarterly, 19*, 99–120.

Stevenson, H. W., & Newman, R. S. (1986). Long-term prediction of achievement and attitudes in mathematics and reading. *Child Development, 57*, 646–659.

Stipek, D. J., & Ryan, R. H. (1997). Economically disadvantaged preschoolers: Ready to learn but further to go. *Developmental Psychology, 33*, 711–723.

Tudge, J., & Doucet, F. (2004). Early mathematical experiences: Observing young Black and White children's everyday activities. *Early Childhood Research Quarterly, 19*, 21–39.

Vygotsky, L. S. (1978). *Mind in society: The development of higher mental processes.* Cambridge, MA: Harvard University Press.

CHAPTER 20

The Early Construction of Mathematical Meanings

Learning Positional Representation of Numbers

Maria G. Bartolini Bussi
Mara Boni

In this chapter we discuss several critical issues in early mathematics education, particularly the use of manipulatives to teach positional representation of numbers. For our prehistoric ancestors, the representation of numbers larger than the ones they could count on their fingers and toes represented a significant challenge. This problem was solved by a brilliant insight of using position to represent and to distinguish large numbers. Some tools have been extremely useful in performing math operations on large numbers. In history, the abacus and the pascaline played a part in implementing and improving the system of positional representation of numbers. These tools can also play a significant role in helping young children understand the role of position. We discuss and provide examples of how teachers can facilitate young children in acquiring strategies for using these tools to represent numbers and to perform arithmetical operations. A point worth noting is that children do not learn simply by accessing and using these tools. Learning depends largely on how thoughtfully these tools are presented and how intentionally they are used. In other words, one simply cannot give children a set of blocks or any other tool and expect access to these tools to produce learning. Teachers must think carefully about what they want children to do and how they might benefit, then structure children's environment and guide them, so that these outcomes are likely to be achieved.

The Didactic Problem

The use of written numbers and knowledge of operational algorithms are required in all school systems, from primary school on. For instance, the National Council of Teachers of Mathematics (NCTM) states that children in pre-K to second grade should learn to "use multiple models to develop initial understandings of place value and the base-ten number system; and develop and use strategies for whole-number computations, with a focus on addition and subtraction" (*http://standards.nctm.org/document/appendix/ numb.htm*) Very early in school, teachers explore "the concept of number" or, as Piaget and Szeminska (1941) label it, "the genesis of number," often to the detriment of teaching the notational domain of numerals (see Tolchinsky, 2003, for a critical discussion of this issue). Yet the notational domain is not easy for students to grasp intuitively. When asked to write numbers in primary school, a common mistake is that in going from number words to Arabic numerals, students write "10013" instead of "113," because they do not overwrite the zeroes on the right (as in 100) with 10's and units (Power & Dal Martello, 1990). This confusion stems in part from the fact that zero has two functions in written Arabic numerals: a referential function (meaning "nothing") and a syntactic function in the positional representation, as a placeholder in multidigit numbers. As Tolchinsky (2003, p. 139) reports, "at age 4, children seem to have a clear idea of the referential meaning of zero – it means 'nothing.' However, they are reluctant to use the numeral zero for notation of absence, preferring to write (or attempting to write) that there is nothing." Later they learn to use the sign "0" to represent emptiness, but it takes still more time to generalize the use of zero to represent lack of units at any level. This happens even if zero has a strong environmental presence in everyday life, similar to that of other numerals. The resistance to using zero with either referential or syntactic functions is documented in the history of human culture (Menninger, 1958).

In some languages (e.g., Chinese, Japanese, or Korean), the formation of oral numerals perfectly fits the written positional notation.[1] These languages are called "transparent," because number positional representations are supposed to show up directly from the verbal expression. Miller and Stigler (1987) found that in transparent languages children understand place value at an earlier age, and more efficiently than in nontransparent languages. Neuroscientists (Butterworth, 1999) consider language transparency to be a likely explanation of this better performance. Yet the better and earlier understanding of number representation seems to depend also on the wider context of family and school social practices. For instance, Cobb and Yang (1995), in their study of children's conception of numbers, found that when Chinese mothers interacted with their children, they often spoke of numbers between 10 and 20 as composites of one 10 and some units, unlike American mothers, who, when referring to those numbers, counted by ones orally or used manipulatives. This common practice makes Chinese children more likely than children in the United States (and in Europe) to use 10's and ones correctly to represent numbers. School practices can make up for this by reinforcing for children the dual functions of zero and the role of position in representing large numbers.

A Successful Teaching Experiment

This chapter describes an experimental approach to teaching that was implemented in first- and second-grade classrooms to overcome children's difficulties in grasping the meaning of the positional representation of numbers. This work is inspired by the concept of semiotic mediation proposed by Vygotsky (1978). To illustrate how theory and practice are linked in our program, we interweave the description of the approach with that of its theoretical foundation. In doing so, we aim to demonstrate how theory may be nurtured by practice, and how practice may be improved by a theoretical perspective. The key insights arising from the concept of semiotic mediation center around the following:

- The use of concrete artifacts[2] to help students understand the positional representation of numbers (e.g., the spike abacus or the "Zero + 1" tool).
- The teacher's role in designing and managing classroom activity.
- The students' semiotic activity, that is, the production of signs[3] (e.g., words, drawings, gestures, written texts) prompted by suitable individual, small-group, or collective tasks.

The Artifacts

Many readers will be familiar with the Slavonic abacus and recognize the spike abacus represented in Figure 20.1. It is set to represent the number 802. However, because readers are unlikely to be familiar with Zero + 1 (Figure 20.2), we have provided a technical explanation of how it works in Appendix 20.1. Zero + 1 is inspired by the pascaline, the mechanical calculator designed by Blaise Pascal in 1642. The first gear to the right represents the unitary position, the second represents the 10's position, the third represents the 100's position. Turning the first gear 10 clicks makes the second gear turn one click, and so on. The upper gears (without numbers) work to transmit motion only. The function is similar to that of electricity, gas, or water counters in the predigital age. Zero + 1 concerns the notational rather than the conceptual domain of numbers. A (moderate) acquaintance with the sign "0" is a prerequisite of activity, yet "0" in the pascaline does not mean "nothing" or "empty," but is a label to represent one of the positions (teeth) in each gear. See Figure 20.2, which shows the pascaline Zero + 1 representing the number 620. In our discussion we use the terms *Zero + 1* and *pascaline* interchangeably.

FIGURE 20.1. A spike abacus (representing 802).

FIGURE 20.2. The pascaline Zero + 1 (representing 620).

The Didactical Cycles

A description of our approach may benefit from an understanding of the notion of *didactical cycle* (Bartolini Bussi & Mariotti, 2008). Teaching experiments produced within the Vygotskian framework often take place over a period of several weeks, or even months. The structure of such teaching sequences may be outlined as iterations of a cycle, whereby students are engaged in different kinds of teaching and learning activities as part of the semiotic process (see Figure 20.3). The activities of the teaching sequence include the following:

1. *Activities with artifacts.* Students are faced with carrying tasks out with the artifact individually or in small-group settings. For instance, students are asked to use a spike abacus to count some items.
2. *Individual production of signs* (gesturing, speaking, drawing, writing, etc.). Students are individually engaged in the process of the production and elaboration of signs related to the previous activities with artifacts. For instance, they are asked to produce either a text or a drawing (or both) to illustrate the previous activity.

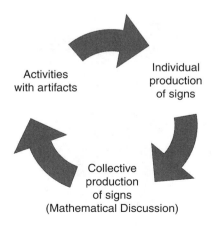

FIGURE 20.3. The structure of didactical cycles.

3. *Collective production of signs* (e.g., narratives, mimics, collective production of texts, and drawings). Students are engaged in classroom discussion under the teacher's guidance about the previous activities (artifact manipulation and sign production) to compare and to share personal signs.

Mathematical discussions with the whole class play an essential part in the teaching and learning processes, and comprise the core of the semiotic processes on which teaching–learning is based. This collective discussion has a special function orchestrated by the teacher and meant as a "polyphony" of articulated voices on a mathematical object or topic. In a mathematical discussion the whole class is collectively engaged in a mathematical discourse, usually launched by the teacher, explicitly formulating the theme of the discussion. In the beginning of the activity with artifacts, when students are engaged in individual production of signs to represent the activity during problem solving, they use a blend of everyday expressions and mathematical expressions. However, it is in the class mathematical discussion that mathematics meanings are often formed and expressed. Therefore, the class discussions are a critical part of the teaching–learning activity.

In the teaching–learning process there are different kinds of signs (Bartolini Bussi & Mariotti, 2008, p. 756): "artifact signs," referring to the context of the use of the artifact; "mathematical signs," referring to the mathematics knowledge; and "pivot signs," that is, artifact signs that are acknowledged by the teacher as potential drivers from the situated context of the artifact toward mathematics and used to foster the shift from the former to the latter. Pivot signs often emerge in the so-called "hybrid" sentences, where the artifact and the mathematical context are joined. For instance, in the case of the spike abacus, students continue to talk about beads and wires, maybe combining these words with mathematical words (units, 10's). Sometimes they use hybrid expression (e.g., *pallina-decina*, an unusual Italian expression that might be translated as "bead-10").

The role of the teacher is crucial; in fact the evolution of signs, principally related to the activity with artifacts, toward mathematical signs is not expected to be either spontaneous or simple, and for this reason requires the guidance of the teacher. We consider the teacher an *orchestrator of polyphony* because he or she is in charge of allowing and fostering the articulation of each voice (including a voice that represents mathematical culture). In mathematical discussion, several communicative strategies are in play, such as mirroring or paraphrasing students' interventions (Bartolini Bussi, 1998; Bartolini Bussi & Mariotti, 2008). As we argue later, the teacher's activity is consistent with a Vygotskian approach.

Activity in the First Grade

Early Activities with Numbers

At the beginning of the first grade, the teacher starts a systematic and intentional activity to encourage the recognition of everyday use of numbers in different contexts, by means of different well-known artifacts: the calendar, dice, the game of the goose, playing cards, the thermometer, the ruler as the actualization of a part of the number line, and so on. In this way, students become more and more familiar with writ-ten numbers, without thinking over the representation rules. The standard design was based on didactical cycles, as explained earlier. Whenever a new artifact is introduced, the students are asked to represent it by drawings, words, mimicry, and so on, before using it.

The Slavonic Abacus

In January, the teacher introduces the Slavonic abacus as a means to improve and control counting. This virtue of the artifact is that it suggests grouping by 10's. The students quickly master the idea that when a number has more than one digit, it is represented by means of beads and at least one line, and vice versa. Each full line is called a "10 line" (*linea da 10* in Italian), meaning that all the 10 beads have been used. The mathematical discussion ends with a shared sentence concerning numbers less than 20: *In the numbers with the 10 line, there is the word* teen. *When there are 10 lines, the number has two digits. The 10 lines are written on the left.*[4] This text is hybrid and shows the intention of the teacher to join the signs produced by the students (e.g., 10 line) to either the mathematical name (the root "teen") or the early idea of positional representation (Bartolini Bussi & Mariotti, 2008, p. 764). Hence, 10 line is used by the teacher as a pivot sign (as we noted in the section of didactical cycles).

The Spike Abacus

In mid-March, the teacher introduces the spike abacus for the first time, assigning stu-dents the task to interpret the representation of the number 13, the exact date on the calendar pad. The activity is carefully orchestrated by the teacher and is successful (for more details, see Bartolini Bussi & Mariotti, 2008, p. 764 ff.).

The Pascaline Zero + 1

At the end of the first grade, the teacher introduces the pascaline Zero + 1 for the first time. The students are first organized into pairs; then each pair is given a pascaline. For the first half-hour, the students are not allowed to touch it; rather, they are invited to describe it verbally and to produce some predictive hypotheses about its function. On the whole, the students are not surprised by this delay in touching the Zero + 1 because it has been standard practice (already used with both the Slavonic and the spike abacus) to become acquainted with the structure of artifacts, paying attention to shapes and spatial organization, before using them. Later, the students are invited to use Zero + 1 freely for some minutes, then to explain what they have discovered to the class. The strongest students understand immediately the possibility of producing the number sequence by iteration, the turning clicks of the first gear. For example, Ales-sia, a particularly adept student, when asked to explain what she discovered about the Zero + 1, recites this "rythmical" song, hitting the right gear with the right forefinger and pointing at the digit with the left forefinger. Figure 20.4 shows Alessia during her explanation.

FIGURE 20.4. Alessia during her explanation.

ALESSIA: From zero, one goes one ahead and one gets Zero + 1. From 1, one goes one ahead and one gets 1 + 1. From 2, one goes one ahead and one gets 2 + 1. ... (*Continues the singsong until ...*) From 9, one goes one ahead and one gets 9 + 1. And in the other gear it has gone one ahead and it has arrived on number 1.

TEACHER: Yes, but what is this number, Alessia? What is the number? What number has come out? Look at it.

VOICE: 10.

TEACHER: 10.

ALESSIA: (*Continues until 30 and more.*)

As soon as the teacher recognizes the potential of the song, she stops Alessia, and asks Alessia's classmates to imitate her gestures. Her classmates do so willingly. She is an affable girl and her classmates enjoy imitating her. Alessia had a very regular rhythm: Her right forefinger just barely hit the more external tooth of the gear at the right; one has the impression that she could go on forever. And each student follows, by means of his or her own pascaline, the realization of the sequence of numbers given by dictation.

This regular rhythm depends on the artifact. Pushing the tooth clockwise is a repetitive action that always requires the same brief amount of time. The sequence is neither interrupted nor slowed down to realize exchanges (which can happen when stringing beads on the abacus). Important traces are left for future development (as is evident from later individual written protocols). After the conclusion of this guided manipulation (guided by a student, yet under the teacher's control), the students are asked to produce a text with individual drawings of the pascaline. No additional activities are possible before the summer holidays. After the summer, the videotape of this activity is shown to the students, now in second grade, to reconstruct the memory of the activity, and so that they can pick up where they left off.

Theoretical Analysis

The Pascaline and Mathematics Knowledge

Before describing the second-grade activities, it is useful to analyze from a mathematical perspective the artifact Zero + 1. This analysis allows us both to interpret the previous episode (in the first grade) and to understand the design and development of the second-grade activities. The representation of numbers is an immense field of research studied by scholars of history (e.g., Menninger, 1958), anthropology (e.g., Crump, 1990), and cognitive theory (e.g., Tolchinsky, 2003). A complete review of this literature is beyond the scope of this chapter. Our discussion of this body of work is restricted to the concepts that are most immediately relevant to this teaching experiment. The abacus and the pascaline (Menninger, 1958) are first and foremost tools to make arithmetic calculations. Both the abacus and the pascaline draw on positional representation of numbers, at least in practice; the abacus was invented in some regions, prior to the complete development of conventions for writing numerals with positional rules. The pascaline, on the contrary, was invented after the positional decimal system was already established in Europe, although before paper-and-pencil representation of operation algorithms were widespread. The history of the pascaline demonstrates well the needs that fostered its invention. In the 17th century, in spite of the existence of paper-and-pencil algorithms, arithmetic operations were still accomplished with the use of counting boards (Menninger, 1958), in which counters representing different values were posed on different strips of the board. This technique was particularly vulnerable to tampering because counters could be moved unintentionally, changing the number represented. The new artifact, the pascaline, was supposed to be more stable, although difficulties in precise construction delayed its diffusion for several centuries more. The use of similar artifacts, however, produced a change in the utilization schemes that affected mathematical meanings and further mathematical development, as we explain below.

The Utilization Schemes of Zero + 1

Zero + 1 may be analyzed as a physical artifact that considers shapes, spatial arrangement, and so on. This kind of analysis is useful for a manufacturer who wishes to reproduce the same artifact. Zero + 1 may be also analyzed from the perspective of the user focusing on how to solve a given task. This distinction, which is very helpful in the field of information and communication technologies, followed Rabardel's (1995) definition of "instrument" (to be distinguished from *artifact*) as a mixed entity made up of both artifact-type components and schematic components called "utilization schemes" (Bartolini Bussi & Mariotti, 2008, p. 748). The utilization schemes are in principle inner representations that may be inferred by means of external traces (words, drawings, gestures, etc.). Next, we describe the utilization schemes of Zero + 1.

When somebody receives a Zero + 1 for the first time and is informed that the original pascaline was for adding and subtracting, it is quite common (even with learned people) to witness the following scene: The user starts with an easy example, adding two 1-digit numbers (e.g., 5 and 7); he or she represents each digit in one gear (e.g., 5 in the gear at left and 7 in the gear at right), then looks for some special button (+) to press, does not find any, and is puzzled. Zero + 1 actually works in another way. To add 5 +

7, the person sets the first addend 5 in Zero + 1 as the initial starting point (on the right gear), then uses +7 as an operator, moving the right gear seven clicks. There is no hidden engine, as one can see by turning the artifact over: Zero + 1 carries automatically, by means of the other auxiliary gears, after 10 clicks of the left gear, and produces 12.

Most activities (with abaci, counting objects, and even pocket calculators) convey the idea of addition as a binary operation, whereas Zero + 1 fosters the construction of utilization schemes related to the meaning of addition as operator. Hence, Zero + 1 is not supposed to be a duplication of already used manipulatives, but something new: Zero + 1 embodies the generation of the number sequence by the iteration of the operator +1.

The most important utilization schemes of Zero + 1 are listed below, with the corresponding task in parentheses:

- **Scheme 1 (counting)**, including two subschemes.
- **Scheme 1a (generating by iteration the standard sequence of numbers)**: *Repeat the operation of pushing the gear at the right one step clockwise.*[5]
- **Scheme 1b (reading)**: *Read directly the resulting number formed by the digits of the different gears.* The artifact suggests the generation of the sequence of natural numbers by the operator +1. This was clear in Alessia's rhythmical song described earlier. This operator has a mathematical counterpart (i.e., Peano's axiomatic system for arithmetics). According to Peano (Boyer, 1991) it is possible to define rigorously the set of natural numbers starting from three primitive terms: "number," "zero," and "successor," identifying the last term with a function or operator (+1) that determines the number immediately following a given number. With a mental experiment, one can reach by iteration every natural number and approach potential infinity.
- **Scheme 2 (counting back)**, including two subschemes.
- **Scheme 2a (one-to-one correspondence)**: *Push the gear at the right one step counterclockwise for each numeral of the standard sequence starting from any number from 1 to 999.*
- **Scheme 2b (reading)**: *Read directly the resulting number.* This is the corresponding scheme for the operator −1. If counterclockwise rotation (one step) is made starting from the initial position (000), the number 999 appears. This contradicts expectations and may be interpreted as follows: In a mental model of Zero + 1, one could imagine a fourth gear on the left. In this case, 000 may be obtained from 1,000, and 1,000 −1 = 999.
- **Scheme 3 (representing a given number by iteration)**: *Rotate the gear at the right clockwise as many steps as the quantity given by the number.* In this way, each number (up to 999) may be produced by iteration of the successor function. This utilization scheme (although correct and theoretically sound) is not very effective for big numbers because it takes a lot of time to repeat +1 as many times as needed.
- **Scheme 4 (representing a given number by decomposition)**: *Find how many units, how many 10's, and how many 100's, then rotate each of the gears clockwise (in whichever order you like) as many steps as the respective quantities given by units, 10's and 100's.* This scheme is more effective than the previous one, but it draws on more advanced competencies and requires a deeper understanding of the decomposition of numbers (e.g., 307 means 3 hundreds, 0 tens, and 7 units).

- **Scheme 5 (addition by recursion or counting on):** *To calculate* n + m, *first represent* n, *then rotate the gear at the right clockwise for* m *steps*. This scheme corresponds perfectly to the recursive definition of addition given in Peano's theory:

$$\begin{cases} n + 0 = n \\ n + (m + 1) = (n + m) + 1 \end{cases}$$

As before (Scheme 3), the procedure is not as effective as the following.

- **Scheme 6 (addition by decomposition):** *To calculate* n + m, *first represent* n, *then decompose* m *in units, 10's, and 100's, and finally add the units in the gear at the right, the 10's in the gear in the center, and the 100's in the gear at the left.* The order of execution is not important: one can start from the right (units), from the left (100's), and even from the center (10's). The fixed conventional order used in the spike abacus (from right to left) is related to the need to string the beads before exchanging 10 units with one 10, 10 tens with one 100, and so on, and is transposed to the written algorithm (where numbers are to be carried). There is nothing sacred in this convention as evidenced by the utilization schemes of the Chinese abacus (where additions and subtraction are made from left to right) because carrying is substituted by other rules (Kojima, 1954). In the case of Zero + 1, carrying is performed automatically by the tool, whatever the order of digit input.

There are also schemes for subtraction that draw on the counterclockwise rotation of gears.

- **Scheme 7 (subtraction by recursion):** *To calculate* n − m *(with* n > m*)*, first represent n *on the artifact, then rotate counterclockwise the gear at the right for* m *steps.*
- **Scheme 8 (subtraction by decomposition):** *To calculate* n − m *(with* n > m*) first represent* n *on the artifact; then decompose* m *in units, 10's, and 100's, and subtract the units in the gear at the right, the 10's in the gear in the center, and the 100's in the gear at the left.*

All of these schemes have been predicted and observed in the pilot experiments carried out in the first and second grade by the teacher Mara Boni, and in another experiment carried out in the fourth and fifth grade by the teacher Franca Ferri (Maschietto & Ferri, 2007). The schemes are reported (verbally, in writing, or with drawings) by the students themselves, in their own situated ways (i.e., referring to the concrete artifact and action of their own spontaneous expressions), that recall the preceding "general" sentences. In this chapter, only the early phases of the first experiment are summarized, concerning the first four schemes.

The Pascaline Zero + 1 in the Second Grade

As we have shown, only a short sequence with Zero + 1 was carried out in the first grade: The students were acquainted with utilization Schemes 1 (counting, i.e., generating the sequence of numbers) and 2 (counting back). After the summer holidays, instruction with Zero + 1 started again. The teacher used the video taken in the first grade to

*Build the number 23 and explain by words
and by drawings how you did (starting from zero).
If I start from zero and I go one ——▶ the pascaline makes the
number 1; from 1 I go one ——▶ and the number 2 comes out
and so on up to 10, that makes* ⊙⬤⬤ *click and you go on up to
twenty that makes* ⊙⬤⬤ *click, then makes 21,22 and comes
to 23 at last.*

FIGURE 20.5. Alessia's protocol (translated by the authors).

refresh children's memories. One of the first new tasks was the construction of a given number. Each child received a personal pascaline. The following task was dictated by the teacher:

"Construct the number 23 and explain by words and drawings how you did so."

Two different utilization schemes emerged. The first and most common was Scheme 3, demonstrated by Alessia (Figure 20.5). She used the same strategy as that in her rhythmical song, beautifully illustrated by the iteration of written sentences, with the same structure and auxiliary drawings. Other students demonstrated the decomposition scheme (Scheme 4). For example, Giancarlo referred both to iteration and to decomposition schemes (*it may be done in two ways*) and produced an interesting hybrid protocol: In the first sentence, he used words related to both the artifact (strike, gear, click) and to mathematics (10's, +1) and shifted from one to the other (see Figure 20.6).

Sharing Personal Signs

Some days, after the individual activity, the teacher orchestrated a mathematical discussion during which different solutions were compared and assessed collectively. The teacher's aim was to bind more and more the personal signs related to the pascaline with mathematical signs. She did not wish to eliminate use of everyday words, gestures, drawings, and sketches (that represented the meaning personally built by the students), but she aimed to link them as strictly as possible to mathematical terms. In this way, the new mathematical terms, on the one hand, acquire the meaning of the personal experience; on the other hand, they are ready to be inserted into the scientific network of mathematical theory. Hence, the teacher compiled the written and drawn signs, onomatopoeic terms, and other helpful strategies from students' protocols into a worksheet to be enhanced and used by the whole class during future tasks.

To make the number 23 one must
strike 3 times the right gear
and in the central gear one must click two tens.

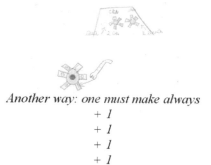

Another way: one must make always
+ 1
+ 1
+ 1
+ 1
+ 1
+ 1

FIGURE 20.6. Giancarlo's protocol (translated by the authors).

The Construction of a Larger Number

A photo of Zero + 1 (see Figure 20.2) representing the number 620 was given to each student with these instructions:

> "Starting from 0, make this number on your pascaline. What number is it? Write it in words. Explain how you did so. You can use the words, numbers, and signs given in the worksheet."

The choice of such a big number aimed at inhibiting the iteration process (it takes too much time to click 620 times!) and fostering the decomposition process. The students were offered the collection of the signs produced by all the schoolmates and shared during previous mathematical discussion. In this way, the most effective signs (from both everyday and mathematical language) were spread among the students in problem solving.

Fast Dictation of Three-Digit Numbers

Some days later, the teacher assessed the students' command of positional representation of numbers by quickly dictating a list of two- and three-digit numbers. This is a difficult task, even for fourth- and fifth-graders (Power & Dal Martello, 1990); hence, the success was not obvious at all. All but a small group of students (7 out of 23) solved the problem without the slightest hesitation. The low performers succeeded with two-digit numbers but made errors with the three-digit numbers. Actually, also with the pascaline, they showed competence mostly for two-digit numbers. These students were then taken out of the classroom by the teacher for a review session. The same assessment task was given again in this session, but the students were allowed to use their pascalines or other artifacts (e.g., the spike abacus), if needed. All the students succeeded in correctly writing the three-digit numbers: The students and teacher compared their performances with and without the artifact. The teacher then led a mathematical discussion comparing the spike abacus and the pascaline.

Mathematical Discussion on Pascaline and Abacus

After the small-group session, teacher and students rejoined the classroom, and the teacher started a mathematical discussion with the entire class, comparing the spike abacus and pascaline. The teacher's aim was to share with the whole class the short discussion from the rehabilitation session: This is important from an affective perspective because, rather than feeling excluded, low performers felt like protagonists of classroom interaction. The teacher carefully monitored students' progression to ensure the participation of all the students, including low performers. In addition, the teacher challenged students to get beyond the relatively simplistic assertion of the "sameness" of the abacus and the pascaline (they are used for similar tasks; show similar spatial arrangements; both represent units, 10's, and 100's, etc.) to consider the utilization schemes of both artifacts and their links to mathematical knowledge. In addition, to avoid a premature shift toward the mathematical signs (which could have been too fast for some of the low performers), the teacher encouraged the use of artifacts and allowed the students to move between the two worlds (artifact and mathematics) continuously.

Subsequently, the students often produced hybrid sentences that also encouraged participation by both high and low performers. Hybrid sentences create a context in which students of different level can participate with understanding. An excerpt of the discussion is reported and commented in Appendix 20.2.

Addition and Subtraction

In the last weeks of the experiment, the pascaline was also used to calculate additions and subtractions. Students were allowed to choose from a variety of artifacts (Slavonic abaci, spike abaci, pascalines, graduated rulers, and also set of straws to be tied in bundles of 10, following the Chinese counting sticks) to solve problems, if needed. The most competent students often solved the problems without any artifacts, whereas low performers were encouraged to use whichever artifacts were most useful to them. As a consequence, the classroom environment was relaxed, with no students feeling awkward. The students walked to the teacher's desk, on which a wide collection of artifacts was available, and chose the ones they needed. No stigma was attached to the reliance on artifacts. As one student said, "Some need glasses to see the blackboard and others need an artifact to make operations." The other utilization schemes were observed, with increasing mastery of the most effective strategies. At the end of second grade, all the students succeeded in performing multidigit additions and subtractions using paper and pencil, without making mistakes. Only one girl still needed an artifact (the ruler) to control the addition and subtraction results for one-digit numbers; however, this was diagnosed by a neurologist as a working memory deficit because the girl had no problems at all in lining up numbers.

Theoretical Analysis II

We claim that the success of the experiment was not coincidental but was instead dependent on the teacher's careful design and strong control of classroom processes. The didactical cycles of the teaching experiment were designed, adjusted to the classroom processes, and carried out according to a theoretical framework that had already been applied to other situations. It is useful to give a brief summary of the theoretical framework, which may be described as *a post-Vygotskian approach to semiotic mediation* (see a complete presentation in Bartolini Bussi & Mariotti, 2008).

Artifacts and Signs in the Mathematics Classroom

A long-established educational strategy is to have students construct mathematical meanings by means of manipulatives (Piaget, 1966). This assumption has often been supported by the implicit or explicit claim that educational manipulatives (artifacts) are "transparent" conveyors of mathematical meanings.[6] Figure 20.7 shows the simplest scheme of classroom activity, which illustrates this simplified idea that, unluckily, is not effective in mathematics classrooms. In other words, one cannot give children a set of blocks, an abacus, a pascaline, or any other tool and expect learning to result simply from access to those tools.

Meira (1998) showed, however, that "artifacts become efficient, relevant, and transparent through their use in specific activities and in relation to the transformations that they undergo in the hands of users." To Meira, transparency is not an inherent (objective) feature of the artifact, but may emerge through the very use of the artifact

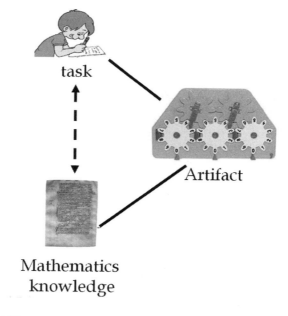

task

Artifact

Mathematics
knowledge

FIGURE 20.7. The simplest scheme of classroom activity.

itself. Hence, the focus is on the analysis of the social practices designed and started by the teacher in the mathematics classroom (Bartolini Bussi & Mariotti, 2008). The scheme of Figure 20.7 needs to be made more complex, by adding a place for the classroom processes carried out under the teacher's guidance. It is necessary to consider that mathematics is a cultural process and product, and it is not likely that the students can reconstruct by themselves the centuries-old process of humankind that produced what is today considered mathematics (see the bottom part of the scheme of Figure 20.8). If small-group work is implemented to solve a mathematical task, even by means of an artifact, then students very often produce situated answers (in the form of texts, drawings, etc.). They can communicate with each other using deictic forms (e.g., pointing at some component of the artifact) and do not feel the need to move to the level of mathematical texts. Sometimes, looking at reports of small-group work, one may guess that mathematics is only in the eye of the observer.

A deep change may be introduced when the teacher interacts with students: The teacher may find in the students' expressions the germs of mathematical meanings and lend them words taken from the mathematical repertoire. For instance, in the case of the pascaline described earlier, the teacher may recognize that in a situated expression such as "with one click on the right gear the number increases by one," the mathematical expression "the operator +1 transforms a number into its successor."

In the mathematical discussion, the teacher is in charge of giving voice to the mathematics culture that might otherwise remain beyond the reach of students. Obviously, the teacher is also in charge of expressing other voices. For instance, if the discussion moves too rapidly toward mathematics, with the risk of abandoning low performers, the teacher may suggest an example or interpret a mathematical expression by means of a

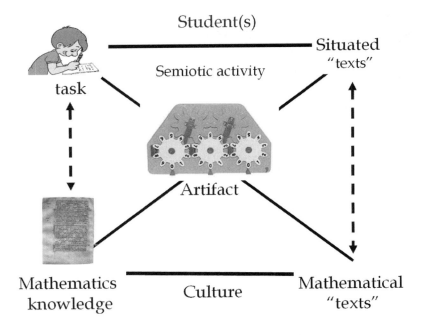

FIGURE 20.8. The scheme of classroom processes under the teacher's guidance.

particular artifact. The artifact itself may be connected with mathematics knowledge. As we said earlier, both abaci and pascalines are part of the history of counting, reckoning, and representing numbers. One might say that pieces of knowledge have been both generated by them and deposited on them because of their social use. These pieces of knowledge are likely to emerge (making the artifact transparent for mathematical meaning) by means of suitable classroom practice (Meira, 1998). Figure 20.8 shows the scheme of the classroom processes under the teacher's guidance.

The transformations mentioned by Meira (1998) say, in a different way, that there is a difference between the *artifact* (i.e., the concrete object) and the *instrument*, as defined in the first part of the theoretical analysis. As we have shown, the same task (addition) with the same artifact (Zero + 1) may produce in different users (but also in the same user) different utilization schemes (e.g., iteration and decomposition). Utilization schemes are personal constructs, yet they may be related to mathematical meanings. For instance, the iteration scheme of the pascaline may be related to the definition of addition within Peano's theory. This last scheme demonstrates one of the motives of teaching and learning activity. In other words, the teacher's aim is not to make students play with the pascaline but to construct the meaning of addition as operator. This piece of mathematics knowledge is deposited on the pascaline: It is likely to emerge for students, by means of suitable classroom activities.

Semiotic Mediation

Vygotsky's construct of semiotic mediation (1978, pp. 38–40) is helpful in clarifying this complex process (English et al., 2008, p. 882). In this chapter we comment on a didactical elaboration of semiotic mediation proposed by Hasan (2002):

> The noun mediation is derived from the verb mediate, which refers to a process with a complex semantic structure involving the following participants and circumstances that are potentially relevant to this process:
>
> [1] someone who mediates, i.e., a mediator;
> [2] something that is mediated; i.e., a content/force/energy released by mediation;
> [3] someone/something subjected to mediation; i.e., the "mediatee" to whom/which mediation makes some difference;
> [4] the circumstances for mediation; viz.,
>   (a) the means of mediation, i.e., modality;
>   (b) the location, i.e., site in which mediation might occur.
>
> These complex semantic relations are not evident in every grammatical use of the verb, but submerged below the surface they are still around and can be brought to life through paradigmatic associations, i.e., their systemic relations: we certainly have not understood the process unless we understand how these factors might influence its unfolding in actual time and space. (*http://lchc.ucsd.edu/MCA/Paper/JuneJuly05/HasanVygHallBernst.pdf*)

In Figure 20.8, most elements of Hasan's model are already represented or at least evoked: the mediator (teacher), the mediatee (student), the mediated (a piece of mathematics knowledge, in this case, the positional representation of numbers), the means (the tasks, the artifact), and the location (the mathematics classroom). The circumstances of mediation (and "the unfolding of the process in actual time and space") are given by what we have called *didactical cycles*.

The teacher's role is twofold. Looking at the scheme of Figure 20.8, one can add the main components of the teacher's actions in the classroom: designing suitable tasks and fostering the transformation of situated into mathematical texts (see Figure 20.9). The teacher in charge of the experiment prepared herself for the job by reading sources (e.g., mathematical, historical, cognitive ones) and discussing these with the other members of the research team; designed a task to foster the semiotic activity, including many different systems of signs (gestures, drawings, speech, written language, etc.); collected the signs produced by the students to share them in the classroom during discussions and also asked students to select from a given list the most effective signs to compose their individual texts; paid attention to the link between the mathematical world and the artifactual world, creating hybrid sentences when the metaphorical expressions used by the students were given value; nurtured metacognition, always asking students to explain and justify the strategy used; proposed that the comparison between different artifacts be explored in depth by the students; took care of low performers, offering them not only training but also occasions to discuss the problems and the features of the different artifacts. In a sentence, one can say that *the teacher used the pascaline (and the other artifacts) as a tool of semiotic mediation* in the Vygotskian sense: Actually, by means of suitable designed tasks calling into play the artifact and by careful management of classroom processes, the teacher was able to make students construct links between their personal meanings (expressed by artifact signs), and the corresponding mathematical expressions and meanings (mathematical signs).

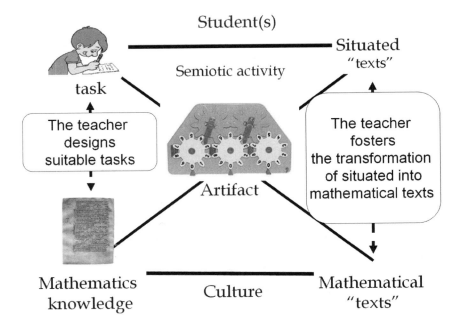

FIGURE 20.9. The two roles of the teacher.

Conclusions

The aim of this complex study is to document in detail effective classroom processes concerning a crucial issue of the mathematics curriculum: the mastery of positional representation of numbers and of the early algorithms of operations. Several different manipulatives were put at the disposal of students, with a careful analysis of the social practices experienced and tasks to be solved, and with the aim of making students conscious of the different utilization schemes and of their links to the mathematical concepts being learned. The didactical cycles of the teaching experiment were designed according to a theoretical framework; conversely, the data collected from the classroom contributed to the development and deepening of the theoretical framework itself, exemplifying the dialectical relationship between theory and practice.

APPENDIX 20.1

The pascaline Zero + 1 (Figure 20.10) is a simple but ingenious tool produced by the Italian company Quercetti (*http://erez.show-360.cz/erez4/fsi4/html/arcastudio_scuola2008.htm*). It is a very robust plastic artifact (27 × 16 cm) with five gears. The 10 digits (0, 1, 2, 3, 4, 5, 6, 7, 8, 9) are written on the teeth of the gears (A, B, C). Three small arrows point at a tooth (digit) on the gears (A, B, C). In different positions, the tool may conventionally represent (by means of the digits to which these arrows point) any number from 0 (written 000) to 999.[7] The gears (A, B, C) function as units, 10's, and 100's, whereas gears D and E are auxiliary driving gears to transmit the motion. Each gear may be rotated by pushing a tooth with one's finger. The rotation is not continuous but step by step (one click is one-tenth of a complete rotation). After a complete rotation of gear A (starting from 000), the bar welded to gear D makes gear B turn one step (producing 010). After a complete rotation of gear B, the bar welded to gear E makes gear C turn one step (producing 100). More precisely, when the gear A rotates clockwise from 0 (000) to 9 (009), all the other gears stay still until a complete rotation of gear A is realized. Then, the tool resists a bit more and requires a stronger push; it produces a louder noise and four gears rotate together (A, D, B, and E), to get 10 (010). From 10 (010) to 99 (099) gears A, D, B and E rotate together. Another functioning change occurs (with an even stronger thrust and louder click) in the shift from 99 (099) to 100 all five gears rotate together and more force is required. When 999 is reached, an additional click reconstructs the starting point (000).

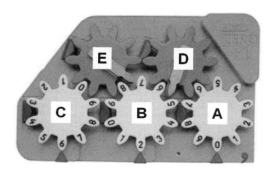

FIGURE 20.10. The pascaline Zero + 1.

Zero + 1 concerns the notational rather than the conceptual domain of numbers. A (moderate) acquaintance with the sign "0" is a prerequisite of activity, yet "0" in the pascaline does not mean "nothing" or "empty"; rather, it is a label to represent one of the positions (teeth) in each gear.

APPENDIX 20.2

EXCERPTS	COMMENTS
1 TEACHER: I remind you that last Friday, Marco said an interesting thing. Marco had used the pascaline and what did he say?	*This first episode is focused on the external features of the artifact. No utilization schemes is evoked yet.*
2 MARCO: That the pascaline is able to use well the abacus. The pascaline knows that in the center there are 10's and on the right there are units, and on the left, 100's.	*Marco suggests a time order: First comes the abacus and then the pascaline. Both are given (metaphorically) human features. The attention is on spatial arrangement.*
3 TEACHER: Is Marco right or not? What do you think? Is your answer like his or not?	*The lack of attention for utilization schemes seems to emphasize the shared mathematical structure of the two artifacts: Both refer to the mathematical knowledge at stake:*
7 SARA: I claim that he is right, as there are units on the right, 10's in the center, and 100's on the left.	

20 Teacher: Is the pascaline similar to or different from the abacus? I wish to hear also from Luigi M., Won, Marco … everybody.	*The teacher aims at:* • *involving all the students.* • *shifting toward the comparison of utilization schemes.*
22 LUISA M.: It carries in the same way. Because beads don't fit, and you squeeze 10 in one.	*Some of the utilization schemes of the abacus (exchange) are recalled with reference to the artifact signs produced.*
23 SILVANA: The pascaline clicks and in the 10's, that are in between, makes 1, and in the units puts zero, then 1 goes always one ahead.	*The artifact signs are different:* • *abacus: to exchange, to squeeze, to empty.* • *pascaline: to click, to trip.*
24 TEACHER: Hence, you say that it behaves like the abacus that empties, that squeezes 10 units in one 10 and put it in the second wire.	*The teacher accepts the students' proposals, emphasizing, however, that the signs are not the same, but they are similar.*
25 MARIA: The abacus is much the same as the pascaline, as it has the same units, the same 10's, the same 100's, and then a 10 … a 100 trips in both.	*The idea is that they are not the same, but they are nearly the same, surfaces.*
28 LUIGI B.: The abacus is the same as the pascaline, as it too has 9 at the end.	*The students try to express the differences in the artifacts. The comparison of instruments (artifacts and utilization schemes) is quite slow. The teacher tries to shift (29) toward the utilization scheme.*
29 TEACHER: Luigi B. is telling us that our abacus also has 9 at the end, ends with 9. You cannot put more than 9.	
30 ALESSIA: The pascaline is different only because it has gears instead of wires.	
31 SILVANA: But the pascaline and the abacus are different: The abacus may go as high as 1,000 and the pascaline, 100.	

32 TEACHER: But there are also pascalines with more gears. You have seen them in the booklet, haven't you? I agree, after having noticed the equal things, too, for differences.

37 MARCO: In the abacus, if there were numbers, beads should have hidden the numbers, but not in the pascaline. In the abacus with beads that cannot be seen anymore.

38 TEACHER: Marco has suggested writing the numbers on the wires. It's a very good idea, but then he says that with beads the numbers cannot be seen anymore.

39 MARICA: Even if you do not write them, you can put only nine there.

40 JOAN: The pascaline is rotated by hand, but in the abacus, beads are strung.

A utilization scheme emerges.

41 DANIELE: But there are two other gears above.

But the students' attention is captured by the different function of the gears, with numbers and without numbers.

42 TEACHER: Why have we spoken always of the gears below?

43 DANIELE: Because there are units, 10's, and 100's.

44 LUIGI M.: The orange gears make the 10 trip and also the 100.

Again, the comparison between the artifacts gets the upper hand.

45 LUCIA: The abacus has four wires and the pascaline has three gears.

46 VALERIA: The pascaline doesn't stand like the abacus; it lies on its back; it is green.

47 LUIGI B.: The pascaline can move also starting from 10's, but we can also go slowly, going one step on.

Luigi B. shifts toward utilization schemes (Schemes 3 and 4) at last, and the teacher immediately mirrors this utterance, stating that it is quite interesting. This piece of knowledge is singled out as being important.

48 TEACHER: What is Luigi B. saying? He is saying a very interesting thing. He said that one may form the numbers by means of 10's and 100's or more slowly, using only units and going always one step on.

49 ANNA: For me it is easier to make numbers with the pascaline.

55 LUIGI M.: With the pascaline you can make the number at once, inputting first 10's and 100's.

56 TEACHER: Can one make the same also with the abacus?

The teacher aims at shifting the comparison between the abacus and the pascaline to the utilization schemes.

57 SILVANA: But with the pascaline, one can make also an exchange, as there are the gears above, and those too rotate and make a "tic" that is as if a bead falls. It is an exchange.

60 ANNA: But the pascaline is more useful, as you can make numbers go on and back, too.

Anna (low performer) introduces another utilization scheme (Scheme 2): The numbers not only go on but also back. The teacher mirrors.
This is reconsidered later.

61 TEACHER: On and back. Silvana has said also another thing. Who remembers it?

62 SILVANA: Also, the pascaline makes exchange as the above gears make "tic" such as when the bead falls.

Silvana also tries to link perceptually the exchange scheme (abacus) to the automatic carrying (pascaline).

63 TEACHER: The exchange, that we make ourselves, is made by the pascaline. But who makes the exchange with the abacus?

The teacher aims at calling attention to a difference: Who is responsible for what?

64 SILVANA: We do, and the pascaline also does itself, when it goes back, but I feel that in subtraction it is not able to exchange (i.e., borrow).

The abacus has to be controlled by the user (exchange), whereas the pascaline has internal control.

65 TEACHER: We shall see. Now we can close with this very important difference.

66 MARCO: That the pascaline, by means of the above gears, make a 10 trip.

The pascaline is a machine!

67 SILVANA: The 10 does not trip; it has exchanges as if a bead falls.

71 VALERIA: The pascaline is a machine because it rotates and trips.

72 TEACHER: Valeria says that the pascaline is a machine because it makes something. Let us listen to the kids that have not yet said anything.

73 WON: The pascaline makes new numbers.

75 SARA: In the abacus we string beads and at nine we have to exchange; it does not trip by itself.

76 TEACHER: This is a good point: after nine, the pascaline trips and exchanges by itself. In the abacus, we decide when to exchange. We are responsible. There, by talking and discussing together we have understood something we had not considered.

And the teacher emphasizes this piece of knowledge as being important.

79 JOAN: Moving the units, you can make always a new different number.

Joan (a good girl) reconsiders Won's utterance and uses Scheme 1 to generate more and more different numbers.

80 TEACHER: Here is another important thing. Joan tells us that going on with units, adding one, one can always form new numbers. Good girl and good kids.
Now we close the discussion.

The teacher mirrors but is aware that this point is not within the reach of all members of the class. She stops the discussion.

Acknowledgments

This research was funded by MIUR (PRIN 2005019721): *Meanings, Conjectures, Proofs: From Basic Research in Mathematics Education to Curriculum* (national coordinator: Maria G. Bartolini Bussi). Maria G. Bartolini Bussi, Mara Boni,[8] Michela Maschietto, and Franca Ferri comprise the research team.

Notes

1. For example, 22 is read "2-10-2"; 37 is read "3-10-7."
2. The idea of "artifact" is very general and encompasses several kinds of objects, produced by humans down the ages: sounds and gestures; utensils and implements; oral and written forms of natural language; texts and books; musical instruments and scientific instruments; and tools of the information and communication technologies. In this chapter we refer mainly to artifacts as concrete tools developed by humans to represent numbers (Bartolini Bussi & Mariotti, 2008).
3. The term "sign" in used in a sense that is deeply inspired by Pierce, yet includes the products of different actions that have an intentional character, such as speaking, writing, drawing, gesticulating, and handling an artifact (Bartolini Bussi & Mariotti, 2008).
4. This refers to Italian numerals in which the root *dici* (teen) appears also in the spoken numerals 11 (*undici*) and 12 (*dodici*).
5. In the experiments, during early exploration, the possibility of using first any of the three gears emerged and the choice of the right one was a result of negotiation with the teacher to comply with the standard convention for number writing. Some time was devoted also to the discussion of the fact that the pascaline has particular conventions and represents all the numbers below 1,000 with three digits, and necessitates writing some unnecessary zeroes on the left (001 instead of 1). However, students showed familiarity with this convention, which is used in some everyday tools, too (e.g., music player counters).
6. Transparency was mentioned in the introduction for languages. "Language transparency," as defined by linguists, may help, but social practices seem to be crucial (Cobb & Yang, 1995). Both languages and tools may seem transparent to experts (e.g., linguists, mathematicians) but are not sufficient to produce the expected outcomes in the mathematics classroom.
7. When we received the pascaline from the company to test it and use it for the first time, we were worried about the number of digits and asked the producer to create a prototype with an opaque cover with three holes to hide all the digits but the three that comprise the number. The prototype was produced but not used because we acknowledged that no student (in first grade) was actually puzzled by the digits: All students (including low performers) succeeded in identifying the intended digit by means of the small arrow.
8. Primary school "G.," Vignola (Modena), *la.mara@libero.it.*

References

Bartolini Bussi, M. G. (1998). Verbal interaction in mathematics classroom: A Vygotskian analysis. In H. Steinbring, M. G. Bartolini Bussi, & A. Sierpinska (Eds.), *Language and communication in mathematics classroom* (pp. 65–84). Reston, VA: NCTM.

Bartolini Bussi, M. G., & Mariotti, M. A. (2008). Semiotic mediation in the mathematics classroom: Artifacts and signs after a Vygotskian perspective. In L. English (Ed.), *Handbook of international research in mathematics education* (2nd ed., pp. 746–783). New York: Routledge.

Boyer, C. B. (1991). *History of mathematics* (revised by U. C. Merzbach). New York: Wiley.

Butterworth B. (1999). *The mathematical brain*. London: Macmillan.

Cobb, P., & Yang, M. T. L. (1995). A cross-cultural investigation into the development of place-value concepts of children of Taiwan and the United States. *Educational Studies in Mathematics, 28*, 1–33.

Crump T. (1990). *The anthropology of numbers*. Cambridge, UK: Cambridge University Press.

English, L. D., Bartolini Bussi, M. G., Jones, G. A., Lesh, R. A., Sriraman, B., & Tirosh, D. (2008). Moving forward in international mathematics education research. In L. D. English, M. G. Bartolini Bussi, G. A. Jones, R. A. Lesh, B. Sriraman, & D. Tirosh (Eds.), *Handbook of international research in mathematics education* (pp. 862–896). New York: Routledge.

Hasan, R. (2002). Semiotic mediation, language and society: Three exotropic theories—Vygotsky, Halliday and Bernstein. Retrieved from *http://lchc.ucsd.edu/MCA/Paper/June-July05/HasanVygHallBernSt.nt13/mediation/semioticmediation.html*. Now published in Jonathan Webster (Ed.), *Language, society and consciousness: The collected works of Ruqaiya Hasan* (Vol. 1). London: Equinox.

Kojima, T. (1954). *The Japanese abacus: Its use and theory*. Tokyo: Charles E. Tuttle.

Maschietto, M., & Ferri, F. (2007, July). *Artifacts, scheme d'utilisation et significations arithmetiques* [Artifacts, utilization schemes and arithmetic meanings]. Paper presented at the CIEAEM 59 Hungary conference, Dobogoko, Hungary.

Meira, L. (1998). Making sense of instructional devices: The emergence of transparency in mathematical activity. *Journal for Research in Mathematics Education, 29*(2), 121–142.

Menninger, K. (1958). *Number words and number symbols: A cultural history of numbers*. Cambridge, MA: MIT Press.

Miller, K. F., & Stigler, J. W. (1987). Counting in Chinese: Cultural variation in a basic cognitive skill. *Cognitive Development, 2*, 279–305.

Piaget, J. (1966). *Psychology of intelligence*. Totowa, NJ: Littlefield, Adams.

Piaget, J., & Szeminska, A. (1941). *La genèse du nombre chez l'enfant* [Genesis of numbers in the child]. Neuchâtel–Paris: Delachaux et Niestlé.

Power, R. J. D., & Dal Martello, M. F. (1990). The dictation of Italian numerals. *Language and Cognitive Processes, 5*(3), 237–254.

Rabardel, P. (1995). *Les hommes et les technologies: Approche cognitive des instruments contemporains* [Men and technologies: A cognitive approach of contemporary instruments]. Paris: A. Colin.

Tolchinsky, L. (2003). *The cradle of culture and what children know about writing and numbers before being taught*. Mahwah, NJ: Erlbaum.

Vygotsky, L. S. (1978). *Mind in society: The development of higher psychological processes*. Cambridge, MA: Harvard University Press.

CHAPTER 21

Applying Developmental Approaches to Learning Math

Beth Casey

This chapter addresses two key controversies relating to pre-K–grade 3 mathematics: (1) the issue of which instructional strategies to use in teaching mathematics content and skills, and (2) the question of relative balance among the different types of math content covered at these grade levels. To consider how to resolve these issues, I present some of the recent theory and research in developmental science that provides guidance for teaching mathematics to young children. At the end of the chapter, several models for teaching preschool through third-grade mathematics are presented. One goal of these different models is to bridge the gap between the different educational approaches to early childhood and early elementary mathematics, and to increase the breadth of children's strategies and tools for solving math problems. Another goal is to shift the content focus away from a primary emphasis on numerical/analytical reasoning when teaching math content by shifting the balance more toward teaching spatial–geometric reasoning.

The Instructional Divide between Early Childhood and Elementary Approaches to Teaching Mathematics

One of the major disagreements between the traditional elementary and early childhood approaches is the choice of focusing on content or process goals. Many early childhood teachers consider children's internal processing and construction of knowledge to be most critical. They are taught to integrate curriculum, to consider the whole child, to do theme-based learning, to consider individual needs of children, and to spend a good portion of the day in small-group activities. Many elementary teachers are taught to focus on content; to structure the day based on these content areas; to develop concepts and skills systematically within a particular domain, such as mathematics, sequentially building concepts over days, weeks, and months; and to spend the majority of the day in whole-group instruction.

The first step in addressing this educational divide is to describe in depth how the goals of math educators and early childhood educators are frequently at cross-purposes. Initially, I list some of the math educators' criticisms about how early childhood math is typically taught in preschool and kindergarten. Then I describe concerns of early childhood educators about the approaches used to teach mathematics in kindergarten and first and second grade. It is important to note that many teachers have found wonderful ways to integrate both approaches—but for the sake of discussion I focus on the distinctions between these two approaches. I then discuss how developmental theories and research can contribute to resolving the differences. Finally, I propose a variety of ways to integrate and incorporate the two approaches into teaching children ages 3 to 8.

Critiques of Traditional Early Childhood Approaches to Mathematics

Early childhood mathematics lessons often are presented as one-shot, isolated activities that are either unconnected to the math taught the rest of the week or only loosely connected to related math topics. In spite of the widening emphasis on curriculum, in many early childhood classrooms, particularly at the preschool and kindergarten level, the integrated curriculum does not effectively include a systematic approach to mathematics (Copple, 2004):

- Even the published early childhood math activity books reflect this lack of a systematic approach. They often provide lots of diverse, fun math activities, loosely organized by math content areas but neither connected to one another in any coherent way or designed to build math knowledge sequentially or systematically.
- Often math activities are chosen because they are fun, hands-on activities, but they lack a coherent scope and sequence.
- An early childhood, theme-based, integrated curriculum often does not extend effectively to mathematics content in any systematic way, and the math content is often selected because it "fits with the theme," not because it develops math concepts in any coherent way.
- Many early childhood teachers do not systematically address the math content recommended by the National Council of Teachers of Mathematics (NCTM; 2000) for this age level.

Some Critiques of Traditional Elementary Approaches to Early Mathematics

In the traditional elementary school approach to teaching grades K–2, math content in particular is often taught with a whole-class, direct-instruction approach based on the scope and sequence chart of a specific math curriculum series for that grade level, with worksheets used to assess learning. One criticism is that this approach does not individualize instruction by taking into account either the varying abilities and deficits of individual children or developmental variations in the cognitive development of children:

- Too often, teachers, simply explain on the board how a simple, one-step problem can be solved. This approach dictates the strategy used to determine the one correct answer. The class then completes a series of very similar "problems," with only the numbers/facts changed. Thus, the emphasis is on learning specific algorithms for solving the math problems.

- The focus is on preparing young math students to learn the procedures and formulas that lead them to the "correct" math answer and how to take tests to prepare for state math testing, which is being introduced at earlier and earlier grade levels because of the No Child Left Behind Act. The criticism is that children are learning rote procedures and do not have a conceptual understanding of the mathematics underlying the procedures taught.

- Many elementary school teachers focus on rewarding the children who get the "right" answer quickly. The problem is that children then learn to feel they are "stupid" if they don't get the answer right the very first time. As an alternative approach, it is important to reward the children who are willing to tackle a difficult task, to persist in thinking hard about a problem, and to try out a variety of strategies—*even if they end up not getting the correct answer.*

- Many elementary school teachers focus on teaching the content of mathematics, ignoring process-based skills, such as teaching diverse strategies for solving math problems and developing math problem-solving skills, as recommended by the NCTM (2000).

- An elementary school approach to teaching grades K–2 does not take into account recommendations for the use of the developmentally appropriate practices (DAPs) for teachers of young children identified by the National Association for the Education of Young Children (Bredekamp & Copple, 1997) as key to young children's learning.

Implications of Research for Developmentally Appropriate Practices in Early Math Education

Reinterpretation and Evaluation of Piaget's Theory of Development

To evaluate the instructional controversy I described earlier, it is useful to examine the most recent research and theories in developmental science to gain some perspective on this debate. Piaget's theory of cognitive development has provided the foundation for many DAPs used by early childhood educators. Therefore, it is important to examine Piaget's theory in light of the recent findings in developmental science. One of Piaget's key ideas was that learning involves the active construction of knowledge, and occurs through both assimilation and accommodation of new information into children's pre-existing concepts or schemes. Some educators in the past misinterpreted Piaget's theory to mean that we should not intervene in children's math learning until they are "ready." However, according to Piaget, for schemes or concepts to change and grow in complexity, accommodation of the schemes must occur as a result of children's *active learning* and manipulation of objects in their environment related to these schemes. Because children are novices at almost everything—lacking schemes for large amounts of information in the world—they need lots of time to interact with the materials around them through play to build up these schemes.

A major contribution by Piaget to the fields of both psychology and education was his focus on the thinking processes that children use to solve problems, rather than an emphasis on output (e.g., whether an answer is correct or incorrect). The result in early childhood mathematics education has been a shift away from stressing "performance" toward an emphasis on children's processing of information in terms of increased understanding and problem solving (Sophian, 2004). Recent theorists and researchers in cognitive science have also incorporated this process-based approach by stressing developmental changes as occurring through the active processing of information (Case, 1985; Siegler, 1996). In 1997 and again in 2007, the American Psychological Association synthesized the research in developmental science to formulate learner-centered psychological principles as a framework for school reform. One of the key principles, drawing on the Piagetian view that children actively construct knowledge, states that "the learning of complex subject matter is most effective when it is an intentional process of constructing meaning from information and experience" (1997, p. 1).

Math Abilities of Young Learners

In a reevaluation of Piaget's view of young thinkers, recent mathematics research has shown that Piaget underestimated young children's abilities. Young children come to preschool and kindergarten with a surprisingly wide range of mathematical concepts that teachers often do not recognize, and that go beyond those described by Piaget for preoperational thinkers (Baroody, 2004; Fuson, 2004). In fact, recent research indicates that a fundamental understanding of quantity occurs in infancy and develops during early childhood (Clements & Sarama, 2009). Herbert P. Ginsburg (Chapter 18, this volume) provides rich examples of the types of mathematical knowledge that children reveal through their play. Thus, one key implication of this new research is that there is a wealth of children's mathematical knowledge on which early childhood teachers can build. The critical issue is that teachers must take advantage of their young students' mathematical understandings by educating themselves about their students' math capabilities, so that they can design activities and experiences that build on these math constructs.

Furthermore, training studies (Field, 1987) have shown that preoperational thinkers are capable of much higher-level thinking than Piaget proposed and that young children can acquire a higher level of understanding through more focused teaching within a specific content area. For example, in a classic study, Rochelle Gelman (1969) investigated what happened when preoperational children were trained to attend to the concept of quantity through a series of learning tasks on number and length, in which they were given feedback on the correctness of their answers. She found that children were able to learn to choose the correct answer based on the concept of quantity, independent of the arrangement of the objects in the array. When retested on the principle of conservation after training, these children showed understanding of conservation of number and length, and they also transferred the principle of conservation to volume.

These finding go against Piaget's stage theory of development. Through training and feedback that directed their attention to the critical cues, preoperational children were able to apply the general "principle of conservation"—that quantity remains the same, when nothing has been taken away or added to a group of objects of a certain size. In fact, researchers have found that development within children does not occur in discrete stages extending across all cognitive domains, as Piaget proposed; instead, it occurs in a more gradual process, with wide inconsistencies in cognitive functioning from task to task on different types of problems.

A New Focus on Executive Functioning

One critical contribution of the new information processing–based approach to learning is the focus on children's executive functioning through central processing of information that involves decision making, organization, and planning. These central processes enable children actively to choose strategies to solve problems. According to the American Psychological Association principles, "Successful learners can reflect on how they think about and learn, set reasonable learning or performance goals, select potentially appropriate learning strategies or methods, and monitor their progress toward these goals" (2007, p. 2). Development is conceived of as involving increased use of more efficient strategies when problem solving (e.g., children searching systematically when approaching a task rather than being controlled by highly salient features of a task). Siegler (1996) proposed an adaptive strategy choice model for understanding children's development that focuses on strategies rather than schemes. He proposed that children can generate a wide variety of strategies to solve problems (depending on the nature of the task and the goals of the child). Certain strategies are selected and used frequently; others are used less often. Multiple strategies exist within a child's cognitive repertoire at any one time. Both early in development and when children are learning new tasks, relatively simple strategies "win." With practice and maturation, children use other, more effortful but efficient strategies with greater frequency. Multiple strategies are available to children across a range of ages, but the particular strategy used on a specific task changes frequently, depending on a multitude of factors, including experience with related tasks.

Overview of Piaget's Contribution

Piagetian theory has been found to be incorrect in some key aspects, especially in the particulars relating to specific developmental capacities of young children and the view of development occurring in a stage-like progression across a broad range of mental processes. However, Piaget's major conceptualization that learning occurs through the construction of knowledge and through children's active interaction with the environment has survived the test of time (Clements & Sarama, 2009). In fact, it is the foundation for many of the more recent conceptualizations of how children learn.

The New View of the Role of the Teacher

A cornerstone of DAPs has been to design a rich environment in which children can actively interact and learn, for example, by providing a wealth of hands-on mathematical manipulatives within the classroom. Within this context, the teacher's role is that of facilitator, enricher, and, cognitive diagnostician. This contrasts sharply with a traditional view of education, in which the teacher's role is systematically to dispense information within carefully prescribed content areas. The recent principles presented by the American Psychological Association are closer to the Piagetian view than to a direct-instruction approach: "Unless new knowledge becomes integrated with the learners' prior knowledge and understanding, this new knowledge remains isolated, cannot be used most effectively in new tasks, and does not transfer readily to new situations" (1997, p. 2).

However, the question remains: What should be the teacher's role within this new constructionist view of learning? Based on recent math research findings compared to the more open-ended DAP approach, educators have argued that the teacher should have a more interventionist role to impart information and to scaffold more systematically children's learning based on the mathematics content they are learning (as well as providing enrichment activities). A key difference from the initial view of DAP is that these curricula are systematically based on the NCTM (2000) Principles and Standards, with a focus on the teaching of the Big Ideas in mathematics (Clements & Sarama, 2009; Griffin, 2004; Klein & Starkey, 2004). They also involve a wide mix of teaching strategies. For example, Fuson (2004) cited a review of the literature (Dixon et al., 1998) that compares recent educational approaches to more traditional direct instruction. Typically, the newer approaches involve an initial orienting phase, in which students are active participants and the teachers' role is to elicit from students their knowledge on particular topics, and to observe the variety of strategies they use to solve math problems. The second phase is more regulated by the teacher, with more structured presentation of information in small and large groups; scaffolding initially provides extensive help that is gradually withdrawn, allowing students to take on more responsibility for their learning. Feedback is given on the correctness of solutions, so that errors are not compounded, and a lot of math language and communication occurs from the perspectives of both teacher and students. In the review, Dixon and associates found that these new methods were more effective than direct instruction.

Integrating Problem-Solving Skills and Content Knowledge in a Systematic Way

One of the problems with research in the field of psychology and education is that it often is designed to pit one model of teaching against another. Surprisingly, this all-or-none perspective arises in part out of standard scientific research methodology. In scientific studies, we often test different hypotheses by designing studies that determine which educational approaches are supported by the data, and which have been shown to be less effective. The effect is that this type of research strategy tends to make us argue in favor of one educational strategy and against another. This approach often gets us into nonproductive, either–or controversies (whole language vs. phonics, direct instruction vs. problem solving, and center-based learning vs. content-based instruction, etc.).

Ask yourself, for example, which has had the most impact on your adult life, the learning strategies you acquired or the facts you learned? The answer probably is "Both." Gaining math knowledge is important during schooling, but learning a range of strategies for solving math problems is particularly important, especially on standardized tests, such as the Math Scholastic Aptitude Test (SAT-M), which requires the solution of novel problems, as well as those based on known algorithms. Acquiring a range of problem-solving strategies is particularly critical for those who choose to enter math–science fields. Effective mathematics learners should be taught from the outset to be creative problem solvers, with a range of strategies at their disposal *and* a knowledge base to draw on when approaching new problems.

Thus, instead of choosing one approach over the other, a powerful alternative is to take elements from these differing educational models and combine the best components of each because this often leads to the most comprehensive and enriched learning for students. A case in point is the ongoing controversy over the usefulness of direct instruction versus discovery learning in teaching students science. Recently, Klahr and Nigam (2004) compared "direct instruction" and "pure discovery" methods in terms of third- and fourth-grade children's effectiveness in learning how to design a science experiment. Note that the children in both cases were actively involved in the design of their experiments and the physical manipulation of the apparatus. The main distinction was that in the direct instruction condition, the instructor gave examples of good and bad designs, explained the differences between them, and told the students how and why good experimental designs work. In the discovery condition, the instructor provided no examples and no explanations, and gave no guidance or feedback. Immediately after, both groups were asked to design four new experiments on their own. A week later, the children were asked to evaluate two science fair posters by making comments and suggestions, based on their experience with designing experiments to help make the poster good enough to enter in a state-level science fair. Not surprisingly, the direct instruction group showed much higher levels of learning and could more effectively evaluate and improve the science posters.

However, the direct instruction condition does not seem to represent a traditional direct instruction approach. With a traditional approach, third- and fourth-grade students would typically have had reading assignments relating both to experimental design principles and the science behind the experiments, and the teacher would have lectured to the whole group on these principles, perhaps demonstrating how the apparatus worked or having students come to the front of the class to do so. The assessment would probably involve worksheets or short-answer exams in which students were asked to rate experiments in terms of whether they showed poor or good designs.

Instead, the instructional model presented under the rubric of "direct instruction" by Klahr and Nigam (2004) presents an approach that beautifully integrates methods found in both early childhood and elementary models of education, and incorporates elements of both discovery and traditional content-based learning. First, the children in both conditions were allowed physically to explore the novel materials. Next, children in both conditions were allowed to do hands-on learning, work with the apparatus, and try to figure out how to design an experiment to test whether steepness and run-length could determine how far a ball rolls on a ramp. Up to this time, both conditions were consistent with developmentally appropriate practices based on an early childhood model of education. At this point in the direct instruction condition, the teacher provided some key content knowledge that enabled the children to have the relevant background to problem-solve effectively on their own in the next session. In contrast, the children in the pure discovery condition were just left on their own to discover the solution—or not.

The type of discovery learning typically used in early childhood classrooms involves "guided learning," in which the teacher poses open-ended questions to their students, and provides a variety of open-ended materials to solve the problem (Casey & Tucker,

1994). Through this open-ended questioning, the teacher *guides* the children to discover the answers for themselves rather than focus on knowing the "correct" answer.

However, it is true that there is much less focus on specific content to be acquired in a typical discovery learning approach. A teacher in a direct instruction classroom might ask students, "What kinds of food does a brachiosaur eat?" This question has a correct and an incorrect response. In a discovery-based, problem-centered classroom, one might ask instead, "How can we figure out what kinds of food a brachiosaur eats by looking at its body?" The many possible answers to the latter question require students to use their reasoning powers, in addition to their memory skills. At the same time, one weakness of the pure discovery approach is that children need a strong knowledge base from which to do effective problem solving to answer questions (Casey & Howson, 1993; Casey & Tucker, 1994).

In teaching a course to early childhood majors on how to facilitate problem-solving skills in children (Casey & Tucker, 1994), it became clear to me that when children do not have sufficient content knowledge, problem-solving lessons become a guessing game. I redesigned the course so that the unit for preservice teachers comprised a content lesson followed by a problem-solving lesson. The critical piece was that the preservice teachers designed the problem-solving lesson *first* to figure out what knowledge base was necessary for the children to do effective problem solving. Then they designed the content lesson based on what background children would need to be effective problem solvers in the second lesson. This combination approach resulted in the children gaining problem-solving skills at a much higher level, and acquiring important content knowledge as well.

Problem-Centered Teaching

Here are some useful suggestions in implementing lessons in which the primary goal is both to develop reasoning skills and problem solving, and to incorporate content lessons. When designing content-based lesson to provide the background knowledge, be sure not to give away the solution to the problem the children will be solving next because it's important to prepare content lessons that give the children the basis for finding solutions but at the same time do not limit their problem solving or direct their solution to one specific answer. It is always important to keep in mind that children's level of reasoning is clearly a function of their developmental level.

During the early years, students are acquiring the hidden curriculum of what will be expected of them in their role as learners within math classrooms. With the introduction of a problem-centered approach early on in their educational lives, students are likely to acquire the very useful expectation that an important part of their role as math learners is to think about and explain the reasoning that underlies the strategies they choose for solving a math problem, and to recognize that different strategies can be used successfully to solve the same math problem.

Another component of the hidden curriculum is to help children learn that failing isn't always a bad thing. Effective learners don't just accept failure; nevertheless, they are *comfortable with failure* and have learned that the road to success is through failure. Children need to be exposed to that wonderful thrill of success that comes only when they have tried and tried, *then* finally succeeded. Conversely, children should not experience excessive frustration due to failure. This can be avoided by helping students reframe their errors and guiding them to possible solutions through the way in which the questions are posed. Thoughtful questioning can be critical when a child is stuck on a problem. Often, if you just ask a general question (e.g., "Why do you think that is happening?"), your students will simply reply, "I don't know." Instead, ask for details that direct their attention toward critical aspects of the problem: "Is there something that is preventing the space capsule door from closing?" Help them to test out their hypotheses. If they are still stuck, you may need to rephrase the question in a concrete way that gives a hint but does not give away the solution: "Are there any materials in this pile over here that might help you solve that problem, or anything in the carpentry area that might help you out?" Work on making your students feel successful at the end of the lesson by focusing on the strategies they tried (even if the problem was not "solved"). Rephrase questions when your students are not responding. Throughout the lesson, pose additional open-ended questions that further probe children's thinking (these suggestions are based on Casey & Howson, 1993; Casey & Tucker, 1994).

Content-Centered Teaching

Conversely, in other lessons in which the emphasis is primarily on acquiring specific content, the teacher can introduce the content itself in a variety of hands-on ways that can be combined with the more direct presentation of information to students. It is quite effective to follow up on the content lesson with an open-ended, problem-solving lesson that allows children to apply and extend their knowledge, and use their reasoning skills to reach a deeper understanding of the content. In fact, that is exactly what Klahr and Nigam (2004) did in the final assessment phase of their study. In a very clever transfer task presented to the students a week later, they asked the children to apply their knowledge of good experimental designs to a real-life, open-ended problem-solving task. The students were asked to critique a variety of science fair projects and to suggest alternative strategies for improving the design of the studies.

In summary, having a process-based discovery classroom does not mean that one abandons content-based learning, or vice versa. The beauty of this approach is the way in which content and problem-solving lessons are mutually enriching. Problem-solving lessons provide wonderful opportunities to teach content at a deeper level and to apply knowledge. In turn, effective problem solving degenerates into a guessing game when children don't have sufficient background knowledge to make educated predictions.

Shifting the Focus in Math Content for Learners Ages 3–8

In the second part of the chapter I turn from the issue of instructional strategies for teaching math to that of math content. I recommend a shift in the balance of math content covered in early childhood classrooms, with less dominance in the area of numerical skills and greater emphasis on developing spatial reasoning skills through geometry and other math content areas. To support this perspective, I present an overview of recent developmental research, showing the importance of introducing spatial reasoning activities to young children at the outset of their first experiences in learning mathematics (see Falcade & Strozzi, Chapter 22, this volume). The literature indicates that this shift is particularly critical for girls. When entering many early childhood and early elementary classrooms where mathematics is taught, it is clear to me that the dominant math focus is on number sense and number skills. Geometry is often placed in a subsidiary position, and the emphasis typically is on shape naming and shape attributes rather than on higher-level spatial reasoning (Clements, 2004). In this chapter, I present research findings indicating that acquisition of spatial reasoning skills through geometry and other types of math activities is an important foundation for the development of effective math learners.

Within the past few years, the NCTM (2000; Clements, 2004) has provided important guidelines on the critical mathematics content to be taught at the early childhood level. The NCTM has recommended a shift in the amount of time spent on numeric content versus other content areas in pre-K to grade 2 mathematics (NCTM, 2000, Figure 3.1, p. 30). The latest NCTM Principles and Standards for these grade levels propose that there should be an equal balance in time given to geometry and number content, as well as increased emphasis on measurement, prealgebra, and graphing. Furthermore, the NCTM (2006) has introduced a set of math curriculum focal points identifying the three most important mathematical topics to be covered at each grade level. The focal points specify the mathematical content a student needs to understand thoroughly for future mathematics learning. For preschool and kindergarten students, geometry is considered one of these three focal points. Within geometry, the key recommendation is that children at these ages should use spatial reasoning to interpret the physical world, with geometric ideas such as the following: (1) identifying shapes and their attributes, (2) exploring the orientation and relative position of objects in space, and (3) observing the spatial relations among shapes and objects in their environment. One recommendation for acquiring this knowledge is to have experience putting together shapes to produce more complex two-dimensional (2D) pictures, designs, puzzles, and three-dimensional (3D) constructions (part–whole relations). Thus, the acquisition of spatial reasoning is clearly a major focus within these NCTM (2000, 2006) recommendations. Yet many teachers in early childhood classrooms still consider counting and number sense to be their primary responsibility when teaching mathematics (Casey, Pezaris, Anderson, & Bassi, 2004; Clements & Battista, 1992).

Spatial reasoning skills involve the ability to think and reason through the comparison, manipulation, and transformation of mental pictures. They are useful for young math learners when putting together 2D shape puzzles, using tangram pieces or pattern blocks, and in building 3D structures with wooden blocks, LEGO® pieces, and so forth. Measurement also involves spatial skills during estimation activities, for example, when estimating the length of an object. Creating diagrams, graphs, and drawings is an important component of math learning that involves spatial thinking. For a thorough review of what young children are capable of learning about their spatial world (see Clements & Sarama, 2009).

Mathematicians report using both analytical, logical–deductive and spatial reasoning when solving mathematics problems, but elementary schools typically approach mathematics primarily using analytical, logical–deductive strategies, without relying on spatial reasoning. Thus, when students reach the higher grades, where spatial reasoning can be used as alternative approach to solving problems, many don't have these types of strategies available to them. A spatial solution to a math problem might involve drawing a diagram of the solution. In contrast, a verbal, logical–deductive solution to the same problem might involve laying out the step-by-step algorithmic solution. We have argued that individuals utilizing *both* spatial and analytical reasoning systems have a problem-solving advantage (Casey, Pezaris, et al., 2004). Thus, it is important to start early to introduce both spatial and analytical strategies for approaching mathematics.

Spatial visualization and mental rotation are two of the key spatial reasoning skills that have application to mathematics learning (Linn & Petersen, 1985, 1986).

> Spatial visualization involves the multi-step processing of spatial information, such as the ability to hold a shape in one's mind and then search for the same shape hidden within a more complex figure (e.g., embedded figures), or to imagine two shapes and then mentally combine them together to create a new design (e.g., pattern blocks). Mental rotation consists of the ability to look at an object or a picture of an object and visualize what it might look like when rotated in 3-dimensional space. A child who figures out that a block needs to be rotated 180 degrees in order to construct the corner of a tower would be using mental rotation. (Casey, Pezaris, et al., 2004, p. 31)

The National Science Foundation recently sponsored a conference on how to introduce spatial reasoning skills into the curriculum, starting at preschool and extending through graduate-level education (Sorby, 2007). At the conference, some of the researchers reported on recent findings related to the acquisition of spatial skills and the effects of experience and training on the development of spatial skills. A group of researchers at the Spatial Intelligence and Learning Center have conducted a meta-analysis of the effects of training on spatial reasoning skills across a wide range of ages (Uttal et al., 2007). This review of the literature showed that experience, education, and training can substantially improve spatial reasoning across ages, even at the preschool and elementary levels; in fact, there was evidence of greater malleability in younger children. One of the most interesting longitudinal research studies presented at the conference showed that toddlers' early play with puzzles predicted for their spatial skills at preschool (Cannon, Levine, & Huttenlocher, 2007). The toddlers (and their caregivers) were observed in their homes six times between ages 26 and 46 months, and those children who played frequently with puzzles performed better on a mental rotation task at 54 months of age.

You might ask, "How does this impact math achievement?" There is evidence for a relationship between spatial reasoning skills and math achievement scores, and this relationship is found most strongly at the middle and high school levels—at the point at which the math curriculum shifts from a primary focus on numerical skills (e.g., addition, subtraction, multiplication, and division) to a wider range of math skills that depend on more diverse problem-solving strategies (e.g., Battista, 1990; Casey, Nuttall, & Pezaris, 1997; Casey, Nuttall, Pezaris, & Benbow, 1995; Delgado & Prieto, 2004; Friedman, 1995).

Some studies of children at the pre-K to fourth-grade level suggest that even at this point in time, there is a spatial–math relationship. One study (Robinson, Abbott, Berninger, & Busse, 1996) that focused on a large sample of mathematically precocious preschool and kindergarten students did find such a relationship, with strong correlations between spatial and math tasks for both boys and girls. Carr, Shing, Janes, and Steiner (2007) reported the results of a longitudinal study of early elementary school students starting at second grade and continuing to fourth grade. She found that mental rotation ability predicted higher subtest scores on a math test at fourth grade for number sense, geometry, statistics, and problem solving (though the relationships were small). Spatial skills also predicted students' use of correct cognitive strategies when solving the math problems that involved the use of *mental representations* of numbers and rapid math-fact retrieval strategies for solving math problems. This relationship is interesting because it suggests the possibility that even in elementary school spatial skills may contribute in part to children's ability to use effective strategies involving mental manipulation of numerical information, which may in turn be influential in determining success on math tests.

Implications for Gender Differences in Math Performance

One reason that the introduction of spatial reasoning skills at an early age is so critical is that an extensive body of research shows that girls across all ages are at a disadvantage in solving spatial problems compared to boys (Halpern et al., 2007; Johnson & Meade, 1987; Linn & Petersen, 1985; Voyer, Voyer, & Bryden, 1995). In a major review of the literature, Halpern and colleagues (2007) concluded that gender differences in spatial skills are implicated as contributing to gender differences on standardized exams in math and science. In our research, we have found that the gender difference on the SAT-M was eliminated in high-ability middle and high school samples when we statistically controlled for mental rotation ability (Casey et al., 1995). We also found that mental rotation ability is a stronger mediator of gender differences on the SAT-M than either math attitudes or math anxiety (Casey et al., 1997).

There is evidence that, even as early as preschool, girls are at a disadvantage on mental rotation and mental transformation tasks (Levine, Huttenlocher, Taylor, & Lanrock, 1999). This finding has recently been replicated (Cannon et al., 2007); using a different type of mental rotation task, we confirmed this effect in kindergartners (Casey et al., 2008). In reviewing the literature more widely on early gender differences in spatial skills, Levine and her associates (1999) found evidence of a male advantage on a range of spatial tasks, including spatial visualization tasks, mazes, block designs, block building, map reading, and mental rotation tasks. Yet when assessing verbal rather than spatial skills, there was no evidence of gender differences in vocabulary. This suggests that the early male advantage may be found primarily on spatial tasks and is not a general pattern.

Also, it is striking that girls at a very early age seem to be more influenced by spatial–environmental input than boys. In their research on early puzzle play in toddlers, Cannon and colleagues (2007) found that girls were more affected than boys by the spatial language used by their parents. While helping their toddlers interact with the puzzles, parents who used a lot of spatial language had daughters who did better on mental rotation tasks later in preschool. This relationship was not found for the boys. The spatial language included references to the size, geometric features, and mathematical names of 2D and 3D objects, with words such as *long–short, corner–straight,* or *square–triangle.* This effect was found even when researchers statistically controlled for parents' own spatial skills, overall amount of speech with their child, and social class level. Thus, the research on the development of spatial thinking has particular implications for the early education of girls.

Researchers have found gender differences in mathematics as early as first grade, when they study students' performance using detailed analyses of their math learning processes instead of test scores. Carr and Jessup (1997) found that young boys tend to use higher-level strategies involving mental representations of numbers and also are more likely to show the ability to retrieve math facts rapidly compared to girls. Girls, on the contrary, are more likely to use concrete manipulatives when calculating solutions to basic mathematics problems. Even when provided with instructions for these more advanced strategies, girls were not able to use them as well as boys (Carr & Davis, 1999). Fennema, Carpenter, Jacobs, Franke, and Levi (1998) also found that first- and second-grade girls used more concrete strategies, such as modeling and counting, whereas boys tended to use more abstract solution strategies that reflected conceptual understanding. By third grade, boys were better at applying their knowledge to extension problems. Thus, understanding the factors that might mediate this early gender difference in strategy use is important for early childhood and elementary educators (Casey, Pezaris, et al., 2004).

We have argued in the past that

> strategies that children choose for solving mathematics problems begin right at the outset of schooling, and that we need to start right at this point in time to introduce spatial as well as analytical strategies for solving mathematics problems. This is particularly critical for girls, since boys appear to be more likely to acquire these strategies on their own during the early years. (Casey, Pezaris, et al., 2004, p. 34)

Thus, introducing spatial reasoning into the early childhood math curriculum should be particularly beneficial to girls, who seem to learn mathematics best within a formal classroom environment (Kimball, 1989). In summary, one purpose of this section of the chapter has been to introduce these spatial research findings, so that early childhood and early elementary educators can recognize the importance of introducing activities that facilitate spatial reasoning skills in their students.

A Supplementary Series for Teaching Early Childhood Spatial Reasoning Skills

It is useful at this point to describe the pre-K–grade 2 math series entitled, 'Round the Rug Math: Adventures in Problem Solving, which was designed specifically to increase children's spatial reasoning skills across a wide range of math content areas. The six-book series includes a variety of mathematics adventure stories that develop (1) an understanding of spatial relations and spatial sense through block building (Casey, Paugh, & Ballard, 2002); (2) an understanding of part–whole relations geometry using mathematical puzzles (Schiro, Casey, & Anderson, 2002); (3) skills in sorting, classifying, and representing 2D and 3D shapes (Casey, Goodrow, Schiro, & Anderson, 2002); (4) visual estimation skills and an understanding of the measurement of length (Anderson, Casey, & Kerrigan, 2002); (5) representational skills through data analysis and graphing (Casey, Napoleon, Schiro, & Anderson, 2002); and (6) prealgebra and patterning concepts through spatial and number patterns (Casey, Anderson, & Schiro, 2002).

I describe two of the books that focus on preschool to grade 1 spatial skills in greater depth to exemplify strategies for teaching these types of spatial skills. Within this framework, a description of the instructional model illustrates one approach for integrating elements of both early childhood and elementary approaches to the learning of early mathematics. One instructional element is that the mathematics concepts are taught to children through the medium of oral storytelling sagas that extend over 8–10 class sessions (Casey, Kersh, & Mercer Young, 2004). The rationale for this approach is based on cognitive research that documents the benefits of a story framework for retention of material (Graesser, Hauft-Smith, Cohen, & Pyles, 1980; Mishra, 2003), as well as the motivational benefits of presenting mathematics content within a meaningful context (Cordova & Lepper, 1996). The teachers use puppets to tell the stories to the children and to pose mathematics problems that arise out of the adventures confronting characters within the stories. The children solve these mathematical problems within this context, often helping a character in the story out of a difficult situation. This problem-centered approach makes the mathematics meaningful and relevant to the children, and facilitates the acquisition of math problem-solving skills. Each story is followed by math activities in which the children participate in hands-on experiences that facilitate the learning of the key mathematical ideas and connect strongly to the stories. In addition to the math–literacy component, teachers are presented with curricular webs that explicitly show how the books may be connected to specific activities across social studies, science, language arts, field trips, dramatic play, and art. This integrated curricular approach is consistent with an early childhood model of teaching and specifically addresses language arts, as well as mathematics, in early childhood competencies.

At the same time, the math content in the series is addressed in a way consistent with an elementary education instructional model. The NCTM Principles and Standards (2000) strongly recommend that students understand how mathematical ideas build upon one another sequentially. To address this recommendation, in the book series, use of storytelling sagas allows the mathematics to evolve and deepen in complexity, in tandem with the evolving story over extended class sessions, and specific geometry objectives are covered within each lesson.

To give an example relating to geometry, the story, *Tan and the Shape Changer*, designed for kindergartners and first-graders, is set in ancient China and focuses on part–whole relations puzzles using isosceles right triangles as the base figure. The character, Tan, in the story accidentally drops a piece of furniture, a tabletop, which he is bringing to the Emperor of China from his parents' home. The square tabletop breaks along the diagonal into two triangles. Tan is upset until he meets the Shape Changer, who encourages him to see what shapes he can make from the table pieces. Within this context, both the character of the Shape Changer (who changes into different forms throughout the story), and the puzzles themselves, involve changes in shapes. At the outset, the character Tan, and the participating kindergartners and first-graders, combine two isosceles right triangles to create a square, a large triangle, and a parallelogram. As the story evolves, they gradually combine more triangles to make more complex shapes. However, as they create these more complex triangle puzzles, they discover that their original three puzzle shapes (a square, a large triangle, and a parallelogram) are actually hidden within these more complex puzzles. Thus, in this storytelling saga on part–whole relations, a strong connection is made from one mathematics lesson to another, through both the ongoing storyline and the developing mathematics. NCTM (2000) geometry objectives for these grade levels are addressed throughout the lessons.

Block building is a dominant activity in most early childhood classrooms. Thus, it is useful to show how block building can be taught in a way that integrates both early childhood and elementary educational goals. The book *Sneeze Builds a Castle* (Casey, Paugh, & Ballard, 2002) was designed for preschoolers and kindergartners, and provides a mathematical focus to the learning of block-building and spatial relations concepts. It is designed as a supplement to the open-ended block-building activities that occur in many early childhood classrooms. The block-building activities in *Sneeze Builds a Castle* are very different from the block building that is typically seen in early childhood classrooms. They are structured around specific tasks, problems, and goals that have been carefully designed to encourage spatial–mathematical thinking rather than open-ended, exploratory play. In this way, they address the content math goals that are a major focus of elementary education classrooms. These goal-specific activities are not intended to replace exploratory block play. Instead, they are intended to complement, enhance, and extend children's block play by helping to foster spatially based mathematical constructs, such as balance, measurement, and estimation. Thus, just like mathematics content involving numbers, these 3D block-building activities are carefully sequenced. Early spatial contents in the initial block-building activities provide the knowledge base for subsequent block-building activities.

To put the activities in context, it is useful to give some background about the development of block-building skills. Research on developmental changes in children's block play indicates that block-building skills emerge hierarchically (Johnson, 1984; Reifel, 1984). First, children make horizontal rows and engage in simple vertical stacking, one block on top of another. The next level of skill is bridging two upright blocks with a horizontal block resting across the top. Children then begin to construct enclosures, positioning blocks to surround and define a space. Subsequently, they gradually incorporate increasing balance and symmetry; their constructions become more complex and elaborate, and block-play becomes increasingly representational.

Extensive developmental changes are seen in children between ages 4 and 7, yet there are wide individual differences in this developmental progression (Reifel, 1984). Some children begin to make bridges, enclosures, and towers on their own, whereas others avoid the block area, or basically use the blocks as props for dramatic play. Typically, designing activities that systematically develop children's skills in constructing enclosures and bridges has not been considered a part of the prekindergarten/early primary mathematics curriculum. Yet there is some evidence that early block-building skills are related to spatial skills (Brosnan, 1998; Caldera et al., 1999), and that they correlate with later math achievement (Wolfgang, Stannard, & Jones, 2001). Given these connections, it would seem that focusing on the development of block-building skills might be an effective way to develop spatial and mathematical thinking in young children (for a review of research relating block building to the development of spatial skills and math achievement, see Kersh, Casey, & Mercer Young, 2008).

Consistent with children's development of block-building skills at preschool and kindergarten, *Sneeze Builds a Castle* begins with the children working in small groups on the construction of enclosures and simple bridges. At this stage of block play, children typically build enclosures that are only one block high (Reifel, 1984)—thereby constructing in only 2D space (walls with length and width but not height). In the book, the children are asked to build enclosures that satisfy specific criteria set by the king and queen for their castle: (1) They must build a castle wall for the royal family that surrounds the entire castle compound to make a complete enclosure, and (2) they are challenged to build the wall at least two blocks high, to prevent the animals in the castle from jumping over the wall and escaping. These requirements encourage the children to construct 3D enclosures that include height, as well as width and length. To facilitate the development of measurement skills, the children are provided with models of farm animals, so they can determine whether the walls are high enough for the animals. Again, the story provides a meaningful context to extend the children's block-building and spatial skills.

As they build their walls, the children are also asked to build a gateway into the castle. The gateway is a simple arch that introduces the concept of balance and bridging. This task also develops measurement and estimation skills; the children must determine how far apart the uprights must be to support the horizontal block. Next, the children are challenged to build more complex bridges with multiple arches, extending these concepts of balance, measurement, and estimation. After children have gained experience constructing enclosures and multiarch bridges, they are asked to construct a complex tower, two or three floors high. In the final story and activity, Sneeze and the students are asked to integrate all their newly acquired knowledge and skills, and to construct an entire castle compound comprising castle wall, gateway, bridge, and tower.

The book demonstrates how it is possible to engage in block building, which is an integral part of the early childhood curriculum, and at the same time achieve focused mathematical goals. The NCTM Standards (2000) relating to geometry are embedded in the activities that children do in *Sneeze Builds a Castle*. These involve investigating and predicting the results of putting together and taking apart shapes, creating mental images of geometric shapes, predicting the effects of transformations on shapes, sorting and classifying based on geometric properties, estimating and measuring, and recognizing and describing spatial relationships (using words like *inside, outside, top,* and *bottom*). The understanding of *enclosure* emphasized in the story is related to an understanding of geometric shapes, open and closed figures, and even to later ideas of perimeter and area.

Evaluations of both the *Tan* geometry book (Casey, Erkut, Ceder, & Mercer Young, 2008) and the *Sneeze* block-building book (Casey et al., 2008) show that storytelling is an effective way to introduce math concepts to early learners. For both geometry and block building, the children improved more in their spatial skills when taught within a storytelling context than in another setting in which they learned the same spatial–math content but received a straightforward, nonstory presentation of the material. The findings from both studies also showed that systematic teaching of these skills (with or without a story context) was effective in transferring children's learning to related spatial reasoning skills.

New K–3 Math Programs Addressing Spatial Skills

It is encouraging that more recent kindergarten to grade 3 curricula, which are based on the newest NCTM standards (2000), recognize the importance of spatial reasoning. Such programs include Investigations in Data, Number, and Space (TERC, 2007) and Everyday Math (Wright Group/McGraw-Hill, 2007). The Investigations curriculum, in particular, addresses geometry and measurement from a spatial perspective, using activities involving hands-on manipulatives. At the same time, these activities are carefully and systematically designed to address the NCTM Standards (2000). Within this curriculum in kindergarten, children construct 2D and 3D shapes, and combine shapes to make other shapes. In first grade, they explore the spatial relationship between 2D and 3D shapes as they match 2D representation to 3D shapes or structures. For example, they make 2D drawings of 3D models of buildings design. They also deepen their understanding of part–whole relations concepts through a paper quilt project, in which they design a quilt by repeating squares made of combinations of triangles and squares. In second grade, they figure out how to use 2D rectangles of various sizes to make a 3D box. In third grade, they make different arrangements of four squares and use them to solve puzzles about area (instead of focusing on the formula for area). They create patterns for boxes to hold a given number of cubes and determine how many cubes will fit into a given box pattern (instead of memorizing the formula for volume). All of these activities involve spatial visualization of shapes and objects in space, as well as mental manipulation and rotation of the shapes as the children flip, turn, and slide the shapes in their minds to figure out how to fit them together.

Throughout the Investigations curriculum, students are encouraged to use hands-on methods and to look for multiple solutions (i.e., to use more than one strategy to solve a single problem). Thus, it is possible to design math curricula for pre-K to grade 3 students that are challenging mathematically, yet developmentally appropriate.

Conclusion

In early childhood/early elementary classrooms, students should become comfortable in solving complex math problems. Greater emphasis should be placed on providing students with open-ended math problems whose solution method is not known in advance, and that can be approached using a variety of strategies, including spatial strategies. This allows students to think in different ways, enabling them to draw on their own cognitive strengths rather than imitating the strategy selected by the teacher. At the same time, students need to acquire experiences using strategies that do not necessarily correspond to their own strengths (e.g., spatial strategies for many girls). Thus, math instruction should emphasize flexibility, so that students can use their preferred cognitive styles for solving some problems and, at the same time, learn to be flexible in strategy selection, with a range of available strategies on which to draw.

One of the difficulties in introducing spatial concepts into the early childhood and early elementary classroom is that many teachers are unfamiliar with the underlying math concepts and the methods of teaching spatial skills to their students (Clements, 2004). "In the future we need more spatially-based mathematics materials for teachers that carefully lay out: (1) the rationale and specific objectives when teaching these spatial/geometry concepts; (2) the specific kinds of motivating activities that teachers can use to develop them, and (3) sequenced problem-solving activities that systematically build upon one another" (Casey, Erkut, et al., 2008, p. 44). It is important for elementary teachers to recognize that teaching math systematically need not be achieved only through worksheets or direct instruction. At the same time, early childhood teachers need to consider how they can teach math content systematically, so that the mathematical concepts build upon one another and children's conceptual understanding of these concepts deepens and grows.

References

American Psychological Association. (1997). *Learner-centered psychological principles: A framework for school reform and redesign.* Washington, DC: Center for Psychology in the Schools and Education, APA Education Directorate.

American Psychological Association. (2007). *Learner-centered psychological principles.* Washington, DC: Center for Psychology in the Schools and Education, APA Education Directorate.

Anderson, K., Casey, B., & Kerrigan, M. (2002). *Froglets do the measuring.* Chicago: Wright Group/McGraw-Hill.

Baroody, A. J. (2004). The role of psychological research in the development of early childhood mathematics. In D. Clements, J. Sarama, & M. A. DiBaise (Eds.), *Engaging young children in mathematics: Results of the conference on standards for pre-school and kindergarten mathematics education* (pp. 173–220). Mahwah, NJ: Erlbaum.

Battista, M. T. (1990). Spatial visualization and gender differences in high school geometry. *Journal of Research in Mathematics Education, 21,* 47–60.

Bredekamp, S., & Copple, C. (1997). *Developmentally appropriate practice in early childhood programs* (rev. ed.). Washington, DC: National Association for the Education of Young Children.

Brosnan, M. J. (1998). Spatial ability in children's play with LEGO blocks. *Perceptual and Motor Skills, 87,* 19–28.

Caldera, Y. M., Culp, A. M., O'Brien, M., Truglio, R. T., Alvarez, M., & Huston, A. C. (1999). Children's play preferences, construction play with blocks, and visual–spatial skills: Are they related? *International Journal of Behavioral Development, 23,* 855–872.

Cannon, J., Levine, S. C., & Huttenlocher, J. (2007, June). *Early play with jigsaw puzzles predicts preschoolers' spatial skill: A longitudinal investigation.* Paper presented at the Spatial Skills Curriculum Workshop, Houghton, MI.

Carr, M., & Davis, H. (1999, April). *Gender differences in strategy use: A function of skill and preference.* Paper presented at the biennial meeting of the Society for Research in Child Development, Albuquerque, NM.

Carr, M., & Jessup, D. L. (1997). Gender differences in first-grade mathematics strategy use: Social and metacognitive influences. *Journal of Educational Psychology, 89,* 318–328.

Carr, M., Shing, Y. L., Janes, P., & Steiner, H. H. (2007, April). *Early gender differences in strategy use: Implications for the emergence of gender differences in mathematics.* Paper presented at the biennial meeting of the Society for Research in Child Development, Boston.

Case, R. (1985). *Intellectual development: A systematic reinterpretation.* New York: Academic Press.

Casey, B., Anderson, K., & Schiro, M. (2002). *Layla discovers secret patterns.* Chicago: Wright Group/McGraw-Hill.

Casey, B., Andrews, N., Schindler, H., Kersh, J., Samper, A., & Copley, J. (2008). The development of spatial skills through interventions involving block building activities. *Cognition and Instruction, 26,* 269–309.

Casey, B., Goodrow, A., Schiro, M., & Anderson, K. (2002). *Teeny visits Shapeland.* Chicago: Wright Group/McGraw-Hill.

Casey, B., Kersh, J. E., & Mercer Young, J. (2004). Storytelling sagas: An effective medium for teaching early childhood mathematics. *Early Childhood Research Quarterly, 19,* 167–172.

Casey, B., Napoleon, I., Schiro, M., & Anderson, K. (2002). *Finding Mathapotamus.* Chicago: Wright Group/McGraw-Hill.

Casey, B., Paugh, P., & Ballard, N. (2002). *Sneeze builds a castle.* Chicago: Wright Group/McGraw-Hill.

Casey, B., Pezaris, B., Anderson, K., & Bassi, J. (2004). Research rationale and recommendations for spatially-based mathematics: Evening the odds for young girls and boys. In C. Greenes & J. Tsankova (Eds.), *Challenging young children mathematically* (pp. 28–39). Golden, CO: National Council of Supervisors of Mathematics.

Casey, M. B., Erkut, S., Ceder, I., & Mercer Young, J. (2008). Use of a storytelling context to improve girls' and boys' geometry skills in kindergarten. *Journal of Applied Developmental Psychology, 28,* 29–48.

Casey, M. B., & Howson, P. (1993). Educating preservice students based on a problem-centered approach to teaching. *Journal of Teacher Education, 44,* 1–9.

Casey, M. B., Nuttall, R. L., & Pezaris, E. (1997). Mediators of gender differences in mathematics college entrance test scores: A comparison of spatial skills with internalized beliefs and anxieties. *Developmental Psychology, 33,* 669–680.

Casey, M. B., Nuttall, R., Pezaris, E., & Benbow, C. P. (1995). The influence of spatial ability on gender differences in math college entrance test scores across diverse samples. *Developmental Psychology, 31,* 697–705.

Casey, M. B., & Tucker, E. C. (1994, October). Problem-centered classrooms: Creating lifelong learners. *Phi Delta Kappan,* pp. 139–143.

Clements, D. H. (2004). Major themes and recommendations. In D. H. Clements & J. Sarama (Eds.), *Engaging young children in mathematics: Standards for early childhood mathematics education* (pp. 7–72). Mahwah, NJ: Erlbaum.

Clements, D. H., & Battista, M. T. (1992). Geometry and spatial reasoning. In D. A. Grouws (Ed.), *Handbook of research on mathematics teaching and learning* (pp. 420–464). New York: Macmillan.

Clements, D. H., & Sarama, J. A. (2009). *Learning and teaching early math: The learning trajectories approach.* Florence, KY: Routledge/Taylor & Francis.

Connor, C. M., Morrison, F. J., Fishman, B. J., Schatschneider, C., & Underwood, P. (2007). Algorithm-guided individualized reading instruction. *Science, 26,* 464–465.

Copple, C. (2004). Mathematics curriculum in the early childhood context. In D. Clements, J. Sarama, & M. A. DiBaise (Eds.), *Engaging young children in mathematics: Results of the conference on standards for pre-school and kindergarten mathematics education* (pp. 83–90). Mahwah, NJ: Erlbaum.

Cordova, D. I., & Lepper, M. R. (1996). Intrinsic motivation and the process of learning: Beneficial effects of contextualization, personalization, and choice. *Journal of Educational Psychology, 88,* 715–730.

Delgado, A. R., & Prieto, G. (2004). Cognitive mediators and sex-related differences in mathematics. *Intelligence, 32,* 25–32.

Dixon, R. C., Carmine, S. W., Kameenui, E. J., Simmons, D. C., Lee, D.-S., Wallin, J., et al. (1998). *Executive summary: Report to the California State Board of Education: Review of high quality experimental research.* Eugene, OR: National Center to Improve the Tools of Educators.

Fennema, E., Carpenter, T. P., Jacobs, V. R., Franke, M. L., & Levi, L. W. (1998). A longitudinal study of gender differences in young children's mathematical thinking. *Educational Researcher, 27,* 6–11.

Field, D. (1987). A review of preschool conservation training: An analysis of analyses. *Developmental Review, 7,* 210–251.

Friedman, L. (1995). The space factor in mathematics: Gender differences. *Review of Educational Research, 65,* 22–50.

Fuson, K. C. (2004). Pre-K to grade 2 goals and standards: Achieving 21st-century mastery for all. In D. Clements, J. Sarama, & M. A. DiBaise (Eds.), *Engaging young children in mathematics: Results of the Conference on Standards for Pre-School and Kindergarten Mathematics Education* (pp. 105–148). Mahwah, NJ: Erlbaum.

Gelman, R. (1969). Conservation acquisition: A problem of learning to attend to relevant attributes. *Journal of Experimental Child Psychology, 7,* 167–187.

Graesser, A. C., Hauft-Smith, K., Cohen, A. D., & Pyles, L. D. (1980). Advanced outlines, familiarity, text genre, and retention of prose. *Journal of Experimental Education, 48,* 209–220.

Griffin, S. (2004). Number worlds: A research-based mathematics program for young children. In D. Clements, J. Sarama, & M. A. DiBaise (Eds.), *Engaging young children in mathematics: Results of the Conference on Standards for Pre-School and Kindergarten Mathematics Education* (pp. 325–342). Mahwah, NJ: Erlbaum.

Halpern, D. F., Benbow, C. P., Geary, D. C., Gur, R. C., Hyde, J. S., & Gernsbacher, M. A. (2007). The science of sex differences in science and mathematics. *Psychological Science, 8,* 1–51.

Johnson, E. S., & Meade, A. C. (1987). Developmental patterns of spatial ability: An early gender differences. *Child Development, 58,* 725–740.

Johnson, H. (1984). The art of block building. In E. S. Hirsch (Ed.), *The block book* (pp. 8–23). Washington, DC: National Association for the Education of Young Children.

Kersh, J., Casey, B., & Mercer Young, J. (2008). Research on spatial skills and block building in girls and boys: The relationship to later mathematics learning. In O. N. Saracho & B. Spodak (Eds.), *Contemporary perspectives on mathematics in early childhood education* (pp. 233–253). Charlotte, NC: Information Age.

Kimball, M. M. (1989). A new perspective on women's math achievement. *Psychological Bulletin, 105,* 198–214.

Klahr, D., & Nigam, M. (2004). The equivalence of learning paths in early science instruction: Effects of direct instruction and discovery learning. *Psychological Science, 15,* 661–667.

Klein, A., & Starkey, P. (2004). Fostering preschool children's mathematical knowledge: Findings from the Berkeley Math Readiness Project. In D. Clements, J. Sarama, & M. A. DiBaise (Eds.), *Engaging young children in mathematics: Results of the Conference on Standards for Pre-School and Kindergarten Mathematics Education* (pp. 343–360). Mahwah, NJ: Erlbaum.

Levine, S. C., Huttenlocher, J., Taylor, A., & Lanrock, A. (1999). Early sex differences in spatial skills. *Developmental Psychology, 35,* 940–949.

Linn, M. C., & Petersen, A. C. (1985). Emergence and characterization of sex differences in spatial ability: A meta-analysis. *Child Development, 56,* 1479–1498.

Linn, M. C., & Petersen, A. C. (1986). A meta-analysis of gender differences in spatial ability: Implications for mathematics and science achievement. In J. S. Hyde & M. C. Linn (Eds.), *The psychology of gender: Advances through meta-analysis* (pp. 67–101). Baltimore: Johns Hopkins University Press.

Mishra, A. (2003). Age and school related differences in recall of verbal items in a story context. *Social Science International, 19,* 12–18.

National Council of Teachers of Mathematics. (2000). *Principles and standards for school mathematics.* Reston, VA: Author.

National Council of Teachers of Mathematics. (2006). *Curriculum focal points for prekindergarten through grade 8 mathematics: A quest for coherence.* Reston, VA: Author.

Nuttall, R., Casey, M. B., & Pezaris, E. (2005). Spatial ability as a mediator of gender differences on mathematics tests: A biological–environmental framework. In A. M. Gallagher & J. C. Kaufman (Eds.), *Gender differences in mathematics: An integrative psychological approach* (pp. 121–142). Cambridge, UK: Cambridge University Press.

Reifel, S. (1984). Block construction: Children's developmental landmarks in representation of space. *Young Children, 40,* 61–64.

Robinson, N. M., Abbott, R. D., Berninger, V. W., & Busse, J. (1996). The structure of abilities in math-precocious young children: Gender similarities and differences. *Journal of Educational Psychology, 88*, 341–352.

Schiro, M., Casey, B., & Anderson, K. (2002). *Tan and the shape changer.* Chicago: Wright Group/McGraw-Hill.

Siegler, R. S. (1996). *Emerging minds: The process of change in children's thinking.* New York: Oxford University Press.

Sophian, C. (2004). A prospective developmental perspective on early mathematics instruction. In D. Clements, J. Sarama, & M. A. DiBaise (Eds.), *Engaging young children in mathematics: Results of the Conference on Standards for Pre-School and Kindergarten Mathematics Education* (pp. 253–266). Mahwah, NJ: Erlbaum.

Sorby, S. (2007). Spatial Skills Curriculum Workshop. *Investigations in number, data, and space.* Retrieved August 28, 2007, from *www. investigations.terc.edu/curric-gl*

Uttal, D. H., Marulis, L., Hand, L., Warren, C., Lewis, A., & Newcombe, N. (2007, April). *What we know and don't know about improving spatial reasoning.* Paper presented at the American Educational Research Association, Chicago.

Voyer, D., Voyer, S., & Bryden, M. P. (1995). Magnitude of gender differences in spatial abilities: A meta-analysis and consideration of critical variables. *Psychological Bulletin, 117*, 250–270.

Wolfgang, C. H., Stannard, L. L., & Jones, I. (2001). Block play performance among preschoolers as a predictor of later school achievement in mathematics. *Journal of Research in Childhood Education, 15*, 173–180.

Wright Group/McGraw-Hill. (2007). *Everyday math: Grade levels pre-K to grade 6* (3rd ed.). Chicago: Wright Group/McGraw-Hill.

CHAPTER 22

Construction and Representation of Space in 5-Year-Old Children

Rossana Falcade
Paola Strozzi

Spatial reasoning, estimation, drawings and representational skills are crucial elements in the teaching and learning of math among preschool children. These skill are highly correlated with the development of language and communication. Teachers can facilitate development of math-related skill by setting up engaging scenarios in which children can use and improve their communicative and representational abilities. The Village Game, an example of a mathematics education scenario conducted with a group of six 5-year-old children at a municipal preschool in Reggio Emilia, Italy, is organized into four main phases: (1) the construction of a village by a child (codifier); (2) a detailed description of this village by the codifier to another child (decodifier), who attempts to reconstruct the same village just from the codifier's description; (3) a class discussion directly comparing the two villages; and (4) drawings of the first village from different points of view by all six children. In respect to the development of spatial and communicative competencies, the Village Game offers children the following opportunities:

- Organize objects (possible components of a village) in a space (table) and in relation to each other (in a microspace).
- Define spatial relations with verbal language and gestures by describing a constructed village to another child, who, without looking, must in turn create the "same" village.
- Assess individually, in pairs, and in groups the similarities and differences between the two created villages, expressing the spatial relationship between elements in the "microspace" (village) and the "macrospace" (the room where the construction of the villages takes place).

The distinction between macrospace and microspace is important in understanding the nuances of what is occurring for the child in the Village Game. The child exists and moves about in macrospace, while being external to microspace. At the same time the child can explore microspace visually and through manipulation.

> Perception through sight in macrospace is not global and so it imposes the assumption of different points of view with consequent use of time (changes in perspectives due to movement are usually slow) of space and of memory (for comparison different perspectives). In microspace we often have the possibility of a relatively global vision from a single (or relatively few) points of view. As a consequence perception is instantaneous and in a relatively short time we have significant changes of perspective. (Bartolini Bussi, 1992, p. 67)

Two other activities of the Village Game include the following:

- Graphically representing some spatial relations by drawing one of the villages from different viewpoints, keeping in mind what can be seen rather than what is known.
- Evaluating and discussing the strategies identified for drawing to render the different viewpoints from which the village has been considered.

These processes of drawing, perceiving, and understanding pictures are important and contribute uniquely to the child's experience of the Village Game. However as Stetsenko (1995, p. 151) has noted:

> The process of drawing should not be treated as isolated from other mental abilities of the child. On the contrary, relating drawing to such processes as language (in both its oral and written form), gestures and symbolic play is equally important, since all these processes are aimed at an overarching task of mastering social semiotic ways of communicating. In fact, such an approach corresponds to Vygotsky's dialectical claim that children's development is a dynamic system of unitary but not uniform, integral but not homogeneous processes.

This "multimodal" aspect is an important feature of the Village Game. In this chapter we focus on how construction activity and language (oral, graphic, gestural) elicited by the Village Game support children specifically in exploring, conceptualizing, and representing spatial relations. We discuss the use of artifacts or manipulatives, the importance of group process, and role of the teacher as mediators. In particular we analyze the following:

- The function of semiotic mediation (Bartolini Bussi, 2007; Bartolini Bussi & Boni, Chapter 20, this volume) offered by artifacts[1] set up by the teacher (the elements of the village) in the process of teaching–learning.
- Cognitive, relational, and communicative processes in individuals and groups.
- The mediating role of teachers (Bartolini Bussi, 1996).

The scenario used in the Village Game was inspired by a research program first conducted in Geneva in 1983 by the research team Groupe Mathématique du Service de la Recherche Pédagogique. This program, originated with a Piagetian approach, made use of not only symbolic elements (house, car, animals, etc.) but also nonstructured material (wooden cubes, parallelepipeds, cylinders, etc.) and was meant to provide teachers with suggestions for teaching practice, without any theoretical framework. In the 1990s, the research group for teaching–learning mathematics in preschools and primary school at the University of Modena, coordinated by Bartolini Bussi, took up the experiment once more with significant modifications (Bartolini Bussi, 1992, 2007). The insights presented here benefit from earlier work (e.g., Arzarello & Robutti, 2008; Bartolini Bussi & Mariotti, 2008) and the educational process within the Reggio Emilia early childhood centers (Bruner, 1966; Edwards, Gandini, & Forman, 1995; Rinaldi, 2006). The work presented here began with an analysis of the "semiotic potential" (i.e., the potential to express the utilization schemes produced in the solution of a given task in mathematical terms, through semiotic activity of the involved objects) (see Bartolini Bussi & Boni, Chapter 20, this volume). Specifically, we investigated the exchanges between coder and decoder in the Village Game activity and teacher effectiveness in facilitating the fabrication, negotiation, and *internalization* of signs[2] (e.g., gestural, linguistic, and graphic) that have spatial significance (Vygotsky, 1931/1978).[3]

Following the paradigm of the *theory of didactical situations* of Brousseau (1997), mostly inspired by Piaget's works, the Village Game is primarily a *didactical situation*.[4] In this *communication game*, knowledge is constructed within a social context as students attempt to solve a problem situation. In particular, validation of the solution comes not from an external, authoritative source (e.g., the teacher) but from the way the situation itself is structured and organized. Like every *adidactical situation*, the game is organized into an "action phase" (the construction of a village by the codifier), a "formulation phase" (description of the village by the codifier to the decodifier, who cannot see the codifier), and a "validation phase" (through direct comparison between the villages constructed by the codifier and the decodifier). In addition to this socioconstructivist structure, the game has a strong semiotic and sociocultural character that comes from the Modena group's post-Vygotskyian[5] revision (Bartolini Bussi & Boni, Chapter 20, this volume).

Because of limited space in this chapter, we present only examples organized around three in-depth foci. A more detailed study is in progress. In this chapter, the results are presented from a teacher's perspective rather than that of a researcher's. The first section of this chapter focuses on analysis of semiotic potential of the objects (artifacts) related to the features of the game. The second section briefly considers the relationships between language and spatial representation, demonstrating that learning of spatial representation categories, as has already been posited by various studies by Stetsenko in psychology (1995), is highly "multimodal," with a systemic nature. In the final section we share observations on the crucial role of the teacher. We present and discuss protocols to support our conclusions.

Experimental Context and the Semiotic Potential of the Artifact

Creating the entire experiment, we placed particular attention on setting up contexts similar to children's everyday experience using materials and spaces with which they were familiar, working in small groups and with durations of playing time similar to those in their everyday school life. The playful and familiar dimension meant that the level of enjoyment shown by the children was always high. After the pilot experiment, described in this chapter, the experience was repeated in many other schools, with similar results. The Village Game was described to a group of six participating children who, in turn, assumed the following roles:

- Codifier (the child who builds the village and then describes it to the decodifier).
- Decodifier (the child who listens and tries to implement the instructions from the codifier to duplicate the village, even asking questions).
- Observer (the child who silently observes the construction and description of the village and participates in the final collective discussion and comparison of the two villages).

The Game comprises a minimum of three and a maximum of six rounds, depending on how long each game lasts. Each game round included the construction of a village, description by the codifier and subsequent reconstruction by the decodifier, and revisitation/comparison by the whole group of the results obtained in terms of similarity–differences between the two villages. Together the children alternated taking the role of codifier and decodifier twice during games. Both meetings lasted about 2½ hours and were filmed with a video camera. The Village Game usually took place in the school *atelier*, or workshop (for a description, see Edwards et al., 1995), in which two square tables were placed so that the tabletop was completely and easily available to the child at arm's length. Tables were placed side by side, facing the same direction, and separated by a movable screen. Each table had a chair at the head. To the side of the two tables, five chairs were set out for the observer children and the teacher (see Figure 22.4, on p. 506). The two children acting as codifier and decodifier sat on either side of the screen, and were each given two identical sets of nine objects whose nature and playful qualities lent themselves to the kind of symbolic narrative that is familiar to preschool-age children. The group included Andrea, Asia, Beatrice, Francesco, Gabriele, and Sharon, who worked together with one of the class teachers, Ilaria. The other adults involved, the teacher Erika, and the authors of this chapter took turns recording the game. The children ranged in age from 5 years, 4 months to 5 years, 11 months.

The choice of giving the children nine objects to build up the village conformed to precise spatial criteria and was inspired by research by Lurçat (1986), who reminds us that

> the child's representation of space is constructed based on fixed objects taken as a reference and this very probably [is] before the constitution of a body schema detachable from her/his organism. . . . The appearance of language, with the formation of concepts, presupposes the possibility of scission of the body schema from the body in order to project it on objects as the start of individuation. Every object . . . structures the space surrounding it, appears as a centre of a geographical map whose polarities are the same ones as the body schema: top–bottom, left–right, front–back. (pp. 17–18)

Hence, when faced with an object, there are three main ways (and combinations of them) to project onto it one's own body schema: by translation, rotation on a central axis, and reflection (symmetry). See Figure 22.1.

We can illustrate these different ways to refer to the position of an object by means of the example shown in Figure 22.2. The map in Figure 22.2 shows a child in front of a square table, where a very little village (a car and two trees) is set down. A football is on the floor, and the teacher is observing the child behind him or her.

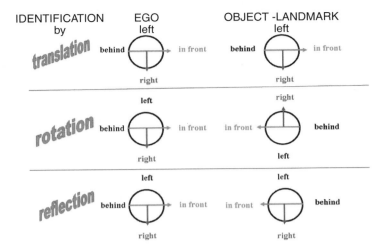

FIGURE 22.1. Scheme translated from Bartolini Bussi (2008, p. 131) based on Lurçat (1986).

Imagine that the child has to describe the position of an object in this village. The child can use the following reference systems:

- An *egocentric* reference system, in which the position of the object depends on the position of the child ("The car is in front of me"), that often implies the use of gestures ("The small tree is on that side").
- An *intrinsic allocentric* reference system, in which localization is totally defined by spatial relationships within the village ("The small tree is behind the car").

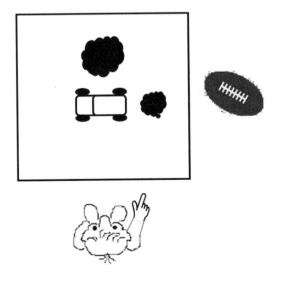

FIGURE 22.2. Map of a child in front of a little village.

- A *situated allocentric* reference system, in which the child considers some physical elements external to the village but present in the room ("The small tree is on the side of the football").
- A *social allocentric* system, in which, instead of the ball, the child refers to a person or an animal that is external to the village but present in the room ("The small tree is on the side of the teacher").
- A *geocentric* reference system, in which the child defines the position of an object in a very abstract way, related to the position of the earth (e.g., the cardinal points; "The car is facing North"). To use this kind of reference system the child needs a very high capacity for abstraction, which can be mobilized if children have been involved in other projects, for example, the observation of different positions of the sun during the day.

In the case of the use of an *intrinsic allocentric* reference system, there are many possible ways to define the position of an object. For instance, the child may not take into account the polarity of the objects and say:

1. "The big tree is behind the car," projecting his or her body schema on the car by reflection. In a projection by *reflection*, the observer defines the position of an object in relation to him- or herself, as if it were reflected in a mirror.
2. "The big tree is in front of the car," projecting his or her body schema on the car by translation. In a projection by *translation*, the observer defines the position of an object in relation to him- or herself as if the object has the same spatial positioning as the observer body.

Otherwise, the child may take into account the polarity of the objects and say:

3. "The small tree is on the right of the car," projecting his or her body schema on the car by reflection or translation.
4. "The big tree is on the right of the car," referring to the intrinsic polarity of the car and projecting his or her body schema on the car by rotation, as if he or she were the driver. In a projection by *rotation*, the observer defines the position of an object in relation to him- or herself, by identifying with it.
5. "The small tree is behind the car," referring to the intrinsic polarity of the car and projecting his or her body schema on the car by rotation.

These are only examples to show the complexity of the task. There is no "right" or "wrong" way of describing the spatial situation. However, there are more and less effective ways for children to communicate meaning to each other.

One feature of an object (i.e., whether it has an intrinsic front and back) is especially useful in the spatial reasoning tasks in the Village Game. Objects with parts that are intrinsically described as front and back are called *canonic*. Those that do not are called *noncanonic*. Canonic objects have this quality because of some feature—direction of movement (e.g., the little car); the presence of organs of perception (e.g., animals, persons, figures, or dolls with human likeness), particularly visible faces (wardrobes, house, mirror, painting)—or because of their adaptation to the human body (e.g., a chair). *Noncanonical objects*, such as a stone, a tree, or a box, are objects without particularly privileged parts. For this reason their orientation or location can only be described provisionally and in a way that requires us to take into account the perspective or position of the subject or viewer.

Canonical objects provided to children included the following:

• A "house" made of cardboard or other material of a sufficient size to totally or partially hide other elements of the village, and with front and back openings allowing the total or partial insertion inside the house of other village elements. The outer walls of the building were different in such a way as to pose the orientation's problems for the children at different times in the game. The hypothesis underlying the use of the house is that it represents an element central to the village from not only a perceptive point of view but also an affective point of view. We thought that the house would be the first object positioned in the village, around which the children would organize various spatial relationships. The house allows a projection of one's own body schema through both reflection and rotation.

• Two human figures (one male and one female): canonical and affective elements given prevalent polarity by the presence of organs of perception. Body schema can be identified with the figures through translation or by rotation.

• An animal: an affective and canonical element with prevalent polarity due to the presence of organs of perception and whose body schema can be identified both by translation and by rotation.

• A means of transportation: a canonical element with prevalent polarity due to the direction of movement and onto which it is possible to project body schema by reflection and by rotation.

• A chair: a canonical element with prevalent polarity because it is an object made for bodies, and it allows projection of body schema by means of translation, reflection, and rotation.

• A ladder: a canonical element with prevalent polarity (top–bottom) that is particularly easy to codify graphically as an isolated element but with increasing complexity in relation to others (e.g., a figure placed on the ladder). This element allows projection of body schema through translation and through reflection.

Noncanonical objects included:

• A low tree: an element that allows projection of body schema by translation and by reflection.

• A tall tree: an element that, because of its size, can obscure or allow only a partial view of another object, and that allows a projection of body schema by translation or by reflection (see Figure 22.3).

The artifact derived from the combination of all these elements can be used by the teacher as a *tool of semiotic mediation* in the process of teaching–learning appropriate spatial categories and signs. Using this artifact, the teacher can support students' production of situated spatial signs. In addition, by using either spontaneously generated or appropriately provided pivot signs described by Bartolini Bussi and Boni (Chapter 20, this volume), the teacher can assist in the transition of signs[6] connected to the world of the artifact toward mathematical signs used in the reference culture. Help is needed because *geocentric* reference systems, which are independent of the particular situation (e.g., not dependent on movable objects), and *intrinsic allocentric* reference systems, which are based on objects' spatial features within a constrained context, are not always easily integrated.

FIGURE 22.3. Elements of the village.

Phases of the Game

Constructing and Dictating the Village

After the teacher has shown the materials to the children and invited them to comment on each element in the set, he or she proposes that a couple of children take turns constructing a village. The codifier first constructs a village, then "describes" it to his or her companion (the decodifier), who, by asking questions, tries to construct an identical village (Figure 22.4) using only the communication from the student codifier. The codifier is usually behind the decodifier.

FIGURE 22.4. First phase of the game; codifier is on the left and decodifier is on the right.

Comparing the Villages

After a child has described the village (codifier) to a friend (decodifier), the screen separating them is taken down and the whole group enters into an exchange discussion about the two villages created (see Figure 22.5). Ideally, the outcome is not someone winning or losing, but an interpretation of a shared learning endeavor. In fact, group evaluation is not limited to counting how many objects are "mistaken" or "correct" but involves "how" oral communication between the codifier and decodifier takes place. The role of the teacher at this point becomes fundamental for guiding the process of validation: supporting the children's expression, reciprocal listening, and memory of expressions used in speech by the codifier and the questions asked by the decodifier. *Annotation, mirroring,* and *paraphrasing* (Bartolini Bussi, 1998a) of speech terms and gestures used by the children are important. In this way, in fact, the teacher is able to create the conditions in order to explore constructed personal meanings to foster the production, sharing, and negotiation of situated signs of a spatial nature, which are significant for the child, and to graft the mathematical signs onto the situated signs (see Bartolini Bussi & Boni, Chapter 20, this volume), which is the long-term objective of this learning–teaching process.[7]

Drawing the Village from a Specific Point of View

After the group discussion, a village is reconstructed on a large table. The children sit around the table on different sides, and are asked to comment, then draw what they see from their specific points of view (see Figure 22.6). Nothing can be taken for granted in this operation at the preschool age. In fact, it means separating ourselves from what we know exists and taking into account only the things we see, which, in some cases, may not be the most characteristic part of the figure or object (as happens with a person's profile or an animal's front or back).[8]

FIGURE 22.5. Second phase of the game: Comparing the villages.

FIGURE 22.6. Third phase of the game: Drawing the village from a specific point of view.

Individual and Group Evaluation of Drawings

After drawing the village from their individual points of view, the children take turns to recount their own drawing to the others, to answer questions, and to observe and comment on other children's drawings (see Figure 22.7). This individual and group rereading of their own drawings and those by others encourages the children to explore more deeply the signs of a spatial, oral, and graphic nature that have already been introduced, thus allowing them to establish new and more vast semiotic connections (Bartolini Bussi, 1993, 1996). Making explicit their personally constructed meanings, and their ways of graphically representing them, facilitates children's distancing themselves from their productions and helps them to become more conscious of their own thinking and to discover possible alternative strategies for representation.[9]

The experiment described in this chapter had a further stage. In fact, the children were asked to move from the microspace of the village constructed on the table to the

FIGURE 22.7. Fourth phase of the game: Individual and group evaluation of drawings.

macrospace of the school playground. The analysis resulting from this phase of the experiment is still in progress. In this chapter we limit ourselves to the first part of the experiment (excluding the macrospace stage in the school playground).

Analysis of the Semiotic Potential of the Artifact Actually Exploited

After the experiments, we analyzed what features of the various objects (previously discussed) were really used in the children's processes of locating the objects in space, which reference systems children used more frequently in relation to the different objects, and whether, based on Lurçat's classification, there was decentralization and, if so, what types of projection of body schema the children used in relating to the various objects.

We observed that, relative to different potential modalities for projection, the children showed a differential ability. They were able to decentralize their points of view relative to front–back orientation (at least for some of the objects), thus localizing one object relative to another using the objects' own polarity. On the contrary, this was not true for lateralization. In the case of left–right orientation of the various objects, the children usually adopted an *egocentric* or *intrinsic allocentric* reference, mainly with reference to the house. In the following section, we summarize what we observed for each object in the village.

The House

The house was the first element to be positioned by all the children. This observation is perfectly consonant with all experiments carried out previously. The house polarizes the space in the sense of inducing an initial *allocentric* reference system, in relation to which all other objects are organized and located successively. Some of the house's features, specifically, a door, windows, and a large door that the children interpreted as a garage, proved to be particularly useful in the clear identification of front and back. The house aided the use of *egocentric* reference systems and *intrinsic allocentric* reference systems, with projection of the body schema by reflection[10] and not by translation (e.g., *295. Andrea: Francesco, I put the house on the right* [indicating the right side with his hand] or *787. Asia:* [pointing with hands and arms joined] *I put the house turned to the left*).

The Automobile

The position of the car was usually described using *intrinsic allocentric* reference systems. The decision to use an *allocentric* reference system, although not exclusive, is supported by the obvious possible connection between car and garage, which offers an "easy" solution to the spatial problem (e.g., *162. Francesco: And I put a car inside the garage*).

The Horse

There was a growing awareness of this object's semiotic potential. Initially the horse was considered globally but later reference was made to its polarity (presence of a differentiated front and back). This generated a great increase in the number of sentences for a more precise localization/positioning. On both days, there was a prevalent use of *intrinsic allocentric* reference systems (e.g., *176. Francesco: After I put the horse on the left side of the house*) and *social allocentric* reference systems (e.g., *344. Gabriele: What about the horse's nose? On Erika's side?; 345. Francesco: No, no, on Erika's side; 346. Gabriele: On Ilaria's?; 347. Francesco: Yes, on Ilaria's side!* And later *352. Francesco: And I put the little tree close to the horse; 353. Gabriele: But where? Against the wall or … or on the other side?; 354. Francesco: No, near to the horse in front of its nose* [Francesco repeatedly brings his cupped hands close to his own face]. *355. Gabriele: Done it!*).

The obvious polarities indicated by the presence of the horse's nose and tail functioned as elements for organizing space. This took place with the children not only at the time of construction/dictation but also, and above all, at the group discussion of the drawings.[11]

The Male and Female Characters

Out of 109 statements for localizing/positioning the human figures, only three statements used an *egocentric* reference system. Most of the reference systems used were *intrinsic allocentric* and connected to front–back polarity. This showed that children are capable of decentering and projection of their body schema relative to front and back (e.g., *568. Andrea: … with her face at the window*). In other cases, the characters were localized in relation to other elements created for the body, such as the chair or the ladder (e.g., *562. Beatrice: But the little woman … the lady … I put her … sitting … on a chair* or *317. Andrea: The builder goes up the ladder*). The children also seemed less willing to accept approximation when defining the position of human elements compared to other types of elements within the village. This led to multiple specifications and questions, and allowed the children to discover the effectiveness of these communication strategies.

The Vegetation Elements

There are two trees in the set of objects, one tall and one short, that for the most part were positioned by children using an *intrinsic allocentric* reference system (e.g., *602. Andrea: The big tree is close to the horse, with its tail touching the tree*) or a *social allocentric* reference system (e.g., *794. Asia: "And then the big tree turned toward the right which is facing just where Erika is*). More than the other elements, and probably because of their noncanonical nature, they seem to raise the question of defined distances for the children, with general qualifiers (e.g., *593. Andrea: Yes … but a little bit far … and a little bit near!* or *595. Beatrice: Medium, do you mean?* and *596. Andrea: Yes. A bit medium*). The left–right spatial relationship was also often brought into play in positioning the trees and was provisionally resolved by children using a generalized "near to" that, however, the children themselves who sought more precise spatial terms began to consider insufficient (e.g., *162. Francesco: … then on the other side of the house on the right I put its trees* or *592. Beatrice: Is it toward the light table?*). In conclusion, we can affirm that, in general, the part of the semiotic potential inherent in the artifact was actualized. However, much potential remains to be more deeply explored, probably by changing the available variables (introducing also a car the human characters may enter, etc.).

Language, Drawing, Gesture: The Need for a Multimodal Approach

In this section, we wish to draw attention to a fundamental aspect of the research project. As we have already said, the hypothesis, inspired by Vygotsky's theory, that runs through the entire experiment is that the process of conceptualization of space is multimodal. Therefore, it is not possible to deal with the issues of children's cognitive processes connected to space without, at the same time, considering all the different systems of spatial signs they utilize. From this perspective, the drawing should not be treated as a separate area of competence. Together with the other sign systems, it contributes to our understanding of the cognitive development of the child. As Stetsenko strongly emphasized (1995), this development is a single dynamic, although it is not necessarily uniform and homogeneous. From the point of view of teaching practice, then, we need to organize activities that mobilize and bring together in various ways the different sign systems. For this reason the sequence of the Village Game includes acting, comparing, drawing, and discussing the drawings. On the other hand, from the point of view of analysis of cognitive processes, it is necessary to consider the child in his or her entirety and complexity, including affective issues. Therefore, we did not limit ourselves to analyzing only the child's linguistic ability. We also collected evidence (not detailed here) of the importance of the narrative aspects (i.e., to describe the village by telling a story) that were not mobilized in similar tasks concerning nonstructured materials.

The case of Gabriele, in contrast with that of Beatrice, is illuminating in this respect. At the end of the second day of the experiment, in the phase of drawing from one's own point of view (see Figure 22.8), Gabriele produced the drawing shown in Figure 22.9. The horse's position represented a significant problem for Gabriele. During the execution of the game, in which he acted as decodifier, Gabriele held a lengthy discussion with the codifier Francesco to understand where Francesco had situated the horse. Gabriele expressed very well the way the horse's position could be communicated, starting from essential elements, such as head and tail (see discussion 431–445).

When he made his drawing, Gabriele first drew the horse and represented it, starting from exactly those elements that were most visible from his viewpoint: the rear

FIGURE 22.8. Gabriele's point of view.

FIGURE 22.9. Gabriele's drawing.

of the horse and the tail. Consistent with this, in the phase where he talked about his drawing, he said:

> 801.   GABRIELE: I can see [the horse's] bottom and the tail and so I drew its bottom and tail!

Gabriele, who was the youngest child, carried out his task effectively, with extremely schematic lines (almost symbolic), in contrast to his companions, who were much more preoccupied with life-like details in their drawings. For Gabriele, the issue of representing the elements of the village from his own viewpoint appeared to be the main priority. If we limited ourselves to this case, then we might infer a linear consequentiality between oral language and graphic language, as if the drawing were nothing other than a translation of what had been said, or as if the drawing posed no difficulties other than those of manual and executive skills.

The case of Beatrice demonstrates a more complex purpose of the drawing. In fact, in the discussion phase preceding the phase of drawing from her individual viewpoint (which also took place on the second day) Beatrice seemed to express her concept of point of view clearly and confidently:

> 675.   TEACHER: ... and what does "point of view" mean in your opinion?
>
> 676.   BEATRICE: That we try to draw what we can see ... them.
>
> 677.   TEACHER: (*writing*) We try and draw what we can see ourselves. ... What do you mean, Bea? Explain it to me properly so that so you can let Gabriele, who is playing, understand as well.
>
> 678.   BEATRICE: That a person is ... a point. ... It's Andrea who can see something.
>
> 679.   TEACHER: A person is in a point that sees something.
>
> 680.   BEATRICE: That in another point sees a different thing, and in another point a different thing from the thing in other point.
>
> 681.   TEACHER: For example, what are the points here?

682. BEATRICE: I can see half the car (*pointing with her right-hand forefinger*), the horse, the little man, and the lady who is there on the chair ...

683. TEACHER: But?

684. BEATRICE: I can't see it ... and then I see the tree.

685. GABRIELE: And the car ...

686. TEACHER: And can you see the car properly?

687. BEATRICE: No, so-so.

688. TEACHER: So-so. ... What can you see of the car?

689. BEATRICE: (*bringing the palms of her hand to within 5 cm of each other*) Half of it.

690. TEACHER: Half ... so what do you have to ... [what] can you draw?

691. BEATRICE: Half!

After this dialogue, we might have expected a "correct" drawing, or a drawing consistent with what Beatrice stated. Instead, at the time of drawing (even though the teacher clearly stated and repeated the request that she draw only from her own point of view), Beatrice could not resist representing the most significant side of the house, the front, and all the other elements of the village (see Figure 22.10). She did this even though her point of view was of the side of the house (see Figure 22.11). At the end of the drawing, in the discussion phase, she explained her choices in the following way:

971. BEATRICE: Even though I couldn't see it, I thought hard and I tried to draw it without seeing.

Evidently, in Beatrice's case there is not a consequential linearity between what she said and what she drew. All the same, to interpret behavior of this kind, as Freeman (1980) has already shown, it is not enough to put forward the argument of Piaget and Inhelder

FIGURE 22.10. Beatrice's drawing.

FIGURE 22.11. Beatrice's point of view.

(1967) that a child represents everything he or she knows in a drawing. Actually, among the things Beatrice knows, although still only in an embryonic form, is what drawing from a certain point of view means. In 1980, Freeman had already proposed analyzing infant drawings in terms of problem solving (i.e., tasks involving the mobilization of a multiplicity of abilities). This view does not conflict with our Vygotskian perspective because it aims to take into account the complexity of the drawing activity and considers this activity in relation to the rest of the subject's abilities. In a sense, spatial thinking is what enables the child to work with images he or she has constructed from personal experiences enacted in physical space, but then manages to transform [sometimes] only in his or her mind (Yakimanskaya, 1991). In the past (and also stemming from Piaget's studies) drawings have often, and sometimes naively, been used as indicators of a child's spatial competence. It was mistakenly thought that the better a child's spatial competence, the better his or her competence in drawing, both for the creation of a photorealistic drawing and the ability to organize the page spatially. In fact, to speak of a child's "spatial competence" means to have different abilities in mind. As Stetsenko (1995) reminds us, the performance we observe must instead be considered as a mixture of competence and of understanding the task, which do not emerge separately as givens. They are built up in a dialectic relationship between action and communication on intra- and interpersonal levels.

The Teacher's Role

In the Vygotskian framework in which this experiment was created, special attention was always paid to the function of the teacher (Bartolini Bussi, 1998b; Falcade, 2006). Apart from managing the *teaching contract* (Brousseau, 1997), the teacher is also of fundamental importance in guiding and supporting the process of semiotic mediation (see Bartolini Bussi & Boni, Chapter 20, in this volume). Rather than a detailed analysis of the teacher's role, we present some points for reflection.

First and foremost, we observe that a fundamental part of the teacher's mediating function is helping with a cooperative and selective reconstruction of the situation (e.g., see 432 and 434 in the following dialogue), that is a shared reconstruction in which the fundamental elements of the activity are highlighted according to the objectives of the teaching project. In particular, through questions of the type, "and what does ... mean in your opinion?" (675), the teacher helps to make explicit and to share the different personal meanings constructed during the course of the activity. Reconstructing and revisiting the activity helps children to generate signs, share them, and negotiate them, thus potentially internalizing them.

Generally, signs generated during a collective discussion *orchestrated* by the teacher (Bartolini Bussi, 1998a) are for the most part situated signs (i.e., directly connected to the activity with the artifact). However, given the deeply educational nature of the proposed activity, these signs have an implicit but strong connection with the mathematical signs of the reference culture. Starting from these situated signs, then introducing new signs or using *pivot signs*, the teacher establishes relationships with the mathematical or culturally pertinent signs that are the objective of her teaching.

Another of the teacher's fundamental roles is to guide the phases of validation and highlight elements that are significantly conflictual. In the phase of comparing the villages, after Francesco's "description" to Gabriele, the teacher helps them to focus on the origin of the wrong location of the horse chosen by Gabriele,[12] due to his improper use of an egocentric reference system by the codifier Francesco:

431. GABRIELE: Oh, because he said ... Francie said the nose is where I am!

432. TEACHER: It's true. He said the horse's nose is where you were ... but instead? ... but I could see Francie. ... He was gesturing, he was doing gestures. ... Francie, what were you doing when you were placing the horse? (*Mimes the gestures Francie made with his hands.*)

433. FRANCESCO: I was here, Gabriele. (*Sits down in his place.*) Gabriele, I was here ...

434. TEACHER: So then? ... What does that mean then ... if you were there?

435. FRANCESCO: (*standing up and going to sit nearby the decodifier's chair*) I could see ... I could see you ... even though there was a screen and I was behind it ... after I could see you on this side.

436. TEACHER: What could you have said otherwise, Francie? Instead of saying "the nose is near where you were," was there another way ... just a minute ... another word?

437. GABRIELE: (*sitting down in his place*) You said the nose was near where I was, not ...

438. FRANCESCO: Oh, I could see you from here. (*Goes back to his place.*)

439. TEACHER: Francie, could you have given him some other help ... in your opinion?

440. ANDREA: (*Says something but it can't be understood.*)

441. TEACHER: (*to Andrea*) Just a minute.

442. GABRIELE: You should have said the tail was where (*with his right hand, pointing to himself*) ... where I am!

443. TEACHER: Should you have said the tail was where I am ... or rather, Asia? (*to Asia, who seems to have suggested something*).

444. ASIA: He could have said that "the face turned toward the light table (*stretching her left arm to point to the light table in front of the two game tables*) and the tail turned toward Gabriele"!

445. TEACHER: What could he have taken? Could he have thought about all the things there are around this space?!

Observe how the teacher, by not only using questions (434, 436, 439) but also gestures that mirror the child's gestures (439), helps Francesco to reconstruct the situation and to become aware of the origin of his mistake. In particular, by redefining and narrowing Francesco's task (439), she helps him to explore other communicative strategies and adopt a more pertinent reference system. Furthermore, the teacher knowingly orchestrates the other children's interventions: She asks Andrea to be silent (441), while giving value to Asia's intervention (443) when she suggests adopting a *situated allocentric* reference system shared by everyone. To finish, she generalizes Asia's intervention (445) by calling attention to the existence of spatial elements other than people (444). In this way, she helps the children to understand the efficacy of different reference systems. The *social allocentric* reference systems, like the one adopted by Gabriele (442, 444), are more comprehensible but more fragile (because of the high mobility of people) compared to *situated allocentric* reference systems.

As Bartolini Bussi (1988a) has observed, this communication strategy of *generalizing*, together with *particularization*, makes it possible for the teacher on the one hand to extend an affirmation's dominion of pertinence (thus helping the process of abstraction and expansion) and on the other to go back to the context of the activity, when a too-general statement is vulnerable to not being fully understood or taken in by the children. Through other opportune communication strategies, such as *mirroring* (432, 443) and *paraphrasing* (Bartolini Bussi, 1998a), the teacher institutionalizes or "relaunches" the discussion and helps to establish connections. In the paragraph relating to the dialogue with Beatrice about what it means to draw from a certain viewpoint, still through *mirroring* (677, 679), the teacher temporarily ratifies the child's statement, thus reassuring her of the direction in which she is going and aiding deeper exploration of what has been outlined.

Conclusion

Analysis of the experiment proposed in this chapter is far from having been concluded. However, results already obtained are extremely rich and have suggested repetition of the same experiment with other children in other schools, in Reggio Emilia and elsewhere. We have seen how the experiment presents vast semiotic potential and allows for mobilization of multiple reference systems, providing an opportunity for generating, utilizing and reinvesting diverse signs of a spatial nature in various contexts (microspace, macrospace) and various semiotic systems (gestural, graphic, and linguistic).

We did not report other results of the research in this chapter, but the Village Game proved very effective in dealing with the challenges related to reference systems and coordination of spatial perspective. These are related to problems of decentration,[13] on which Piaget himself was the first to work (see the celebrated Three Mountains Task), and to several interpretations about development of children's spatial competencies in terms of a linear, step-by-step process. The data gathered, even if they concern a very small group, allowed us to refute an overly simplistic view espousing a linear development of children's spatial competencies from an egocentric reference system to an absolute, objective reference system.[14] As already demonstrated in established studies (Pontecorvo & Pontecorvo, 1986), it can be observed that the choice of reference system does not appear to be connected so much to cognitive development of the subject as to the type of task. Therefore, these are not depending on cognitive development competencies but are "domain-specific" competencies (i.e., deeply connected to the type of situation and context in which they are mobilized) (Karmiloff-Smith, 1992). From our point of view, the concept of "reference system," on the one hand, is a tool allowing access to cognitive processes of a spatial nature in an individual and, on the other hand, given its centrality and versatility in not just mathematics, is a fundamental object of teaching–learning in primary schools. In particular, we believe that the construction of representations of spatial categories should be one of the fundamental objectives of early childhood education. From an educational point of view, the situation provides a significant learning context. From a research point of view, it provides a possibility for further exploration of links between not only gesture and language but also language and drawing in processes of spatial conceptualization. Furthermore, from a social implications point of view, it can be efficiently reinvested in teachers' professional improvement during inservice training, using the vast collection of videotaped sessions as training tools. The situation is also robust, having been transposed several times both in preschool and primary school contexts, and also outside the Reggio Emilia institution, by both teachers and prospective teachers during school apprenticeship.

The situation opens up various possibilities. For example, the difficulty in quantifying relative distances between the various objects in the village, manifested in many of the children's interventions, suggests that we should work on new educational journeys to approach issues connected with either measuring or estimating distances. On the other hand, the transition from a 3D situation to its 2D representation, which is not straightforward, posed for the children the interesting problem of perspective drawing. From this point of view, it would be interesting to construct an activity using digital photo cameras for quick comparison of children's own drawings. Finally, it could be advantageous to set up a transition to the macrospace of the school playground. In fact, when we carried out such an evolution of the game in our experiment, it showed a lot of potential. For example, we could observe how drawing in this new dimension contributed to further clarification of what it means to observe and to draw from a certain viewpoint, and led some children to become aware and to evaluate their own personal implicit reference system, as well as supported the explicit and negotiated adoption of a shared reference system, which is a first step toward the idea of an absolute reference system.

The situation described in this chapter also shows indirectly the robustness of the theoretical framework (previously used only in primary school) in which the reference system was developed and analyzed, and contributes to clarifying processes connected with using an artifact as an instrument for semiotic mediation on the part of the teacher. The theoretical framework proved to be easily accessible to teachers, as well, and improved their ability put the theoretical concepts into practice.

Notes

1. According to the Vygotskian perspective, by "artifact" we mean a particular object with its intrinsic characteristics, designed and realized for purpose of accomplishing a particular task.
2. Vygotsky distinguishes between the mediation of technical tools and that of psychological tools (signs, tools of semiotic mediation). Both are part of the cultural heritage of humankind, and were produced and used by human beings, evolving over the centuries but maintaining their functions. Although clearly distinguished, "signs and tools" are assumed by Vygotsky (1931/1978, p. 53) in the same category of mediators. As for their function, the difference between signs and tools rests on "the different way that they orient the human behaviour" (Vygotsky, 1931/1978, p. 54). The tool's function is externally oriented; it is to serve as the conductor of human activity aimed at mastering nature. The sign's function is internally oriented; it is a means of internal activity aimed to master oneself.
3. For applications at the elementary school level, see *www5.indire.it:8080/set/set_linguaggi/ul/o/lingomat/pres.html*.
4. In his text *Theory of Didactical Situations in Mathematics*, Brousseau (1997) states the following:

> The modern conception of teaching therefore requires the teacher to provoke the expected adaptation in her students by a judicious choice of "problems" that she puts before them. These problems ... must make the students act, speak think and evolve by their own motivation. ... The student knows very well that the problem was chosen to help her to acquire a new piece of knowledge, but she must also know that this knowledge is entirely justified by the internal logic of the situation and she can construct it without appealing to didactical reasoning. Not only can she do it, but she must do it because she will have truly acquire this knowledge only when she is able to put it to use by herself in situations which she will come across outside any teaching context and in the absence of any intentional direction. Such a situation is called an adidactical situation. ... This situation or problem chosen by the teacher is an essential part of the broader situation in which the teacher seeks to devolve to the student an adidactical situation which provides her with the most independent and most fruitful interaction possible. ... She is thus involved in a game with the system of interaction of the student with the problems she gives her. This game, or broader situation, is the didactical situation. (pp. 30–31)

5. We can consider the Modena group's approach to be post-Vygotskian because of the reference not only to Vygotsky but also to other post-Vygotskian authors, such as Luria, Leonti'ev, Stetsenko, and so forth.
6. Because of the post-Vygotskian vision of this chapter, it is not possible to separate the production of signs and the process of conceptualization accompanying it. Our view, then, like Vygotsky's (1934/1986), is that to speak of sign construction is the same as speaking of meaning construction.
7. Each game lasted about 5–7 minutes. Our experiment examined, in 2 days, nine rounds of games in which all the children played both codifier and decodifier. The nine episodes of comparison, one for each game, lasted an average of 5 minutes.
8. In the 2 experiment days, the two drawing sessions from individual points of view lasted about 20 minutes each.
9. This phase of the experiment lasted from 5 to 10 minutes for each child. Because all six children were present both days, the total length of this phase was 100 minutes.

10. In reality these two systems (*egocentric* and *allocentric* with projection by reflection) are not distinguishable in the case of the house. In fact, when we say, "I placed the house facing right," this can mean "I placed the house with the facade turned toward the right of the person positioning it" (*egocentric*) or "I placed the house with the facade turned toward the house's right-hand side" (*allocentric* with projection by reflection).

11. One part of an episode related to a group discussion of the horse's position is covered in more detail later (430–444).

12. Figure 22.4 shows Gabriele, the decodifier, in front of Francesco, the codifier.

13. To characterize/define the position of an object, it's important for children to learn not only to use egocentric spatial reference systems but also to mobilize multiple points of view ("decentration").

14. This step-by-step interpretation, at least in Italy, is a widespread misconception shared at preprimary and primary levels by most teachers, who transpose it in a normative sequential approach to the teaching–learning of spatial competence.

References

Arzarello, F., & Robutti, O. (2008). Framing the embodied mind approach within a multimodal paradigm. In L. English (Ed.), *Handbook of international research in mathematics education* (2nd ed., pp. 720–749). New York: Routledge.

Bartolini Bussi, M. G. (1992). *Lo spazio, l'ordine, la misura* [Space, order, measure]. Bergamo, Italy: Juvenilia.

Bartolini Bussi, M. G. (1996). Mathematical discussion and perspective drawing in primary school. *Educational Studies in Mathematics, 31*(1–2), 11–41.

Bartolini Bussi, M. G. (1998a). Joint activity in the mathematics classroom: A Vygotskian analysis. In F. Seeger, J. Voigt, & U. Waschescho (Eds.), *The culture of the mathematics classroom: Analyses and changes* (pp. 13–49). Cambridge, UK: Cambridge University Press.

Bartolini Bussi, M. G. (1998b). Verbal interaction in mathematics classroom: A Vygotskian analysis. In H. Steinbring, M. G. Bartolini Bussi, & A. Sierpinska (Eds.), *Language and communication in the mathematics classroom* (pp. 65–84). Reston, VA: National Council of Teachers of Mathematics.

Bartolini Bussi, M. G. (2007). Semiotic mediation: Fragments from a classroom experiment on the coordination of spatial perspectives. *ZDM: The International Journal of Mathematics Education, 39*, 1–2.

Bartolini Bussi, M. G. (2008). Matematica: I numeri e lo spazio [Mathematics: Numbers and space]. Bergamo, Italy: Junior.

Bartolini Bussi, M. G., & Mariotti, M. A. (2008). Semiotic mediation in the mathematics classroom: Artifacts and signs after a Vygotskian perspective. In L. English (Ed.), *Handbook of international research in mathematics education* (2nd ed., pp. 746–783). New York: Routledge.

Brousseau, G. (1997). *Theory of didactical situations in mathematics*. Dordrecht: Kluwer Academic.

Bruner, J. S. (1966). *Toward a theory of instruction*. New York: Norton.

Edwards, C., Gandini, L., & Forman, G. (1995). *I Cento Linguaggi dei Bambini: L'approccio di Reggio Emilia all'educazione dell'infanzia* [Hundred languages: The Reggio Emilia approach to child education]. Bergamo, Italy: Junior.

Falcade, R. (2006). *Théorie des situations, médiation sémiotique et discussions collectives dans des séquences d'enseignement qui utilisent Cabri-géomètre et qui visent à l'apprentissage des notions de fonction et graphe de fonction* [Theory of situations, semiotic mediation and collective discussions in teaching and learning sequences involving the use Cabri-géomètre and aiming to the construction of function and graph notions]. Doctoral thesis, Université Joseph Fourier de Grenoble e Università, Torino, Italy. Available at *http://tel.archives-ouvertes.fr/docs/00/08/52/02/pdf/these.pdf*

Freeman, N. H. (1980). *Strategies of representation in young children.* London: Academic Press.

Groupe Mathématique du Service de la Recherche Pédagogique. (1983). *Approcher la mathématique à cinq ans.* Geneva: Département de l'instruction publique.

Karmiloff-Smith, A. (1992). *Beyond modularity.* Cambridge, MA: MIT Press.

Lurçat, L. (1986). *Il bambino e lo spazio: Il ruolo del corpo* [The child and the space: The role of the body]. Scandicci. Florence, Italy: La Nuova Italia.

Piaget, J., & Inhelder, B. (1967). *The child's conception of space* (F. J. Langdon & J. L. Lunzer, Trans.). New York: Norton.

Pontecorvo, C., & Pontecorvo, M. (1986). *Psicologia dell'educazione: Conoscere a scuola* [Education psychology: Learning at school]. Bologna, Italy: Eds. Il Mulino.

Rinaldi, C. (2006). *In dialogue with Reggio Emilia: Listening, researching, and learning.* London: Routledge.

Stetsenko, A. (1995). The psychological function of children's drawing: A Vygotskian perspective. In G. Thomas & C. Lange-Kuttener (Eds.), *Looking and drawing: Theoretical perspectives* (pp. 147–158). London: Simon & Schuster.

Vygotsky, L. S. (1978). *Mind in society: The development of higher psychological processes.* Cambridge, MA: Harvard University Press. (Original work published 1931)

Vygotsky, L. S. (1986). *Thought and language* (A. Kozulin, Ed. & Trans.). Cambridge, MA: MIT Press. (Original work published 1934)

Yakimanskaya, I. S. (1991). *The development of spatial thinking in schoolchildren* (R. H. Silverman, Ed. & Trans.). Reston, VA: National Council of Teachers of Mathematics.

CHAPTER 23

Enhancing Mathematical Problem Solving in Primary School Children:

Lessons from Design Experiments

Erik De Corte
Lieven Verschaffel
Fien Depaepe

Although educational research in general, and research on learning and instruction specifically have expanded greatly over the past decades (e.g., National Research Council, 2005), and although investigators often aim to contribute to the improvement of education, complaints about the deep gap between theory and research, on the one hand, and educational practices, on the other, are still commonplace. The urgency of this challenge is underscored by the pressing need to reform education to keep pace with the ongoing rapid developments in today's society (see Berliner, 2006). There is an especially great need for innovation in math and science education. A report of the European Round Table of Industrialists (ERT; 1995) attempted to alert society to "an ever-widening gap between the education that people need for today's complex world and the education they receive" (p. 6). This gap is widening as a consequence of globalization, an exponential explosion of knowledge, and the introduction of multiple new information and communication technologies.

Researchers themselves are well aware of this situation. For instance, in her Presidential Address to the 1994 Annual Meeting of the American Educational Research Association, the late Ann Brown argued: "Enormous advances have been made in this century in our understanding of learning and development. School practices in the main have not changed to reflect these advances" (p. 4). Similarly, Weinert and De Corte (1996) have noted: "Although research and educational practice have changed substantially since the beginning of the twentieth century, the question of how research can actually contribute to the solution of real educational problems continues to be controversial" (p. 43). Glaser, Lieberman, and Anderson (1997) have pointed to the continuing difficulty of translating educational research into practice: "We've had various models of the proper relationship between research and practice. None of the models work very well" (p. 25).

One area of mathematical education that could benefit from the integration of research and practices is problem solving. The National Council of Teachers of Mathematics (1989, 2000) has argued that student acquisition of problem-solving skills, particularly heuristic and metacognitive strategies, is a critical skill that might develop from more rigorous mathematics training. The application of mathematical knowledge to solve problems is an important skill with both practical and intellectual benefits, but it may be a deficit in some children's development. *Problem solving* is "cognitive processing directed at achieving a goal when no solution method is obvious to the problem solver" (Mayer & Wittrock, 2006, p. 287). For instance, the task "How much is 297,297 divided by 13?" is not a problem for most adults; they can routinely find the answer by applying the division algorithm or by using a calculator. However, the following task represents a problem for many adults: "Why are all numbers with the structure abc,abc, like 297,297, divisible by 13?" The claim of the National Council of Teachers of Mathematics about the importance of problem solving, especially heuristic and metacognitive strategies, is supported by research that shows the significance of these skills for enhancing students' mathematical proficiency (e.g., Mayer & Wittrock, 2006; National Research Council, 2001, 2005; Schoenfeld, 1985). For instance, the National Research Council (2001) considers "strategic competence" to be a key component of mathematical proficiency and defines it as "the ability to formulate, represent, and solve mathematical problems" (p. 5). However, at the same time, research demonstrates that these strategic aspects of proficiency are currently lacking in many students' problem-solving activities (De Corte & Verschaffel, 2006; Janssen, De Corte, Verschaffel, Knoors, & Colémont, 2002). Therefore, designing powerful, theory-based learning environments that are realizable, workable, and sustainable in educational practice, represents a real challenge for scholars in the field of mathematics education.

In this chapter we briefly discuss the use of design experiments as a lever for the simultaneous pursuit of theory building and practice innovation. Then, we present two related design experiments whose aim is to enhance the mathematical problem-solving proficiency in upper primary school students, especially their strategic competence. In the next section, the critical issue of the broader dissemination and upscaling of innovative learning environments is addressed. We end the chapter with some comments.

Design Experiments: A Lever for the Joint Pursuit of Theory Building and Practice Innovation

Design experiments in educational settings represent a promising approach to forging a stronger relation between theory and practice. A robust design theory should guide the implementation of educational innovations by identifying the variables influencing their success or failure. Accordingly, design experiments have two goals: to advance theory building about learning from instruction and its effects, and at the same time to innovate and to improve classroom practices. Because they are motivated by a desire to improve practice, design experiments are correctly classified in Stokes's (1997) quadrant model of scientific inquiry in Pasteur's quadrant representing use-inspired basic research (Phillips & Dolle, 2006). According to Collins (1992), the mandate of design experiments is to "determine how different designs of learning environments contribute to learning, cooperation, motivation, etc." (p. 15).

Although use of the term "design experiment" is relatively new, this intervention approach to research on learning and instruction is not at all new. This kind of inquiry has been typical in Russian educational psychology for quite a while. In the United States as early as 1976, Glaser made a plea to conceive of instructional psychology as a science of design that aims at the development of more efficient educational programs and teaching methods. Kalmykova (1966) distinguished between "ascertaining" and "teaching" experiments. Whereas ascertaining experiments mainly describe how learning occurs under given conditions of instruction, teaching experiments are characterized by an intervention of the researcher. In this approach, a teaching–learning environment is designed and implemented based on notions of what the optimal course of a learning process should be. In a continuous recursive cycle of analysis and theory reformulation, examination of learning activities and student outcomes either support the initial notions or are used to revise them. Thus, design experiments design, implement, and evaluate novel and powerful learning environments (Brown, 1992; Collins, 1992; Phillips & Dolle, 2006).

A major reason that this kind of research has at the time fallen into disuse is the dominance of cognitive psychology in the United States in the late 1970s and the 1980s. Indeed, in the early days of cognitive instructional psychology, the focus of research was on the knowledge structures and the processes underlying human competence. As a consequence, study of the learning environments and processes necessary to acquire competence was pushed to the background (Glaser & Bassok, 1989). The situation has gradually changed. Substantial progress in our understanding of the knowledge structures, the skills, and the processes underlying expert performance has contributed to a reemergence of interest in the processes required to acquire such competence and, consequently, in the instructional arrangements that can support and facilitate acquisition. The initiation of design experiments in the early 1990s in the United States was in line with this renewed interest (see also Phillips & Dolle, 2006). However, strong pleas in favor of design-based research rose also in Europe at that time, especially from scholars studying mathematics education. For instance, the so-called "developmental research projects" of the Dutch Freudenthal Institute in Utrecht, The Netherlands (see, e.g., Gravemeijer, 1994), and of the Dortmund Institute for Mathematics Education in Germany (see, e.g., Wittmann, 1995) are typical examples of this approach.

But, the important question that now has to be answered is: How and under what conditions should design experiments be carried out if they are to build theory and improve educational practices? In this respect the design of powerful learning environments should take into account our present understanding of learning as a constructive, cumulative, self-regulated, goal-oriented, situated and collaborative, and individually different process of knowledge building and meaning construction. However, to have a reasonable chance of success in making psychological theory applicable to education, it is necessary to develop a strategy for conducting design experiments that are holistic, collaborative, and transformative (De Corte, 2000; see also National Research Council, 2000):

- To be "holistic" means that it incorporates not only relevant learner and teacher variables but also important aspects of the social and physical environment.
- To be "collaborative" means that it relies on two-way communication with practitioners and translates the goals, approaches, and outcomes of research in a format that becomes accessible, palatable, and useful to teachers.
- To be "transformative" means that it induces a fundamental change of teachers' belief systems and value orientations with respect to the goals of education, good teaching, and productive learning (in line with the conception described above).

To simultaneously pursue theory building and practice innovation successfully, design experiments must incorporate an understanding of effective learning processes and high-powered learning environments. Reflecting that understanding, design experiments must create complex instructional interventions and evaluate them in real classrooms. Such attempts at fundamentally changing the classroom environment and culture cannot be undertaken without a partnership between researchers and educational professionals. This partnership is essential not only to promote mutual and felicitous relationships but also to modify and reshape teachers' beliefs about education, learning, and teaching. Finally, if the innovations resulting from design experiments are to be disseminated widely, then their implementation should be feasible in existing classrooms. Therefore, the idea of a partnership between researchers and practitioners is also crucial to achieve a cross-fertilization of ideas between research and practice. Whereas practitioners can help in translating theory into practice, thus making classroom teaching more research-based, their partner role can also contribute to more practice-driven research (De Corte, 2000).

In the next section we review two related studies carried out in the Leuven Center for Instructional Psychology and Technology (CIP&T), whose aim was to promote upper primary school students' proficiency in mathematical word problem solving. In the first intervention study, researchers designed and evaluated an innovative, constructivist, and collaborative learning environment that focused on the development of a mindful, strategic, and self-regulated approach toward mathematical problem solving. In the second study, this learning environment was technologically enriched by embedding in it Knowledge Forum, a software tool designed to facilitate and foster a research team approach to learning that supports collaborative inquiry and knowledge building.

Study 1: Designing a High-Powered Learning Community for Mathematical Problem Solving

In the Flemish part of Belgium, new standards for primary education were instituted in the 1998–1999 school year (Ministerie van de Vlaamse Gemeenschap, 1997). With respect to mathematics—and in line with other recent reform documents, such as the *Curriculum and Evaluation Standards for School Mathematics* (National Council of Teachers of Mathematics, 1989) in the United States—these new standards place increased emphasis on mathematical reasoning and problem-solving skills, their applicability to real-life situations, and the development of more positive attitudes toward mathematics. To help implement those new standards we designed a powerful learning environment and evaluated the extent to which it promoted competence in mathematical problem solving and elicited positive mathematics-related beliefs in upper primary school children.

In line with the strategy we described in the previous section, the learning environment in the classroom was fundamentally changed, and its design, implementation, and evaluation involved the cooperation of the teachers of four participating experimental classrooms and their principals. The learning environment comprised a series of 20 lessons, taught by the regular fifth-grade classroom teachers (for a more detailed report about study design and measures, see Verschaffel et al., 1999; see also De Corte & Verschaffel, 2006).

This design experiment focused on fundamentally changing the following components of the math learning environment: the content of learning and teaching, the nature of the problems, the instructional techniques, and the classroom culture.

First, in terms of content, the students were taught a general metacognitive strategy for solving real-life problems mathematically. This metacognitive strategy comprises five steps: building a mental representation of the problem, deciding how to solve the problem, making the necessary calculations, interpreting the outcome, and evaluating the solution. Embedded within the first two steps are heuristic strategies that specify alternative ways for the students to carry out those steps (see Table 23.1). To acquire and implement this problem-solving strategy successfully students must (1) become aware of the different phases of a competent problem-solving process (awareness training); (2) monitor and evaluate their actions during the different phases of the solution process (self-regulation training); and (3) master the eight heuristic strategies (heuristic strategy training).

Second, a key pillar of the learning environments was the development of a varied set of carefully designed and open problems; by "open problems" we mean that they can be conceived, approached, and/or solved in different ways. These problems differ substantially from traditional textbook tasks. For instance, they are presented in different

---

TABLE 23.1. The Competent Problem-Solving Model Underlying the Learning Environment

Step 1: Build a mental representation of the problem.
  Heuristics: Draw a picture.

Make a list, a scheme, or a table.

Distinguish relevant from irrelevant data.

Use your real-world knowledge.

Step 2: Decide how to solve the problem.
  Heuristics: Make a flowchart.

Guess and check.

Look for a pattern.

Simplify the numbers.

Step 3: Perform the necessary calculations.

Step 4: Interpret the outcome and formulate an answer.

Step 5: Evaluate the solution.

formats: a text, a newspaper article, a brochure, a comic strip, a table, or a combination of several of these formats. The following example illustrates the kinds of tasks used in the learning environment.

School Trip Problem[1]

The teacher told the children about a plan for a school trip to visit the Efteling, a well-known amusement park in The Netherlands. But if that turned out to be too expensive, another amusement park might be an alternative.

Each group of four pupils received copies of folders with entrance prices for the different parks. The lists mentioned distinct prices depending on the period of the year, the age of the visitors, and the kind of party (individuals, families, groups).

In addition, each group received a copy of a fax from a local bus company, addressed to the principal of the school, that gave information about the prices for buses of different sizes (with a driver) for a one-day trip to the Efteling.

The first task of the groups was to determine whether it was possible to make the school trip to the Efteling given that the maximum price per child was limited to Euro 12.50.

After finding out that this was not possible, the groups' second task was to find out which of the other parks they could visit for the maximum amount of Euro 12.50 per child.

The third task was to create a learning community through application of a varied set of activating and interactive instructional techniques. The basic instructional model for each lesson period comprised the following sequence of classroom activities: (1) a short, whole-class introduction in which the teacher explained the objective of the lesson and introduced the problems to be solved; (2) two group assignments solved in fixed heterogeneous groups (three to four pupils), both of which were followed by a whole-class discussion; (3) an individual task, also with a subsequent whole-class discussion. The working groups were heterogeneous in terms of general mathematics achievement. The whole-class discussion focused on articulating and discussing the problem-solving strategies of the different groups and the individual students. Due to the intensity of these discussions on the solution processes and the problem-solving strategies, only a couple of problems, and sometimes only one problem, were treated. Throughout the whole lesson the teacher's role was to encourage and to scaffold pupils to engage in and reflect on the kinds of cognitive and metacognitive activities involved in the model of skilled problem solving. These instructional supports were gradually faded out as pupils became more competent and aware of their problem-solving activity, thus taking more responsibility for their own learning and problem-solving processes.

The fourth task was to create an innovative classroom culture through the establishment of new social and sociomathematical norms (Yackel & Cobb, 1996) about learning and teaching problem solving, aimed at fostering positive mathematics-related attitudes and beliefs in not only the children but also the teachers. Typical aspects of this classroom culture included (1) stimulating pupils to articulate and reflect on their solution strategies, (mis-)conceptions, beliefs, and feelings relating to mathematical problem solving; (2) discussing what counts as a good problem, a good response, and a good solution procedure (e.g., there are often different ways to solve a problem; for some problems a rough estimate is a better answer than an exact number); (3) reconsidering the role of the teacher and the pupils in the mathematics classroom (e.g., the class as a whole deciding which of the generated solutions is optimal after an evaluation of the pros and cons of the different alternatives).

In line with the standpoint taken above, this learning environment was developed in partnership with the four teachers of the participating experimental classes and their principals. The teachers were involved at each phase in the research process, from pre-intervention planning to postintervention evaluation, and meetings were held to encourage reflection and input by all members of the research team, the teachers, and their principals. The adopted model of teacher development emphasized the creation of a social context wherein teachers and researchers learn from each other through continuous discussion and reflection on the basic principles of the learning environment, the learning materials developed, and the teachers' practices during the lessons. This has resulted, for example, in a set of 10 general guidelines for the teachers, comprising specific actions they should take and ways they should be involved with students before, during, and after the individual and group assignments to strengthen the power of the learning environment (see Table 23.2). In the teachers' guide, each of these 10 guidelines was accompanied by an explanation of its purpose, as well as several worked-out examples of its implementation. For instance, the following support was given with respect to implementation of the guideline *Avoid imposing solutions and solution methods onto pupils*:

> In traditional classroom practice it is mostly the case that the teacher decides which is the correct (or the best) response and the right (or the most appropriate) solution method. In our learning environment these decisions should be the outcome of discussion and deliberation with the students. As a result of the discussions, the students should themselves come to the conclusion that one solution is better than another, and that a certain solution strategy or method is more efficient, more elegant than others. In these discussions, you, as a teacher,

TABLE 23.2. General Guidelines for the Teachers before, during, and after the Group and Individual Assignments

Before

1. Scaffold new information onto the old. Relate the new aspect (heuristic, problem-solving step, etc.) to what has already been learned before.
2. Provide a thorough orientation to the new task.

During

3. Observe the group work and provide appropriate hints when needed.
4. Stimulate student articulation and reflection.
5. Stimulate the active thinking and cooperation of all group members (especially the weaker ones).

After

6. Demonstrate the existence of different appropriate solutions and solution methods for the same problem.
7. Avoid imposing solutions or solution methods onto pupils.
8. Pay attention to the intended heuristics and metacognitive skills of the competent problem-solving model, and use this model as a basis for the discussion.
9. Encourage as many students as possible to participate in the whole-class discussion.
10. Address (positive as well as negative) aspects of the group dynamics.

play a crucial role. First of all, you act as discussion leader, making sure that the discussion takes place in an orderly way; furthermore, you guide the discussion in the right direction with regard to its content. But you take into account that your students may need some time to adjust to this new classroom norm.

In view of contributing to theory building, the effects of the learning environment on students were evaluated by researchers in an experiment with a pretest–posttest–retention test design for an experimental group and a comparable control group, thereby using a wide variety of data-gathering and analysis techniques. To assess the fidelity of implementation of the learning environment by the teachers of the experimental classes, a sample of four representative lessons was videotaped in each class and analyzed afterward in terms of an implementation profile. The results of the study can be summarized as follows.

According to the experimental group scores on a self-made, written word problem pretest and a parallel posttest and retention test, the intervention had—in comparison with the control group—a significant and stable positive effect on experimental students' skills in solving mathematical application problems (see Figure 23.1).

The learning environment also had a significant, albeit small, positive impact on students' pleasure and persistence in solving mathematics problems, and on their mathematics-related beliefs and attitudes, as measured by a self-report questionnaire employing Likert-type scale items. The results on a standard achievement test showed that the extra attention during the mathematics lessons for cognitive and metacognitive strategies, beliefs, and attitudes in the experimental classes had a significant positive transfer effect on the learning outcomes for other, more traditional parts of the mathematics curriculum. Indeed, the experimental classes performed significantly better than the control classes on this standard achievement test. Analysis of students' written notes on their response sheets of the word problem test showed that the better results of the experimental group were paralleled by a very substantial increase in spontaneous use

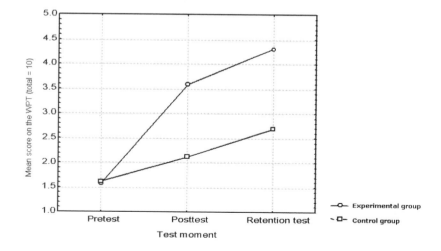

FIGURE 23.1. Mean scores of the experimental and the control group on the three versions of the word problem test (pretest, posttest, and retention test).

of the heuristic strategies taught in the learning environment (see Figure 23.2). This finding was confirmed by a qualitative analysis of videotapes of the problem-solving processes of three groups of two children from each experimental class, before and after the intervention.

Finally, as shown in Figure 23.3, we found that not only high- and medium-ability students but also low-ability students benefited significantly—albeit to a smaller degree—from the intervention in all aspects just mentioned.

In terms of theoretical perspective, these results show that a substantially modified learning environment, combining a set of carefully designed word problems with highly interactive teaching methods and the introduction of new sociomathematical classroom norms, can lead to the creation of high-powered learning communities that significantly boost pupils' cognitive and metacognitive competency in solving mathematical word problems.

From the perspective of contributing to the innovation of classroom practice, it is first of all important to report—based on the analysis of the videotaped lessons in each class—that all four experimental teachers implemented the learning environment in a satisfactory way, although clear differences were observed among them on the distinct components of an implementation profile. In addition, the following conclusions, derived from an extensive interview with the four experimental teachers after the intervention, but before they knew their children's results, are promising: First, they considered the five-step competent problem-solving strategy as appropriate and attainable for fifth-graders. Second, they evaluated the content and the organization of the learning environment very positively, and were greatly satisfied with the support and help during the implementation of the intervention. Finally, they were very enthusiastic about their active involvement and participation in the project. That this was more than just a momentary feeling is demonstrated by the fact that three of the teachers were imme-

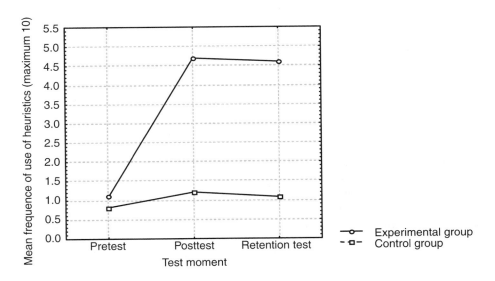

FIGURE 23.2. Mean frequency of the use of heuristics in the experimental and the control group on the three versions of the word problem test (pretest, posttest, and retention test).

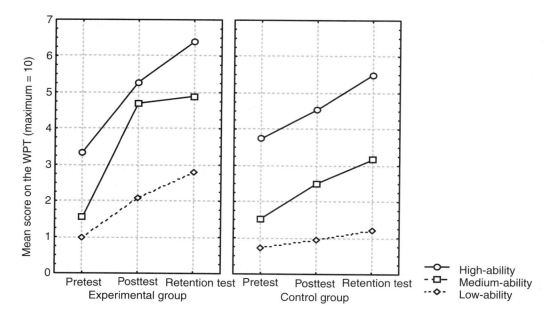

FIGURE 23.3. Mean scores of the high-, medium-, and low-ability students of the experimental and the control group on the three versions of the word problem test (pretest, posttest, and retention test).

diately willing to participate in a subsequent similar, and again very demanding, design experiment, and that fellow fifth-grade teachers at their respective schools continue to apply the basic principles of the learning environment in their mathematics teaching. Subsequent to the first design experiment, the lesson materials have been revised and transformed into a format that makes them appropriate for use in classroom practice and in teacher training. Moreover, the reform-based ideas underlying the learning environment we just described have led to a new generation of textbooks for mathematics education in Flanders (as we illustrate later on).

Study 2: Networking Minds in a High-Powered Mathematics Learning Community

The results of the previous study encouraged us to combine in a second investigation the theoretical ideas and principles relating to socioconstructivist mathematics learning and teachers' professional development with a second strand of theory and research focused on the (meta-)cognitive aspects of computer-supported collaborative knowledge construction and skills building. Taking into account available empirical evidence showing that computer-supported collaborative learning (CSCL) is a promising tool for the improvement of learning and instruction (Lehtinen, Hakkarainen, Lipponen, Rahikainen, & Muukkonen, 2001; see also Lehtinen, 2003), we assumed that the learning environment in the previous study could be made more powerful by enriching it with a CSCL component, namely, Knowledge Forum.

This study was part of the more comprehensive CL-Net (Computer-Supported Collaborative Learning Networks in Primary and Secondary Education) project funded by the European Union. The overall aim of the CL-Net project was to examine how knowledge construction and skills building can be fostered by immersing primary and secondary school pupils in computer-supported collaborative learning networks (CLNs) under the guidance of a teacher. CLNs can be characterized as powerful learning environments in which technology-based cognitive tools are embedded as means and resources that in a community of networked learners can elicit and mediate active and progressively more self-regulated processes of collaborative knowledge acquisition, meaning construction, and problem solving. The project combined the relevant expertise available in eight research centers spread over five European countries. The shared expertise related to aspects such as software development, teacher preparation for the implementation of CLNs, design principles for technology-supported powerful learning environments, and the construction of assessment instruments.

Within this broader framework of the CL-Net project, our aim in the present investigation was to design, implement, and evaluate a CSCL environment that facilitates the distributed learning of solving and posing complex mathematical application problems in upper primary school students. As in the previous study, the learning environment focused on students' acquisition of the same five-step metacognitive strategy and the embedded heuristics for solving problems, as well as on affecting positively their beliefs and attitudes toward mathematical problem solving. In addition, the CSCL environment aimed to foster students' communication and collaboration skills relating to problem solving and problem posing on the one hand, and computer skills on the other, especially proficiency in working, learning, and communicating with CSCL software. The basic hypothesis of this investigation was that technological enrichment of the learning environment from the preceding intervention study by embedding in it the CLN cognitive technological tools would lead to a significant improvement in the quality of upper primary school students' problem-solving and communication processes and skills, and, in doing so, would result in greater learning effects. In addition, we intended the study to explore and elaborate an effective strategy to guide and support teachers in the embedded appropriate use of cognitive technological tools in their teaching of mathematical problem solving (for a more detailed report of the study, see Verschaffel, De Corte, Lowyck, Dhert, & Vandeput, 2000).

We used the same basic design principles as in Study 1 in developing the CSCL environment:

- A focus on students' acquisition of the five-stage metacognitive strategy for solving mathematical application problems.
- Use of a varied set of (nontraditional) complex, realistic, and challenging word problems that elicit and enhance the application of heuristic and metacognitive strategies (an example is given in Figure 23.4).
- Application of highly interactive and collaborative instructional techniques (i.e., small-group activities followed by whole-class discussion).
- Creation of a fundamentally changed classroom culture based on new social and sociomathematical norms established through negotiation in the community of learners in the class.

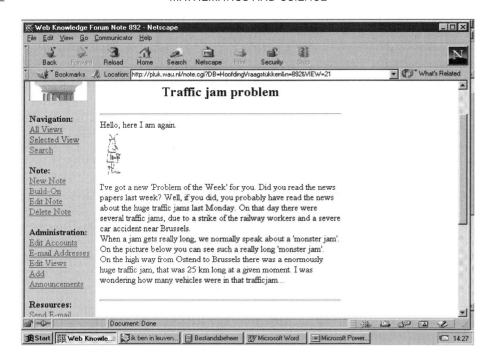

FIGURE 23.4. The traffic jam problem presented by FIXIT in KF.

However, this environment was enriched by embedding in it Knowledge Forum (KF), a software tool—like its predecessor CSILE (Computer-Supported Intentional Learning Environment, Scardamalia & Bereiter, 1992)—designed to foster a networked research team approach to learning that supports knowledge building, collaboration, and progressive inquiry. Key features in KF include a series of cognitive tools for constructing and storing notes, for sharing notes and exchanging comments on them, and for scaffolding students in their acquisition of specific cognitive operations and particular concepts (Scardamalia & Bereiter, 1998). Although in most other studies the communication through KF is entirely open and unstructured, students' use of KF in our CSCL environment was initially quite restricted and teacher-regulated. More intensive and self-regulated involvement with KF increased gradually as pupils became more familiar with the software and the expert five-step model of solving mathematical application problems.

For the teachers, introduction of the CLN approach amounted to the adoption and implementation of a fundamentally new role and pedagogy based on a technology-supported, collaborative and self-regulated perspective on learning. Taking into account that many interventions that attempt to drastically shift teachers' instructional behavior, beliefs, and attitudes run into difficulties (see e.g., Huberman, 1993; van den Berg, 2002), substantial attention was paid to cooperation with the teachers, and their guidance and support. Another important consideration was ensuring that the researchers and teachers collaborated throughout the process (De Corte, 2000); therefore, the preparation of the teaching materials (including all instructional interventions by a comic strip character called FIXIT, who permanently interacted with the students via KF, as illustrated below) was done by the researchers in consultation with the teachers. However, the lessons were taught by the regular classroom teachers, who also were responsible for coaching the students during small-group activities and for the leadership of the whole-class discussion. In that perspective, a substantial part of teacher preparation took place in training sessions that involved the researchers and teachers, with each group taking turns acting as teacher and student in simulating the new computer-supported approach.

The designed learning environment was implemented in two fifth-grade and two sixth-grade classes of a Flemish primary school over a period of 5 months. A computer was available in each classroom; in addition, teachers and students had access to a classroom with a large number of computers, all networked to a common server. Each of the participating classes spent about 2 hours a week in the learning environment over a period of 17 weeks. The series of lessons can be divided into five phases.

- *Phase 1 (2 weeks)*: Introduction by the teacher and exploration by the students of the same five-step problem-solving strategy developed and used in the previous study, and the KF software tool.
- *Phase 2 (3 weeks)*: In the beginning of each week, the students in groups of three solved a problem presented in KF by the comic strip character FIXIT; an example of a problem was given in Figure 23.4. Initially they could use scaffolds provided by FIXIT in the form of KF notes with strategic help for solving the problem in a mindful way (see Figure 23.5 for the first screen page of the help note relating to the Traffic Jam Problem shown in Figure 23.4). Taking turns, the students imported not only their solution but also their solution strategy in KF, on which FIXIT then commented in KF before the second lesson at the end of the week (for an illustration see, respectively, Figures 23.6 and 23.7). During that lesson a whole-class discussion was organized around the solution and solution strategies of the different groups, and the role and use of KF in problem solving, taking into account FIXIT's comments.
- *Phase 3 (6 weeks)*: Students continued to work on complex application problems (2 weeks per problem) presented by FIXIT through KF. However, in this phase, the scaffolds and comments by FIXIT were gradually withdrawn as the students made progress, and they were encouraged to read the work of the other groups and to comment on it in KF before the whole-class discussion at the end of the second week.
- *Phase 4 (4 weeks)*: In the beginning of each of two 2-week periods the group members themselves had to pose an interesting mathematics application problem they imported in KF. As usual, this problem-posing task was introduced by means of a KF note from FIXIT, who also made a help note for groups that experienced great difficulty with the problem-posing task. Because students had little or no experience with posing problems themselves, and also because the instructional time was restricted, each class was given as a starting point for posing a problem, a folder with copies of photographs and short articles from recent newspapers or other popular publications (e.g., the well-known *The Guinness Book of Records*), all dealing with remarkable quantities or measurements. Furthermore, the groups had to solve at least one problem posed by another group. Each group acted as coach for the other groups with respect to the group members' own problem. The products of that work (problems posed, solutions given by the groups, and possible comments, all imported in KF) were again the object of whole-class discussion and reflection at the end of the 2-week period.

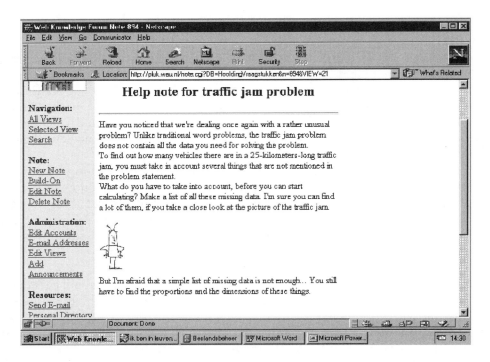

FIGURE 23.5. First screen page of FIXIT's help note relating to the traffic jam problem.

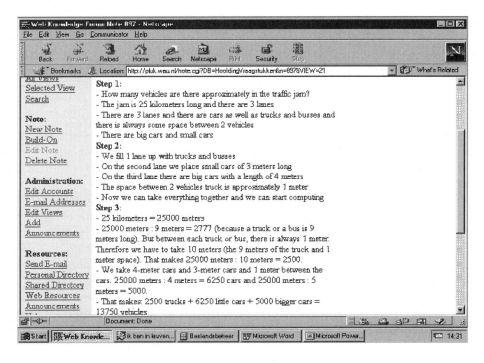

FIGURE 23.6. First screen page of the answer of one group of students to the traffic jam problem (relating to Step 1 [Build a mental representation of the problem], Step 2 [Decide how to solve the problem], and Step 3 [Execute the necessary calculations] of the five-stage strategy for solving problems).

534

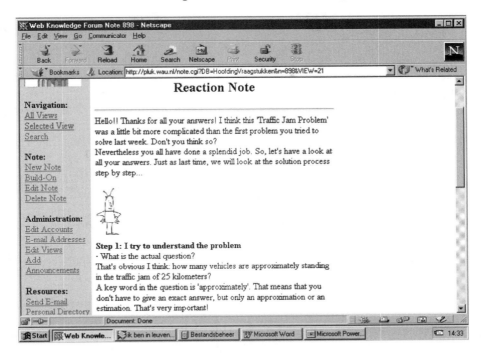

FIGURE 23.7. First screen page of FIXIT's comment to the students' solutions of the traffic jam problem (relating to Step 1 of the solution process).

- *Phase 5 (2 weeks)*: All four participating classes got involved in an international, 2-week exchange project with students from an elementary school in Amsterdam, The Netherlands, during which pairs of Flemish and Dutch children exchanged problems and problem solutions in a manner similar to that in Phase 4.

A pre–posttest quasi-experimental design was used to evaluate the cognitive, metacognitive, and affective effects of the learning environment on the participating students, using a variety of instruments: a word problem test, several questionnaires, logfiles analysis, classroom observations using video registration, and interviews with students and teachers. In addition to these quantitative measures, qualitative data about the implementation of the learning environment, and about the changes in students' and teachers' mathematical thinking and communication processes were gathered. The findings derived from the analysis of all these data can be summarized as follows.

The cognitive, metacognitive, and affective effects of the CLN environment on the students were mixed. According to the results of the word problem pretest and posttest, the learning environment had a significant positive effect on the problem-solving competency of the sixth-graders but not the fifth-graders. Contrary to what was observed in the previous technology-lean study (Verschaffel et al., 1999), questionnaire data revealed no significant positive impact of the intervention on children's pleasure and persistence in solving mathematical application problems, or on their beliefs and attitudes toward learning and teaching mathematical problem solving. However, the CLN environment yielded a significant positive influence on students' beliefs and attitudes toward (collaborative) learning in general. Finally, a significant effect of the intervention was students' beliefs and attitudes toward computers in general and computer-supported learning in particular.

The study has shown that it is possible to create a computer-supported learning community for teaching and learning mathematical problem solving in the upper primary grades. From the data of the teacher evaluation forms administered throughout the intervention, and the answers during the final interviews, we concluded that the teachers were very enthusiastic about their participation and involvement in the investigation. Their positive evaluation of the learning environment related to both the approach to teaching problem solving and the use of KF as a supporting tool for learning; for instance, they observed several positive developments in their students, such as a more mindful and reflective approach to word problems. Furthermore, the implementation profiles, based on the analyses of videotaped lessons of the two sixth-grade teachers, indicated a high degree of fidelity in implementation of the learning environment. Finally, the CLN environment was also enthusiastically received by most of the students. Throughout the lessons, and in reaction to FIXIT's farewell note at the end of the intervention, students expressed that they liked this way of doing word problems much more than the traditional approach. Many of the children also reported that they had learned something new about both information technology and mathematical problem solving.

The two design experiments presented in this and the previous section were carried out with a twofold goal: to advance theory building about learning higher-order cognitive and metacognitive skills for mathematics problem solving from instruction on the one hand, and to contribute to innovation and improvement of educational practices in line with a new conception of the goals of mathematics education on the other. With respect to the first goal, the results of the two intervention studies support the hypothesis that our present understanding of productive learning as an active, constructive, collaborative, and progressively more self-regulated process can guide the design of not only novel but also practical, applicable learning environments that effectively boost students' competency in an important domain such as mathematical problem solving. We obtained similar findings in an investigation in which we designed a powerful learning environment for strategic reading comprehension in fifth-graders (De Corte, Verschaffel, & Van de Ven, 2001). But, how about the potential of those studies to change mathematics learning and teaching?

Implementing and Upscaling New Learning Environments: A Major Challenge

The outcomes of the two design experiments are very promising from the perspective of innovating educational practice. Indeed, as we reported earlier, participating teachers were very positive about the new approach to teaching and learning mathematical problem solving; moreover, they succeeded in implementing this new approach with a high degree of fidelity. Furthermore, the students in the experimental classrooms were enthusiastic about this novel learning environment. However, the significance of these intervention studies for the innovation and improvement of classroom practices should not be overstated. In this regard, it is interesting and useful to consider our two studies from the perspective of the interplay between theories of learning and educational practice put forward by the Cognition and Technology Group at Vanderbilt (1996).

More specifically, the Group has elaborated an interesting framework for looking at the research on educational technology in the context of learning theory and educational practice (see Figure 23.8). Their LTC (Looking at Technology in Context) framework comprises two dimensions: (1) research contexts ranging from *in vitro* laboratory settings over individual classrooms to connected sets of classrooms and schools; and (2) theoretical contexts ranging from the transmission model of learning over constructivist models applied during a part of the school day to constructivist approaches used during all of schooling.

The challenge not only for educational technology research but also for research on learning and instruction in general is to move toward the second and even third rows of the LTC framework. The interventions designed and implemented in the studies presented previously fit in Cell 5 of the LTC framework, which refers to innovative, constructivist-oriented learning environments that relate to only a part of schooling. This is still a long way from covering the whole (mathematics) curriculum in line with the approach underlying the basic principles of the intended powerful learning environments.

Moreover, we should realize that an effective implementation of learning environments like the ones developed in our design experiments is not an easy task. This is, for instance, illustrated by a recent video-based study in which we analyzed the teaching of mathematical problem solving in 10 Flemish sixth-grade classrooms (Depaepe, De Corte, & Verschaffel, 2007). As we mentioned earlier, over the past years, the reform-based ideas reflected in our design experiments have already been integrated into some new textbook series for primary mathematics education. A major example of such a

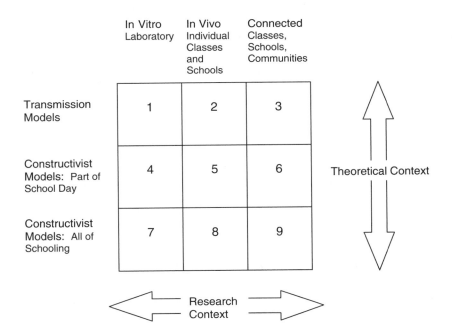

FIGURE 23.8. LTC (Looking at Technology in Context) framework. From Cognition and Technology Group at Vanderbilt (1996, p. 809). Adapted by permission of the author.

reformed textbook is *Eurobasis 6* (Boone, D'haveloose, Muylle, & Van Maele, n.d.). This textbook, which is now widely used as a basis for mathematics teaching in Flanders, attempts explicitly to integrate the four pillars of the design experiment of Study 1 (Verschaffel et al., 1999) discussed earlier: the content of learning and teaching, the nature of the mathematics problems, the instructional techniques, and the classroom culture.

First, with respect to content, the textbook authors adopted the acquisition by students of the five-stage metacognitive strategy for solving mathematical application problems (see Table 23.1) and a number of heuristics embedded in it as a main objective of mathematics education in general and of learning to solve problems in particular. In the teacher's manual that accompanies the textbook, the five-stage strategy is mentioned, together with a series of important heuristics to which teachers should pay attention, such as distinguishing relevant from irrelevant data; rewording the problem; contextualizing the problem; drawing a picture; making a scheme/table; guessing and checking; evaluating the solution; and interpreting the outcome. In addition, throughout the textbook, references are made to the strategy and the heuristics, for instance, by means of symbols, such as *S* for making a scheme. Second, the introductory part of the textbook explicitly states that students' involvement in mathematics learning can be fostered by adapting the problems and contexts to their experiential world by using appropriate materials; it also claims to provide realistic problems. Third, the authors argue that teachers play an important role in implementing the textbook materials. In both the general introduction of the textbook and in the guidelines of particular lessons they recommend and promote the application of powerful instructional techniques (e.g., coaching students, articulating and reflecting on solution strategies and procedures), as well as the use of activating and interactive classroom organization forms, such as partner and group work. Fourth, relating to the establishment of a new classroom culture in view of fostering the development of positive mathematics-related beliefs in students, the authors argue that it is important to let students experience success, to balance between attention to the solution process of a problem and to the solution itself, and to discuss meaningful alternatives to solve a problem. In addition, the authors acknowledge that children differ not only with regard to their knowledge (e.g., whether they know what *tare* means) and their skills (e.g., whether they are able to distinguish relevant from irrelevant data) but also with respect to their attitudes (e.g., their persistence while solving mathematical application problems). Being able to solve a mathematical problem is dependent on students' competencies on all three aspects. We investigated (Depaepe et al., 2007) whether teachers using the textbook *Eurobasis 6* succeeded in establishing classroom practices that reflect appropriately these pillars of Verschaffel and colleagues' (1999) design experiment. Therefore, we videotaped the same two problem-solving lesson periods (of about 60 minutes) in 10 sixth-grade classrooms.

An in-depth analysis of these videotaped lessons revealed that regarding the first pillar of the learning environment (i.e., the content of mathematical learning and teaching) some heuristics were frequently addressed, such as distinguishing relevant from irrelevant data (17) and making a scheme or a table (16).[2] To the contrary, teachers (almost) never referred to other heuristics, for instance, to guess and check (0.5). Overall, we observed that the participating teachers demonstrated a fair tendency to address a variety of heuristic skills, but these skills were hardly integrated in the five-stage metacognitive strategy for mathematical problem solving (represented in Table 23.1). Moreover, substantial differences between the teachers were observed; for instance, whereas some teachers did not even mention the successive phases of this metacognitive strategy, another teacher explicitly referred to it 11 times over the two lessons.

With regard to the realistic nature of the problems used during the two lessons, we found that almost all of them referred to contexts that fit into students' experiential worlds (95.2%). However, this does not imply that all teachers explicitly used and handled these tasks as examples of reality. For instance, while solving the same problem (i.e., measuring the length of a car presented in the textbook and calculating its real length by using the scale), students in two classrooms made the same remark: "6.6 m is very long." One teacher stimulated his students to interpret that outcome ("Indeed that is not a small one; that is right. But you can see it on the picture, it is a monovolume, a family car"). To the contrary, the other teacher prevented his students from interpreting the outcome and, consequently, also from making realistic considerations ("Stop it! All your comments are not relevant here"). Obviously these different ways in which teachers treat the problems may have an impact on students' engagement and interest in solving mathematical problems.

As far as the third pillar of the learning environment in the design experiment of Verschaffel and colleagues (1999) is concerned, we observed that the teachers succeeded in applying a variety of powerful instructional techniques. We used the teaching methods distinguished in the cognitive apprenticeship model (Collins, Brown, & Newman, 1989) as coding categories. However, we split coaching into two subcategories and added to the list the technique of praising, which relates to the motivational side of learning. This resulted in the following coding categories: modeling, nondirective coaching, directive coaching, scaffolding, articulation, reflection, exploration, and praising. With respect to classroom organization we distinguished between whole-class instruction, group work, individual work, and a combined organizational form. Notable was the importance given by the teacher to articulation of (42) and reflection on solution strategies and processes (13.8); these two activities certainly foster students' problem-solving competency. To the contrary, exploring (2.9), modeling (1.7), and scaffolding (0.8) were rarely observed. Again, we noticed substantial differences between teachers' use of these instructional techniques. With regard to classroom organization forms, the textbook *Eurobasis 6* argues, in line with the research literature (see e.g., Good, Mulryan, & McCaslin, 1992), that group work has to play a central role in problem-solving instruction. However, we found that only three of the 10 participating teachers used group work frequently during the two problem-solving lessons.

Finally, the 10 participating teachers paid little or no attention to the deliberate establishment of an innovative classroom culture by explicitly addressing and negotiating classroom norms in view of promoting the development in students of positive mathematics-related beliefs. In our analysis of the video material, we looked for instances wherein teachers referred to the following classroom norms: Solving problems is agreeable; students are competent to solve (unfamiliar) problems; other, and more controllable factors than gift and luck, such as effort, play an important role in solving problems; solving problems is also time-consuming for smarter students; it is worthwhile when students solve a problem themselves; a problem can be solved in different ways and/or may have different solutions; it is worthwhile to listen to the ways that other students solved a problem; it is worthwhile when students articulate how they solved a problem; mathematics, as well as the things that are learned in mathematics lessons, are worthwhile, useful, and/or play an important role in everyday life; and one can always learn from errors. Only to a very small extent did some teachers emphasize that a problem may be solved in different ways and/or may have different solutions (e.g., "There is also another solution process possible, but probably a more difficult one"). Most of the other norms were never even articulated by the teachers.

The overall conclusion that derives from this study is that although classroom practices of the participating teachers manifest a moderate positive trend, in line with a reform-based approach to teaching and learning mathematical problem solving, the findings obviously show that introducing reform-based textbooks does not easily and automatically result in a high-fidelity implementation of the innovative ideas. This observation is in line with previous research in which researchers claim that teachers play an active role in the implementation of curricular materials: They interpret—often unconsciously—the new ideas through their existing prior knowledge, beliefs, and experiences (Remillard, 2005; Spillane, Reiser, & Reimer, 2002).

Final Comments

The intervention studies we have presented show that under certain conditions design experiments can result in highly innovative and sustainable mathematics teaching practices in the classrooms of the participating teachers. A first condition is that the reform-based learning environments embedded in the interventions are designed and elaborated in narrow cooperation with the teachers as educational professionals. A second major condition is that those teachers are provided with substantial guidance and support in implementing these learning environments. Under these conditions, design experiments can make a significant and important contribution to bridging the gap between theory and practice in mathematics education. But, as illustrated by the in-depth analysis of classroom practices based on a reform-based textbook, upscaling the novel learning environments presents a major challenge. One obvious reason why broader implementation of the reform-based classroom practices turns out to be problematic is that it puts extremely high demands on the teachers, requiring drastic changes in their roles and their teaching practices. As observed by the Cognition and Technology Group at Vanderbilt (1997), the changes we are asking the teachers to make are "much too complex to be communicated succinctly in a workshop and then enacted in isolation once the teachers returned to their schools" (p. 116). Instead of being the main, if not the only, source of information—as is often still the case in average traditional educational practice—the teacher becomes a privileged member of the knowledge-building community, who creates an intellectually stimulating climate, models learning and problem-solving activities, asks thought-provoking questions, provides support to learners through coaching and guidance, and fosters students' agency and responsibility in their own learning. Disseminating this new perspective on learning and teaching mathematics appropriately and widely in educational practice will require intensive professional development; it will take a long time and much effort in partnership between researchers and professionals. Indeed, it is not just a matter of acquiring a set of new instructional techniques; this new perspective calls for a fundamental and profound change in teachers' beliefs, attitudes, and mentality (van den Berg, 2002). Such an endeavour transcends the field of research on learning and instruction, and constitutes a challenge for collaboration among educational researchers with a variety of areas of expertise; for instance, it is indispensable to take into account the contextual, social, and organizational dimensions of classrooms and schools wherein reforms are induced (Stokes, Sato, McLaughlin, & Talbert, 1997).

Notes

1. The problem is not presented in its original format because it takes a lot of space. Moreover, translating it from Flemish to English is somewhat cumbersome.
2. The numbers in parentheses represent the average frequency that a particular (meta-)cognitive skill was explicitly referred to by the teachers over the two problem-solving lesson periods.

References

Berliner, D. C. (2006). Educational psychology: Searching for essence throughout a century of influence. In P. A. Alexander & P. H. Winne (Eds.), *Handbook of educational psychology: Second edition* (pp. 3–27). Mahwah, NJ: Erlbaum.

Boone, M., D'haveloose, W., Muylle, H., & Van Maele, K. (n.d.). *Eurobasis 6*. Brugge: Die Keure.

Brown, A. L. (1992). Design experiments: Theoretical and methodological challenges in creating complex interventions in classroom settings. *Journal of the Learning Sciences, 2,* 141–178.

Brown, A. L. (1994). The advancement of learning. *Educational Researcher, 28*(8), 4–12.

Cognition and Technology Group at Vanderbilt. (1996). Looking at technology in context: A framework for understanding technology and education research. In D. C. Berliner & R. C. Calfee (Eds.), *Handbook of educational psychology* (pp. 807–840). New York: Macmillan.

Cognition and Technology Group at Vanderbilt. (1997). *The Jasper Project: Lessons in curriculum, instruction, assessment, and professional development.* Mahwah, NJ: Erlbaum.

Collins, A. (1992). Toward a design science of education. In E. Scanlon & T. O'Shea (Eds.), *New directions in educational technology* (NATO-ASI Series F: Computers and Systems Sciences, Vol. 96, pp. 15–22). Berlin: Springer-Verlag.

Collins, A., Brown, J. S., & Newman, S. E. (1989). Cognitive apprenticeship: Teaching the crafts of reading, writing, and mathematics. In L. B. Resnick (Ed.), *Knowing, learning, and instruction: Essays in honor of Robert Glaser* (pp. 453–494). Hillsdale, NJ: Erlbaum.

De Corte, E. (2000). Marrying theory building and the improvement of school practice: A permanent challenge for instructional psychology. *Learning and Instruction, 10,* 249–266.

De Corte, E., & Verschaffel, L. (2006). Mathematical thinking and learning. In K. A. Renninger & I. E. Sigel (Series Eds.), & W. Damon & R. M. Lerner (Editors-in-Chief), *Handbook of child psychology: Vol. 4. Child psychology and practice* (6th ed., pp. 103–152). Hoboken, NJ: Wiley.

De Corte, E., Verschaffel, L., & Van de Ven, A. (2001). Improving text comprehension strategies in upper primary school children: A design experiment. *British Journal of Educational Psychology, 71,* 531–559.

Depaepe, F., De Corte, E., & Verschaffel, L. (2007). Unraveling the culture of the mathematics classroom: A videobased study in sixth grade. *International Journal of Educational Research, 46,* 266–279.

European Round Table of Industrialists (ERT). (1995). *Education for Europeans: Toward the learning society.* Brussels: Author.

Glaser, R. (1976). Components of a psychology of instruction: Toward a science of design. *Review of Educational Research, 46,* 1–24.

Glaser, R., & Bassok, M. (1989). Learning theory and the study of instruction. *Annual Review of Psychology, 40,* 631–666.

Glaser, R., Lieberman, A., & Anderson, R. (1997). "The vision thing": Educational research and AERA in the 21st century: Part 3. Perspectives on the research–practice relationship. *Educational Researcher, 26*(7), 24–25.

Good, T. L., Mulryan, C., & McCaslin, M. (1992). Grouping for instruction in mathematics: A call for programmatic research on small-group processes. In D. A. Grouws (Ed.), *Handbook of research on mathematics teaching and learning* (pp. 165–196). New York: Macmillan.

Gravemeijer, K. (1994). *Developing realistic mathematics education.* Utrecht, The Netherlands: Freudenthal Institute, University of Utrecht.

Huberman, M. (1993). *The lives of teachers.* New York: Teachers College Press.

Janssen, R., De Corte, E., Verschaffel, L., Knoors, E., & Colémont, A. (2002). National assessment of new standards for mathematics in elementary education in Flanders. *Educational Research and Evaluation, 8,* 197–225.

Kalmykova, Z. I. (1966). Methods of scientific research in the psychology of instruction. *Soviet Education, 8*(6), 13–23.

Lehtinen, E. (2003). Computer-supported collaborative learning: An approach to powerful learning environments. In E. De Corte, L. Verschaffel, N. Entwistle, & J. van Merriënboer (Eds.), *Powerful learning environments: Unraveling basic components and dimensions* (Advances in Learning and Instruction Series) (pp. 35–53). Oxford, UK: Elsevier Science.

Lehtinen, E., Hakkarainen, K., Lipponen, L., Rahikainen, M., & Muukkonen, H. (2001). *Computer-supported collaborative learning: A review* (The J.H.G.I. Giesbers Reports on Education, No 10.). Nijmegen, The Netherlands: University of Nijmegen.

Mayer, R. E., & Wittrock, M. C. (2006). Problem solving. In P. A. Alexander & P. H. Winne (Eds.), *Handbook of educational psychology* (2nd ed., pp. 287–303). Mahwah, NJ: Erlbaum.

Ministerie van de Vlaamse Gemeenschap. (1997). *Gewoon basisonderwijs: Ontwikkelings-doelen en eindtermen: Besluit van mei '97 en decreet van juli '97* [Educational standards for the elementary school]. Brussels: Departement Onderwijs, Centrum voor Informatie en Documentatie.

National Council of Teachers of Mathematics. (1989). *Curriculum and evaluation standards for school mathematics.* Reston, VA: Author.

National Council of Teachers of Mathematics. (2000). *Principles and standards for school mathematics.* Reston, VA: Author.

National Research Council. (2000). *How people learn: Brain, mind, experience, and school* (J. D. Bransford, A. L. Brown, & R. R. Cocking [Eds.], Committee on Developments in the Science of Learning and Committee on Learning Research and Educational Practice). Washington, DC: National Academy Press.

National Research Council. (2001). *Adding it up: Helping children learn mathematics.* (J. Kilpatrick, J. Swafford, & B. Findell [Eds.], Mathematics Learning Study Committee, Center for Education, Division of Behavioral and Social Sciences and Education). Washington, DC: National Academy Press.

National Research Council. (2005). *How students learn: History, mathematics, and science in the classroom.* (Committee on *How People Learn*: A Targeted Report for Teachers, M. S. Donovan & J. D. Bransford [Eds.], Division of Behavioral and Social Sciences and Education). Washington, DC: National Academy Press.

Phillips, D. C., & Dolle, J. R. (2006). From Plato to Brown and beyond: Theory, practice, and the promise of design experiments. In L. Verschaffel, F. Dochy, M. Boekaerts, & S. Vosniadou (Eds.), *Instructional psychology: Past, present and future trends: Sixteen essays in honour of Erik De Corte* (pp. 277–292). Oxford/Amsterdam: Elsevier.

Remillard, J. T. (2005). Examining key concepts in research on teachers' use of mathematics curricula. *Review of Educational Research, 75,* 211–246.

Scardamalia, M., & Bereiter, C. (1992). An architecture for collaborative knowledge building. In E. De Corte, M. C. Linn, H. Mandl, & L. Verschaffel (Eds.), *Computer-based learning environments and problem solving* (NATO-ASI Series F: Computer and Systems Sciences, Vol. 84) (pp. 41–66). Berlin: Springer-Verlag.

Scardamalia, M., & Bereiter, C. (1998). *WebKnowledge Forum: User guide.* Santa Cruz, CA: Learning in Motion.

Schoenfeld, A. H. (1985). *Mathematical problem solving.* Orlando, FL: Academic Press.

Spillane, J. P., Reiser, B. J., & Reimer, T. (2002). Policy implementation and cognition: Reframing and refocusing implementation research. *Review of Educational Research, 72,* 387–431.

Stokes, D. E. (1997). *Pasteur's quadrant: Basic science and technological innovation.* Washington, DC: Brookings Institution Press.

Stokes, L. M., Sato, N. E., McLaughlin, M. W., & Talbert, J. E. (1997). *Theory-based reform and problems of change: Contexts that matter for teachers' learning and community.* Stanford, CA: Center for Research on the Context of Secondary Teaching, School of Education, Stanford University.

van den Berg, R. (2002). Teachers' meanings regarding educational practice. *Review of Educational Research, 72,* 577–625.

Verschaffel, L., De Corte, E., Lasure, S., Van Vaerenbergh, G., Bogaerts, H., & Ratinckx, E. (1999). Learning to solve mathematical application problems: A design experiment with fifth graders. *Mathematical Thinking and Learning, 1,* 195–229.

Verschaffel, L., De Corte, E., Lowyck, J., Dhert, S., & Vandeput, L. (2000). *Supporting mathematical problem solving and posing in Flemish upper elementary school children by means of Knowledge Forum* (TSER Project No. 2019, Computer-Supported Collaborative Learning Networks in Primary and Secondary Education, final report of the Leuven site). Leuven, Belgium: Center for Instructional Psychology and Technology, University of Leuven.

Weinert, F. E., & De Corte, E. (1996). Translating research into practice. In E. De Corte & F. E. Weinert (Eds.), *International encyclopedia of developmental and instructional psychology* (pp. 43–50). Oxford, UK: Elsevier Science.

Wittmann, E. C. (1995). Mathematics education as a design science. *Educational Studies in Mathematics, 29,* 355–374.

Yackel, E., & Cobb, P. (1996). Sociomathematical norms, argumentation, and autonomy in mathematics. *Journal of Research in Mathematics Education, 27,* 458–477.

CHAPTER 24

Science Education for Young Children

A Conceptual-Change Point of View

Stella Vosniadou

One of the most important missions of education is to enable students to understand the ways of thinking of the various disciplines, particularly disciplines such as the physical and biological sciences. Yet this is the area in which schools fail most. Many students do not succeed in acquiring basic science knowledge or cannot apply what they learned in school in everyday, out-of-school situations. An overwhelming body of educational research has also documented students' misconceptions, inert knowledge, lack of critical thinking, as well as low achievement motivation in the learning of science (see, e.g., Novak, 1987).

In this chapter I argue that one important reason why schooling has not produced good results in the case of the learning of science is because it has not dealt adequately with the problem of *conceptual change*. Most theories of learning assume that learning is cumulative and domain-general, and that instruction should be based on the enrichment of prior knowledge. These theories find it difficult to explain the considerable reorganization of conceptual knowledge that takes place with learning and development. However, to understand the advanced scientific concepts of the various disciplines, students need to learn how to reorganize their naive, intuitive theories based on everyday experience and lay culture. In other words, they must undergo profound conceptual change. This change concerns both the content and organization of existing knowledge, as well as the various specific mechanisms of learning. How does this change take place? What can schools do to make conceptual change easier and more accessible to most students?

In the pages that follow I outline some of the basic tenets of a theoretical approach to the problem of conceptual change and discuss its implications for the design of instruction for young children ages 3–8. I argue that teaching for conceptual change must be based on careful choices about the selection of science curricula, so that they can gradually build on students existing knowledge. I also argue that it is important to help young students develop conscious and deliberate mechanisms for intentional learning by creating a social classroom environment that supports deep and enduring comprehension activities for a prolonged period of time.

Characteristics of Science Learning That Need to Be Explained and Existing Theoretical Approaches

Many science educators adopt a primarily empiricist approach to the learning of science. They give a great deal of importance to experience and consider learning to consist mostly of the enrichment of existing knowledge. According to this approach, science learning proceeds along a continuum, where ideas become gradually more abstract and more widely applicable as a result of increased experiences.

Piaget also gave a great deal of attention to experience, but he has also argued that cognitive development proceeds through a series of stages, each of which is characterized by a different psychological structure. The Piagetian stages are considered to be the product of a natural process of spontaneous psychological development achieved through the constructive activity of the individual but not the product of explicit learning. The implication of this approach for instruction is that we should encourage the constructive activity of the learner by providing access to rich experiences, but that systematic science learning should start after the stage of formal operations in early adolescence.

Vygotskian and other sociocultural approaches, on the other hand, consider knowledge acquisition primarily as a social activity influenced by the situational and cultural contexts in which it takes place. According to these approaches, children learn by internalizing or appropriating the culturally relevant practices of adults; thus, such approaches pay a great deal of attention to informal teaching or apprenticeship types of activities. What this implies for science education is that we need to worry about making science activities meaningful by relating them to authentic experiences and scientific practices in the culture.

All of the previously mentioned approaches have important implications for learning and instruction. I agree that science education must enrich children's experiences in ways that are appropriate for their age and their sociocultural environment. But I also believe that these perspectives by themselves are not adequate to explain certain well-agreed-upon characteristics of science learning that need to be taken into consideration for the design of more effective instruction. These phenomena are the following:

- *Science learning is difficult.* Students have great difficulties in understanding fundamental science concepts even after many years of science instruction. This difficulty is experienced even by students whose performance on standardized tests and teacher evaluations is above average. In one of many examples, diSessa (1982) has shown that MIT undergraduates with at least 1 year of college physics still had great difficulty understanding Newton's three laws. Similar findings have been reported by Clement (1983).
- *Science learning is inert.* The term "inert knowledge" has been used to describe the phenomenon of knowing something but failing to use that knowledge when doing so is relevant (Bereiter, 1984; Bransford, Franks, Vye, & Sherwood, 1989). Inertness is

exhibited when knowledge is restricted only to certain settings or situations in which it could be applied. Science and mathematics are areas in which the phenomenon is observed more. Students learn how to solve science and math problems at school but fail to apply this knowledge to everyday situations outside the school context. They also forget what they learned in school soon after graduation, if they do not continue to study physical and/or mathematical sciences in college.

• *Science learning is characterized by misconceptions.* Misconceptions have been noted in practically all subject-matter areas of science. For example, in the area of light, children (and some adults) believe that they perceive objects directly through their eyes, and that color is a property of the objects themselves (Anderson & Smith, 1987). In the area of electricity, some novices believe that a switch is like the trigger of a gun, that it sends an impulse to a battery to trigger current flow from the battery to a light bulb (Collins & Stevens, 1983). Kempton (1987) has shown that many adults use a folk "valve theory" to deal with home heating thermostats. These individuals believe that the thermostat controls the rate of heat flow and that the higher a thermostat is set, the more heat will flow and the faster the house will heat up.

In the area of elementary astronomy, research has shown that many children do not understand the spherical shape of the earth and the scientific explanation of the day–night cycle (Baxter, 1989; Nussbaum, 1979; Nussbaum & Novak, 1976; Vosniadou & Brewer, 1992; 1994). As shown in Figure 24.1, some children believe that the earth is like a flat rectangle or disc, supported by the ground below and covered by the sky above. Others believe that the earth is a hollow sphere, with people living on flat ground deep inside it. These misrepresentations of the earth are not rare. In fact, only 23 of the 60 (third and fifth grade) children in the Vosniadou and Brewer (1992) study gave evidence of some initial understanding of the scientifically accepted model of the earth as a rotating sphere in a heliocentric solar system, and none could provide a full explanation of the day–night cycle.

As I mentioned earlier, theories of learning and instruction cannot explain why science learning is difficult and produces inert knowledge and misconceptions. To be able to account for students' particular difficulties in learning science and the presence of misconceptions, we need to move from domain-general learning theories to domain-specific theories that provide more specific information about the content of knowledge and the knowledge acquisition process.

Piagetian and Vygotskian approaches, information-processing and sociocultural theories are all *domain-general.* They focus on principles, stages, mechanisms, strategies, and so forth, that are meant to characterize all aspects of development and learning. In contrast, cognitive-developmental psychologists have recently argued that it makes sense to study learning and development within a domain-specific approach (Carey, 1985; Keil, 1994). Domain-specific approaches examine distinct domains of thought and focus on the description and explanation of the changes that take place in the content and structure of knowledge with learning and development. Domain-specific approaches should be seen as complementary rather than contradictory to domain-general approaches. It is very likely that both domain-general and domain-specific mechanisms and constraints apply in development and learning (Keil, 1994).

The area of physical knowledge is one such important domain. I believe that we need specific research on the knowledge acquisition process in this domain and, in addi-

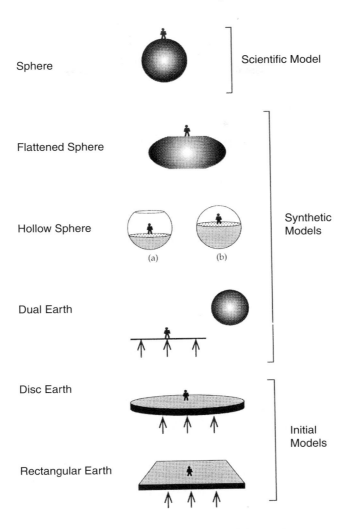

FIGURE 24.1. Mental models of the earth.

tion, argue that we need to consider seriously the possibility that knowledge acquisition in this domain requires considerable *conceptual change*. In the next section I outline the *framework theory approach to conceptual change* and describe how it can explain better than other perspectives students' difficulties in learning science.

The Framework Theory Approach to Conceptual Change and the Learning of Science

Let us stop for a moment to examine the misconceptions of the earth presented in Figure 24.1. A careful look reveals that these misrepresentations of the earth have some common elements. All include in some way the information that the earth is round and flat at the same time, and all portray people as living either on flat ground on the earth or inside the earth. For example, the children who believe the earth to be a flattened sphere think that the earth is spherical but also flat, and that people live on its flat top. The children who think that the earth is a disc also think that the earth is round and flat, and believe that people live on its flat top. The children who adhere to the hollow sphere model seem to understand that the shape of the earth is spherical but believe that people live on flat ground inside this spherical earth. Children who adhere to the dual-earth model believe that there are two earths: a round one that is a planet in the sky, and a flat one, supported by ground, on which people live.

All the misconceptions of the earth obtained in various cross-cultural studies (Brewer, Hendrich, & Vosniadou, 1987; Bryce & Blown, 2006; Diakidoy, Vosniadou, & Hawks, 1997; Mali & Howe, 1979; Nussbaum, 1979; Nussbaum & Novak, 1976; Sadler, 1992; Samarapungavan, Vosniadou, & Brewer, 1996; Sneider & Pulos, 1983; Vosniadou, Archontidou, Kalogiannidou, & Ioannides, 1996), can be accounted for as attempts on the part of the children to synthesize two inconsistent pieces of information: the information they receive, usually through instruction, that the earth is a sphere, and their initial belief in a flat, supported, and stationary earth.

It appears that young children start by forming an initial model of a flat, supported, stationary physical object, with the sky and solar object located above its top (Vosniadou & Brewer, 1992), which is embedded within a larger "framework theory" of physics that forms a relatively coherent (although narrow in its scope) explanatory structure.

The term "theory" is used here to denote a relatively coherent body of domain-specific but implicit knowledge that can give rise to explanation and prediction. It does not refer to a well-formulated, explicit, and socially shared scientific theory. In fact, researchers claim that children do not have metaconceptual awareness of their beliefs, and rather than consider these beliefs to have a hypothetical, theoretical status, believe that they represent true facts about the world.

Studies of physical learning in infancy have indeed shown that the process of knowledge acquisition starts immediately after birth and proceeds rapidly toward the construction of certain fundamental principles or presuppositions that characterize physical objects (that they are stable, they do not move on their own, they fall "down" when not supported, etc.). Children originally categorize the earth as a physical object (Vosniadou & Skopeliti, 2005) and attribute to it all the properties of physical objects located in the physical world, including presuppositions such as that the organization of space is in terms of the directions of up–down, and that unsupported objects fall "down" (the so-called up–down gravity presupposition). Such presuppositions in turn constrain children's understanding of the information that the earth is a sphere, and become the main cause for the formation of misconceptions, or "synthetic models," as we call them (Baillargeon, 1990; Spelke, 1991). Figure 24.2 shows a representation of some of the beliefs and presuppositions that underlie the mental representation of a flat, supported earth, which we assume to form children's initial representation of the earth.

As we know, categorization is a powerful learning mechanism (Bransford, Brown, & Cocking, 1999; Chi, 2008; Chi & Koeske, 1983; Medin & Rips, 2005). Knowing that an object belongs to a given category allows us to infer certain characteristics of the object that can either support learning or hinder it, if the category to which the object is

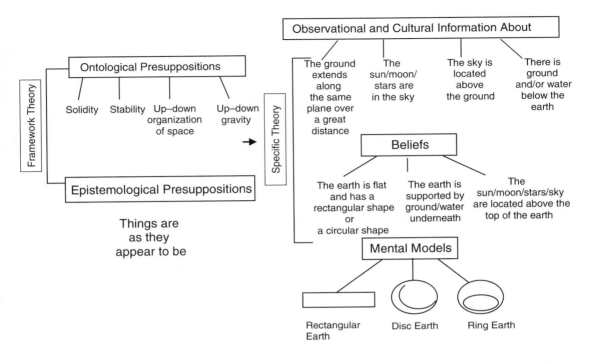

FIGURE 24.2. Hypothetical conceptual structure underlying children's mental models of the earth.

assigned is inappropriate. In the case of the earth, its categorization as a physical object allows young children to infer a host of interpretations about the way observational evidence is received from experience and to draw conclusions regarding certain inaccessible, unobservable properties of the earth (e.g., that it is supported, or that it has an end). These inferences are not subject to conscious awareness and can stand as powerful presuppositions that constrain the process of learning science.

An examination of children's alternative models of the earth, as well as their internally inconsistent responses, suggests that children use enrichment types of learning mechanisms to add new (scientific) information to their initial concept of the earth. Although the use of such mechanisms may be very appropriate in most situations in which new, to-be-acquired information is consistent with what children already know, their use is not very productive when the new information belongs to a scientific concept embedded within a theoretical framework that is incompatible—incommensurate, we might say—with children's initial concept of the earth.

As shown in Table 24.1, the scientific concept of the earth is embedded within a different explanatory framework, that of an astronomical object, a framework whose many presuppositions differ from those of the initial concept of the earth, which is categorized as a physical object, and is embedded within a naive physics. In such cases, when the new information conflicts with what is already known, the use of additive, bottom-up enrichment mechanisms can only lead the learner into small changes that may either fragment what he or she already knows, creating internally inconsistent pieces of knowledge or, at best, lead him or her to create alternative models or misconceptions.

TABLE 24.1. Concept of the Earth

Initial	Scientific
Earth as a physical object:	*Earth as an astronomical object (planet):*
Flat	Spherical
Stationary	Rotating around its axis
	Revolving around the sun
Supported	Unsupported
Up–down gravity	Gravity toward the center of earth
Geocentric system	Heliocentric system

We have interpreted the alternative models of the earth to be "synthetic models" because they seem to result from children's attempts to synthesize information that comes from the scientific concept, and particularly that the earth is a sphere, with aspects of the initial concept of the earth (i.e., that it is a solid, stable, supported physical object, with an up–down organization of space and gravity). If we look carefully at all the alternative models of the earth in Figure 24.1, we see that in all cases they represent children's attempts to solve the problem of how the earth can be spherical and flat at the same time, and how it is possible for people to live on this spherical earth without falling down.

To avoid the creation of synthetic models the learner must first of all become aware of the incongruity between the incoming information and his or her prior knowledge. Metaconceptual awareness and intentional learning are required to achieve conceptual change. Learners must also avoid the use of simple, additive mechanisms. Conscious, intentional, and top-down learning mechanisms, such as the deliberate use of analogy and cross-domain mappings, are much better mechanisms for producing radical conceptual change. I discuss these issues in greater detail in the last section of the chapter. In other words, instruction-induced conceptual change requires the restructuring of not only students' naive theories but also their modes of learning, and the creation of metaconceptual awareness and intentional learning (Sinatra & Pintrich, 2003; Vosniadou, 2003).

Promoting Conceptual Change in the Classroom

The realization that students do not come to school as empty vessels but instead have naive beliefs and explanations about the way the physical world operates that are difficult to change has important implications for the design of science instruction. Teachers must be informed about students' initial ideas about the physical world and learn to take their points of view into consideration. Curricula need to be based on the results of research that shows how students acquire science knowledge. In addition, instructional interventions need to be designed that aim toward making students aware of the theoretical nature of their beliefs and capable of engaging in hypothesis testing and conceptual restructuring. In the pages that follow I discuss some of these issues in greater detail.

Designing Science Curricula for Young Children

It is often the case that science curricula designed for young children cover a great deal of material in a superficial way. My view is that it is better to design curricula that focus on the deep exploration and understanding of a few key concepts rather than cover a great deal of material in a superficial way. The superficial coverage of a great deal of information does not give students enough time to achieve a qualitative understanding of the new ideas and explanations that are being taught. On the contrary, it encourages the casual memorization of facts, which is likely to lead to inert knowledge and misconceptions. It also makes teachers very anxious about covering all the material, with the result that not enough attention is paid to the quality of students' understanding.

Another consideration is to design curricula based on available research that provides information about how children acquire knowledge in the subject-matter area. There is a great deal of research on children's conceptual development in the areas of biology (Carey, 1986; Inagaki & Hatano, 1996; Keil, 1992), the nature of matter (Wiser & Smith, 2008), and observational astronomy (Vosniadou & Brewer, 1992, 1994; Vosniadou, Vamvakoussi, & Skopeliti, 2008), and these seem to be good areas in which to begin systematic science education for young children.

Table 24.2 provides an example from experimental curricula we designed in observational astronomy for elementary school children (Vosniadou, Ioannides, Dimitrakopoulou, & Papademetriou, 2001). The curricula focus on the explanation of certain counterintuitive aspects of the scientific information that according to research causes children particular difficulty. For example, research has shown that children have difficulty reconciling their perception of a flat earth with information they receive from

TABLE 24.2. Examples from Experimental Curricula in Observational Astronomy

Sequence of concepts/ theoretical framework	Basic questions/ entrenched beliefs	Instructional interventions
Earth shape	Perceived flatness	C: model of earth Q: perception of flatness IM: globe, video demonstrations E: toy ship on the globe
Earth shape and gravity	Up–down gravity	C: drawing of a man in Australia Q: life at "bottom" of the earth E: magnetic globe
Earth, moon and sun	Relation between size and distance	C: models of earth, sun, moon Q: perception of sun/moon IM: scale models E: balloons near/far
Solar system and gravity	Geocentric solar system	C: drawing of the solar system IM: slides, video, maps E: demonstration of revolution of earth using a toy car (earth) and a ball (sun)
Earth movements, day–night cycle	Movement of earth, sun, moon	Q: explanation of day–night cycle C: acting out the movements of the earth E: demonstration of day–night cycle
Creation of universe, galaxy and solar system		Visit to the planetarium

Note. C, constructions; Q, questions; IM, instructional materials; E, experiments.

adults that the earth is spherical. They also have trouble understanding how it is possible for people to live on a spherical earth without falling "down." In our curricula we have designed specific activities to help children understand these counterintuitive pieces of information. These activities include the construction of models of the earth, demonstrations of the shape of the earth from space using video, explicit verbal explanations, reference to historical cases, and the use of experiments.

In general, in designing curricula and instruction, it is important to distinguish between new information that is consistent with prior knowledge and new information that runs contrary to prior knowledge. When new information is consistent with prior knowledge, it can be incorporated easily into existing conceptual structures. This type of information will most likely be understood, even if it is presented as fact, without any further explication. However, when the new information to be learned is inconsistent with what children already know, simply presenting the new information as a fact may not be adequate. In this situation, students seem to have two courses of action available to them. One is simply to add the new fact to their existing knowledge, creating inconsistencies and fragmentation. The other is to distort the new fact to make it consistent with what children know, creating misconceptions.

Designing Instruction to Promote Conceptual Change for Young Children

Instruction for conceptual change often makes use of "cognitive conflict," an instructional strategy that uses experiments to produce results different than those predicted by the students. As students' confidence in their explanations decreases, they are more likely to understand the need for a new and different explanation. Cognitive conflict has been criticized, however, on the grounds that it is not consistent with constructivist approaches, in the sense that it does not build on what students know (Smith, diSessa, & Rochelle, 1993).

My colleagues and I think that cognitive conflict can be useful in an overall program of science instruction, if it is used carefully. A problem is that cognitive conflict often targets a specific misconception, leaving untouched the fundamental problems children may have in understanding the scientific concept. For example, even when we provide undeniable proof that the earth is a sphere, we are still not solving children's problems. Children create misconceptions not because they do not believe that the earth is a sphere, but because they cannot reconcile this fact with their remaining beliefs about the earth, such as their belief in up–down gravity. Needed is systematic instruction that answers all the implicit questions children have in the context of their naive physics.

Conceptual change is not about replacing a "wrong" concept or explanation with a "correct" one. Rather, it is a process that requires students to be able to understand different perspectives and to move to higher degrees of abstraction. For example, from the point of view of someone on the earth, it is rather rational to believe that the earth is flat and stationary. However, when the earth is looked at from space, its spherical shape cannot be denied. It took many years of scientific discovery and many mistakes for scientists to understand the shape of the earth and its location in the solar system. For this reason the use of cases from the history of science can be very useful.

Another problem is that traditional instruction moves students very quickly into verbal definitions or problem-solving procedures, without teaching them the qualitative models that the scientists themselves use to support their reasoning (see, e.g., Nersessian, 1992, 1995). Physical reasoning depends on rich representations of the physical world—representations that need to be constructed slowly as children's science knowledge develops. Linguistic explanations do not provide all the detail needed to construct complete, explanatory models. Models and external representations can be used to clarify aspects of a scientific explanation that are not apparent when the explanation is given in a linguistic form. For example, our research on children's explanations of the day–night cycle has revealed the many different interpretations that can be given to the information "the earth rotates around its axis" by children with different models of the earth (Vosniadou & Brewer, 1994). The visual qualities of a model are useful in making an explanation more easily understood and memorized (e.g., Mayer, 2003/2007).

However, because models may be rather memorable, they may also be a source of misconceptions and misrepresentations. A common misconception related to the explanation of the seasons, namely, that the earth is closer to the sun during the summer, is often attributed to a picture used in textbooks showing the earth in an elliptical orbit around the sun. Thus, models have to be used with great care.

In addition to using models to demonstrate explanations in science, it is also important to teach children how to make their own models, and to provide model-based explanations. In the process of making a model, children can start making explicit their implicit and largely unconscious beliefs, while they are also being exposed to the theoretical nature of science making. Such activities may be time-consuming, but they are important to ensure that students become aware of what they know and understand what they need to learn.

Students often do not see the reason to change beliefs and presuppositions that provide good explanations of their everyday experiences, function adequately in the everyday world, and are tied to years of confirmation. To persuade students to invest the substantial effort required to become science-literate and to reexamine their initial explanations of physical phenomena, we need to provide an environment that motivates them to make such changes and relates to their social and cultural environment outside the narrow context of the school. Students need meaningful experiences in the form of systematic observations, hands-on experiments, and classroom discussion that persuade them that the explanations they have constructed are in need of revision. If we want these experiences to be useful in the process of conceptual change, we need to select them carefully, so that they are theoretically relevant. What I mean by "theoretically relevant" is that these experiences should address the underlying presuppositions and beliefs that constrain students representations and influence the way they interpret scientific information, and show students that these presuppositions do not adequately explain the known empirical facts.

Although students are relatively good interpreters of their everyday experience, they do not seem to be aware of the explanatory frameworks they have constructed and of the presuppositions that constrain them. Even when they start to achieve this metaconceptual awareness, they do not understand that their explanations are hypotheses that can be subjected to experimentation and falsification. Therefore, their explanations remain implicit and tacit. Lack of metaconceptual awareness of this sort prevents students from questioning their prior knowledge, and facilitates the assimilation and distortion of new information. This type of assimilatory activity seems to form the basis for the creation of synthetic models and misconceptions, and lies at the root of the surface inconsistency so commonly observed in students' reasoning.

To help students increase their metaconceptual awareness, it is necessary to create learning environments that allow them to express their representations, and beliefs. As I mentioned earlier, building models and providing explanations can be one way of creating the necessary metaconceptual awareness. Metaconceptual awareness is also promoted in learning environments that facilitate group discussion and the verbal expression of ideas.

Hatano and his colleague Inagaki have conducted a number of educational studies to show how individual cognitive mechanisms can combine with sociocultural constraints to promote instruction-induced conceptual change (Inagaki & Hatano, 2008). They pay particular attention to the use of classroom dialogue, which they believed can foster individual cognitive change through constructive processes. Most of these studies are conducted using the Japanese science education method known as hypothesis–experiment–instruction (HEI), a method utilized extensively by Hatano and his colleagues. It is a promising method for helping students achieve exactly the kind of metaconceptual awareness required for the deliberate and intentional belief revision needed for instruction-based conceptual change.

The design of HEI presents to students a multiple-choice problem with conflicting alternatives, some of which represent students' common misconceptions. This method creates the necessary conditions for producing cognitive conflict. Hatano believes that cognitive conflict is important in inducing "cognitive" or "epistemic" motivation in students to evaluate their prior knowledge, but it may not be enough to create conceptual change. To amplify students' motivation, a teacher needs to create a sociocultural environment that favors prolonged comprehension activities—what Hatano calls a "collective comprehension activity" (Hatano & Inagaki, 1991).

One way a teacher can provide the sociocultural environment to encourage collective comprehension is to ask students to participate in whole-class discussions. Classroom dialogue can be effective because on the one hand, it ensures that students truly understand the need to revise their beliefs instead of engaging in local repairs (Chinn & Brewer, 1993) and on the other, that they spend the considerable time and effort needed to engage in the conscious and deliberate belief revision required for conceptual change (see also Miyake, 2008). Students can also break up into smaller groups that compete to discover the correct solution and support it with the best arguments.

In conclusion, I have argued that to understand the advanced scientific concepts of the various disciplines, students cannot rely on simple memorization of facts. They must learn how to restructure their naive, intuitive theories based on everyday experience and lay culture. In other words, they must undergo profound conceptual change. This type of conceptual change cannot be achieved without systematic instruction that builds gradually students' existing knowledge, while making students more metaconceptually aware of their beliefs and presuppositions. Teachers must find ways to enhance individual students' motivation by creating a social classroom environment that supports the creation of intentional learners who can engage in the deep and enduring comprehension activities required for the revision of conceptual knowledge.

References

Anderson, C. W., & Smith, E. (1987). Teaching science. In V. Richardson-Koehler (Ed.), *The educator's handbook: A research perspective* (pp. 84–111). New York: Longman.

Baillargeon, R. (1990). *The development of young infants' intuition about support.* Paper presented at the 7th International Conference of Infant Studies, Montreal, Canada.

Baxter, J. (1989). Children's understanding of familiar astronomical events. *International Journal of Science Education, 11,* 502–513.

Bereiter, C. (1984). How to keep thinking skills from going the way of all frills. *Educational Leadership, 42,* 75–77.

Bransford, J. D., Brown, A., & Cocking, R. (Eds.). (1999). *How people learn: Mind, brain, experience and school.* Washington, DC: National Academy Press.

Bransford, J. D., Franks, J. J., Vye, N. J., & Sherwood, R. D. (1989). New approaches to instruction: Because wisdom can't be told. In S. Vosniadou & A. Ortony (Eds.), *Similarity and analogical reasoning* (pp. 470–497). New York: Cambridge University Press.

Brewer, W. F., Hendrich, D. J., & Vosniadou, S. (1987, January). *A cross-cultural study of children's development of cosmological models: Samoan and American data.* Paper presented at the 3rd International Conference on Thinking, Honolulu, HI.

Bryce, T. G. K., & Blown, E. J. (2006). Cultural mediation of children's cosmologies: A longitudinal study of the astronomy concepts of Chinese and New Zealand children. *International Journal of Science Education, 28*(10), 1113–1160.

Carey, S. (1985). *Conceptual change in childhood.* Cambridge, MA: MIT Press.

Carey, S. (1986). Cognitive science and science education. *American Psychologist, 41*(10), 1123–1130.

Chi, M. T. H. (2008). Three kinds of conceptual change: Belief revision, mental model transformation, and ontological shift. In S. Vosniadou (Ed.), *International handbook of research on conceptual change* (pp. 61–82). New York: Routledge.

Chi, M. T. H., & Koeske, R. D. (1983). Network representation of a child's dinosaur knowledge. *Developmental Psychology, 19*(1), 29–39.

Chinn, C., & Brewer, W. F. (1993). The role of anomalous data in knowledge acquisition: A theoretical framework and implications for science instruction. *Review of Educational Research, 63,* 1–49.

Clement, J. (1983). A conceptual model discussed by Galileo and used intuitively by physics students. In D. Gentner & A. L. Stevens (Eds.), *Mental models* (pp. 325–340). Hillsdale, NJ: Erlbaum.

Collins, A., & Stevens, A. L. (1983). A cognitive theory of interactive teaching. In C. M. Reigeluth (Ed.), *Instructional design theories and models: An overview* (pp. 247–278). Hillsdale, NJ: Erlbaum.

Diakidoy, I. A., Vosniadou, S., & Hawks, J. (1997). Conceptual change in astronomy: Models of the earth and of the day/night cycle in American-Indian children. *European Journal of Psychology of Education, 12,* 159–184.

diSessa, A. (1982). Unlearning Aristotelian physics: A study of knowledge-based learning. *Cognitive Science, 6*(1), 37–75.

Hatano, G., & Inagaki, K. (1991). Sharing cognition through collective comprehension activity. In R. Resnick, J. M. Levine, & S. D. Teasly (Eds.), *Perspectives on socially shared cognition* (pp. 331–348). Washington, DC: American Psychological Association.

Inagaki, K., & Hatano, G. (1996). Young children's recognition of commonalities between animals and plants. *Child Development, 6,* 219–231.

Inagaki, K., & Hatano, G. (2008). Conceptual change in biology. In S. Vosniadou (Ed.), *International handbook of research on conceptual change* (pp. 240–262). New York: Routledge.

Keil, F. C. (1992). The origins of an autonomous biology. In M. Gunnar & M. Maratsos (Eds.), *Minnesota Symposium on Child Development* (pp. 103–137). Hillsdale, NJ: Erlbaum.

Keil, F. C. (1994). The birth and nurturance of concepts by domains: The origins of concepts of living things. In L. A. Hirschfeld & S. A. Gelman (Eds.), *Mapping the mind: Domain specificity in cognition and culture* (pp. 234–254). New York: Cambridge University Press.

Kempton, W. (1987). Two theories of home heat control. In D. Holland & N. Quinn (Eds.), *Cultural models in language and thought* (pp. 222–242). Cambridge, UK: Cambridge University Press.

Mali, G. B., & Howe, A. (1979). Development of earth and gravity concepts among Nepali children. *Science Education, 63,* 685–691.

Mayer, R. E. (2007). *Learning and instruction* (2nd ed.). Upper Saddle River, NJ: Prentice-Hall. (Original work published in 2003)

Medin, D. L., & Rips, L. J. (2005). Concepts and categories: Memory, meaning, and metaphysics. In K. J. Holyoak & R. G. Morrison (Eds.), *The Cambridge handbook of thinking and reasoning* (pp. 37–72). Cambridge, UK: Cambridge University Press.

Miyake, N. (2008). Conceptual change through collaboration. In S. Vosniadou (Ed.), *International handbook of research on conceptual change* (pp. 453–478). New York: Routledge.

Nersessian, N. (1992). How do scientists think?: Capturing the dynamics of conceptual change in science. In R. N. Giere (Ed.), *Cognitive models of science: Minnesota studies in the philosophy of science* (Vol. 15, pp. 3–44). Minneapolis: University of Minnesota Press.

Nersessian, N. J. (1995). Constructive modeling in creating scientific understanding. *Science Education, 4,* 203–226.

Novak, J. D. (Ed.). (1987). *Proceedings of the Second International Seminar: Misconceptions and educational strategies in science and mathematics* (Vols. I–III). Ithaca, NY: Cornell University, Department of Education.

Nussbaum, J. (1979). Children's conceptions of the earth as a cosmic body: A cross-age study. *Science Education, 63,* 83–93.

Nussbaum, J., & Novak, J. D. (1976). An assessment of children's concepts of the earth utilizing structured interviews. *Science Education, 60,* 535–550.

Sadler, P. M. (1992). *The initial knowledge state of high school astronomy students.* Doctoral thesis, Graduate School of Education, Harvard University, Cambridge, MA.

Samarapungavan, A., Vosniadou, S., & Brewer, W. F. (1996). Mental models of the earth, sun, and moon: Indian children's cosmologies. *Cognitive Development, 11,* 491–521.

Sinatra, M. G., & Pintrich, R. P. (2003). The role of intentions in conceptual change learning. In G. M. Sinatra & P. R. Pintrich (Eds.), *Intentional conceptual change* (pp. 1–18). Mahwah, NJ: Erlbaum.

Smith, J. P., diSessa, A. A., & Rochelle, J. (1993). Misconceptions reconceived: A constructivist analysis of knowledge in transition. *Journal of Learning Sciences, 3,* 115–183.

Sneider, C., & Pulos, S. (1983). Children's cosmographies: Understanding the earth's shape and gravity. *Science Education, 67,* 205–221.

Spelke, E. S. (1991). Physical knowledge in infancy: Reflections on Piaget's theory. In S. Carey & R. Gelman (Eds.), *The epigenesis of mind: Essays on biology and Cognition* (Jean Piaget Symposium series) (pp. 133–169). Hillsdale, NJ: Erlbaum.

Vosniadou, S. (2003). Exploring the relationships between conceptual change and intentional learning. In G. M. Sinatra & P. R. Pintrich (Eds.), *Intentional conceptual change* (pp. 377–406). Mahwah, NJ: Erlbaum.

Vosniadou, S., Archontidou, A., Kalogiannidou, A., & Ioannides, C. (1996). How Greek children understand the shape of the Earth: A study of conceptual change in childhood. *Psychological Issues, 7*(1), 30–51. (in Greek)

Vosniadou, S., & Brewer, W. (1992). Mental models of the Earth: A study of conceptual change in childhood. *Cognitive Psychology, 24,* 535–585.

Vosniadou, S., & Brewer, W. F. (1994). Mental models of the day/night cycle. *Cognitive Science,* *18,* 123–183.

Vosniadou, S., Ioannides, C., Dimitrakopoulou, A., & Papademitriou, E. (2001). Designing learning environments to promote conceptual change in science. *Learning and Instruction,* *11*(4–5), 381–419.

Vosniadou, S., & Skopeliti, I. (2005). Developmental shifts in children's categorizations of the Earth. In B. G. Bara, L. Barsalou, & M. Bucciarelli (Eds.), *Proceedings of the XXVII Annual Conference of the Cognitive Science Society* (pp. 2325–2330). Mahwah, NJ: Erlbaum.

Vosniadou, S., Vamvakoussi, X., & Skopeliti, I. (2008). The framework theory approach. In S. Vosniadou (Ed.), *International handbook of research on conceptual change* (pp. 3–34). New York: Routledge.

Wiser, M., & Smith, C. (2008). Learning and teaching about matter in grades K–8: When should the atomic–molecular theory be introduced? In S. Vosniadou (Ed.), *International handbook of research on conceptual change* (pp. 205–239). New York: Routledge.

CHAPTER 25

Improving Science Teaching for Young Children

Mark Enfield
Dwight Rogers

Persons who wish to reform educational practice cannot simply tell teachers to teach differently. Teachers themselves must make the design changes. To do so, they must acquire rich knowledge of subject matter, pedagogy, and subject specific pedagogy; and they must come to hold beliefs in these domains. Successful professional development efforts are those that help teachers to acquire or develop new ways of thinking about learning, learners, and subject matter, thus constructing a professional knowledge base that will enable them to teach students in more powerful and meaningful ways.
—BORKO AND PUTNAM (1995, p. 60)

In the foregoing quote, Borko and Putnam argue powerfully for the central agentic role of teachers in pedagogical reform and curricular innovation. Moreover, they suggest that the goal of professional development is to support teachers' agency by strengthening their professional knowledge base of the critical elements of the teaching and learning process. In this chapter we consider these assertions in light of research findings from cognitive and developmental fields, as they apply to the area of early science education. We review how fully these findings have been implemented in professional development and, finally, draw several conclusions about what should be done in terms of professional development for teaching science to young learners. Thus, the chapter examines training for teachers of young children and considers how insights from cognitive and developmental science can guide, enliven, and transform the design and content of preparation for teaching science.

Before proceeding, it may be helpful to address why we should be concerned about early learning of science, as well as teacher professional development in science. Early science learning is important for several reasons. American competitiveness in a global economy requires an educational system that is capable of preparing citizens who are highly competent in mathematics and science (National Commission on Mathematics and Science Teaching for the 21st Century, 2006). Economic competitiveness is not the only reason to advocate for rigorous preparation of the populace in math and science. Other benefits include personal fulfillment, as well as being prepared for productive engagement as citizens of an increasingly connected and interdependent global society (Settlage & Southerland, 2007). Because children begin to form commitments to careers in science, technology, engineering, and mathematics at an early age, "we should pay close attention to children's early exposure to science" (Tai, Liu, Maltese, & Fan, 2006, p. 1144). Finally, research presented in this volume and arguments based on research syntheses (e.g., Gelman, 1999) suggest that by developing substantive science learning in young children and then building on that in subsequent grades, it may be possible to overcome problems of student performance science (Valverde & Schmidt, 1997, 1998, 2000).

Assuming agreement on the importance of early science learning, we are led to wonder what might comprise science learning in an imaginary classroom of young children. A common science learning goal focuses on children developing the ability to describe and explain the motion of objects. Typically, children investigate the motion of objects through activities in which they observe motion of different objects. Specifically, the activities might focus on the motion of balls and provide places for children to roll, bounce, toss, and observe the motion of balls. Most often, children engage in these activities independently and undirected by a teacher. The assumption is that through their experiences children develop understandings of the motion of objects. Teachers might ask children to describe the motion of the objects they observed and/or to draw those objects. Children are rarely asked to explain their own thinking or how their ideas relate to those of others in the group. Similarly, teachers are rarely asked or encouraged to explain their own thinking about the same concepts. Furthermore, teachers are implicitly encouraged to let children construct their own understandings independently; thus, many early childhood teachers labor under the mistaken notion that they should not introduce concepts or ideas to children. Finally, if the imaginary teacher in this classroom is asked why he or she did not include an explanation or comparison of ideas, then he or she likely will say that either there wasn't time, or that it is not developmentally appropriate to ask children to discuss their reactions, rationales, or understanding of scientific concepts. Furthermore, the teacher might argue that "hands-on" experiences with phenomena are the most important aspect of young children learning science.

Although this description of classroom practice may seem somewhat simplistic, naive, and stereotyped, it is not far from the reality of what happens in most early childhood classrooms. The research reviewed in this volume points to severe limitations in the teaching of science for most children. First, the emphasis on discovery through firsthand experiences with phenomena is an ineffective approach to teaching science. Research has compared approaches to science instruction identified as traditional, discovery, and conceptual change. This reason showed how in classrooms that followed traditional and discovery approaches, children retain naive and inaccurate conceptions of phenomena. However, in classrooms where the teacher followed the conceptual change approach, children began to move toward scientific conceptions (Roth, 1991; Smith, 1991). The reasons for students' failure to learn scientific conceptions have many explanations. One problem focusing on a discovery approach is its assumption that children will naturally discover a scientific explanation of phenomena based on their experiences. The development of scientific understandings involves logical and creative analysis of observations, consideration of a variety of explanations, and coming to a conclusion about which explanation is most plausible—which rarely occur in discovery learning. Another shortcoming of discovery approaches is revealed by research that shows how children's conceptions of phenomena impact their interpretations of experience with new phenomena (Roth, 1991; Smith, 1991). Children interpret their experiences with phenomena in discovery learning settings based on their prior conceptions (Posner, Strike, Hewson, & Gertzog, 1982). These limitations of discovery learning connect with findings from developmental science research that suggest (1) children come to science learning with experiences and explanations about phenomena in the world; (2) they are capable of complex and abstract reasoning that allows them to develop and argue over explanations of those phenomena; and (3) their engagement with representational and metacognitive activity is important in developing their understandings of ideas.

If we agree that this is problematic, we are led to wonder about teachers' professional development in science teaching and learning. Several arguments favor careful consideration of the professional development of teachers of young learners in science. In recent years, research has improved our understanding of science learning, and has led to new recommendations about teaching and learning in science (National Research Council, 2007). Whereas these developments are important and lead to improved understandings, it is not clear that they are reflected in the teaching of young children. Although training is important, teachers with the least amount of training in mathematics and science are most likely to teach young children (Bogard, Traylor, & Takanishi, 2008; Johnson, 1999). To have practitioners and newly trained educators share common visions and understandings about young children's science learning, professional development remains an important consideration. As a result of these issues, the professional development of educators working with young children is simultaneously vital and challenging.

Another argument for improving and increasing professional development in science concerns the possibility to interpret conflicting information in the various curricular reform documents. For example, the "goals for learners" section of the Head Start Child Outcomes Framework (available at *www.hsnrc.org/CDI/Outcontent.cfm*) includes scientific skills and methods focusing on observation and description of phenomena. Based on these goals, recommendations for classroom practice focus on providing experiences for children, as well as having them observe, ask questions, and explore phenomena. The National Science Education Standards (NSES; National Research Council, 1996) suggests a similar set of goals but includes communication of results, which implies that young learners might be expected to engage in explanation. The NSES goals also imply that children should learn to connect abstractions with concrete experiences. In summary, some standards focus on young children having concrete experiences to develop concepts and potentially move toward abstraction. But the documents implicitly disagree about not only the degree to which abstraction is developmentally appropriate but also the role of communicating and theorizing about knowledge. Regardless, the largest challenge is that relatively few professional development programs are documented for early childhood teachers in science (Copley & Padron, 1999). Although questions remain about the nature, content, and form of the most effective professional development, this chapter summarizes guidelines for young children's science learning based on ideas generated from cognitive and developmental science.

Design of Professional Development

In this section we present ideas for designing a sustained professional development program to facilitate early childhood educators' deeper understanding of science and to enhance their teaching of science. To begin with, we know what does not work. For example, a "one-shot workshop," from the perspective of workshop participants and organizer, is not generally regarded as an effective approach to professional development (Kennedy, 1999). These ubiquitous "one-shot," "hit-and-run," professional development workshops do little to change teachers' practices or beliefs (Day & Sachs, 2004; McLaughlin & Talbert, 2006).

A challenge in thinking about the design of professional development to facilitate teaching science to young children is that there is limited knowledge about professional development of teachers of children ages 3–8 years. Few professional development programs focus on science learning for teachers of young children (Copley & Padron, 1999). There are more professional development programs for the elementary grades, yet the findings remain limited. Kennedy (1999) cites only two studies that relate professional development of elementary teachers in science and document outcomes for student learning. Unfortunately, these studies offer limited insights about aspects of the design of those programs that contribute most to programmatic effectiveness. Professional development that involves multiple efforts over a long period of time is regarded as more effective. Banilower, Heck, and Weiss (2007) examined 42 National Science Foundation professional development projects, occurring over 7 years, that focused on kindergarten through eighth-grade teachers. The studies report modest gains in the amount of time spent on teaching science, on teachers' attitudes, and on teachers' sense of efficacy in teaching science. However, they point out that there is still much to be learned about the most effective models of professional development (e.g., their design). This research was important and helped to clarify the impact of national efforts. However, it offers neither insight into the design of effective programs nor information about teachers of children ages 3–5 years. A review of recent literature revealed one study that focused on professional development in science with teachers of young children. Of relevance here, and described by Howes (2008) as being important and effective, professional development occurred in the context of a learning community model. Therefore, we can infer from these findings that long-term exposure learning community models are important. Because there is a fairly limited body of evidence about teacher professional development for young children's learning of science, we describe general principles of professional development, based on research findings from other areas, that we believe to be effective.

We believe that several general principles, which we found in the literature, are important for effective professional development. For professional development to be effective it must be *collaborative*, *inquiry-oriented*, and *long term*. It should be designed as a joint problem-solving venture, not just as a few "training" sessions delivered by "experts" with limited connection to teachers, children, and schools. There is clearly a place for expertise in professional development experiences, but we suggest that teacher learning (and professional developers' understanding) would be better served if professional developers took on a role similar to that of a consultant rather than attempt to play the part of an expert with knowledge to impart. The professional development process should be designed to draw on the pedagogical and experiential knowledge of participating teachers, as well as that of the professional developer. We believe that new knowledge of children's learning and teacher practice must be co-constructed by teachers and professional developers alike, and not simply be delivered passively to teachers by experts. A more collaborative and inquiry-oriented approach to professional development requires that the two parties work together to co-construct new and deeper understanding by building on their collective experience and expertise. Thoughtful and meaningful professional development must be an active and demanding intellectual activity for all involved, one in which everyone is both teaching and learning.

These general principles for design of professional development are grounded in premises set forth by Grundy and Robinson's (2004) review of the research literature on professional development. They found that to deepen teachers' knowledge, strengthen individual practice, build collective capacity for improvement of teaching and learning, and create a culture of inquiry though professional development, the process must be

- Relevant to the needs identified at the school level by teachers.
- Controlled by the participants.
- Collegial and collaborative.
- Grounded in action learning principles (i.e., development is a learning process that is in turn grounded in investigations of practice and critical reflection upon change processes).
- Extended time frames to allow development through cycles of action and reflection.
- An acknowledgment of the need for school reform and restructuring as a basis of improvement, as well as professional development and change. (p. 158)

Additionally, Day and Sachs (2004) contend that the research investigating successful professional development "points to the complexity of teacher development which mirrors the complexity of the purposes and practices of teaching" (p. 16). Child development researchers and scholars concerned about furthering the knowledge and understanding of young children's science learning, improving teachers' ability to affect that learning, and generating new knowledge about science teaching and learning should engage in a professional development program situated in models or approaches in which the conditions for learning are equally as complex and complicated as those in a classroom of young children. Therefore, we argue for a general principle of professional development that prioritizes training within a classroom context, as opposed to being at a distance from classrooms, so that the complexity of purposes and practices of teaching is apparent. King and Newmann (2001) suggested that chances for real teacher learning are greatly increased when teachers can concentrate on teaching and student learning in the schools and classrooms in which they teach, and not in a laboratory or other alien setting.

Day and Sachs (2004) also found that gaining a better understanding of teachers' perspectives and exhibiting sensitivity to their personal agendas are critically important for successful professional development. For example, in a 4-year study focused on school district recommendations for differentiated instruction, Valli and Buese (2007) reported, "[We] did not find the kind of pedagogical improvement desired by the school district in our examination of differentiation" (p. 553). However, they also cited the research finding that teachers will make changes in practice if those changes are aligned with their personal agendas, and if they have sufficient support. Such research suggests that teachers are committed to improving practice to the extent that professional development reflects issues, problems, and ideas that are of concern to them. In terms of science learning of young children, this is potentially problematic. Few teachers of young children are concerned with science teaching (Johnson, 1999) or feel efficacious in that area (Ramey-Gassert, Shroyer, & Staver, 1996). Yet were these teachers to appreciate the affect and motivation of science for children (Anderson, 2003; Hogan, 2002), they might be more likely to believe in the importance of science teaching. Science teaching and learning can become part of teachers' perspectives and agendas when professional development highlights the personal and "psychic" rewards (Lortie, 1975) to be gained from students' interest, affect, motivation, learning, and understanding of science.

Consistent with Grundy and Robinson's (2004) findings, Day and Sachs (2004) strongly suggest that

> teacher learning needs to be inquiry oriented, personal and sustained, individual and collaborative, on and off site; ... that these [factors] need to be supported by school cultures of inquiry ... where evidence is collected and interrogated which acknowledges the complex worlds of teaching and learning, teachers and learners; and, that if it is to be effective its direct and indirect results need to be systematically evaluated. (p. 26)

For example, this might involve new forms of professional development that focus on understanding intellectually demanding ideas and executing subtle, sophisticated teaching strategies. Such forms of professional development would require sustained programs designed to impact the understandings, beliefs, attitudes, and practices of individual teachers, while thoughtfully considering the cultures and contexts of schools. In such a design, it is critical for teachers to have the support and encouragement of researchers, school administrators, and colleagues to permit them to build a "culture of inquiry" that allows the creation of continuous opportunities for honest discussion, deep reflection, and experimentation and ongoing chances to master new practices (Sparks & Hirsch, 1997). Developing new forms of professional development seems particularly important in light of the findings from developmental science described in this volume. The ideas based on recent developmental science research are intellectually demanding and socially challenging. Teachers enacting pedagogies that reflect the findings reported here may find it necessary both to reinvent their own teaching and to teach against the grain (Cochran-Smith, 1991); professional development should recognize and support them in that effort. Fullan (1993) suggests that "learning teachers" are the cornerstone of any learning organization. To ensure that teachers are learning in schools requires opportunities for meaningful collaboration with others through well-designed teacher professional development projects. This follows McLaughlin and Talbert (2006), who contend that

> even the highest quality professional development will falter unless teachers can work together on new ideas and reflect on practice and its implications for students' learning. ... External knowledge resources can be vital ingredients to improve student learning, but they cannot be enough to meet society's goals without opportunities for teachers to situate them in their own classrooms and school contexts. (p. 3)

Such thinking builds on the notion that the possibilities for teacher learning are heightened when teachers have the chance to experiment with and receive assistance and thoughtful feedback on innovative practices and curricular materials (King & Newmann, 2001).

Complementing the recent reconceptualization of professional development is a robust movement that encourages school and school district educators to establish and sustain *professional learning communities* and/or *communities of practice in schools*. Professional learning communities are built on the elements of good professional development detailed earlier. Much like the professional development structures we have presented to this point, professional learning communities are typically defined as spaces where "teachers work collaboratively to reflect on practice, examine evidence about the relationship between practice and student outcomes, and make changes that improve teaching and learning for the particular students in their classes" (McLaughlin & Talbert, 2006, pp. 3–4). Bolam and McMahon (2004) also cite arguments and research that attest to the potential of establishing collaborative, school-situated, sustained professional development learning communities designed for teachers and researchers. For example, Smylie (1995, 1996) synthesized a wide range of adult learning theories associated with powerful learning in the workplace, arguing that human capital is an important aspect of school effectiveness. Investment in human capital can be achieved through development of professional learning communities. Research supports this argument by showing that provision of continuous opportunities for teachers to learn collaboratively with peer colleagues in school through open communication, experimentation, and feedback was critical to enhancing an intellectual climate. This new school climate in turn provided impetus and support for more pedagogical experimentation, and open and honest dialogue, while encouraging personal and professional learning (Briscoe & Wells, 2002; Howes, 2008; King & Newmann, 2001).

Authentic school reform and genuine school change are dependent on schools becoming learning communities for both teachers and students. In this same vein, if teachers are to continue to learn how better to educate children, and if researchers are truly concerned about how to put into practice basic research regarding children's learning of science, then teachers and researchers must work together in a sustained fashion in schools to investigate how to enhance young children's conceptual understandings of science and advance our knowledge of the learning process in school settings.

Little (2004) points to an innovative design for professional development that she terms "looking at student work." This design may offer an example of the type of practice-focused, collaborative, school-based professional development strategies and processes that provide the kind of sustained, collaborative professional development necessary to promote genuine teacher, student, and researcher learning. Looking at student work, an example of what Ball and Cohen (1999) term "learning in and from practice," is based on the deep and sustained study of student work samples, classroom tasks and assignments, videotapes of teacher–student interactions, and other forms of classroom activities. Central to the various looking at student work projects are the sustained, serious conversations prompted by the systematic investigation of the impact of curricular materials and activities, teacher instructional practices, and teacher–child interaction on student learning. Little (2004) contends that compared to the traditional, expert-led, in-service workshops, professional development programs grounded in learning in and from practice are rare. However, she maintains that the available evidence does provide support for professional development activity in which looking at student work occupies a prominent place. Although the body of relevant research is small, findings from the available studies indicate that the collective examination of student work, where it is designed to focus teachers' attention closely on children's learning, may have a positive affect on outcomes of interest: teacher knowledge, teaching practice and (some cases) student learning. (p. 105)

Although these conclusions must be subjected to additional empirical investigation, given the relative paucity of evidence in terms of developmental science–based professional development for teachers of young children, we believe that these ideas suggest a reasonable course of action and warrant testing and application.

Some examples of these types of learning in and from practice professional development projects in science do exist, such as Science Education for Public Understanding Program (SEPUP), which focuses on secondary science learning. There are more substantial and relevant findings in the field of mathematics, including projects such as Integrating Mathematics Assessment (IMA) and Cognitively Guided Instruction (CGI). Studying CGI, Kazemi and Franke (2003), in their yearlong, in-depth study of 11 teachers at one school, found that teachers' deeper understanding of student thinking and problem solving was a product of sustained, close, and careful analysis of student work samples combined with classroom talk. In this study, it seemed that teachers' inferences derived from analyzing the work samples were challenged when they carefully analyzed students' words and actions as the activity played out in the classroom. Little (2004) argued that in this and other CGI studies,

> student work was employed consistently by the organizers of the professional development activity as a means of opening up new insights into subject matter and learning. ... These studies demonstrate that simply convening teachers to look at student work may have a modest effect on teachers' understanding and practice (p. 109). ... Where research has delved inside the practice of looking at student work, it reveals what might be summed up as meaningful variations in "opportunity to learn" the level of practice. Together, these studies reveal how groups and events vary in their ability to bring student work onto the table for consideration in the first place. They also depict how groups vary in their resources for opening up and sustaining generative discussion of student learning and related questions of teacher knowledge and practice. In doing so, they illuminate some of the characteristic problems that arise in translating the notion of "learning in and from practice" in formal [continuous professional development] programs. (p. 111)

Such research on teacher learning communities adds additional insight into the power and potential of having groups of teachers working collaboratively to study their classroom practice seriously and systematically as it relates to student learning. Research on teacher learning communities suggests that teacher participation has the potential not only to deepen their knowledge of teaching and learning but also to serve as a vehicle to develop new norms and communication patterns conducive to disclosing problems of practice and encouraging teachers to express their uncertainties through thoughtful and constructive public criticism and disagreement (Grossman, Wineburg, & Woolworth, 2001; Pfieffer & Featherstone, 1996). Establishing an atmosphere of trust and support through the creation of an inquiry-driven, school-based, teacher–researcher learning community encourages teachers to work collaboratively with peers and university researchers on common problems of practice. Central to this process is the opportunity to engage in serious dialogue with one another as "critical friends," which in turn provides an ideal context for teachers and researchers to work together to explore more deeply how better to assist young children's science learning.

Content of Professional Development

The preceding discussion focused on the design of professional development. It is also important to consider the content, or what teachers should learn from professional development. In the following section, we consider both the research findings on professional development in science teaching and those from developmental science–based research as they relate to science learning. Our goal is that these findings will help us elaborate on recommendations for the content of professional development. Naturally, a problem with this is that such findings can become abstract and distant from classroom practice. Therefore, we revisit the imaginary classroom described at the beginning of the chapter to "put a face" on the recommendations for professional development based on past research.

• *What is known about the ideas and practices included in teacher professional development in early learning of science?* Asking what is known about the broad topic of teacher professional development in early learning of science may seem overwhelming and impractical. However, as previously stated in this chapter and elsewhere (e.g., Copley & Padron, 1999), there is a relative paucity of research in this area. Nevertheless, important insights about science teaching and learning can be gleaned from the work that has been conducted. This section surveys concepts that research findings have already shown to be effective in professional development contexts. Unfortunately, little of this research has been done with teachers of children ages 3–8 years. Also missing from this survey of research are studies that focus on implementation of new or innovative curriculum or strategies. Rather, we focus on conceptual issues and theoretical ideas related to science teaching that might suitably be learned in professional development, and that have been documented through research. These include teacher subject knowledge, inquiry-oriented instruction, pedagogical knowledge, and issues of equity.

Subject-matter knowledge of science has been a perennial problem for teachers of young children. Research focused on elementary teachers has shown that many teachers lack adequate subject-matter knowledge in science to be effective teachers (Kennedy, 1998; Smith & Neale, 1989). There are many explanations for this issue, but the importance of subject-matter knowledge for teaching seems to relate to positive outcomes for students (Wilson, Floden, & Ferrini-Mundy, 2002). It seems reasonable to infer that if elementary teachers lack subject-matter knowledge of science, then preschool teachers would have similar deficiencies. Because subject-matter knowledge is related to positive outcomes for students, attention to development of teachers' subject-matter knowledge is important. Furthermore, both the findings presented in this volume and implications described in greater detail below require substantive understanding of subject-matter knowledge.

Another issue that has received considerable attention in science education has to do with instructional models of inquiry and their relationship to developing understandings of the nature of science. Teachers' core conceptions of teaching influence how they adopt and enact inquiry pedagogies (Lotter, Harwood, & Bonner, 2007). We believe there is a relationship between inquiry pedagogies and teachers' understanding of the nature of science. Teachers' conceptions of the nature of science have been well documented (Abd-El-Khalick, 2005; Abell, Martini, & George, 2001; Akerson, Abd-El-Khalick, & Lederman, 2000), and the impact of professional development related to the nature of science is beginning to emerge (Akerson & Hanuscin, 2007). The challenge is that this literature focuses on upper elementary and secondary teachers. We assume that if teaching young children followed principles of inquiry and the Nature of Science, then this would be the first step in a trajectory of participation in science that would enable continued success.

An issue receiving increased attention in terms of professional development of science teachers concerns efforts to address issues of access and equity. Access and equity are substantial and complex problems in science education, and involve many ways to theorize about what problems exist and how to resolve those problems. Similar to other areas, the research base on professional development is not fully conclusive in this area. However, we do know that professional development in some of these issues is productive. For example, Lee, Luykx, Buxton, and Shaver (2007) have described efforts to develop teachers' cultural and linguistic competence in the context of science teaching. Working with upper elementary teachers, the researchers concluded that after a 2-year professional development program, teachers made few, if any, changes toward engaging in culturally relevant practices in their teaching. Although this outcome seems disappointing, it highlights the complexity and challenge inherent in addressing issues of culture and linguistic differences in science teaching and professional development.

• *Based on cognitive science research, what content should be the focus of professional development for early learning in science?* Preceding chapters in this volume have considered several developmental perspectives on young children's learning. These chapters have asked us to reexamine some common notions about cognitive development and to develop an empirically based theoretical model that accounts for these findings on young children's cognitive development. Ultimately, though this section is not a review of theories of cognitive development, we attempt to reflect on perspectives of learning and development, and attempt to move from generalized notions about cognitive development to specific proposals that relate to young children's learning of science.

There are assumptions about learning and development that are important to specify. This chapter assumes that learning and development are social activities that rely on less knowledgeable individuals (learners) interacting with more knowledgeable individuals (teachers) (Collins, Brown, & Newman, 1989; Rogoff, 1995). Relating to a constructivist perspective, teachers can plan experiences and encounters that challenge the conceptual frameworks of learners (Posner et al., 1982; Smith, 1991; Watson & Konicek, 1990). Furthermore, it is assumed that particular modes of reasoning and representation/description are situated in social contexts (Gee, 1997; Lemke, 2001). Finally, connecting these assumptions is the notion that teachers and learners bring conceptual frameworks and modes of reasoning and representation to learning that are socially constructed through interactions with others and based on interpretation of individual lived experiences (Hogan, 2002; Warren, Ballenger, Ogonowski, Rosebery, & Hudicourt-Barnes, 2001). In the following pages we consider two perspectives that have potential as specific implications for developmental science–based professional development: children's abilities to theorize about the world, and how children's reasoning is mediated by the limitations in their representational and/or metacognitive abilities.

• *Children have sophisticated and theorized ideas about the world.* Simplistic interpretations of Piaget's (1929) ideas can be interpreted to mean that the thinking of children is limited by the developmental stage of the child. As a result, most young children are thought to be concrete thinkers whose knowledge of the world is directly attributable to their experiences with phenomena or ideas. However, recent research challenges the simplistic notion that children are bound to concrete thinking (Bullock, Gelman, & Baillargeon, 1982; Metz, 1995). This research suggests that there is no clear progression from concrete to abstract in children's development (National Research Council, 2007). It further suggests that children develop sophisticated notions about the world at early ages. Recent research shows that young children can identify improbable events and demonstrate abstract thinking (Bullock et al., 1982). This leads to a new understanding of cognitive development, suggesting that stage theories, although useful, do not adequately account for young children's development. We know that children are capable of engaging in abstract thinking.

Similarly, a simplistic interpretation of Piagetian theory is that young children are incapable of theorizing about phenomena or representational systems (e.g., that addition is a more sophisticated way to think about counting, or that numbers represent more than their symbols). Although this is not conclusive, evidence suggests that young children are capable of more sophisticated reasoning than might be assumed if we restrict our images of children's thinking to the bounds of sensorimotor activity. Research has shown that even as early as 1 year of age, infants demonstrate ability to consider the consequences of events (Kotovsky & Baillargeon, 1994). This research suggests that children are thinking from a perspective of causal reasoning. However, such reasoning is limited to operations that require a limited number of steps. Thus, young children do not seem to be as able to coordinate and to consider causally a sequence of actions or events (National Research Council, 2007).

There is robust research in the field of science education on children's conceptions about phenomena. The conceptual change theory is described well by Vosniadou (Chapter 24) in this volume. A challenge for the conceptual change literature is limitations of available information about young children (National Research Council, 2007). Furthermore, some researchers argue that findings about children's conceptions may be misleading (Smith, diSessa, & Roschelle, 1993). Regardless, the growing consensus is that teachers should not view students as coming to school with merely batches of misconceptions that need changing. Rather, these conceptions represent complex notions about the world that are grounded in students' interactions with phenomena, people, and ideas. Furthermore, children's conceptions of phenomena are powerful forces in their development of understandings of scientific conceptions of phenomena. Finally, as described by Vosniadou (Chapter 24) in this volume, children's conceptions are developed through social interactions and also situated in cultural norms and values. Thus, the development of children's conceptions is impacted by multiple factors (e.g., experiences and interactions with others). Regardless of these issues, it is clear that children's development of conceptions reflects their ability and willingness to engage in sophisticated and theorized ways of both understanding and considering others' understandings of phenomena in the world.

• *Children's reasoning is mediated by abilities to represent and be metacognitive.* Some have argued that an explanation for the inaccurate use of stage theory developmental perspectives has to do with limitations in young children's abilities to represent their knowledge and theories about the world, which can in turn lead adults to make inaccurate assumptions about young children's cognitive capacities (National Research Council, 2007). Clearly, there are limitations to students' abilities at early ages that are related to fine and gross motor skills development (e.g., young children's drawings and representations of phenomena and ideas can be difficult to interpret based on their abilities to generate representations). Oral and written language is a fundamental communicative tool that children develop (Jordan, Snow, & Porche, 2000; Papafragou, Massey, & Gleitman, 2002). Because many young children are just developing their abilities to use language as a communicative tool, this can also impact our impressions of their cognitive reasoning ability and lead to inaccurate impressions of those abilities.

Many young children's reasoning practices are implicit (Gopnik, Sobel, Schultz, & Glymour, 2001) and, as a result, it is difficult to for them to describe their ideas metacognitively. This has a couple of important implications. First, would there be a benefit to explicit modeling of these processes? For example, could the "think-aloud" protocols that yield positive results in literacy do the same in science? The second implication is that implicit reasoning practices are difficult to represent. Because children do not think explicitly about their reasoning, being asked to represent their thinking in some way (e.g., writing, drawing, or talking) may be difficult for them to accomplish. In terms of metacognition, Klahr (2000) argues that it may be important for young children to develop an understanding of psychology. Such understanding relates to scientific thinking. For example, children must understand that knowledge that can be subjectively formed also can potentially be distorted through communication to consider metacognitively the validity of explanations of phenomena and ideas.

Developmental Science–Based Professional Development: Classroom Impact

The significance of the research we have described might be minimized by arguing that some developmental science–based perspectives and practices are already being implemented in early childhood and elementary classrooms. One could also argue that, while potentially valid, many developmental science–based perspectives and practices are not feasible in regular classrooms. However, before a preemptive rejection of the praxeological implications of developmental science research findings, we should identify specific recommendations for practice. Then, by connecting those recommendations with the imaginary classroom earlier in this chapter, it becomes possible to engage in a rational discussion of how research findings might relate to practice. Furthermore, such an exercise helps to highlight how it is easy to consider something as good practice that may not reflect the findings of developmental science research.

Practice Recommendations

What does current evidence from cognitive and developmental science say about effective practices for teaching young children about science? First, teachers should acknowledge and engage with young children's abstract and theorized reasoning about the world. This requires that they appraise children's understanding and engage them in talking about their newly formed conceptions, ideas, and theories. Second, young children should be given opportunities to represent their thinking using different modes of communication (writing, speaking, reading, drawing, etc.). This may require teaching children new strategies to present their conceptions and also engaging them in thinking about developing new ways to represent their ideas. Finally, teachers should engage and support young children in evaluating the accuracy of their own conceptions in comparison with the conceptions of their peers. Young children should be provided opportunities to engage in metacognition, so that they can begin to appreciate the limitations of their conceptions and the affordances of alternative conceptions.

What Would the Imaginary Classroom Look Like That Followed These Recommendations?

Based on the recommendations summarized here, lets revisit the imaginary classroom and consider how it differs given these recommendations. The activity would most likely change very little. The teacher would intentionally choose balls that were different masses and different diameters. In addition, some of these balls would also be the same diameter but made of different materials, and also be solid or hollow. Initially, students might try out different ideas or "play" around with the different balls. Eventually, the teacher would ask students to share their observations and interpretations of the motion of the balls. The teacher would listen closely, trying to understand the children's ideas and explanations about the motion of the balls. Through scaffolding by the teacher, the students would co-construct an investigation of the motion of the balls. Ideally, this would involve comparing two or more students' conflicting explanations about the motions of balls. The students would be expected to represent, through writing or drawing, or some other means, their new ideas based on their observations from the co-constructed investigation. The class would revisit their explanations, talking about whether one explanation made more sense, and how the two explanations differed.

Obviously, this is neat and clean, and as naively presented as the previous imaginary example. But the differences are important to consider. First, the engagement of the teacher and students around concepts and ideas enables consideration and challenge of students' conceptions. The point is that although experiences with phenomena are important, teaching must move beyond providing experiences. Cognitive science research tells us that children are theorizing about the world; therefore, teaching should engage that theorizing. In addition, the communication, both between student and teacher and among students, enables children to build representational systems that tap into their ongoing linguistic and conceptual development. Children need practice and opportunities to invent effective representational systems. Finally, the comparison of ideas enables the teacher to lead students to become metacognitive about the explanations and ideas that they hold. This connects back to an earlier point, but the central point, again, is that developmental science research is challenging the field to begin to recognize the importance of metacognition in children's cognitive development.

Professional Development and Developmental Science–Based Practice

The question driving this section arises out of the implied differences between the two imaginary classrooms. The differences between the two seem clear. But what will support teachers in transforming their practice to reflect the findings of developmental science research? To answer this question, it helps to begin clarifying the distinctions between the classrooms described earlier, then describe the design and content of professional development that we speculate would facilitate teachers' transformation of practice.

The differences between the two classrooms include many ideas rooted in findings from developmental science research. To begin with, the role of children's conceptions of phenomena is different in the two classrooms. In developmental science–based teaching, children's conceptions are made explicit in classroom interactions. Another way the classrooms are different involves the role of children's representations of phenomena. The classroom that follows developmental science–based teaching involves children in representing their conceptions of phenomena. Similarly, having children's representations be part of classroom interactions allows the teacher to discuss students' thinking. This enables teaching to reflect developmental science–based research about the role of metacognition. Finally, the presence of children's work is reflective of effective professional development, which we describe below.

Particularly with regard to science, the Committee on Science Education has established a number of goals for K–8 science learning (National Research Council, 2007) that should drive inquiries and activities that are the focus of this professional development. These goals reflect many of the findings of cognitive science research reported earlier in this volume. However, to be clear, we find the following connections between these recommendations and the findings from professional development research and developmental science–based research described in this chapter:

1. In terms of design, the preceding pages lay out an argument that the design of professional development should include opportunities for teachers to have extended experiences in inquiry-oriented activities in professional learning communities. Furthermore, the focus of the professional development should be children's attempts, through writing or other forms of representation, to describe and explain phenomena. In addition, given the limitations of existing research, it is important that this work be documented to develop greater understanding about professional development of the teachers of young children. Furthermore, this professional development should be rigorous, addressing the following issues, but productive and meaningful to teachers. This builds on notions about the power of professional learning communities in teacher learning (Bolam & McMahon, 2004; Howes, 2008; McLaughlin & Talbert, 2006).

2. Professional development of teachers should build on the robust body of knowledge about children's conceptions of phenomena in the natural world. However, attention to children's conceptions should be situated in the larger sociohistorical context of the child and recognize that children have more complex abilities to think and reason about phenomena. Thus, professional development should focus less on "correcting misconceptions" and more on engaging with children's thinking, reasoning, and theorizing about phenomena.

3. Professional development of teachers should consider the multiple ways that children have to represent and communicate about the world. Engaging children in graphical, symbolic, and linguistic efforts to represent their conceptions of phenomena facilitates both conceptual and language development. Through professional development, research on professional development, and student learning, we may be able to develop a better understanding of learning trajectories for children learning to represent and communicate ideas that represent and challenge disciplinary norms (Roth & Barton, 2004).

4. Finally, the role of metacognition seems vital in children's conceptual and academic development. Yet there is limited understanding of how professional development around teachers' metacognitive talk in science learning may facilitate young children's development of scientific reasoning. Thus, we suggest that this may be an important addition both to professional development practice and the research base on early science learning.

A question that emerges requires us to think about how professional development can support teachers in reacting, responding, and planning instruction based on children's conceptions. The second recommendation, based on recommendations from the Committee on Science Education at the National Academy of Science (Duschl, Schweingruber, & Shouse, 2007) makes reference to this common question and concern of teachers. These questions and concerns are rooted in a crucial issue that may need further research and exploration in terms of professional development for early childhood science teachers. This issue involves analyzing and interpreting children's reasoning, thinking, and conceptions of phenomena in science. Although a robust body of literature documents children's conceptions, and the many inroads being made are helping teachers recognize that "correcting misconceptions" is not necessarily an effective strategy, a limitation is that we have yet to develop robust models for developing teachers' abilities to assess and interpret students' conceptions. Furthermore, richer understanding is needed in terms of helping teachers learn to plan instruction in response to the unique constellation of student conceptions in their classroom. In other words, how does professional development help teachers learn to plan effective instruction that challenges all students, especially their conceptions of phenomena; supports students in developing explanations; develops students' abilities to represent and think metacognitively about their ideas; enables formative assessment of children's conceptions; and allows space for teachers to offer students alternative, preferably accurate and scientific explanations?

In conclusion, we prefer to think about moving toward a conclusion rather than stating a final answer. Moving toward something implies our recognition that both the path and the obstacles may not be entirely clear. The challenge is that although robust evidence is emerging from the fields of cognitive and developmental science, and similar evidence in terms of general notions about effective professional development, we lack adequate knowledge and understanding to know that these recommendations will respond to the specific situation that is the focus of this chapter. We believe the recommendations offered here will facilitate progress toward more effective science learning for young children through more effective models of professional development. Although we hope that these recommendations will serve as guidance for those engaged in the professional development of early childhood educators, our greater hope is that future professional development of early childhood educators will be more fully documented and researched.

References

Abd-El-Khalick, F. (2005). Developing deeper understandings of nature of science: The impact of a philosophy of science course on preservice science teachers' views and instructional planning. *International Journal of Science Education, 27*(1), 15–42.

Abell, S., Martini, M., & George, M. (2001). "That's what scientists have to do": Preservice elementary teachers' conceptions of the nature of science during a moon investigation. *International Journal of Science Education, 23*(11), 1095–1109.

Akerson, V. A., Abd-El-Khalick, F., & Lederman, N. A. (2000). Influence of a reflective explicit activity-based approach on elementary teachers' conceptions of the nature of science. *Journal of Research in Science Teaching, 37*(4), 295–316.

Akerson, V. A., & Hanuscin, D. L. (2007). Teaching nature of science through inquiry: Results of a three-year professional development program. *Journal of Research in Science Teaching, 44*(5), 653–680.

Anderson, C. (2003, May). *Teaching science for motivation and understanding.* Retrieved May 2006 from *www.msu.edu/~andya/tescience/index.htm*

Ball, D. L., & Cohen, D. K. (1999). Developing practice, developing practitioners: Toward a practice-based theory of professional development. In L. Darling-Hammond & G. Sykes (Eds.), *Teaching as the learning profession: Handbook of policy and practice* (pp. 3–32). San Francisco: Jossey-Bass.

Banilower, E. R., Heck, D. J., & Weiss, I. R. (2007). Can professional development make the vision of the *Standards* a reality?: The impact of the National Science Foundation's Local Systemic Change Through Teacher Enhancement Initiative. *Journal of Research in Science Teaching, 44*(3), 375–395.

Bogard, K., Traylor, F., & Takanishi, R. (2008). Teacher education and PK outcomes: Are we asking the right questions? *Early Childhood Research Quarterly, 23,* 1–6.

Bolam, H., & McMahon, A. (2004). Literature, definitions, and models: Towards a conceptual map. In C. Day & J. Sachs (Eds.), *International handbook on the continuing professional development of teachers* (pp. 33–63). Berkshire, UK: Open University Press.

Borko, H., & Putnam, R. T. (1995). Expanding a teacher's knowledge base: A cognitive psychological perspective on professional development. In T. R. Guskey & M. Huberman (Eds.), *Professional development in education: New paradigms and practices* (pp. 35–66). New York: Teachers College Press.

Briscoe, C., & Wells, E. (2002). Reforming primary science assessment practices: A case study of one teacher's professional development through action research. *Science Education, 86,* 417–435.

Bullock, M., Gelman, R., & Baillargeon, R. (1982). The development of causal reasoning. In W. J. Freidman (Ed.), *The developmental psychology of time* (pp. 209–294). New York: Academic Press.

Cochran-Smith, M. (1991). Learning to teach against the grain. *Harvard Educational Review, 61*(3), 279–310.

Collins, A., Brown, J., & Newman, S. (1989). Cognitive apprenticeship: Teaching the crafts of reading, writing, and mathematics. In L. Resnick (Ed.), *Knowing, learning and instruction: Essays in honor of Robert Glaser* (pp. 453–494). Hillsdale, NJ: Erlbaum.

Copley, J., & Padron, Y. (1999). Preparing teachers of young learners: Professional development of early childhood teachers in mathematics and science. In American Association for the Advancement of Science (Ed.), *Dialogue on early childhood science, mathematics, and technology education* (pp. 117–129). Washington, DC: American Association for the Advancement of Science.

Day, C., & Sachs, J. (2004). *International handbook on the continuing professional development of teachers.* Berkshire, UK: Open University Press.

Duschl, R. A., Schweingruber, H. A., & Shouse, A. W. (Eds.). (2007). *Taking science to school: Learning and teaching science in grades K–8* (Report of the Committee on Science Learning, Kindergarten Through Eighth Grade, Board on Science Education). Washington, DC: National Academies Press.

Fullan, M. (1993). *Change forces.* London: Cassell.

Gee, J. P. (1997, March). *Science talk: Language and knowledge in classroom discussion*. Paper presented at the annual meeting of the National Association of Research on Science Teaching, Chicago.

Gelman, S. A. (1999). Concept development in preschool children. In American Association for the Advancement of Science (Ed.), *Dialogue on early childhood science, mathematics, and technology education* (pp. 50–61). Washington, DC: American Association for the Advancement of Science.

Gopnik, A., Sobel, D. M., Schultz, L., & Glymour, C. (2001). Causal learning and mechanisms in very young children: Two-, three- and four-year-olds infer causal relations from patterns of variation and covariation. *Developmental Psychology, 37*, 620–629.

Grossman, P. L., Wineburg, S., & Woolworth, S. (2001). Toward a theory of teacher community. *Teacher College Record, 103*(6), 942–1012.

Grundy, S., & Robinson, J. (2004). Teacher professional development: Trends and themes in recent Australian experience. In C. Day & J. Sachs (Eds.), *International handbook on the continuing professional development of teachers* (pp. 146–166). Berkshire, UK: Open University Press.

Hogan, K. (2002). Small groups' ecological reasoning while making an environmental management decision. *Journal of Research in Science Teaching, 39*(4), 341–368.

Howes, E. V. (2008). Educative experiences and early childhood science education: A Deweyan perspective on learning to observe. *Teaching and Teacher Education, 24*, 536–549.

Johnson, J. R. (1999). The forum on early childhood science, mathematics, and technology education. In American Association for the Advancement of Science (Ed.), *Dialogue on early childhood science, mathematics, and technology education* (pp. 14–25). Washington, DC: American Association for the Advancement of Science.

Jordan, G. E., Snow, C. E., & Porche, M. V. (2000). Project EASE: The effect of a family literacy project on kindergarten students' early literacy skills. *Reading Research Quarterly, 35*(4), 524–546.

Kazemi, E., & Franke, M. L. (2003). *Using student work to support professional development in elementary mathematics*. Seattle: Center for the Study of Teaching and Policy, University of Washington.

Kennedy, M. M. (1998). Education reform and subject matter knowledge. *Journal of Research in Science Teaching, 35*(3), 249–263.

Kennedy, M. M. (1999). Form and substance in mathematics and science professional development. *NISE Brief, 3*(2), 1–8.

King, M. B., & Newmann, F. M. (2001). Building school capacity through professional development: Conceptual and empirical considerations. *International Journal of Educational Management, 15*(2), 86–93.

Klahr, D. (2000). *Exploring science: The cognition and development of discovery processes*. Cambridge, MA: MIT Press.

Kotovsky, L., & Baillargeon, R. (1994). Calibration-based reasoning about collision events in 11-month-old infants. *Cognition, 51*, 107–129.

Lee, O., Luykx, A., Buxton, C., & Shaver, A. (2007). The challenge of altering elementary school teachers' beliefs and practices regarding linguistic and cultural diversity in science instruction. *Journal of Research in Science Teaching, 44*(9), 1269–1291.

Lemke, J. (2001). Articulating communities: Sociocultural perspectives on science education. *Journal of Research in Science Teaching, 38*(3), 296–316.

Little, J. W. (2004). Looking at student work in the United States: A case of competing impulses in professional development. In C. Day & J. Sachs (Eds.), *International handbook on the continuing professional development of teachers* (pp. 94–118). Berkshire, UK: Open University Press.

Lortie, D. C. (1975). *Schoolteacher: A sociological study*. Chicago: University of Chicago Press.

Lotter, C., Harwood, W. S., & Bonner, J. (2007). The influence of core teaching conceptions on teachers' use of inquiry teaching practices. *Journal of Research in Science Teaching, 44*(9), 1318–1347.

McLaughlin, M., & Talbert, J. (2006). *Building school-based teacher learning communities: Professional strategies to improve student achievement*. New York: Teachers College Press.

Metz, K. E. (1995). Reassessment of developmental constraints on children's science instruction. *Review of Educational Research, 65*(2), 93–127.

National Commission on Mathematics and Science Teaching for the 21st Century. (2006). *Before its too late: A report to the nation from the National Commission on Mathematics and Science Teaching for the 21st Century*. Washington, DC: U.S. Department of Education.

National Research Council. (1996). *National Science Education Standards*. Washington, DC: National Academy Press.

National Research Council. (2007). *Taking science to school: Learning and teaching science in grades K–8*. Washington, DC: National Academies Press.

Papafragou, A., Massey, C., & Gleitman, L. (2002). Shake, rattle, 'n' roll: The representation of motion in language and cognition. *Cognition, 84*, 189–219.

Pfieffer, L. C., & Featherstone, H. J. (1996). *Toto, I don't think we're in Kansas anymore: Entering the land of public disagreement in learning to teach*. Lansing: National Center for Research on Teacher Leaning, Michigan State University.

Piaget, J. (1929). *Child's conception of the world* (J. & A. Tomlinson, Trans.). Totowa, NJ: Littlefield, Adams.

Posner, G. J., Strike, K. A., Hewson, P. W., & Gertzog, W. A. (1982). Accommodation of scientific conception: Toward a theory of conceptual change. *Science Education, 66*(2), 221–227.

Ramey-Gassert, L., Shroyer, G., & Staver, J. R. (1996). A qualitative study of factors influencing science teaching self-efficacy of elementary level teachers. *Science Education, 80*(3), 283–315.

Rogoff, B. (1995). Observing sociocultural activity on three planes: Participatory appropriation, guided participation, and apprenticeship. In J. V. Wertsch, P. D. Rio, & A. Alvarez (Eds.), *Sociocultural studies of the mind* (pp. 139–164). New York: Cambridge University Press.

Roth, K. J. (1991). Learning to be comfortable in the neighborhood of science. In W. Saul & S. A. Jagusch (Eds.), *Vital connections: Children, science and books* (pp. 143–161). Washington, DC: Library of Congress.

Roth, W.-M., & Barton, A. C. (2004). *Rethinking scientific literacy*. New York: Routledge/Falmer.

Settlage, J., & Southerland, S. A. (2007). *Teaching science to every child: Using culture as a starting point*. New York: Routledge.

Smith, D. C., & Neale, D. C. (1989). The construction of subject matter knowledge in primary science teaching. *Teaching and Teacher Education, 5*(1), 1–20.

Smith, E. L. (1991). A conceptual change model of learning science. In S. Glynn, R. Yeany, & B. Britton (Eds.), *Psychology of learning science* (pp. 43–63). Hillsdale, NJ: Erlbaum.

Smith, J. P., diSessa, A. A., & Roschelle, J. (1993). Misconceptions reconceived: A constructivist analysis of knowledge in transition. *Journal of the Learning Sciences, 3*(2), 115–163.

Smylie, M. A. (1995). Teacher learning in the workshop: Implications for school reform. In T. R. Guskey & M. Huberman (Eds.), *Professional development in education: New paradigms and practices* (pp. 92–113). New York: Teachers College Press.

Smylie, M. A. (1996). Bureaucratic control to building human capital: The importance of teacher learning in education reform. *Educational Researcher, 25*(9), 9–11.

Sparks, D., & Hirsch, S. (1997). *A new vision for staff development*. Alexandria, VA: Association for Curriculum Development and National Staff Development Council.

Tai, R. H., Liu, C. Q., Maltese, A. V., & Fan, X. (2006). Planning early for careers in science. *Science, 312*(26), 1143–1144.

Valli, L., & Buese, D. (2007). The changing roles of teachers in an era of high-stakes accountability. *American Educational Research Journal, 44*(3), 519–558.

Valverde, G. A., & Schmidt, W. H. (1997). Refocusing U.S. math and science education. *Issues in Science and Technology, 14*(2), 60–66.

Valverde, G. A., & Schmidt, W. H. (1998). *First lessons from the Third International Mathematics and Science Study: Policy challenge of cross-national comparisons*. East Lansing: Michigan State University.

Valverde, G. A., & Schmidt, W. H. (2000). Greater expectations: Learning from other nations in the quest for "world-class standards" in U.S. school mathematics and science. *Journal of Curriculum Studies, 32*(5), 651–687.

Warren, B., Ballenger, C., Ogonowski, M., Rosebery, A. S., & Hudicourt-Barnes, J. (2001). Rethinking diversity in learning science: The logic of everyday sense-making. *Journal of Research in Science Teaching, 38*(5), 529–552.

Watson, B., & Konicek, R. (1990). Teaching for conceptual change: Confronting children's experience. *Phi Delta Kappan, 71*(9), 680–685.

Wilson, S. M., Floden, R. E., & Ferrini-Mundy, J. (2002). Teacher preparation research: An insider's view from the outside. *Journal of Teacher Education, 53*(3), 190–204.

PART VI

CONCLUSION

In this final section, Odom, Barbarin, and Wasik return to the initial purpose of this handbook to consider the lessons or compelling insights provided by developmental research and theory. They identify and selectively review important ideas introduced in the prior chapters and comment on the lessons that might be derived and applied to initiatives such as the First School specifically and to pre-kindergarten to third education generally. Beginning with emerging knowledge on brain and biological development, they distinguish the implications that cut across multiple domains of literacy, numeracy, language, and behavior from those that are specific to a particular domain. However, the chapter is more than a backward-looking summary. It is also forward looking in that it identifies continuing gaps in our knowledge and proffers a set of conditions needed to make to help designers of early childhood curricula, pedagogy, and professional development programs that take advantage of and benefit from the guidance developmental research and theory offers for practice. In addition, the authors identify promising areas for reflection and application that will advance the translation of developmental theory and research into applications that improve the effectiveness of early education.

CHAPTER 26

Applying Lessons from Developmental Science to Early Education

Samuel L. Odom
Oscar A. Barbarin
Barbara Hanna Wasik

Not since the 1960s, when it was one of the strategies for fighting the War on Poverty, has there been as much interest in early childhood education in the United States. Early childhood education has been widely identified as a good investment of economic resources by politicians, Nobel Prize–winning economists, and federal banking associates (Bernanke, 2007; Heckman, Stixrud, & Urzua, 2006). A great momentum that exists in the United States is also present internationally (Clifford & Crawford, 2009).

A difference between the heightened interest of individuals in the 1960s and the perspectives of the 21st century is that application of early childhood education is increasing seen as applying to all children, not just as a remedy to social problems and poverty (Zigler, Gilliam, & Jones, 2006). Public officials are extending the age of public education downward, as has happened in state prekindergarten (pre-K) programs now offered in states such as California, Florida, and Georgia. Yet a discontinuity exists between early childhood education for prekindergarten-age and kindergarten-age children through third grade. These differences are more than cosmetic; they are fundamentally different perspectives about teaching and learning for young children.

To address the discontinuity and even the professional tensions that have arisen, we have looked to developmental science for guidance. The goal of the authors of this handbook is to glean from developmental science theory the research implications for the education of young children from age 3 to grade 3 (P–3). Ritchie, Maxwell, and Bredekamp (Chapter 2, this volume) identified the many concerns facing P–3 education, especially for the areas of language and literacy, math and science, and socioemotional functioning. Nevertheless, because educational policymakers, administrators, and practitioners are recognizing the importance of bridging the chasm between the two, there is still a great need to integrate philosophy and practice in early childhood programs with that of elementary education.

In the sections that follow, we describe lessons learned from the developmental science that are reported in chapters in this book and other literature that may inform the design of practices and educational systems for young children. We first review new and emerging knowledge reported about brain and biological development. In the main section of this chapter, we highlight implications for developmental science that are "domain general" and "domain specific." In our conclusion, we propose important factors for moving scientific research from the lab and literature to practices in early childhood education programs for young children.

Biological and Neurological Bases for Education

An expanding brain science and its linkage to behavior and development provide glimpses into the developing and evolving infant and young child. A clear message from this science is that much of the neurological system is laid down before the age of 3 (Fusaro & Nelson, Chapter 4, this volume). Maternal nutrition and prenatal care; the early caregiving environment in the home and/or infant child care centers; the security established through attachment to a primary caregiver; the exposure to a rich and responsive oral language environment; and early exposure to print, book reading, and numbers are experiences in the first 3 years of life that influence the physiological development of the brain, the growth and pruning of neurons, and the formation of synaptic pathways and neural networks (Kagan & Herschkowitz, 2005). In a recent national conference on preschool readiness (National Center on Children in Poverty, 2008), leaders in the field of developmental science summarized the most recent research on preschool intervention programs. A primary topic of discussion was the necessity of beginning work earlier than age 3 years, as happens with Early Head Start because of the massive brain development that occurs during those earlier years. When children enter child care and preschool programs at age 3, it is not too late to support their positive trajectory of development or to provide support to influence the trajectory in a more positive way, but those children arrive with more than a 1,000 days of learning, development, and experience which teachers and caregivers have to consider in their plans for early education.

Although humans do not have the clearly defined critical periods found in some species (Bruer, 2001), early experience has major effects on some developmental skills. Fusaro and Nelson (Chapter 4, this volume) note the *experience-expectant* nature of some abilities; that is, during certain points of brain development, specific experiences are essential. Visual perception is one very specific example for humans, in that without sufficient visual stimulation during the first year of life, features of the visual cortex will not develop (Horton, 2001). Language development is a second example. Wells (Chapter 13, this volume) noted that humans are phylogenetically ordained to develop language, but such development is based on the availability of a language environment and/or language system during the second year of life, when both neurological and oral language growth accelerates (Neville & Bruer, 2001).

In contrast, *experience-dependent* abilities evolve over time and although tied to brain development, their temporal impact is not as dramatic or specific. Learning to read requires a coordinated set of skills (Wasik & Newman, Chapter 14, this volume) and processing capacity of coordinated brain centers (Furusco & Nelson, Chapter 4, this volume). As such networks come "on line" the component skills merge into the capacity to decode and understand written text. But having the brain capacity is not enough for most children, in that an intentional set of experiences must be planned.

A second example of an experience-dependent ability is self-regulation. Calkins and Williford (Chapter 9, this volume) describe well the interplay between neurological maturation of the frontal cortex and the increased ability to self-regulate over time. However, the child's self-regulation skills depend on both this capacity and experiences in which self-regulation is modeled and expected.

In summary, brain science and development science are sisters in their description and explanation of the unfolding human organism. To date, we understand more about the capacities of young children because of discoveries about the way the brain works. This understanding provides general guidance in how early educators might plan for children and families, but specific recommendations from brain science, filtered through developmental science, still comprise a potential to be realized in the future. As one of the great developmental neuroscientists, the late Elizabeth Bates (2002) once said in a keynote presentation (to paraphrase), "If a child's behavior changes, then, of course, brain processes are going to change." The challenge for the field, which will be realized in the future, is how information about brain development and functioning can be translated into practical guidance for teachers and caregivers.

Domain-Specific and Domain-General Implications of Developmental Science

The compendium of knowledge about developmental science presented in this handbook has much to offer individuals charged with the education and care of young children. Ritchie and colleagues (Chapter 2, this volume) noted that the findings of developmental science may be "domain general" (i.e., they may apply across developmental areas) or "domain specific" (i.e., they may apply to specific developmental areas or processes, such as language or memory). The conceptualization of children's abilities as being both general and specific was the foundation of Bornstein's (Chapter 7, this volume) theoretical and empirically supported conceptualization of the Mind of the Child assessment. Extending the classic work of Spearman, Guilford, and Gardner, Bornstein's identification of both specific and general abilities (e.g., linguistic, interpersonal, numerate/spatial), which he calls first- and second-order skills (respectively), supports the potential for thinking about educational practices that may have specific or more general effects. The other implication drawn from Bornstein's work is that children may have strengths or needs in specific skills areas, so teachers need to assess children to determine individual needs and to plan for children individually. Although the whole child is more than his or her constituent parts, nevertheless there are still important constituent parts.

Domain General

Domain-general lessons learned from developmental science apply across development capacities and skills areas. The implications apply to issues of classroom physical and social ecology, theoretical and conceptual orientation of the program, specific pedagogy, and assessment.

Classroom and School Environment

A primary part of the ecology of early childhood programs is the classroom physical and temporal environment. J. Thompson and Twibell (Chapter 10, this volume) and Wasik and Newman (Chapter 14, this volume) have highlighted particularly important features, such as predictable routines and schedules that also have some flexibility, a balance between physically active and passive activities, a mix of large-group and small-group experiences, furniture and equipment that is physically and developmentally appropriate, designated learning areas, and opportunities for child choice and child-initiated learning. Although these features convey a pre-K philosophical approach, they have relevance for designing classroom environments in the K–3 age range (Ritchie et al., Chapter 2, this volume). Many of these variables have been included in measures of early childhood development quality, which in turn have been linked to child outcomes at the pre-K level (Burchinal, Peisner-Feinberg, Bryant, & Clifford, 2000). Indeed, there is a national movement to establish quality rating systems to assess the quality programs for young children in states providing pre-K services (National Association for the Education of Young Children, 2008). The provision of a high-quality classroom physical ecology serves as a foundation for learning experiences that may occur across domains.

Teacher–Child Interactions

The types of teacher interactions with children and the relationships that develop between teacher and child may also have a general effect on development. From an active program of research, Mashburn and colleagues (2008) have documented the variance in the quality of teacher–child interaction, the association with overall class climate, and the effect on child outcomes. In an elegant set of studies that combined both descriptive and experimental work, Ornstein, Coffman, and Grammer (Chapter 6, this volume) documented the positive impact of teachers' elaborative interactions on children's memory. For the development of social competence, R. Thompson and Goodman (Chapter 8, this volume) noted the importance of a facilitative teacher with whom students develop a positive relationship. Wasik and Newman (Chapter 14, this volume) emphasized the essential features of instructional conversations between teachers and children that engage both in extended conversations.

Across chapters and areas of research, a common image of an effective teacher for young children emerges. An effective teacher is one who manages a classroom day so that there are consistent, extended, well-modulated interactions with individual children. Such interactions elaborate on children's thoughts, ideas, and interests, and lead to positive relationships between the adult and child. Often, but not always, the interactions are responsive, although such interactions may at times, and for some content, take on a group, didactic form (e.g., when introducing a general topic to the class or managing a transition in the daily routine, such as going to lunch).

Theoretical Approach

An interesting trend in early childhood education has occurred over the past few decades. Many early childhood educators and probably most authors of chapters in this book would characterize themselves as constructivists. Constructivist theories are based primarily on the works of Piaget and Vygotsky, with each having different but not antithetical views of development. Piaget proposed an image of early childhood in which the children act on their environment and build their intellect through direct experiences and observations. Vygotsky proposed that children's development is fostered by mediation through social interaction with adults (or other, more cognitively advanced individuals). The role of the teacher and other adults in these two approaches is different. In the former, the adult is the constructor of learning environments and perhaps the elaborator of child-initiated activity. In the latter, the adult fills both of these roles but also takes an active mediational role in engaging the child in meaningful learning (Stetsenko & Vianna, Chapter 3, this volume). Although most authors have not dogmatically aligned themselves with either of the constructivist camps, the developmental science conveyed by authors in these chapters appears to favor the Vygotskian form of constructivism. But, in reality, teachers pick and choose among theoretical approaches and construct for themselves a "theory of teaching" that may guide their actions (Odom & Wolery, 2003). There is much wisdom in the adage attributed to several authors (Siegler, Chapter 19, this volume) that "there is nothing so practical as a good theory" (p. 429), and the elaboration by Stetsenko and Vianna (Chapter 3, this volume) that "at the same time, there is nothing more theoretical than a good practice" (pp. 38–39).

Didactic Instruction versus Exploration

As noted previously, a primary distinction between pre-K and K–12 education is found in the extent to which each emphasizes teacher-led large- and small-group didactic instruction versus teacher-orchestrated child-initiated engagement in learning with teacher feedback. Whereas the former is more characteristic of K–3 education, the latter is more likely to be observed in pre-K programs. Teachers in programs for younger children are more likely to utilize projects, demonstrations, cooperative activities, and tasks to promote learning over and above strictly didactic methods.

A developmental science perspective may question whether this dichotomy is universally appropriate for all types of learning. Rather, there are situations in which intentional and explicit instruction is appropriate for a child's learning needs and, alternatively, when it is appropriate and effective to foster children's self-guided engagement and discovery. Teachers should consider using intentional instruction when (1) children lack basic information they need to understand a phenomenon or problems; (2) knowledge is sequential and/or hierarchical; and (3) successful acquisition of new knowledge, skills, or abilities is dependent on access to prior information. For example, much of early mathematics builds on an understanding of terms used in spatial representation (e.g., *behind*, *above*, and *under*), or comparative terms (e.g., *bigger* or *longer*). When children lack such terms, explicit instruction and practice in the use of these terms is a prerequisite for their learning in areas such as measurement and geometry (Casey, Chapter 21, this volume). Similarly, for social problem-solving tasks, children may first need to have a vocabulary for and awareness of emotions such as anger, frustration, and relaxation (Gallagher & Sylvester, Chapter 11, this volume; R. Thompson & Goodman, Chapter 8, this volume).

Child-initiated engagement and discovery may be useful when (1) knowledge to be gained is abstract and outside of children's prior experience, and (2) actual experience of a fact or phenomenon can make it real and accessible to a child. For example, in introducing some concepts related to quantity and numeracy, actual physical manipulation may be particularly instructive (Ginsburg, Chapter 18, this volume). Similar, when introducing a science concept, such as different forms of matter, experimentation with basic elements (e.g., as ice, water, and water vapor) may be most facilitative (French, 2004). Experimentation should of course include teacher or peer support in the experience, and in fact teachers' elaborative conversations that perhaps build from errors that children may provide important "teachable" moments (Ornstein et al., Chapter 6, this volume). Stetsenko and Vianno (Chapter 3, this volume) noted that perhaps the dichotomy in this discussion should not be didactic versus child-initiated instruction, but rather the inert versus generative knowledge that instructional procedures foster.

Scaffolding

Wasik and Newman (Chapter 14, this volume) make the bold proposition that scaffolding underlies all that we are about in early childhood education. They describe scaffolding as "structure for a child to move from an existing skill level to a more advanced, sophisticated level" (p. 317). As applied individually to children, a teacher takes the role of expanding, stretching, and facilitating new learning by any child and associating it with existing knowledge. From a Vygotskian perspective, the teacher identifies the child's "zone of proximal development" and supports his or her learning into the next level. This differs from the standard, didactic large- and small-group instruction in some classrooms. The dichotomy between lecturing and scaffolding, between telling the child and allowing the child to discover, is one of the pedagogical issues at the heart of the tension between pre-K and K–12 education.

From the Wasik and Newman perspective, scaffolding may also be viewed as a conceptual framework for what we do as a field of education. We, as teachers, identify the next steps in learning and organize learning environments that supports their developmental progress. Embedded in this process is the need for assessment and a plan for instruction that leads to the next level.

Assessment

When assessment is discussed in early childhood professional communities, images emerge of adults keeping young children in testing situations for long hours to measure their IQs with standardized, norm-referenced test. Although there are purposes for which such assessments are necessary (e.g., diagnosis of a disability, research) and appropriate ways to conduct such assessments, this type of assessment process is often viewed as antithetical to early childhood education. An exception, perhaps, is Bornstein's Mind of the Child assessment, which might be used as an initial planning instrument early in the school year to help practitioners plan around the general strengths and needs of children in their class. There is, however, a more fundamental formative assessment process that should be inherent in the work of early childhood practitioners. Ongoing assessment of children's current developmental performance to make judgments about instruction should be an inherent part of the early childhood education process. Wasik and Newman (Chapter 14, this volume) point out that this formative assessment of children's current functioning is a necessary part of the scaffolding process. From a Vygotskian perspective, an adult mediator must know about a child's current development to determine the "zone of proximal development." In planning elaborative conversations to promote memory, Ornstein and colleagues (Chapter 6, this volume) emphasized the need to gather information for planning from the child. Importantly, their research revealed that the way such information was gathered affected the type of information obtained, with an elaborative assessment process being more productive than a traditional assessment style.

Informal assessment systems that allow continuous progress monitoring for children have been developed and are used widely for literacy assessment in early elementary programs (e.g., Dynamic Indicators of Basic Early Literacy Skills) (Good, Gruba, & Kaminski, 2002). Similarly, McConnell, McEvoy, and Priest (2002) reported on a process for developing individual measures of growth and development for infants and young children, and researchers have established a variety of these measures (Luze & Hughes, 2008). Systematic and feasible assessment tools that build on developmental science, and inform teachers about current performance and next steps in development, should be essential features of early childhood education programs.

Consolidation

Consolidation and reconsolidation are concepts from developmental science that provide a window onto how children learn and retain information. Bauer (Chapter 5, this volume) explained that memory traces of what has been learned are usually unstable until they are integrated into long-term storage and connected with prior knowledge. "Consolidation" is a process by which memory of new information is stabilized, associated with related information, and stored for long-term retrieval and use. As a part of this process, recently acquired information is connected with bits of old information on the basis of having some elements in common. "Reconsolidation" occurs when new learning is linked to and integrated with previously learned information.

The concept of consolidation may be informative for early childhood education. The recommendation by J. Thompson and Twibell (Chapter 10, this volume) that intensive instruction or activities be alternated with quiet or less intense activity might provide immediate opportunity for consolidation. Providing multiple examples, opportunities, and contexts for learning concepts or information may allow for the reconsolidation of information in memory (Bauer, Chapter 5, this volume). This practice of scaffolding, described previously, is very consistent with the process of reconsolidation, in that it connects new information or more advanced concepts (in the zone of proximal development) with current knowledge or abilities.

Self-Regulation

Although often thought of in a social context, "self-regulation" may be defined more broadly as regulation of not only emotions and social behavior but also attention and cognitive strategies. R. Thompson and Goodman (Chapter 8, this volume) and Calkins and Williford (Chapter 9, this volume) define "self-regulation" (combining elements of both definitions) as children's ability to suppress a dominant response to the environment to cope with environmental demands. The latter authors proposed a developmental framework for progressively greater self-regulation, from biological regulation to regulation of attention, emotions, behavior, and cognitive skills. These forms of self-regulation culminate in children's increasing ability to work independently, to follow rules rather than to behave on impulse, and to focus attention on learning tasks for increasing amounts of time, to name but a few. These skills apply to learning across literacy, math, science, and social learning. Specific curricula (e.g., Bodrova & Leong, 2007; Webster-Stratton & Reid, 2008) and particular styles of teacher interaction (Calkins & Williford, Chapter 9, this volume) may foster children's acquisition of self-regulation skills.

Culture and Family

Although they differ, culture and family are included together because, we propose, it is the family that mediates the understanding and expression of culture for children at a young age. Vygotsky and followers are clear in their proposition that cultural learning is a primary part of the developmental process and is inseparable from teaching. Barbarin and Aikens (Chapter 17, this volume) detail the ways in which families from different cultures have different perspectives and influences on children's acquisitions of literacy skills. The specific friendships that children develop in early childhood education programs are directly affected by the cultural, racial, and gender factors. Interestingly, Amendum and Fitzgerald (Chapter 16, this volume) note that we still do not have all the information we need about the effect of cultural and linguistic factors on children's development, as revealed by their finding that Latino children in their reading project made as much progress as native-English-speaking children on most indicators of literacy. Implications for teachers and practitioners include fostering a culturally respectful environment that includes, when appropriate, cultural representation in materials and activities. Barbarin and Odom (Chapter 12, this volume) note that a primary outcome for early childhood programs should be social acceptance and respect for diversity, which is discussed more specifically in a subsequent section on social competence but also applies across developmental domains.

Domain Specific

Language and Literacy

At the forefront of the attention of federal policymakers responsible for early childhood education is the need to prepare young children to become literate members of society, which, specifically, means that children become competent readers by the end of their elementary years in school. At that point, and even earlier, the school curriculum shifts from learning to read to reading to learn. One might take issue with this distinction, however, if we conceptualize writing as another form of literacy (Wells, Chapter 13, this volume), that extends across the school years.

A significant program of research in developmental and education science has in the last two decades identified a set of skills or abilities that underlie the development of literacy. Wasik and Newman (Chapter 14, this volume) noted that the following are frequently listed as the key early literacy abilities at the preschool level: oral language, concepts of print, phonological awareness, and alphabetic knowledge at the early literacy level. For children in early elementary grades, phonemic awareness, phonics, fluency, vocabulary, and comprehension are typically identified as the main skills. Rather than separate these early literacy skills into these two sets, Wasik and Newman propose putting all these early literacy skills within the same framework across the pre-K–3 range to assist teachers as they plan for individual children. This more comprehensive framework helps teachers recognize the wide range of skills acquisition by young children. Although it does not suggest a pedagogy, this identification provides a focus for assessment and instructional planning.

Another clear implication of the developmental science reported in this book is that support for the acquisition of literacy is a joint affair, shared by family and school. Barbarin and Aikens (Chapter 17, this volume) note that early in children's lives, families provide key literacy learning experiences in the words they speak, the modeling of interest in reading they provide, and the time they take in reading storybooks to their children. The power of book reading can be enhanced by the type of questions parents ask their children about books they read together, such as open-ended rather that yes–no questions, and the elaborative ways they respond to children's answers (Barbarin & Aikins, Chapter 17, this volume; Wasik & Newman, Chapter 14, this volume). In addition, parents may enhance early literacy abilities in more intentional but playful ways with songs and word games.

Developmental and educational science have contributed much knowledge that may be used to support literacy skills in early childhood education settings. As it is in families, book reading is an important learning activity in classes, and teachers focus on highlighting the print features of the book being read, facilitative questions that lead children to cognitive and linguistically rich responses, and instructional conversations before, during, and after the story. For example, Wells (Chapter 13, this volume) noted the elaborative process of supporting children through conversations about planning, acting, and reviewing, which are key elements of several early childhood curricula (e.g., High/Scope). Again, incorporating writing in the literacy learning process is useful. Although the fine motor skill feature of writing adds a developmental feature not present in reading, the combined reading–writing approach to literacy may create an interesting "multimodal" dimension to literacy learning that allows the teacher to present similar concepts in different formats. As noted previously, Bauer's work (Chapter 5, this volume) suggests that such an approach may well support the consolidation and reconsolidation process.

Explicit skills instruction may be necessary for children who do not have the developmentally necessary component skills of reading. Most authors would agree that large-group, undifferentiated didactic instruction is not a pedagogy of choice for young learners. Teachers, however, can be intentional, focused, and individualized in their instruction. Such approaches may include a balance among child-directed engagement in literacy experiences enhanced by teacher conversation and scaffolding (e.g., independent writing activities), and small-group, teacher-led, differentiated instruction that focuses on key early literacy skills (e.g., phonemic awareness, comprehension). In addition, literacy skills can become a recurrent theme in the early childhood education classroom through integrated curricula that focus on literacy skills in other content areas (e.g., vocabulary development during science activities) or elaboration of literacy concepts during transition routines in the classrooms (e.g., "All children sitting on the letter A mat, line up for recess").

An approach that has gained increasing visibility in the early childhood education community is called "response to intervention" (RTI; Wasik & Newman, Chapter

14, this volume). Although originally for children who might be at risk for learning problems or those with disabilities, the concept of RTI applies to all children in early childhood education classes. RTI is a tiered approach that progressively increases the amount of instructional support provided to children based on their need. The foundation, or first tier, of any program is a literacy-rich classroom and facilitative teacher whose interactions support the literacy of all children. Using an ongoing system of progress monitoring for all children, practitioners identify children in need of greater support that may be provided in a Tier 2 level of instruction through perhaps small-group experiences (as noted earlier) or individual teacher scaffolding in the routine activities of the class. For children who continue to need greater support, teachers may provide more focused literacy experiences on specific skills or abilities. Although originating in the older elementary grades, models for RTI, such as the recognition and response model developed by Coleman, Buysse, and Neitzel (2006), have been developed for early childhood education and are consistent with many of the approaches identified through developmental science (Stetsenko & Vianna, Chapter 3, this volume; Dickinson et al., Chapter 15, this volume).

The effect of English as a second language on the development of literacy is a significant issue in early childhood education. Amendum and Fitzgerald (Chapter 16, this volume) have summarized a literature suggesting that Spanish-speaking children (i.e., children with Spanish as their first language) may be at risk for poor academic performance, but they also acknowledge that, for this population, there is little systematic research on the association of oral English development and the acquisition of key literacy skills (in English) for children in the early elementary years. In their research, which began in first grade, Spanish-speaking children initially had delays in key literacy skills compared to their English-speaking peers. Over the 2 years spanning the first and second grade, they "caught up" with those English-speaking peers on important indicators such as instructional reading level, word- and sound-level understanding, and comprehension and fluency. A question might arise about how Spanish-speaking children in this study could do so well when a general prediction might be that they would perform poorly in comparison to their peers. One may reflect back to this earlier discussion of RTI, in that a solid and high-quality literacy learning experience in the classroom may enable most children in the class to perform well. Amendum and Fitzgerald described the literacy instruction in the classrooms in their study as being excellent, and the Mexican children in the study appeared to benefit, as did the English-speaking children.

Mathematics

As in literacy, consensus exists among developmental and educational scientists about topics that should be covered in early childhood mathematics (Ginsburg, Chapter 18, this volume; Siegler, Chapter 19, this volume). These topics include number and operations, geometry (shape and space), measurement, and algebra (particularly patterns). Although teachers in many early childhood programs make an effort to cover numbers and operations, they pay too little attention to geometry, spatial representation, and spatial reasoning. As Ginsburg notes, spatial reasoning skills involve the ability to think and reason through the comparison, manipulation, and transformation of concept, which children may develop through a range of play activities, such as putting together two-dimensional shape puzzles, using tangram pieces or pattern blocks, and building three-dimensional structures with wooden blocks or LEGO® pieces. In addition, Ginsburg notes that measurement skills can be fostered by creating diagrams, graphs, and drawing. Spatial visualization can be developed through embedded figure tasks, in which the child searches for a figure hidden within a more complex ground or by imagining two shapes, then mentally combining them to create a new design.

In early childhood programs, number sense is a key developmental ability that teachers should foster. Siegler (Chapter 19, this volume) defined "number sense" as the ability to approximate numerical magnitudes of specific dimensions of objects, events, or sets. It may involve estimating the number of marbles in a jar, the number of cars that pass an intersection in a given time, or the size of an object or the outcome of a large numerical operation. Number sense is developed through experiences with counting, but counting alone is not sufficient. Siegler has provided evidence that playing numbered board games, such as Chutes and Ladders, can significantly improve children's number sense.

The intentionality and focus of math instruction in early childhood programs is open for debate. Ginsburg (Chapter 18, this volume) notes that experience with math learning does not necessarily have to be integrated into other activities and recommends that teachers spend at least 20 minutes of their day focusing specifically on math in a developmentally appropriate manner. His recommendation does not preclude a broader, integrated approach that might be a salient dimension of projects, and Bartolini Bussi and Boni (Chapter 20, this volume) and Falcade and Strozzi (Chapter 22, this volume) present examples of how mathematic concepts and abilities may be fostered through such child-constructed, teacher-mediated projects and activities. Casey (Chapter 21, this volume) also emphasizes that the two approaches—focused, domain-specific math content and broader integrated approaches—are not antithetical. Citing work by Klahr and Nigam (2004), Casey notes that often the problem-solving process necessitates that children have some content knowledge as a foundation, without which the elaborative questioning and problem-solving process may become a "guessing game" rather than a learning experience. Such content knowledge may well be introduced through intentional, teacher-led activities.

Several authors note the lack of math emphasis in early childhood programs and speculate that such underrepresentation may be because early childhood educators do not feel comfortable or knowledgeable about math content (Siegler, Chapter 19, this volume), outside of perhaps traditional number naming and identification. Curricula containing information about child developmental skills, important early math content, and teacher facilitation processes may provide essential support in early childhood programs. Fortunately, the development, quality, and efficacy of early math curricula are the strongest of any domain-specific pedagogical area in early childhood education. To name a few, Big Math for Little Kids by Ginsburg, Greenes, and Balfanz (2003), Building Blocks by Clements and Sarama (2007), Number Worlds by Griffin (2007), and Pre-K Mathematics Curriculum by Klein and Starkey (2002) provide excellent guidance for early childhood practitioners.

Science

If organized and elaborated emphasis in early mathematics is underrepresented in early childhood education, then a systematic focus on science is nearly invisible. The dilemma again involves the comfort level of early childhood educators with the content and familiarity with the problem-solving process that is implicit in developing a "scientific method" approach to early learning (Enfield & Rogers, Chapter 25, this volume). Often approaches in early childhood education have included science as a ritualized part of the curriculum (i.e., discussion of the weather at circle time) or to expose children to a panoply of topics, all touched on very lightly, without very deep knowledge. This fundamentally flawed strategy should be replaced by curricula that containing focused and conceptually organized content as well as a teacher-mediated problems solving process (Vosniadou, Chapter 24, this volume). An example of such a curriculum is Science Start!, developed by French (2004). A year-long curriculum involving four conceptual foci (Measurement and Mapping, Color and Light, Properties of Matter, Neighborhood Habitat), the curriculum model includes teacher-led introduction of concepts, exploratory and hands-on activities in small groups or independently, and an elaborative, interactive approach for teachers organized around four progressive levels of conversation: reflect and ask, plan and predict, act and observe, and report and reflect.

Socioemotional Competence

Unlike early literacy and mathematics abilities, the component skills that make up socioemotional abilities and, more broadly, social competence are less well established. We know it when this goes wrong, such as through disruptive behavior, aggression, and social withdrawal, and we understand the long-term negative implications of aberrant behavior or disrupted peer relationships (Ladd, 2005). The component skills, however, are not as discrete as naming all alphabet letters, writing one's name legibly, counting, detecting one-to-one correspondence, or identifying spatial relationships. Because social engagement draws on several domains (e.g., cognitive, language) and varies infinitely in form and context, socioemotional development is in many ways a more complex subdomain than others.

Developmental science does provide guidance. Most developmental scientists would agree that socioemotional development for preschoolers and early elementary school children is influenced by attachment relationships and early caregiving experiences that occur during the first three years of their lives (R. Thompson & Goodman, Chapter 8, this volume). The attachment literature is one of the most active in all of developmental science. It provides a convincing argument that attachment between caregivers and children is strongly associated with the interactions and relationships that develop between children and their peers and nonparent adults during the preschool and early elementary years (Sroufe, Egeland, Carlson, & Collins, 2005). Similarly, early caregiving may establish routines or patterns of behavior that are more or less responsive to a classroom setting. Given that early education practitioners receive these children in their classrooms after children have had these experiences, two lessons are important: (1) being aware of attachment, and aware that an early caregiving experience may help practitioners understand children's behavior in classroom; (2) realizing that even a poor early caregiving experience or attachment relationship does not doom a child to ongoing social failure. Building a program to support early social and emotional competence is a worthy goal of early childhood education.

As noted previously, researchers do acknowledge that self-regulation is a fundamental capacity that has implications across domains, but it has specific and perhaps more direct implications for socioemotional development (Calkins & Williford, Chapter 9, this volume). R. Thompson and Goodman (Chapter 8, this volume) propose more broadly that the development of "self"—as reflected through self-awareness, socioemotional understanding of others, empathy and caring, and self-regulation—is a major developmental achievement of the early years. They emphasize that learning to meet expectations of adults and understanding how to cooperate with peers are two developmental tasks of early childhood. More specifically, establishing at least acceptable social status in a peer group and making at least one or two reciprocal friendships appear to be indicators of early social competence (Odom, McConnell, & Brown, 2008).

One of the mediators of socioemotional competence during early childhood education is the interaction with teachers and the development of a positive teacher–student relationship. J. Thompson and Twibell (Chapter 10, this volume) note that facilitating features of teachers' interactions with children in their class are consistency, nurturing support, modeling socially positive behavior and attitudes, and using specific rather than general praise. They also noted how infrequently these positive social behaviors occur during a school or classroom day. In a consistent program of research, Pianta and colleagues (Hamre & Pianta, 2005; La Paro, Pianta, & Stuhlman, 2004) have examined teachers' interactive styles with students and the emotional climate they create in the classroom, documenting associations with students' social and academic behavior. A special feature of the teachers' work that facilitates positive interactions in the classroom is creation of predictable and secure classroom environments, although Gallagher and Sylvester (Chapter 11, this volume) note that for children with major socioemotional needs, this is a necessary but insufficient feature of the early childhood education program. For those children, more focused approaches may be necessary.

Fortunately, more intentional and focused approaches exist in manualized, organized, and empirically supported early childhood curricula that often are delivered to all children in the classroom to promote prosocial behavior. They generally also have specific skills instruction for children with challenging behavior. Examples of such curricula identified by Gallagher and Sylvester (Chapter 11, this volume) and Calkins and Williford (Chapter 9, this volume) include Promoting Alternative Thinking Strategies (Domitrovich, Greenberg, Cortes, & Kusche, 1999), Second Step (Committee for Children, 1989), Incredible Years (Webster-Stratton & Reid, 2003), and Tools of the Mind (Bodrova & Leong, 2007). These curricula vary in the theoretical and pedagogical orientation, but most include a combination of teacher-delivered content, child participation around social problem-solving situations, and teacher facilitation of social problem-solving, emotional literacy, and/or prosocial interactions across the school day.

A common assumption is that by providing a nurturing social environment with curricular content that intentionally fosters prosocial behavior, children will naturally be socially accepted by members of their peer group and develop reciprocal friendships. However, individual variations in children's characteristics affect social acceptance and friendship formation (Odom et al., 2008). A well-established finding is that, early in life, boys and girls exhibit a preference for interactions and friendships with peer of their same sex (Gallagher & Sylvester, Chapter 11, this volume). For children with disabilities, there appears to be a higher rate of social rejection, at least in inclusive preschool classes, relative to nondisabled peers (Odom Zercher, Li, Marquart, & Sandal, 2006). Similarly, children appear to prefer as friends and to accept socially peers within their same racial/ethnic groups rather than peers from other groups. Teachers' modeling and facilitation are the key to supporting "cross-group" social acceptance. Yet Barbarin and Odom (Chapter 12, this volume) propose that social acceptance alone is not sufficient, that it may have a neutral affective valence; rather, teachers and early childhood programs should strive for a broader goal of social acceptance and respect for diversity (SARD). This goal of SARD extends beyond a "bias-free" curricular approach that occurs often in early childhood education, and specifies more proactive outcomes of positive rather than neutral, attitudes, and friendships with children across groups in the classroom.

In Summary: Challenges to Moving Developmental Science into Practice

The differences between applying a beautifully designed project model for promoting math skills in the Reggio Emilia preschool in Italy (e.g., Falcade & Strozzi, Chapter 22, this volume) and implementing such a program in a state prekindergarten or even first-grade classroom in an urban school in the United States are great. Cultural, pedagogical, philosophical, and fiscal degrees of separation make such an application unlikely or at least improbable. Besides the figurative (and sometimes literal) translations that may be necessary for strategies described by chapter authors, what needs to happen? We propose, briefly, several necessary steps in moving developmental science to early childhood education practice.

Translation Process

For the scientific findings reported by chapter authors in this volume (e.g., consolidation proposed by Bauer [Chapter 5]; elaborative questions and commenting described by Ornstein et al. [Chapter 6] and Dickinson et al. [Chapter 15]; Vygotskian techniques and content suggested by Bartolini Bussi & Boni [Chapter 20] and Falcade & Strozzi [Chapter 22]), the first step in a research-to-practice process is to design applications that can occur in the classroom or other practice settings. Such procedures must be specified clearly and precisely enough that other individuals can replicate them. In clinical psychology and medicine, in a process called "manualization," a set of procedures is documented in a manual or treatment guide (Smith et al., 2007). Because some of these early education procedures involve interactive strategies rather than just specific content, a comprehensive curriculum manual many not always be an appropriate form of documentation, and more dynamically oriented procedural guides may be an alternative. But, at a minimum, innovative pedagogical techniques must have a process for clearly documenting implementation.

A key feature of this process is practitioners' involvement (e.g., early childhood educators), which may take different forms. First, practitioners may become research partners (Enfield & Rogers, Chapter 25, this volume). In their discussion of design experimentation, which is an underutilized and potentially valuable technique in developmental science, De Corte, Verschaffel, and Depaepe (Chapter 23, this volume) highlight researchers' partnership with teachers in determining effects of variations in curricular or procedural applications in classrooms. Alternatively, practitioners may be viewed as expert consumers whose guidance is sought initially in determining the research questions to address, evaluating the acceptability and feasibility of teaching strategies they designed to address the issues, and judging the social importance of the results of the procedures (Wolf, 1978). Last and perhaps most important, practitioner from the pre-K and the K–3 early childhood communities are the individuals needed to bridge the pedagogical and philosophical divide between the two professional communities (Ritchie et al., Chapter 2, this volume).

Validation

A science of early childhood education requires verification that pedagogical procedures based on developmental theory and research have efficacy in promoting the intended outcomes for children (e.g., oral vocabulary, problem solving, math knowledge). In the United States and other countries, there is a great emphasis on evidence-based practice (Whitehurst, 2004), and although leaders in the field have noted that evidence-based practice includes practitioners' and families' expertise and values (Buysse & Wesley, 2006), there still must be an empirical validation of efficacy. As noted previously, for some curricular and instructional procedures, developmental and education scientists have documented procedures in a replicable form, designed tools for assessing implementation, and conducted research studies to document their efficacy (e.g., Bierman et al., 2008; Clements & Sarama, 2008; Webster-Stratton, Reid, & Stoolmiller, 2008). However, studies from the Preschool Curriculum Evaluation Research Consortium (2008) have documented how many of the commonly used early childhood curricular and procedural models, most based on developmental science, show few effects on children's development. The challenge for developmental science and early childhood education is to persist in the very difficult process of conducting rigorous evaluation research in settings in which there are many factors to be controlled or built in to the research design.

Enlightened Professional Development

The verification process should communicate the effect of early childhood education procedures on children's development, but it is rare that receiving a curriculum manual will result in practitioners' implementation of practices with the same form or intensity as the published efficacy studies. Professional development and training are almost always necessary, and the field has become much more knowledgeable about strategies that may effect change in teachers' practices. Enfield and Rogers (Chapter 25, this volume), along with others (Fixsen, Naoom, Blase, Friedman, & Wallace, 2005; Joyce & Showers, 2002) have stated that "one-shot" workshops without follow-up and traditional didactic, lecture-style presentation of procedures do not lead to teachers' sustained use of new practices. A challenge for developmental science and early education is to design effective elaborations or alternatives to this traditional form of professional development.

In fact, there are emerging professional development practices that one might called "enlightened" (Odom, in press), in that they build on current knowledge of adult learning, group dynamics, and information technology. These practices include models for team building (Hayden, Frederick, & Smith, 2003), procedures for coaching and consultation (Wesley & Buysse, 2006), communities of practice (Buysse, Sparkman, & Wesley, 2003), online instruction, Web-based video and visual access (Pianta, 2006), and Web-based video systems (Buysse, Winton, & Rous, 2009). Space constraints preclude descriptions of these techniques, but for more information, the reader may consult Winton, McCollum, and Catlett (2008).

Institutional Support

A future challenge in moving developmental science into practice, even after countering the translation, verification, and professional development challenges, is garnering the necessary institutional support for effective, sustainable use of practices. The most current models from implementation science (Durlak & DuPre, 2008; Fixsen et al., 2005) are built on an ecological systems conceptual framework (Bronfenbrenner, 1979). Organizational support, a feature of the system, has proven essential. Examples of such support include funding for training and essential materials, time for planning, and administrators' advocacy of the change. Although distant from the developmental science laboratory, these underlying organizational supports are just as critical if the science is to move into practice.

Conclusion

A challenge of early childhood education is to bridge the gap between the very early childhood years (pre-K) and the early elementary years of schooling. Developmental science can serve as a foundation for designing early childhood education practices that are continuous across the early years of school and respond well to the academic and social development of all students. To move this research into practice, a systematic process involving translation, verification, professional development, and institutional support is required.

References

Bates, E. (2002, February). *Brain science, early childhood development, and early intervention.* Keynote presentation at the biannual Conference on Research Innovation in Early Intervention, San Diego, CA.

Bernanke, B. S. (2007, February). *The level and distribution of economic well-being.* Speech given to the Greater Omaha Chamber of Commerce, Omaha, NE. Retrieved from *federalreserve.gov/newsevents/speech/bernanke20070206a.htm*

Bierman, K. L., Domitrovich, C. E., Nix, R. L., Gest, S. D., Welsh, J. A., Greenberg, M. T., et al. (2008). Promoting academic and social–emotional school readiness: The Head Start REDI Program. *Child Development, 79,* 1802–1817.

Bodrova, E., & Leong, D. J. (2007). *Tools of the mind: The Vygotskian approach to early childhood education.* New York: Merrill/Prentice-Hall.

Bronfenbrenner, U. (1979). *The ecology of human development: Experiments by nature.* Cambridge, MA: Harvard University Press.

Bruer, J. T. (2001). A critical and sensitive period primer. In D. Bailey, J. Bruer, F. Symons, & J. Lichtman (Eds.), *Critical thinking about critical periods* (pp. 2–26). Baltimore: Brookes.

Burchinal, M. R., Peisner-Feinberg, E., Bryant, D. M., & Clifford, R. (2000). Children's social and cognitive development and child care quality: Testing for differential associations related to poverty, gender, or ethnicity. *Applied Developmental Science, 4,* 149–165.

Buysse, V., Sparkman, K., & Wesley, P. W. (2003). Communities of practice: Connecting what we know with what we do. *Exceptional Children, 69*, 263–277.

Buysse, V., & Wesley, P. W. (2006). Evidence-based practice: How did it emerge and what does it really mean for the early childhood field? In V. Buysse & P. W. Wesley (Eds.), *Evidence-based practice in the early childhood field* (pp. 1–34). Washington, DC: Zero to Three.

Buysse, V., Winton, P. J., & Rous, B. (2009). Reaching consensus on a definition of professional development for the early childhood field. *Topics in Early Childhood Special Education, 28*, 235–243.

Clements, D. H., & Sarama, J. (2007). *Building Blocks—SRA Real Math, Grade Pre-K*. Columbus, OH: SRA/McGraw-Hill.

Clements, D. H., & Sarama, J. (2008). Experimental evaluation of the effects of a research-based preschool mathematics curriculum. *American Educational Research Journal, 45*, 443–494.

Clifford, R. M., & Crawford, G. M. (Eds.). (2009). *Beginning school: U.S. policies in international perspectives*. New York: Teachers College Press.

Coleman, M. R., Buysse, V., & Neitzel, J. (2006). *Recognition and response: An early intervening systems for children at risk for learning disabilities: Research synthesis*. Chapel Hill: FPG Child Development Institute, University of North Carolina.

Committee for Children. (1989). *Second Step violence prevention program*. Seattle, WA: Author.

Domitrovich, C. E., Greenberg, M. T., Cortes, R., & Kusche, C. (1999). *Manual for the preschool PATHS curriculum*. South Deerfield, MA: Channing-Bete.

Durlak, J. A., & DuPre, E. P. (2008). Implementation matters: A review of research on the influence of implementation on program outcomes and the factors affecting implementation. *American Journal of Community Psychology, 41*, 327–350.

Fixsen, D. L., Naoom, S. F., Blase, K. A., Friedman, R. M., & Wallace, F. (2005). *Implementation research: A synthesis of the literature* (FMHI Publication No. 231). Tampa: University of South Florida, Louis de la Parte Florida Mental Health Institute, National Implementation Network.

French, L. (2004). Science as the center of a coherent, integrated early childhood curriculum. *Early Childhood Research Quarterly, 19*, 138–150.

Ginsburg, H. P., Greenes, C., & Balfanz, R. (2003). *Big math for little kids*. Parsippany, NJ: Dale Seymour.

Good, R. H., Gruba, J., & Kaminski, R. A. (2002). Best practices in using Dynamic Indicators of Basic Early Literacy Skills (DIBELS) in an outcome-driven model. In A. Thomas & J. Grimes (Eds.), *Best practices in school psychology* (Vol. 1–2, pp. 699–720). Washington, DC: National Association of School Psychologists.

Griffin, S. (2007). *Number Worlds: A mathematics intervention program for grades pre-K–6*. Columbus, OH: SRA/McGraw-Hill.

Hamre, B. K., & Pianta, R. C. (2005). Can instructional and emotional support in the first-grade classroom make a difference for children at risk of school failure? *Child Development, 75*, 949–967.

Heckman, J. J., Stixrud, J., & Urzua, S. (2006). The effects of cognitive and noncognitive abilities on labor market outcomes and social behavior. *Journal of Labor Economics, 24*, 411–482.

Horton, J. C. (2001). Critical periods in the development of the visual system. In D. Bailey, J. Bruer, F. Symons, & J. Lichtman (Eds.), *Critical thinking about critical periods* (pp. 45–66). Baltimore: Brookes.

Hayden, P., Frederick, L., & Smith, B. J. (2003). *A road map for facilitating collaborative teams*. Longmont, CO: Sopris West.

Joyce, B., & Showers, B. (2002). *Student achievement through staff development* (3rd ed.). Alexandria, VA: Association for Supervision and Curriculum Development.

Kagan, J., & Herschkowitz, N. (2005). *A young mind in a growing brain*. Mahwah, NJ: Erlbaum.

Klahr, D., & Nigam, M. (2004). The equivalence of learning paths in early science instruction: Effects of direct instruction and discovery learning. *Psychological Science, 15*, 661–667.

Klein, A., & Starkey, P. (2002). *Pre-K mathematics curriculum*. Glenview, IL: Scott, Foresman.

La Paro, K. M., Pianta, R. C., & Stuhlman, M. (2004). The Classroom Assessment Scoring System. *Elementary School Journal, 104*, 409–426.

Ladd, G. W. (2005). *Children's peer relations and social competence: A century of progress*. New Haven, CT: Yale University Press.

Luze, G. J., & Hughes, K. (2008). Using individual growth and development indicators to assess child and program outcomes. *Teaching Young Exceptional Children, 12*, 31–41.

Mashburn, A. J., Pianta, R. C., Hamre, B. K., Downer, J. T., Barbarin, O. A., Bryant, D., et al. (2008). Measures of classroom quality in prekindergarten and children's development of academic, language, and social skills. *Child Development, 79*, 732–749.

McConnell, S. R., McEvoy, M. A., & Priest, J. S. (2002). "Growing" measures for monitoring progress in early childhood education: A research and development process for individual growth and development indicators. *Assessment for Effective Intervention, 27*(4), 3–14.

National Association for the Education of Young Children. (2008). *NAEYC Quality Rating and Improvement Systems (QRIS) toolkit*. Washington, DC: Author. Retrieved November 30, 2008, from *www.naeyc.org/policy/state/pdf/webqrstoolkit.pdf*

National Center on Children in Poverty. (2008, October). *A working meeting on recent school readiness research: Guiding the synthesis of early childhood research*. Washington, DC: Author.

Neville, H. F., & Bruer, J. T. (2001). Language processing: How experience affects processing and organization. In D. Bailey, J. Bruer, F. Symons, & J. Lichtman (Eds.), *Critical thinking about critical periods* (pp. 151–172). Baltimore: Brookes.

Odom, S. L. (in press). The tie that binds: Evidence-based practice, implementation science, and early intervention. *Topics in Early Childhood Special Education*.

Odom, S. L., McConnell, S. R., & Brown, W. H. (2008). Social competence of young children: Conceptualization, assessment, and influences. In W. Brown, S. Odom, & S. McConnell (Eds.), *Social competence of young children: Risk, disability, and intervention* (pp. 3–29). Baltimore: Brookes.

Odom, S. L., & Wolery, M. (2003). A unified theory of practice in early intervention/early childhood special education: Evidence-based practice. *Journal of Special Education, 37*, 164–173.

Odom, S. L., Zercher, C., Li, S., Marquart, J., & Sandall, S. (2006). Social acceptance and social rejection of young children with disabilities in inclusive classes. *Journal of Educational Psychology, 98*, 807–823.

Pianta, R. C. (2006). Standardized observation and professional development: A focus on individualized implementation and practices. In M. Zaslow & I. Martinez-Beck (Eds.), *Critical issues in early childhood professional development* (pp. 231–254). Baltimore: Brookes.

Preschool Curriculum Evaluation Research Consortium. (2008). *Effects of preschool curriculum programs on school readiness* (NCER 2008–2009). Washington, DC: U.S. Government Printing Office.

Smith, T., Scahill, L., Dawson, G., Guthrie, D., Lord, C., Odom, S., et al. (2007). Designing research studies on psychosocial interventions in autism. *Journal of Autism and Developmental Disorders, 37*, 354–366.

Sroufe, L. A., Egeland, B., Carlson, E., & Collins, W. A. (2005). Placing early attachment experiences in developmental context: The Minnesota Longitudinal Study. In K. E. Grossmann, K. Grossmann, & E. Waters (Eds.), *Attachment from infancy to adulthood: The major longitudinal studies* (pp. 48–70). New York: Guilford Press.

Webster-Stratton, C., & Reid, M. J. (2003). The incredible years parents, teachers, and children training series: A multifaceted treatment approach for young children with conduct problems. In A. E. Kazdin & J. R. Weisz (Eds.), *Evidence-based psychotherapies for children and adolescents* (pp. 224–240). New York: Guilford Press.

Webster-Stratton, C., & Reid, M. J. (2008). Strengthening social and emotional competence in young children who are socioeconomically disadvantaged: Preschool and kindergarten school-based curricula. In W. Brown, S. Odom, & S. McConnell (Eds.), *Social competence of young children: Risk, disability, and intervention* (pp. 141–164). Baltimore: Brookes.

Webster-Stratton, C., Reid, M. J., & Stoolmiller, M. (2008). Preventing conduct problems and improving school readiness: Evaluation of the Incredible Years teacher and child training programs in high-risk schools. *Journal of Child Psychology and Psychiatry, 49,* 471–488.

Wesley, P. W., & Buysse, V. (2006). Making the case for evidence-based policy. In V. Buysse & P. W. Wesley (Eds.), *Evidence-based practice in the early childhood field* (pp. 117–159). Washington, DC: Zero to Three.

Whitehurst, G. J. (2004). *Making education evidence-based: Premises, principles, pragmatics, and politics.* Paper presented to the Institute for Policy Research, Northwestern University. Retrieved November 30, 2008, from *ies.ed.gov/director/pdf/2004_04_26.pdf*

Winton, P., McCollum, J., & Catlett, C. (Eds.). (2008). *Practical approaches to early childhood professional development.* Washington, DC: Zero to Three.

Wolf, M. M. (1978). Social validity: The case for subjective measurement. *Journal of Applied Behavior Analysis, 11,* 203–214.

Zigler, E., Gilliam, W. S., & Jones, S. M. (2006). *A vision for universal preschool education.* New York: Cambridge University Press.

Author Index

Subject Index

Page numbers followed by *f* indicate figure; *n*, note; and *t*, table